Sander, Mae E.
    Jewish time-travel.

Date Due

JEWISH TIME-TRAVEL

JEWISH TIME-TRAVEL

A Travel Narrative and Guide to Jewish Historic Sites in Europe and Israel

MAE E. SANDER

JASON ARONSON INC.
Northvale, New Jersey
Jerusalem

This book was set in 10 pt. New Baskerville by Pageworks of Old Saybrook, CT and printed and bound by Book-mart Press, Inc. of North Bergen, NJ.

10 9 8 7 6 5 4 3 2 1

Library of Congress Cataloging-in-Publication Data

Sander, Mae E.
   Jewish time-travel : a travel narrative and guide to Jewish
historic sites in Europe and Israel / by Mae E. Sander.
       p.   cm.
   Includes bibliographical references and index.
     ISBN 0–7657–6099–1
       1. Israel—Description and travel.   2. Jews—Palestine—History.
   3. France, Southern—Description and travel.   4. Jews—France,
Southern—History.   5. Spain—Description and travel.   6. Jews—
Spain—History.   7. Italy—Description and travel.   8. Jews—Italy—
History.   9. Abravanel family.   I. Title.
   DS107.5.S263   2000
   914.04'559—dc21   00–13419
                                                                               CIP

Printed in the United States of America on acid-free paper. For information and catalog write to Jason Aronson Inc., 230 Livingston Street, Northvale, NJ 07647–1726, or visit our website: www.aronson.com

DEDICATION

I dedicate this book to Lenny,
who traveled with me on every voyage,
and to my friends who traveled with me,
who listened to me,
and who read what I was writing.

LIST OF FIGURES

CONTENTS

Part 2
Medieval Jews in Southern France

Part 3
Iberian Voyages

Part 4
Italy, Renaissance Voyages

Appendices
Practical Information and References

Introduction—Traveling
Backward in Time

I invite you to share my reading, my travels, and my search for interesting Jewish communities in European history. My motive for travel and for reading is to connect with such communities—to understand how they fit into familiar tourist destinations where, until recently, I always found them to be invisible. I looked for books that treated characters and events in the history of Mediterranean Europe and Israel and that suggested where I might look for traces of their communities. I am curious about the good times: what they accomplished, how they survived, and in what manner they led their lives beyond observing Jewish obligations and keeping the familiar calendar of Jewish holidays. Successful communities are the most interesting; I want to stay away from the frequent characterization of Jews as permanent victims.

I have always loved to travel. For years, I have taken conventional sightseeing trips and extended business trips to major European cities and European rural attractions. Magnificent cathedrals, romantic castles, and well-preserved medieval villages pointed me to the history of the mainstream Christian majority. Famous artists, sculptors, architects, and writers documented the progress of Classical civilizations, medieval times, the Renaissance, the assimilation of wealth from the New World, and the French Revolution. Famous books, paintings, and monuments all spoke eloquently to me. Today's living Tuscan villages appeared just like the ones in Renaissance frescos and in the background of medieval altar-pieces. Landscapes in Provence dissolved into the works of the Impressionists and Van Gogh. Modern paintings informed my vision of the Paris skyline. The Forum in Rome, the Roman aqueducts in southern France, the palaces of the Medici in Florence, the cathedrals of Chartres and Rouen, the Invalides where Napoleon is buried, the Eiffel tower, and the new Grand Arch at La Defense outside Paris took their places in history, which I often learned by reading guidebooks.

A few years ago, I started on a reading project about the Jews of the Renaissance, and a new view of history began to affect my travel plans. I turned from conventional tourism to a search for signs of Jewish life before the major expulsions at the end of the Middle Ages. I was aware that Jews had once lived in many of the places I had visited and that a few survivors still did. In medieval times, I vaguely knew that they led a different life, much less settled. But pre-nineteenth-century Jewish history was never vivid and was rarely even mentioned in the brief summaries I read. Because much earlier European history had always interested me, I found the usual concern with merely the last hundred years of Jewish history, and the focus on the Holocaust, to be frustrating. I developed many questions about how early Jews had migrated around the Mediterranean, where they had lived, when they had left, and where they had gone.

Once such questions began to concern me, I searched for relevant history books and then visited cities and villages in France, Spain, and Italy where I thought I might find answers to my questions. As I learned about the wanderings of Jews in the Middle Ages and in the Renaissance, I also became curious about what had attracted their ancestors to Europe or had driven their ancestors from Israel. The history books that I read began by mentioning the spread of Jews under the Roman Empire and with the destruction of Jerusalem by Rome in 70 c.e. Slowly, I developed a mental time-line, following the Jews from Israel to sites in Roman cities, a long though deteriorating relationship with the other inhabitants as Goths and Visigoths conquered Roman territory, and a series of persecutions and expulsions that rearranged Jews in Europe at the end of the Middle Ages. Finally, the famous expulsion of the Jews from Spain destroyed the last of the long-term communities.

I combined reading and travel, beginning with a search for Jews in the southwest of France. I was curious to know if any traces in villages there could help me to visualize Jewish living there eight hundred years ago. I found a few traces of medieval Jews—a street, a house, an arcade, a memory. In Italy, where Jewish communities remained after the late

Middle Ages and where they were joined by Jews expelled from other European countries, the traces are stronger: Italy has many magnificent synagogues in Renaissance and Baroque styles, and several impressive Jewish museums. When I had the opportunity to spend several months traveling in Israel, I explored historic sites that offered insights into the Diaspora. Israel naturally has many monuments where the physical traces of Jewish history are easy to locate and very well documented, though more emphasis is placed on the biblical era than on the era when the Diaspora was beginning. Israel also presents the challenge of identifying modern myths that re-interpret historic events, but my end result was increased understanding of the roots of the Jewish communities that had spread across Europe in the first centuries of this era.

Searching for ancient and medieval Jews fits in with their own habit of being wanderers. From the first exile in Babylonia, Jews outside Israel always had a sense of being from elsewhere. While a medieval Christian typically remained within a day's voyage of his village, medieval and Renaissance Jews often made long journeys for commercial or religious reasons. Beginning at the end of the Middle Ages, frequent expulsions forced whole communities to move from one place to another. Sometimes the search for Jewish connections led me to follow a particular traveler, such as the famous Benjamin of Tudela, who explored much of the known world, leaving his native Spanish town in 1165. Sometimes I could follow a family for several generations as they moved onward, as I did with the Abravanel family, whose members lived in Castile, Portugal, and several Italian cities.

As an American Jew of Eastern European descent, I claim no personal connection with any of the European communities that became my subject for travel and research. My father used to tell me about the village in Eastern Europe where he was born, but he felt no desire to go back to a place whose identity had intentionally been obliterated and whose Jewish inhabitants had all been slaughtered. He communicated to me the love of travel, but for him it was California and the West—the New World—that had the appeal. He always said, "I've been to Europe," dismissing it as if it were simply an extension of his birthplace and its destroyers. Brought up like this, with a standard education about art and culture, for years I felt the closest to the monuments of Western Europe, the gothic churches, palatial museums, and the monuments of recent European culture—a culture from which Jewish participation was principally barred. However, though nothing in my own family history offers me the slightest relationship, I consider myself connected to these Jews of the past on the basis of being one of the Jews who still survives in this world; I hope that you can find your own reason to connect to them as well.

TRAVEL NARRATIVES IN THIS BOOK

In this book, I will describe my search for the evidence of Jewish communities in several Mediterranean countries: France, Spain, Italy, and Israel. I will introduce you to a number of historic Jewish figures from Roman times through the Renaissance, and explore the conditions that make them so obscure in current consciousness. Throughout my narrative, one particular characteristic of Jews is important: our tendency to travel and to move around. While most Europeans remained incredibly stable for over a thousand years, many Jews took long, dangerous, and very interesting voyages—sometimes willingly, sometimes not. By following them, I hope to help you visualize the lives and times of Jewish communities that flourished in the Mediterranean region long ago.

In describing my voyages, I will describe how you can engage in your own journeys, real or imaginary. Thus, I have organized my material both as a travel narrative and as a guide. Each narrative focuses on a different country, on a different period of history, and on specific travelers and families. I have selected what I feel to be the most interesting moments in the lives of the Jews of each region and have tried to select lives of people who represent important strains of Jewish culture and a variety of interests, as well as to provide historic and cultural background. I have especially tried to trace the secular lives and accomplishments of the members of these communities.

Israel in Roman Times

The first itineraries in this book visit the sites in Israel where communities participated in the start of the Diaspora. Through them you will discover when and why the Jews left Israel. The Diaspora began, according to tradition, at the fall of the Temple in 70 C.E. Jews in the Middle Ages, for example, sometimes upheld this tradition by expressing their birth dates as a number of years since the Temple's fall, which they called "the Exile." Today the Diaspora Museum in Tel Aviv, at the start of their presentation of Diaspora history, displays a replica of a panel from the Arch of Titus. In the panel, the victorious Romans march in a triumphal procession, bearing the most valuable possessions of the Temple, most visibly, the *menorah.* Having seen so much of this symbolism, I imagined a sudden invasion, battles, destruction, a vacant Jerusalem, a scattered people, a lost culture. When I traveled in Israel, I planned to find the evidence and learn the history of this calamity, hoping to understand how the collision with Rome connected Israel to the later Jewish communities of the Mediterranean. I discovered—predictably—a reality that is more complex.

While the fall of the Temple was a catastrophe, the "Exile" was a slow process, not an abrupt event. As I toured in Jerusalem and other historic places I gave up my simple vision of the Exile and assimilation of the Jews in exchange for a much more interesting one. I saw ancient buildings and archaeology sites where Greek, Roman, and Jewish architecture, alphabets, languages, and symbols coexisted side by side for over six hundred years. As I read more and saw more, I began to visualize a Jerusalem that by 70 C.E. was as much Roman as biblical. While medieval accounts of the fall of the Temple talked about rudderless ships taking the refugees from the ruins of Jerusalem, I never heard of them when visiting the numerous Israeli archaeology sites. However, I learned a much more interesting story, which I will tell in three itineraries:

- Visiting Roman sites in Jerusalem, Judaea, and the Dead Sea
- Touring the coast from Ashdod to Akko
- Exploring Roman-era cities in the Galilee

Languedoc and Provence

My next voyage jumps forward from the slow dispersal of the Jews of Roman times to the Middle Ages, in France. My French itinerary begins with a retracing of the journey of a Jewish traveler named Benjamin of Tudela (1127–1173). Benjamin described six cities that are now in modern France: four in Languedoc, west of the Rhone; and two in Provence, east of the Rhone. He named the most prominent Jewish scholars and rabbis that lived there and told a little about their accomplishments. In fact, Jewish scholars, scribes, and translators of this era were important in transmitting classical culture and Arab learning from the Arabs to the Christians. They also gave birth to a new Jewish mysticism, which inspired the body of knowledge called the Kabbalah. Not long after Benjamin, rabbis and scholars of Languedoc participated actively in a debate over the works of the famous Maimonides. The communities also had many ordinary people: textile workers, butchers, bakers, jewel and spice merchants (perhaps like Benjamin), dealers in agricultural products, money-lenders, and manual laborers, whose lives I enjoyed discovering.

Benjamin followed established trading routes that were well-known to Jewish merchants of the day, and his book provided information about much of the known world. Travel was unusual in his time, and he was nearly the only contemporary to leave an account of a journey of that extent—he was substantially earlier than the much more famous Marco Polo (1254–1324). Thus, Benjamin has always been important to both Jews and Christians who wanted to learn about the medieval world. Even today, he represents a unique source of knowledge of medieval travel: a recent issue of *Mercator's World: The Magazine of Maps, Exploration, and Discovery* reprinted an excerpt from his travels under the heading "Field Notes: The Travels of Rabbi Benjamin." The editors marked this excerpt only by a brief introduction, which concluded: "His itinerary provides a rare glimpse of a rich, diverse medieval world, prior to the Jews' expulsion from much of western Europe" (*Mercator's World*, September/October 1998, p. 11).

In following Benjamin's voyage, I found that of the six cities he visited in France, all but one have retained their medieval names, and most contain at least a building or a location traditionally associated with the distant Jewish scholars whom Benjamin named. Like many French cities, most still have a "Rue des Juifs," or Jews' street, despite the length of time that has passed since their expulsion. One wonders at the exact function of this preservation, when one learns that for hundreds of years, long after the expulsion of all Jews, some townsmen preserved the custom of throwing stones at these, the Jews' former houses, during the Easter season. Details like this suggest that one will never fully grasp the complex situation of medieval Jews, but as I describe each French town on Benjamin's itinerary, I will relate some of the specific history of the Jews of that place and try to build a picture of their lives.

In addition, I will describe several other places in Provence that continued to be important until slightly later. Provence was independent of the French kings, who lived in Paris. Beginning the centralization that characterizes France to this day, these Parisian kings conquered the Languedoc region between 1200 and 1250 and expelled the Jews from France between about 1305 and 1395. Provence was a logical place for these Jews to go; the rulers were more tolerant, and the culture was similar to what they had known. They established several communities there or joined existing ones such as Arles and Marseilles, where Benjamin visited.

Later, France also acquired Provence and by 1501 also expelled the Jews from there. After this expulsion, a few small communities remained in a few towns that continued to be ruled by the Pope rather than by the kings of France, in an area called the Comtat Venaisson. I will point out those towns, where you can see much more evidence of Jewish history, including the eighteenth-century synagogues of Carpentras and Cavaillon and the nineteenth-century synagogue of Avignon.

Spain, 1391 to 1492

In Spain today, there are so few Jews that they are viewed as a medieval holdover. So much seems mythological that I began to wonder about my own impressions of Jewish history in the Iberian peninsula. Was there ever a Spanish Golden Age for Jews, or is it a myth? How numerous and powerful were the Jews during the Moslem rule in Spain? How did Jews behave during the long struggle between Christians and Moslems for control of the peninsula? Were Jews at all associated with the still-more-mysterious Knights Templar? Did King Ferdinand and Queen Isabella expel the Jews because of religious fanaticism? Because they wanted their wealth? Or because Ferdinand needed to solidify his support among the Jew-hating masses in order to control the nobles in Castile and Aragon? Was the secret practice of Judaism by Marranos a reality or a fabrication of the Inquisition? My doubts about these questions grew as I toured Spain, and I began to seek some solid historical details.

The history of the Jews in Spain for the century before the expulsion in 1492 provides a frame for comparing myth and history. My travel narrative follows the lives of the illustrious Abravanel family of the Spanish kingdom of Castile, whose members lived through this century of persecution and expulsion. I begin with a focus on Samuel Abravanel, born in the mid-fourteenth century, who served the kings of Castile for decades, and—typically for his era—converted to Christianity. Samuel's son Judah remained Jewish; he left Castile at the beginning of the fifteenth century to serve the more tolerant rulers of neighboring Portugal. In 1484, the family's most famous member, Isaac Abravanel, returned to Castile, where he achieved great power at the court of King Ferdinand and Queen Isabella—only to be expelled in 1492. In the context of this family's history, I have tried to create a picture of the last century of active Judaism in Spain: of the pogroms and mass conversions that occurred from 1391 until 1412, of the growing anti-Jewish and anti-convert sentiment, of the initial impact of the Spanish Inquisition, and of the agony of the expulsion.

Three Italian Renaissance Families

My Jewish-historical visit to Italy concentrated on Renaissance Jews, a diverse group of people with origins in a number of places. I focused on the lives of three families and on ordinary people in the Ghetto of Venice. I visited cities and towns that presented a variety of memories of Jewish communities and individuals from that period.

In a continuation of the narrative about Spain, I followed Isaac Abravanel and his sons after their expulsion from Spain in 1492. The accomplishments of the oldest son, Judah Abravanel, are particularly important. He achieved wide recognition as a Renaissance poet among Christians as well as among Jews and was influenced by some of the most famous humanist scholars of Florence.

Next, I traced a family whose origin was in Speyer, Germany. In the mid-fifteenth century, they moved to Italy, assimilated to life in the Duchy of Milan, and adopted the name of the town that welcomed them, Soncino. Several generations of this family made a major contribution to the development of Hebrew printing—books from the Hebrew press in Soncino are still famous for their beauty and accuracy. While most people have an idea of the dramatic changes worked by the new technology of printing on Christian letters, Renaissance humanism, and European politics, Jewish uses of printing are more obscure. In describing the Soncino family, I will illustrate how Jews rapidly adapted this technology to their own culture and literature. I will particularly concentrate on the voyages of Gershom Soncino, who founded presses in various cities in Italy and later in the Turkish empire.

A native Italian-Jewish family named Norsa, descendants of Jews who came to Italy during the time of the Roman Empire, provided my next focal point. The Norsa family lived in various small towns in the southern part of Italy during late Roman times and throughout the Middle Ages; their family name refers to Nurzia, a village where their ancestors lived. In the fourteenth century, branches of the family took up residence in at least two northern Italian towns, Mantua and Ferrara, where they were bankers and merchants participating in the growing commercial development of the Renaissance. For several generations, they were prominent members of a growing and flourishing Jewish community fostered by the exceptional tolerance of the rulers of these towns. I will describe the impressive Jewish and civic monuments that still stand there, in depicting Jewish life in these towns during the Renaissance.

FURTHER INFORMATION

In the appendices to this book, you can find practical information and a chapter-by-chapter list of the books that I used as sources. I have kept references in the text to a minimum, to improve readability, but my debt to these books is enormous. I would like to express my appreciation and admiration for the authors, translators, and editors of these books, whose labors of scholarship and of study of the primary sources have supplied me with so much information and enjoyable reading.

The most important practical point that you will find in the appendices is this: European tourist information bureaus are the best and most convenient source of city maps, local guidebooks, up-to-date museum and monument schedules, hotel availability, and local current events. The route to the local office is usually marked with the letter i on placards along the roads leading into most town centers. In friendly places, especially in Italy, the personnel often speak English, and they frequently are willing to make phone calls to help you arrange visits to sites (such as synagogues), as well as to reserve hotel rooms. Where possible, I have noted tourist office addresses in the text when discussing individual cities and towns.

PART 1

Israel and the Romans

Overview—Ancient History

In 1997, I traveled for the first time to Israel. I had often visited Europe, had toured the United States, had taken vacations in the Caribbean, and had visited Japan and Australia, but had never been in Israel before. I arrived with much curiosity about the modern country and its people and political problems. I also wanted to learn, through tourism, about the event or events that had scattered Jews throughout the Mediterranean after the fall of the Temple. I expected to discover a defining moment, which had suddenly created the Diaspora. My most important realization, as I toured historic sites in Israel, was that no drama of expulsion or war caused their Exile; rather, a long process dispersed the Jews to many other lands.

Historic sites in Israel illustrated this process for me. I saw the places where Jews lived throughout the centuries, and I learned about the evidence that they moved away, sometimes returning, sometimes simply keeping in touch with Jewish life in Israel, until no center remained there. Major factors in the history of Jewish Exile from Israel:

- After the destruction of Solomon's Temple in the eighth century B.C.E., some exiles never returned from Babylon, though within a century Cyrus the Great, the new ruler of the region, officially allowed the resumption of Jewish life in Jerusalem and the rebuilding of the Temple.
- When Alexander the Great conquered the Near East during the

fourth century B.C.E., many Jews adopted aspects of Greek culture.
As hellenized Jews began to travel throughout the eastern empire,
Jewish communities formed in Alexander's city of Alexandria, in
Antioch in neighboring Syria, and in other hellenistic cities.

• As the Romans began to dominate these areas during the first
century B.C.E., a Roman-Jewish state emerged in Israel, creating firm
relationships between the two cultures. Jews began to make longer
commercial voyages and to live in the western Mediterranean. They
established themselves as a minority in Rome and probably participated in trading and commerce in northern European colonies as
well.

• In 70 C.E. after several years of Jewish rebellion, Roman troops
destroyed the Second Temple and sacked Jerusalem. Traditionally,
this is the point of sudden departure of Jews from Jerusalem. In
fact, although it triggered more emigration, many Jews remained
in Israel, hoping for permission to rebuild the Temple and restore
the priestly institutions, and keeping this hope alive in the exile
community.

The period of Roman occupation witnessed the most important
steps that led to more definitive exile. After the war, the Jews lost
political power and influence with the Roman rulers. Organization-
ally, the Romans made the land into a province of Syria, canceling
its former autonomy. Financially, Jews throughout the empire owed
to Imperial Rome the tax that had previously supported the Temple.
Religiously, Jewish survivors created new rituals and leaders; the
unifying force of the Temple, with its priestly leadership and focus
on sacrifice, was never restored.

• In 135 C.E. Romans put down the Bar Kochba rebellion. They
banned Jews entirely from Jerusalem and implemented many other
repressive measures. Jews who remained in the area took refuge
in small obscure towns in Galilee or moved toward the desert,
becoming marginal members of society in Roman Palestine.

For several centuries afterward, Jews increasingly felt the push
of hostile conditions in Israel and the pull of opportunities in the
Roman and later the Byzantine empire. At this time, Jews were
allowed a special status as Roman citizens. Cities that already had
Jewish communities were especially attractive to new refugees from
deteriorating conditions in Israel. Consequently, Jewish migration
to Spain, Provence, Italy, and North Africa grew. Hope that the

Romans would soon grant permission to rebuild the Temple became obviously unrealistic.

• After the Byzantine Empire ended, decline was irreversible. The Moslem conquest of the area in the seventh century destroyed more Jewish communities, and the Temple Mount became the site of mosques. Christian Crusaders from 1099 onward killed many Jews; the Knights Templar converted the Temple Mount to a Christian holy site. In the twelfth century, the Jewish traveler Benjamin of Tudela reported very few Jews still in residence in Jerusalem or outlying towns. Hope for a restoration of the Temple by this time stemmed from religious faith in the arrival of the Messiah.

In modern Israel, I found many sites to help me to understand the changes and interactions between Jewish and Roman culture: this era of drastic religious re-definition, political and cultural domination by Rome, loss of power to Christians throughout the empire, and migra-tion. The Temple Mount in Jerusalem, today rep-resented by the Western Wall, serves as a power-ful symbol of this pro-cess, but many other monuments also illus-trate it, particularly the post-Temple synagogues and villages that lie off the beaten track, where the frightened and per-secuted Jews took ref-uge, until eventually the combined impact of centuries of Moslem conquerors and Crusad-ers wiped them out entirely.

Fig. 1-1: Map of Israel Showing Places Mentioned in the Text

Masada

Masada was my starting place for understanding the interaction of Jewish and Roman culture. Masada has for generations been one of the most famous Israeli tourist sites. When I visited the National Park there, I became aware of a sequence of myths and truths about Masada. I heard the inspiring rendition of a very articulate guide telling the history of the site. I learned how the site related to the building mania of Herod the Great in the first century B.C.E. I learned about its role in the rebellion against the Romans and about the dramatic finale in 73 C.E. when Jewish fighters and their families made a famous last stand in the fortress and how, once they lost hope of a victory, all committed suicide.

I followed up the visit by reading two essential books. The first was the *Jewish War* by Flavius Josephus, written a few years after Masada's fall, and the only contemporary account. Second, I read *Masada* by Yigael Yadin, the archaeologist who, in the 1960s, excavated the site, hoping to verify what Josephus said. I'll tell you about these two intriguing figures: Josephus and Yadin. Later, I read other books, and I learned not only about the history of Jews and Romans at the site, but also about their importance to modern Israelis. The myth and meaning of what happened there helped to shape modern Israeli identity, and for several generations of Israelis, the trip to Masada has had the status of a pilgrimage. But this was later. Let me start with my first impressions and introduce you to these many ideas a little at a time. (See the list of references at the back of the book for complete bibliographical details.)

DISCOVERING MASADA

Less than a week after arriving in Israel, in January 1997, we visited Masada with our friends Phil and Roberta and their four-year-old daughter, Caroline. The trip was their idea, and they knew much more about Masada than we did; in fact, Roberta, in her college days, had taken a course from Yigael Yadin himself; she told us that his first-hand descriptions of the dig and what he had found there were charismatic—much more so than his book. I had only the vaguest knowledge of the significance of this site, of Yadin, or of the occupation and final resolution that had taken place during the Jewish war against Rome in around 70 C.E.

We drove from our temporary Israeli home in Rehovot through orange groves and then through winter fields, still dry as the winter rains hadn't yet begun. After Beersheva, the cultivated land gave way to more barren-looking hills—Bedouin country. Some Bedouins live in concrete apartment blocks in urban areas such as Rahat, while others live in camps of black tents and trailers, with flocks of sheep and goats. We saw occasional tethered camels, boys or girls leading donkeys and tending sheep, and adults in long robes and traditional head coverings. In the same encampments, we saw parked cars, pickups, and youngsters on bicycles.

At the Dead Sea, after the four-hour ride and the impressive twisting road down into the rift, we were struck by the incredible barrenness of the landscape. The Dead Sea mirrors the sky with a shimmery light, perhaps because it's so far below sea level. Its surface reflects the craggy flat-topped hills on the opposite side—that is, in Jordan. After dinner we drove into an open, unpopulated area at the foot of Masada to see the Milky Way and the stars, and to look at the lights on the far side of the sea. Places that had looked uninhabited by day were full of bright lights at night. I was a little startled to see that the main building at this location was the youth hostel, which I found puzzling. Since then, I have learned that the Zionist youth movement was the driving force behind the creation of Masada as a legendary place and now as a tourist destination.

The next day, having seen the sun rise with a strange orange reflection in the sea and having tried to do justice to the generous breakfast buffet served at our hotel, we went up to Masada, which stands on a huge craggy mountain not far from the seashore. For obvious reasons, Roberta, Caroline, and I took the cable car up to the citadel while the men walked up the famous Snake Path to the top. Flavius Josephus mentions the difficulties of this path, which he names the Serpent. It's now much improved—

its reputation probably also owes something to the former need to carry heavy packs and water supplies up the winding and steep route in blazing hot weather. Because we were there on a January day that was only warm, the walk up required only 45 minutes instead of the 75 minutes we had expected, so we weren't at the designated meeting place right away. As a result, the men started to listen to a tour, which was just getting started, and we decided that we would all join politely and follow at a slight distance to hear the excellent guide. After a few stops, a burly body guard accompanying this tour questioned us a little but seemed to decide that we were not any danger to his charges. We also noticed that a professionally equipped photographer was taking pictures, not of the sights but of the people on this tour.

The guide, we realized, had an obvious agenda: to link the events of ancient Masada to the current situation in Israel. We were very impressed with how he did this. We were even more impressed when we learned that one of the participants on this tour was a U.S. congressman, possibly from one of the southern states. Later on our trip we tried to find out who the guide was; we asked the U.S. consul, who arranges these things. However, he explained that almost every U.S. congressman visited Israel, including approximately fifteen of them that January, so we have never successfully identified the guide who made such an impression on us.

An important claim that the guide expounded was that in antiquity, the Jews had not focused on impressive monuments and beautiful buildings as had the Romans; their accomplishments, he proposed, were more intangible. At Masada, the stones are old and it requires imagination to see what was there, he explained, also pointing out how the Jewish occupiers of 68 C.E. to 73 C.E. consciously disrupted the aesthetic intent of Herod's skilled architects. He illustrated this by pointing out a crudely built bread oven placed on top of a stunning mosaic floor. This evidence supported his claim that beautiful lasting monuments are not in keeping with a Jewish spirit.

Interestingly, the guide's group did not climb down to Herod's summer palace in the shade of the north side of the rock face, where floral and geometric motifs carved in pale-colored stone, a remarkable circular room, and half-columns set in the rock are still beautiful and impressive. The Jewish-Roman builders of this palace seemed to contradict the guide's generalization about abiding monuments. These possibly contradictory sights of Masada illustrate the core conflict of Roman times in Israel, which pitted those who wanted to accommodate to "modern" times and to live and prosper under Roman rule, against the rigid opposition, who wanted to keep Temple worship pure and to prevent any weakening of the old traditions. This conflict contributed to the destruction of Jerusalem just before the famous Masada story. I will come back to it.

Around 66 C.E., the guide explained, the Jews had refused a variety of Roman demands to introduce Roman Emperor worship into the Temple. Relations had deteriorated, and the revolt ended with the final destruction of Jerusalem in 70 C.E. Early in this war, the small band of Jews called Sicarii had overrun Herod's fortress, then a small Roman outpost. The community of just under one thousand men, women, and children camped in Herod's palaces and barracks. On top of the Roman structures, they built crude structures to meet their needs—our guide pointed out the subdivisions of Herodian barracks to accommodate the Jewish families, simple cooking ovens built over elegant mosaic floors, a synagogue that faces Jerusalem, and the ritual bath.

After Jerusalem fell, the Romans declared Judea fully conquered and pacified, but this little band of Jewish outlaws held out, to the embarrassment of the Roman rulers. Eventually, they sent a huge force of Roman troops to wipe them out, as witnessed by the outlines of Roman camps still visible on the bare mountains below Masada. The Romans waited a while, perhaps expecting the rebels to run short of food or water, but Herod's design goal—an impregnable and carefully stocked fortress— ensured that supplies were unlikely to run out.

The tour continued with a dramatic visit to Masada's synagogue, during which the guide emphasized its importance and uniqueness. He had us all face in the direction that the ancient worshipers had faced: toward Jerusalem, whose hills are almost in sight. This told us that synagogue orientation to the Temple Mount was established before the Temple was itself destroyed, a connection of modern and ancient Jewish practice. His tour group sat down on the stone benches that go around the synagogue wall. He explained that this synagogue was considered the oldest synagogue in Israel, dating from Herod's time. He did not mention subsequent excavations that have unearthed older ones—I recently read of the current "oldest" near Jericho, from 75 B.C.E. which, after an earthquake, was built over by a Herodian structure; the next archaeology report could bring news of still older remains, of buildings upon buildings. All the pieces of the myth must fit together.

Our guide was most dramatic in encouraging his audience to imagine the feelings of the last rebels who worshiped at this synagogue one hundred years later, during the Roman siege. Perhaps the rebels knew that the Temple had just been destroyed—or perhaps, not really knowing, they hoped that these were false rumors. Above all, he communicated the emotion of the excavators, as described in Yigael Yadin's book, upon their discovery of papyrus scrolls with the biblical text of Ezekiel's story of the valley of dry bones. He gestured toward the spot where the discovery occurred.

We walked on, along the walls facing the other side of the hills, opposite the Dead Sea lookout. Eventually, the Romans built a ramp on the foundations of the old aqueduct and brought up siege engines to destroy the walls. At the site of this ramp, our guide gave a dramatic summary of the last days of Masada in 73 c.e. before the defenders accepted their fate. He pointed out that the Roman legions brought in Jewish slaves, victims of the recent battle over Jerusalem, and made them work on the siege ramp, asking whether the defenders were able to bring themselves to shoot at their brethren on the other side of the barricades. (After having read more about the last stand, I think he made this up, as the actual defenders were from a totally different subgroup, but at the time it seemed overpowering.) Let's imagine life in Masada at the final moment.

A Last Holdout against the Romans

First, try to picture modern Masada. You are in an open courtyard surrounded by ancient stone walls and ruined watchtowers, at the top of a craggy peak. Beyond and far below you can see a severe and barren landscape stretching toward the Dead Sea, the sun relentlessly beating down. The rough stone walls each have a line that shows which parts stood there for two thousand years and which parts were reconstructed in the 1960s. Beyond the walls on the mountain's steep slopes you can see faint outlines of the Roman siege camps and sentry towers that once threatened the final defenders. The fortress still looks nearly inviolable, surrounded as it is by steep and rugged mountain crags.

Now project yourself back in time at the end of the Jewish War, three years after the fall of the Temple in 70 c.e. The buildings are complete and have been standing in the preserving desert air since Herod built them a century earlier. You have shared them with your fellow rebels since you all arrived and overpowered the Roman outpost here a few years ago. Men, women, and children of your group live in the former Roman barracks, and in Herod's hundred-year-old palaces, which you and your comrades have rearranged to suit your needs. You spend much of your time in practical tasks, but also carry on the traditional rituals. (The ruins of the ritual bath and the synagogue of Masada today indicate that these final Jewish occupants of Masada were actively following Jewish practices.)

During the final war, in which Jews fought bitterly against other Jews and in which the Roman destruction was a response to inter-group struggles, you and your band of assassins were rejected among the factions of Jerusalem and throughout the Jewish territories. Despite your overthrow of the Roman garrison that was stationed here, the Romans seemed to ignore your presence at first. Now, they have completed the destruction of Jerusalem, and you are the last mop-up operation: the siege camps outside the walls are full of soldiers, and you can see and hear them day and night. First, they built stone walls delineating their camps, and they are now constructing a makeshift ramp, preparing to breach the wall that still protects you.

How do you pass your time until the inevitable attack of these Roman troops? Perhaps you take your turn at work as a metal smith, making arrowheads for the archers' bows, which you and your fellow defenders will need to fight back when they attack. (In one area of the fortress, archaeologists discovered charcoal, metal, and a variety of arrowheads that indicated a smith's workshop.) If you are an archer or a fighter, you will also need to make sure your armor and your shield will withstand attack. (Additional archaeology finds were the metal scales that were affixed to soldiers' armor and one or two leather shields.) After a rain, everyone on the mountain top has the duty of carrying water up from the catch basin to fill the cisterns inside the fortifications, but the Roman attackers now make that impossible; fortunately, the water supplies are enough to last several years. Food supplies are also adequate for now.

If you are a woman, you take your turn minding the children, grinding the stores of grain, which, legend has it, were originally put away when Herod built the fortress, and baking bread in the ovens that were built when your community occupied the site. You may have brought some skeins of wool along, which you can work, spinning, mending, or making fringes for men's garments. (In an excavation of the caves of En Gedi, Yadin's expedition found that some women traveled with supplies of yarn to continue this important work wherever they went.)

According to Flavius Josephus, during the years your group spent in the fortress, there was at least one unsavory episode, when your food ran low. Armed members of your band conducted a raid on the little town of En Gedi, not far away. You took their food and massacred your fellow Jews who lived there. Do you think of that at night, when you look over the barren wasteland around you? Or do you recall the time when you and your fellow defenders were bandits up in Galilee?

During the last several months, none of you have been able to leave the fortress, as the Romans have surrounded the entire mountain with their siege wall and constantly staffed watchtowers, preventing any exit. Down in the Roman camps, the conscripts who are getting ready to fight you have to pass the time, too; in the evenings when you and your comrades—men, women, and children—sit around communal fires or perhaps in darkness, you can see the lights of their camps below. They may pass the time by playing at dice or other games. Nineteen hundred years later, you can still see the outlines of the siege walls, which cast visible shadows as you look down from the top of the fortress. And, in the debris of the Roman camp, excavators have found Roman dice made of bone—the spots on the dice are placed in the same order as those on modern dice.

Imagine how by day you may have little time to look out toward the shimmering waters to the east and northward to Jerusalem—the Dead Sea in the first century came much closer to the foot of the fortress than it does now. Boats on the sea can bring supplies and reinforcements nearly to the Roman camps at the foot of your stronghold. You and your fellow rebels must know, by now, that the Temple, toward which your synagogue faces, has been destroyed, and nothing remains of its splendor but a smoldering ruin, sacked and desecrated. The priests' palaces are rubble, the priests are dead or refugees, and the gold *menorah* from the Temple has been paraded through Rome in triumph. In a ceramic pot in your small corner of the barracks you still hoard the coins that proclaim your cause—rebellion against the Romans. Do you know that in Rome, and throughout the Empire, the triumphant Romans have made coins that proclaim the fall of the Temple? These Roman coins depict the vanquished Judea as a pathetic woman, embellished with the words "Judea Capta."

The Last Stand

One afternoon, according to our guide, the Romans finally breached the walls. Clearly, their forces were positioned to march with hugely superior firepower into the citadel. That night, the leader of the Jewish zealot band spoke dramatically to the doomed community. He pointed out that they were about to meet a fate worse than death and that only one way was left for them to make a statement to posterity: to seize the joy of victory from Rome by a mass death before the victors could enslave, rape, and humiliate each of them. The Jews agreed to die honorably by one another's hands, avoiding suicide, which was forbidden by their faith. Parents cut their children's throats, and by agreement, a few men put all the others to death, finally drawing lots to see who would be last. The lots consisted of potsherds with a special mark—Yigael Yadin's archaeology expedition found a hoard of such marked potsherds, which he presented as proof that these were the very objects used that night. In the end, everyone died except for some women and children who hid from the leaders and told the tale. The last to die burned all the group's possessions, except for symbolic grain reserves that demonstrated that they had the wherewithal to continue their resistance. The next day, when the Roman troops marched in, they found only corpses.

Our guide concluded by reading the dramatic words of Flavius Josephus's description of the last night and the persuasion of the rebels to die rather than accept defeat.

FLAVIUS JOSEPHUS'S STORY

Flavius Josephus wrote the only contemporary historic account of events from the Hasmoneans until the fall of the Temple. The story of the fall of Masada, as I have told it here, is related in no other source. Josephus, like Herod, represents a successful fusion of Roman and Jewish culture in a single life. Born into the priestly class of Jerusalem, and educated in both Jewish and Classical Roman studies, he had been a military leader during the early years of the revolt, before the Romans destroyed the Temple in 70 c.e. During the revolt, he went over to the Roman side and became a favorite of Emperors Vespasian and Titus. During his later life, in Rome, he wrote several books, all directed toward the aim of making the Romans understand the Jews, fostering Roman respect for Jewish religion and culture, and justifying the revolt and his role in it.

I read about the history in Flavius Josephus's book, the *Jewish War*, which I had purchased in Masada's souvenir stand. Josephus's detailed account of the causes of the war and its factions and battles gave me a number of insights. His fusion of Jewish and Roman attitudes and cultures pointed me to the Jewish–Roman relationship of which I had been mainly ignorant and influenced me to want to know more. The book itself is simple and direct. Josephus is addressing a Roman (or hellenized) audience. He seems motivated neither by a wish to exhort people to religious acts nor by a wish to make or proliferate myths, but by a spirit of curiosity and need to know, which I feel also motivates many modern writers, myself included. At the same time, he's a Jew, from the community that he describes, and a participant in some of the events, with a need to justify his own actions and those of his fellow-Jews; he thus has a point of view as both insider and outsider. Most of all, he presents direct observations of the countryside, the cities, the people, the rulers, some of the battles, and the religious disagreements that otherwise seem so distant in time and spirit. Even his account of the three main religious factions —Pharisees, Saduccees, and Essenes—seems to come from personal acquaintance with members of these groups.

Secondary sources all use and comment about Flavius Josephus. To them, he represents a variety of important things; in particular, he wrote just between the biblical and the mishnaic traditions. Thus, his books constitute the last Jewish writing before the very different approach of the rabbinic tradition. Of course, there could have been other writers whose works were lost due to not being as interesting to later Christians, but that's no use to me. In a modern book, *Zakhor*, the author Yosef Hayim Yerushalmi summarizes Josephus's work: ". . . after the close of the biblical canon the Jews virtually stopped writing history. Flavius Josephus marks the watershed. Writing in a not-uncomfortable Roman exile after the destruction of the Second Temple, sometime between 75 and 79 C.E., Josephus published his account of the *Jewish War* against Rome and then went on to an elaborate summation of the history of his people in the *Jewish Antiquities*."

HEROD AND ROME

At the beginning of this story is Herod the Great, the first Roman client King of Judea, whose reign began in 37 B.C.E. Herod applied enormous vision, organizational talent, and determination to create a Jewish-Roman state. A vast and famous restoration of the Second Temple was his most conspicuous public work. Today, the Western Wall—actually a fortification of the Temple platform—is the last trace of this Temple and probably the most famous Herodian structure still standing. However, Herod's influence remains visible throughout Israel in the form of many other buildings and monuments, which extend from Mediterranean ports in the west to the borders of the Palestinian territories and Jordan in the east; from Galilee in the north to the ancient trade routes between Arabia and Egypt across the Negev desert in the south. Beyond Israel, Herod built more, but my narrative remains inside Israel's current borders.

The story of Herod's reign is a key to understanding the Jewish-Roman interaction and how it propelled the migration of Jews throughout the Mediterranean and later throughout Europe. During most of his reign, Herod succeeded in keeping the Jews happy by observing Jewish taboos in Jerusalem and kept the Romans happy by building cities with pagan Temples and institutions elsewhere. However, from his death in 4 B.C.E. until the rebellion in 66 C.E., the Romans did not handle things with the same level of skill and tact. By practicing their standard treatment of a colony, they had infuriated most of the Jews and increased friction between Judea (the Jewish state) and Rome.

Roman colonizers, who put Herod in power, handled their conquests like Wall Street raiders handling a merger of two corporations. Sometimes they came in by invitation or at least without much of a struggle; sometimes they sent in the legions and performed a hostile takeover. Colonization, with all its economic and social implications, developed during the time of the Roman republic—which ended during Herod's lifetime—and flourished as the republic gave way to the empire, and motives of profit, power, and capital investment drove Roman expansion.

As a part of each takeover, the Romans introduced their advanced technology throughout their new domain and also leveraged whatever technology they discovered there. Two such interchanges illustrate technology-sharing in Roman Judea:

- *Water systems.* Herod borrowed from the Romans' ingenious inventions for irrigation and for urban water supplies to create Roman-style systems of aqueducts, underground pipes, cisterns, reservoirs, and water-powered mills. Meanwhile, in desert areas south of Jerusalem, the Romans encountered the Nabateans, whose original systems of terraces conserved the rare but copious desert rainfall for later irrigation. Romans added this technology to their repertoire, introducing similar systems into their colonies in North Africa. Today the traces of such Roman water systems are still visible in Masada, Sepphoris, Emmaeus, and Caesarea.

- *Glass blowing.* Artisans in Sidon and Tyre in the first century B.C.E. based their invention of glass blowing on older glass-forming techniques. Romans and their subject peoples immediately loved blown glass because they found it beautiful, affordable, and practical. Artisans elsewhere in the empire adopted the processes, and so a product from a colony became a commercial success for the "parent corporation." Today, glass appears in almost every museum of Roman art and civilization; the Eretz Israel Museum in Tel Aviv includes not only a collection of glass objects, but also information on the technology, including the remnants of a glass-blowing shop and crafts demonstrations.

The Romans also had a habit of identifying and co-opting the existing power structure; that is, a certain class of rich and powerful people in each culture. If the old top management (say, a king) didn't want to give in, they were willing to get rid of that part of the structure and work within the remaining system to ensure profitability and compliance. Often, the co-opted class ended up richer and more powerful in the expanded context than they had been before the takeover. Loyal members of this class also received Roman citizenship, which meant they could rise in the corporation (excuse me, empire) at large. Often, this strategy meant that very few Roman troops were needed to rule an area; the local management could be trusted to keep the tribute taxes coming in. Occasionally, able individuals of non-Roman ancestry were even able to rise to be CEO (excuse me, emperor). Septimus Serverus, born in Africa, managed to come up through the ranks in this way, and rise to emperor, because the earlier emperor, Marcus Aurelius, befriended him.

As in a corporate takeover, the Romans expected conquered people to adopt not only their government and technology, but also to follow their corporate culture, adopt their values, and buy into their mission. At the same time, the Romans were completely willing to tolerate a certain continuity of old customs and values. The most important obligation was to accept the cultural elements that the Romans thought the most *civilized*—in particular, to accept Roman gods and (later) the Roman cult of worshiping the emperor. In most places, conquered people happily added new gods and new practices to their old ways without conflict. This strategy didn't work as expected when the Romans under Pompey conquered Jerusalem in 63 B.C.E. and began to control the weak and ineffective Hasmonean kings. Within a few years the Romans deposed the Hasmonean king and appointed Herod; this worked for a while, but not indefinitely. The Jews were categorically unwilling to worship the Roman gods or add their symbols and images to Jewish holy places— especially not the Temple. Unlike Greeks or Celts or Assyrians, who didn't mind adding Roman gods to their list or building a few new cult sites, the Jews were utterly unreceptive to the Roman process called syncretism; that is, combining a variety of religions and forms of worship and adding Roman gods to the local mix.

Even when the Romans gave up demanding to place statues of

pagan gods in the Temple, they had difficulties. The most respected class in Judean society was the priests, who weren't necessarily tempted by the rewards the Romans offered. Some priests took advantage of their position to make money and live high, but many were idealistic, and wealth and Roman-style power couldn't buy their loyalty. The Hasmoneans, formerly known as the Maccabees, were both kings and priests. About one hundred years earlier they had fought for their independence (you know, the Chanukah story), and since then had been doing quite a bit of conquering on their own. Still earlier, the Jews had begun their experience with hellenistic ideas, beginning with the conquest of Alexander the Great almost three hundred years earlier. Ever since, Jewish factions had argued for and against the introduction of new ideas, especially Greco-Roman ideas and philosophies. All this created an environment hostile to the Roman colonial practice of developing an indigenous class of ambitious nobles or merchants eager to adopt Roman ways, support Roman goals, and work for Roman rewards.

Nevertheless, as they marginalized the Hasmoneans, the Romans expected their usual strategy to work. First in Herod's father and then in Herod, they found the type of flexible but firm management they were used to. Herod tried to keep the Romans happy by placing Roman Temples in peripheral cities outside the sacred range of Jerusalem—particularly in his new Mediterranean port Caesarea. He tried to keep the Jews happy by protecting the sacred Temple from incursions by Roman gods (with a few slip-ups). Mostly, he did keep them all happy, at least as long as he lived.

Herod's Reputation

Archaeologists who dig in Israel often present the contrast between their findings and Herod's traditional reputation as a terrible tyrant. Herod's negative reputation particularly results from his late-life paranoia and jealousy of his sons, as well as from various Christian traditions and myths (where he also tends to be confused with one of his successors, also named Herod, who allowed Salome to dance for the head of John the Baptist among other things). Modern writers find much to admire about his building projects, his introduction of Roman architecture and engineering, and his success at organizing the kingdom and developing the Judean economy. He kept up a delicate balance among conflicting interests, particularly between the various Jewish factions and the demands of his Roman overlords. His strengths balanced serious weaknesses—he lacked legitimacy, he often put loyalty to Rome above consideration for Jewish tradition, he was indisputably ruthless in holding power, and he believed relatively exaggerated accusations against his wife and sons, which led him to kill them.

Herod's rise to power had begun when his father Antipater attained great power as the highest subordinate and political ally in the struggle for succession of the last Hasmonean king. Antipater was an able leader, whom the Romans slowly entrusted with more and more power. This power allowed him to appoint Herod and his other son Phaesal to high positions; Herod began his career as administrator of affairs in the Galilee. During this time, as the Romans lost confidence in the Hasmoneans, Herod's demonstrated ability and ambition caused them to trust him. In 44, Julius Caesar died. From 40–37 Antigonus, a Hasmonean, served as both high priest and king, but he was weak. Herod, who had sided with one of the other Hasmonean claimants to power, fled with his family first to Masada, then to Petra, on to Alexandria. As the last Hasmoneans were quarreling, Herod went to Rome, where Antony had Herod proclaimed King of Judea by the Roman Senate.

At this point, Herod demonstrated his willingness to work with his Roman sponsors, the general Mark Antony and the young Octavian. In a procession up the Capitoline Hill, Herod participated in a sacrifice to Jupiter, Juno, and Minerva, placing the senate's decree in their temple. Mark Antony and Octavian led the procession. When he got back to Jerusalem, Herod had to fight to take over the Judean kingdom. He also survived challenges from Rome. As Antony and Octavian slugged it out for control, Herod stayed loyal to Antony, but managed to patch things up when, in defeat, Antony and Cleopatra committed suicide. He went to Rhodes, where humbly, he once again met Octavian, who accepted him and even enlarged his kingdom.

The Jews of Herod's kingdom had religious problems with his appointment. There was always a concern because his mother was not Jewish, and Antipater had come to Judea from Idumaea, a region that the Hasmoneans had conquered and subjected to forcible conversion a generation earlier; thus the ultra-orthodox of the day referred to him as "half-Jewish." Herod's participation in the pagan rites in Rome was another problem. During his reign, he sometimes contributed to the construction of pagan temples in other parts of the Roman Empire, and tolerated or encouraged the building of pagan as well as Jewish institutions in his own kingdom—Herod's constructions at Banias, in the northern Golan area, represent such pagan projects. These acts aroused skepticism about Herod's commitment to the religion. The question of his commitment is still unresolved. Some current scholars see in Herod's private palaces a commitment to Jewish culture because he used no human or animal forms, and dismiss his behavior elsewhere. Others say that although his building projects within the Jewish state conformed to a Jewish identity, his pagan temple projects are evidence of insincerity.

Herod replaced the last contenders from the Hasmonean line. Almost from the start, Herod's power was enormous, as the Romans entrusted him with all responsibility for civil administration, taxation, law courts, military leadership, and control of the religious establishment; as a client-king, he lacked only independent control of foreign policy and full rights to mint coins. Economically, Herod immediately began vast building projects in support of his trade policies. In turn, the wealth coming in from the expanding trade with Rome and the East enabled him to afford more and more new building projects. Under the Hasmoneans there had been much territorial expansion, and Herod presided over an ever-increasing land area, including Judea/Jerusalem, the coastal plain and port cities, the Galilee, areas east of the Jordan River (now a part of modern Syria and Jordan), and the Nabatean and Idumaean desert regions.

Herod's personal life included some things that improved his position, and others that antagonized his subjects. Herod's marriage to the Hasmonean princess Mariamme was supposed to confirm his legitimacy and secure the succession. Her noble ancestry—her father was an heir to the Hasmonean kingship—was also supposed to help make up for his own questionably Jewish background. But he distrusted her relatives and the marriage thus caused friction with them. He executed quite a few of them as coldly as he had executed many members of the old Council of Elders, or Sanhedrin. Finally, he gave way to mad rages and murdered his wife and her sons.

Herod was a great economic innovator and political maneuverer. He developed commerce between various local parts of the empire, creating new trade routes through his territory. He appointed priests who did not threaten him, but he protected and expanded rituals and sacrifices as he rebuilt the Temple. Although he destroyed or weakened the old power structure, even arranging the execution or assassination of many of its members, his dynastic alliance with Mariamme was a recognition of their popular appeal and residual power. Herod also was very savvy about the political situation in Rome and managed to stay allied with the changing cast of Roman leaders; his time in office corresponded with the transition from republic to empire, and he worked the changes in his favor. His policies fully supported the Roman reward and tribute system, with spoils distributed both locally and to Rome.

The Madness of Herod the Great

Herod had directed the creation of Masada's impressive palaces, baths, storehouses, cisterns, and, above all, fortifications, for which Josephus gives two reasons. First, he feared that the Jewish masses might depose him and restore his predecessors, so he wanted a place where he could flee. Second, he feared that Antony, the Roman now in Egypt, would agree to Queen Cleopatra's demand that he give her the Judean kingdom for her own, so he wanted a secure citadel. Despite these seemingly rational motives, the fortress mentality revealed at Masada also suggests Herod's obsessions and fears.

In the end, Herod messed it all up. He became insanely jealous of his wife and of two of his own very popular sons. Driven by this mania, he ordered her death. Flavius Josephus provides much detail on the madness of Herod, particularly on the specifics of his assassination of Mariamme. First, Herod developed wild suspicions, having her watched and harassed. He seemed out of control even to his loyal supporters. After a struggle with his own divided feelings, he ordered her death. Immediately regretting his action, he sat beside her decaying body and talked to it, unable to accept the finality of his act. He continued to act out his jealousy of her sons, who, after all, had a better claim to the throne than he did and who fulfilled the ancient view that nobility of behavior and demeanor is inherited along with nobility of blood lines.

Herod's final, disastrous destruction of Mariamme's sons during his last illness also provides insight into his mad streak. Although he had sent the sons to be educated in Rome, giving them an opportunity to continue his connections to the real power structure there, he never forgave them for their natural and inherited gifts. He was especially infuriated because the public loved them for their Hasmonean ancestors and for their personal charisma. At the end of his life, they showed enormous promise as the popular successors of his power and leadership. Unfortunately, he had other sons who were neither good nor well-liked.

When it became apparent that Herod soon would die, his various sons had a sort of race to see who could turn the mad old man against the others and thus take over the kingdom. At the very end, the oldest and most jealous, ambitious, unpopular, and, above all, disinherited son prevailed. This son of Herod's first wife, left over from Herod's pre-kingly days, convinced King Herod to kill his and Mariamme's aristocratic and popular sons—his own half-brothers—so that he could replace them in the line of succession. With the half-brothers out of the way, this son successfully exploited Herod's madness. Herod not only made his will in favor of this schemer and other less popular and not-so-well-connected sons, he specified that his relatively solid kingdom be divided among them.

During his long reign, Herod had cultivated no Judean leadership to maintain future productive interactions of the two cultures. His legacy thus was not a solid Jewish–Roman synthesis. The weak, unpopular son who followed him was only the beginning in a series of ineffective kings, who had little influence with appointed Roman rulers. The basis for the disaster of the rebellion of 66–70 c.e. was in place.

Herod's Fortress

Herod's fortress at Masada reflected his character as a sometimes-mad, sometimes-brilliant leader. As indicated in Flavius Josephus, the threat from Queen Cleopatra of Egypt, another Roman client, was real, not a madman's imagined danger. Herod apparently hoped that he could use Masada as an escape refuge if she invaded. He also prepared the fortress for the eventuality of a civil insurrection directed against him; in this, he appears to be verging on a more paranoid view of his relationship with his subjects. At Masada, Herod evidently was concerned with both security and comfortable living in his refuge from his potential enemies. The site of Masada was in the desert, conveniently close to Jerusalem and not far from Herod's ancestral lands. Earlier, during the confusing year before his trip to Rome and his appointment as the Roman client king, he had already used the site as a refuge. Herod also built another major palace and refuge at Herodium. (Although I would have liked to see it, its position inside Palestinian Authority territory makes it impractical to visit in today's political environment, where tourists' cars are often stoned by hostile locals.)

Masada's builders constructed an incredible palace on the side of the cliff, with a single entry that would also enable a defense against his own troops if even they attacked him. Who knows if this was mad or realistic? At Masada today, beyond the fortifications, you can visit this secluded pleasure palace. You descend a long, steep stairway to a series of beautiful terraces placed in sequence down the side of the cliff. Half-columns are carved into the vertical rock faces, with open platforms supported by tour-de-force Roman engineering. The terraces occupy the cliff-side where the angle of the punishing afternoon sun would be most favorable, so that the royal family could sit in the shade enjoying the view of the Dead Sea and the rugged landscape.

On top of the cliff, water-storage tanks held water collected from nearby wadis. Herod's builders devised a method whereby an aqueduct crossed the deep valley from the higher hills opposite from the Dead Sea–side of Masada. Occasional heavy rains pelt the area, and Roman engineering contrived aqueducts to channel water from nearby streams. During rainstorms, the aqueducts carried the water to underground reservoirs controlled from the cliff-top fortress. Soldiers from the garrison, rather than sitting idle, could spend the days hauling the water up from these reservoirs into several cisterns within the fortress walls, which held several years' supply. Today these appear as cavernous holes in the rock.

Also on top of the plateau, a maze-like network of enormous store rooms, now reconstructed, held grain, weapons, raw materials for making more weapons, and other essentials, while additional luxuries abounded in the administrator's palace as well as in Herod's private quarters. A traditional Roman bath with hot and cold tubs, tiled floors, and other Roman amenities ensured that he and his loyal troops could comfortably hold out for a long siege. You can see the elaborate arrangement of tile and pipes that carried steam to heat the bathing and steambath areas, which resemble the Roman baths at many other sites throughout the former Empire.

The double exterior walls with lookouts and garrison barracks inside them protected the whole fortress—another classic Roman design. Only a highly visible path, the Snake Path, was really feasible for access. The last defenders put Herod's plans to the test. They used the large supply of food Herod had stocked, which had been preserved by desert conditions; the water cisterns enabled them to store a supply good for several more years. They also used some of the weapons that Herod had stockpiled. The walls and ramparts protected them from attack by anything but major force. In 73, when the Romans finally attacked the last Jewish rebels there, their only route into the fortress was a massive build-up of the ramp on the high side opposite the Dead Sea. Thus, Herod's plan for an emergency refuge seems to have been a very effective one, even if these palaces and fortifications also reflected the paranoid feelings that eventually overwhelmed him.

Probably Herod never visited the vastly improved fortress at Masada in his later life, to see its marvel of engineering and Roman architecture, but perhaps knowing it was there gave him some relief from the stress that overtook him in the final, mad days of his reign. His fortresses expressed both strains of his personality—he was simultaneously a skillful leader and planner, and a fearful, insecure tyrant.

MODERN SYMBOL AND MYTH

Like a series of Russian dolls, Masada provides a new face each time you probe, yielding insights into Israeli history, culture, and politics. Initially, Masada impressed me simply as a first-class historic tourist attraction in a splendid natural setting. The once-inaccessible site now features a very good archaeology park surrounded by lots of amenities, such as a large parking lot, a snack bar, a restaurant, and clean rest rooms with running water. Using the cable car allows visitors to skip the walk up the Snake Path, but even the path is now smoothed and leveled.

Tourists like us see Herod's palaces and the site of the Jews' last battle with the Romans, but like everything in Israel, they're invested with other layers of meaning, as well. People and books refer to the slogan "Masada will not fall again." However, interpretations of this phrase often conflict with one another. Masada symbolizes a last refuge where enemies besieged the Jews. Masada inspires a fight to the death for freedom rather than the acceptance of slavery. Masada generates a cry to stand up to tyrants, to fight rather than compromise, or to make an ultimate commitment to an ideal. Sometimes the final suicide is central to the symbolism; sometimes it is de-emphasized. For some, the victory of Rome symbolizes the impotence of Masada's defenders. For others, the important symbol is the strength of purpose of the last nine hundred holdouts, whose defeat required a major commitment from the world's mightiest empire. Many symbolic references are intentionally vague, leaving the choice to the hearer or reader. Like our guide, many writers like to call the last-standers "Zealots" even though Flavius Josephus calls them "*Sicarii*"; that is, they de-emphasize that, although pious Jews, the defenders were not only religious fanatics, but also bandits.

Several roads lead to the literal Masada. The map around Masada reflects recent history. The road we took in 1997, leading from the south end of the Dead Sea, is magnificently engineered. This was the only land route before 1967, when Jordan held the northwestern shore of the Dead Sea. The road we took in 1998, from the north, comes from Jerusalem and Jericho and follows the Dead Sea shore line, which is continually receding as Israeli irrigation projects deplete the waters of the Jordan River and the Sea of Galilee that feed it. A major purpose of this road is access to Masada, although it serves a number of bathing spas along the seashore as well. Whether you come along the Dead Sea shore from the north or from the south, you must first descend into the amazing depth of the rift to well below sea level, and then follow a final spur of road to the parking lots surrounding the very steep Masada hilltop. Finally, you must either climb the Snake Path or take the cable car.

Less obvious tracks, perhaps not suitable for ordinary passenger vehicles, crossed the Judean hills and provided access to Masada before the independence war. These are now unmaintained, and probably dangerous, because they are in Palestine Authority territory. Another approach to the high side of Masada, a back road from Arad, takes a completely different route, with a parking lot near the Roman siege ramp. No automobile route joins the two sides, which are separated by the extremely steep cliffs. I have heard or read various stories about the different roads and tracks. Sometimes the early Zionist youth organizations came by boat across the Dead Sea and then climbed from the shore up the mountain.

The touristic nature of the place obscures the history and symbolism. On ordinary days, the parking lot on the Dead Sea side is full of tourist buses. The arduous Snake Path that challenged generations of Israeli pioneers, even taking some lives, is now paved with stair-steps, water fountains, and modern conveniences. The cable car ascends in ten minutes, not counting the wait in line. At the top, huge crowds follow tour guides or wander alone among the restored excavations: Herod's splendid palace, Roman mosaics, the Roman baths, cisterns, defense walls, the Jewish ritual bathing pool, the synagogue, Roman storehouses (where our guide said the defenders of 73 found hundred-year-old supplies perfectly preserved by the un-earthly Dead Sea climate), and a Byzantine monastic church, all documented in the National Park brochure you receive when you pay your admission. The artifacts and coins from the excavation are displayed in museums elsewhere, but you can buy copies or books about them at the gift shop at the foot of the cable car.

From an ancient perspective, Masada presents a concrete example of the intersection of Roman and Jewish culture over the period from Herod to the destruction of the Temple. Masterful Roman engineering produced the fortress-like walls and a cliff-hanging palace, and Herod's Roman taste inspired beautiful Roman-era buildings and mosaics—without representations of human or animal figures, because of Herod's piety. The Israeli National Park Service and guides like the one we followed provide considerable information about this perspective, including many reminders of the small band of Jews who defied the Romans after the destruction of the Temple, but the brochure doesn't have space for the other levels of the story.

Historic Attitudes

On the literal level, also, the history of Masada from Herod to the revolt was recorded uniquely by Flavius Josephus. However, Flavius Josephus himself is a bit of a paradox, and there are various ways of interpreting his credibility. His presentation is dramatic and vivid, particularly the speech of the leader at the final hour. Unfortunately, Flavius himself was a renegade. He had once served the Jewish cause, but had changed his loyalty and become a Roman military man after a failed suicide pact with his beleaguered colleagues. His sympathy for the rebels is notable, and he always refers to them as *Sicarii*, assassins. Conventional wisdom is that history is written by the winners. In the case of Flavius Josephus, it's more complicated than that—not wanting to be a loser, he changed sides, and he wrote to justify himself and his people both to other Jews and to Romans.

Recent preoccupation with Masada began in the last century, when people looked for the "real" Masada in Flavius Josephus's account. First, Christian explorers satisfied themselves that the particular rocky point overlooking the Dead Sea was the site in the history books. Later, Zionists used the idea of Masada as a rallying point. Zionist myth-makers created versions of the Masada story to be taught in the earliest years of school. From the 1920s to the 1940s, adolescents climbed up as a life-risking rite of passage. Its importance crystallized when a Zionist poem, written in 1927, provided the slogan "Masada shall not fall again." Several generations of pioneers from the 1930s to the 1950s toiled up the un-improved Snake Path to make their commitment to the Zionist ideals they believed to be embodied there. This gave rise to the attitude that is reflected in the park's documentation. The holdouts at Masada became a model for the "new Jews" who took up arms in their own defense, part of the Zionist reproach to the old ghetto mentality.

The myth developed along with Zionism. It occupied the center of Zionist youth organizations in the 1940s and helped motivate the Jewish armies, many of them outgrowths of the youth groups, as they struggled in 1948. In the new state, these stories combined with other tales of patriotic heroism, and despite the danger from the Jordanians nearby, difficult treks continued. Archaeological exploration of Masada energized the myths. From 1971, the National Park with its new cable car access to the site enabled more Israelis to see Masada and encouraged foreign tourists to be exposed to its important message. At the same time, the challenge of climbing up the mountain was vastly reduced to the point where a tourist guide's manual suggested that guides slow the hikers down to help them feel they have accomplished more.

The myths helped the citizens of the new nation forge a sense of identity. In the context of the Holocaust, they saw Israel as the last hope of the Jews of the world, emphasizing the struggle, not the suicide, of the ancient last-standers. Still more recently, the mentality that the Holocaust must never be allowed to happen again has emphasized the suicide as the only dignified choice, rather than focusing on the struggle of the last defenders. Because of Masada's significance to the Israelis and because of its history for Zionist youth outings and pre-military training, inductees of the Israel Defense Forces, between about 1950 and 1991, marched up the mountain to take their oath of loyalty. Today, you can see an amphitheater beyond the hills on the Arad side, where military functions still take place. Because virtually every Israeli serves in this force just after high school, the Army experience unites and socializes Israeli young people, and thus the oath-taking represents an important symbol for every citizen. However, other venues have joined Masada in today's military rituals.

Yigael Yadin: Mythical Myth-Maker

Yigael Yadin (1917–1984) contributed to the myth and also played a role in it. Yadin's first reputation was as a war hero; he served as military adviser and strategist to Ben-Gurion during the Independence War from 1947–1948. After the war, Ben-Gurion charged him with secret negotiations with several Arab rulers. Later, in the seventies, he held high political office and played a controversial role in Israel's multi-party system.

Between these periods of public service, Yadin studied archaeology and became an influential archaeologist—which was how he helped create the myth about Masada. As a professor at the Hebrew University in Jerusalem, he led famous expeditions to the ancient Canaanite and Israelite city of Hatzor, to Dead Sea caves where he found Bar Kochba's letters, and, most dramatically, to Masada. He effectively publicized his findings in Israel and also worldwide, through books, visiting professorships, and lecture tours. He translated and interpreted the "War Scroll" and other Dead Sea Scrolls, and conducted a successful negotiation to obtain three Dead Sea Scrolls that had been taken out of Israel.

Yadin, through his archaeology, lectures, and publications, consciously contributed to Israel's emerging national identity. He made sure that his expeditions served as documentation of Masada's fall in 73 c.e. and of

Bar Kochba's revolt ending in 135. He demonstrated a driving resolve to discover consistency between archaeological evidence and his expectations. His personality and some of his accomplishments almost certainly contributed to Mitchner's portrayal of an archaeologist in *The Source*— thus providing another element of legend for the worldwide reading public.

Unaware as I was of Israeli culture, I first heard of Yadin when I visited Masada at the start of my trip. Later, on a visit to Hatzor I gained additional insight into his influence and reputation. We visited the small museum on the kibbutz adjacent to the Hatzor National Park, across from the partially excavated tell—that is, a mound with the remains of a multi-level ancient city. Although nineteenth century archaeologists had identified this tell with the biblical site Hatzor, Yadin's expedition was the first to conduct a major exploration there. The subject of the museum, in fact, is not only ancient Hatzor, but also Yadin and his expedition. The museum's ground floor displays poster-sized photos of Yadin and his team as they appeared in the mid-fifties during the excavations. The upper floor presents the history of the site, including local artifacts and copies of the most valuable finds (originals are in the Israel Museum in Jerusalem).

The museum is run by members of the kibbutz across the highway. When we arrived, the attendant volunteered to keep the museum open for at least half an hour after closing time, because he clearly wanted us to see it. He described how he and other kibbutz members had participated in the digging efforts around forty years ago, and identified the people in the photos of Yadin and his now-famous associates. His reverence for this great man demonstrated Yadin's reputation and went far beyond my expectations of what ordinary people might think about archaeology. When I read more about Yadin and his accomplishments, I discovered that his personality and deep commitment to biblical archaeology had indeed inspired Israelis from all levels of society to identify with his searches and to incorporate the archaeological findings into their identity and their sense of ownership of their country's distant past. During the early sixties, hundreds of volunteers participated in the Yadin's Masada excavations. Hundreds of thousands of fans awaited his claim to have validated the myths about the Zealots' last stand.

I read Yadin's book to learn more—what parts of the Masada legend were true? All was true, said the book. The expedition, it said, discovered the physical evidence to support Flavius Josephus's information, which, before archaeologists excavated the site, was considered rather suspiciously to be a literary legend. Yadin described how his expedition was much publicized, with a huge number of volunteers. He described how during the expedition, he announced findings of incredible confirmation of Flavius Josephus's story. He found hoards of coins with the legend "Freedom of Zion" explicitly dated from the revolt period, piles of partially burned personal belongings, religious scrolls related to the Zealot brand of Judaism, and several burned bodies, which he identified as the last-standers. He interpreted the writing on several potsherds as proof of Flavius Josephus's tale that the last-standers had drawn lots to see who would be the last to die—stating that these were the very lots that had determined the Zealots' final destiny. He dramatically described three bodies found in the ruins.

While Flavius Josephus identified the holdouts on the mountain as members of the Sicarii, a band of terrorist assassins, the Zionist myth called them Zealots and turned them from bandits to heroes. And while scholars have searched other contemporary Jewish and Roman sources— such as other historians or the *Mishnah* and the Talmud—for further references to the siege and suicides, their search has been without success. Yadin never dwelt on these questions. He ignored the distinction between Sicarii and Zealots, their dubious past as bandits and assassins, or their raids on the neighboring village. He explained away why only a few bodies, not the full nine hundred, were still present. He ignored the fact that scientific age-determination of the few skeletons showed it to be implausible for them to have been Zealots. Despite arguments from other scholars, he prevailed in convincing the public that he had found what he wanted to find.

But now for more of the curmudgeon's view. Flavius Josephus is the only source of the story of the mass suicide at Masada, but he is not the only writer from that time—no other Roman or Jewish historian of the first century or soon afterward so much as mentions this event. Yadin and many others insisted that Masada was a symbol for our time, the symbol of a refusal to live as slaves. But the critics point out that similar suicide stories are repeated in many accounts of contemporary events other than those of Flavius Josephus, making it possibly just a literary convention. Critics point out how several parts of the contemporary legend are over-interpretations or even distortions of the evidence that is available. From a variety of viewpoints, Yadin's colleagues and critics dispute his belief that the suicides occurred as Flavius Josephus recorded. They question his view that the marked pottery fragments were the exact objects used by the desperate and besieged garrison to determine the order of their suicide, and question his claim that the skeletons he excavated were members of this last holdout. Recently, some of his former colleagues at Masada have revealed that they expressed these doubts even during the expedition. The transcripts of the discussions that took place each evening among the staff show how he persisted in interpreting facts to suit his theories and myths, even when his peers pointed out serious difficulties with these views.

From the point of view of an outsider, even with the understanding of Jewish customs, I find the oddest part of the Israeli mythopoeic behavior to be the state funeral that was held for the bodies that Yadin's expedition found. Somehow, such public ceremony for people whose death took place nineteen hundred years ago seems to turn the usual rationale upside down. Since the main beneficiaries of a funeral are the survivors, it's an indication of how modern Israelis view themselves. Perhaps the need to believe has prevented the modern proponents of this legend from carefully examining the evidence. Perhaps, indeed, the Roman legions and auxiliary troops marched up their siege ramp and defeated the last holdouts by their superior force, and the suicide tale is simply a good story for our time.

In the last few years, sociologists and journalists have examined the discrepancies between Flavius Josephus's account and the myth that galvanized the Zionists, tracing its origins and its power to inspire them. The intellectual heirs of Yigael Yadin have quietly expressed their doubts about his claim to have proved the truth of the myth and have re-evaluated some of his evidence. New articles are constantly being published, and the park curators are working on new ways to present the site to the numerous visitors. If you go to Masada, you'll find that there is always another way to look at this story—like another tiny doll nested in the Russian souvenir.

Background of
the Diaspora

Before I continue my travel narrative, I want to offer some general background about Israel's history, geography, languages, and cultures, and how the relationships of people in this hotbed of conflict over a crucial crossroads was at the root of the eventual Diaspora. It's difficult to identify a logical start for the contemplation of this broad topic, so I'm starting at the beginning—that is, if you will, when Abraham and Sarah arrived in Israel—but in a brief version of the story.

ISRAEL BEFORE THE ROMANS

You are probably familiar with at least some of the history of the Jews. Biblical histories describe Abraham and Sarah's start in Mesopotamia and follow tribal wanderings, rivalries, dynasties, hostile neighbors, conquests, a period of exile in Babylonia, and the rebuilding of the Temple. After that, historians trace more rivalries, dynasties, hostile neighbors, conquests by Greeks, a brief freedom under the Hasmoneans, and then conquest by the Romans.

Biblical stories begin with an account of how a nomadic, pastoral people conquered the land, overcame the Canaanite rulers, and began to lead a settled farm life there. A conflict always existed between the settled people and the Jews to whom the land had been promised—as they said. The Bible itself says that Abraham came from far away, that the Jews left during a famine, lived in Egypt, came back and conquered the land once more, held it for some centuries, and were dispersed after a conquest by Babylon.

Scholars report that reasonable evidence indicates that such shepherds and farmers inhabited the region at the time, but their exact relationship to later Jewish history is subject to debate. Archaeological evidence tells us that the early occupants lived in fortified cities at Gezer, Hatzor, Meggido, Dan, and Arad—all places you can visit, incidentally. Eventually, a Jewish kingdom with its capital in Jerusalem emerged to dominate the land of Israel and all of these strongholds. There is not only material evidence of these biblical cities but also Egyptian inscriptions that mention the cities and the Pharaohs who conquered them. Although the biblical Exodus story cannot be scientifically supported, contact between the peoples is well documented. The Egyptians dominated the area and threatened Jewish interests because the Jews occupied a critical crossroads between the Egyptians and the centers of civilization farther East.

Archaeologists today agree on the broad outlines and dispute most of the details. Whether the Jews were entirely "foreign" to the Canaanites and how they took over the territory is not clear, although during the second millennium B.C.E. there were clearly a number of different people, including diverse Jewish tribes, in the region. By about the tenth century B.C.E., archaeology shows that the fortified cities of the region were rebuilt under a centralized authority and further consolidated in the following hundred years. Many experts believe that this tenth-century unification was centered in Jerusalem, although there is some dispute about whether there were "really" kings named David and Solomon in that century. But by the ninth century, they say, Jewish domains definitely existed in the region, including a major Temple cult and central authority in Jerusalem.

Modern archaeology has shown the extent of this kingdom, which was quickly lost by the successors of the ninth-century rulers. At the Israeli National Park sites of Hatzor, Meggido, and Gezer I saw huge stone gates of the same type in each city, said to be evidence of the centralized planning of these kings. Several Canaanite temples with "horned" altars in biblical style have come to light. At Tel Dan, a Canaanite gate is near the altar where King Jeroboam supposedly sacrificed to a Golden Calf. At Jaffa, there is evidence of the port through which Solomon's men imported the cedars of Lebanon for the Temple and carried on commerce with Egypt. Similar evidence exists in the southern city of Maresha, which later reverted to the Edomites, as well as in the north toward the border with Sidon and Tyre. As I write this, archaeologists are at work at Tel Dor, near Haifa, unearthing remains of a port city with a similar gate, demonstrating new evidence for the power and extent of this briefly lived kingdom.

The First Diaspora: Babylon

In the seventh century B.C.E., Babylonians destroyed Jerusalem and initiated the "captivity" of biblical record—evidence from Babylonian archaeology supports this story. Less than a century later, Cyrus the Great of Persia conquered the region and allowed the Jews to return and rebuild the Temple in Jerusalem, though they did not regain their independence. However, not all of the Jews left Israel, and not all of the exiles returned: the Babylonian Jews can thus be regarded as the first Diaspora community. Subsequent biblical history is supported reasonably well by archaeological evidence, although there is something of a gap during the Persian period, just after the return from Babylonia, when the initial Second Temple was built.

Alexander the Great and Hellenism

In the fourth century B.C.E., Alexander the Great conquered much of the known world, spreading Greek culture throughout and beyond Asia Minor. As the aftermath of this conquest, Alexander's generals founded dynasties to rule the lands he had conquered, and generations of Greeks and Greek-influenced people began to dominate the cities of the region. Hellenism—that is, the influence of Greek culture—became the norm throughout Asia Minor and Egypt. Hellenistic cities based their civic life on Greek ideals for philosophy, education, sports, democracy, and general culture. The Jews were recognized for having a unique philosophy, and their ideas contributed to the continued development of Hellenistic culture at this time.

This cultural background is essential for understanding Jewish attitudes in Roman times. The Jews were affected by contact with the Greeks in the following ways:

• In Judea, Greek ideas and philosophy attained an important influence. Ruled by Alexander's successors, Judean cities, including Jerusalem, became hellenized. Successive governments recognized the hereditary high priest (selected from appropriate candidates, with the foreign rulers' approval) and the associated Council of Elders as the local supreme authority, but these hand-picked priests generally cooperated with the Hellenistic rulers and thus even the Temple rites seemed subject to Hellenistic ideas. A variety of protest groups and purist sects developed in response to this situation. In a sense, the conflict between Greek and Jewish ideas was never resolved.

• Judeans became victims of the conflicts between the various major powers of the region. In particular, the Seleucids to the east and the Ptolemies in Egypt competed to rule the Jewish state, and competing factions within Judea formed shifting alliances in pursuing their own power struggles.

• Outside Israel, Jews joined Greeks in forming colonies in the major cities of the region and developed an expatriate life. In Alexandria, Greek was the language of the Jewish community to such an extent that the Bible was translated into Greek. In this atmosphere, also, Jewish philosophy achieved an external reputation among other Hellenists.

The Maccabees, or Hasmoneans

After two centuries of Hellenism, in 150 B.C.E., for a number of reasons, the Jews rebelled against Alexander's successors, and the Maccabees, also called the Hasmoneans, assumed the role of both priests and kings. After a long struggle, they achieved independence for a state in Judea. They attempted a restoration of the ancient Jewish state, dominated by a religious life that centered around the Temple in Jerusalem and its festivals. The priestly class emerged as a major force and, like modern Israel, based ideals and national identity on earlier biblical traditions. At the same time, a variety of dissidents from the official religion interpreted biblical commandments in their own ways and therefore formed sects and factions that challenged the priestly authority.

Under the Hasmoneans, the Judeans conquered a variety of neighboring political units, expanding their borders and forcing a number of people to convert to Judaism and pay tithes to the Temple. To the south, they conquered Idumea, converted the peoples who had replaced its ancient Jewish inhabitants, and made the capital, Maresha, a Jewish city for the first time since the defeat of the ancient kingdoms. To the north, they strengthened their hold on Galilee. Meanwhile, a variety of great powers outside Judea were engaging in conflicts, and internal factions competing for rule of Judea made alliances with these external powers. Eventually, the Roman Empire became the supreme power in the area.

THE JEWS IN THE ROMAN EMPIRE

After a period of peaceful interference and alliances with various Hasmoneans, the Romans, under Pompey, finally conquered Judea, taking Jerusalem in 63 B.C.E. (Pompey sneaked a look into the guarded "holy of holies" of the Temple, but was disappointed.) The Romans began to exert control over the choice of Judean rulers, although they allowed a succession of contentious Hasmoneans to continue in power. However in about 40 B.C.E., they chose the non-Hasmonean King Herod, as we have seen—and Herod's appointment as king kicked off the maximum interaction of Jewish and Roman cultures.

Construction and Destruction

From Herod's time until the fall of the Temple, religious disputes, factionalism, and disagreements over principles divided Jewish society and disrupted civil and religious order in the state. The conflict was ongoing from the time of Alexander the Great, when the Jewish people initially came in contact with the Greeks. Some Jews wanted to absorb new ideas, modernize their lives, adapt the religion to changing times, and accommodate to the ways of their conquerors. Other factions always pushed back, insisting on one or another strict interpretation of Jewish law and custom (while often bitterly disagreeing with each other). The ruling parties varied in their points of view and in the effectiveness with which they could resist superior force. There were always many opportunists whose decisions were based on greed and desire for power—the fatal rivalry among Herod's sons was the most destructive of these competitions.

Occasionally, an extreme provocation—such as a demand that idolatry be practiced in the Temple—unified the Jews for a time. But often, the Jews reached a state of open warfare among themselves, including just before the Romans marched in, besieged, sacked, and practically leveled Jerusalem and destroyed the Temple in 70 C.E. A huge percentage of the Jews in Judea were killed or exiled by the war, and, at its end, their wealth and way of life were nearly destroyed. Many crafts and trades were never revived.

Herod's Two Cities

The contrast between Jerusalem and Caesarea illustrates how Herod separated Jewish from Roman culture, while promoting both. In building each city, he exploited the genius of Roman engineering, but with different sensitivities. In Jerusalem, he avoided all possible offense against Jewish tradition. He arranged for members of the priestly class to serve as construction workers to ensure ritual purity of the inner sanctum of the rebuilt Temple. To ensure that no hidden graves rendered the Temple platform impure, Herod's engineers either placed it on bedrock or built up a series of arched vaults, as you can see today in the tunnels near the Western Wall. Neither architectural decorations nor coins from the mints in Jerusalem showed his image. In contrast, in the new city of Caesarea, targeted for a primarily pagan population, Herod set no similar restrictions. He sponsored temples to Roman gods, built structures for Roman entertainment and bathing, and encouraged Roman sports that were distasteful or even hateful to the Jews. Statues, mosaics with human images, coins with pictures of gods, and other violations of the "graven image" prohibition appeared freely in this magnificent non-Jewish city, as you can still see when you visit Caesarea today.

During Herod's reign, many other cities in Judea besides Jerusalem underwent lavish construction projects, thus developing Roman cities and Roman infrastructure: walls and watchtowers, column-lined shopping malls, improved drainage, water supplied by Roman aqueducts, Roman baths, and a network of Roman roads. In cooperation with their Jewish clients after Herod, the Romans continued to build and embellish Jerusalem to their taste and standards, using the highest Roman engineering skills, while allowing the Jews, by special exemption from normal Roman law, to preserve certain independent religious and cultural customs.

After Herod's death in 4 B.C.E. there was an outbreak of chaos, with extremely weakened kings, and by 6 c.e. the Romans began to rule directly. His much less vigorous heirs were replaced by Roman appointees who lacked the cultural insight needed for long-term order. These individuals were sort of like Dilbert's pointy-haired boss—not too bright, but much too gullible about unconditional support for the policies of the management. Under their power and excesses, the Jews became harder and harder to govern.

Looking onward to the year 66 c.e., Caesarea was again at the heart of history when the situation in Roman Israel reached a flashpoint. Caesarea's Jews demonstrated against the erosion of their rights by the emperor Nero. Riots began, and non-Jews massacred large numbers of Jews in Caesarea. Violence rapidly spread to other cities. Jewish groups began an open rebellion, although most Jewish leaders encouraged peace and supported Rome. The rebel groups slowly gained political and popular support; however, until the last moment, the Jews remained bitterly divided. After a terrible struggle among these factions, Roman troops marched in and destroyed the Temple and all of Herod's accomplishments in Jerusalem. Meanwhile, in Caesarea, by now the major Roman administrative center, the gentiles prospered.

Thus in destroying Jerusalem, the Romans destroyed a Roman city. Afterward, the Romans reconstructed Jerusalem as a Roman-Pagan center, more Roman than ever. The Romans no longer recognized Judea as a separate province of the Empire, but administered it as part of the surrounding territories. They continued to maintain the centers of Roman administration and trade in the region and increased development of Roman cities such as Caesarea on the Mediterranean coast, and Tiberias, Sythopolis, and Sepphoris near the Sea of Galilee, and permitted Jews to worship outside the Temple as before, but the Jewish center was lost. In the travel narrative, we will see what is left of these cities.

From Hellenistic times until the fall of the Temple, increasing numbers of Jews took up residence outside of Judea and the adjacent territories such as Galilee. By the first century c.e., fair-sized Jewish communities lived in Babylon, Egypt, North Africa, Rome, and elsewhere. As a result, Jewish rituals to replace the annual pilgrimages to the Temple began to develop long before the Temple fell, external Jewish communities developed an identity, and non-Jews around the Mediterranean began to be at least somewhat aware of Jews and their differences. After 70 c.e., although Jews also still lived in Judea, the number of dispersed Jews increased and their customs slowly adapted to the loss of the Temple.

The Bar Kochba Revolt

A second rebellion, in 132 C.E., took place in the time of Hadrian. Under the leadership of Bar Kochba, Jews fought because Hadrian announced the plan to put a temple to Jupiter atop the ruined Temple Mount. The aftermath of the rebellion was that the Romans expelled the Jews from the ancient Judean kingdom, particularly banning them from Jerusalem. Many more Jews joined the dispersed communities around the Mediterranean or joined the Jewish communities in nearby Galilee just north of Judea. From the Bar Kochba revolt onward, the major sites of Jewish religious activities and rabbinic authority, dealing with issues such as the consolidation of the Talmud, were Galilee and Babylon.

Changes in the empire affected the Jews during these times. The Romans reorganized Herod's former independent jurisdiction as three provinces subordinate to the eastern Roman empire. Roman legions were quartered in these provinces to prevent uprisings and to fortify the eastern boundaries of Roman power, and Romans assumed control of commerce and growth, expanding important towns like Sythopolis and Caesarea. Jerusalem became a sort of a backwater. Even the name Judea was abolished: the Romans adopted the name Palestine to emphasize that Jews had no claim on their former kingdom. Elsewhere in the empire, the barbarian raids were starting, and the Roman capital moved from Rome to Byzantium under the Emperor Constantine in the fourth century C.E. The move brought the seat of power closer to Jerusalem, and as Christianity became the religion of the empire and of more and more of its people, Christians created pilgrimage sites and churches in Jerusalem and Galilee. With this Christian power, persecution of Jews emerged as a policy.

Finally, another series of conquests brought the end of Byzantine rule of Asia Minor. In the seventh century C.E., first Persians and then, almost immediately, Moslems conquered the entire region. Most of the Jews were expelled from Palestine and joined existing Jewish communities throughout Asia Minor and the Mediterranean region. Organized Jewish life in Israel as it existed under Romans and Byzantines effectively came to an end.

Sacred Books

For religious Jews and Christians, the production of sacred books and books that shed light on the sacred books was one of the most important trends of Roman times in Jerusalem, Galilee, and the Dead Sea region. From a religious person's point of view the most important process of the era occurred around the first and second centuries B.C.E., when respected authorities among the Jews determined which of the books from ancient times were to be regarded as sacred. This process, called canonization of the Bible, resulted in the definitions that are still in place. The five books of Moses were frozen in an accepted form and content. These sages also specified which remaining books of writings, psalms, wisdom, prophets, and so on were sacred, and which were not. Some books that the Jewish sages omitted, however, became part of the Christian canon later on.

Once the biblical decisions firmed up, Jewish writers of the period began to write other types of literature. These sources provide scholars with insights about the daily life and thought of the residents of Israel in Roman times. These other writings include several forms of literature:

- Pseudepigraphica represented the ongoing commitment to create sacred literature, knowing it was too late to be in the canon. To improve credibility, authors attributed their works to existing ancient authors. (*Pseudo* means "false" and *epigraphica* means "attribution.")

- The *Mishnah*, traditionally identified as the recording of ancient oral traditions going back to Moses, was written in the second century.

- The Christian New Testament has some sections that are in the Jewish tradition; later sections are in the emergent Christian tradition.

- Religious cult works, inscriptions, letters, and grave markings provide a variety of insights. These include works pertaining to the rule of the Essenes and other works found in caves near the Dead Sea since 1948.

- Secular writers of the later parts of this period also created works of Roman-Jewish history—particularly, Flavius Josephus and Philo of Alexandria.

From my point of view, both the process of writing and the product are interesting and important. I can't begin to absorb the huge number of primary sources, so I have relied on secondary sources. Scholars whose works I used are expert in sorting out lots of textual problems, the dates of the works (problematic indeed when it comes to pseudepigraphica), the accuracy of the works, the intention of the ancient authors, the classical and Hebrew sources, the question of lost originals and saved translations, and much more.

Contentious Date Labels

There are two ways to refer to dates before and after the beginning of the Christian era. For current dates, the choices are "A.D.," short for "Anno Domini," which means "the year of our Lord," or "C.E."—"Common Era." The date when the Second Temple fell could thus be designated "70 A.D." or "70 C.E." Similarly, "B.C." stands for "Before Christ" while "B.C.E." means "Before the Common Era." Thus, the death of King Herod could be expressed as either "4 B.C." or "4 B.C.E." (The Jewish calendar, with its totally different months and years, is confusing and unfamiliar.)

The B.C.–A.D. convention (obviously) is more common, representing, as it does, the Christian religious viewpoint. Some Christian authors, especially in academia, use the B.C.E.–C.E. convention, while some Jewish authors use B.C.–A.D. I have read that some Christians think that people who use B.C.E. and C.E. to label dates are engaging in some sort of denial. As far as I know, those who choose the alternate designation don't deny the existence of the Christian era or Christian beliefs, we just don't need to participate in Christian dogma every time we specify a date. But there is no way to get agreement on an issue that touches religious faith as this one does. A recent article on the subject in the *New York Times* inspired a variety of emotional letters. The magazine *Biblical Archaeology Review* allows each author to make his own decision and often publishes letters from readers criticizing this tolerance—sometimes criticizing it with great emotion.

I'm using B.C.E. and C.E. in this book. I'm aware that it will never replace the standard, but I have a soft spot for lost causes.

ISRAELI GEOGRAPHY, CLIMATE, AND GEOLOGY

Although Israel is a small country, it has a startling diversity of geography and climate, from Mediterranean coastal plains to rugged mountains, from fertile farming valleys to arid, sterile desert. Israel's desert scenery and small oases keep alive the connection to the early biblical stories and remind one of the ancient conflicts between nomadic herders of sheep and goats and more settled agricultural people. This memory fueled the commitment of fanatics in Herod's time and I think it continues to fuel the fanatics of today. Moreover, the beautiful roads that wind through the rugged territory, linking the valleys and avoiding the deserts, have also imposed a strategic value on this location. The borders with Egypt, Syria, Jordan, and Lebanon—or their predecessors—have always been disputed, and the relations with the neighbors were thus always important. The ancient roads of Israel linked major cities in Egypt, Asia Minor, and the Mediterranean, so geography has always driven the course of historic events and generated conflicts over the territory.

The most striking of Israel's geographical features is the rift valley— that is, the Syrian-African Rift. In geological terms, the rift is at the joint between two of the earth's huge tectonic plates and thus is a sort of deep crack in the earth's surface. Its lowest point—the Dead Sea—is the lowest point on earth's surface. The sea is currently receding from these shores as irrigation projects take more and more water from its tributary, the Jordan. The need for water is unlimited, and thus the deadly saltiness of the Dead Sea is increasing, while the shore becomes more and more eerie and barren-looking, piled with white salt formations. In ancient times, the Dead Sea region, an extreme desert, offered a refuge to those who fled from civilization into rugged oases such as Qumran and En Gedi, or who used the huge mountain of Masada as a fortress; you can thus see many archaeology sites in the hills. Today, bathing resorts and spas for tourists, cosmetic factories, and industrial chemical plants line the shores of the Dead Sea, all making use of the strange mineral resources concentrated in its toxic waters.

North of the Dead Sea is the Jordan River, coming down the rift valley from the mountains in the north through the Sea of Galilee (also called Lake Tiberias or the Kinneret). The entire valley from the Sea of Galilee past the Dead Sea lies below sea level, surrounded by rugged cliffs. Earthquakes shake this region from time to time, because of these geological conditions.

Around the Sea of Galilee and the northern Jordan valley, with its end at Mount Hermon, are well-watered agricultural areas. The need to hold the high points that overlook this region has dominated military objectives for millennia. I found myself thinking of this particularly as I stood on the foundations of the old Crusader castle known as Belvoir, which looks from the heights above the western edge of the rift over the southern part of the Jordan River valley, from Israel into the modern kingdom of Jordan. In the river is a shared territory, which had become a symbol of peace between these two countries at the time I was staying there. Nevertheless, at one point, a terrible violent attack by a Jordanian soldier at this site left a number of Israeli schoolgirls dead or wounded.

I also thought about this as I visited the northeast side of the Galilee, standing where the Golan Heights overlook the rift valley on one side and look into Syria on the other side. From the high point, you can look down into "no man's land," patrolled by United Nation troops. The power of the high ground leads Israelis to claim that these strategic Heights must always be their security zone. I repeated the experience again, in the far north, as I stood on the slopes of the Tel Dan refuge, where a now-abandoned bunker looks right into Lebanon.

Returning to the south of the Sea of Galilee, the other half of the Jordan River flows past Jericho, through increasingly dry regions, and finally into the Dead Sea. South of the Dead Sea, though the rift continues, a wall of barren mountains separates the valley from the Red Sea and further isolates the region. Beyond this ridge, the rift continues through the Negev Desert to the Red Sea and then onward, under water, to Africa. Here, at Eilat, the Negev and Sinai deserts separate Egypt from Israel. This region has thus always been a meeting place of the two cultures; at the ancient mines of Timna near the modern port of Eilat, you can see the world's oldest copper mines, which once supplied Solomon's cities, and you can see graffiti by Egyptians who also once mined the minerals there.

The Romans, too, exploited the area. They found it occupied by the Nabateans, who had already started to be an important ally, and later a conquest, of the growing Hasmonean state. Herod's mother came from the ruling family of this region, and thus he also had some strong alliances there. The Nabateans had achieved a high level of use of the desert, irrigating desert valleys by terracing the wadis of their region. I earlier pointed out how, in North Africa, the Romans used the Nabatean method of storing water behind a series of dams in an area that was dry most of the time but sometimes received violent rainstorms. As the Romans developed the area, Petra (an important tourist attraction in today's country of Jordan), became an important trade center, able to develop routes directly from the East across the desert to Gaza and down to Egypt. Trade routes for spices, minerals, and other commodities led through Petra. Various Roman-era sites in the Negev Desert, particularly the city of Avdat, are preserved, and you can visit them today.

Going another direction, the Judean hills and Jerusalem are just to the east of the Dead Sea, with spectacular roads linking Jerusalem to the Dead Sea to the west and to the coastal plain on the east. Jerusalem itself sits in a sort of saddle in the mountains, with roads going up and roads going down, but very few ways in or out of the city. The road to the coast, particularly, has seen battles for control of the area for as long as history records them. The modern intersection of the north-south road with the road from Tel Aviv to Jerusalem is at a hilltop site named Latrun that was most recently contended in 1948 and 1967; when you see it, there's no question of its strategic value.

The coastal plain beyond the Judean hills once belonged to the Philistines but is now the backbone of Israel; on it lie the cities of Tel Aviv, Ashdod, Jerusalem, and Haifa, and the agricultural areas east of the hills. In Roman times, Caesarea and Jaffa were the main points on the Mediterranean coast, and the Via Maris, or coast road, was critical for trade. Now, it's the main route for tourists traveling from Tel Aviv to Haifa and for beginning a trip from Tel Aviv to central cities such as Tiberias on the Sea of Galilee or Nazareth in the middle of the fertile agricultural plain.

The ancient road along the coast from Egypt through Gaza and Jaffa and eventually to Damascus went past the ancient cities of Meggido and Hatzor, which commanded access in ways that were critical until approximately Roman times. These roads allowed travelers to bypass the deserts. There weren't many alternate choices for avoiding the Arabian desert, so the major powers of the time were always interested in controlling, if not actually conquering the territory. During Roman times, there were links between these northern sites and the Negev, Gaza, Sinai, and the Nabatean desert.

The climate also plays a role. Recent studies have tracked the changes in climate that in some eras created a more accessible Negev Desert, allowing trade routes to connect Egypt with cities like Petra, now in southern Jordan, and in some eras caused the desert to be a total block to trade, forcing travelers to go north through the populated areas of Israel. During Roman times, a change in the climate provided the inhabitants with cooler, more humid weather, mitigating the punishing desert heat and dryness for a few hundred years.

Due to all this geographic variety, a visit to Israel without seeing a single religious or historic site could still be memorable. To the south and east, Israel includes the world's lowest point at the Dead Sea, strange salt formations and caves, desert oases and canyons with beautiful hiking trails, several unique desert erosion craters in the Negev known as Makteshim, and world-class coral reefs in the Red Sea at Eilat. On the west coast are sandy Mediterranean beaches. And to the north are ancient volcanic hills, splendid fertile plains, beach resorts on the Sea of Galilee, and rugged Mount Hermon with its ski slopes and marvelous mountain springs.

Geography and Conflicts

The ancient states and ethnic groups of the area—Egypt, Canaan, Judea, Israel, Samaria, Edom, Ammon, Nabatea, Idumea, Phoenicia, Philistia, Babylonia, Persia, and eventually Greece under Alexander the Great—fought over domination of the territory and the various regions I have described. David's kingdom united the Jewish tribes of Israel and Judea, with Jerusalem at the center. The Jewish kingdoms fell, as the importance of the location caused the great powers of the day—Egypt and Babylonia, later Persia—to covet the land. Mostly, the same great powers continued in Hellenistic and Roman times.

Under the heirs of Alexander the Great, the major powers—Egypt, Syria, and Babylon—alternately conquered the territory. Then Hasmonean kings established a small Jewish state in a portion of the territory, which they managed to enlarge by various conquests. With his Roman sponsorship, Herod the Great ruled more territory than any king since the division of Judea and Israel in the ninth century B.C.E.; his nearest neighbors were called Egypt, Coele-Syria, and Phoenicia. He ruled both halves of the ancient kingdom, with the center in Judea, Jerusalem, and also the territories conquered by the Hasmoneans—Idumea, Galilee, the Philistine cities of the Plain, Gaza, and the Nabatean desert. These are also, more or less, the modern neighbors—Egypt, Jordan, Syria, Lebanon.

Fights over land and resources never stop. Both Israel and its neighbors have always wanted the plains near the Mediterranean and the Sea of Galilee, seaports such as Jaffa, the mineral riches of the Negev Desert, the fertile valleys and hillsides, and control of scarce roads across the mountains. The formidable desert barrier to the south and east enhanced the strategic value of the land for trade routes or for military strength. The Via Maris already existed in the time of King David, linking the cities of the coast with Egypt and other parts of the Near East. Damascus, Ur, Sidon, Tyre, and the Mesopotamian cities further east, many founded four thousand years ago or more, saw the value of this crossroads. Meggido, also called Armageddon, was the scene of ancient battles, Roman battles, and of an important battle in the Palestinian campaigns of World War I. And both ancient and modern religions valued the religious significance of Jerusalem, Hebron, Jericho, and Galilee, so that the boundaries of the old kingdoms of Judea and Samaria often become a subject of demands by orthodox Jews who oppose the "land for peace" trade with the Palestinian Authority.

Contentious Place Names

Even the names of the territories of the region create confusion, because they reflect political positions in today's conflict and because they derive from ancient historical conflicts and embody a variety of border disputes. A complete discussion is too complex and contentious, but here is a brief summary:

> **ISRAEL**, a name used since biblical times, has a range of meanings. It can refer to the patriarch Jacob, to the northern biblical kingdom, to the union of the two kingdoms under David and Solomon, or can serve as a collective name for the entire Jewish people. Based on these meanings, the Zionists chose this name for the new Jewish state when they achieved independence from the British in 1948. The ancient Jewish people were called Israelites, while citizens of modern Israel (no matter what their religion) are called Israelis.

> **JUDEA** refers to the Jewish kingdoms centered in Jerusalem during antiquity. Variants: Judea, the Latin form, is also spelled Judaea; Judah is the Hebrew form.

> In biblical times, Judah was the southern kingdom, including the tribe named Judah. Later, the name Judea referred to the reformed and more extensive Jewish state founded by the Hasmoneans (or Maccabees) around 150 B.C.E., to Herod's kingdom, and to the province later ruled by the Romans. When the Romans destroyed the Jewish identity of the province and dispersed the people, the ethnic designation "Jews" replaced the nationality "Judeans."

> **PALESTINE** is a name that derives from the ethnic group the Philistines, who in biblical through Roman times inhabited the cities in the southwest of the current state of Israel. The *Encyclopedia Judaica* attributes its invention to the fifth-century B.C.E.-historian Herodotus, explaining that no one else adopted this term until the Romans, after the fourth century C.E., chose the name Palestine for three provinces of the former kingdom of Judea. The new name emphasized that the Jews had been expelled.

> Later, Moslem conquerors ruled the region as a subsidiary part of their larger territory, using the names of capital cities to refer to provinces. The next rulers, the Crusaders, used the Roman designation of three provinces named Palestine. After the Crusaders were driven out, Arabs and Turks ruled—although they used the name Palestine for general reference to the region, no political entity bore the old Roman name.

The *Encyclopedia Britannica* of 1926 states that the term Palestine refers to "a geographical name of rather loose application . . . conventionally used as a name for the territory which, in the Old Testament, is claimed as the inheritance of the pre-exilic Hebrews." According to this source, "The extension of the name of Palestine beyond the limits of Philistia proper [i.e., the narrow strip of land along the Mediterranean coast] is not older than the Byzantine period." The *Oxford English Dictionary* (supplementary section) dates the first English-language use of the term *Palestinian* to 1875.

Under the British Mandate, beginning in 1922, the English ruled the territory west of the Jordan River under the name Palestine, while the kingdom on the other side of the Jordan River was named Transjordan. In 1949, after the Arab troops forced the location of the boundaries of the new state of Israel, Transjordan annexed part of the former British territory and changed its name to Jordan.

This terminology has been a matter of much contention in the last fifty years, as a result of the conflict over the ownership of the territory. As more Arab states have recognized Israel, the tendency to refuse to mention Israel by name has declined, and the name Palestine tends to be used for the land under the authority of Yassir Arafat (at least in English—the Arabs make different statements in Arabic). The borders of present-day Israel, including the West Bank territories conquered in the 1967 war, are very similar to the kingdom of Solomon or the kingdom of Herod, although the Jews now occupy the coastal plain, whereas in ancient times the Jews occupied the hills and valleys toward the center.

It seems to be anachronistic to use the term Palestine to refer to any state or territory before the fourth century when the Romans brought the name into use. During the Hellenistic and Roman periods, the state or province was named Judea, whereas, throughout history, the entire area has often simply been called Israel, and, therefore, when I talk about the pre-Byzantine era, I will use these two terms as they seem appropriate.

Also difficult, though slightly less political, are the spelling and usage of other place names. Some names have persisted for two thousand years or more, and in other cases, the Israelis have restored the use of ancient or biblical names. Spelling them is an entirely topsy-turvy mess. Every author, every map maker, every translator, every commentator, and every street-sign and road-sign painter in Israel seems to have his or her

own conventions. I have seen different spellings on a sequence of otherwise consistent road signs pointing to the same place. (Although I am
very grateful that the Israelis have English-language road signs, not just
Hebrew ones!) In this book, with place names as with proper names,
I have done the best I can to pick a reasonable and recognizable spelling
for each place and to stick with it.

Jerusalem

Jerusalem is the center of any trip to Israel. It's a focal point of the common history of Jews and Romans during the Herodian, Roman, and Byzantine eras that I am describing. From Roman times until this century, Jerusalem was a small city contained inside a wall. The wall fortified the natural and artificially enhanced contours of the hilly site; these fortifications frequently played a role in violent struggles over this "old city." Now a vast modern city surrounds the walled area, but the nerve center is still inside the walls, and in some ways, especially for tourists, this is the "real" Jerusalem.

THE OLD CITY AND ITS BURIED TREASURES REVEALED

Our second big trip after our initial arrival in Israel was a guided tour of Jerusalem's Old City. Along with friends named Sheila and John, we hired a guide named Moshe, who in a single day taught us a great deal of history, as well as various interesting items from his own life and experiences. He made me realize that in 70 C.E. Jerusalem had been a Roman city destroyed by Romans. As a native of modern Jerusalem, born in 1929, he also made me aware of the results of the more recent Israeli Independence War of 1948. He explained how excavations of the Hasmonean and Roman city became possible after the Israelis took the city in 1967, because the Jordanians, in the previous war, had leveled the buildings of the Jewish Quarter and left them as rubble. As a result, there was an opportunity to excavate underneath the current street level before a new Jewish Quarter was rebuilt, and to uncover enormous amounts of new information about the building and the destruction of the Second Temple and the Roman city.

The tour was full of contrasts. On one side of the city, Moshe pointed out the bullet holes from the 1948 war in the Zion gate and the sloping hills down to the original city of King David; on the other side of the city, he showed us Christian holy sites and an Arab pastry shop whose owners he has known for three generations. In the Jewish quarter, he showed us the excavations of the Herodian priests' houses, accompanied us to his favorite falafel restaurant for lunch, and recalled the beauty of the now-ruined Huerva synagogue before it was destroyed in 1948. By the time we were finished with our tour, I felt that this brief introduction had left me enormously curious about at least three thousand years of history.

We started our tour at the Jaffa Gate. Moshe first showed us through the main street of the Arab quarter and then, by way of exotic pedestrian streets, to the Church of the Holy Sepulcher. As it was early morning, we saw Arab shop owners hanging embroidered shirts, hand-woven tablecloths, long skirts, tourist-oriented T-shirts, bolts of cloth, and other merchandise out in front of their shops, as we were passing through the cloth market. As we walked, we learned that the Israelis had vastly improved the infrastructure of this quarter, such as paving and drainage, after conquering the territory in the 1967 war. In particular, this project had reused huge ancient Roman paving stones dating from the first century B.C.E.

In the courtyard of the church, our guide explained the geography of Jerusalem at the time of the crucifixion and the arguments for and against believing this church to be the actual site of this event. He showed us the many chapels in this bizarre structure, each in a different style, dating from a different era and belonging to a different Christian sect. In one chapel, we ducked through a narrow opening into a first-century tomb—actually, a sort of hole burrowed into the bedrock and blackened by centuries of candle flames. He led us to an Ethiopian monastery on the roof by way of a stairway that we never found again. Finally, we took a back stairway down from the roof into a covered street lined with narrow market stalls. Suddenly, instead of icons and incense, we saw and smelled open trays of fragrant spices, bins of dried fruit, towers of sticky pink and green Arab pastry, piles of fresh fruit, and huge hot griddles sizzling with fresh pancakes. Between the food shops were men with sewing machines making and mending a variety of goods side by side with stacks of ordinary mass-produced items: plastic buckets, detergent, sewing notions, canned goods, packaged cereal, instant soup packets, and other things for home and pantry. Not far away we walked down the Via Dolorosa for a while. Occasional processions of Christian pilgrims passed by us, sometimes carrying religious objects, sometimes just an ordinary guidebook.

We continued farther along the pedestrian street through the butchers' market. Numerous stalls specialize—lamb, poultry, fish, frozen meat, or offal lie in bins of chopped ice next to the narrow, ancient pavement. Huge hanging carcasses, buckets of guts, and trays of unrefrigerated meat contributed to the strong smell, in contrast to the fragrance of spice and pastry a few hundred yards away. Groups of African women tourists passed these stalls with their faces covered in the corners of their colorful native dresses, avoiding the odors, while families of American tourists went by, complaining loudly. Merchants on nearby streets have abandoned the local community and cater to the huge numbers of tourists; they often combine several of the narrow storefronts into a single emporium offering olive-wood carvings, decorative ceramics, Christian religious objects, reproductions of Roman lamps, inflatable Yassir-Arafat dolls, inlaid-wood boxes, postcards, or slogan-imprinted T-shirts. We saw all sorts of clothing—the African women's long, tight batiks; Catholic priests' black cassocks; Greek orthodox priests' high mushroom-like hats; local Arab tea-towel-type head coverings for men; Arab women's embroidered dresses; and European or American tourist uniforms of raincoats and sturdy shoes. Local Arab women sometimes balance heavy bales of goods on their heads, while the children wear American-style T-shirts and baseball caps.

Some of the pedestrian streets are actually indoors, under common roofs above a large number of internally separate buildings. The entire city goes up and down steep slopes in the rock on which the streets are built. Streets are too narrow for cars or trucks, and men or boys push handcarts that rumble up and down the narrow ramps beside the steep stairways. Small, agile tractors bring in loads of heavy building materials and follow a daily route to collect the garbage; from time to time, a donkey carries a huge burden of flour sacks or similar bulky commodities. Our guide gave us clues about the existence of a separate life on the roofs above the market and above the houses. Imagine the complexity of titles to land with centuries worth of independent buildings built one above the other! The overall impression is of a topography that is very hard to visualize, so that one senses incredible mystery and exotica.

The Western Wall: Remains of the Temple

From the market, a few turns of the narrow streets and a walk down a steep stairway took us to the security kiosk beside the large plaza before the Western Wall, known outside Israel as the Wailing Wall. Like the Israelis today, I call this the Western Wall because its actual function was not as a wall of the Temple, but as the western fortification of the enclosure in which Herod's Temple stood. As we approached, crossing the sloping plaza, we saw the domes belonging to the mosques on the Temple Mount. These domes, especially the huge gold Dome of the Rock, tower above the wall, which in turn dwarfs the small figures of praying Jews at its base. Beside the wall, our guide explained, young men read the Torah for their *Bar Mitzvahs* on certain days of the week. We saw them as we looked over the barrier that prevents women from entering the area reserved for male worship. As of my visit, the huge plaza in front of the wall is open to all, day and night, though controlled by security booths with guards and metal detectors. A sudden rainstorm caused a moment of near abandonment in the constant hum of activity, and we moved on to get out of the storm.

The wall offered my first exposure to Roman-Jewish construction and inspired my curiosity about the intersection of Roman and Jewish culture. Like other Herodian structures, the wall consists of huge blocks of stone up to several yards long. Each block has a chiseled band on its edge, amplifying the visual boundary with the next stone. Although the construction uses no mortar, these boundaries trick the eye: the chiseled band imitates mortar between the blocks. These immense stones reinforce the awe that I think almost anyone brought up in Jewish tradition would feel at seeing the wall, no matter what their religious inclinations. It's irresistible just to walk up and touch the stones, and you see many people doing just that.

I came back to the wall many times and always found intense activity. Anyone may enter the enclosures beside the wall, observing the required segregation of the sexes. Large numbers of pious Jews leave tiny notes, which fill up the cracks between the stones and flutter around when dislodged by wind. Men and women on the two sides of the barrier sway as they read from prayer books or recite their prayers. Beggars ask for donations. Hasidic cult members in eighteenth-century European dress are everywhere and on Friday night converge from all over the Old City to dance in the Sabbath.

Standing on bedrock, the wall's construction seems impossible. The stones are too big. In fact, I learned later, archaeologists have explanations of the incredible effort and organization that it required. Each massive stone, technically called an ashlar, was planned carefully by the masters of Roman engineering who worked for Herod, and individually quarried at quarries not far from the Temple Mount. Using teams of oxen and log rollers or axles and wheels, the workers slowly moved each stone into its planned location. The commitment of manpower, beasts of burden, resources, and equipment must have been amazing, and in fact there are hints that Herod's priestly fund-raisers, like Solomon's, supplemented public resources by soliciting individual contributions to a Temple Building Fund.

While today the gold Dome of the Rock occupies the site of the Temple, it's still possible to imagine how it looked in Herod's time. The approach that you take when entering the Temple Mount today is probably the location at which Herod allowed the Romans to place an image of the Roman Eagle (offending the spiritual ancestors of the folks who throw rocks at cars on Jewish holidays nowadays). On my many trips back there, I thought about the pilgrims that marched through the bazaar-lined streets of Jerusalem and filled the Temple at major festivals. Only Jews could be pilgrims and enter the inner courtyards, but non-Jews participated as well, entering only the outermost "gentiles' courtyard." The Jewish pilgrims came from Jewish communities throughout the Roman empire: from nearby Galilee, from across the Jordan in Syria, from Damascus, Carthage, Rome, Alexandria, perhaps even Spain and Roman Gaul. Tithes came to the Temple from all these communities, supporting the lavish priestly expenditures and the huge bonfires roasting the animal sacrifices. The pilgrims celebrated the big agricultural festivals by participating in Temple sacrifices: they came to celebrate fall harvests at Succoth, to sacrifice lambs for the Passover festival in spring, and to celebrate grain harvests in early summer at Shavout.

The Western Wall and the Temple Mount have political, mystical, symbolic, religious, and historical significance. The Jewish longing for the Temple, the Arab denial of Jewish connection to the holy place they appropriated, and everyone's political use of the mystical insights are compelling. While not religious, I nevertheless sense the reasons why Jews want to pray at the wall (but I don't understand why they want to send faxes to be stuck in the crevices along with the pilgrims' handwritten notes to God). Like many other people, I worry about today's deep disagreements concerning religious control of the wall, which may lead soon to total control of the area by the ultra-religious factions, reducing the access that all others have at present. In 1998, I talked to an Arab who expressed the wish for restoration of his childhood football game, which he said took place just at the foot of the wall, before the 1967 war—his idea of the only appropriate use for the area.

Archaeology at the wall is of the greatest interest, as well as being another focus of considerable controversy. Orthodox Jews fear disturbance of ancient bones, and Arabs fear the sanctity of their mosques. When long-known tunnels that revealed far more of the wall were made more accessible to the public in the fall of 1996, immense riots broke out among the Arab residents of the territories, and access was again restricted. I regret that I didn't manage to tour this evidently magnificent area, with its Moslem-built vaults, Roman water system, the Herodian street including half-pillars along the walls, and ancient secret passageways. Perhaps I shall see it on a future trip.

The Jewish Quarter

After looking at the wall, we climbed another stairway to the Jewish Quarter of the Old City. On the steps we met a crowd of orthodox Jews in knee-breeches carrying a Torah and singing into a microphone. Their song was one we had known as a camp song as children, though I had never realized it was in Hebrew. Our guide told us about the history of this quarter from 1948 until the 1970s. A few Jewish soldiers in the Independence War had tried to hold the Old City against the Jordanian army but had been routed, and over the next week, the Jordanians in revenge had blown up the synagogues and most of the Jewish buildings. The Jordanians left all this as rubble until Israel recaptured it in 1967. They didn't even bury the bodies after they blew up the synagogues and Jewish schools. After the Israeli army took back Jerusalem from the Jordanians in the 1967 war, the government arranged for archaeologists to dig under the foundations before reconstructing the Jewish Quarter as a modern city, with housing, restored synagogues, and schools. Our guide mentioned his early memories of the beautiful Huerva synagogue, whose ruined arch still stands alone in the ruins of its walls, a reminder of that time.

This part of the city contains evidence of ancient sieges as well as of the recent destruction by a vindictive enemy—a reminder that it's a city of barely controlled emotion that can become a war at any time and has been causing wars for thousands of years. The Canaanites, the armies of David, the Babylonians, Romans, crusaders, Turks, British, Jordanians, Israeli independence fighters, and the 1967 armies—the city walls, massive defenses, remind you that so many have been willing to fight. The numerous uniformed, armed police and the gun-carrying guards who accompany school trips and tourists reinforce this impression.

Today, anti-Jewish violence is always a threat; the Arabs of the city can change their usually peaceful attitude at a moment's notice, and there is a certain amount of risk each time you go there. From time to time, worshipers at the mosques above begin to hurl stones down at the Jews below, as in May 1998, when TV coverage showed Jewish worshipers fleeing from the wall. And just waiting for the opportunity are the intolerant, black-clad orthodox Jews, whom the Israelis call Haredi; they, too, are capable of violence when they decide to throw stones to impose their practices of Sabbath observance or make women sit at the back of the bus to enforce their prejudices against women.

The Temple Priests' Houses

The Wohl Archaeology museum, which we toured next, occupies the subground-level floors of a number of the new buildings in the Jewish Quarter overlooking the wall. In the museum are displays of the buildings that the archaeologists of the 1970s uncovered. Three meters below modern street level, you can see the Roman-style homes and palaces where the Temple Priests lived in Herod's time and that were destroyed by the Romans in 70 C.E.

As our guide introduced us to this history, he impressed us with how well the priests had lived. They had private cisterns to supply their large baths; the bathing rooms had beautiful mosaic floors and comfortable bathtubs, as well as ritual baths for Jewish purification activity. In the cellars you can still see huge Roman amphoras, once filled with wine, oil, and grain. All was burned in the final destruction, so you can still see the soot on the reddish frescos and broken pottery that may have been left by Roman looters. Clearly, the inhabitants of these enormous houses included numerous servants or slaves as well as the families of the priests.

The artifacts from the excavations mainly appear in the Israel Museum, rather than the onsite museum. These include many coins, stone vessels, pottery, and fragments of furniture. The stone vessels were probably used for meat from the animal sacrifices at the Temple, from which the priests were entitled to take choice cuts for their own tables. The archaeologists found a *menorah* sketched on one wall, a sort of schematic image (in the Israel Museum, with a facsimile at the site), and also a few coins depicting the *menorah*. Because these date before the destruction of the Temple, they reveal unique images of the famous Temple *menorah* made by someone who may have seen the real thing inside the Temple.

What is available today tells much about the Temple priests and their life. During the century between the time Herod built up this area and the destruction in 70 C.E., a raised bridge or causeway led from the Jewish Quarter to the Temple Mount. At this point now you see the security kiosks, where everyone going to the Western Wall must be checked over by Israeli police. Besides the causeway, in the days of the Temple secret tunnels linked the Temple Mount with various parts of the city; today, with the city divided between the hostile groups, I'm curious to know if anyone is making use of them.

For the ancient Temple priests, as perhaps for today's leaders, religion was inseparable from politics. Many of them were ruthless in their commitment to winning power. Flavius Josephus related that not long before Herod's final takeover, several of the Hasmonean priests were fighting it out for high-priesthood and kingship. After one of them, Antigonus, won a battle, he received the defeated contenders, Phasael and Hyrcanus, in fetters, as his prisoners. Josephus continues: "Antigonus himself also bit off Hyrcanus's ears with his own teeth, as he fell down upon his knees to him, that so he might never be able, upon any mutation of affairs, to take the high-priesthood again; for the high-priests that officiated were to be complete and without blemish" (Flavius Josephus, *The Wars of the Jews*, translated by William Whiston, London, J. M. Dent & Sons, 1915, p. 47). The other prisoner immediately committed suicide by dashing himself head-first against a convenient rock.

The Roman Cardo

In the Jewish Quarter, beyond the priests' houses, our guide also showed us the excavation of the old Roman Cardo, built in the second century C.E., a colonnaded area where Roman shoppers once bought local oil and grain, Eastern spice, aromatics, exotic foods, and trade goods from the Mediterranean Roman Empire. A long-known mosaic from a pavement in Syria had baffled scholars because it showed a long, column-lined street dividing the walled city of Jerusalem, but our guide explained that the 1970-era excavations had resolved this puzzle when the archaeologists discovered the Cardo. We looked down into shafts sunk far below the level of the column bases, where you can see older layers of historic ruins, back to the days of Solomon's Temple.

The Cardo now mainly consists of a line of classical columns below the level of the modern street. The Romans built the Cardo after the Bar Kochba revolt, when they expelled all the Jews and rebuilt Jerusalem as a Roman city. Thus, the Cardo demonstrates not the intersection of Jewish and Roman culture, but Roman culture to the exclusion of the Jews. Roman intentions to remake Jerusalem had already contributed to the Bar Kochba disaster, as Hadrian, on his trip to Judea in 129–130, had announced his intention to rebuild Jerusalem under a new name: Aelia Capitolina (a name chosen in his own honor). He planned a classical temple to Jupiter on the site of the Jewish Temple, which of course had been in ruins for sixty years. This announcement incited Bar Kochba. Hadrian never built his own temple as planned, but the other improvements took place after the revolt was put down. Eventually, a temple to Roman gods stood on the site.

The original Roman columns, discovered under the ancient city in the excavations of that time, line the Cardo today. As a result of these efforts, you can easily picture what may have been there in the second century, particularly as small shops again line the covered walkway, many offering reproductions or antiques from that period. Trade and culture among the Romans must have brought an enormous selection of goods from all over the Roman empire. The Cardo's modern jewelry shops probably offer comparable goods to the shops of Roman days: rings, seals, precious and semi-precious stones, gold laurel crowns, necklaces, and brooches for holding Roman garments shut. Glass vessels big and small came from Sidon, Egypt, and parts of Israel—the first-century B.C.E. development of glass blowing had increased the market for the finest clear glassware. Merchants in the Cardo no doubt sold less expensive colored glass and pottery as well. Roman shoppers bought cosmetics and perfumes in glass bottles; shops also sold instruments for using them— stygils for spreading oil on the body, perfume bottles with long stoppers for applications, and droppers of various types. Clay oil lamps and pots for all purposes were a more mundane item—pots were the wrapping materials for all kinds of shipping, sort of like today's corrugated cardboard, so there would have been plenty in sight. All sorts of food and raw materials also had a place in the Roman market. The fragrances of today's spice market and less pleasant odors of the butchers' street not far from the Cardo might suggest the ancient atmosphere, while a visit to the Roman section of the Israel Museum will show you some of the unperishable Roman goods.

We have often gone back to the old city, but my first impression remains fresh in my mind. Like almost every Western tourist, Jew or

Christian, I am almost overwhelmed by the omnipresence of the distant past, and by the contrasts of modern violence with the exotic and romantic aspects of the present.

The City Wall and the Citadel

Our first one-day tour of the Old City didn't leave time for the city walls or the museum that is inside them, the Citadel Museum, but we later returned for a closer look at these. The wall surrounding the Old City is of Ottoman Turkish construction, as is much of the Citadel, though the city has always had a wall and a citadel or fortress of some sort has always stood on the site. On the east and west, the wall is in a very similar place to that of Herod's day, while reconstructions suggest that to the north and south, the city was then larger, extending particularly down into the area known as King David's city.

We visited the Citadel and the walls on a Saturday afternoon in March. A sort of double gate and drawbridge just inside the Jaffa Gate to the city leads to the Citadel Museum. We liked the Jaffa gate entrance to Old Jerusalem because of the large modern parking structure where one feels a car will be safe. At the museum, we briefly waited in line with a number of Israeli families with children, adolescents, and even baby carriages. A number of displays showing costumes, warfare, and simplifications of history make this museum attractive to children.

Once you pay your admission, you enter a huge central courtyard in which excavations have revealed fragments of stone work from Hasmonean, Herodian, Crusader, and Turkish periods, demonstrating the strategic value of this piece of real estate. The towers and roofs of the fortress provide views over the city that are unlike any other and also look down into the courtyard. You can also walk around the moats and huge stones called ashlars from Hasmonean city wall fragments; you can see the footings of one of Herod's towers and small elegant garden areas. Julius Caesar, who visited the city in 47 B.C.E., gave Hyrcanus, one of the last Hasmoneans, permission to rebuild the city wall, and some of these stones may thus date from that time, some from a little later when King Herod took over.

The displays in the museum include a lot of scale models of the Citadel at various times, video presentations with cartoons showing various historic events, and many historic costume displays that appeal to kids and adults alike. You can see department-store dummies dressed as Teutonic knights, Arab water carriers, Turkish soldiers, British gents, and so on.

It's fun. I know many children, too, who would love something else we found: there are huge numbers of connected rooms inside the fortress walls that wind around and up and down so that you never know exactly where you will come out. You see a video of Isaiah's dream of peace for the city that's still fighting three thousand years later.

From the museum we moved on, paying another admission for a walk along the walls going toward the Zion Gate. Our guide's only warning when we asked about security had been that we shouldn't walk toward the Damascus Gate. Both sides of the walls are built up to protect sentinels walking along against attacks from below, so you peer down through the narrow slits, down into streets, yards, rubbish dumps, cemeteries, and parking lots. (But the narrow, confined walkway gives opportunities to modern thieves or politically motivated muggers.)

Beyond the Zion Gate, the city is protected by a natural escarpment so the wall is lower on the city side, where there is only a railing, and very high above a sort of cliff on the outside, dropping down in the direction of the Kidron Valley and the ancient site of the Canaanite town. As you walk, you look across the street into the Armenian quarter and the so-called Armenian gardens that look more like a neglected rubbish dump to me. This corner of town was Herod's palace before the destruction of Jerusalem, and the Roman legions' camp afterward. We could see the other Saturday afternoon tourists walking along this street, but I felt something that I have also felt in other well-preserved walled cities: a sense of isolation in time and place, as if I wouldn't be surprised to see a chain-mail-clad Roman sentry or a Crusader on the wall, guarding the top of the gate, instead of several flack-jacketed young Israeli men and women with Uzis watching over the real conflict in the here-and-now. The Bar Kochba revolt protested Roman development of a neighborhood near the old city; last year or yesterday, Arab demonstrators are protesting the same thing.

The gates of the city of Jerusalem are subjects of songs and legends, but like much about the place are also quite palpably real. The sense of peace on a quiet Saturday contrasts to fortified walls, watchtowers, battlements, modern police barricades, bullet holes from 1948 in Turkish walls, and occasional views of the Temple Mount. You must descend from the wall before reaching the portion that overlooks the site of the Temple Mount; you never get to the last gate. This, the Golden Gate, was long ago walled up, because the Moslems don't want a Jewish Messiah to fulfill a traditional prophesy that through it he would enter Jerusalem.

I mentioned that in many cases, the historical significance of a place is complemented by the story of the archaeological digs and analyses that brought the history to light. The Citadel and the wall nearby are a good example. For over one hundred years, a sequence of excavations have been revealing the history. Almost every new team finds new towers that successive builders and fortifiers of the city put into place. Herod, according to Flavius Josephus, made three, and the tower that forms part of the Citadel, which is called the "Tower of David," is actually one of Herod's towers. Some say it's the one he named Phaesel, but the modern excavators believe it to be the one he named Hippicus.

In the 1980s, careful excavations disclosed that in Hellenistic times there was a single, isolated tower outside the more modest city walls. Although the towers are mainly located on bedrock, meaning that the previous constructions on the site were cleared away, a small portion stands on rubble; as a result, inside the courtyard of the Citadel, archaeologists in the 1980s found a hoard of weapons that they date from the time of the siege of Antiochus VII in 133 B.C.E. Just outside the walls and under the gardens of the Citadel there have been finds of coins, pottery fragments, and organic material that show the site of a city rubbish dump and of sewers, also from the time of the Second Temple.

The history disclosed by these excavations a little further toward the Zion Gate begins with the Hasmoneans (also called the Maccabees). High priests Jonathan and Simon Maccabee, in 144 to 141 B.C.E., built a new wall, the first to take advantage of the natural slope down toward the valley outside the Old City. In building they increased the steepness by quarrying stone from the outside slope. Their efforts to fortify the city started before their position was totally secure, and they were able to finish only after they expelled the last Seleucid occupiers from the fortress, called the Akra, which stood next to the Temple.

Around 25 B.C.E., King Herod rebuilt this fortification, adding more towers, as an integral part of his grand project of a magnificent palace that occupied the space near the modern Citadel. Contributions to the rubbish dump just outside the wall seem to have stopped at this point, perhaps because Herod said "not in my back yard." Herod's palace stood where the current Armenian quarter is located, and his construction workers built special gates to allow access to his palace, and foundation walls eight meters thick and very strong, to support the outer walls of the palace. In 70 C.E., much if not all of this was destroyed, and the Tenth Roman Legion built quarters on the site. Archaeologists in the 1980s identified a number of segments of red clay water pipes and roof tiles as the traces of this Roman encampment, as well as signs of barracks life such as dice.

By the end of Byzantine times, these walls were probably forgotten, and the current walls were built on top of them by the Ottoman Turks. Since the Israeli takeover of the Old City in 1967, the Turkish wall has been restored, and the archaeologists have been able to explore the area.

THE VISION OF HEROD THE GREAT

Let's get back to Herod, and his vision of the greatly expanded Temple and greatly empowered Jewish state. He earned the title "the Great" because his kingdom, expanded from recent Hasmonean conquests, eventually occupied more territory than any Jewish state since David and Solomon. Although he paid tribute to Rome, he governed with a fair degree of independence. Above all, he built the sort of infrastructure— cities, roads, ports, aqueducts, agricultural developments, and commercial investments—for which the Romans are still famous, and his subjects thus enjoyed unprecedented prosperity. Herod must have been a man of enormous vision and energy before he became a mad old man whose fearful and insane actions consumed everything he had accomplished.

When Herod started his ambitious urban renewal project in Jerusalem, there was already a Temple—the Second Temple—that for several centuries had stood on the correct spot as designated in the days of David and Solomon. Apparently, it did not impress anyone enough to result in a surviving description, so we really don't know exactly what Herod had to work with. The sanctuary's dimensions specified in the Bible suggested a building that would be puny by first-century international standards. Herod set out to create a Jewish religious center capable of becoming the spiritual and physical symbol of a major religion in an important Roman provincial capital. Lavish materials and monumental architectural features placed the new Temple complex in competition with the shrines of other world religions.

Herod respected the ancient traditions; he did not alter the God-given dimensions of the inner sanctuary but expanded only the surrounding wall, external structures, courtyards, and approaches. He developed the still-existing large, flat surface inside the monumental retaining walls. Courtyards inside of courtyards enabled the non-Jews, the ordinary Jews, the pious Jews, the women, and the high priests to penetrate to their appropriate level of sanctified ground. He rebuilt much of the city to ensure good traffic flow of the hundreds of thousands of Temple pilgrims who came for the various festivals, and whose tourist shekels contributed to the economy of the city. He planned the approaches with numerous shops in the walls to tempt the pilgrims to buy necessities or luxuries,

he created access to financial centers and law courts, and he generally
improved the entire city's attractiveness. He exploited a labor surplus to
undertake this massive government building project and simultaneously
to keep the people prosperous and out of trouble.

Every Jew in the world paid a tithe to support the Temple, including
Jews living in Rome itself and in other Roman territories. However, this
tithe and other local taxes were inadequate for the level of effort of
Herod's building projects, and thus he developed several other sources
of revenue. First of all, he managed a great expansion of the international
trade routes through his domain. This was the principal source of revenue
for all his lavish projects, exceeding by far the revenue from taxes on
the local farmers and artisans. Profits and tolls on the caravans of spices
and other luxury goods flowing from the east toward the expanded ports
of Jaffa and especially Caesarea directly benefited Herod, who was the
first Judean ruler to realize their potential.

The author Ben-Dov describes the extent of this crucial commerce:

> The main beneficiaries of this bounty were the Arab tribes and the Nabateans
> living on the marches of Judea. The Hasmoneans had tried unsuccessfully
> to cash in on this flourishing branch of commerce, but Herod succeeded
> where they had failed. The "spice trade" was undoubtedly the real motive
> behind his wars, the regional friction, and Herod's ties with the Nabateans.
> It also explains Herod's territorial expansion . . . to the north and east.
> Though the ostensible reason for this annexation of territory was to protect
> the Jewish pilgrims coming from Babylonia, in retrospect it was more like
> an outstretched fist that dominated the commercial route from Damascus,
> making it impossible to bypass Herod's kingdom. This was also the reason
> for Herod's penetration into Moab (Transjordan). . . . As a matter of fact,
> the construction of the large harbor at Caesarea should also be seen in
> the same light, as the small harbors of Jaffa, Gaza, and Ashkelon were
> swamped by the volume of trade.

Herod's second source of income was from huge farms that he
developed in the Jordan River valley. Ben-Dov describes these areas as
"a gigantic hothouse for the cultivation of spices, medicinal plants, and
dates." Under Herod's ingenuity and leadership, his subordinates applied
Roman military metal-working technology to making farm implements
and borrowed Roman city-water aqueduct techniques for irrigation projects
in Judean fields, resulting in improvements in agricultural yields. To
suggest the enormous size of the income of Herod's farmlands, Ben-Dov
describes how Mark Antony "gave" Cleopatra Herod's farm in Jericho;
she leased it back to Herod and he still made money. Later Antony

returned it to him (Meir Ben-Dov, *In the Shadow of the Temple: The Discovery of Ancient Jerusalem,* Jerusalem, Keter Publishing House, 1982, pp. 81–83).

Consider the jobs that Herod must have created to conduct the massive rebuilding of the Temple and enlargement of the Temple precinct. First, he employed agents to plan and negotiate for permission to demolish existing structures. He needed highly skilled engineers and project managers to plan the construction. They had to be experts in determining how to construct the enormous walls that still stand today and in estimating need for labor and materials. When archaeologists who have studied the site say that every giant stone block was measured and cut for its exact location in the walls, they imply that the project planners were very able. Herod's urban redevelopment also included improvement of streets, water systems, and sewers, which required engineers, plumbers, and laborers. As in similar modern construction projects, fund-raisers and accountants also played their role; tradition is that a standard contribution to building the Temple was the cost of quarrying and moving in one of the massive stones.

Actually erecting the enormous Temple platform and rebuilding the infrastructure required an organization of foremen, skilled craftsmen, and unskilled workers. Stone cutters extracted the blocks from quarries, masons dressed the stones at the quarry, and other stone workers carved capitals for columns and other decorative elements. To move the stones required carters, which implies wheelwrights and cart makers; the effort would include animal drivers and manual laborers to participate in the huge job of transporting blocks of stone up to thirteen meters long and five hundred tons. Workers combined skill and hard labor to build the scaffolds and earthen ramps needed to drag or cart the stones into place. Finishing and decorating were the work of plasterers, painters, fresco makers, workers in precious stone and metal, and others. In order to preserve the holiness of the site, Herod arranged for members of the priestly class to be trained as builders, and these unusual dual-specialists were the only workers allowed to work on the sanctuary. Flavius Josephus doesn't say if the Temple was built within the original budget, but I'll bet there was some accountant who knew at the time.

The Temple Mount today, in spite of the dominant presence of the later Dome of the Rock and several other Moslem holy buildings, still reflects the vast resources that went into Herod's project. For non-Moslems there is only one entry way allowed: a sloping walk adjacent to the plaza in front of the Western Wall. This is directly across from the Jewish Quarter and probably at the location of a bridge or causeway that linked the priests' houses with the Temple Mount. Once you have entered the enclosure itself, you can't help being impressed by the sheer size of the project. Although the mosques that stand on the site today have totally obscured the ancient purpose of the area, the vast openness of the area retains what is perhaps its original spirit and grandeur. You can only speculate about what archaeological treasures might be under the paving.

Social Classes

Let's move forward several generations and consider the situation just before the revolt. Herod's economic expansion and the resulting building projects were a generation in the past. However, his civic improvements were still foremost in the economic well-being of the city, upholding the Roman policy of keeping the masses employed and entertained. Although Roman appointees had replaced Herod and his family, the upper class of Jerusalem continued to include several classes of priests and wealthy merchants. The excavations of their palatial homes, on view in the Wohl Archaeology museum, indicate their luxurious lifestyle. To grasp how they lived, we can also read Josephus, who describes his life experiences as a member of this class. During his career, he successively acted as a priest, a military officer on the Jewish side, an officer on the Roman side, and finally, as an expatriate writer in Rome.

Both literary and archaeological sources discuss the several classes among the Jews of the time. Upper classes, particularly the top Temple priests, lived in the luxury befitting similarly placed officials throughout the Roman Empire. I have described the large palaces in Jerusalem where the storerooms were full of wine, oil, and grain, and where the banquet tables offered up luxurious meals in beautiful glass and ceramic dishes. Servants and slaves waited on them, and in some cases, they acquired a taste for Roman baths, Roman theater and entertainment, and so on. The high priests in Hasmonean times, particularly, were wealthy men and later Herod could not completely disable their importance.

Herod's economic innovations and new sources of funds changed the situation of the upper classes, who had previously lived on the rents from the land they owned. They had to adapt to the formation of wealth through the new international trade that was developing under Herod's skillful leadership. Merchants of various classes began to deal in all sorts of goods, particularly spices and luxury products from Arabia and agricultural products from the developing farms in Israel. Herod's innovations included changes in farming, which successful entrepreneurs exploited to make more money on commodities like grain, oil, and wine.

A growing middle class lived in the cities, similarly enriched by exploiting land in new ways, engaging in trade in the east and throughout the Roman Empire, taking advantage of the wealth created by Herod's building boom and trade expansion, and making and selling the goods for which demand was being stimulated. Excavated artifacts suggest the wide variety of skilled craftsmen—glass makers, ceramists, stonemasons, painters, plasterers, mosaicists, jewelers, armor and weapons makers, textile-, rope- and leather-workers, and more. The craftsmen employed native technology, for example, manufacturing stone vessels on huge lathes and blowing fine glass bottles. They also used Roman technology such as Roman metal-working techniques for making farm implements. This urban middle class included less successful merchants, shopkeepers, small landowners who lived on rents from tenants, lower-level priests, scribes, and Temple functionaries. Trade and commerce created a need for bankers and coin-changers, as well as shopkeepers, specialized merchants, and middlemen. Agricultural products required processing, meaning there were jobs pressing olives, making wine, refining perfume and cosmetic products such as the "balm" of En Gedi, and extracting "honey" from dates. Women working at home turned raw material into finished goods—for instance, by grinding grain, baking bread, spinning, dyeing, and weaving wool or flax, and by overseeing the labor of servants or slaves.

When you start thinking in terms of the labor needs originally created by Herod's building projects, his developing of industry, trade, and commerce, and the ordinary daily life of a highly populated and urbanized country, it's clear that by a few generations later, the middle class was varied and possessed many skills. They also needed a place to live, and extensive building of housing areas was proceeding; this included a sort of gentrification of various neighborhoods in Jerusalem, such as the old valley below the Temple Mount, which was becoming more "respectable." Many skilled workers depended on the nearly constant construction projects for employment, and consequently, the government could never afford to get out of the construction business.

A major source of profit in Jerusalem throughout the lead-up to the rebellion continued to be religious tourism. Herod's Temple never ceased to attract and serve the hundreds of thousands of pilgrims from Judea, from the Diaspora Jews of Alexandria, and even those from the more distant parts of the empire. Jews theoretically came to Jerusalem for three festivals a year. In practice, those from far away attempted to make at least one pilgrimage in their lifetime. By the time of the rebellion, Herod's city had grown, with massive hotel-like buildings that appear to have offered shelter, food, and ritual bathing facilities to the pilgrims, and massive commercial enterprises to allow them to do what we all do on vacation: shop for souvenirs. Besides the wealthy and aristocratic members of the hereditary priestly class, middle-class priests and Levites also made a living from ordinary people's religious obligations. Up to eighteen thousand priests served the Jerusalem Temple, as well as rotating into the provinces. The vast public religious and secular buildings employed not only priests, but also scribes, Temple functionaries, judges and clerks for law courts, and general administrative personnel.

Life was not so good for the lower classes: day laborers, unskilled construction workers, common soldiers, and at the very bottom, under-employed and unsavory beggars, criminals, and recipients of public charity. Among the huge numbers of manual laborers employed in building the Temple or in other building projects, the lowest were poorly paid and overworked. Mines, such as the copper mines at Timna near the Red Sea or the salt works near the Dead Sea, used up people in excruciatingly hard and dangerous labor. Forging furnaces, pottery kilns, glass-blowing shops, and other crafts demanded heavy labor to haul wood, stoke their fires, and clean the ash. Outside the urban centers, tenant farmers' poor livelihood depended on the wealthy or middle-class land-owners, while very small landholders and many village artisans lived in rural poverty.

In farming areas and villages, artisans and agricultural workers were slowly being displaced by a variety of economic conditions. Dislocations of both middle-class city people and farmers, caused by concentration of land and capital in hands of the wealthy, constantly created newly poor people. Semi-settled herdsmen undoubtedly tended sheep and goats on the rocky hillsides then as they do today, and were no doubt sometimes forced out by one landowner or another—farmer-herdsmen conflicts had been a constant since early biblical times. These displaced rural workers contributed to a large and disaffected class in the cities. The urban poor included this continually increasing mass of displaced agriculturalists and unemployed laborers as well as beggars, charity cases, and also thieves. From a modern perspective, the lives of slaves also seem particularly depressing, although there were mechanisms—particularly under Jewish law— for slaves to attain freedom.

Josephus provides a great deal of information about the growth of rural bandit gangs, who acted as a sort of anti-Roman, Robin-Hood class. These bandits had already existed in Herod's time; in fact, his first act as his father's appointee in Galilee was to put a bandit leader to death, for which some people condemned him. Josephus uses the word *bandits* to refer to the rebels, betraying the condescension of the Jewish aristocracy and of the Romans for whom he wrote the book. Each "bandit" episode seemingly resulted in more brutal repression and in laying waste to villages; in turn, their popular support grew.

The situation of the lowest classes, especially in the growing cities, was always precarious. The consolidation of agriculture and the displacement of farmers drove up prices, so that poor people could ill afford food even when harvests were good. During crop failures, urban masses are always more vulnerable than peasants, who can at least gather wild plants or consume their livestock, and hence there were numerous famines. Taxes were high, as Herod and his successors needed money for their construction projects, required tributes to send to Rome, and owed money to support Roman legions quartered locally. The high Temple tithes on top of the civil taxes for Rome also promoted unrest. Disillusionment and dislocation contributed to the success of some of the sects of the time and to strengthening support for outlaw organizations such as the Sicarii. Some outbreak of civil unrest always seemed possible, if not immanent. Herod managed to keep the lid on, but the roots of the revolt were set in his time.

THE DESTRUCTION IN 70 C.E.

The Roman destruction of the Temple, the resulting redefinition of Jewish religious practice, and the eventual exile of the Jews from the land have made 70 C.E. the defining moment in Jewish history. By the end, just before the rebellion, Jerusalem was a city full of crafts, commercial ventures, and activities of religious tourism. Despite much dissatisfaction, Jews possessed an enormous investment in the wealth and religious importance of Jerusalem and the region. Why didn't the many highly invested people find it in their interest to maintain the status quo, instead of engaging in a violent internal struggle with such disastrous consequences?

One contributing factor was the cultural discrepancy between how the Romans habitually ruled their colonies and how the Jewish people were willing to be ruled. The Romans had become more and more worried about Jewish insistence that their religion couldn't bend or concede to Roman imperial cults and demands. The priests grew ever more greedy, with higher priests stealing tithes from lower priests. Resentment had grown as a result of a famine in 46 to 48 and a series of incompetent Roman functionaries. Taxes were high and burdensome, full employment always seemed threatened, and a variety of economic and social factors had caused a great deal of unrest. Stupid mistakes by a new procurator

named Florus, who initiated more provocations than any of his predecessors, set the stage and triggered the events.

The Zealots and the Sicarii emerged as the two most violently
competing factions. The Sicarii had adopted urban terrorist tactics, hiding
daggers under their robes and stabbing random people in the crowds
of pilgrims going to Jerusalem. The ultra-religious Zealots, whose leaders
were mostly priests, claimed religion on their side, as well as economic
resentment—the famine had strengthened their popular appeal. While
the Zealots were allied with the Jewish establishment, the Sicarii were
allied with the various bandit movements. A vast modern scholarly discussion hones the fine points of the terms Zealot, bandit, and Sicarii
and attempts to sort out Josephus's truths about them from his alibis
about his own part in the rebellion.

In 66, riots started in Caesarea when anti-Jewish rowdies sacrificed
a cock in front of a synagogue whose members already were in a feud
with some neighbors. These riots in turn touched off violence throughout
the country—at first, Jews rioted in protest of their rights, and then the
Roman police turned their backs while the gentile population in numerous cities massacred the Jews. Twenty thousand Jews—the entire community—died in Caesarea, according to Flavius Josephus.

Then Jews began to organize. Bands of Jewish rebels fought back,
bringing more and more of the "establishment" Jews to their side. At
the beginning of the open revolt in 66 C.E., the rebels of Jerusalem
destroyed the archives recording the bonds to money-lenders, captured
the Antonia fortress that stood next to the Temple, and took over the
palace. Representatives of the Jewish community met in Jerusalem and
established at least some central plan, designating military districts,
commanders, and responsibilities. They began minting coins dated with
the Year One of the rebellion, such as those with the legend "Freedom
of Zion." This currency was a symbol of Jewish independence and rebellion and also enabled the Jewish self-appointed government to pay
for weapons and salaries for the troops and to continue Temple sacrifices,
which persisted until the last possible moment in the war.

There was a brief burst of Jewish success, but the Romans reacted
quickly. While rebels were becoming strongly entrenched in Jerusalem,
Roman armies marched through the country, putting down the Jewish
effort and terrorizing various districts and cities. First under Vespasian,
then under his son Titus, the Fifth, Tenth, and Fifteenth Roman Legions,
a formidable force, put down the Jewish forces. Sepphoris declared loyalty
to Rome; other cities became factionalized. The troops in Galilee—led
by Flavius Josephus—suffered defeat. Josephus himself changed his loyalty

and went over to Rome. While these campaigns took place outside Jerusalem, the city itself was occupied by several competing Jewish factions. Fighting in Jerusalem for most of the revolt was between Jews and other Jews; not until the end did the Romans engage in battle there. Roman troops retreated to the city towers when the rebel leader Menachem entered the city. Josephus's account catalogues a great deal of detail about the individual campaigns and battles of the first several years of the war, including a pause while Rome itself experienced a year of chaos after the death of Nero.

By 69, the Romans had pacified most of the country, and Vespasian had become the emperor, ending the Romans' own difficulties. (We have already discussed the exceptional band of Sicarii holdouts that were in control of the fort at Masada.) In Jerusalem, there were two major factions, one under the leadership of Flavius Josephus's old rival John of Gischala, who had fled from Galilee, and one under Simon bar Gioras who came from Idumaea to "liberate" Jerusalem from John. Josephus mourned the desecration caused by the in-fighting among the Zealots and other factions. He mentions the missiles—launched by Jewish factions in other parts of the city—landing among the Zealots who held the Temple Mount. Meanwhile, he says, pilgrims continued to visit and make sacrifices, but among them disguised members of other factions came into the precinct to work more mischief. Josephus writes:

> O most wretched city, what misery so great as this didst thou suffer from the Romans, when they came to purify thee from thy intestine hatred? For thou couldst be no longer a place fit for God, nor couldst thou long continue in being, after thou hadst been a sepulchre for the bodies of thy own people, and hadst made the holy house itself a burying-place in this civil war of thine. Yet mayst thou again grow better, if perchance thou wilt hereafter appease the anger of that God Who is the author of thy destruction. But I must restrain myself from these passions by the rules of history, since this is not a proper time for domestical lamentations, but for historical narrations. (*Wars of the Jews*, Whiston translation, p. 326)

In the early summer of 70, after putting down the rebellion in virtually all the rest of the country, Romans broke through the outer walls, destroyed much of the surrounding city, built a siege wall and an attack rampart, and prepared to defeat the last defenders. Josephus presented vivid descriptions of the rapid construction of walls and siege engines, of Jewish attempts to burn or destroy the Roman works, and of the inexorable progress of Roman battering rams; he reported what he had witnessed, as he was present in the Roman camp. As Roman control of access to the city increased in effectiveness, real starvation set in. Jerusalem was always dependent on food imports. In the earlier days of the revolt, the road from the direction of the Dead Sea and Galilee was still passable, allowing scarce provisions. Even then, people had begun to forage for weeds and grass or to eat nauseous substances. As time went on, hunger and diminishing confidence caused more and more people, including some of the leaders, to desert Jerusalem and surrender to the Romans. Josephus recorded the suffering and desperation of hungry people who brutalized one another in search of the remaining food, even the least morsels. At the extreme, he documented the pathetic and horrifying case of a woman who murdered and cannibalized her own baby. During this time, the priests maintained the daily sacrifices of lambs and grain, in an effort to symbolize the continuity of Temple practice and demonstrate that the Temple had reserves, but at the end, food ran out even for sacrifices.

In July, the Romans re-took the Antonia fortress adjacent to the Temple. In August, on the traditional anniversary of the First Temple's destruction, in a final battle, the Romans destroyed the Second Temple and the upper city where the priests' residences were located. I am intrigued by the regret that Flavius Josephus attributes to the Roman rulers at what they viewed as a tragedy—they had to destroy their own handiwork, Jerusalem, and they had to destroy such valuable property. Treading the usual thin line between the two audiences he had in mind, Josephus credits the Romans with giving the Jews ample opportunity to give in and spare the Temple, and he praises the valor and effective fighting of both Roman troops and of the Jewish fighters who tried to save the Temple. Despite their efforts, Jerusalem, defended by groups that couldn't agree with each other, was sieged, sacked, burned to the ground, totally devastated; its defenders were punished utterly. Rome was triumphant. Both of the rival Jewish leaders ended up in Rome to march, defeated, in the victory procession depicted on the Triumphal Arch of Titus, after which they were put to death.

After the destruction, despite a third of the Jews killed, the priesthood destroyed, and the former free farmers now the tenants of the emperor, there was a period of time when everyone thought the Romans, confident in their victory, would soon allow the rebuilding of the Temple. The Temple platform remained intact although the buildings and structures had been burned and sacked. The surviving priests were in disorder, but their identity was known, and they had the potential to return to their former priestly duties. To make sure that all would be in order when they returned, rabbis and scribes of various schools began recording the Temple customs; they relocated to small cities of Judea and bided their time. However, each administration in Rome had its own reasons to prohibit the reconstruction. The preservation of information about Temple customs became a habit, not a necessity. Eventually, the recording rabbis began to give Temple practices a symbolic or allegorical meaning—they developed symbolism of keeping the dietary laws, reading the Torah, setting a table as a substitute for Temple sacrifice; that is, they redefined the sacred obligations into effectively a new religion.

After the Temple fell, the Jews experienced major social disruptions. The effect of the destruction penetrated all areas of life and changed even obscure details. Artisans fled, and their handiwork was never the same again, as summarized in the following quote about a particular form of stone-molded lamp:

> After the destruction of the Second Temple . . . the urban population, including artists and craftsmen, fled and was dispersed throughout Judea, a rural region whose inhabitants were occupied mainly in agriculture. Among the refugees were most certainly stone-carvers, whose magnificent work, unearthed in Jerusalem, was abruptly halted by the destruction, and who made the stone moulds in which the lamps . . . were produced. And indeed, no lamps of this type have been discovered in the many excavations in Jerusalem and other sites in which Jewish settlement ceased with the destruction of the Second Temple. The special ornamentation of these lamps reflects the longing for Jerusalem and the destroyed Temple, the ceremonies performed within it, and its sanctified vessels, as well as a portrayal of an agricultural way of life. (Yael Israeli and Uri Avida, *Oil-Lamps from Eretz Israel,* Jerusalem, Israel Museum, 1988, p. 48)

When the Bar Kochba rebellion resulted in even Judea being off-limits to Jews, one more retreat took some of the Jews to Galilee, some to obscure towns in the Hebron hills, and dispersed many more throughout the Mediterranean. The fall of the Temple became a symbol for the scattered Jews everywhere; eventually, it was also used against them by the Christians, who viewed the ruins as a symbol of the Jews' loss of status as the chosen people and of their own superiority.

SEEING JERUSALEM

Stone. This one word describes Jerusalem, both ancient and modern. I have seen a seemingly eternal landscape of stone terraces on the approach

to Jerusalem, new apartment buildings and hotels of stone, modern
shopping centers of stone, British government buildings made from stone,
Turkish fortifications and watch-towers of stone, ancient streets paved with
stone, the huge stones in Herod's Western Wall, stone tombs and ancient
stone vessels, and natural crags of stone where no man-made structure
has been built. The color of the stone ranges from yellow to peach to
nearly rosy pink, beautified by the clear light of the sun or the artificial
lights that shine on the city walls at night. Building in stone is enforced
by tradition, available materials, and city building codes.

Ancient Jerusalem's residents and pilgrims kept many stone workers
busy. Stone vessels for food-use were by definition ritually pure, incapable
of ritual contamination. Large stone tables and stone vessels have been
found in the houses of the rich priests of Jerusalem, while small cups
with ear-like handles are common in a variety of sites, including Qumran
where the Essene sect lived. These, the most common variety of stone
vessels, which look as if they hold between one and two pints, are called
"measuring cups." They may have been used for measuring or may have
served as containers for "pure" water to perform ritual hand-washing.
Other stone items included ossuary boxes for burial of human bones,
Roman statues, and small architectural decorations for homes or public
buildings.

The manufacture of such stone items required challenging technology—a stone cutter's shop, such as archaeologists have found outside
the center of Old Jerusalem, made use of chisels, polishing tools, and
at least two kinds of stone-cutting lathes. In addition to tables, vessels,
and containers, stone cutters made molds for clay lamps and ossuary
boxes; shops produced both workman-like, plain objects and elaborately
decorated objects. You can see many examples of stone cups, tables, and
ossuaries in the Israel Museum.

Construction stone, particularly the enormous stones called ashlars,
also clearly required highly skilled workmen. These monumental stones
are still visible throughout Old Jerusalem in many buildings and pavements. The ashlars of the Western Wall tower over the worshipers, who
stick their little notes into the ancient mortarless cracks between them.
One still-existing stone within the tunnel beside the Temple wall weighs
over five hundred tons.

When you walk down the streets of the Old City, your feet tread
on stones cut in Herod's time. In the ancient Cardo, you can see Roman-
style columns from a few centuries later. The quarries still produce this
stone for new buildings, contributing to the continuing beauty of the
golden city.

Views of the Old City

Because of the odd geography, the choppy, rocky hills, there is no dominant skyline along the in-out roads between Jerusalem and the coast or Jerusalem and the Dead Sea—the Old City skyline depicted in ancient and modern images is as seen from the south, from the road to Bethlehem. Although traditional images give the impression that the city is on a hill top, it's actually a little protrusion at a sort of saddle point. On the west, the new quarter of Jerusalem toward the Israel Museum slopes upward from the Old City. On the north, there are irregular hills, and to the east the Mount of Olives towers over the city. Only toward the south does a downward slope afford the view of traditional artists and photographers. Seeing the city this way helps us to understand the challenge of King Herod's architects: making the small Solomonic Temple into an impressive sight that would compete with the grandeur of monumental architecture in the Roman world while working with the sacred and unmoveable site in such a difficult location.

Two promenades, named the Haas Promenade and the Sherover Promenade, offer wonderful views. These are adjacent to one another and a short distance from the main road toward Bethlehem. (You can find them on a good map, near the neighborhood of Talpiot; there are also restaurants and cafes for the promenaders.) The promenades zigzag through a hillside park, facing the walls of the old city. At dusk, we were greatly impressed by the view of the glowing gold Dome of the Rock atop the Temple Mount. The winding pedestrian paths hug the side of a hill and slowly curve down into the valley. As you walk through the peaceful gardens of the promenades, the gold dome dominates the view, but you also have unobstructed views into the Kidron Valley where King David's city began, of the part of the city called Silwan, and toward the Mount of Olives.

The promenades are surrounded by new apartment blocks and houses on the west. To the east is the Kidron Valley on the other side. People walking on the paths come from both neighborhoods, so this is one of the only places I have seen where there appears to be a peaceful coexistence of Arab and Jewish families, young couples, elderly people, kids on bikes and roller skates, and teenagers on skateboards, without the evident tension of most urban places or the total segregation of the coastal towns. I was only a casual observer, one Saturday at dusk as Orthodox families were obviously waiting for the sun to set and the *Shabbat* to end. Tension had existed there in the past; perhaps my view was wishful thinking.

The Kidron Valley and Just Outside the Temple Mount

The area just east of the Temple Mount, the Kidron Valley, and the village of Silwan are, in my view, Arab territory, and I didn't much explore this area. There are a number of sites with traditional names from the Bible: Absalom's Pillar, the Tomb of Jehosaphat, the Tomb of Zechariah. All of them, in fact, are from Roman times, and the archaeological excavations in them yielded a vast amount of important information, particularly stone ossuaries (bone boxes) with useful inscriptions. Most of the findings are displayed in the Israel Museum or the Rockefeller Museum, and the tombs themselves are less impressive than many other sights of the city.

Jerusalem Scale Model

A scale model of the entire Roman city as it is thought to have appeared in 66 C.E. at the beginning of the revolt against Rome is on display at the Holyland Hotel in Jerusalem. The scale is dramatic: the Temple Mount model is about three feet high and five feet across, and the whole city occupies about a 100-foot square area; the scale measures 1:50. The management makes revisions when archaeologists make new findings. They use local stone, wood, copper, and iron to imitate what is thought to have been the original building materials. In my opinion, the most useful choice of the designers of this exhibit is that it is entirely three-dimensional. Because of the accurate contours of the city's hills, it's much easier to mentally compare it to the real city as it is today.

The modern, actual Old City is entirely inside of a wall built around five hundred years ago by the Turks, but the model helps you visualize how this relates to the city of Jerusalem in the first century, as these walls primarily follow the Roman walls to the east and west, with a wider north-south axis projected for Roman times. The details are of great interest, particularly to those who wish to reconstruct the events surrounding the Crucifixion, and for this reason, the site is popular with Christian tour groups.

Basically, the Roman city was contiguous with the Old City; the city wall represents approximately the area where the Romans and their predecessors had their city, including the area of Solomon's Temple and the expanded area of the Second Temple, which were on the Temple Mount. You can see in the model that next to the Citadel was Herod's palace, that the Antonia fortress that looked down into the Temple area was just beside the Temple Mount, and you can see where the various pools and markets were. You can see how the pedestrian traffic was routed around the walls and through the city to ensure that pilgrims walked past many bazaars and also see that they were properly impressed by the imposing size and construction of the ancient Temple.

The Zoo

The format and content of the Jerusalem Zoo are not directly connected to King Herod or Roman times, but the zookeepers make an effort to display animals native to the region, many of which have long-since disappeared—like lions—or that are hard to see—such as hedgehogs or leopards. Many animals are labeled with a biblical quotation to put them in the local context, a help to me in identifying one mystery. In touring around the Sea of Galilee, I had been baffled by the sight of a strange brownish animal sitting on a rock and sunning himself. Later, at the zoo I got a good look at this animal, the hyrax, which in biblical translations is called a cony. The experiences of travelers in ancient times, who feared snakes, leopards, or other beasts, is also easier to picture when you see the zoo. The recently remodeled enclosures and animal houses are very well organized and nicely presented. The zoo is not far from the Holy Land Hotel, the site of the scale model of Jerusalem.

Ascent and Descent: Roads to Jerusalem

When a fellow-visitor to Rehovot asked me my opinion of a 1970-era Volvo she thought of buying, my first question was "could it make it up to Jerusalem?" Ancient sources refer to going "up to Jerusalem"—this is not metaphor. Stone mountains isolate Jerusalem on all sides. From where we stayed, in Rehovot to the west, you must approach Jerusalem by a steep and dangerous road blasted from this stone. From the east, the ascent is greater, as the road comes up from the deep rift and the Dead Sea. From the south, there is a slower climb, up from Bethlehem and the Judean hills. To understand Jerusalem, and its isolation, you must picture these roads as they are now and imagine how much more isolated the city must have been in the distant past and how dependent on these few arteries to bring the wealth of the land, the Temple pilgrims, and almost all necessities.

Along these roads, there are terraces—old and etched into the rock and stone almost as if a natural occurrence. Facades on the old villages, Moslem domes, minarets, and farm buildings, made from locally quarried stone, contribute to the uniqueness of the landscape. Until the modern urban development, these terraces were the only agricultural land in the area; clearly, Jerusalem depended on the rich produce of the valleys of Judea and Galilee for commodities like grain, oil, animals, and flax. The light on the terraces and stone buildings is beautiful in all seasons, as countless writers from every epoch have remarked.

Most of the buildings outside of the Old City are modern despite the stone facades, which a forward-looking British ruler required as part of the building code earlier this century. Two hundred years ago, you would have seen only individual isolated villages and the ancient stone-terraced fields. One hundred years ago there were a few settlements uneasily clustered around the city wall. Some were inhabited only during the day, because there were bandits and other dangers outside the wall at night. Now all the hills are covered with urban sprawl. Although some people who have spent their lives in Jerusalem tell us the atmosphere has been destroyed by the pace of recent construction, I—having never seen it till 1997—find that the stone is beautiful.

From the West, Jerusalem's most critical road joins the routes from the cities of Jaffa, Tel Aviv, Rehovot, and Beer Sheva. These roads meet at the monastery at Latrun, a strategic crossroads. Roman troops preparing for the final battle in 70 A.D. no doubt marched by here as they came from the ports at Caesarea or Jaffa. Caravans carrying the rich cargo from the East toward the Mediterranean had already been using the road for centuries. Another road comes to Latrun from Ramalla, now in Palestinian Authority territory, by way of Park Canada, named for its sponsor, the Canadian Jewish Agency. In this park near the crossroads, you can walk down a long valley beside the rocky channels and cisterns of a Roman water system that served the town of Emmaus, of New Testament importance, also often mentioned in Flavius Josephus's strategic accounts of troop movements.

Immediately past Latrun the modern road begins to ascend eastward toward Jerusalem. It follows a deep valley, or wadi, for a while. The road goes past an inn that was the last stop in the several-day foot and donkey trip from Jaffa until a hundred years ago. (In 1997, the inn was a ruin, in 1998, a building project, so perhaps it will soon be serving tourists or pilgrims again.) The climb becomes steeper, and the road alternately seems to cling to the hillsides or lies in a trench blasted from the rock. Pine forests, planted by the early Israeli reforestation efforts, grow sparsely on top of the hills. Across the valley the ancient stone terraces divide the hillsides like a cubist painting. Along the road you see the rusted hulks of makeshift armored cars that the irregular Israeli freedom fighters hacked together to fight the professional, British-trained and -led Jordanians in 1948—hulks left as they were abandoned, as a monument to the numerous casualties of the battle for the strategic road.

The road is four lanes wide and amazingly engineered. The traffic is heart-stopping. As a driver, I was always impressed by other passenger cars, decrepit pickups, minivans, buses, garbage trucks, and even construction vehicles that would try to pass me—to the left or to the right— on the steep grades. Sometimes road graders and other non-road vehicles moving between Jerusalem's ubiquitous construction sites delay the traffic. If you are unlucky, the forty-minute trip can become much longer. But finally, around a bend, you are in city traffic and city neighborhoods. You have reached modern, urban, sprawling Jerusalem; however, you must continue through the traffic-filled streets and over several more hills to reach the ancient walled city.

An obscure alternate two-lane, much less dramatically engineered route takes even longer, winding up and down through the stony countryside and past several villages, perhaps providing more insight about the once-difficult trip on foot or by pack animals, but the main road carries almost all of the traffic into the city.

East of Jerusalem, a spectacular road winds toward the Dead Sea, Jericho, and the Rift Valley. In Herod's time, pilgrims from the Galilee area climbed up or down this way to or from the Jordan valley. They brought their sheep, their grain, and their first fruits to sacrifice at the Temple and went home, no doubt, with souvenirs from the exotic markets of the big city. Enterprising pilgrims no doubt also brought practical foodstuffs to sell in these markets. Herod's camel caravans from the East followed the road, carrying spice and luxury products, dates, and other produce from his farms and groves at Jericho; some of this material was destined for Jerusalem, other items were headed onward to Mediterranean ports to supply the rest of the Roman Empire. By this route, supplies came to the besieged Jerusalem in Flavius Josephus's history, until the Romans blockaded the entire city and food supplies were exhausted. Later, Bar Kochba loyalists may have fled down this route as they escaped to the caves along the Dead Sea.

We traveled this road from Jerusalem on a day trip to the Dead Sea. We picked up the road to the northeast of the Old City, where it's very poorly marked, even presenting a challenge to our Israeli host on our first trip and continuing to challenge us when we repeated the trip. If you go, be sure to watch the map carefully. The signs when we traveled did not mark the Dead Sea as a destination, but listed an intermediate village named Ma'ale Adumim. (There could be political reasons for missing signs, who knows?)

This road winds through Jerusalem's dense apartment neighborhoods—on Saturday in these times you have to be careful because this road passes quite near the ultra-orthodox neighborhoods where zealots throw rocks at cars. Outside the urban area, the apartments give way to barren hillsides, and you descend very rapidly. When you pass the large sign labeled "sea level" you still have a long way to go, all downhill into the rift valley, all craggy, barren landscape. Just north of the Dead Sea, there is another strategic crossroads. Here, you can go north, past Wadi Quelt and Jericho toward the Galilee, continue east toward the Jordan River and the country of Jordan (if the border crossing is open), or south, along the shore of the Dead Sea toward En Gedi, Masada and eventually, if you follow the rift for several hours more, to Eilat and the Red Sea.

Jerusalem's surroundings are so mountainous that there is no large level terrain for a modern airport. The Lod International Airport, which serves both major Israeli cities, is on the Tel Aviv side. Helicopters are reserved for the military and rich or distinguished visitors. All others have the choice of a bus, a van, or a car. *You must take the road up to Jerusalem.*

THE ISRAEL MUSEUM—LAMPS, COINS, SCROLLS

There are several ways to learn more about the land and its ancient history. Archaeologists dig and analyze. Museums and other modern displays present the findings. Some people say the stones themselves are the witness of history. For them, Jerusalem is a mystical experience, the heavenly city made manifest. If you want a more material view, though, the museums of Jerusalem offer it. The main museums showing objects from Roman times are the Israel Museum, the Rockefeller Museum, and the Bible Lands Museum. Here, I will concentrate on the Israel Museum. For opening times and days, admission fees, and special exhibits consult the entertainment section of the Friday English-language newspapers. (Current pressure for public facilities to close on Sabbath and religious holidays makes hours subject to change. In any case, be aware that even if a museum is open on Saturday, there is likely to be no food served in the cafeterias.)

Most of the important finds from the archaeology digs in Jerusalem and many from elsewhere are on display in the Israel Museum. They relate to a number of the historic and archaeological facts I have mentioned in this chapter. From the time of Herod and the later Roman period there are statues, mosaics, oil lamps, coins, priestly riches, glass, stone vessels, Roman soldiers' helmets, chain mail, spears, and fine iron work. In the Shrine of the Book you can see the papyrus religious scrolls, letters, and personal items of the Essene sect and of the fleeing supporters of Bar Kochba. The Roman artworks are masterpieces of their type. The smooth marble statues, graceful glass vessels, stone architectural fragments, and many other items help you to picture the magnificence of the city. The stone tables and vessels from the priests' houses in the Old City provide clues to the religious practices of the Temple and to the opulence of the priestly lifestyle.

The museum also helps you put the Herodian city, which you can see at the Citadel, the Western Wall, and in other archaeology sites, in the context of the rest of history. Only imagination can really reveal the splendors of the city of David; there just isn't enough evidence in buildings in the city, only a few tombs. The museum presents the available evidence so that you can try to imagine it. A few stones and a bit of a relief in one of Nebuchanezzar's palaces provide a clue, but nothing to compare with the eyewitness account and the archaeology of the Roman city. Luckily, the Israel Museum in Jerusalem reproduces this relief, showing the procession of captives.

Objects of Daily Life

Material culture as dug up in recent archaeological excavations commonly includes coins, glassware, stone vessels and architectural fragments, mosaics, bone objects such as buttons, ceramic objects such as tableware, storage vessels, and lamps. Occasionally, especially in desert caves, discoveries include more perishable objects such as papyrus documents (most notably the Dead Sea Scrolls), textiles, ropes, shoes, baskets, and metal objects such as armor, arrow tips, or vessels. Funeral objects often supplement the objects left from actual use. The Israel Museum, which includes the Shrine of the Book, is particularly rich in examples of all of these types of objects. The Rockefeller Museum in another part of Jerusalem, the Eretz Israel Museum in Tel Aviv, and the historic museum in Jaffa also have good exhibits of such archaeology finds.

Even before modern archaeology, there were reminders that the Romans had built and decorated elaborate buildings. Travelers of all eras saw at least the fragments of mosaics, carved stone, columns, and frescoes. Sometimes these elements were recycled into buildings of the Moslem era, like Caesarea's columns that now decorate the mosques and public buildings of Akko. Recent excavations of Roman and Byzantine cities have unearthed public bathhouses, theaters, race tracks, gymnasia, aqueducts, fountains, shopping centers, paved streets, and inter-city roads, which the Romans left in Judea as they did throughout the Roman Empire. Excavations around the Temple Mount in Jerusalem have mainly provided insights into Roman times, particularly disclosing Herod's shaping of the Temple's physical appearance.

Coins

Several specific types of items appear in so many digs that they are of special significance. First of these are coins, invented in Asia Minor during the early biblical era and by Roman times in use throughout the Mediterranean. The coin room at the Israel Museum and the collection at the Eretz Israel Museum each help you to realize how, for a number of reasons, coins are incredibly useful to scholars. These reasons—still true of modern coins—include the following:

- Coins are common. People often amassed them, left them in hiding places, and never came back. As a result, hoards of ancient coins have resurfaced in the hands of modern farmers, construction workers, archaeologists, and treasure hunters, and several such hoards are displayed in the museum.

- Coins are small. People often lost them in building foundations, in rubbish dumps, and in sewers. Shipwrecks, earthquake rubble, burned-out buildings, and graves almost always contain some well-preserved coins, no matter what happened to the other stuff that was there—a major excavation may produce tens of thousands of examples.

- Coins have labels or images to indicate the date and location of their origin. Ancient coins often identified the current ruler or commemorated historic events. Each museum offers several cases where coins are arranged chronologically.

- Coins are mass-produced. Mints made many copies of each design, and the coins from a particular mint usually had recognizable features. This allows modern comparison and tracking methods to identify a coin's origin. The Bar Kochba rebellion's coins had an even more complex history. These were overstruck using already minted Roman coins instead of clean blanks, showing the lack of full manufacturing capability by the rebels. Museums can also choose the best and cleanest examples of almost every type of coin to display.

• Coins—because they are metal—are both durable and detectable. A coin made during the Roman Empire frequently circulated for as long as two hundred years and traveled great distances in Roman commerce. Yigael Yadin's expedition to the Dead Sea caves used military mine detectors to detect a hoard of coins hidden for nineteen hundred years in a crack in the rocks.

In the case of the ancient Jewish state, coins additionally reveal information about the political situation and about Jewish attitudes. Coins minted in Sepphoris had names of Roman emperors on one side and Jewish symbols on the other side, showing the double cultural identity of that time and place. At times, a client state, even one as independent as Herod's, lacked the right to mint coins, and thus the coins in use during an occupation were those of the distant Roman, Egyptian, or Persian ruler. During the few independent periods, Jewish rulers minted their own coins—significantly, in 37 B.C.E., the Hasmonean King Mattatias Antigonus issued a coin depicting the *menorah* that stood in the Temple, one of very few representations of the *menorah* before 70 C.E. During certain eras, pious Jews refused to use coins with "graven images." Authentic Jewish coins thus never represented such subjects as human faces, human figures, pagan gods, birds, or animals. From a modern perspective, this is disappointing. It's intriguing to see an image of an ancient ruler that was actually manufactured during his own lifetime—too bad there's no coin with Simon Maccabee or Herod the Great.

When Jews engaged in defiance, one of their first acts was to begin minting their own coins: both the rebels of 66–70 C.E. and Bar Kochba in the 130s produced coins proclaiming their revolts. Similar motives, of course, existed on the opposite side: in Rome, coins minted in the early 70s celebrated Titus's victory over Jerusalem, showing a symbolic captive chained under a tree and bearing the words "Judea Capta." I found the sight of this coin to be one of the most fascinating points of the museum's coin display.

The vast abundance and non-uniqueness of ancient coins means that you not only see them in the museum, but it's still possible to buy them legally for entirely affordable prices. I'm no expert, and I've never bought coins, but I saw them for low prices in shops that were supposed to be reliable. A serious buyer has to be aware of what he's doing, as there are evidently lots of ways to fake antiquities, but it's a fun idea.

Oil Lamps

Like coins, Roman oil lamps are discovered in great numbers in most archaeology digs, and reveal a variety of cultural facts to scholars. The lamps are generally made of reddish, low-fired clay, simple or ornamented, and are around three inches long, with a spout for a wick and a hole through which oil was added. Rich and poor people alike used these lamps, which were almost considered disposable—if your lamp broke, you would throw it on the trash heap or down the privy and buy another. For much of the period, burials also included new lamps for the use of the dead, providing another source for modern collectors. Buried or discarded lamps do not disintegrate, so they are well preserved.

Anywhere you go around the Mediterranean, you will see at least a few Roman lamps in every museum dealing with Roman times, a testimony to the unified nature of the Roman government, the great appeal of the Roman Empire and its culture, and wide-ranging trade routes that connected Rome with the most distant outposts. The Israel Museum has many cases of lamps on display. In some of these cases they show several examples of the same model to illustrate how some were made more carefully than others. You can even see molds used for the mass production of lamps, such as the stone molds used uniquely in Jerusalem before the fall of the Temple. Lamps in the display also illustrate how some Jewish owners intentionally damaged their lamps, breaking out the central medallion, perhaps because the design depicted a human face (which made it objectionable to the pious) or perhaps because it was too hard to fill a lamp with a small hole.

The Roman oil lamp in its characteristic form developed in about the first century B.C.E. In Israel, clay oil lamps already had a long history when the inhabitants began to produce lamps of the Roman type. When you first see a collection, such as in the Israel Museum, Roman lamps all look very similar. In fact, according to the book that I quoted earlier, the shape of the Roman oil lamp was more stable than that of any other type of pottery used by Mediterranean peoples. I found as I looked at case after case of them, that lamps of various types from various times and places begin to have a noticeable character, particularly with respect to the designs molded on them.

Lamp designs reflected their owners' identity. The tiny details of flowers, fruits, faces, and symbols suggest the people whose nights were lit up by the burning olive oil. Jewish symbols appeared on lamps that were intended for Jewish customers. Such symbols include depictions of the "seven species," that is, wheat and barley, grapevines, date palms, and pomegranate, fig, and olive trees, as listed in Deuteronomy 8:7-8. Other Jewish lamps depict *menorahs*, *lulav* and *etrogs*, and characteristic rosettes. A "Sabbath" lamp in the Israel Museum was made so as to burn longer without the addition of oil or an extra reservoir (which were prohibited for the Sabbath). Early Chanukah lamps on display in the Israel Museum's Judaica collection (as opposed to the archaeology section) consisted of eight clay lamps, in contrast to today's fixture with open oil reservoirs and wicks.

The museum collection continues past the fall of the Temple with Christian lamps whose religious symbols show objects such as a cross or a fish. Lamp-owners could also express other tastes. A dig in an ancient barracks outside the Jerusalem city wall revealed that the Roman legionnaires used lamps depicting explicit sexual scenes. I did not notice any of these on display in Jerusalem, but I saw a lamp with an erotic scene in a traveling exhibit about Sepphoris, which appeared in the United States just after my return from Israel. I believe that in Israel recently, there was a controversy about displaying or depicting these objects.

With reservoirs that held no more than an ounce, a Roman lamp must have emitted a tiny flame compared to the amount of light we expect today from an electric bulb. Also, greasy smoke from the lamp made quite a mess on walls and supporting tables or fixtures. Enhanced versions of the lamp, such as hanging fixtures with a big reservoir and several wicks to be lit at once, probably still cast rather dim light.

If antique lamps appeal to your collecting instinct, you can buy them from antique dealers, particularly in the Old City and in Jaffa, or buy reproductions—then maybe you could experiment with the light level they produce. I saw lots of frankly modern oil lamps for sale for a few dollars in the market in Jerusalem, while documented reproductions are available in museum shops. Again, to antique buyers, I say *Caveat Emptor*— let the buyer beware! Not only might some unscrupulous dealers offer forged or mis-labeled lamps at authentic antique prices, but others (according to one article I read) add rare decorative motifs to boost the value of ancient—though uninteresting—lamps.

Of course, there are many other ceramic objects beyond the lamps. Every dig presents vast numbers of fragments of pottery, and the museum offers cases of them as well. Pots served as packaging material, such as amphoras used for wine and oil. There were special vessels for sacrificial meat, pots that farmers used for bedding young plants, ceramic tableware, tools, building materials such as drain tiles and pipe, and many other objects. When pots broke, the shards could be used the way we use note paper or scrap paper; thus, often the shards have additional interest because of hastily written texts that appear on them. There's much more in the museum; I have only tried to whet your appetite.

The Dead Sea Scrolls and Other Finds

From the time of their discovery in the late 1940s, the Dead Sea Scrolls have inspired enormous interest and subsequent activity. Numerous publications have discussed the meaning of the scrolls and the scholarly fights over who will eventually publish them. The politics of the Dead Sea Scrolls have occupied scholars for decades. I have no interest in even summarizing the rival positions, the petty quarreling, and the race for academic credit that have led to public perception of some sort of conspiracy to suppress the "truth" of the scrolls. If you can't get to Jerusalem, I recommend an exhibit on the World Wide Web (if it is still available) describing a recent U.S. Library of Congress exhibit of scrolls and artifacts.

In Jerusalem you can see many original and copied scrolls, tools, artifacts of various kinds, and personal objects from Qumran on display in the Shrine of the Book, a separate building in the campus of the Israel Museum. The exhibits of non-text objects change from time to time, so specific objects vary. On the lower level of the rotunda dedicated to the scrolls, they often display objects from caves where the last of Bar Kochba's soldiers hid.

In the long entrance hall leading to the rotunda, the museum presents a few objects at a time. They organize varied exhibits from their collections from Qumran and the wadis where Bar Kochba's men took shelter and where various refugees died during the rebellion. On one visit, I was impressed to see the sandal of a woman named Babata, whose personal effects and papers were hidden there from the time of Bar Kochba until this century and Yigael Yadin's expeditions. It's a rather small sandal, with a flat leather sole and a thong strap that went around the foot. Most of us, that is, American women of my generation or younger, have at one time or another owned a pair of sandals almost identical to this. Babata's documents include bills of marriage and divorce, papers for the sale of a house or portion of a house, outlining in simple, legal language the terms of the sales agreement, and other things. Above all, the exhibit showed letters from Bar Kochba himself.

On another visit, the entrance hall presented artifacts and documentation about daily life in the Qumran community. Agricultural tools, fittings from scrolls, and fragments of scrolls complemented photos of the current site. One case explained how the inhabitants had constantly lost nails from their sandals as they walked around the site, and presented several such nails. I enjoyed seeing the old, very plain pottery vessels, particularly a small, rather crude cylindrical ink well.

The displays of personal objects also help answer a simple question: What did people wear in Jerusalem in Herod's time? Trying to picture the ancient Jews is difficult because of all the representations of Bible stories in European art. Before the nineteenth century, people didn't seem to worry so much about development of dress style, and subjects of biblical pictures and statues usually appeared to have dressed as if they were slightly exotic contemporaries of the artist—like Rembrandt's biblical subjects. During the nineteenth century and sometimes earlier, European Christians wanted to know what people really wore in biblical times. They often modeled their mental and literal images on the dress of the Arab and Bedouin inhabitants of the Arabian deserts, and it's sometimes hard to separate these fictions from reality. The prohibition against creating images of human beings makes it even harder to find out what the Jews of ancient times or Roman times wore. The Jewish captives depicted on the Arch of Titus don't help much, as they are captives being humiliated.

The most detailed discussion of this question of dress is in Yigael Yadin's book *Bar Kokhba*, which documents his finds in desert caves near En Gedi. Among the personal effects of the refugees from the revolt, Yadin's expedition found several articles of clothing in very good condition, preserved by the very dry conditions inside the caves. These findings were so well preserved that even the colors were vivid, and experts could even perform a chemical analysis of the dyes and an analysis of the fiber content, which revealed pure fabrics complying with biblical prohibition against fabric blends. These now belong to the Israel Museum, and appear periodically in the rotating exhibits at the Shrine of the Book.

Yadin compared the clothing he found to the images from the third-century synagogue of Duro Europa (now in Syria but available in reproduction in books or in Tel Aviv's Diaspora Museum). This synagogue is considered to be one of the oldest examples of representational Jewish religious art, and its decorations include many panels with figures from biblical and other scenes. The figures wear a variety of clothing in interesting styles, mostly resembling robes and togas. However, Roman togas were circular in shape, while the dress of the Jews was made from rectangular strips of cloth.

Yadin shows how the clothing he found was quite similar to that in the Duro Europa portraits, with stripes and certain geometric figures that appear in the images. The clothing was woven carefully and sewed together with a minimum of cuts in the weave, leaving the selvage edges inside the seams and leaving simple slits for arms. A few sewing baskets found in the caves demonstrate the constant work, presumably by women, of spinning and weaving cloth or making fringes for the garments. He also found evidence of women's jewelry, leather sandals, and cosmetics, allowing the reconstruction of the ensemble that a woman might have worn.

Also in the caves, Yadin's workers found many personal articles, metal ewers and incense shovels, straw baskets, and other objects. My favorite is a glass plate wrapped carefully in straw mats. The protective mats and the twine used to tie them up are perfectly preserved, and successfully protected the plate for its long stay in the cave. The plate is around fifteen inches in diameter, with a very simple circle of decorations, in the form of simple raised dots; the caves are so dry that the glass is still clear, with little or none of the iridescent patina that one associates with ancient glass. This beautiful object stuns you with its impressive state of preservation. You can picture the owner of the plate carefully tying up the twine, presumably as she gathered her most valuable possessions in order to flee to the caves in the desert as the events of the rebellion disrupted her life. I was disappointed that the plate and its wrappings were not currently on view when I revisited the museum.

In later Roman and Byzantine times, mosaics representing human forms became more acceptable even in synagogues, and thus there are more frequently indications of people's dress. In the Israel Museum you can see many Roman statues, and a Roman soldier's clothing from an archaeology dig, with his chain mail vest tucked into his helmet as he must have put it down somewhere and never returned; you can also see many mosaics depicting Jewish scenes and even human figures.

Evidence of Alphabets and Languages

Many objects in the Shrine of the Book and in the general archaeology collection of the museum suggest the various languages and alphabets in use in Roman times: Aramaic, rabbinic Hebrew, and Greek were spoken by the people and used for religious ritual, while Roman Latin served aspects of public life. Evidence about these languages comes from the Dead Sea Scrolls, from the Bar Kochba letters, from inscriptions, graffiti, and potsherds, and from mosaics on display. In particular, in the Israel Museum's archaeology section, in a series of rooms adjacent to the displays from the time of the First Temple, you can find an exhibit explaining the history of alphabets and writing in the Middle East. Across the parking lot from the Israel Museum, the independent Bible Lands Museum also has extensive displays about the development of the alphabet.

During Roman times, formal religious writings were frequently in rabbinic Hebrew, while official correspondence of the Roman Empire was in Latin or, in later times, in Greek. Inscriptions in the Greek, Latin, and Hebrew alphabets appear on public buildings and tombs. In Byzantine times, many Jews used Greek epitaphs, suggesting that Greek became an important local language. Writings of the period that have come down to us are often in Aramaic or Greek, as Hebrew became more and more obscure and specialized. Numerous stone architectural objects with such inscriptions appear throughout the museum.

Hebrew remained a second language for the Jews throughout the period of exile. Zionist theorists brought it back to life a hundred years ago. Yadin demonstrated the zeal of Zionists for Hebrew when he described his presentation, in the early 60s, of the newly discovered letters from Israel's president from 134 c.e. to Ben Gurion, who had the same title— *Nasi*. Ben Gurion's reaction was to ask why the letters were in Aramaic rather than Hebrew—Yadin, in his account in the book *Bar Kokhba*, compared his reaction to the way he might reprove his staff if they failed to use Hebrew. Less dramatically, Yadin related how one of the letters, written in Greek, contained an explanation by its writer that there was no one present who could write either Hebrew or Aramaic. These letters, rotated into displays in the Shrine of the Book, thus give insight into the distribution of language in that period.

The Land of Judea

From the Hasmoneans through the Bar Kochba rebellion, Jerusalem was the center of Judea and the focus of national consciousness. Today, Jerusalem covers hills and valleys that were rocky and barren a generation ago, and it dominates the surrounding territory even more than it did in ancient times. In other areas that belonged to ancient Judea, several of the Jewish cities of Roman times are now predominantly Arab, governed under the ever-changing agreement with the Palestinian Authority. The modern, primarily Jewish coastal cities such as Ashkelon, Tel Aviv/ Jaffa, Haifa, and Akko lie in the area that in Roman times was principally Philistine-occupied; modern history has made them firmly Israeli. As a result, my travel narrative about the Judean hills and Herod's most Jewish lands is limited by the problems I had in wanting to avoid travel in hostile areas. Several important places have been impractical destinations for my personal travel style during the times I have been in Israel.

Leaving Jerusalem, each direction offers you a different climate and landscape. To the northwest, the village of Abu Gosh offers Arab hospitality; further in that direction, you will be in Palestinian Authority territory. If you drive southeast on the non-freeway route, you get to the beautiful Soreq valley, whose center is the small town of Bet Shemesh. Nearby, you can tour the Soreq limestone cave, discovered in the course of quarrying rock in the late 1960s, with huge caverns filled with stalactites and stalagmites. At the enterprising Tzora kibbutz not far away, you can buy local wine, cheese, and bread to eat at handy picnic tables or you can have beer and a hamburger at the kibbutz pub. The kibbutz even has an international gift shop with Scandinavian and Far Eastern knick-knacks directed at Israeli shoppers.

Beyond the kibbutz, the valley continues toward Beth Guvrin, also called Maresha, an ancient Hellenistic site, as the Hebron hills begin. The beautiful area varies from hilly to genuinely mountainous. Beyond Maresha are Hebron and the cities of the Palestinian Authority, which now occupy much of the old kingdom. In this valley and to the west, past the Latrun junction, large irrigated farms and fields are under modern cultivation. You could picture goats and sheep on the hillsides as they must have been in ancient times. Similarly to the west in Rehovot, which was on the border of Judean territory, in suburban Bedouin villages, almost daily we watched young boys chasing scraggy sheep and goats across land that's waiting for development by the Weizmann Institute of Science. Rehovot and its neighbors Gadera and Nes Ziona are at the edge of the highly urbanized coastal area, where modern high-rises and shopping centers dominate the landscape.

To the east of Jerusalem are many sites along the Dead Sea, also within easy driving distance for a day trip, and much more accessible, except for Jericho, which is entirely Palestinian.

FOOD AND AGRICULTURE IN JUDEA

In Roman times, as today, the produce of Israel's farms included olive oil, wine, grain, and fruit. In addition, imported spices and luxury goods were traded in sophisticated markets in the urban areas. The biblical passage about "seven species" provides a key to the continued self-image of Jewish agriculture through Roman and Byzantine times. These plants produced important food. Wheat and barley produced bread. Grapevines supplied wine and fruit. Figs could be dried and used as a portable food supply, as well as eaten fresh. Pomegranates produced juice and fruit. Olive oil was critical for lamplight and cosmetic use, as well as for food. And dates were eaten fresh or dried and processed to make date honey, an important sweetener, as refined cane or beet sugars were not yet known.

The Bible Lands Museum in Jerusalem, with its emphasis on the common elements in Near Eastern civilizations, mounted a very effective exhibit about the seven species in 1998; for each of the seven there was a collection of objects and photographs from ancient and modern times, including many artifacts decorated with images of these plants. Of particular interest, the exhibit displayed actual organic remains of items from each of the seven, such as grape seeds, olive pits, date pits, and wheat or barley grains that had been preserved in desert refuse piles. One interesting item on display was a large urn full of figs that had been strung on strings, dried, and stored; the storehouse had burned down, carbonizing the figs but leaving them completely recognizable.

In Roman times, residents of Israel continued to use the traditional seven species and many other foods mentioned in the Bible, such as Esau's lentil porridge or the fish and cucumbers that the Israelites complained were preferable to manna in the desert. Foods mentioned in biblical passages were also important to other people throughout the Mediterranean. Greeks and Romans used olive oil, made grapes into wine, and sweetened their food with honey from beehives or extracted from dates. Israeli produce was exported, and Roman consumers appreciated such delicacies as Jericho dates.

Herdsmen with cows, sheep, and goats appear in stories and on artifacts from biblical times and Homeric or prehistoric Greek times onward. Throughout the Mediterranean, milk and fermented milk products from such herds were important sources of nutrition. I imagine white cheeses and yogurts that resemble what Israel's dairies produce now. (They just didn't market them in little aluminum foil wrappers or plastic tubs.) Producing many types of white cheese, but not much aged cheese, probably is a response to Israel's hot climate. White cheese and yogurt need a short fermentation period at relatively high temperature; aging cheese needs months or years in a suitably cool damp place like a basement in France, where natural organisms occur but don't go wild and cause the food to rot. The same conditions probably applied in Roman times. Herd animals also provided meat for food and sacrifices. Also, columbariums, or houses for raising doves, appear at several sites, which I will mention—doves, too, made tasty dinners and ritually approved sacrifices.

The celebration of wheat and barley harvests by the major Temple pilgrimages points to the significance of grain. Threshing, grinding grain for bread, and toasting it for porridge, were critical food-processing activities. Much of the grinding of grain took place in the home; people employed hand mills to grind what was needed on a daily or other short-term basis from the supplies stored in amphoras or from just-in-time purchases of grain. Mass production of grain was rarer, though archae-ologists have excavated a Roman grain mill, driven by water power, on the Crocodile River near Caesarea, indicating the potential for mass production of flour in Roman times. (This is one of only three known Roman water mills; the others are near Arles, France, and in Tunisia. Water-powered flour mills along streams on the upper Jordan river and at En Gedi date from much later eras.)

The Passover taboo on leavened bread similarly reflects its nutritional importance to ancient Israel. Bread had a place in both daily life and in the Temple ritual, as illustrated by the Temple's "shewbread" tables on which bread loaves were displayed—you can see a similar table, from the priests' houses in Jerusalem, now on display in the Israel Museum. Baking was principally a domestic activity; often bread was prepared at home and baked in communal ovens or small, local bake shops. Often the loaves probably resembled today's pita bread.

As time went on, a number of Jews were influenced by the Romans, cultivating more refined taste and customs. During this era, Mediterranean peoples first began to adopt citrus fruits, which came via Arab traders from the Far East, and to try other new exotic foods and spices. Herod evidently set the stage for Roman-style consumption and encouraged the trade with both East and West. Wealthy, Roman-influenced Jews may have hosted lavish banquets where a set number of guests reclined on couches to be entertained and over-fed. Presumably, the Roman description of a meal "from eggs to apples" began to influence them as well, as suggested by the Roman dining room in a wealthy home in Sepphoris. Set in the floor is a fine mosaic with scenes from the story of Dionysus and a face known as the "Mona Lisa of the Galilee," as well as a large blank space where the archaeologists assume the diners placed their tables and reclining couches in typical Roman fashion. Possibly the Jewish banqueters skipped the Roman delicacies that were strictly taboo, such as roast hedgehogs or flamingo tongues, but there were many luxuries available to them. Shipwrecks outside the harbor at Caesarea have revealed amphoras and other vessels containing Roman foods, particularly *garum*, a type of fermented fish sauce that was beloved by the Romans. Special Jewish *garum* omitted shellfish and other prohibited sea creatures from the preparation and was available in other parts of the Roman Empire where Jews demanded it.

While some Jews assimilated, many followed the dietary laws in varying degrees. As today, these laws regulated the slaughter of animals and food preparation for home or communal consumption, as well as food taboos. Before the end of the Temple, people who wanted to obey the laws also concerned themselves with farmers' obligations to contribute to Temple sacrifices and to observe the seventh-year sabbatical year when many foods could not be grown. The religious avoided all "libation" wine, that is, wine that had been used in pagan rituals. They also defined special ways of handling oil, though this was later deleted from ritual requirements.

Temple sacrifices of roast oxen, sheep, and poultry allowed the priests to take a large share of the meat produced, as well as tithes of grain and fruits. A man who contributed a sacrificial animal was allowed to take away certain portions in special pottery vessels—another priestly monopoly. Ritually slaughtered meat other than sacrificial animals could also be used for food but only by those who could afford it. Tithing demanded contribution of the first fruits, a set percent of the grain and wine production, and the first animals. Tithes could be presented to any priest (no need to travel to Jerusalem). Tithing was enforced by the powerful priestly establishment and was also considered essential to make a farmer's produce acceptable to the religious.

After the Romans destroyed the Temple, Roman government replaced the priestly power structure, and disputes arose about just which rules were still binding. Strict Jews tried to impose continued tithing on farmers in the Galilee, who were less rigorous about their commitment—or too poor to carry it out. During the sabbatical year, farmers were still expected to leave some fields fallow and to refrain from cultivating certain produce. A sixth-century mosaic found in the Rehov synagogue near Bet She'an gives a list of species in this prohibited category—watermelon, mint, onions, garlic, beans, dates, nuts, plums, rice, wheat, oil, wine, and others that couldn't be interpreted. (This mosaic and the translation were on display in the garden of the Israel Museum in 1997 and 1998.) In some cases, famine broke out when stored-up food for a sabbatical year proved inadequate, or when the harvest just afterward failed and left people without reserves.

In the extreme, the food rituals governed every aspect of a highly religious person's life. Flavius Josephus mentioned the strenuous taboos of the Essenes, who consumed only food and drink that they raised and prepared themselves, particularly bread, but also (at least at Qumran) dates, date honey, dairy products, and meat, and a grape beverage called *tirosh*, which may or may not have been fermented. They were much more concerned about who had touched the food than about the taste or nutrition. The cult at Qumran was particularly strict. Members ritually purified themselves before *each meal*. Essenes, Josephus claimed, were so worried about attention to ritual purity that neophytes were only allowed to eat at the members' table after a two-year probation period. They swore an oath never to eat outside their community, and when the group expelled an errant member, he was likely to starve to death rather than break this oath.

A meal could itself serve as a religious ritual even for less stringent Jewish cults. Both before and after the destruction of the Temple, groups of men formed societies called *haverim*. These groups met from time to time for a ritual banquet that very strictly followed the dietary laws, using food that had been planted, harvested, prepared, and handled according to religious requirements. The members considered themselves more holy than ordinary farmers, whose piety they questioned—a set of attitudes that were reflected in later religious writings. After the Temple's destruction, some people developed beliefs that they could fulfill the now-impossible obligations concerning Temple sacrifices by participating in a ritually prepared meal with family or friends, saying appropriate prayers and blessings over traditional foods.

VISITING THE DEAD SEA

East of Jerusalem, a desert road descends into the rift valley, branching south to the Dead Sea and north toward Jericho, the world's oldest city (now in Palestinian Authority territory). At the Dead Sea, you can visit several sites. The first, as you come from the north, is Qumran, where a park shows the site of the ancient community. Further along the Dead Sea, you can walk through the oases and see the ancient synagogue at En Gedi. Along the shoreline, you can visit bathing beaches and resorts to relax in the beating desert sun and dip yourself into the saltiest water on earth. A day trip from Jerusalem can conclude with Masada, farther south along the Dead Sea. The barren desert beauty of these areas is well worth seeing, along with the historical sites.

Religious Conflicts and Sects

As a background to a visit to Qumran, you need to know about Jewish sects that emerged in Roman times. Three strains of Judaism, the Pharisees, the Saducees, and the Essenes, emerged in early Hasmonean times. There were many other splits and distinctions, resulting from religious rivalry or religious conviction or arising from conflicts of interest among various social classes. People who called themselves hasids existed before King Herod. We have already encountered the Zealots and the Sicarii in discussing the fall of the Temple and the last stand at Masada.

The dominant religion of Judea was like many dominant religions: there was room for merely formal observance; control by a rich, powerful, and self-serving priestly class; and simultaneous moral outrage by stricter practitioners. Social pressure and economic dislocations encouraged the success of sects that promised better times in exchange for purer belief, more rigorous practice, and commitment to their way only. The Jews' insistence on a single God, of course, caused a unique sort of conflict with Romans, and it defined the struggle between them.

Until the destruction of the Temple in 70 C.E., worship occurred both in the Temple and in local synagogues. The synagogues' form was just developing in Herod's time. The worshipers faced Jerusalem sitting on benches built around the outer edge of the structure. In these synagogues, there may also have been the beginnings of rituals conducted without the presence of the "holy of holies" associated with the Temple in Jerusalem. The synagogue at Masada is among the oldest of such synagogues, dated with certainty from before the Temple's destruction in 70 C.E.

Christianity, of course, established its foundation during the Roman period. In fact, very little archaeological evidence from that time pertains to the Christian story as the pilgrimage sites in Jerusalem and the Galilee area were identified and laid out in the fourth century, after the official adoption of Christianity by the Empire.

Qumran and the Essenes

Reclusive communal sects, especially the Essenes, lived in the desert and at various other strategic places. The Essene communities occupied sites at Qumran by the Dead Sea and just outside the gate of Jerusalem right near the Temple; there may have been another community in Egypt, where Jews already lived at the time. According to Philo and Josephus, there were around four thousand Essenes. There has been a great deal of speculation, as early wishful thinking attempted to identify the Essenes as the immediate intellectual ancestors of Christianity. Many modern scholars have refuted some of the more extravagant theories of the past and simply identify the Essenes as one of the more extreme versions of the huge number of second- and first-century B.C.E. Jewish splits. However, various scholars may have other—highly contentious—interpretations of the activities, beliefs, and life of the Qumran community.

The Essene cult and lifestyle represented an effort to isolate the Jews from external influences and corruption, particularly from the combination of Roman and Jewish culture. Like any extremist stance, the Essenes' viewpoint was shaped by their need to react against what they abhorred: any synthesis of the two cultures. The sect consciously distinguished its practices from those of Herod's Temple or from the priests' self-aggrandizement. The Essenes reflected Jewish hatreds going back to the assimilation of Hellenistic culture originally brought by Alexander the Great. They had started originally as members of another ancient group, the hasidim, splitting off during the Hasmonean kingdom, that is, around the second century B.C.E. They rejected priests, Temple sacrifices, and other mainstream Jewish practices in favor of an obsessively pure community lifestyle. Other elements of the communal rule required them to make a living by agriculture, as they forbade members to engage in commerce or to manufacture weapons.

The Essenes modeled their communal houses on the organization of ancient Israel—they defined twelve "tribes" of priests, Levites, and Israelites. The "priests" made the sect's decisions and also engaged in private sacrifices, replacing their participation in the sacrifices in the Temple. Full membership was open only to adult men who had to serve several years of initiation stages. This membership gave a man the right to share the food and work of the sect, particularly to eat at the common table, where the strictest rules of ritual food purity were observed. Initiates promised to turn over all their present and future property and earnings to the group. They had many religious customs and rituals, and according to most sources, they never married but only kept up membership by recruitment. (There is some discussion about whether women and children also lived in the Qumran community.) In an age when slaves were common, they rejected slavery. Members who violated the rules were expelled, while those in good standing were cared for throughout their lives, even in old age or sickness.

The most famous accomplishment of the Essenes was to write and deposit the Dead Sea Scrolls at Qumran. For two thousand years these scrolls lay hidden in a number of caves where their owners had secreted them. Qumran National Park at the north end of the Dead Sea includes the site where first, Bedouin shepherds, and later, archaeologists, discovered the scrolls in the late 1940s and early 1950s. The site includes the remains of buildings where the sectarians cooked and ate their communal meals, ground their grain, and copied and bound their manuscripts. The water system, scriptorium, and several of the caves disclose reminders of that distant time. The landscape, the solid rocky cliffs and tiny pools and dribbles of scarce water and scarcer vegetation seem even more vivid reminders of the experience of life in the community. The vistas down sheer cliffs toward the shimmery surface of the Dead Sea increase the atmosphere of isolation in the desert. The site inspires you to picture the extremely austere and isolated life of the Essenes.

The National Park brochure summarizes the history of the commune: "The Essenes arrived at Qumran toward the end of the second century B.C.E. . . . In 31 B.C.E., during the reign of Herod, there was a serious earthquake in the area and the sect abandoned the site. But a quarter of a century later, during the rule of Archelaus, Herod's son (4 B.C.E.–6 C.E.), the Essenes returned to Qumran and rebuilt it. In 68 C.E., during the great Jewish revolt, the Romans conquered Qumran and dispersed the sect. The last known inhabitants of Qumran were members of a Roman garrison stationed there during the Bar Kochba revolt . . ." (Israel National Parks Authority, "Qumran National Park," December 1997).

Besides a visit to the national park at Qumran, a variety of tours allow the visitor to see this part of the desert. A friend participated in such a group outing, which we missed because we had already returned home. He described how they spent an entire moonlit night, from around midnight to dawn, being driven over impossible inclines and traveling over rocks in "comical" desert vehicles big enough for fifty passengers and in Land Rovers. At 3 A.M. they reached a ravine that was once the site of a fifth-century C.E. monastery. They continued to a high point over a ravine from which, traditionally, the biblical "scapegoat" was tossed down to its fate. At Qumran they left the vehicles for a final, two-hour descent on foot, down to Dead-Sea level, where I assume that prearranged transportation was waiting to return them to Rehovot.

An exhibit about the Qumran sect appeared in the entryway to the Shrine of the Book in 1998. It described their calendar, which was a solar calendar resulting in different days for celebration of festivals and which displayed two sundials with indications for determining both the time and the season. Vessels for food in the exhibit included nested pottery bowls and stone cups. Modern scholars speculate that the earthquake that interrupted the sect's habitation of the site occurred immediately after kitchen workers had washed all the dishes, which thus were preserved under the toppled building in large numbers, all neatly stacked up and evidently ready for the next meal. Other artifacts illustrated their work as farmers, as potters, as makers of leather fittings for scrolls, and as scribes. The display included an inkwell, as well as other artifacts and photos of the current site.

En Gedi and Its Desert Springs

Further south of Qumran, in the Nature Reserve of En Gedi, we took some wonderful hikes. The area offers both natural beauty and historic significance. The documentation posted along the trail at the En Gedi springs explains its biblical significance, but when we climbed through the beautiful spring at Wadi Arugot, the oasis next to En Gedi, I was only awed by the dramatic blue of the desert sky, the cool spring-fed streams and cascades, the warm sulfurous water welling up beneath overhanging rocks, and the vivid red cliffs towering above the wadi. (Note that the words *wadi* and *nahal* are used interchangeably to refer to an oasis-like canyon where a spring has eroded a channel through the desert.)

I learned later that it was in caves within the cliffs at Wadi Arugot that Yigael Yadin's expedition in 1960 found many important artifacts and documents that revealed much about the historical character of Bar Kochba. Yadin explored with the assistance of the Israeli armed forces, using mine detectors to find hordes of bronze vessels, using army generators to light the recesses of the cave, and using army personnel to scrutinize the niches of the cave, which had already been looted by Bedouins for whatever they could sell on the international black market in antiquities. Yadin captured the drama of his discoveries by describing them slowly in the order they happened. The background is that some of Bar Kochba's soldiers hid in these caves with their wives and children, who concealed certain possessions with the evident hope that they would return when their luck changed. Unfortunately, the Romans defeated this temporary Jewish state shortly afterward, and the memory of the refugees in the cave was lost. In fact, Bar Kochba had seemed more like a legend than a historical reality until Yadin's expedition.

The packages of letters to his followers, written in Aramaic, Hebrew, and Greek, were the first indication of his first name, Simon, and the first definite knowledge of the spelling of the name Kochba, which tradition preserved in two versions, Bar Kochba, "Son of a Star," or Bar Kosiba, "Son of a Liar." The truth was closer to Bar Kosiba, though originally the meaning may not have been negative. Yadin and his volunteers learned much about the culture and daily life of the area from the objects, and much about the war from the letters. The expedition findings now belong to the Shrine of the Book in Jerusalem. (For a full description, see Yadin's *Bar Kokhba*.)

On our second trip to En Gedi, we set three goals. First—climb the spring beside the waterfalls and visit the cave where the Bible tells us that young David once hid from the powerful and jealous King Saul. Second—go up to the cacolithic temple on the heights above the springs, completing the walk we interrupted on our previous visit. And third— continue to the ancient town of En Gedi, where the village and the synagogue have been excavated. We accomplished what we set out to do with great pleasure. Despite all kinds of posted warnings, the round trip was under two hours in length.

The main springs and waterfalls along the lower parts of the trail were very crowded with kids and adults in bathing suits, each presumably adding a little organic matter for the algae to grow on. It's sad, as Israel doesn't have lots and lots of other such sites—just this one and Wadi Arugot in the next ravine. The cacolithic temple stands at the peak of one of the lower hills between these two oases. Just down the hill is a smaller spring, beautifully clear. The water bubbles out of a hole between some rocks into a quiet, shallow pool under low-hanging trees. Dense rushes form nearly solid walls around it. Although it was fortunately not a hot day, the spring area was a respite from the desert air. While the trail going up was extremely steep, the trail going down is very easy, partly following a reasonably maintained dirt road.

On the other side of the mountain, the archaeological site is a rubble-strewn mound without documentation, but the spacious Byzantine synagogue is preserved under a huge canopy (owned by the National Park Authority). The mosaic floors and surrounding dwellings are clearly documented. The inscription part of the mosaic, naming synagogue donors and other information, is a copy, though the rest is supposed to be original. Beautiful birds and geometric figures fill the mosaic space, with the zodiac represented only by names, no images. An older synagogue stood on this site when the Masada last-standers raided the town around 72 C.E.

BET GUVRIN, MARESHA, AND SUSSIA

The Judean hills southwest of Jerusalem have a long history in biblical and Roman times. The major site in this area, Hebron, has associations going back to the Matriarchs and Patriarchs, with Jewish sites drenched in emotion and continual conflicts. Herod's palace at Herodium is also in this area. Two sites are more accessible to timid tourists and are also relevant to the Roman and Byzantine periods: Bet Guvrin and Sussia.

Bet Guvrin

Bet Guvrin National Park is almost on the border of the Palestinian West Bank, not far from the road to Hebron. The park at first glance offers a strange scrubby desert landscape, but this area contains the foundations of the Hellenistic city of Marisa, or Maresha, a hilltop that was once a more ancient fortress with the ruin of a biblical-era tower, and some Moslem-era stone quarries called the Bell Caves. Points of interest in the park are well marked and documented, and the ancient houses, cellars, and quarries are easy to visit because the park management has installed effective electric lights beside the well-maintained stairway routes through them. They even provide hardhats for walking through the sometimes-crumbly Bell Caves.

The history of Maresha incorporates many of the important historical connections between Jews and outside influences of the Greeks and the Romans. At the beginning of Hasmonean times, Maresha belonged to the state of Idumea and was populated with people from the ethnic groups called Edomites and Sidonians, although long before, in biblical times, it had been inside the territory of Judea. The Hasmoneans conquered the territory, which, you may recall, was the original home of Herod's father, Antipater. The Hasmonean policy dictated that these conquered people be forcibly converted to Judaism, regardless of their historic ethnic origins. By Hellenistic times, Jews, pagans, and people from other parts of the empire lived in the city, so that the architecture and implied lifestyle combined a variety of Mediterranean influences.

Two burial caves from Hellenistic times contain a number of impressive tombs. The paintings in these caves are vivid—because they have just been restored to the state in which they were first discovered in 1902 and soon after. Mythical animals join almost-realistic hippos, hedgehogs, and lions on the walls of one cave, while a statue of a musician playing a reed pipe is the most impressive decoration of the second one. Greek inscriptions and geometric decorations also appear in the frieze-like panel above the tomb niches.

The ancient city of Maresha was destroyed in 40 B.C.E., and another city was founded nearby. In Byzantine times, Septimus Severus gave it the privileges of a Roman city, renaming it Eleutheropolis, which means "city of free men." This city, as a regional center, enjoyed the rights of coinage and taxation and thus amassed great wealth. Its jurisdiction, the Talmudic "Darom," covered Edom, Hebron, and En Gedi. The city remained important through the Byzantine and Arab eras; at the time of Benjamin of Tudela's visit, it still had three Jewish families. Today the city exists only as an archaeology site.

Bet Guvrin National Park presents you with many details of life from Hellenistic and Roman times. Soft limestone, a particularly good building material, comprises the entire top layer of the ground on which the city rests. As a result, the inhabitants built their houses by digging stone blocks from their basements, thus creating large underground spaces where they stored goods, lived, raised livestock, and worked. While the above-ground portions of their city disappeared over time, the cellars still provide a good look at olive oil presses, storage rooms, baths, arched roofs, and cisterns from these times. Several of these cellars have numerous niches in the walls, forming columbaria, or dove cotes. The doves raised here provided meat and eggs for the tables of the affluent occupants. Farmers used the doves' droppings for fertilizer. In addition, according to biblical prescription, doves were appropriate sacrifices for the Temple; non-Jewish residents of the city probably also used them in pagan sacrificial rites.

The residents cultivated olive trees, and the city was famous for its olive oil. As in many cities, the olive presses have survived in very good condition, thanks to the fact that pressing olives required huge pressing stones. The restored press at Bet Guvrin offers diagrams and documentation to help you visualize its use. Wooden beams for leverage to operate the press have been reconstructed, attached to the ancient pressing stones with systems of ropes, and positioned in the trenches through which the oil once flowed, so that you can understand the process of extracting the oil. The residents also made a substantial industry of quarrying the excellent stone for export to other locations. Archaeologists have identified stone from the Bet Guvrin quarries in buildings as far away as Ashkelon and Lod. For all this heavy work, the occupants must have had many slaves.

Sussia

Not far from Bet Guvrin, just into the Palestinian Authority territories, are the remains of another Byzantine-era town called Sussia. Founded after the fall of the Temple, Sussia provided a refuge where Jews could escape from the eyes of Roman legionnaires in the more traditionally populous parts of the country. Houses, craftsmen's shops, and a synagogue have been restored for public viewing. The synagogue once had a zodiac mosaic, but its current state is more traditional; that is, at some point during the several hundred years of Jewish occupation, residents remade it to omit the human figures. Synagogue inscriptions commemorate donors to the building funds. To see some of the finds, you must visit the Israel Museum as well as the site.

Architectural fragments that I have seen in museums and special exhibits suggest that various other communities of Jews lived in several places among the Hebron hills during Byzantine times, after the Bar

Kochba rebellion. A column capital here, a lintel there, and pretty soon you'd think there were lots of synagogues. I suspect that the sites from which these fragments came have never been turned into parks or tourist sites, and in fact, many dig areas may be covered up or no longer accessible.

The Roman
Coast Road

The old Roman road—the Via Maris— carried important traffic the length of Judea. When the Romans arrived, a road had existed here for approximately two thousand years. The route had always been much coveted by whatever factions were most powerful in the region. Just north of Egypt, it crossed through Gaza and the Philistine cities of Ashdod and Ashkelon. Further north, it went through Jaffa. After Jaffa and after the road toward Jerusalem, a little north of the present Tel Aviv metropolitan area, the road has two branches. One branch turns inland and goes toward Damascus: this is the start of the most accessible' way through the mountains and across the Syrian-African Rift. The other branch continues along the coast, north through current Akko, then toward the Phoenician cities of Sidon and Tyre, and on in the direction of Anatolia. This now belongs to Turkey but was then occupied by the old colonies of ancient Greece. See the map at the beginning of this chapter for the relative locations of Ashkelon, Jaffa, Tel Aviv, and Akko.

From earliest times until the Crusades, this road carried the trade between Egypt and the various civilizations in Anatolia, in Mesopotamia, and farther east. The road often enabled armies to reach the sites of major battles. The road had always made local inhabitants wealthy and powerful because its many hilly stretches afforded local people strategic places where they could stop travelers or entire caravans. They could prevent access by enemies and could collect tolls or taxes in exchange for the use of the roads. Cities and hamlets along the road offered commercial travelers and their pack animals inns and stables, and thus the inhabitants could share the wealth that went by. When times were more chaotic, their strategic location enabled them to rob the caravans. When the Romans began to dominate the region, the ancient biblical strongholds still played a major role in controlling the road from Egypt to Damascus. Meggido (also called Armageddon) and Hatzor dominated the tops of two hills, each standing at an important crossroads. As Roman-style defense and attack became the norm, these old hilltop fortifications became obsolete and were replaced by a different sort of city. As a result, today you see Roman construction on flat areas and much older cities or areas of the cities on tops of hills such as at Sythopolis/Beth She'an.

The Romans, naturally, developed the coast road and built more ports. Under Herod, Roman policy created an enormous increase in trade between the East and the Mediterranean. Ships sailed between Jaffa and Caesarea and ports in Phoenicia, Egypt, Carthage, Greece, Crete, Anatolia, Sicily, and Italy, and to Roman colonies as far away as Spain and France. Caravans went from Ashkelon toward Petra across the Nabatean lands and desert. Farther north, traditional land routes allowed travel from the coast toward the Decapolis—ten Roman and Hellenistic cities in Syria and Eastern Israel. The Romans conquered and held most of the territory in the Middle East during the time of Herod. The Via Maris was a strategic Roman road, as it had been strategic throughout history, because it connected several superpowers of the time—Egypt, Babylonia, Syria, and Phoenicia.

ASHKELON

Along with Ashdod, Ashkelon was an old Philistine city of importance in biblical days; the importance continued during the times of Herod because it was the first city north of the Egyptian-dominated Gaza strip and thus essential to defense against potential attacks from Egypt. Major Roman building activity made it into an important city on the Via Maris. After the period we are talking about, the city returned to importance during the Crusades, when its strategic location again became an issue. The current archaeology park is disappointing compared to Caesarea or Masada.

Throughout the Roman occupation, hostility continued between the Jews and the Philistines who occupied this area. Flavius Josephus describes how the riots in Caesarea first touched off anti-gentile riots in a number of cities in the province of Syria—"Philadelphia, Heshbin, Gerasa, Pella, and Sythopolis. Next they swooped on Gadara, Hippus, and Gaulantis . . . Then on to Kedasa near Tyre, Ptolemais, Gaba, and Caesarea. There was no resistance to their onslaughts in either Sebaste or Ascalon, both of which they burnt to the ground" (Josephus, *The Jewish War,* translated by G. A. Williamson; revised by E. Mary Smallwood, London: Penguin Books, 1981, p. 169). The Romans accordingly gave carte blanche to anti-Jewish activity, and in revenge, non-Jews in Ashkelon massacred 2,500 Jews, drove others from their homes, and pillaged Jewish property.

Later on, when the Jews formed an army, Jewish troops first defeated Cestius, the ruler of Syria, and then "as if carried off their feet by this stroke of luck they determined to send their armies further afield. Without loss of time all their most warlike elements joined forces and marched to Ascalon. This is an old town sixty miles from Jerusalem, though the Jews hated it so bitterly that when they made it the object of their first attack it seemed much nearer than that!" (*Jewish War,* Williamson translation, p. 190). The Romans defeated them very badly.

Today, the seaside park at Ashkelon displays a number of Roman columns and other architectural fragments set up in an almost random way. The archaeologists who dug there a century ago seem to have restored things haphazardly. They mingled Crusader ruins with the Roman ruins. A line of capitals from variously styled columns controls traffic flow into a parking lot. Other architectural elements seem to be placed at odd intervals to delimit picnic sites or playing areas. In a special exhibit at the Israel Museum, I saw a stone carving from the ancient synagogue at Ashkelon, which belongs to a collection in Europe, suggesting that early archaeologists removed the most valuable artifacts from the site. Modern visitors seem attracted more by the sandy Mediterranean beach adjacent to the Roman ruins.

Very active archaeology expeditions continue there now, though they are closed to the public. When I was there, the archaeologists had reserved most of the Roman site, which therefore was inaccessible to tourists, particularly the restored Roman theater. The National Park Web site and the web site sponsored by the archaeology team would be good sources of current information, if you hope to see more on your own visit.

Caution: Almost all of the nonviolent thefts I ever heard of in Israel took place in the parking lot of the National Park at Ashkelon, which is administered by locals, not by the more reliable Park Authority. Apparently, petty thieves watch the behavior of arriving tourists, particularly with rental cars, and break the windows and open the trunks when they know the owners are swimming in the sea.

JAFFA, THE OLDEST PORT

Jaffa was the only port for biblical Judean trade with the entire Mediterranean, and it may be the world's oldest port still in use. References to Jaffa occur in ancient Egyptian documents, as the Egyptians liked to control this coast and its communicating routes in strategic directions. The Jaffa port used the only natural harbor in a long stretch of the coast; thus ships from far and wide wanting to trade with the ancient Jews came to do business there. Ashkelon to the south and Akko to the north belonged to other peoples. Although there were efforts to create alternative ports, such as the Roman development of Caesarea, only in the twentieth century has Jaffa's port become totally unimportant: modern freighters and military ships put in at the artificial harbors of Tel Aviv, Ashdod, and Haifa. I love to go to Jaffa today, because of the historic setting and the pleasant atmosphere.

Roman Views of Jaffa

The Romans associated Jaffa with the Greek mythical figure Andromeda. The story tells how the hero Perseus rescued her from a sea monster in the harbor after her mother, Cassiopea, had boasted that she was more beautiful than the mermaids—an act that inspired the god Poseidon to send the sea monster to devour her. One rock formation in the harbor is even today named for Andromeda. Flavius Josephus provides a description of the "haven," or harbor of Jaffa and the rock formation of Andromeda's Chair that still seems quite accurate:

> Joppa [Jaffa] is not naturally a haven, for it ends in a rough shore, where all the rest of it is straight but the two ends bend toward each other, where there are deep precipices, and great stones that jut out into the sea, and where the chains wherewith Andromeda was bound have left their footsteps, which attest to that antiquity of the fable. But the north wind opposes and beats upon the shore, and dashes mighty waves against the rocks which receives them, and renders the haven more dangerous than the country they had deserted.

Although Herod had essentially replaced Jaffa with Caesarea, the port still had strategic importance during the rebellion of 66 to 70. During this time, the city was taken twice. The second time, Vespasian marched unopposed into Jaffa. The people fled to their ships in the harbor as

Vespasian approached. Flavius Josephus continued the previous passage with a description of the disaster:

> Now as those people of Joppa were floating about in this sea, in the morning there fell a violent wind upon them; it is called by those that sail there the black north wind, and there dashed their ships one against another, and dashed some of them against the rocks, and carried many of them by force while they strove against the opposite waves into the main sea; for the shore was so rocky, and had so many of the enemy upon it, that they were afraid to come to land; nay, the waves rose so very high that they drowned them; nor was there any place whither they could fly, nor any way to save themselves, while they were thrust out of the sea, by the violence of the wind, if they stayed where they were, and out of the city by the violence of the Romans. . . . the Romans came upon those that were carried to the shore and destroyed them; and the number of the bodies that were thus thrown out of the sea was four thousand and two hundred. The Romans also took the city without opposition and utterly demolished it. (*Wars of the Jews*, Whiston translation, pp. 244–45)

After defeating the Jews, Vespasian established a camp from which the Romans plundered the towns in the area.

Tourism in Jaffa

Jaffa offers a number of very pleasant activities, including attractive seaside restaurants, an exotic flea market, and a visitor center and museum that present the history of the town. Up above the old port, on the high ground, the Romans built an area they called the Acropolis. Today, many buildings, the visitor center, the museum, several historic churches, a restaurant with a dramatic view of the coast, and a park occupy this site. I recommend that you begin at the visitor center, which is under the main plaza, where you can obtain a map locating the other tourist attractions.

The visitor center is located in a carefully preserved archaeology site. You can view the ruins of a house that was destroyed in 68 C.E., when the Romans put down the Jewish rebellion. In addition to the excavation, a number of placards illustrate the highlights of Jaffa's history. One placard mentions that Jonah, the biblical prophet, put out to sea from Jaffa. Another mentions a tale in the book of Maccabees about a massacre of the Jews of the city. Still another placard tells the story of Nicanor, one of the richest Jews in Alexandria in Herod's time. By Herod's time, it was almost a legend that the cedars of Lebanon for the First Temple had entered Solomon's Kingdom through the ancient port.

The museum, which occupies an old Turkish building about two blocks from the visitor center, begins its display with artifacts from the stone age and includes items found in Jaffa throughout prehistoric and historic times. From Roman and Hellenistic times, you can see the gravestones and ossuaries of Jews who were buried in Jaffa. By the time of the rebellion in 68 C.E., many of these people (according to the epitaphs) had already begun to disperse through the Roman Empire and were originally from Alexandria, Anatolia, or elsewhere. Today, Jaffa is rather quiet, while the ancient city must have been really busy with the commerce of the country.

The museum displays many coins, pottery items, glass flasks, bottles, and drinking cups, and a few brass bangles and glass beads. The coins illustrate how many other countries have ruled Jaffa, which only once in history had its own mint. The Romans left coins showing Judea Capta, and the Jews left coins of the revolt. The museum presents one oil lamp from each period of Jaffa's history, starting with one from before the age of bronze. From the graves, there are also a number of Roman and Byzantine lamps with various bands of designs, some still showing the soot from the burning wicks that illuminated the darkness in the buildings beside the only harbor of the time. Jaffa's own coins show Athena's owl.

The Jaffa port now serves only small craft such as fishing dinghies and pleasure-boats. Instead of cranes and dry docks on the waterfront, you will find pleasant outdoor cafes, restaurants, and shops catering to weekend sailors and yacht owners, as well as a few sheds where fishing nets are hung up to dry. At the harbor, quiet men and women line the ancient breakwater, casting their lines into the waves and waiting for the fish to bite, while the waves break on the natural rock barriers. Thus, the old port still serves vessels the size of those that the Romans built.

The fish restaurants and the picturesque walk along the breakwater beside the port are targeted toward sightseers as well as middle-class visitors from Tel Aviv. Quite a few of the restaurants do business on Friday night. Because the owners are Arabs, they can serve the secular community, whereas the religious minority forces many businesses in the city center to remain closed on the Sabbath. Many of the restaurants specialize in the fish caught from the small boats you can watch in the harbor, a few yards from your table. A few of them do rather innovative cooking; most serve traditional Middle-Eastern dishes. To select a good restaurant, I recommend that you consult the *Gault-Millau* guide (as mentioned in the appendix on practical travel tips).

Just beyond the row of restaurants you can watch as Andromeda's rocks create huge splashing ricochets, and higher waves break right over the twenty-foot-tall breakwater even on fairly nice days. The small Roman, Egyptian, and Judean ships of two thousand years ago must have had a challenge negotiating the rocks and shallows in the channel leading to this little port. Looking north, you see Tel Aviv's modern skyline and waterfront promenades a few miles away. On a clear day, you can see as far as the modern port of Tel Aviv. A bit to the south along the coast, fish restaurants line the beach. You can try delicious fried Mediterranean squid rings, shrimp, grilled fish, and the ever-present hummus or egg-plant salads in semi-outdoor settings.

The Jaffa flea market, not far from the old port, stirs with sales of old furniture, old clothing, old electronic parts or appliances, souvenirs like jewelry and ceramics, expensive antiques, oriental rugs, pita-bread sandwiches, snacks, and fresh Middle-Eastern pastry. Indoor shops com-pete with outdoor stalls and with people selling a few items spread on the hood of a car or out of a tailgate. The oriental bazaar atmosphere includes the smells of frying falafel and french fries, the cries of street vendors, and the call to prayers echoing from the mosque near the seashore. Many of the buildings that house the market date from Turkish times, and a few from Crusader times, but it's possible to imagine how the town may have looked at a number of times in the past, perhaps going back to the neolithic age when people first inhabited the hill overlooking the natural port.

The clock-tower near the flea market is a major Jaffa landmark. Past that are the winding streets of the Arab quarter, a few mosques, Turkish public buildings, and the huge flea market. Beyond the tourist area, many of Jaffa's buildings are in a very bad state of disrepair, illustrating the stalemate between the Israeli–Arab community and their country with regard to rebuilding. The streets wind around, dead-end unexpectedly, and are often one-way, and we only once succeeded in driving in and out of Jaffa without becoming lost.

ERETZ ISRAEL MUSEUM, TEL AVIV—GLASS BLOWERS AND GLASS TECHNOLOGY

Let's make another diversion into understanding the material culture of the Jews under the Romans. Tel Aviv, just north of Jaffa, wasn't a city during the Roman period. I am sure you will want to spend some time in the modern city, but details of its attractions are outside the timeframe to which I have limited my description. However, the Eretz Israel Museum on the site of the archaeology dig called Tel Quasile (once a Canaanite city) has very important evidence about the Roman-Jewish interaction. In the Glass Pavilion, the Ceramics Pavilion, and the Numismatic Pavilion, you can see vivid examples of authentic objects that in the Roman era (and other eras) individuals in Israeli towns used in their daily lives. Even in the Philatelic exhibit, mainly concerned with the history of the Israeli Post Office and its predecessors, there are a few indications of how the ancients communicated as well. I have mentioned several of these collections in the context of discussing the Israel Museum in Jerusalem. The museum also offers technology and crafts demonstrations, recreating how people made some of these artifacts or used certain items, such as the full-scale olive presses in the courtyards of the large museum campus (you must obtain a schedule to learn when particular crafts are demonstrated).

The Glass Pavilion shows the development of glass, which originated in the region around three thousand years ago. Middle-Eastern glass makers in Sidon and Tyre, as well as at sites in Israel and Egypt, were always among the world's best and were important to the Greeks and Romans. The museum displays original glass bottles, beads, and other artifacts from the area and explains the process of glass blowing, invented during the Roman period.

The displays illustrate the earliest glass from Egypt and the Middle East. In these ancient times, glass objects were formed around a core. Glass makers could manage only small beads, icons, and vials, which were opaque with a sort of matte finish. They imitated colors of gem stones—deep blue, lapis, yellow, and quartz colors. Later, they added a technique of draping a glass object around a mold, which allowed a larger size and more varied appearance. Around 150 B.C.E., the Phoenicians invented the process of blowing, rather than passively forming, glass, and the technique took off. Large plates, bowls, vases, and bottles could be made from glass that was completely clear or somewhat tinted. Though perishable, many objects of glass remain from ancient Israel because it was so often used in burials; most of the delicate vessels with their ribbon-like handles and fanciful, thin necks come from graves, not from ordinary city ruins.

The museum exhibits show how glass was manufactured and shipped in large unformed blobs to glass shops where workers heated it until molten and glass blowers at their kilns and forges formed the final product. Glass shops of the Middle East supplied the entire Roman Empire, where glass was widely popular. From this time onward, every Israeli archaeology site yields many glass fragments as well as other artifacts, as glass was a valued commodity, though not in the least rare in Roman times. Glass blowers were important artisans in Galilee in later Roman times, and there are examples of glass fabrication plants (where they made the raw slabs of glass) and evidence of glass blowers in many shops. Glass blowers used a sort of a forge and kiln, the heavy industry of the time. There was even recycling—broken glass could be melted down along with the slabs of glass from the factories.

On display are glass objects of incredible beauty. Bowls, beads, tiny perfume vials, large pitchers, and carved and blown vessels were made in clear glass and light colors. The handles take on fanciful or graceful shapes. Although some people say that the Jews were less interested in material culture than in spiritual and philosophic activities, the glass that they owned or that was buried in various local burial sites seems to contradict this. Particularly interesting is a first-century c.e. Classical vase, signed by the glass maker named Ennion. It's deep blue, in a very graceful shape, like a Greek vase, with a single high handle. A perfect, restored copy is in the Eretz Israel museum, while a twisted and damaged version, found in the ruins of the priests' houses, appears in the Israel Museum in Jerusalem. The possession of so Roman an object reinforces the idea of how the priests accepted many amenities of the Roman lifestyle.

Later during the period when Jews lived in Galilee, glass blowing became a common activity in the Jewish cities there, and there was much glass production for Jews and with Jewish themes. Rabbis in Galilee during the third and fourth century made their living as artisans, and quite possibly glassblowing was the trade of at least a few of them. Items made from glass became more and more common and inexpensive. From the earliest times, glass beads had been cheaper than precious stones. By Roman times, technology improvements lowered costs even more. From the excavations of Sepphoris I saw several colored glass bangle-bracelets, some in children's sizes, labeled as the jewelry of the less well-to-do classes of Byzantine times.

The rest of the Eretz Israel museum is also very interesting and includes some mosaics installed outdoors and the ongoing archaeology dig at Tel Quasile. The Ceramic Pavilion has a number of Greek and other Mediterranean vases, but in my view is less well organized than the Glass Pavilion; its presentation mixes up regional, thematic, and manufacturing concepts, even including descriptions of modern African and South American village crafts. Another pavilion displays ritual objects from Diaspora communities, including art objects from an Italian synagogue. Finally, although I usually find coin displays tedious, the Numismatic Pavilion of this museum is very enlightening. It's exciting to see the faces of Roman emperors and rulers of the area on objects that were made in their time. The coins of the various Israeli uprisings and revolts are well represented: coins from the time of the Maccabees, coins dated from the various years of the anti-Roman uprising that ended with the fall of Masada in 73, and coins from the Bar Kochba revolt. Each case documents one small period in history, amply illustrated by many coins.

Within walking distance of the museum, on the campus of Tel Aviv University, is the Diaspora Museum, where you can find a brief summary of Jewish life outside of Israel during the last two thousand years. There is little or nothing about Roman times, but you might want to look at the computer databases of information about current and past Jewish communities throughout the world. The museum's collection of recordings and videos of Jewish music, and a database of family names and their origins are also interesting. Their archives also include family trees that people have contributed, but their data retrieval system is quite inadequate, and they do no verification on what people give them.

CAESAREA, HEROD'S PAGAN CITY

The site of Caesarea contains no modern city. Nearby housing and a kibbutz are discretely arranged to preserve the ambiance of the ancient harbor. Ruins dominate the beautiful seashore for several miles—ruins from the eras of Herod, the Byzantines, the Arabs, and the Crusaders, and a city founded by the Turks one hundred years ago to house Bosnian refugees. The tall stacks of a power plant in the middle distance present a modern counterpoint to the vast views of a ruin so large that decades of archaeology have not completed the reconstruction. National Park ticket booths, makeshift shelters for current archaeology digs, and souvenir stands and restaurants housed in the Turkish village structures are the only other evidence that you are still part of the twentieth century.

After buying your ticket, good for entry to both the theater and the separate area of the ancient city, the main entrance takes you through a covered crusader gate and down the main street of the ruins. In the main seaside area you can tour reconstructed city walls and gates from several eras, the foundations of civic buildings, the marketplace, and the Roman baths, and the ruins of an amazing Roman breakwater and port. The highest structure is the tower of an old minaret from the Turkish town that stood here a century ago. You can wander around where the digs are taking place, seeing little bits of mosaic scattered on the ground and sandbags protecting the more valuable findings. We saw the work in the bath house in the Roman area. They seemed to be unearthing and restoring mosaics. We never saw anyone actually at work, as we were there on Saturday out-of-season—like most Israeli archaeology projects, most of the exploring takes place during Israeli, American, and European universities' summer vacations to accommodate the schedules of researchers and volunteer workers.

The reconstructed Roman theater just to the south has its own gate with another snack bar and traffic patterns that permit concerts and presentations to take place with controlled seating and ticket taking. The theater was excavated and restored by Italian archaeologists between 1959 and 1963. Its perfect modern bleachers were clearly redone to accommodate modern audiences. From behind the bleachers, you can see that now, the seats are reinforced with modern concrete under the Roman stones. When you climb up these bleachers, there is a magnificent view out to sea and down the coast to the town and port area—a view that must have been an asset to Roman performances. At the modern entrance to the theater area you can find the area's most photogenic item: a giant marble foot, at least a yard in length, with carefully sculpted toes, arch, heel, and so on, broken off at the ankle—perhaps from one of the giant statues that Flavius Josephus mentions. After all, if a foot is a yard long, the whole figure must have stood five or six yards high to be proportional. Several torsos of beautiful Roman statues also stand beside the foot, decorating a small garden. If you miss this photo opportunity, you can always stop at the many souvenir shops to get postcards.

Beyond the walled city you can drive on toward a Byzantine forum in which there is a Roman pavement lined by fragments of massive statues propped up oddly against some pillars. The jumble of ruins from various times, the sight of ancient stones set up in traffic circles to decorate the new vacation neighborhoods, a restaurant called "The Statues" that stands at the site where a huge red statue rests in the Byzantine forum, and the power plant with tall cooling stacks up the shore combine into a sort of parody. In the park, you might see the capital of a Roman column turned sideways to support a Crusader wall, or other Roman stones incorporated into Gothic arches. Caesarea's businesses: "The Crusader Restaurant," "Herod's Restaurant—Kosher," or "Caesarea Art Gallery" reinforce this sense of dislocation. It's all somewhat like the intentional anachronisms of the TV series "Hercules," where ancient Greek heroes and gods often spout later Greek philosophy or Medieval European ideas, or eat modern Greek food or kiwi fruit, or use Renaissance technology.

Several miles farther down the beach stands the Roman aqueduct, partly covered by drifting dunes and beach grass, framing ordinary twentieth-century beach activities: noisy dune buggies, family barbecues, and sunbathing teenagers. The combination of stone ruins, deep blue seascape and clear, light sky is breathtaking. The aqueduct is nearly swamped by the sand dunes, but the arches still stand in beautiful symmetry. Because Caesarea was a seaside town, it didn't require the really spectacular feats of Roman aqueduct engineering, carrying water across deep valleys, such as the one still standing in Segovia, Spain, but this is nevertheless a beautiful sight. Once as we walked along the top of the aqueduct, looking at the ancient water carrier, we thought it seemed to sway in the wind: later, we found, we had felt the motion of a slight earthquake.

Caesarea is amazing in the long extent of its ruins, including Herod's harbor, with practically no modern city in the area. A line of massive red marble pillars lies in low water like a strange logjam, suggesting the beauty of the ancient construction, as well as its practical side. Engineering was state of the art, including the first use of concrete poured and cured under water, a new Roman invention of the time. Above all, I think Caesarea supports the greatness of King Herod, his broad vision for his country, and his ability to take advantage of Roman engineering and administrative ability. As I have said, it's interesting to contrast the pure Romanness of Caesarea with the compromises and syntheses of Jerusalem.

The surroundings also give many clues as to how dramatically Caesarea improved the freight transfer capacity of Herod's commercially emerging state. Jaffa is still visibly a harbor for small craft, which must require considerable navigation skill to bring boats around the breakwater and past the large rock formations. Just south of Jaffa near Bat Yam we walked on the beach with the sand dunes behind us and watched the long rolling waves that break far out beyond the wide sand beach. There were once dunes like this all along, where Tel Aviv is today and up and down the coast. Looking at these dunes and the long beach, you can picture what Flavius Josephus had in mind when he described the treacherous coast. A small sailing ship with a deep ocean keel would certainly founder if it approached such a beach. The only watercraft at Bat Yam was a wind surfer, riding the waves and going well past them for long reaches. A very skillful surfer indeed, young, strong, dressed warm, and able to hike way out and wrestle with his sail. It's no place for cargo ships, ancient or modern. Herod's city was indeed a contribution.

History

Let's turn back the clock to Herod's time. Flavius Josephus provides much information about Caesarea and Herod's interest in it. He thus describes how Herod developed Caesarea:

> And when he observed that there was a city by the sea-side that was much decayed (its name was Strato's Tower), but that the place, by the happiness of its situation, was capable of great improvements from his liberality, he rebuilt it all with white stone, and adorned it with several most splendid palaces, wherein he especially demonstrated his magnanimity; for the case was this, that all the seashore between Dora and Joppa, in the middle between which this city is situated, had no good haven, insomuch that everyone that sailed from Phenicia for Egypt was obliged to lie in the stormy sea, by reason of the south winds that threatened them; which wind, if it blew but a little fresh, such vast waves are raised, and dash upon the rocks, that upon their retreat the sea is in a great ferment for a long way. But the king, by the expenses he was at, and the liberal disposal of them, overcame nature, and built a haven larger than was the Pyreeum at Athens; and in the other retirements of the water he built other deep stations . . . he enlarged that wall which was thus already extant above the sea till it was two hundred feet wide: one hundred of which had buildings before it, in order to break the force of the waves, whence it was called Procumasia, or the first breaker of the waves; but the rest of the space was under a stone wall that ran round it. On this wall were very large towers, the principal and most beautiful of which was called Drusium, from Drusus, who was son-in-law to Cæsar. (*Wars of the Jews*, Whiston translation, pp. 70–71)

Mediterranean port development, intended to create an international maritime industry to connect with other Roman colonies, was foreign to the Judeans. Before Herod, Caesarea was a small, decayed town called Strato's Tower. The seagoing towns to the south along the coast—Ashdod, Ashkelon, Gaza—were Philistine towns and weren't associated with the people of Judea and the other Jewish kingdoms, as were the Phoenician cities to the North. Jaffa, virtually the only port into the Jewish kingdoms, simply was inadequate for Herod's ambitious commerce.

Herod was a great investor—recall that even the Temple was a draw for the lucrative Jerusalem tourist trade catering to rich pilgrims from all over. His profit motive was very much in keeping with his tendency to combine Roman and Jewish culture. He conceived Caesarea as a non-Jewish city, which would mainly fulfill the need for a bigger port to carry his enormously developed trade with the Far East. It would allow him to develop markets for the agricultural products of the Jordan valley and the coastal plain, as well as for exotic products like balm and dates from his desert plantations near the Dead Sea. Jaffa, with its small natural harbor, could not be enlarged, but Roman engineering could create an artificial port.

Caesarea's construction and the technology applied to it were remarkable examples of Roman design and Herodian determination. Herod employed the most highly skilled architects and engineers to create a city plan and to build the city. The project required only thirteen years, beginning in 22 B.C.E. These leaders hired thousands of slaves and wage-workers and created a classical city with a grid of streets and public squares, marble temples and public buildings, theaters, an aqueduct, and a sewer system. The local water supply was supplemented by water from Mount Carmel, brought down the coast along the aqueduct. Above all, using Roman technology for pouring concrete under water, they created the vast harbor with "docks, warehouses, breakwaters, a lighthouse, and six colossal bronze statues to guard the entrance and welcome seafarers seeking haven. Herod dedicated this city to Caesar Augustus—he was a 'faithful client of Rome and its ruler'" (Kenneth G. Holum, *King Herod's Dream: Caesarea on the Sea,* New York: W. W. Norton, 1988, p. 22).

These skillful Roman engineers made pioneering use of underwater concrete construction at Caesarea, as suggested in the quote from Flavius Josephus. Roman concrete was composed of stone rubble bound by lime and a special volcanic ash—the archaeologist-divers, exploring the foundations of the harbor, determined that this ash was imported from Italy for use in Caesarea. The Romans had already determined that the special hardening properties of this concrete made it excellent for bridge and harbor construction, and thus they used it effectively, building special forms under water and then filling them with the concrete. A characteristic block that the archaeologist-divers have studied measured 11.5 by 15 by 2.4 meters. Traces of the wooden forms were still in place. Carbon 14 dating and botanical analysis showed that the forms were truly from the Roman era and that the wood included spruce, pine, fir, and poplar of European origin, implying that Roman engineers probably brought these materials with them.

Herod could choose the inhabitants of this new city, ensuring their loyalty and thus strengthening his hold on his domains. He populated the new city with a mix of Greek-speaking pagans, local pagans, Samaritans from the neighboring region, and Jews from Judea. Perhaps he even thought he might compete with Alexandria. In *Herod's Dream,* the author summarizes Herod's motive for building the city: "Herod willed Caesarea into being, for reasons of policy, to make a profit, and as a colossal act of self-expression. The city figured prominently in his career, a manifestation of his personality and his dreams" (*Herod's Dream*, pp. 55–56).

Holum, like many archaeologists, explained that his excavations contradict many historic stereotypes. One of these is the claim that Herod avoided giving offense by allowing no coin to represent human forms. In fact, images of gods appeared on Caesarea's coins, and the city had its own goddess, or Tyche, whose image appeared on local coins in the ruins. In 1972, the archaeologists discovered her statue, enabling them to understand the image on these coins. Herod also built several temples and statues to other Roman gods, including a temple to Roma and to Augustus, bringing home that this was a totally Roman city where Jews were always foreigners, not natives. Caesarea was both a pagan and a Jewish city, leaning toward the pagans and with much in it to offend the Jews.

The building of Caesarea continued after Herod's death, as did the rivalry between the Jews and the non-Jews. All did not go well for the Jews, and Caesarea was the site of the quarrel between the members of a synagogue and their neighbors, which started the war against Rome in 66. Flavius Josephus set the death toll in the subsequent riots at twenty thousand, which suggests the size of the city. We have already discussed the subsequent war and its disastrous effect on the remainder of the country.

Caesarea remained mainly a non-Jewish city during the aftermath of the revolt and during the Bar Kochba revolt. Eventually, toward the end of the next century, the Jewish population began to grow again, in response to the continuing prosperity of the port. Later, both ordinary people and prominent rabbis lived in the city, along with members of the increasingly influential Christian sect. "Ancient sources mention Jews in many trades—goldsmith, shopkeeper, potter, fish merchant, baker, and weaver. One Caesarean Jew was an 'engineer,' perhaps responsible for the city's aqueducts, and at least one is known who served on the governor's staff" (*Herod's Dream*, pp. 196–197).

The National Park at Caesarea today is also the site of a major archaeology expedition, a joint Israeli-American undertaking. Each summer professionals and volunteers perform digs and also underwater diving exploration of the site to bring up shipwrecks and to learn more about the Roman technique for pouring concrete under water. Their discoveries have been rich and varied. You can see photos and learn more by examining the WorldWide Web sites, which report on recent findings and recruit volunteer labor for the next summer's activities.

AKKO, A STRATEGIC LOCATION

The road to the north stays along the coast, past the biblical site of Tel Dor, now an archaeology excavation and a pleasant bathing beach. The Roman road continued through Akko and on into Lebanon. Flavius Josephus knew Akko by its Greco-Roman name, Ptolmais. His descriptions of the Roman campaigns during the war of 66 to 70 often include Roman troop movements through this city, whose strategic location near Lebanon was then very critical. If you drive to Akko, you must decide whether to brave the traffic of the large modern city of Haifa or whether instead to try to detour around Mount Carmel. If you choose, you can make a circle through Galilee and come back down the coast through Akko. Every route, whether by sea or by mountains, is beautiful. And every route has historic resonance, whether from ancient, classical, or more modern wars and battles.

Like Caesarea, Akko was an important Crusader city, shared by famous crusading kings and famous monastic orders such as the Hospitallers and Templars. The main places of tourist interest today are the Mosque, built over a destroyed Crusader church, the big Crusader halls, and a labyrinth of Crusader tunnels beneath the markets and houses of the old city. For modern history, you can see one of the principal prisons where the British held Zionist underground fighters. You can supply your own fantasies about hidden Templar treasures or heroic battles. New excavations are making additional historic sites accessible all the time. The old Arab squares and buildings incorporate many classical marble columns taken from the ruins of Caesarea. The market offers enormous local color, with fragrant spices and appealing fresh fruit, fish, and vegetables. Our Israeli friends also rate the hummus in Akko as the best in Israel, so presumably the best in the world. I have as yet failed to become a full-fledged hummus gourmet, but I pass the information on for your meal planning on any trip to the area.

Galilee and
the North

GALILEE, PLACE OF RABBIS AND EMPERORS

Galilee and the northern part of Israel contain the country's most beautiful green hills and farmland, in contrast to the southern desert landscapes. The farms, villages, towns, and parks of this region are more relaxing than the intense cities of Tel Aviv and Jerusalem. The heights surrounding the below-sea-level Sea of Galilee (also known as Lake Tiberias or the Kinneret) create peaceful and expansive views. South of the Sea of Galilee, the Jordan River, the boundary between Israel and Jordan, provides water for prosperous farms in a wide valley sloping down toward the Dead Sea. To the north, an abrupt ridge separates the sea from another fertile plain, which stretches to the slopes of Mount Hermon on the Lebanese border. Among Mount Hermon's foothills are extraordinary springs from which the Jordan River flows. Grapevines and fruit trees grow on the sloping hillsides, and kibbutzes raise large dairy herds. These natural features provide opportunities for varied recreation—water sports, hiking, bird-watching, and even skiing.

The unique appeal of the region is in the variety of historical sites, which date from every era: prehistoric villages; the Canaanite cities of Hatzor, Meggido, and Dan, which became part of Solomon's kingdom; the Herodian city of Caesarea Philippi, also called Banias; Byzantine cities full of glorious art and sculpture; synagogues and Jewish towns where talmudic rabbis lived; Crusader-era castles with Medieval moats, towers, and dungeons; Turkish buildings and city walls in Tiberias; and modern kibbutzes whose members fought heroic battles in several recent wars. Galilee also has a promise for the future: the apocalyptic battle at the end of the world—according to tradition—will occur on the plain of Armageddon, which lies beneath the walls of the city of Meggido.

While Jerusalem has been destroyed thirty times, according to some sources, and has been rebuilt each time on bedrock, the ancient cities of Galilee contain numerous layers of historic debris. Typically, after wars, earthquakes, or fires, ancient builders simply smoothed over and rebuilt on the old site, until the characteristic mound-shaped tell with its layers of debris accumulated. These tells were often the only hint of ancient occupation until nineteenth- and twentieth-century archaeologists began digging, restoring, and collecting from the sites.

Roman cultural treasures have been unearthed from many sites in Galilee. They enable us to gain additional insight into the interaction of Jewish culture with that of Rome. A few cities dominated the region in Roman times and still provide imposing remains: Sepphoris was mainly Jewish, while Beth She'an and Tiberias were dominated by non-Jews. Small Jewish villages housed most of the Jewish population of the time. Archaeologists have excavated several of these villages and their ancient synagogues, which illustrate Jewish life in those times. In Byzantine times Christianity became important in the area. Today, churches in Nazareth, Capurnaeum, and elsewhere commemorate events of Jesus' life and early Christianity, so the area also attracts many Christian pilgrims.

Rabbis and Emperors

Before I describe specific places and their past, let me provide some historic background. Galilee achieved its highest importance for Jews in late Roman and Byzantine times, after the fall of the Temple and the Jews' exclusion from Jerusalem and Judea, when this was the last part of their traditional country in which the Romans tolerated their presence. Two rather dramatic types of characters made an impact on Jewish history of the time: rabbis and Roman Emperors. Such an unlikely pairing of figures actually occurred—at least, according to Jewish tradition.

Several catastrophes concentrated Jewish life into Galilee and contributed to its character: the destruction of the Temple following the Jewish rebellion in 70 c.e., the now-mysterious rebellion in Alexandria and other North African Jewish communities around 117, and the Bar Kochba rebellion, which ended in 135. Although by rabbinic tradition, rabbis were always present in Jewish life from the time of Moses, scholars present a progression of rabbinic history punctuated by these disasters. In the following paragraphs, I have summarized the major periods of history after the fall of the Temple, to highlight the growing rabbinic culture and influence on the Jewish people.

From Herod until Bar Kochba

Beginning in Herod's time, schools of rabbis under Hillel and Shammai formed to study law, participate in developing literature, and comment on law. The supreme authority and control of worship continued to be held by the temple priests until the fall of the Temple, and the Sanhedrin, a group of elders (not rabbis), held supreme judicial authority. Sects like the Essenes, Sicarii, and so on claimed various sorts of religious authority.

After the Temple fell, large numbers of Jews moved to Galilee, while others decided to join existing communities throughout the Roman Empire. Others established new Jewish centers in developing Roman cities such as Narbonne and Vienne. The refugees were often demoralized by the destruction and death they had witnessed. The Jewish communities of Galilee had to exert some effort to help them settle in, as well as creatively developing their institutions to fit their changed circumstances. Eventually, these events left Galilee in a position of leadership with respect to the world's Jewish population, including local Jews and those in the growing Diaspora. The schools of rabbis left Jerusalem and settled elsewhere in Judea and Galilee. In particular, Rabbi Johannan ben Zakkai was carried from the besieged Jerusalem in a coffin and set himself up as an ally of Rome, repudiating the rebellion.

By the second century, Judaism and Jewish leaders, especially in Galilee, were responding to the loss of the Temple as a permanent condition. Synagogues enlarged their existing functions as the community center, house of study, collector and distributor of charity, and travelers' hospitality center. Worship and celebrations in synagogues emerged as a substitute for temple worship. Rabbis began to attain local respect by the end of the first century, particularly for taking over the maintenance of the calendar from the temple priests. At least two competing types of Judaism existed, although the rabbinic form later dominated so much that very little is known about its competition. Because they wrote the record, the rabbis are much better known—even their names have come down to us along with the many stories and legends of the *Mishnah* and Talmud. (The winners always write the history books!) Ironically, the archaeological record seems to offer more information about the synagogues, which were to a great extent the "property" of the non-rabbinic strain. By the end of the second century, the rabbis began to influence the course of synagogue worship, as well as fulfilling other functions.

In the aftermath of the 66–70 rebellion, a group of rabbis assumed the title of Sanhedrin, but they did not have the supreme judicial authority of the former body; over time, the title remained but the function altered. Most of the sects disappeared (except the Christians), leaving the rabbis more important than they had been before. These rabbis' principal importance derived from their assumption of the priestly duty of setting the calendar, which required knowledge of astronomy and mathematics. Whatever else the rabbis did, the calendar remained their responsibility.

During this time, Rabbi Gamaliel was a very prominent rabbi. His associate Joshua ben Hananiah was famous for his wisdom—so much so, that he is supposed to have influenced the Emperor Hadrian while the Emperor was in Judea and Galilee. There were some actual chances for them to have met. Rabbi Joshua was born at least thirty years before the revolt of 70, as he was one of the pallbearers of Rabbi Johannan ben Zakkai's false coffin. After escaping from Jerusalem, he worked as a blacksmith in a town in the area of today's Lod Airport; eventually, he became the mentor of Akiba. He was eighty years old when Hadrian first arrived in the area as governor of Syria, and older yet when Hadrian traveled there as the emperor. However, the legend also states that the rabbi traveled to Rome and there discussed science with Hadrian.

Some modern scholars have devoted a great deal of work to classifying which of the various legends about the rabbis reflect actual events, which are dubious, and which are impossible. When the legend says the rabbi talked with Moses, no one has any problem classifying it: impossible. When the legend says the rabbi talked with the Roman emperor, the scholars have a harder job. I accept the word of the *Encyclopedia Judaica* and of scholars who have figured it out, and I will make no effort to reconstruct arguments about the credibility of the claims.

The Bar Kochba Rebellion

Hadrian played an interesting role in starting the Bar Kochba rebellion. As emperor, he traveled widely, seeing his domains and initiating the building projects and the team-building exercises that gave him the reputation of a wise and good man—at least in non-Jewish sources. His determination to render all people equal, and thus to establish uniform worship of Roman gods alongside local cult figures, may have suited many of his subject peoples, but it was bad for the Jews. His order to rebuild Jerusalem with a Temple to Zeus on the vacant Temple Mount, along with social measures such as a ban on circumcision, infuriated the Jewish population. This reaction drove the revolt of 132 to 135, which was led by Bar Kochba and supported by the famous Rabbi Akiba.

Many members of rabbinic schools died during the war. Rabbis and laymen lost homes and possessions and fled from Judea to Galilee. During the war, the term *Nasi* referred to Bar Kochba, the military leader, rather than to the head rabbi. About this time, the rabbis lost the last remnants of power as judges.

The revolt was messy for the Romans, too. The Roman general had to send a message that omitted the standard formula about the welfare of troops and general: all had not gone well. In fact, Hadrian later had to come back to see that all the unrest was properly put down. The Romans felt it necessary to repress all Jewish activity in Judea; thus, they banned the Jews completely from Jerusalem and drove most of them to the Galilee or to more distant points throughout the empire. In consequence, Hadrian is known in Jewish sources for his wickedness and cruelty.

If Herod represents the most successful effort to unite Jewish and Roman traditions, Hadrian, in my view, represents a complete replacement of the synthesized version with a purely Roman version—a reaction against the principle of syncretism. Hadrian's public buildings, civil engineering projects, and artworks survived the rebellion, and, in fact, they remain on view in Israel today, in archaeology sites, parks, and museums. These still can impress and awe you with Roman taste, power, and engineering skill. The park at Caesarea contains many public works of his era. At Beth She'an, which he called Sythopolis, modern archaeologists discovered a magnificent statue of him. Sepphoris, which he called Diocaesera, and Jerusalem's Roman Cardo both contain splendid buildings dating from his renovations.

The Aftermath of the Bar Kochba Rebellion

Historic evidence suggests that the Jews of Galilee were very little involved with the Bar Kochba rebellion; they thus suffered little compared to Jews in Judea, where the Romans took furious revenge. Moreover, in Judea's devastated cities, official policy prohibited Jews from continued residence and barred them from Jerusalem even as visitors. The Romans formally changed the name Judea to Palestine, meaning country of the Philistines, and ruled it as a province of Syria, not as an independent or separate territory.

Expelled from Judea, many rabbis settled in Galilee. Rabbi Judah ha-Nasi, traditionally born at the death of Rabbi Akiba, inherited the office of patriarch. The title *Nasi* assumed the meaning "prince" or "patriarch," and traditions ascribed to the *Nasi* a descent from the house of King David. Beginning with his traditional birthdate at the death of Rabbi Akiba, Judah ha-Nasi's biography sounds more like a legend than history. However, my sources all seem to take him seriously, and so I will also. Judah ha-Nasi lived in Beth She'an, Bet She'arim, and Sepphoris and is best known as the compiler of oral legends into the *Mishnah*. In the context of this book, the most interesting elements of his biography are stories of how he was respected and consulted by the Roman Emperor "Antoninus"—never mind which emperor this means, or how they met.

Having been forced out of their homes in Judea by the Roman decree, most rabbis were poor. They earned their living as craftsmen or artisans such as blacksmiths or glass blowers in Sepphoris. In contrast, legend tells us of awesome riches belonging to Judah ha-Nasi and praises his superhuman wisdom and goodness. Like most rich people, he was highly practical. While earlier rabbis had insisted on a strict application of many laws, he was willing to compromise with the times and therefore won wider support. He declared that the Jews of mainly Roman Beth She'an should be exempt from tithes, because payment of tithes made them uncompetitive. He suggested the cancellation of rigorous observation of the sabbatical year, because it caused hardship or famine.

Judah ha-Nasi's decision to be buried at Bet She'arim inspired a large number of others to follow him. Today, the burial caves of this small town in Galilee are a point of interest because of the various caves in which you can still see elaborate sarcophagi. The interesting inscriptions on the tombs reveal a variety of facts about the nationality and occupations of the many Jews who had their bones sent back to rest in Israel until the Last Judgment wakes them.

By the fifth century, the synagogues, previously run by the people independently, became more dominated by the rabbis' influence and pronouncements. Archaeologists have excavated many synagogues from this period, in Tiberias, Sepphoris, Beth She'an, Bet Alpha, Katzrin, and outside Israel, such as at Dura Europa in Syria and even at Ostia Antiqua near Rome. Many of them seem to violate rules about graven images; these suggest an interesting situation in the nature of the religion of that era. These synagogues used vivid mosaics and frescoes to present Temple symbols such as the *menorah* and incense shovels, holiday symbols, biblical stories such as the sacrifice of Isaac, and even Greek mythological figures to the presumably ignorant worshipers; the rabbis' decisions about representative art became increasingly permissive.

SEPPHORIS AND ITS ANCIENT "MONA LISA"

Sepphoris—Zippori in Hebrew—was one of two big and important cities in Galilee throughout Roman and Byzantine times. Details about Sepphoris can provide a window into the history and social life of the region. Located at a crossroads between the exterior Mediterranean ports of Akko and Caesarea and the interior Sea of Galilee, Sepphoris was important to administrators from Rome and Jerusalem, to military occupiers, to local villagers and farmers, to developing rabbinic institutions, and to the Byzantine-era Christians. During the two periods of revolt in Judea, Sepphoris managed to maintain a degree of neutrality. After each revolt, people fleeing from devastation and disorder particularly tried to get to Sepphoris.

Sepphoris was home to many craftsmen such as potters, glass makers, and metal workers. The city's marketplaces served as a point of exchange, where people from the surrounding rural areas sold the produce from their prosperous farms and bought the craftsmen's goods. When Herod got his start as the administrator of Galilee, Sepphoris was the region's capital. Just after Herod's reign, his son Herod Antipas founded Tiberias, which temporarily replaced Sepphoris as the capital, but not for long. The city was continually being ornamented with new buildings, both Jewish and Roman. Many of these buildings are visible today in the extensive restored archaeology site, offering insight into life in ancient times—the site received attention when the excavators found a beautiful woman's face in a mosaic, now called "Mona Lisa of the Galilee."

Sepphoris Today

After winding around on narrow, barely paved country roads, we reached the national park, site of ancient Sepphoris. The park opened only in 1992, and the road seems little improved, passing through very small farming hamlets. From the restored city center, which stood on a hilltop, we enjoyed extensive views in all directions. While modern Israel is usually crowded with farms, orange groves, or apartment houses, the landscape around Sepphoris seems almost deserted, with quiet cultivated fields, pine forests planted by the Jewish National Fund, and only a few cows on the hillsides. A little way down the hill is a small historic church dedicated to Saint Anne, whose family traditionally originated in the city. Subsequently, I learned that before 1948 there had been an Arab village on the hill surrounding the current archaeological site.

Numerous buildings and streets of the ancient city are open for viewing: a Roman theater, a residential neighborhood, a vast commercial center, a large basilica-type building, and a series of underground cisterns that once supplied water to the inhabitants. Clearly, non-Jews and Jews shared the city. In the center of the ancient residential area, a tall building, once a Crusader citadel, houses a small museum exhibit and gift shop affiliated with the Israel Museum of Jerusalem. At the time of my trip, one of the major recent finds—an elaborate mosaic of the zodiac and Jewish religious symbols and scenes from the synagogue—was on display at the Israel Museum. If you don't have time to go to the park, you might also be able to see some of the Sepphoris artifacts in Jerusalem. There are constant new discoveries and new buildings created to house the finds.

Sepphoris is particularly rich in mosaics, including this zodiac, in which Jews were uninhibited with the representation of human, mythological, and animal subjects. In an elegant Roman villa that is believed to have been owned by a rich Jewish merchant, you can see the most famous one, called the Dionysus mosaic. After its discovery in the mid-1980s, the remarkably lifelike woman's face in the border received much attention as the "Mona Lisa of the Galilee." This name seems arbitrary—I find the resemblance to the famous painting tenuous, though the face is indeed beautiful. Other images in this masterpiece include Dionysus's horse-drawn chariots, floral motifs, and groups of mythical dancers. A large empty space toward one end provided a location for the tables and couches used for the traditional Roman banquet, demonstrating that the inhabitants of the house followed Roman customs.

Other rooms in this house have also been restored, including the room we all wonder about: an indoor bathroom with a toilet. The other rooms surround the dining room, which must have been very important to the inhabitants. The neighborhood surrounding the house was the site of many other private houses and mansions. While the restoration includes a roof (to protect the art), little but the cellars remain from the surrounding houses; you can see the storage areas where, below ground, the people stored wine, oil, grain, and other staple products for household use. The very skilled workmanship and taste of these buildings illustrate the lives of wealthy Jews at the time.

It's a pretty good distance on foot from this residential neighborhood to the marketplace. Along colonnaded walks you follow a stone-paved street, rutted from Roman chariot wheels; perhaps the inhabitants of the house were in the habit of riding to their central city activities. A number of public buildings, which the modern discoverers have restored, make it easy to imagine the bustling city life that once existed there. Mosaic pavements decorate almost all of the public buildings. One mosaic shows battle scenes, with dogs and horses engaged by mail-clad Roman soldiers. Another, the "Nile Mosaic," shows an elaborate allegorical depiction of the Nile river with the gate and lighthouse of Alexandria. The river emerges from the mouth of the Nile Beast, and various river gods and river creatures surround the image. Nearby is the Nilometer, a column for the measurement of the annual high point of the river. (Several centuries later, Benjamin of Tudela described the use of this Nilometer to predict the size of the next year's harvest. His description of a marked column sounds like the object in the mosaic, and he also mentioned large, fat fish, as depicted.) In the lower part of the mosaic, hunting scenes depict all sorts of wild animals. The Nile themes point to communication between the Jews in Galilee and the numerous Jews of Alexandria.

Outside of the central site, you can drive for a while, following a carefully marked driveway. You pass several fields of modern cows and then you can see the recently restored urban water system. It once supplied the entire large city, another feat of Roman engineering. Channels and underground cisterns—some natural, some artificial—provided storage capacity. You can walk down a stairway and pass through these cavernous reservoirs. There is no remaining trace of the aqueducts that once crossed the valley, bringing the water from the surrounding hills.

After leaving the park and driving back down the narrow road, where passing the oncoming tourist buses is an adventure, we rejoined a more major road and continued to Nazareth, just a few miles away. Arriving at lunch hour, we found that traffic was backed up all around the town; however, we managed to get to the Diana Restaurant, which Israeli friends had recommended with the statement that the hummus there is poetic. We enjoyed eighteen automatically served special salads, including hummus, freshwater fish from the Sea of Galilee, and dramatically prepared minced lamb kabobs, all served with great style in a pleasant atmosphere. Travel is not limited to the exploration of history.

Sepphoris and the History of Galilee

When Herod first arrived in Sepphoris as the district administrator, he was a very young man with a very powerful father. He found himself in charge of a district with social and economic problems. In the century before his arrival, Sepphoris had emerged while the hilltop fortified cities of the area were declining; these cities, Meggido and Hatzor, had once been Canaanite towns and then magnificent outposts of Solomon's kingdom. Changing methods of warfare made obsolete the need for walled and fortified cities, and some time in the second century B.C.E., Sepphoris had replaced them as the critical crossroads town, probably becoming the capital of the region in approximately 100 B.C.E. By 55 B.C.E., the Roman proconsul officially designated it capital of the newly created district of Galilee to which Herod was soon appointed administrator.

According to Flavius Josephus, Herod's first act was hunting down certain bandits who were plaguing the area and ordering the execution of their leader. Flavius Josephus hints that there were various points of view about these bandits. The urban dwellers in Sepphoris, rich Jews and pagans, clearly despised the bandits. Flavius Josephus also condemned them but acknowledged a certain level of popular approval for their activities. They represented an anti-government and anti-tax faction of the rural Jewish population, which resented the oppressive priesthood and its heavy demands for produce, livestock, and money for the Temple. There was probably quite a bit of local support for the bandits, who lived in caves and rural hiding places. They interacted with relatives who continued to be respectable farmers or villagers and, according to Josephus, persisted in the region throughout the time of Herod and his successors. Some scholars believe these early Robin Hoods were allied with Jewish sects that were later involved in the 66 to 70 C.E. revolt. They may have been the precursors of the Sicarii who were finally defeated at Masada.

A few years after his initial period as district administrator, in 37 B.C.E. the newly appointed King Herod had to come back to Sepphoris to fight for control of his dubiously acquired domain. During this campaign, his troops conquered Sepphoris from the last Hasmonean king. As Herod's reign continued, a class of Jewish peasants and villagers in the area became less observant in their practice of Judaism. These less-educated people grew lax about paying what the Judeans thought they owed to the Temple; this opened them up to criticism by the priests and richer urban people. In principal, every Jewish man had to make a Jerusalem Temple pilgrimage and sacrifice at the three harvest festivals—Passover in early spring, celebrating the harvest of winter-raised grain and first-

born animals; Shevout in early summer, when the barley and first fruits
came in; and the fall fruit harvest at Succoth. These tri-annual pilgrimages
played a growing role in Jerusalem, as Herod rebuilt the Temple and
expanded its economic significance. At the same time, pilgrimages
threatened the small farmer from Galilee with increasing difficulty, danger,
and cost. The responsibility to give or send the tithe was so burdensome
that farmers became lax about sending cattle, grain, and fruits to the
distant, aristocratic, and greedy Temple priests.

A related social problem was that farmers, fearful of bandits, burdened
by heavy taxation and tithes, and coping with rapid inflation that devalued
their produce, began to leave the land and head for areas of heavier
population. This was a source of conflict as peasants and urban dwellers
came into closer contact. Famines occurred when the loss of farmhands
caused inadequate agricultural production or when poor harvests followed a sabbatical year, when land was held out of production. Social
dislocation and discontent grew, along with the perception that the priests
were placing unbearable responsibilities on the people.

During the reigns of Herod and his immediate successors, Romans
and Romanized Jews expanded the Galilee area's infrastructure, developed existing cities, and founded new cities. Herod's will divided the
kingdom into much the same divisions that had existed before his
unification of the territory. Herod's son Herod Antipas became the ruler
of the Galilee area. His new city, Tiberias, temporarily replaced Sepphoris
as capital. Also, just after Herod's death there was widespread unrest,
and Sepphoris was involved in a rebellious action that resulted in its
destruction. The inhabitants were sold into slavery. However, Herod Antipas
also rebuilt Sepphoris.

Eventually, social conditions, leadership problems, and actions by
the Romans led to the 66 revolt. Early in the war, when Josephus, as the
commander of the region, fortified several cities, he invited the citizens
of Sepphoris to build a wall on their own responsibility: Josephus said
that he "saw that they had ample means and that their enthusiasm for
the war needed no stimulus" (p. 180). However, when the Roman troops
marched in, the residents of Sepphoris sided with them, and in 67, they
opened the city gates to Vespasian, the general who was attempting to
put down the Jewish rebels. Flavius Josephus at that moment was a general
on the Jewish side; he changed over to Rome after failure to prevail in
Galilee. This was a decisive moment in the career of Flavius Josephus,
the turning point that everyone remembers when assessing the quality
of information and his motives for writing his various histories. Throughout the rest of the war, the Roman troops often were very punitive toward

the residents of Galilee, attempting to threaten the major holdouts in Jerusalem and near the Dead Sea. However, Sepphoris did not suffer total destruction and reprisals in the extremes experienced by Jerusalem and Judea.

After the fall of the Temple in 70 c.e., Sepphoris grew in importance. At first, people thought that the change was temporary, but in time, the likelihood of restoring the Temple shrunk. With Jerusalem and the Temple in ruins, Jews wouldn't even walk on the Temple Mount (as is still true of some orthodox); a substitute for Temple worship emerged in the synagogues. As they had when the Temple stood, synagogues like that in Sepphoris faced Jerusalem. Their builders decorated them with reminders of the Temple and its functions—pictures of the holy Ark, the incense shovels, and the *menorah*. These had already provided year-round sites of worship, supplementing the responsibility of men to make pilgrimages; now they became the only organized worship. When rabbis from Judea began to settle in Galilee after the Bar Kochba rebellion, many of them naturally settled in Sepphoris because it was one of the largest cities; Judah ha-Nasi lived in Sepphoris for much of his active life as the compiler of the *Mishnah*.

At the end of the first century c.e., new buildings and public works were in progress in Sepphoris, as it continued to grow in importance. Romanized rulers built the theater that is still visible at the entrance to the National Park site and the new buildings in the residential area nearby. Most inhabitants were Jews; even the Romanized rulers were Jewish deputies appointed by the Roman government. Sepphoris's schools of rabbinic thought prospered as they codified Jewish ideas for a post-Temple society.

In 129–130 c.e., Emperor Hadrian's critical tour of the province started in Caesarea and included Sepphoris. He spent the winter in northern Jordan and then returned to Judea for the spring and summer. During Hadrian's progress through the region, he initiated many projects, such as roads from Judea toward the borders with the neighboring regions and other building projects. He built a Roman temple at Tiberias, which was dedicated to Zeus but which clearly equated his own personality with that of the deity, and he left statues of himself in major cities. He refounded Sepphoris, renaming it Diocaesarea in his own honor.

Hadrian's plans for increasing the importance of pagan worship, for standardizing laws and customs in the Empire (such as a universal ban on circumcision), and for making himself a deity to be worshiped at the former site of Jerusalem's Temple, touched off the rebellion of Bar Kochba from 132 to 135. As in the earlier revolt, the Galilee was less rebellious than Judea to the south, although, like many facts about Bar Kochba and his war, the position taken by Sepphoris is unknown. Arrival of the exiled Judeans, as I have mentioned, made the Galilee the default center of Jewish life during the subsequent period. After the war, although its population was primarily Jewish, Sepphoris was run as a Roman city; scholars are unsure whether Jews were always included in the ruling council. The already less-devout Jews there became more and more assimilated to Roman customs. Romans equipped their cities with Roman baths, theaters, marketplaces, gymnasia, race courses, and temples dedicated to pagan gods and the Emperor cult. In all these buildings, idols offended pious Jews. Nevertheless, Galilee from 150 C.E. until around 600 was effectively the last Jewish state until 1948.

The economy of Sepphoris and the surrounding agricultural lands and villages depended mainly on internal markets, with food, ceramics, glass, and building materials produced locally. Only oil and a few other foodstuffs were exported in exchange for metal, salt, and some luxury goods. You can see the foundations of the courtyards and covered buildings of the marketplace at Sepphoris. The shops are in a circular arrangement. Once they offered olives, wine, oil, eggs, locusts, honey, cooked vegetables, and baked bread. Jews ate more fish than meat at the time, though both were luxuries. Sepphoris had many glass blowers as well as metal workers, blacksmiths, carpenters, weavers, dyers, tailors, and tanners (whose shops were located downwind). These local craftsmen sold directly from their workshops, while middlemen dealt in flax, wool, and other commodities. The roads were bad, so people had to carry the products to market in baskets supported on their heads or shoulders.

On a neighboring hill, archaeologists have identified the town of Shikhin, which was a center of pottery manufacture in the Roman period, according to tradition in rabbinic literature. Shikhin was particularly recognized because of its storage jars, which were so consistent that their volume was considered a standard. Comparison of potsherds from elsewhere with rejects found in the excavation at Shikhin shows that these jars were traded throughout the region.

The activities of the city also required many service occupations. Because Roman Galilee had a money economy, not a barter economy, another type of commercial activity at Sepphoris was money changing. Moneychangers were needed to ensure that people coming to trade in the city's markets received a fair exchange between the many new and old coins in circulation. In another sort of service, scribes offered to create papers for loans, sales, divorce, rents, and other transactions; they maintained a library of standard forms to enable these to be completed efficiently. Other service workers such as barbers and doctors also had shops or workspaces in the market. Women had a nearly separate life inside the courtyards and inner rooms of the houses, with responsibilities for spinning and weaving textiles like wool and flax, and for other household tasks.

By the end of the century, rabbis were making Sepphoris an important site for the development of religious writings. Rabbi Judah ha-Nasi, recognized as a leader of this effort, lived in neighboring Bet She'arim for some years but moved to Sepphoris in approximately 200 c.e., living there for the last years of his life. During this time, there were said to be eighteen synagogues in the area, though only a few fragmentary remains of synagogues from this early era have been found.

Judaism at this time became focused in religious practices in homes and in public synagogues where prayers and communal meals took the place of Temple sacrifice. Synagogues assumed public responsibilities, providing for lodging of strangers and collection and distribution of charity for poor members. In synagogue rituals, there was new emphasis on sounding the *shofar* for Rosh Hashana, displaying the *lulav* and *etrog* on Succoth, and the Purim reading about Esther and the downfall of persecutors of Jews. In these new practices, the Jews in Galilee added their own ideas to earlier changes in religion developed by Jews in Babylonia, Alexandria, and other cities of the Diaspora. Some people also participated in the societies called *haverim*—they would scrupulously prepare meals according to laws of ritual purity that had once pertained to priests and Temple rituals.

Many of the commonly respected religious practices, such as these holiday ceremonies, observance of *Shabbat*, and circumcision, were perpetuated without help from the rabbis. Other laws and customs became too burdensome and fell out of use, like the rules about unkosher mixing of various substances, the practice of paying the tithe, and the observation of the sabbatical year. The rabbis performed some services that might be viewed as magical, like the release of people from oaths or praying for rain. The unique rabbinic service was to observe the moon and the planets and figure out the calendar, determining when to celebrate the holidays. Also, common people generally accepted the moral superiority of the rabbis, who thus attained some level of prestige despite usually not being rich or otherwise powerful. Rabbi Judah ha-Nasi's great wealth seems to have been an exception to this—or a myth.

Scholars describe that conflicts arose between the pious Jews who came from Judea and the more relaxed Jews in Galilee. Jerusalem rabbis, scribes, and former members of fanatic sects such as the Essenes considered the produce of Galileean farmers who didn't contribute tithes to be impure—even after there was no longer a Temple cult. Their writings contain many cutting remarks about these farmers, although they slowly softened some of their attitudes. After seeing the contrast between the rough, stony hillsides in Judea and the much richer agricultural valleys in Galilee, I also wonder whether the refugees weren't already feeling like aliens in an area that didn't remind them of the biblical stories and the connections with the land.

As more and richer people began to decorate their homes with Roman-style art, Jews in Galilee found ways to get around the "no graven images" command. In villages and cities, synagogues themselves began to display representational mosaics; several of these are among the master finds of archaeologists in the region, particularly a magnificent zodiac mosaic on the floor of a synagogue in Sepphoris, found just a few years ago. During this period, the locals must have been aware of the expanding importance of the dispersed Jews far and wide, such as the community in Babylonia where rabbis were writing the authoritative Talmud, or the large communities of merchants and businessmen in Rome and Alexandria.

The perennial problem of "Who is a Jew?" reappeared during this time. In the Diaspora communities the former Temple tax was now a tax owed to Rome, earmarked for the principal Roman cult. Thus, all Jews in the Roman Empire had to decide if open commitment to their faith was worth the extra money! The rabbinic writers sought clarification of the issues of conversion, intermarriage, and denial of one's Jewish heritage. They originated the still-observed convention that the mother's Jewish heritage determines that a child is Jewish. Their writings often criticized heretics, in which group they included communities of "Jewish Christians" who observed all Jewish commandments yet also subscribed to the orthodox view of Jesus, the Messiah, who had been resurrected to save them. These groups were equally unpopular with the nonobservant gentile Christians, and they may have later moved from Galilee to the Golan area to escape the disapproval of the traditional Jews of Sepphoris and the smaller towns.

A dramatic interruption in the progress of building Sepphoris occurred when many buildings fell in an earthquake in 363. It is to this earthquake that we owe the remarkable state of preservation of some of the dramatic mosaic floors; the buildings in which they lay were heaped up as rubble, and the rebuilding effort simply covered up the ruins.

Archaeology at Sepphoris

The earliest modern expedition to Sepphoris was sponsored by the University of Michigan in 1931. At that time, the principal archaeological remains were underneath the houses of the Arab village. The archaeologists dug in the school courtyard, which is adjacent to the old Crusader tower that now houses the museum, and they excavated the theater and explored the water system. Their efforts made it clear that much more could be done, but the efforts were only resumed long after Israeli Independence.

Archaeology expeditions have been particularly busy at this site in the last twenty years, with enormous discoveries and insights about the consistency of the finds with ancient sources. Glass and pottery workshops and large numbers of mosaics have almost all come to light during this time. In the last ten years, this has been most spectacular: finds include the synagogue mosaic and the "Mona Lisa." According to the current report on the Web, one current dig is disclosing a large basilica-like structure, which we looked at as we were leaving the site. Since the various archaeology teams all report their progress on the Web, you can find current information with an appropriate search, as described in the appendix.

BET SHE'ARIM, A BYZANTINE BURIAL SITE

The necropolis of Bet She'arim, approximately ten miles from Sepphoris, contains tombs of people from a wide number of places, who sent their bodies, or at least their bones, back for burial in their holy land. By the second century C.E., Jews of the Diaspora were beginning to accept their status as outsiders, without their own country and without a central religious authority. They retained the desire to be in the right place at the moment of the Last Judgment. Rabbi Judah ha-Nasi began the practice and inspired the others. Over time, visiting these tombs also became a tradition— Benjamin of Tudela mentions this in his *Itinerary* in the twelfth century.

You can see the tombs, a small museum, and a number of catacombs with interesting carvings in this well-presented National Park on a winding back road. The main attraction is the necropolis where numerous bodies from many countries were buried in impressive tombs with carving that indicated who they were and where they had lived. Above the site of the necropolis, on a hill, once stood the city to which the rabbis once fled from Judah, but this city is in nearly unrecognizable ruins. I don't know if it could potentially be reconstructed the way the more dramatic ruins have been or if the stones have all disappeared. The hill overlooks the valley that extends toward Meggido.

At the necropolis, a small kiosk sells refreshments, maps, souvenirs of Israel, and postcards: basically the same merchandise that is offered at every Israeli National Park. On the day we visited, there were very few visitors, and the young woman at the kiosk was sitting on a lawn chair, looking terribly bored and listening to the radio. The sound of the radio was particularly discrepant with the surroundings: as we read the documentation about the ancient burial caves, we heard the song named "She Wore an Itsy-Bitsy Teeny-Weenie Yellow Polka-Dot Bikini."

One cave is now the location of a small exhibit of archaeological finds from the site. A huge circular slab of raw glass several feet in diameter is one of the interesting artifacts that have been discovered at the site; it illustrates how glass was made. The material was manufactured in the place where needed minerals were available and then was shipped elsewhere to be remelted and formed into bottles, storage containers, and whatever other glassware was needed. Based on this discovery, Bet She'arim appears to have been the site of a glass-making industry. The rabbis at that time didn't make their living as scholars; they worked as artisans. Perhaps some of them worked as glass blowers in the workshop that owned this slab of glass.

The catacombs of Bet She'arim have massive stone doors cut in the side of a steep hillside. There are both natural caves and excavated niches for burial sites. Large stone coffins inside the catacombs display elaborate carvings, some of them representational or even using mythological subjects, and often have detailed inscriptions in various languages. Various burial places have separate doors and served a particular family or national group. The tomb inscriptions and the iconography of decorative work carved on a wall or sarcophagus often tell the name, country, and occupation of the person whose body—or at least whose bones— must have made the journey to be laid to rest in the networks of caves and niches. We saw lions, garlands, *menorahs*, and many other carved symbols. Near the refreshment kiosk, the park provides a series of placards and plastic-covered documentation that summarizes the information gathered from the tombs.

Ancient Burial Customs

How did this happen? First, look back to the customs of burial that prevailed in Jerusalem prior to the fall of the Temple and perhaps also in the period just afterward, when there was hope that the Temple might be rebuilt.

Each family, or at least important well-to-do families, had a family tomb. The bodies of newly deceased family members were placed, along with certain material objects such as new lamps, in the tomb. As these bodies decayed, they were moved aside to make room for others. Eventually, tombs had to be enlarged by carving new niches in the rock. (You can see a tomb like this in one of the side chapels in the Church of the Holy Sepulcher.)

Customs developed further with the introduction, in early Roman times, of ossuaries—that is, stone boxes the right size for the bones of an individual. The long dimension had to be as long as the femur, one's longest bone, and as wide as the pelvic girdle, one's widest bone. Some ossuaries were plain, and some were incised with decorations. The deceased person's name was written on the box. Both men and women might be treated this way. Large numbers of ossuaries appear in Jewish burial sites, and thus you can see them in many museums.

Ossuary-making was one of the important activities of Jerusalem's stone-cutting industry. Ossuaries in Jerusalem were decorated in a restrained way, following the prohibition of making images of human or animal forms. Before the destruction of the Temple, there were few religious symbols in current use; after the Temple was destroyed, stonecutters in other places used a larger variety of symbols. The *menorah* became more and more common, eventually becoming a sign that the ossuary contained the remains of a Jew. Also, as time went on, many other symbols were adopted for Jewish use. For this reason, there is a wide variety of interesting carving on the tombs at Bet She'arim.

Bet She'arim from the Second Rebellion Onward

When the Romans expelled the Jews from Judea, certain schools of rabbis moved to Bet She'arim. After 70 c.e., in hopes that the Romans would soon allow the priests to rebuild the Temple and restore its sacrificial role, the rabbis already had begun the habit of writing down everything they knew about Temple practice. By the end of the first century, it became obvious that no restoration would soon occur in Jerusalem. Bar Kochba's troops hardly set foot there—of fifteen thousand extant coins with his logo for the revolt, only four have been dug up in Jerusalem, the rest in other areas of Judea. And after the second rebellion, Jews were not allowed in Jerusalem at all. In this context, rabbinic writings and customs began to emerge first at Bet She'arim, which was also heavily influenced by Greco-Roman ideas.

Under leaders called *Nasi*, the old title for Patriarch, these rabbis and others in the region continued their work of preserving the oral law. The first famous rabbi to arrive was Judah ha-Nasi, who settled there in 175 C.E.

It was very desirable to be buried in Jerusalem, because the concept of resurrection that developed in some strains of Judaism during Hasmonean times claimed that at the final awakening of the dead, those buried in Jerusalem wouldn't have to travel underground to be reawakened. The rabbis, deprived of Jerusalem, developed the theory that those buried anywhere in the former Jewish state, including in Bet She'arim, would be similarly resurrected, and so the custom developed.

Bet She'arim was subject to all the social factors I described previously—the conflicts between urban people and farmers, the religious disputes, and so forth. Another revolt in the 350s may have caused its destruction, but little is known about this revolt.

BET SHE'AN OR SYTHOPOLIS

The big ten cities of the Roman Middle East were called the Decapolis. Most of the Decapolis cities stood in the territory of modern Jordan and Syria, but Bet She'an, the Roman Sythopolis, was the capital of this league. A biblical city had formerly occupied a tell above the expanded site. The ancient city, once the stronghold of an Egyptian occupation that left hieroglyphic inscriptions and statues of Egyptian gods alongside biblical and Canaanite artifacts, disappeared in the eighth century B.C.E. In the fourth century, Alexander the Great founded a new city at the location. Hadrian re-established it and proceeded with major building projects; the city had two rivers and dominated a rich agricultural region at the foot of Mount Gilboa, on the border of Galilee and Judea.

While Sepphoris was known as Galilee's primarily Jewish city, Bet She'an was primarily pagan. After Hadrian visited on his progress through the region, his building mania caused a great deal of rapid improvement in the city. Within a century after Hadrian's visit, there were major shopping centers, baths, Roman temples, a theater, and elegant residential quarters, principally occupied by Roman and pagan inhabitants. An important bronze statue of Hadrian is among the magnificent archaeological finds of the area, along with statues of Dionysus and other gods.

Today, the Israeli National Park at Bet She'an is vast and full of impressive late Roman art and architectural elements, tumbled into ruins by a violent earthquake in the eighth century c.e. I was impressed by the theater, rows of columns lining the Cardo, shops and public buildings with mosaic floors, a Roman bath on a hilltop, and an ancient fountain with a half-circle of columns. We walked through on a rainy day, with only glimpses of blue sky. Children on high-handlebar bikes were plowing down the sloping stone streets where, I suppose, Roman chariots or carts once drove. We wondered if that meant there were gaps in the surrounding fence: the children looked like unlikely candidates to pay the National Park admission or own an annual pass for free entry! Some of the mosaics in the marketplace have been removed (in fact, we had seen them at the Israel Museum in Jerusalem) for this reason: at some time someone had stolen some of them by entering the nearly unguarded park at night. The town located there now is much smaller than the archaeological area, illustrating how in Roman times, as scholars believe, the Galilee was more heavily populated than today.

BET ALPHA AND THE ZODIAC

As you drive from the coast toward the Sea of Galilee, you follow a valley near beautiful mountains. If you follow the signs to Bet Alpha National Park, you drive through a working agricultural kibbutz. Eventually, you will find a shed-like structure, which protects the foundations of a building from Byzantine times: this is the National Park. The floor plan and the stunning mosaic of the ancient remains indicate that this was a synagogue. It once had an outer area surrounded by columns, an inner area decorated with a mosaic, and a niche or Ark for the Torah scrolls that faces toward Jerusalem, which, in fact, is not terribly far away.

The mosaic itself is dramatic. Its style is very primitive compared to the mosaics of Caesarea or Masada. There are three panels in the design. In the center is a zodiac with recognizable images showing the signs that modern astrologers still use—the ram, the crab, Virgo, Libra, and so on. In the center is the face of the sun, Helios—it's hard to grasp what he's doing in a synagogue, but there he is! Each corner illustrates one of the four seasons, also represented by human figures. Hebrew labels identify the various signs and symbols; people who know Hebrew and the orthography of the time have determined that these letters are so badly formed that it's likely the mosaic artist was not literate in Hebrew; perhaps he knew Greek or was unable to read at all. Above, at the end that faces toward Jerusalem, are several images representing the Temple of Jerusalem (which had been in ruins for centuries when the mosaic was made): the doors of the holy Ark, the incense shovel, and the *lulav* of Shevouth. Two lions of Judah look like big dogs. Below is a scene with several human and angelic figures, which quite clearly depicts Abraham about to sacrifice his son Isaac. Above, the hand of God waves from a cloud, and the ram, sort of waiting in the wings, appears hanging from a tree. The whole presentation has the primitive freshness that's always completely appealing, rather than the skillful sophistication of works influenced by high Roman art such as the Dionysus mosaic and the Nile mosaic at Sepphoris.

As you walk around on a special catwalk designed to allow viewing of the mosaic without endangering it, you can also see an amusing film that "reenacts" the search conducted by the village elders to find a mosaic-maker who would not charge too high a price to make a mosaic for their synagogue. They hire an apprentice, who clearly didn't have much independent experience but had worked on the elaborate and sophisticated mosaics of nearby Bet She'an. He wants to put in a zodiac, and they agree, if he'll also put in the Temple symbols. The video is supposed to clean up all the mysteries and explain to you why the mosaic is so primitive, why it has such an odd combination of symbols, and why it was found so far from any reasonably large metropolitan area. Well, there's no way to find out whether the video makers were wrong, so have fun and watch this "reenactment."

Flavius Josephus mentioned the signs of the zodiac in association with the symbolic objects within the Temple. Although he specified that the pagan signs of the zodiac were not depicted, this passage might help explain why later, this seemingly pagan imagery began to appear alongside the other symbols of the Temple:

> There was a veil . . ., a Babylonian curtain, embroidered with blue, and fine linen, and scarlet, and purple, . . . Nor was this mixture of colors without its mystical interpretation, but was a kind of image of the universe; for by the scarlet there seemed to be enigmatically signified fire, by the fine flax the earth, by the blue the air, and by the purple the sea. . . . This curtain had also embroidered upon it all that was mystical in the heavens, excepting that of the twelve signs, representing living creatures. [In the Temple were] three things that were very wonderful and famous among all mankind, the candlestick, the table of shewbread, and the altar of incense. Now the seven lamps signified the seven planets, for so many there were springing out of the candlestick. Now the twelve loaves that were upon the table signified the circle of the zodiac and the year: but

the altar of incense, by its thirteen kinds of sweet-smelling spices with which the sea replenished it, signified that God is the possessor of all things that are both in the uninhabitable and habitable parts of the earth, and that they are all to be dedicated to his use. (*Wars of the Jews*, Whiston translation, p. 346)

Bet Alpha and Changing Times

One of the noticeable features of the mosaics in Masada was the use of only geometric and floral patterns, not the normal Roman representation of birds, animals, and people. Jews in earlier times had protested the figure of an eagle on a gate of the Temple precinct. Jews had refused to use coins that showed a human face, even when it represented an emperor who was not the object of cult worship. Yet at Bet Alpha (and other synagogues in the region) there are not just images of Abraham sacrificing Isaac as the Angel watches, but all the zodiac signs appear, and even the god Helios. Such a depiction would have previously been anathema to Jewish houses of worship. Of course, the fact that this is the same zodiac that we still use makes it all the more intriguing. The representations of the Temple symbols facing toward Jerusalem increase the certainty that this was indeed a synagogue.

How did images become accepted in Jewish houses of worship like Bet Alpha? Or is it a mystery? In discussing the loss of this taboo, scholars cite the writings of the rabbis who lived in the period. More and more, perhaps making a virtue of the necessity of recognizing the way things actually were (instead of how they wanted them to be), they found reasons why images were not necessarily to be shunned. Only images that were being revered as gods or images that had been used in actual pagan worship were condemned; eventually, even former idols could become Jewish property if their owners were sure never to allow them to be worshiped again. During this changing time, rabbis conceded that Jews could own ordinary household goods such as lamps or pots and pans with images on them, or use them as personal seals. Bar Kochba's seal had a lion on it, which would have been prohibited a century before, and some rabbis used seals with faces on them. Eventually, the Talmud permitted mosaics with images in them, and even the prohibition on images in synagogues crumbled. By the time of the Bet Alpha mosaic, the only prohibition seems to have been against actual worship of the images.

The Discovery of the Mosaic

The national reaction to the mosaic at Bet Alpha also illustrates changing times in the history of Zionism and the era before the state of Israel. In the late 1920s, some kibbutz members unearthed the mosaic while digging an irrigation ditch in a then-undeveloped agricultural area. These young men and women were the most hardened of non-religious Zionists. Their first reaction was that this ancient expression of Jewish sentiment had little or nothing to do with them and their commitment to build a modern state; they needed a ditch, not an ancient work of art. However, not long before, the kibbutzniks had heard a lecture from a man named Eleazar Sukenik, an aspiring archaeologist. Sukenik had convinced them that the history of Israel, particularly this region of the Galilee, was important. He himself believed that the evidence of ancient synagogues could serve two critical purposes: first, it could substantiate the Zionist claim to the land, and second, it could help to create a national idealism— if you like, a myth—of the sort that was needed to found a state under the prevailing circumstances. Because of this lecture, they called in Sukenik to see what they had found, although they were very impatient to resume their digging.

Sukenik convinced them to allow him some time to excavate and restore the mosaic, which explains its strange location among the cattle barns. He enlisted their support in his efforts, which were rather poorly funded. (The big-time archaeologists of the era were all Christians, supported from abroad, while he was a semi-amateur without major sponsors.) As he explored, he attracted national and international attention and indeed contributed to the myth and to the conviction that the Jews had an ancient claim to the land, just as he had hoped. His efforts created a passionate interest in archaeology and history that persisted for much of Israel's existence, only abating after the 1967 war, modern economic reality, and massive new immigration created new concerns. Sukenik's son, then around eleven years old, assisted him in his efforts. Later, the son himself, under a new Hebrew name, also became an archaeologist. His new name was Yigael Yadin.

TIBERIAS AND THE SEA OF GALILEE

If you want to visit the Sea of Galilee, it's inevitable that you will go to Tiberias, the main center of seaside resort facilities, restaurants, and the like. I found it to be a fairly tacky beach resort with a typical big-city waterfront, full of hustlers inviting you to come into their restaurants, big ostentatious hotels, and lots of souvenir shops. The atmosphere varies from shoddy to seedy, though inside the big hotels things are probably better than on the street. In the immediate area of the city, the beautiful landscapes have been overbuilt and the lake views spoiled. There is one Roman bathhouse and a Roman-era synagogue that you can visit. There are other types of places to stay besides the big resort hotels. On our visit, we stayed about fifteen minutes down the road from Tiberias at a kibbutz guest house in the oldest kibbutz in Israel, Kibbutz Dagania; this means we saw a very different side of modern life in that area.

In addition to the natural attractions around the lake, there are various shrines and hostels, including churches—formerly synagogues— where Jesus is thought to have preached. For Christians, the greatest significance of the lake is the ministry of Jesus in this area—his home, Nazareth, is about a half hour's drive from Tiberias. Like many Christian shrines, the Roman-era buildings have frequently been replaced by later buildings, leaving only a trace of the original.

One big tourist attraction on the lakeshore is a two-thousand-year-old boat that was preserved in the mud at the bottom of the lake. A fisherman found it, and it somehow became the property of a kibbutz that runs a large luxury hotel. After the discovery, experts first soaked the boat in a vat of preservative to stabilize the ancient wooden planks, and they are now completing its restoration in a little workshop beside the lake. Now, in order to capitalize on tourists' interest, the kibbutz is in the process of building a huge structure to house the boat. So far, they have completed a gift shop with an extensive selection of T-shirts, table mats, framed cards, illustrated maps, and other merchandise memorializing their treasure. Although the boat's main tourist appeal derives from perceived connections to the story of Jesus' apostles who fished in the lake, it's worth stopping if you have half an hour.

Fortunately, most of the scenery around the Sea of Galilee remains more unspoiled and attractive than the city waterfront; perhaps the shore has not greatly changed since Josephus enthusiastically described the lake, which he called Gennasareth, and its beauty. He wrote: "Now this lake of Gennasareth is so called from the country adjoining it. Its . . . waters are sweet and very agreeable for drinking, for they are finer than the thick waters of other fens; the lake is also pure, and on every side ends directly at the shores and at the sand . . . here are several kinds of fish in it, different both to the taste and to the sight from those elsewhere." I assume that he was referring to the St. Peter's fish, which you can order at any fish restaurant in Tiberias or find in an American grocery under

the name *tilapia*. He also expressed his admiration of the surrounding
countryside, to which attributes a wonderful natural beauty; he says that
its "soil is so fruitful that all sorts of trees can grow upon it . . . particularly
walnuts, which require the coldest air, flourish there in vast plenty; there
are palm trees also . . .; fig trees and olives grow near them, which yet
require an air that is more temperate. . . . [The region] supplies men
with the principal fruits, with grapes and figs . . . and the rest of the
fruits as they become ripe together through the whole year" (*Wars of the
Jews*, Whiston translation, pp. 253–254).

To see and appreciate the sea, we drove all the way around it. This
requires a couple of hours. Because the Sea of Galilee is in the Syrian-
African rift, lake level is in fact quite far below sea level. As a result, higher
ground is everywhere around the lake. We enjoyed the very beautiful
views, as we followed the road up the surrounding hills and descended
to stretches of road adjacent to the water's edge. We crossed the Jordan
River both on its entry and exit from the lake. From the eastern shore,
the lake looked very deep and cold, but the weather didn't encourage
wading or swimming. At the north end, we found the river to be almost
undistinguishable from the low-lying swamp, as it meanders through a
marshy territory. We were amused by the rabbit-sized animals called hyraxes
that were sunning themselves on rocks not far from the wildflower-covered
shoreline, although we were unable to identify them.

Tiberias under the Romans

Tiberias had been founded by Herod's son Herod Antipas as an alternate
capital city for the region instead of Sepphoris. Later, Nero gave Herod
Antipas's son Aristobulus lesser Armenia and he gave four cities to Agrippa,
one of which was Tiberias. The city was founded on the site of an ancient
burial ground, which for a long time made Jews shun it, but eventually
they consented to live there. It was always small in comparison to Jerusalem and Caesarea, but was one of the larger centers of the Galilee, which
was mostly villages. Eventually, the city became one of the sites where
the rabbis lived after the Bar Kochba rebellion.

Josephus summarized his role in defending Tiberias during the
rebellion. First he included it in the most defensible positions, which
he fortified as soon as he began his duties as commander. During the
war, John of Gischala, Josephus's rival, devised a plot to cause trouble
between various cities that should have been allies. When Josephus began
to exert his influence over the inflamed citizens, John was angry and

jealous, and he again plotted against Josephus. Feigning sickness, he sent a letter begging his permission to seek a cure by taking the hot baths at Tiberias. Unsuspecting, Josephus instructed his representatives in the city to allow John to take the cure. Although Josephus caught John, John slipped away and Josephus was afraid to persecute him for fear of stirring up trouble.

Along with other cities, Tiberias went over to John, but Josephus got them back. Tiberias revolted again even though John was confined to Gischala. Josephus was furious at wasting efforts on his supposed allies. Finally, Josephus allowed the soldiers to plunder the disloyal cities of Tiberias and Sepphoris. But he then gave the people back their goods to obtain their goodwill and kept peace for the moment. Eventually, Vespasian arrived in Galilee, and Josephus's troops—camped at Sepphoris— fled to Tiberias without a fight.

In Tiberias, Josephus continues to describe his own role: "Josephus' hurried arrival produced panic in the city he had chosen as a refuge. The people of Tiberias concluded that if he had not completely written off the war, he would never have taken to flight. In this they were perfectly right about his opinion; for he saw the inevitable end awaiting the Jews, and knew that their one safety lay in a change of heart" (*Jewish War*, Williamson translation, p. 200).

While waiting in Tiberias, Josephus wrote a justification for a Jewish decision at this point to seek terms and sent it to Jerusalem. Meanwhile, Vespasian was about to sack Jotapata, and Josephus went there to defend it. Upon Vespasian's victory, Josephus hid with others and eventually, after a suicide pact, turned himself over to Rome instead of keeping his part of the pact. Shortly afterward, Vespasian came back to the neighborhood of Tiberias to fight again, at the end of the campaign. The final battle at Tiberias saw the death of 6,700 Jews.

The city of Gamla, on the eastern side of the Sea of Galilee, was the site of another major Josephus-era battle. This site also has been restored for visitors.

Capernaeum

Capernaeum, a site on the northern shore of the Sea of Galilee, has a well-preserved fourth-century synagogue. The splendor of this synagogue, which is made of white stone that had to be brought from elsewhere, is mysterious. Capernaeum appears to have been a relatively poor village, yet this is a magnificent building with tall, well-carved columns, three imposing entrance doors, and generally fine workmanship. The rows of stone benches around the sides are still beautiful and smooth, and invite the pilgrims to sit down. There are a few excavations below the floor, which is plain marble and doesn't appear to have had a mosaic design like many others. These disclose the base of a first-century B.C.E. synagogue, where Christian tradition believes that Jesus preached some of the Gospels. One theory about the very fine synagogue is that early Christians, who retained Jewish traditions as well, built it as a memorial to the preaching of Jesus to enhance the experience of the pilgrims who were starting to arrive from various parts of the Byzantine empire. Another theory says that Jews enlarged it as a kind of answer to St. Peter's shrine a few yards away.

Capernaeum has been a Christian pilgrimage site since the first century, and the tradition that one house, now preserved under a sort of floating modernistic church, was the actual residence of St. Peter doesn't entirely lack credibility. Currently, the site is owned by a Franciscan monastery. Numerous carved stones line the walkways, presented in straight lines without much evident order or documentation. One is a milestone from the Via Maris, others came from the synagogue and have skillful geometric and floral motives, including both five-pointed and six-pointed stars, wreaths, and other Roman-style decorative elements. Voices singing masses inside the church fill the air.

ROMANS IN THE GOLAN

In Hellenistic through Herodian times, Greeks and Romans maintained a presence in the north of Israel, on the slopes of Mount Hermon. The Greeks placed temples at the sources of the Jordan River in a city called Panias (for the god Pan). Later, Herod and his successors developed the city, which they called Caesarea Philippi. The site remained important until the Crusades, and the name evolved to its present spelling, Banias.

During post-Bar Kochba times, although officially governed by Roman officials and controlled by Roman legions, the Golan Heights provided another somewhat inaccessible area where Jews tried to keep a low profile. Although the Golan was part of the northern kingdom that had been lost to Judaism in the First-Temple period, it became a site where Jews lived later. Over time, conditions became more difficult, as Jews competed with the growing number of Christians who by the later Byzantine period were no longer of Jewish descent and who became hostile to those continuing to practice traditional Jewish religion.

The Golan is a volcanic region. The hills are round volcanic humps rather than worn-down craggy mountains, except for the Mount Hermon region, where granite and limestone dominate. As a result, the local building stone is black basalt, a lava stone. In the Israel Museum's permanent collection and in a special exhibit there, "In the Light of the Menorah: Story of a Symbol" (May 1998), I saw a variety of synagogue remnants and gravestones from the Golan area, many of them made from this easily identifiable material. Some of these objects belong to European or Turkish museums, as they were collected long ago. The vast number of items suggests that a high number of Jewish settlements existed in the area during Byzantine times, though only a few sites now offer access to this archaeology.

Banias and Nahal Hermon

First, I want to describe several interesting sites in the far north. The Nahal Hermon Reserve includes the ancient city of Banias, also called Caeserea Philippi. It's also a wonderful natural area and contains some of the springs that feed the Jordan River. The Tel Dan Nature Reserve includes the other springs at the source of the Jordan, as well as ancient remains of the city of Dan. Not far away, the medieval fortress called Nimrod's castle dominates a strategic hilltop. Much of this area was contested in the 1967 war, and there is occasional evidence of the international tensions that seem to be a permanent feature of the region. You will also find frequent mention of conflicts there if you read a history of the Crusades.

In Herod's time, Banias was the site of a complex of Hellenistic temples. Now it's a beautiful walk along the rushing spring to the ruins of these buildings. The principal temple, sacred to Pan—as indicated by the original name Panias—includes a shrine where dancing goats were used in the rituals. At the spring now, placards note how archaeologists excavating the site discovered the bones of the goats in the rubble. Adjacent structures were sacred to related gods such as Nemesis. Archaeology is problematic, as earthquakes have reconfigured the sources of the springs and have collapsed the caves onto some of the shrines. The existence of these Greek gods here seems to be an interesting indicator of the presence of pagan religions along with Judaism and underscores Herod's position as a Jew for Jews and a loyal servant of Rome and its preoccupations when he dealt with those outside Jerusalem.

Near these pagan shrines are the remains of a Herodian palace or temple. Josephus mentions Herod's building project in Banias, which the Romans gave him. The area had not recently been part of the Jewish domain because it was in the northern kingdoms that had long since been lost. Herod's activity here again demonstrates how he was thoroughly Jewish in his projects in or near Jerusalem but apparently had few or no scruples when building outside the Jewish boundaries.

Walking through the trails (next to barbed wire fences with warnings about adjacent minefields), you go under the modern road and then under a Roman bridge, which suggests that the course of the road is approximately the same as in Roman times. The path under the bridge is easy to walk because of a boardwalk that allows you to keep your feet dry. The park brochure states that the Romans had a similar arrangement carrying the path under the bridge.

Flour mills and towers along the stream make use of both Roman- and Crusader-era worked stones, as these building blocks were consistently reused when the new inhabitants rebuilt the settlement according to their needs. The current flour mills seem to date from the Turkish period and use a system with a sort of chimney down which the water falls to turn the millwheels. There is no specific mention of Roman use of the waterpower available from the beautiful rapids of the rushing mountain river, but it seems likely that they would have done so here as they did elsewhere. In places, the path goes along old and broken-down mill races, which could easily have begun their existence as Roman watercourses.

The Katzrin Synagogue and Village

During Byzantine times, Katzrin (or Qasrin), not far from the Sea of Galilee and Capernaeum, appears to have been a thoroughly Jewish village. The site was excavated by Shmaria Guttman after the 1967 war and belongs to the regional council, which means that it's presented quite differently from sites controlled directly by the Antiquities Authority. Several houses have been restored, in an attempt to present a direct understanding of life at that time. In addition, the movie at the entrance presents an emotional, patriotic argument that Israel should never give up the Golan in any negotiations. Beautiful aerial helicopter shots illustrate how Israel has developed agriculture and tourism, and how essential it is for Israel to control the strategic high ground in their own defense.

As for the ancient village, in one house the restored sleeping loft contains a low cot equipped with a mattress and patterned blanket. In the kitchen, a restored beehive-shaped oven, appropriate utensils, and large baskets containing fuzzy wool and a spindle (like those found in the Bar Kochba caves and displayed at the Shrine of the Book) suggest the household's activities. A storeroom contains more earthenware pots, pitchforks, and other agricultural tools. Wooden ladders link the rooms, lofts, and rooftop areas. One other realistic touch: sooty oil lamps flicker in stone niches blackened by their greasy drips. The dimness of their illumination provides instant insight into the vast improvement offered by gaslight or electricity. At the lowest point in the town, the ancient water source, a natural spring, still runs into a rectangular pool, though an unattractive greenish scum covers the surface of the water.

The synagogue at Katzrin is modest in comparison to Capernaeum: it's much smaller, with only one entrance way, and has columns with less expertly carved capitals. Like the other buildings in town, the ancient residents built the synagogue from the locally available black basalt, not imported white stone as in Capernaeum. The building faces directly south to Jerusalem. A typical double row of benches around the walls accommodated men for worship or study (women were not allowed, I presume). The lintel of the synagogue has a decorative carving, and the stone is somewhat lighter in color, perhaps having been carefully selected. Other major decorative stones and artifacts must have been lost or removed and taken to museums, especially to the one in the modern town across the road.

THE END OF AN ERA

The end to Jewish life in Israel was slow. Christians persuaded Jews to convert. Byzantine emperors engaged in occasional persecutions. Moslems officially tolerated the "people of the book," but their conversion efforts made inroads as well. Each invasion—Persians, Moslems, Crusaders—terminated a little more of the life of the small and struggling Jewish communities in Galilee and Judea: Katzrin, Bet Guvrin, Sussia.

For a time toward the end of their rule in Galilee, the Romans recognized the patriarchs and delegated certain powers to them, including the right to obtain money from the Jews of Galilee and from the Diaspora. This recognition ceased between 415 and 429 c.e. In this period, the rabbis became still more popular with the uneducated and less-observant public. As the Byzantine era continued, the Christians more and more dominated the area, and Jews became marginalized. Finally, the Persians and then, almost immediately, the new Moslem troops conquered the region. In some towns, their conversion policies prevailed, and Jewish residents converted along with Christian and pagan neighbors. Some small Jewish villages and communities persisted until the era of the Crusades, which eliminated almost all those who still survived.

Subsequently, when the Crusaders were expelled, the Moslems put pressure on the Jews. Several Arab families from the now-destroyed Arab village on the site, interviewed in the 1930s, retained a tradition of having descended from Jews who lived there in the Byzantine era. One family's oral tradition sets their conversion date in the tenth century. Another family became Christian during the rule of the Crusaders and converted to Islam after Saladin's expulsion of the Crusaders and the destruction of their state in 1187.

Benjamin of Tudela, visiting in about 1170, wrote of a visit to several Jewish and Samaritan communities in Israel. In the northern part of the country, he mentioned two hundred Jews in both Akko and Ceaesarea, and only one in Lod (or Lydda). He also named several villages where he found no Jews at all, and at Sepphoris, he mentioned finding many Jewish graves. In Jerusalem, he saw numerous "knights," or Crusaders, and he found two hundred Jews living near the Tower of David. He also referred to two Jewish dyers at Bethlehem, a few caretakers in Hebron, and three Jews at Bet Guvrin. Clearly, by this time, the Jewish population was at its lowest.

PART 2

Medieval Jews in Southern France

A Search for the Jews Who Lived in Languedoc and Provence in the Twelfth through Fifteenth Centuries

Looking for Forgotten Places

On the picturesque streets of Lunel, France, we made a search for the building where the "Sages of Lunel" had once met, eight centuries ago. From the tourist office, we walked through an open square, full of traffic, and then down a small street, hardly large enough for the numerous cars and trucks speeding by. Uneven stone blocks paved the street, which zigzagged between well-kept stucco walls. On the sills of second-story windows, pink and red flowers bloomed, reflecting the bright southern sunlight of the June day. Occasional doorways with a single solid stone stoop offered a place to avoid the speeding cars, small delivery vans, bicycles, and motor scooters. The few other pedestrians carried briefcases or shopping bags with lumpy grocery packages and long, thin French loaves with their golden crust.

Following the rough pen marks on the map we had just obtained from an enthusiastic young woman at the tourist office, we soon turned a corner and found the building: white stone, older-looking, and larger than the neighboring houses. I viewed its stone facade and wooden gate from across the street. Then I approached the gate and peeked through a tiny gap between its wooden slats, feeling uncomfortable for this mildly anti-social behavior. Beyond the gate I saw a small boy playing in the shade of some trees; there were toys in the yard, including a large rubber ball for a child to straddle and then bounce on it. An asphalt parking area separated the green yard from the courtyard side of the building. Two stone doorways with stout wooden doors stood open, linking the

building and the courtyard. While the green garden and open doors
contrasted pleasantly with the stark white wall facing the street, the yard
was not remarkable.

Nothing about the building or its surroundings suggested what we
knew: this place had once been a medieval center of Jewish learning.
Almost a thousand years before our visit, this building, the property
of an already ancient Jewish community, had housed the school where
medical doctors, makers of astronomical tables, skilled scientific and
philosophical translators, and other scholars lived and worked. This
community left Lunel before 1400, so it's amazing that the building still
retains its identity, even vaguely. The woman in the tourist office
had warned us that the building is completely private and shows no
signs of its history. The most that the owners might do to acknowledge
the history of their home, she had said, was that next summer or some
time in the future they might decide to allow the archaeologists from
a historical museum and research center in Lattes, around thirty miles
away, to do some exploration in their cellar. A particular researcher, a
specialist in the history of Lunel, hoped to discover some remains of the
building's long-forgotten inhabitants, who had lived there from Roman
times until the fourteenth century. The woman thought that other archaeology digs with similar goals had taken place in Lunel but didn't
know any details.

By the late Middle Ages, I learned, Languedoc was the home of
a vibrant multicultural society in which Jews participated fully in the
social and commercial life. In the fourteenth and fifteenth centuries,
the kings of France, rejecting the tolerant attitude of their predecessors, expelled them, first from the western part of Mediterranean
France, later from the east. Since their expulsion, both intentional
and accidental actions have destroyed nearly all of their homes, synagogues, school buildings, and cemeteries. Their daily lives, relationships
with neighbors, and their overall identity remain rather mysterious,
and these are what intrigue me. Our trip to southern France was
specifically intended to see if I could find any memories of these long-
lost people. In telling you about my travels there, I would like to share
my sense of history, my attempt to see what was there long ago, behind
the few remaining facades. Languedoc was my first experience with
the search for a historic Jewish presence in the Mediterranean; experiences such as this one inspired me to continue seeking and reading
history.

THE JEWS, THE ROMANS, AND THE DARK AGES

Medieval legend defined the destruction of the Temple as the exact moment when Jews dispersed throughout the Roman Empire. Stories described three rudderless ships that left Jerusalem at that time and wandered from port to port, looking for a home for their cargo of Jewish refugees; the legend says these unfortunates settled particularly in the Roman colonies in the south of France. In reality, of course, the Diaspora began before the destruction and proceeded slowly. Jewish travelers and traders took advantage of the established lines of communication within the Roman Empire, settling in more and more of the Roman colonies in Spain, France, North Africa, and the Middle East. As Jews and early Christians dispersed around the Mediterranean, they competed for converts from other religions. Although in Roman times there were converts from paganism to Judaism, and even from Christianity to Judaism, by the Middle Ages, most of the identifiable Jews were descended from the original refugees from the kingdom of Judea.

Due to the Jews' constant travel in pursuit of business or scholarship, scattered Jewish communities throughout the Mediterranean and the Middle East never lost touch with one another. In later times, because of the need to flee persecution or seek better lives, the communities often merged, so that their traditions never fully diverged. Among the Europeans, Jewish scholarship and contacts with the superior Arab culture contrasted with the widespread illiteracy and isolation of the Christian community. Jewish linguists, medical practitioners, merchants, and scholars were commonly fluent in both European languages and Hebrew, and often in Arabic. In the era predating the humanists of the early Renaissance, Jews helped to preserve and teach medicine, the sciences (including alchemy), music, and literature. Jewish diplomats and translators served a number of European rulers, because Christians, even nobles, were rarely educated in languages or culturally flexible. In the ninth century, Charlemagne employed a Jewish diplomat as his representative on a diplomatic mission to the Middle East. Later, Jews contributed to humanist efforts to restore the lost knowledge of classical antiquity to Europe. They translated and transmitted knowledge from the much more active intellectual culture in Islamic countries of the period, including the Arab-ruled Iberian peninsula, the Middle East, and North Africa.

The Jewish community played an important role in Mediterranean commercial and political life throughout the Dark Ages. They lived through the reigns of Visigoths, Saracens, and Franks under Charles Martel and Charlemagne. They were tolerated more in Moslem Spain and in Narbonne and the southwest of France than in many other cities and countries of Europe, enjoying a great deal of freedom and political power there, as Charlemagne's unified Europe broke up into various disunited principalities. In the seventh century, additional Jews from Babylonia established a special Jewish center of learning in Narbonne, based on the Babylonian school, which continued to be important until the twelfth century. Throughout this time, Jewish identity became more and more distinct, as reflected in Benjamin's consciousness of a united Jewish presence throughout the known world.

EUROPE IN 1165

The date 1165 is the start of the travels of Benjamin of Tudela, which we will follow in the remainder of this chapter. The territorial divisions, linguistic divisions, and political relationships in Europe at this date were substantially different from those in Europe today. Many conditions of life that Benjamin experienced would be utterly unfamiliar to a modern visitor to the courts, castles, farmhouses, or bourgeois homes of the era.

Politics

In Languedoc and neighboring Spain, a number of independent nobles ruled small and nearly independent principalities, dukedoms, kingdoms, and other states. Formally, most smaller rulers, such as counts, viscounts, dukes, and seneschals, owed feudal loyalty to other rulers, in a complex network of relationships and obligations. Many individual rulers held several titles that could each require different ties of feudal loyalty, and their constant power struggles were reflected in arranged marriages between noble families, in a variety of conflicts, and even in open wars.

The king of France in 1165 was competing with other rulers to consolidate the various principalities that eventually united to become modern France. It was the era of Eleanor of Aquitaine and her complicated marriages. Her two royal husbands each wanted her vast inheritance, including Poitou and Aquitaine, and hoped to secure these territories for their posterity by having children by her. Eleanor's first husband was Louis VII, King of France, whom she divorced after the birth of one daughter. Eleanor's second marriage took place just before her husband, Henry Plantagenet, became Henry II of England in 1154. Besides England, Henry ruled various territories in France, both through Eleanor and in his own right. He and their sons Henry, Richard the Lion Hearted, and John were in general more occupied with their French possessions and with Crusades to the East than with their English territories. Besides her sons, Eleanor's children included the daughter by King Louis and two daughters by King Henry. Of these, Joanna married one of the rulers of Languedoc, and the other daughter married into the family of Louis. The aftermath of claims of succession to Eleanor's territories continued long after her death in 1204.

At the time of Benjamin of Tudela, France under Louis VII had no claim to the vast territories that now make up the southwest of modern France. When Louis and Eleanor divorced, he lost his claim on her inheritance, and his heir, Philip Augustus, was the son of his second wife. These quasi-independent territories were, in fact, allied with Louis's enemies and rivals, such as the English and the adjacent Christian principalities in Catalonia. During the next hundred years, however, successive French kings, by war and by marriage, consolidated most of these territories into a powerful kingdom, shrinking the English kings' power in the north and toppling most of the independent rulers of the south and west. In particular, for the first half of the thirteenth century, the French kings waged a destructive war against the various counts, viscounts, and other nobility of Languedoc. Their excuse was to eradicate a religion that had become a rival to the Catholic church. Believers in this religion called themselves "Bonshommes"—that is, Good Men. They also called themselves Christians, believing their viewpoint to predate the Catholic interpretation of Christianity. Their enemies called them Cathars, Albigensians, Bogomils, credentes, or heretics. The war is thus known as the Albigensian Crusade, and the most common name for the members of the religion is Cathars. We will come back to the Cathars, their religion, and the French destruction of their way of life.

In general, Europe in the twelfth century consisted of rather weak, small countries. In the Iberian peninsula, the territories were divided between Christians and Moslems. Italy's many small political units were ruled by the Pope or by foreign or native dukes, kings, or princes. Germany's rulers divided the land under complex feudal inter-relationships. The Holy Roman Emperor, successor to one of Charlemagne's heirs, had his main seat in Vienna, and was at least the nominal overlord of various northern Italian, German, and Balkan rulers. Byzantium was still the eastern outpost of Christianity, and its rulers considered it to be the successor to the original Roman Empire; it remained Christian until the conquest by the Turks in 1453. Outside Europe, North Africa was firmly in Moslem hands. In the Middle East, Christian Crusader kingdoms and Moslem rulers were competing over several kingdoms, particularly Jerusalem.

Jews lived in virtually all of the countries of twelfth-century Europe, North Africa, and the Middle East, under varying conditions. An important Jewish community lived in Oxford, England, where times were good for them. Several Jewish communities in cities in the north of France experienced persecutions, restrictions, and occasionally expulsions during this time. Many Jews lived in the Rhineland and other parts of Germany, though Jerusalem-bound Crusaders, starting in 1096, had massacred large numbers of Jews in German cities and towns, causing unbearable suffering. In Italy, especially around Rome, Jewish communities had lived fairly peacefully from the time of the Roman Empire; after his voyage in France, Benjamin of Tudela visited several of them. Jews in the Islamic territories in Spain, North Africa, and the Middle East enjoyed many privileges despite occasional periods of persecution. In particular, in the twelfth century the Almohades in Spain and elsewhere had recently reversed previous Moslem policies of tolerance, creating problems for local Jews. Among the Europeans, the Jews of Languedoc enjoyed exceptionally good relations with their Christian neighbors.

Quality of Life

For Jews and Christians alike, streets and houses were crowded, sanitation was minimal, clothing was expensive, working hours were long and hard, and food was limited by the success of the harvest as well as by what was in season locally. Import of food, textiles, and wine was very costly, so luxuries such as furs, silk or other imported cloth, spice, and sugar were privileges of the very wealthy. Most common men did a great deal of manual labor. Women even in the nobility spent vast amounts of time spinning to provide weavers with thread. Cloth remained a scarce luxury item, and used clothing was continually recycled, until the industrial revolution six centuries later made textile production more efficient. People worked hard and had few of the material comforts we now expect.

At court, life may have been a little easier, the food may have been slightly better, and at least there was less chance of starvation. But even castles were far from meeting today's standards. Quarters were crowded, with little of what we would call privacy or sanitation. Winter nights were long, dark, and cold. Summer brought flies, heat, damp, easily spoiled food, or perhaps disease or a war. However, court entertainment included the songs of the Troubadours, the most famous cultural accomplishment of that distant time. There probably was at least one Jewish Troubadour among the many who wandered between the fortified castles of many small counts, dukes, princes, and even bishops, providing songs and tales of courtly love. Singing, telling stories, dancing, and playing instruments—flutes, lutes, tambours—was also a major pleasure for common people, though they worked long and hard and probably had little time or energy for such distractions.

Languages

Twelfth-century Jews in Languedoc were usually bilingual in their local vernacular and Hebrew. Besides speaking various languages, they could read and write in Hebrew and often in Latin, as well as in the local languages. Jewish scholars, traders, and liturgical poets of the time used Hebrew as a common language for both religious and secular purposes. Many of the scholarly Jews of the time studied in Spanish or North African Moslem countries and thus also knew Arabic, a language of scholars, philosophers, scientists, and preservers of Greek learning. The surviving manuscripts of Benjamin's *Itinerary* are in medieval Hebrew, but he wrote with many Arabic forms, and Arabic may have been his native language.

Christians in France in the twelfth century employed two major vernacular languages, both descended from Latin. In Languedoc and Provence, people spoke Langue d'Oc, which gave its name to the region. This language was barely intelligible to the northern French, particularly the Parisians, whose language was the forerunner of modern French. While speakers of Langue d'Oc could not communicate well with the northerners—that is, the French—they could understand the language of the people of Catalonia, the adjoining region of Spain, with whom they also shared cultural similarities. The Troubadour poets, who originated in the courts of Languedoc in the twelfth century, sang in Langue d'Oc. They were innovators in this respect, as European vernacular literature did not emerge elsewhere until a century or two later. In France, as in all of Europe at the time, the written and spoken language of government, Christian education, the church, and diplomatic communication was Medieval Latin.

Langue d'Oc, later called Provencal, persisted in the south of France until a generation ago. Provencal has been a focus of various regional political movements for at least the past two centuries. It has now nearly been eradicated by the French educational system; what remains is standard French with a regional accent. As a traveler in Provence and the southwest of modern France, you will see restaurants, farms, and towns with Provencal names and may hear elderly people—or activists—speaking it.

Work and Study

The vast majority of the population in the twelfth century worked in agriculture, engaging in some subsistence farming and raising some crops for barter such as wine, wool, and cheese. Trades for both city and country people included carding, dyeing, weaving, carpentry, ceramics, metal working and blacksmithing, baking or tending communal bakery ovens, slaughter and butchering of animals, and artisanal work. Common people everywhere did their share of ordinary hard labor, such as work on roads, town walls, and fortifications, and young men were, of course, conscripted into various military services. Along the coast, a man might also find work as a fisherman, a boat builder, or a sailor. In towns and on the farm, men and women worked side by side, sharing much of the labor, as the family unit was also the work unit. Women and girls, even among the upper classes, spent every free moment spinning fleece into thread. Women generally either bore and tended many children or died in the attempt.

Jews engaged in a variety of occupations, including agriculture, dealing in grain and other agricultural products, and making and selling textiles or dealing in old clothes, as well as in intellectual occupations such as medicine and translation. The less-fortunate Jews often served as porters, carrying heavy loads along the roads. Individual Jewish communities also variously supported rabbinical scholarship, talmudic centers, or groups of dedicated religious practitioners sometimes called *perushim*, as well as schools for their own sons and extended learning for men. I have found no information about Jewish learning for women at the time.

Jewish involvement in finance and money-lending emerged in this period as a result of prohibitions on their earlier, more varied occupations. Because Christians believed that taking interest on loans was immoral, all money lending was officially prohibited. However, the emergence of various new forms of capitalism placed enormous pressure on the economy, and merchants and artisans were frequently desperate for cash to facilitate trade and develop commerce. As a result, the heads of small states often invited Jews to come to town and become moneylenders, defying the global prohibition but relieving the rulers of some of the burden of their sin. A specific case occurred in Perpignan, where Jews were invited to settle and engage in small-loan activities around the thirteenth century. As the Middle Ages proceeded, guild movements and other social forces pressured rulers to prohibit Jews from engaging in other professions or owning and farming the land. The Jews were more and more channeled into the financial occupations, which ultimately came to be their main source of support.

Although lending money at interest was against church law for anyone—Jew or Christian—the established way to get around this prohibition was for the civil authority to permit Jews to violate it and to profit by taxing the Jewish business. Since they were thus required to violate a law, the Jews were extremely vulnerable, although they often did make a lot of money in their endeavors. The highest interest rate (often set by local statute) was usually 20 percent, which by modern standards is a fair return, when taking into account frequent defaulted loans as well as the ones that were repaid, and also the fact that when people became restless, the rulers often canceled debts and expelled the Jews. When Christians did engage in loaning money, they often asked higher rates than those that were legally set for Jewish moneylenders.

A Jewish household was distinguished above all by ownership of books. Handwritten manuscripts (remember, printing was not invented until the fifteenth century) were rare and comprised a scholars' most valuable possessions. Often, scholars had difficulty obtaining what they needed, and several documents from the period describe the loving care that scholars lavished on their books, organizing them, cataloging them, and noting when someone borrowed one. Since each book had to be copied by hand, each one was immensely valuable—a scholar had to collect all the books he needed for his work, as the invention of lending libraries was centuries in the future. A scholar who was willing to share a manuscript or allow it to be copied was admired.

Much of the learning in school was rote learning, since a text might be available for only a limited time, and thus memory was essential. Writing materials even for letters or compositions were scarce, and writers prepared their drafts on tablets of wax before they wrote them on expensive media—paper or parchment (vellum). The Torah was ritually copied then in exactly the same way as it is now; that is, with extreme care to avoid transcription errors.

Food and Dining

At table, people ate with their fingers from a common plate or from trenchers made from bread, perhaps taking out their own knives to cut off pieces of meat or bread. The few medieval ceramic vessels I have seen in museums include wine jugs, drinking mugs, and platters, roughly glazed in brown or green, and fired at rather low temperature; each household probably also owned at least some brass, iron, wood, or copper cooking and serving utensils. These were probably scarce and valued possessions. I believe that vessels of glass were reserved for the rich, as were objects made from precious metals.

Among the poorer classes, the diet of Jews and Christians would have been about the same—a very limited selection. The main sources of nutrition were bread and porridge made from wheat, buckwheat, oats, barley, or millet flour. Even in those days, there appear to have been professional bake shops, although often, a baker simply tended the shared oven, baking the bread that people made from their own supplies of flour. Individual dwelling places rarely had a private bread oven. During times of bad harvests, various undesireable substitutes, such as a weed called tares or horse chestnut flour, would be added to bread in desperation. Jews would have maintained their own ovens wherever they could, particularly special ovens for Passover.

When times were good, people added a wide variety of foods to their bread. Seasonal fruits and vegetables, wild fruits, herbs, mushrooms, dairy products, eggs, meat, and fish expanded the taste and nutritional value of their meals. In the south of France, local produce frequently included cheese, wine, and olive products. Rural people (particularly Christians) hunted any wild birds or animals they could find, to whatever extent allowed by the law, which reserved the most valued game for the nobles. The bourgeois in cities and other rich people ate quite large quantities of meat, and towns often had a number of butchers. Rich and middle-class people, both Jewish and Christian, celebrated feasts and festivals by making special dishes such as pies filled with mincemeat or cheese. The choices needed for a varied diet were scarce among poor, common people.

Wine, which was always safer than drinking water, was important to both Jews and Christians. Jews in Narbonne and other cities often owned vineyards in order to make their own wine, which they increasingly kept from any contact with Christians. Distinctions in wine quality of various regions already existed. The Christian contemporary of Benjamin, Aimery Picaud, included wine tips in his guidebook of the pilgrimage from France to Santiago de Campostela in Spain. He listed wine as one of the important attractions in a town called Estella, along the pilgrim route, and mentioned the excellent wine of Bordeaux.

The range of available crops for food and beverages was far smaller than in Mediterranean countries today; coffee and tea arrived much later from the Orient, and New World produce like tomatoes, corn, potatoes, and chocolate still waited for Columbus and the other explorers to bring them to Europe. Most citrus products were not widely available in Europe, although the Jews grew or traded in citrons because of their ritual use in the Succoth festival. Benjamin of Tudela did not describe the produce on his European itinerary—this would be no news to his audience; however, his description of Egypt mentions the cultivation of "cherries, pears, cucumbers, and gourds in plenty, also beans, peas, chickpeas, and many kinds of vegetables, such as purslane, asparagus, pulse, lettuce, coriander, endive, cabbage, leek, and cardoon."

An important luxury item was imported spice from distant places in the Orient. Ginger and pepper were among the most popular. Jews often were spice dealers, as evidenced by frequent taxes they paid on spices. In some places, they even paid their taxes directly in pepper. Perhaps this gave them more opportunity to use the spices, as well. Since meat spoils within a day of slaughter without refrigeration, spices were obviously valued for covering up bad tastes, but they were also valued for the same reasons we like them today. Onion, garlic, and wild herbs offered some of the same attractions and also were less expensive and locally grown.

A history of the resistance to French invasion by the Cathars, the heretical sect of Christians, described a few specific products in the context of the French siege of the city of Toulouse. During this siege, the residents lost much of their property and: "they were left neither flour, nor cheese, nor ciclatoun [i.e., cloth of gold] nor purple nor any fine raiment." Followers normally made gifts of food and produce to the Cathar religious leaders, including "bread, flour, honey, vegetables, raisins, figs, nuts, apples, hazelnuts, strawberries; fish, either fresh or, sometimes, baked or stewed; wine, loaves, cakes, and various cooked dishes, some plain, some positively luxurious. The latter were prepared by local peasant women, who could, without arousing suspicion, either go into the forest themselves, or send their children instead. The richer *credentes* [Cathar believers] would supply the heretics' hide-outs with bushels of wheat and kegs of wine—and the best wine in their cellars, too." Note that the Cathars were vegetarians, which means that their supplies could include no meat, eggs, or dairy products; people of other faiths might have also made use of some of these forbidden products (Zoe Oldenbourg, *Massacre at Montsegeur*, New York: Pantheon Books, 1961, pp. 192 and 314).

Information for the fourteenth century and afterward is more abundant than earlier information, because later archives are much better preserved. These archives document how Jews made special requests of market regulators, in order to observe Jewish dietary laws. They often had a hard time obtaining permission to ensure supplies of ritually slaughtered meat, unleavened bread for Passover, and ritual wine. Jewish communities frequently negotiated over rights to have a kosher butcher stall in the market, to maintain a kosher wine maker, and to keep a separate oven for baking their own bread. As craft guilds formed in towns and cities, and authorities granted them exclusive rights to the trades of butchering, baking, and wine-making, the potential for conflict of interest increased. In another context, Jewish customs inspired superstitions—they suffered because Christians sometimes suspected witchcraft or other diabolical practices when they witnessed the Jewish custom of throwing a small piece of dough into the oven before baking bread.

Jewish holidays provided the occasion for enjoying a number of special foods. A writer and satirist named Kalonymos ben Kalonymos described twenty-seven Purim dishes, including macaroni, tortellini filled with nutmeg-flavored meat filling, spicy stews, and other meat, poultry, and game dishes. He mentioned a ladder-shaped honey cake for Shavout and wrote a poem praising Chanukah pancakes fried in oil. The customs in 1165 were probably very similar to those Kalonymos experienced 150 years later—but remember, potatoes came from the New World, after 1492, so he wasn't talking about potato latkes. Cakes flavored with ginger and honey and marked with special verses or magic words were a Jewish tradition for little children's first day of school in Languedoc. The ritual of offering sweets to encourage a child's learning was of deep significance, and included a number of other elements, such as writing verses in honey on a slate for the child to lick. This custom emerged in the Middle Ages; later, the celebration of first learning to read was replaced by the ritual of *Bar Mitzvah*. Also, Passover customs were emerging during this period, along with special food habits.

Rabbis of the twelfth and thirteenth century were still establishing the details of kosher law, and their disputes provide some insight into which foods were available. Rabbi Asher ben Saul of Lunel, early in the thirteenth century, declared a then-controversial prohibition on eating beans during Passover—he said they fermented so thus were not allowed. Later, the prohibition became standard for Askenazic, but not Sephardic,

Jews. Rabbis in Narbonne, where Jews owned vineyards and made their own wine, extended earlier rules for kosher wine, which had no explicit biblical basis. Their prescriptions included forbidding a Christian, such as a servant, to participate in wine making or even to handle an open bottle. In the academies of Languedoc, the sages also pondered the permissible ways to serve a hot meal on the Sabbath. There might be a relationship between the slowly cooked Jewish Sabbath stews, called *cholent*, and the signature dish of Languedoc, cassoulet.

Dress and Distinguishing Marks

Few verbal descriptions record exactly what people wore as early as 1165. Still fewer details tell us exactly what distinguished the dress of Jews from that of Christians. Manuscript illustrations and other depictions require interpretation, but they are the principal source. Certainly, for poor and laboring people, clothing was very plain, draped, coarse cloth, with little distinction between groups, while richer people could afford more warmth, more self-expression, and more ostentation.

Here is a summary of general trends in clothing until the year 1200:

> The European scheme for costume since late antiquity had dressed men and women in similar bag-like garments without curved seams, either for armholes or to create any fit around the body. Three-dimensionality was not built into the construction of the garment, but came into existence as the fabric fell around the wearer and was variously wrapped, belted, and fastened. . . . During the early Middle Ages men's tunics might sometimes be shorter than women's, but both sexes wore draped clothing still fundamentally like those of the ancient Greeks and Romans, who had also allowed men shorter tunics for active war, active labor, and active leisure. Men wore long gowns, too, on all formal civil occasions. The main new medieval difference between the sexes was that with their shorter tunics, men wore separate leg-coverings loosely drawn up and attached to a waistband, and loose-fitting underpants tied around under those, both arrangements well adapted to the European climate and deriving from the original Northern and Northeastern invaders of the Mediterranean world (Anne Hollander, *Sex and Suits*, New York: Kodansha International, 1995, pp. 41–42).

There is little specific information about the dress of the medieval Jews of Languedoc; most imagery comes from Spain or Northern France. Many books and pamphlets reproduce the same drawing from a manuscript, which shows a fourteenth-century Jewish man from Languedoc. He displays the distinguishing round Jewish badge on his draped cloak, which reaches his feet. His head is covered by a long hood with a point touching his shoulder: the hood also probably marked him as a Jew. His face is solemn, and he wears a short beard. His right hand is extended, in a gesture that I can't interpret. A *Haggadah* copied in Avignon at the end of the fourteenth century depicts men in capes with long armholes, short hoods, and full beards.

Pictures from manuscripts show Jewish men from Spain wearing similar cloaks and hoods. During this era, men in Spain wore either a long or a short cloak, while women and girls wore long, unfitted tunics or capes with a cord to tie the waist. Sleeves were wide, because they served as our pockets do—to carry a coin purse or handkerchief inconspicuously. The poorest people wore a single garment, lacking even shoes and head coverings. Girls wore their hair long and loose, while Jewish married women wore a veil or tall hat to cover their hair.

The Jewish badge, special headwear, and other distinguishing marks were under development in the period. The badge was a round circle of varying size, either red or yellow. The hats were often pointed, and sometimes the color red was also required. The Arabs had had the idea of special badges to identify various foreign groups living in their countries, and the Christian kings began to adapt this idea for their own purposes in the twelfth century. In 1215, the Lateran council that mainly dealt with the Cathar heresy declared that rulers in all Catholic countries should require Jews to wear the badge. For centuries after this, Jews made various deals with individual rulers. Some bought themselves out of the obligation, some received permission to make the badge smaller (even just a thread), some requested dispensation for wearing it while traveling, but for all it was an ever-present fact of life.

When times were bad, Jews sometimes determined their own additional restrictions to avoid attracting undesirable attention. They often established prohibitions on furs, luxurious clothing, or displays of jewelry for this reason. Also, they tended to wear black clothing to be inconspicuous. Use of bright colors marked wealthier people in that era. Sometimes the rulers demanded that Jewish men or women wear articles of red or yellow for further distinction.

Besides matters of dress, observation of dietary laws, and their religious and scholarly practices, Jews were distinguished by their custom of washing their hands before meals. The general practice in the Middle Ages was that people rarely if ever washed themselves. In fact, a few centuries afterward, the Inquisition considered washing a dangerous sign of secret

Jewish tendencies and persecuted anyone who behaved in this suspicious way.

Architecture, Streets, and Living Quarters

The monuments of the south of France present a visual history of architecture. You can see elegant buildings and triumphal arches designed by Roman masters of classical style. Practical engineering produced the famous bridge of Avignon and the Roman aqueducts near St. Remy de Provence. Much cruder—though inspired—churches and abbeys illustrate the Romanesque style with its round arches and oddly smiling statues. Some cities also have monuments that date from Gothic, Baroque, and later eras. The southwest is unlike northern France, where a smooth transition occurs between Romanesque and Gothic. The conquerors from the north imposed the Gothic art and its severe Catholic message, as they forced their rule on the southerners, especially in Carcassone and in Narbonne.

For housing ordinary people, the late medieval builders often provided arched doorways and arcades facing the street. Arcades and porches seem natural as a way to shelter from the Mediterranean sun of the region, although arcades as such were prohibited and destroyed during a later epoch in Provence. The outer walls of the houses lean precipitously into the street, some say in order to shelter pedestrians from the rain, perhaps just to make a little more use of the crowded and protected village center. The few remaining medieval streets, as we see them today, can give us some idea of the former appearance of streets, houses, and public buildings such as churches, castles, and fortifications.

All of the problems of crowding and sanitation were worse in the Jewish parts of town because over the ages they were allowed less and less freedom to choose their dwellings, and also because of poverty. In earlier times, before the tenth century, many Jewish communities had enjoyed the freedom to obtain land or buildings and use their property as they wished. In some places they had owned farmland or rental properties. As the Middle Ages progressed, they chose or were forced more and more into segregated quarters. Although the strictly enforced ghetto with its locked gate and frightful overpopulation was the invention of a later age, by the thirteenth century the Jews normally lived near to one another. Some towns, such as Narbonne and Marseilles, had two Jewish quarters because of political or geographic divisions in the municipality. Several facilities attracted Jews to live close together: the synagogues, the kosher butcher shops, ritual baths, bakeries for bread and *matzoth*, a market, a hospital building, or, in some cases, a fountain reserved for Jewish use, such as in Montpellier. Need to protect themselves during anti-Jewish uprisings or riots would also motivate Jews to live together, even if the ghetto were not legally required. By the mid-1500s, the Popes required enforcement of the ghetto by any city that still permitted Jews to live there. In France this Papal decree was only relevant in the four small Jewish communities that survived the expulsions, and this quarter was called the *carriere*.

Medieval streets were never straight and rarely met at right angles. Street cries, people bargaining over wares, animals, and constant foot traffic contributed to congestion and noise. Sanitation was frightful. A gutter in the center of each narrow winding street served as an open sewer, carrying filth from industrial processes like tanneries or butcher shops, household garbage, or human and animal waste. The archives reveal complaints against people who abandoned unwanted building materials in the street or used the street to dispose of the waste cleaned out of their stables. The smells of those streets is unthinkable to a modern person, accustomed as we are to hot and cold running water, municipal waste treatment plants, and refrigeration. In the Jewish quarters, streets were almost always even narrower than the rest, sometimes with tall buildings arching across the right-of-way to make use of the scarce land. In many of the locations where Jews lived before the expulsions, these very streets still retain names such as Rue des Juifs or Rue Juiverie even now, an echo of their long-ago presence. As you wander the narrow winding streets of the medieval areas still preserved in many French cities and small towns, you can watch for them.

Try to picture the interior of a school of Jewish scholars all those years ago. The great academy of Narbonne was large and had rooms for many purposes, but it was exceptional, and in many towns, the study room is the same room used as a synagogue on Sabbath and holidays, perhaps even rather bare. Books and scrolls, like those of Christian monks, are probably stored on their sides on shelves or tables, with several sloping lecterns designed to support material in current use for reading and writing. Perhaps each man has a small brazier of coals to warm his hands and make writing easier in the winter, but who knows? Somewhere would be a room where the smallest boys received instruction, presumably advancing until they could join the men in the study.

As times grew harder and space became scarce, Jewish communities often could manage only one crowded building for all communal activities, including worship, study, and other activities. The ritual bath was frequently in the cellar, as in the surviving buildings in Carpentras, Cavaillon, and Montpellier. Ovens for *matzoth* and everyday bread were often in the same building: in Cavaillon, this oven also heated the water for the bath. These buildings often housed a depository reserved for discarded religious books: the museum of the synagogue of Cavaillon displays several scrolls and bound volumes rescued from this "book cemetery," discovered under the roof. Space limitations forced some of the communities to locate the women's separate seating in a room below the synagogue, where they would have probably had a rather difficult time hearing the services. You can see one such women's section in the synagogue-museum in Cavaillon, where crowding also required them to use a balcony to build a communal *Sukkah*, the only one possible in their over-crowded neighborhood.

As to the interiors of the homes, we can only imagine them. Furniture was primitive, with trestle tables and many wooden chests, perhaps equipped with large iron locks. Richer people would have used carpets or tapestries on the walls, to keep out the cold and damp, and only the rich had the luxury of candles or oil lamps. Poor and even middle-class people relied mainly on a fire for light, cooking, and heat; the central room in each house no doubt served as kitchen, living room, and bedroom for at least some members of the household. Women probably spent much of their lives in this room, cooking, spinning, tending babies, and talking to each other. In the poor homes, there would be little distinction between Jews and Christians.

For most people, there was no separation of home and workplace. Children must have helped to whatever extent they could in their parents' occupations. Many Jewish women were seamstresses and dress designers, or did fine needlework, all certainly done within the home with the help of even the smallest fingers. Seamstresses and other women who worked with textiles were very likely members of families where men bought and sold cloth; Jews were often in wool and silk trades. In the poorer families, a single table would serve as the work table, the dining table, and the study table for the little boys. I think wishfully that maybe even the girls at least learned their letters; perhaps they, too, received a taste of honey or sweet gingerbread when they began to learn the letters at around the age of three. Otherwise, I imagine, little girls at that age began to sit around the family table and use a needle or a spindle, as their mothers, aunts, or older sisters would have been doing. In the poorest homes, whose breadwinners made their living as porters, day-laborers, or mule drivers, the life of men, women, and children would have been more difficult than that of the seamstresses.

Following the Route of
Benjamin of Tudela

Now I will relate my effort to retrace the visit to France of Benjamin of Tudela. He started in Spain and reached Languedoc and Provence about 1165. Every city on his route through France still exists, all but one still under the same name that he used. (Medieval Posquieres is now called Vauvert.) After leaving France, he covered virtually all of the known world.

To start this chapter, I have provided some information on the life and later influence of Benjamin, which should explain why I decided to look into the places that he traveled. In describing the cities along the route, I have tried to contrast past and present. To start each description, I quote what Benjamin said, using a translation from Hebrew into English by Marcus Nathan Adler, published in 1907. Then I describe what I found on my own trip there, more than eight hundred years later, in 1996, including some addresses of the places to visit and the location of the tourist offices, and provide some historical background, with special efforts to tell about the lives of individual people who lived there. For the cities in Languedoc, my cutoff date is the end of medieval Jewish history at the expulsion of the fourteenth century. For Arles and Marseilles, on his itinerary further to the east, in Provence, Jews were allowed to remain until about 1500, so my historical descriptions are somewhat longer-ranging.

THE LIFE AND INFLUENCE OF
BENJAMIN OF TUDELA

Benjamin's native city, Tudela, is on the Ebro river, many days' travel from the more famous centers of Iberian Jewish life, such as Toledo, Grenada, or Gerona. The exact date when Jews arrived in this ancient Roman colony is not known, but Tudela is considered the oldest Jewish settlement in the region. The Ebro provided the major artery for commerce and voyaging to and from Tudela.

During Benjamin's lifetime, the city belonged to the kingdom of Navarre, which had become a part of Christian Aragon in 1115 when the King of Aragon defeated Navarre's Moslem rulers. Throughout the century, the city had a large Moslem and Jewish population and had not yet been heavily repopulated with Christians under the policies of the "reconquering" Christian kings. Tudela was also the native city of two other famous Jewish writers of the previous generation: Judah Halevi (born approximately 1075) and Abraham Ibn Ezra (born 1092).

Tudela's Jewish residents primarily earned a living in crafts, wool trading, textile production, and agriculture. After the Christian victory over the former Moslem ruler, the new king allowed them to return to their lands and homes, taxing them at the same rates that they had paid to the conquered Moslems. Evidently, the Jews held fields, vineyards, farms, and estates, as well as homes inside the city. During Benjamin's lifetime, the Jews of Tudela probably continued to speak Arabic and to have cordial relationships with their Moslem neighbors.

Later in the century, in 1170, King Sancho IV granted the Jews a bill of rights—and restrictions—whose content suggests the conditions of their lives there. One limitation applies to the Jewish occupation of slave trading: the document prohibited Jews from purchase of Moslem prisoners of war. Suggesting that they had had administrative authority earlier, the document also prohibited them from serving as officials with jurisdiction over Moslems and from molesting Moslems in word or deed. However, they received a guarantee that they could sell their houses to any buyer, they received permission for a cemetery, and they were exempted from a previous tax in exchange for a promise that they would maintain the city fortress.

Benjamin's travel account provides the only information about his life. His name, Benjamin ben Jonah of Tudela, is the only identification of the writer. He gave no indication of his past life in Tudela, nor did he specify the motive for his trip, give his age, or identify his traveling companions, if any. These facts remain unknown, open to speculation.

Benjamin began his account by mentioning several cities in the Iberian peninsula: Saragossa, Tortosa, Tarragona, Barcelona, and Gerona. He specified little information about them. His next visit, to the coastal cities of Mediterranean France, is the subject of the remainder of this section. Afterward, he continued to Italy, Greece, Constantinople and the Byzantine Empire, Jerusalem and other cities of Israel, the Middle East, and Egypt. His information about the Far East, northern France, and Germany is considered to be hearsay, though of considerable importance.

Benjamin's Reputation

Benjamin of Tudela's work has served historical and modern scholars, both Jews and Christians, as an important primary source. Many of his observations about Jewish communities provide very important details and population figures, and his accounts of Jerusalem and of the Samaritans are very important, as mentioned earlier in this book. According to *Encyclopedia Judaica*, his work is more objective than travel documents by Christian pilgrims to Israel. His observations about non-Jews, such as about Roman monuments, wars between Pisa and Genoa, life in Constantinople, conditions in the Byzantine Empire, the assassins of Lebanon, and other details, make his work essential to any modern scholars who study the times and places where he traveled (*Encyclopedia Judaica*, "Tudela," v. 15, p. 1423; "Benjamin of Tudela," v. 4, p. 535).

Jewish scholars from the fourteenth century onward evidently read his book with great respect for its authority. In 1368, Samuel Zarza may have been the first to refer to him; in the fifteenth century, Isaac Abravanel summarized the extent of his voyages. The first printed editions appeared in Constantinople in 1543 and in Ferrara in 1556. A Latin translation came out in 1575, an abridged English version of this in 1620, a German translation in 1691, and a French translation in 1729—throughout this era, his Christian reputation among scholars and travelers was increasing.

An exchange of letters between Joshua ha Lorqi and Pablo de Santa Maria in 1400 illustrates how knowledge of Benjamin's voyage was assumed, for a literate Jew. Writing about conversion, Joshua speculated that perhaps Pablo had seen the "destruction of our homeland" (Palestine) and the oppression that recently had come upon the Jews in fifteenth-century Spain as a sign of God's "hiding his face," and he feared that "the name of Israel will no longer be remembered." In his discussion of possible reaction to circumstances, Joshua reminded Pablo of "what is known from writings of travelers"—specifying Benjamin of Tudela as one example, and as another, "the Epistle to Yemen of Maimonides." He cited his friend's assumed knowledge of these sources as proof of the awareness that many Jews lived outside Christian lands (Norman Roth, *Conversos, Inquisition, and the Expulsion of the Jews from Spain*, Madison: University of Wisconsin Press, 1995, pp. 139–142).

For a long time, there was little corroborating evidence of Benjamin's descriptions, particularly of the Middle Eastern countries. During the eighteenth and early nineteenth century, the result was that scholars, especially Christians, often questioned the accuracy of his reports. However, support for Benjamin's observations appeared among the letters, documents, and literary texts found in the Cairo Genizah, a storehouse of worn-out books discovered in the synagogue at Cairo between 1860 and 1896, and today, his accuracy again receives respect.

Beginning in the nineteenth century, various authors or fictitious characters have made themselves out to be the symbolic heirs of Benjamin:

• Israel Joseph Benjamin (1818–1864) called himself "Benjamin the Second." After failing in business in his native Romania, he went in search of the ten lost tribes. In 1856, he published a book about the Jewish communities he had seen in the Middle East, North Africa, and Asia, giving information about their livelihoods, folklore and customs, and population data.

• In 1878, classic Yiddish author Mendele Moykher Sforim published "The Brief Travels of Benjamin the Third," a satire about two foolish men who go off like Don Quixote and Sancho Panza to find faraway places, lost tribes, and other wonders. Benjamin, a Jew from a village, wants to be like ancient travelers, especially Benjamin of Tudela, whom he quotes—or misquotes. (S. Y. Abramovitsch—pen name, Mendele Moykher Sforim, "The Brief Travels of Benjamin the Third," in *Tales of Mendele the Book Peddler*, New York: Schocken Books, 1996).

• In the 1970s, Israeli poet Yehuda Amichai wrote a long poem about the experiences of a modern Israeli, comparing these experiences to those of Benjamin of Tudela (Yehuda Amichai, "Travels of a Latter-Day Benjamin of Tudela," *Webster Review*, vol. 3, no. 3, [Summer 1977]).

• In 1995, Sandra Benjamin published *The World of Benjamin of Tudela*. Writing in the first person, as if she were Benjamin himself, she expanded each of his "letters" for every city and country, adding

all the information that she was able to find and extrapolating to
show his decisions and observations to satisfy modern curiosity.

• I leave it to you to decide if I belong in this list—or if I am a
fool like the characters in "Benjamin the Third."

TRAVEL TODAY AND IN 1165

Benjamin started his travel narrative with the words: "I journeyed first
from my native town to the city of Saragossa, and thence by way of the
river Ebro to Tortosa." He implies two means of transport: by road and
by water. But here, and for the remainder of the book, he provides no
details of the mechanics of the journey or of his motives. To begin, let's
briefly compare conditions and motives of travel then and now.

Modern modes of transportation make most voyages today short
and painless. Benjamin of Tudela probably found no attraction in adventure for its own sake, as many modern travelers do; rather, his unstated
travel motives probably included commerce, study of dispersed Jewish
communities, and desire to see the holy sites in Israel. The *Encyclopedia
Judaica* points out that his attention to the coral industry may suggest
that he was a gem dealer. The content of his book suggests that he also
wanted to learn about the dispersed Jewish communities throughout the
world and present a report on their well-being, as well as to visit the tombs
of holy Jews in Israel. These motives were all consistent with Jewish attitudes
of the time.

Some people still travel for commerce and study, but in general,
motives for travel now are different from those of medieval travelers,
particularly the modern popularity of tourism for its own sake. My challenge
to you is for a more intellectual sort of adventure than is popular with
modern tourists—that is, to try to picture how various sites may once
have appeared, and to imagine what once went on in these places.

Today, many tourists visit the south of France because of the beautiful
beaches and spectacular, mountainous coastal landscapes. In the past,
beaches didn't seem particularly attractive. Areas now crowded with high
rises and sun bathers were left to the poor fishermen, who had no choice
but to work on the sea and live beside it, suffering from dampness, winter
winds, damaging storms, and occasional pirate raids. You can still see
the remnants of old fishing harbors side by side with the sea-walls that
protect the sandy beaches. The roads that Benjamin took were set back
from the sea. They followed the coastal mountains and thus were difficult

and dangerous to negotiate: the highways in the region that make all the resorts accessible now are less than one hundred years old. Travelers like Benjamin had to pay high tolls and customs duties to travel even these poor roads. They also faced hostility from strangers, a chance of being caught in local wars, danger of robbery by pirates or brigands, loneliness as they moved farther from their peers, and other problems.

During the Middle Ages, despite the challenges, travel was popular among both Christians and Jews. Christians most frequently traveled in order to make pilgrimages, while Jews, as I mentioned, frequently traveled for business or study. Jewish traveling merchants, presumably including Benjamin, traded in precious stones or metals, wine, silk, spices, or books. Scholarly Jews traveled to study medicine, science, or religious subjects. They sought out famous scholars in centers such as Safed (in Israel), Cairo, Gerona (in Spain), Narbonne, Montpellier, Lunel, or elsewhere. Troyes, near Paris, had been the home of the famous talmudic academy of Rashi (1040–1105) and was still a center of learning. No doubt there was often a combination of reasons, since scholars usually had to have a way to earn a living, and even for a rich man, the smaller trade goods like spices and jewels were more easily exchanged than money. Jews recognized their need to travel, and a local Jewish community generally would grant written permission to a community member who left, as long as he paid his debts and his taxes. This document could be presented to communities along the route, to demonstrate the traveler's good faith and trustworthiness—if someone left home under suspicious circumstances, his community could also spread word to try to capture the fugitive.

For Jews, there was another, less pleasant reason to be on the road: Jewish communities were often forced to leave their homes temporarily or permanently because their ruler found an excuse to expel them and confiscate their goods. When medieval Jews went into exile from one or another of their home bases, they preferred to move only as far as neighboring cities. Unlucky exiles, especially those who had to travel far from home, lost their possessions or even their lives. They might succumb to illness or accidents or become lost on the journey. They might be captured and sold by slave-traders. They might be shipwrecked. Dishonest sea captains or guides might kill them in order to steal their belongings. The lucky ones might manage return to their original homes when conditions improved or relations with the local authorities changed, but most suffered irreversible losses.

Jewish commercial travelers had an advantage because of their common culture and ability to use Hebrew as a common language. (Theoretically, Latin was such a language for Christians, but fewer were educated.) They had a disadvantage, as well, which was their obligation to stop their voyage and commerce each week to observe the Sabbath. In a situation in which a trader depended very much on the respect of his peers, Sabbath observance was an important commitment to maintaining one's good name and thus couldn't be overlooked or treated casually. Jewish travelers depended on finding Jewish traveling companions and on staying with Jewish people, who felt obliged to welcome them, whatever local Jewish community they belonged to. The differences in synagogue rites, food habits, and other geographic and cultural splits between Sephardic and Askenazic Jews were already beginning to arise— Benjamin's description of Germany equates "Alemannia" with "Ashkenaz." However, in that era, there were many more categories; Italian, French, North-African, and Middle-Eastern Jews were all distinct. The French Jews were called Zarfati, referring to Zarfat, the Hebrew name for France, which Benjamin mentioned as extending from Paris to Auxerre.

Although, in general, the Moslems were more open-minded than Christian rulers, even certain Jewish communities of Moslem Spain had problems in Benjamin's era. Around 1150, the Almohades had begun a persecution of Jews in their Spanish domains, and as a result, many had been in transit, seeking new homes not long before Benjamin's travels. Thus, as he visited Languedoc, Benjamin met representatives of various Spanish families who had escaped from these places. This included the Kimhis in Narbonne and the Tibbons in Lunel.

Christian pilgrims en route to Santiago de Campostela in Spain visited several cities that Benjamin described. St. Gilles, Arles, and Montpellier were important sites on the route from Italy and Marseilles to the very popular shrine of St. Jacques (as he was called in French), Saint James (in English), or Sant Iago (Spanish). Although Benjamin is silent about any meetings with such pilgrims, you could imagine him traveling side by side with men and women wearing the St. Jacques pilgrim's scallop shell in their hats as proof that they had been to the famous site. He could have met passing caravans of pilgrims on their way toward Spain as well.

Aimery Picaud, a contemporary of Benjamin, wrote a travel guide for this pilgrimage—perhaps the first-ever travel guide. His work, written in 1150, provides an alternate perspective, not only because he described Christian holy sites, but also because he offered more detail about the conditions of travel than Benjamin. In a section called "Rivers, Both Good and Bad," Aimery warned of certain rivers along the route whose waters were so bad that thieves sat beside them waiting to skin the horses of pilgrims who died of their waters and named other rivers that were safe for drinking. He described hostels, mainly run by religious orders, that were comfortable and locations where the services were deficient. He spent more time describing the character of the people along his route than Benjamin—he distinguished the Gascons for their hospitality, despite the fact that he considered them "frivolous, talkative, full of mockery, debauched, drunken, greedy, dressed in rags," and without money. (An abridged translation of Picaud's work appears in T. A. Layton, *The Way of Saint James,* London: Allen & Unwin, 1976; the quotation is on page 203.) A few adventuresome travelers today still try the walk from France to Santiago; it's a popular subject for some travel writers.

Christian pilgrims, like Jews, could have mixed reasons for their journeys. The Crusaders often went off to the East in search of booty and glory, not just spiritual adventures. Travelers from the East sometimes also came to the West: for example, a prelate of the Cathar religion traveled from the Byzantine Empire to Languedoc for a Cathar summit meeting in 1167. Many medieval travelers, I think, showed a sense of curiosity and adventure comparable to the spirit of many modern voyagers. Shopping, which is so appealing today, was also a tourist attraction then: someone in Santiago must have noticed this and invented the souvenir scallop shell to sell to pilgrims as a sign to put on their hats (of course, they invented a myth to explain its significance, too, but that's not important now).

Travelers looking for food and shelter, as Aimery implied, often had a choice between monasteries, Christian hostels, and commercial inns; the inns had the reputation of being both dirty and dangerous. A Jewish community always offered food, shelter, and emergency aid such as medical care to Jewish travelers. Benjamin consistently commented on the generosity of his hosts in various cities. In later centuries, anti-Jewish writers, who used Benjamin's work because it was the only account known of that period, commented that the generosity he noted was in conflict with their stereotyped view of Jews!

As for the means of transportation, in contrast to modern travelers' options of modern highways, planes, and bullet trains, twelfth-century travelers rode on both horses and mules and also used them as pack animals. Most of them also had to walk at least some of the time, as roads were very rough. Travelers banded together on the road because of danger from various brigands or wild animals. When possible, boat travel was preferable; it was faster and usually more comfortable than road travel, though it was also physically taxing. Despite advantages, boat passengers faced dangers from pirate raids or dishonest captains, as well as dangers from storms at sea. In general, at that time, only the able-bodied could manage a substantial trip. If a traveler became ill, as sometimes happened, he had to stop; there were special hospices along the Santiago route for pilgrims who became ill and died on their way, and even formal provisions for disposal of their possessions. Jewish communities took responsibility for sick or injured Jewish travelers.

The major roads between the cities of Languedoc still follow more or less the same routes as the roads that Benjamin traveled. In the twelfth century, these roads were bad. There were still many Roman roads in use, such as the Via Domitia, that went through Narbonne. The Roman road-builders had wanted to carry salt and agricultural products and to make transportation feasible for their occupying armies, so their roads accessed the coast only if there was a port. A thousand years after the Romans built the roads, they were still the best Benjamin would have found, but sometimes the local peasants tore up the paving stones for other purposes, leaving a difficult situation for the traveler. In his account, Aimery Picaud also notes that there were many rapacious toll collectors who demanded exorbitant fees, threatening the travelers who refused, and ferrymen whose boats were scarcely capable of carrying the many pilgrims they crowded into their crafts. Some, he noted, would allow the boat to capsize so that they could pillage the possessions of their drowned clients.

Benjamin measured distance by the parasang, which was equal to 2.4 miles. An average traveler's daily distance was 10 parasangs, when the roads were good and not too rough: 30–40 miles a day was the maximum possible. Today, along these same routes, you will find major roads, primarily limited-access toll roads. It's therefore easy to follow Benjamin's entire itinerary in modern France in a day and even see some of the towns where he stopped. You will find that several of the towns that were seaports in the twelfth century have since lost their harbors through the silting up of the rivers and are now land-locked, and thus some that were well known and important in the past, such as Narbonne and St. Gilles, are now obscure and no larger than they were back then. In contrast, Montpellier and Marseilles have grown enormously in population from that time to the present. If you are interested, you might allow yourself quite a bit of time in the area, especially as there is much of interest beyond the few traces to link you with Benjamin.

Despite all the difficulties with roads, food, shelter, and dangerous conditions, many medieval Jews traveled widely on journeys that could take years, and thus there was much communication and awareness of the wider Jewish community that Benjamin wrote about.

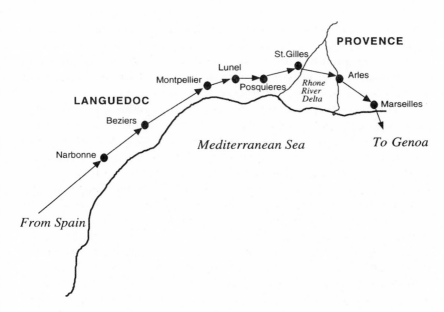

Fig. 2-1: Map of Benjamin of Tudela's Voyage in France

NARBONNE, CENTER OF JEWISH LIFE

Benjamin of Tudela wrote:

> [From Gerona, Spain] A three days' journey takes one to Narbonne, which is a city pre-eminent for learning; thence the Torah [Law] goes forth to all countries. Sages, and great and illustrious men abide here. At their head is R. Kalonymos, the son of the great and illustrious R. Todros of the seed of David, whose pedigree is established. He possesses hereditaments and lands given him by the ruler of the city, of which no man can forcibly dispossess him. Prominent in the community is R. Abraham, head of the Academy: also R. Machir and R. Judah, and many other distinguished scholars. At the present day 300 Jews are there.

What You Can Find There Today

When you set foot in Narbonne, you start your connection to the past. You will find reminders of the Romans, of the Visigoths, of Kings Pepin and Charlemagne, of the counts of Toulouse, and of the lively court of Ermengard whose troubadours sang of courtly love in Benjamin's day. Next to the huge but unfinished cathedral, sharing its walls, a few old buildings tell this story—a Carolingian tower, medieval cloisters, newer palaces, and municipal buildings that Viollet le Duc restored in the nineteenth century. Surrounding all this, you will find an early department store and modern shops around the cathedral compound.

Narbonne can be the center from which you can get to far more intriguing old ruins. Within a few hours' drive, you can find a large number of crumbling castles commanding the still-rugged countryside. Instead of wide tollways or even small, tree-lined nineteenth-century roads, tiny roads wind dangerously up steep hillsides and through nearly deserted woodlands. These are probably as close as you can come to the way things looked when Benjamin of Tudela traveled through the region. The beautiful castle ruins were once the Cathars' fortified strongholds, during the long struggle against French takeover of the region and destruction of their religious way of life. The countryside around these old ruins remains quite undeveloped and sparsely populated. A major Cistercian monastery that dates from the time of Benjamin is near Narbonne as well.

Queribus was the very last of the Cathar castles to fall to the French, and it still seems to be proud to command its sweeping view all the way to Spain. Its tallest tower contains a ruined spiral staircase. Walk up and you will suddenly see that the uppermost treads have crumbled away, and you look up, breathless, past their worn-away stumps into the blue sky. You can imagine how the embattled Cathars, from these heights, might have signaled to castles visible on many surrounding mountaintops, as they watched the invading French armies pass in the wild craggy valleys and uneven farmlands. On the hilltop path of the stronghold, the ruin of a chapel has a single white column that still supports the eerie walls.

Beyond these strongholds, an hour from Narbonne by tollway, you will find Carcassonne—another triumph of Viollet le Duc's restoration. Carcassonne's stunning double walls, its Gothic cathedral, fortified palace, winding streets, and impressive towers replaced an older citadel, mainly destroyed in the wars between the old rulers of Languedoc and the French invaders. Inviting outdoor restaurants and less appealing souvenir and postcard shops occupy the historic buildings. Although it hosts enormous busloads of tourists, parking lots full of private cars, and even bicycle tours, the city still seems to present a convincing demonstration of what life was like there when it was in its prime.

Carcassonne, like Narbonne, was the home of a large number of Jews until about the time of the French conquest and their resulting expulsion. The medieval Jewish quarter, including all its buildings and its cemetery, disappeared when the French rebuilt the city in the fourteenth and fifteenth centuries, and comparing an old map of Jewish sites with the modern map, we discovered that nothing whatsoever remains of the former Jewish quarter. We inquired about our quest at the tourist office, which resulted in an interesting conversation with the tourist office representative about the destruction of the independent local society as it existed before the French conquest. We were fascinated by this young woman, who described her regret of the loss of the open, multicultural environment where Jews, Cathars, and free-thinkers once co-existed, and her renewed resentment of the French imposition of orthodox Catholicism. We found several other people who shared this view as we traveled through the region.

Not far from Narbonne is an ancient wine region, still a good place to see today's vines growing. Here the Romans introduced grape cultivation into France. From Roman times, also, there were Jews who owned vineyards there, and rabbis of Narbonne contributed to the concept of kosher wine.

Narbonne itself is a rather small town, scarcely different now than it was in the Middle Ages. We sensed a lack there of a really lively nighttime center. We reluctantly ate in the same restaurant—though a good one—two nights in a row, because we couldn't find any others; our selected alternative, supposedly open that day (according to the Michelin guide), looked as if its owners had abandoned it.

The major tourist attraction is the grandiose cathedral, which the French built after the conquest of Languedoc. They rebuilt almost the entire city of Narbonne in the fourteenth century. The expression of the power and oppression of the conquering French in this rebuilding seems to be Gothic style, and its force is nowhere more evident than in the cathedral of Narbonne. Beginning not long after the French conquest, these builders began a cathedral so enormous that it was never feasible to finish it; before they could do so, circumstances changed and the fortunes of the city declined irreversibly. Only the ambulatory and the part of the church that would have been behind the transept are complete. The building's height is an overpowering fifty meters, almost as tall as it is wide and long. Outdoors, you can see a sort of stub of a transept and a few columns soaring into nowhere. To complete the church in proportion to Gothic standards, the builders would have been obliged to tear down the city wall, and they didn't yet have the confidence to do that, at least not at the time when their finances still could have sustained their too-ambitious endeavor.

In the morning, Narbonne traffic seems to pick up. We saw a very lively covered market on the opposite side of the river from the cathedral. Near the cathedral we saw many small and not very chic shops, crowded with people carrying baskets and bags. The shopping area appears to have been built in the nineteenth century and from my map of Jewish Narbonne as it was in 1200, these shops and a big Monoprix department store are on the site of some of the old Jewish streets. The medieval city walls have long since disappeared. The Lapidary Museum, which contains a funerary stone with a Hebrew inscription from the sixth century, according to my sources, is only open in July and August.

Unfortunately, while Narbonne has the most interesting Jewish historical background, it has no distinctive Jewish historic sites to see today. It would really be wonderful if the old Jewish school were redis-covered somehow. I hope that my lack of "finds" there is just my fault and that some day I will discover where there is more to see.

Narbonne from the Romans until the Time of Benjamin

There were Jews in Narbonne from Roman times onward, with concrete archaeological evidence (the tombstone that I mentioned) as early as the sixth century. The earliest Jews arrived after the destruction of the Temple in Jerusalem. The Jewish community continued to be an impor-tant element of the population throughout the Visigoth period and into the Middle Ages.

At the end of the Dark Ages, the Saracens—that is, Moslems from North Africa—conquered Narbonne from the Visigoths. Pepin, the king of the Francs, conquered the Saracens, chased them out of that part of France, and established himself as ruler of the city. Jewish residents as well as Visigoths cooperated with his troops to help him take the city; in turn, he recognized many rights of the Jews to own property and pursue their trades. Later, this series of events was translated into legend, and one of the medieval books of *Gestes* said that Narbonne had actually been divided into three kingdoms: one Visigoth, one Frankish, and one Jewish. This story, written centuries later, also attributed the three-way division to Charlemagne, rather than his predecessor. In fact, although he had recognized the rights of the Jews of Narbonne, Charlemagne apparently had not allowed them to have an independent kingdom.

A perspective on Narbonne's history of this time appears in a frankly fictitious family history, Marek Halter's *La Memoire d'Abraham* (Paris: Robert Laffont, 1983; an English translation was available, but I have never located a copy). Halter places his imaginary ancestors in Narbonne during the eighth and ninth centuries. He follows their descendants through Jewish history, including several of the times and places in the later chapters of this book.

In other parts of Europe at the time of Benjamin of Tudela's visit, the condition of the Jews was deteriorating, and in many places they became subject to ritual humiliation and degrading practices, especially at Lent and Easter. In Narbonne, the decline in tolerance of the Jews was less rapid. Jews continued to exercise a wide variety of trades and were often allowed to pay a tax instead of submitting to humiliations, such as having the faces of the Jewish elders slapped on Palm Sunday. In fact, from Roman times until the end of the independent era of the counts of Toulouse, Jews were relatively well treated in Narbonne. In the earlier times, Jews were not formally restrained as to the neighborhoods where they could live. Later, after the French conquest, they became restricted and suffered from overcrowding and its problems. From the French conquest in the 1220s to the end of the century, their state declined, ending with their expulsion in 1306.

Twelfth-century Narbonne was a city of about 30,000, with a Jewish population of about 1,500. When Benjamin says there were 300 Jews, he means heads of families. The viscount—or in the time of Benjamin, Viscountess Ermengard—of Narbonne was a subject of the count of Toulouse, who was allied with the house of Aragon. City government included both the viscount's civil government and a religious administration, headed by a bishop. They each administered parts of the city, and some Jews fell under the auspices of each administrator: thus, there were "the viscount's Jews" in the Grande Juiverie and "the Bishop's Jews" in the Petite Juiverie. The Bishop's Jews were poorer and less numerous than those of the viscount. This sometimes meant they disputed whose Jews were whose, especially for tax purposes: the Jews were responsible for many more taxes than the Christians. Some of the taxes applied to Jewish individuals and some applied to the community as a whole.

The head of the Jewish community was called the *Nasi*, or prince. Benjamin mentions that members of his family traditionally were considered descendants of the house of the biblical King David. Their more recent ancestors, the family Kalonymos, were scholars who had come to Narbonne from Babylonia, a center of learning, a few centuries earlier. These *Nasis* even enjoyed official recognition. Other branches of the

family spread to many other parts of Europe, where they also obtained
respect and positions of religious leadership.

Scholars

Narbonne was a center of intellectual leadership, associated with the
school, or academy, that Benjamin mentioned. Three styles of thought—
kabbalistic mysticism, talmudic hair-splitting, and Maimonidean rationalism with its revival of Greek philosophy—provide a dramatic contrast in
thought among the writers of the age. In addition, there were many
students and original thinkers in secular disciplines, particularly astronomy,
astrology, and medicine. Throughout the various academies and rabbinical schools of southern France, there were proponents of these varying
points of view, and the tensions and disputes among them made Jewish
intellectual life during that age very lively.

Several families of talmudic and secular scholars and important
translators lived in southwestern France at the time, including the Kimhis,
the Tibbons, and the Kalonymos family. Joseph Kimhi (1105–1170), a
teacher, translator, and author of works on Hebrew grammar and biblical
commentaries, settled in Narbonne in 1148 after persecutions by the
fanatic Almohad Moslems drove him from his native Spain. His book
Sefer ha-Berit, written during his years in Narbonne, provided source material
for Jews who had to engage in disputes with Christians or who were
troubled by doubts about their Jewish convictions. Kimhi's descendants
were active in Narbonne for many years. Scholars based in Narbonne
engaged in a great deal of communication with rabbinical institutions
throughout the Jewish world at the time, from Babylonia to Spain, and
from North Africa to England.

The most famous Jewish scholar of the age was Maimonides, who
was born in Cordoba, Spain, in 1135, fled from the Almohades' persecutions, and ended his life as the physician of the rulers of Egypt. He
died in Cairo, Egypt, in 1204. Although he was never in France, he was
well known there, both for his works of philosophy and for his works
on medicine, and he encouraged the scholars of Provence who translated
his works from Arabic into Hebrew. Scholars from Narbonne were among
the first to recognize Maimonides, who corresponded with members of
several schools of Jewish learning in France. A Narbonnese translation
of his work was eclipsed by that of the scholars of Lunel. Later, members
of the academy of Narbonne, such as members of the Kimhi family,
participated actively in the thirteenth-century controversy over Maimonides'

works. The scholars of Montpellier were particularly active in this controversy, which is discussed at length later in this chapter.

The head of the school in Narbonne in the twelfth century was Rabbi Abraham ben Isaac. His followers believed that he had a vision of Elijah, the prophet, who served as a spiritual guide to Jewish mystics. Rabbi Abraham's family continued in his tradition. His son-in-law Abraham ben David, known as the Rabad, was a talmudic scholar and also the first to publish criticism of Maimonides' fusion of Greek and Hebrew traditions. His grandson Isaac the Blind, who lived in Posquieres, extended existing mystic traditions to create important new ideas and thus is considered the "father" of the Kabbalah. Isaac's disciples Ezra and Azriel returned to their home in Gerona, Spain, which became the later center of kabbalistic thought; the author of the *Zohar*, at the end of the fourteenth century, was indebted to the earlier French thinkers. (Modern scholars don't even bother to mention that the schools were for men only; it goes without saying.)

A large complex of buildings formed Narbonne's academy. Unfortunately, nothing of the complex remains today. Old city plans show that the academy stood in what is now Narbonne's main shopping district, which appears to date from the nineteenth century. The school resembled a modern college campus—although the institution of a university for Christians, from which we get the modern concept, was extremely rudimentary at that time. The school's buildings included the local synagogue, benevolent societies to help the poor, and the Rabbinical Court, where rabbis discussed or settled points of religion and law cases that didn't require secular intervention. Scholars at the academy had studied with famous teachers in Gerona, Spain, another great center of learning. Their discussions and comments were recorded in various rabbinical documents and *responsa*.

The library at Narbonne received particular recognition and the level of education was very high compared to the standards of the day. The Jewish school was also unusual, as there were few Christian schools or institutions of higher learning in the region: the university of Toulouse was not founded until 1229, and Montpellier was mainly a medical school.

Making a Living

Industry in medieval Narbonne included production of salt, wine, and textiles, and trade in grain and other agricultural produce. Genoese ships carried Narbonnese products throughout the Mediterranean, exchanging goods among Europe, Asia, and North Africa. Narbonne also sent and received a number of products to and from Bordeaux, just across the narrowest part of France on the other coast and onward to England.

For Jews, money lending, pawnbroking, and dealing in precious stones and metals had become their major occupations in Mediterranean communities by this time. However, Narbonne, with its older traditions, continued to offer a wider freedom of occupation for Jews. Exceptionally, the Jews owned a substantial amount of land in and around the city, including farms and vineyards. Although they sometimes acquired real estate as a result of defaulted loans, land and buildings also belonged to long-time resident families, who had established themselves as farmers and wine-growers before the era of restrictive laws. Jewish owners of agricultural land sometimes farmed and sometimes rented out the land to others for a share of the produce. As a result, many Jews were dealers in grain (especially wheat and millet) and wine. Beyond agriculture, a few Jews were employed in the textile-making crafts (for example, a dyer), and many were textile dealers. Jews provided administrative services to the Christian rulers, as well as court entertainment—one record lists a Jewish troubadour in Narbonne. The poorest Jews engaged in manual labor, working as porters, as mule drivers, and at other types of back-breaking jobs. Finally, Jews provided services to other Jews as butchers, bakers, wine makers, notaries, scribes, rabbis, scholars, and teachers in the schools.

Narbonne from the Albigensian Crusade until the Expulsion of the Jews

Among the Christian population in the twelfth century, the Cathar religion was strong and growing, opposed, of course, by the Catholic church. Narbonne was strongly affected by the French wars against the Cathars between 1200 and 1244, but unlike many other cities, was not directly attacked, besieged, or sacked. The crusade against the Cathars also made a difference to the Narbonnese Jews. In 1227, a church council in Narbonne decided on strict enforcement of the limitations on Jewish rights that had been specified at the fourth Lateran Council in Rome in 1215. In addition, they declared that Jews must not appear on the streets during Holy Week, the week before Easter. Reaction among the Jews was to become more conservative and worried about heresy among themselves. The problems became worse when the treaty of 1229 gave full jurisdiction to the French king.

The condition of the Jews deteriorated throughout the thirteenth century, ending with their expulsion in 1306. From 1306 until 1308, the authorities of Narbonne auctioned off the confiscated property of the expelled Jews, including the buildings of the academy and the elementary school. The sales record suggests the affluence of the community, listing palatial homes and goods evaluated at five thousand livres, a large amount of money. Despite the occasional reopening of Narbonne to the Jews in the course of the fourteenth century, the community never reestablished itself.

Although the conquering French did not destroy Narbonne and seemed to have expected to keep up its wealth, the city experienced a severe decline beginning in the fourteenth century. This decline occurred for three reasons. First, during that century, the port silted in, and thus the city was cut off from the Mediterranean trade that had created much of its wealth. Second, the plague killed so many of its occupants that many activities were destroyed. And third, the expelled Jews had been one-third of the population and had been major contributors to the economic life of the city; their loss was critical. Narbonne never recovered.

BEZIERS AND THE HISTORY
OF A SLAP IN THE FACE

Benjamin of Tudela wrote:

> [From Narbonne] it is four parasangs to the city of Beziers, where there is a congregation of learned men. At their head is R. Solomon Chalafta, R. Joseph, and R. Nethanel.

What You Can Find There Today

The road between Narbonne and Beziers is not far from the old Roman road that Benjamin probably traveled. Rolling hills covered with brush, which flowers in spring and early summer, probably have changed very little, and today, as then, there are occasional gaps in the rocky landscape that allow the traveler to catch sight of the horizon where the Mediterranean joins the very deep blue sky. When you are rushing along at modern freeway speeds, it's challenging to imagine how it must have been to go on foot, perhaps accompanied by a few pack animals.

Any buildings that Benjamin actually visited were surely destroyed when the French sacked the city in 1209 and burned the cathedral, where most of the victims perished. In the nineteenth century, the city discovered the mosaic pavement of the twelfth-century synagogue, but I don't know where it is now. The museum owns the oldest stone inscription from the city's history, written in both Latin and Hebrew. (I can't verify if it is displayed.) The Jewish quarter stood near the present place de la Revolution and rue Boudard; in the thirteenth century, a Jewish school occupied a location on the current rue du 4-septembre.

Historical Background

Jewish inhabitants of Beziers were known in Hebrew as Bedersi; even after they left Beziers, the term continued in use as a surname. The earliest record of these Jews was in the sixth century, the date of the stone inscription that still remains in the museum. Earlier in the Middle Ages they had become an important part of the economic life of the town; they paid a tax on honey, cinnamon, and pepper, which might indicate that they traded in those goods. The archives provide several references of importance in learning about this community. The synagogue was built in 1144 or 1164. The famous translator Abraham ibn Ezra visited Beziers in 1155; it was also the home of a number of liturgical poets. The Jews' high socioeconomic position is indicated by the presence of a Jewish bailiff named Nathan some time in the twelfth century and by the Viscount Raymond-Roger's appointment of a Jew named Samuel as an official of the town in 1204.

Beziers' archives include evidence about a very old display of disrespect for Jews, which may have been widespread in the Dark Ages. On Good Friday, or even throughout the entire Easter weekend, European Jews were required to stay inside their houses or within the Jewish quarter of towns. During this period, especially in response to inflammatory sermons, Christians in some towns habitually threw stones at the Jews' houses or at any Jewish person in the streets; these stones were often large and dangerous. Alternately, in other towns, an elder of the Jewish community had to endure a public slap in the face; in 1018, at Toulouse, the Jewish elder died of the blow. In 1160, Raymond Trencavel, viscount of Beziers, convinced the bishop to abolish the custom of stoning the Jews in Beziers, replacing it with a payment of "200 . . . sous outright and an annual tribute of four livres for the ornamentation of the church"

(Cecil Roth, *Gleanings: Essays in Jewish History, Letters, and Art.* New York: Bloch Publishing Company, 1967, pp. 2 and 82).

At the time, Jews—especially moneylenders—were considered property of the rulers. This was the case in Beziers, where the rulers' protection seems to have had a large element of self-interest. Jews could loan money, while Christians could not, and the money that they loaned was openly regarded as an extension of the wealth of the ruler who profited by taking a very high tax on the loans. Noble dowries or wills in Catalonia and Languedoc sometimes listed a Jew by name, as one of the assets—which meant that the bride's father or the estate was disposing of the right to tax a Jew and profit from his moneylending activities. This view gave rise to the strange fact that if the Jew converted to Christianity, so that he was no longer eligible to loan money, his goods would all revert to the ruler. As a result, both the Jews and their rulers had an economic incentive for the Jews to keep their own faith. On occasion, when the church noticed this, they proposed the solution of canceling all Christian debts to Jews and taking their money as an incentive to their conversion.

A major war in the first half of the thirteenth century caused a period of decline of the Jewish community. The most important event in this war, for both Jews and Christians, was the sack and destruction of the city in 1209. Late in the century, the community flourished again before the expulsion of Jews from all the realms of the King of France in the fourteenth century. For a time, a Jewish poet named Abraham Bedersi adopted the troubadours' custom of challenging other poets to poetry contests. According to the historian of Jewish literature Zinberg, Bedersi's many works of satire, parody, and songs of praise suffer from a lack of true inspiration.

Background: The Cathars and the War against Them

To understand what was behind the sack of Beziers, it's necessary to go back to the roots of the anti-Cathar crusade and trace the French Crusade against these people, whom they viewed as heretics. The Cathar movement was dangerous to Catholic teachings, but what's more important is that it threatened the power of the Catholic church. Jews were grouped with Cathars for persecution by many Papal Bulls and other decisions at the higher levels. The Lateran Council of 1215, which was directed mainly against the Cathars, incidentally created much important law regarding the Jews. It ordered the Jews to wear the round badge and other distinctive clothing and placed restrictions on their professional and personal activities. Equally important, the Inquisition emerged during this time as a weapon against the Cathar religion and was honed and improved even more over the years in ways that deeply affected the Jews. The conflict between Catharism and the dominant Catholic church had a persistent effect on the Jews, and the defeat of the rulers of Languedoc by the Kings of France led directly to the Jews' expulsion.

When Benjamin traveled through Languedoc, the Cathar domination of the religious life of the region was in full swing. The Cathars had many adherents among the nobility as well as among peasants and workers, especially among itinerant weavers, who spread the Cathar philosophy as they traveled. Believers in this faith were so common that in some parts of Languedoc, there were no Catholic masses said for close to a century, churches were neglected, and tithes not paid. The counts and other rulers of the region tended to protect both Jews and Catholics; both Jewish and Cathar strength in Languedoc bears witness to the multicultural and open-minded atmosphere of the time.

A high point of Catharism was in 1167, when the prelate of Constantinople's Cathar organization attended a congress of Cathar leaders in Languedoc. Besides the group from Constantinople, the Languedoc Cathars were allied with a variety of contemporary religious sects, also considered heretics by the Catholics, such as the Bogomils of Bulgaria and sects in other parts of the Balkans. The Cathars also had ties to ancient Manicheans, Gnostics, and those from other philosophic movements. Theory aside, the Cathars earned the respect of the people because of their self-denying lifestyle and consistent rejection of the rampant materialism of many priests and bishops of the time.

By around 1200, Cathar believers became so numerous and so open that the Pope determined to fight the practice and attack its proponents, first sending St. Dominick and other churchmen to persuade them to return to Catholicism and, when persuasion failed, convincing the king of France to use force in a campaign now known as the Albigensian Crusade. Once he started to fight, the French king became quite enthusiastic about conquering the rich territory of the Counts of Toulouse and their vassals, and he joined his wider ambitions to his religious duties. All-out war resulted, and French armies began to attack cities in the area. The war soon went over the line from an effort to bring Cathars back to the Catholic faith. Soon it became an assault on the power of the southwestern principalities and an effort to add their rich land to the domains of France. The military leader of the French forces, Simon de Montfort, still today seems to be detested by the citizens of the area for the brutality of his killing and destruction, as we learned when talking to people in Carcassonne and elsewhere.

The Sack of Beziers by French Troops

The French attack on Beziers in 1209, along with the destruction and sack of the city, was a crucial event of the campaign against the region and its native rulers. Simon de Montfort's massacre of twenty thousand Christians, many of them gathered for safety in the cathedral, inspired widespread horror even in a violent and warlike age. The ruthless killing served as a warning of the real intentions and the atrocities the French were capable of committing in the name of the Crusade against the cities of Languedoc. A verse account of the battle, written a generation later, expressed the bitterness of feeling against the French, with their undisguised territorial drives and mere pretense of religious motivation. According to this account, Simon de Montfort, when asked how his troops were to know the true Catholics from the heretics during the siege, replied, "Kill them all, God will know His own."

Another troubadour song recounted that the city's Jewish community was saved because the count, who fled from the city before the attack, took his valued Jews with him. Unfortunately, this seems to be a legend; only a few of them may have accompanied him. Thus, besides the twenty thousand Christians, the victims included two hundred or more Jewish residents of the city. After the destruction of the city, Jewish survivors fled to Narbonne and to Olot and Gerona in Catalonia, returning to Beziers later when things improved.

The war against Languedoc eventually succeeded in eradicating the Cathar religion. The combined forces of the church and the ambitious French kings repeatedly resumed their actions. In the 1240s the final Cathar strongholds fell, and the resulting conquest served the interest of the French in uniting the territories that now make up France. The Jews of the region suffered almost incidentally, as French kings who valued religious purity assertively replaced the more tolerant Catalan power structure.

Cathar Beliefs and Kabbalist Parallels

Catharism was a "dualist" religion, believing in equivalent powers of good and evil. Cathars interpreted the different historical views of God in the Old Testament as evidence of two different gods or powers. The Old Testament creator was in their view evil because they believed that all material things were evil, and for this reason, some Cathars were anti-Jewish. The more sophisticated God of some of the biblical prophets corresponded to their good deity. Christ was not in their view material, and the suffering on the cross was for them symbolic or illusory. It's difficult to trust some of the recordings of the Cathars' beliefs, because the Catholic monks and priests who wrote these accounts represented the Inquisition and clearly wished to put the Cathars in a bad light.

One rare Cathar document, *The Vision of Isaiah,* describes the dualist vision, which was imported from the Bogomils via Italy around 1190. The document explains how Isaiah reaches the seventh heaven, and he sees the Old Testament God. Another document, *The Secret Supper of John the Evangelist,* describes the origin of the world, the devil's role, and predicts the last judgment. The Cathars also wrote glosses on their main prayer: a slightly altered version of the Catholic Lord's Prayer. Cathar practice included monastic orders who took oaths of extreme self-denial. Ordinary believers observed varying degrees of commitment to a vegetarian diet and ascetic lifestyle.

Several authors suggest a connection between the emerging Jewish beliefs known as the Kabbalah, which were in the process of development in Languedoc at this time, and the tenets of the Cathar religion. No one has documented specific evidence of influence or contacts between Cathars and Jews, such as direct references or recognizable quotes. However, in the intellectually free atmosphere of the time, the wide variety of new ideas and religious practices may have included communication between the various dissenting communities of the area.

In the development of Jewish mystic beliefs, Isaac the Blind, who was born in Narbonne in the 1160s and lived in Posquieres until the 1230s, made essential innovations to the existing Jewish traditions of the time, developing the foundation of the Kabbalah. Considering that most of the Christians during the time were at least sympathetically aware of Catharism, various writers have attempted to draw parallels between the two philosophical systems. Parallels include that both Cathars and kabbalists drew inspiration from the Old Testament prophets, both Cathars and kabbalists believed in the transmigration of souls, both believed in the creation of new souls in some individuals, and both possibly had similar origins in the work of the Gnostics.

According to Gershom Scholem:

The details are very different. The Cathars regarded the higher souls as those of fallen angels that must continue to wander until they reach the body of a Cathar perfectus. This connection between psychology and the myth of the angels who fell away from the good God, of major import for the Cathars, is totally absent in the Kabbalah. (Gershom Scholem, *Origins of the Kabbalah*, Princeton: Jewish Publication Society: Princeton University Press, 1987, p. 237)

Scholem discussed the early mystic book, the *Bahir*, as a source:

Different details of a gnostic character entered into the Book *Bahir* through an internal Jewish tradition, just as a number of gnostic details turn up here and there in Cathar doctrine. Thus the Cathars recognize four elements as composing that supreme world, in a manner reminiscent of the circle of Isaac the Blind. The Creator God or demiurge, who for the Cathars is identical with Satan, has a form and a figure in which he appears to his prophets; the good and true God, on the other hand, is imperceptible to the eye. We may also detect a certain resemblance between the doctrine in the *Bahir* of Satan as the seducer of souls, as the prince of *tohu* and the material world fashioned from it, and the conceptions of the Cathars with regard to the role of Satan. (*Origins of the Kabbalah*, p. 235)

In addition, Scholem mentions the common influence on mystics of Provence in the period around 1180–1220 and on the Cathars of Scotus Erigena, particularly the doctrine of the "first cause," which is a unity of divine wisdom (*Origins of the Kabbalah*, p. 314).

Eventually, the major element in common between Jews and Cathars was their threat to the power and prestige of the Catholic church. Cathar religious leaders, called Perfecti, were inspired essentially by religious motives, while Catholics acquired the role of priest, bishop, or other church offices for social and financial reasons more often than for religious reasons. Cathar religious ties were less formal and despite the informal ties to other sects, their church was not a major international political institution as was the Church of Rome. The Catholic church was tied to the upper classes and run for the benefit of the wealthy, while the Cathar's political power and what little hierarchy they had belonged to bourgeois and even peasants. Because of this, the Cathar faith appealed to people craving religious honesty and sincerity, and also to local loyalty as now defined by terms like civic pride, nationalism, or patriotism. This clearly increased the desire of the institutionalized church to crush them. Over time, the church view of the Jews acquired much of the same institutional antipathy, which combined with the many strains of anti-Jewish sentiment already in the philosophy and rhetoric of Christian thinkers.

MONTPELLIER, HOME OF A CONTROVERSY

Benjamin of Tudela wrote:

> [From Beziers] it is two days to Har Gaash which is called Montpellier. This is a place well situated for commerce. It is about a parasang from the sea, and men come for business there from all quarters, from Edom, Ishmael, the land of Algarve [Portugal], Lombardy, the dominion of Rome the Great, from all the land of Egypt, Palestine, Greece, France, Asia, and England. People of all nations are found there doing business through the medium of the Genoese and Pisans. In the city there are scholars of great eminence. . . . They have among them houses of learning devoted to the study of the Talmud. Among the community are men both rich and charitable, who lend a helping hand to all that come to them.

What You Can Find There Today

In Montpellier in 1986, archaeologists restored the old ritual bath, whose traces survived under a building in the city on Rue de la Barralerie. The same site once also held the medieval synagogue and other Jewish buildings. For the dedication of the restored bath, the current Jewish community and the scholars of the university prepared a book of articles on the history of the Jews of Provence, including the scholarly study of the Jews' role in the foundation of the Montpellier medical school. The book offers a very detailed history, including many names of the Jews who lived in Montpellier in the Middle Ages (Carol Iancu, *Les Juifs a Montpellier et Dans Le Languedoc A Travers l'Historie du Moyen Age A Nos Jours*. Montpellier: Centre de Recherches et d'Etudes Juives et Hebraiques, 1988).

A suburb of Montpellier, Lattes was also a Jewish center and has an interesting archaeology museum, though not concerned with Jewish subjects. Lattes was the home of a family of Jews who later went to Rome and became the popes' doctors.

In Montpellier today you can find scholars of great eminence, doing research on the history of the Jews of France. They work for the University of Montpellier and for the French scientific establishment, the CNRS. Times are different now, however, and the Jewish traveler no longer expects to look up the community of scholars and profit from their generous hospitality. If you want to visit them, your method today is the WorldWide Web, where they present a description of their current publications. (Because the organization of the Web changes constantly, I have decided not to specify exact addresses, but to suggest that you use a current search engine to find the up-to-date location.)

Also now, at the end of the twentieth century, a great medical school still exists in Montpellier. At the gates of this school is an inscription that commemorates its twelfth-century founders, including several Jewish doctors.

To visit the ritual bath, which has no clearly stated hours, check with the Tourism Office, 30, allée Jean de Lattre de Tassigny, 34000 Montpellier, phone, 04-67-60-60-60.

Historical Background

Montpellier was a rather quiet city from its founding in the tenth century, throughout medieval times, and up until the present. The first explicit mention of a Jewish community is in 1121, when Guilhem V prohibited his heirs from employing Jewish bailiffs; evidently, this had been an earlier practice of the rulers there. Around the time of Benjamin's visit, a trade agreement between Montpellier and Agde mentions Jewish merchants. Later, Jewish men and women were active in trade in wool and silk, as well as loaning money. In 1208, they promised to furnish arrows for defense of the city. There are also various records of the imposition of the *rouelle*, or Jewish badge, on members of the community, following the Papal decree of 1215 that required it. In the fourteenth century, there were twenty-eight Jewish families who owned vineyards around Montpellier, as well as Jewish butchers, manual laborers, and, above all, medical practitioners.

The Medical School

Tradition attributes the founding of the medical school of Montpellier in the twelfth century to various Jewish doctors of the area, including those from Lunel. In 1181, Guilhem VIII made a declaration recognizing the liberty to teach medicine. However, modern scholarship challenges the details of this story of the founding of the university. The *Encyclopedia Judaica* states that there is no valid reason to attribute its founding to Jews even though, beginning in 1272, a formal decree required Jewish physicians to take an examination to prove their credentials. The Jewish physicians of Montpellier participated in a network of Jewish medical professionals who formed a sort of elite among medieval Jews of Provence and Languedoc. Montpellier belonged to the Kings of Majorca for a time, and they protected the Jews until the end of the fourteenth century; contemporary statutes show regulation of Jewish moneylending, as well as items relating to medicine.

For several centuries after Benjamin's visit, Jews in Montpellier indisputably served the medical school as medical and scientific translators, particularly making Arab sources accessible to a Christian community that was typically ignorant of Arabic. Moses ibn Tibbon, in the second half of the thirteenth century, translated at least a dozen medical works, including those of Maimonides and Avicenna. Around 1300, Tibbon's nephew, Joseph Makir, called Profacius, was an enthusiastic exponent of scientific thought in both Montpellier and Lunel, where he had studied. Makir contributed to the theory of medicine, to the knowledge of specific cures, to the advancement of astronomy, and to astrology, and he participated in the interchange of ideas between Jews and Christians. His name appears on the placard at the gates of the medical school.

Just before their expulsion in 1394, Jews were prohibited from even owning medical manuscripts. Right before this time, Jewish scientific translators, such as Solomon and Abraham Avigdor, engaged in a final burst of activity. The medical community, when expelled, moved on to Spain, where they were able to spend another hundred productive years before they were again exiled.

The final end of the Jews of Montpellier and the end of their participation in its intellectual life occurred despite the Majorcan king's opposition. He was weaker than the French, who were then expelling all of the Jewish communities from the region. When he eventually agreed to expel them from his territory, both kings shared the booty left behind by the fleeing Jews.

Montpellier and the Maimonidean Controversy

In the first half of the thirteenth century, the Jewish communities of the region disagreed over the interpretation and acceptance of Maimonides' work, particularly his *Guide for the Perplexed*. A bitter controversy erupted, causing a great deal of trouble within the Jewish community. Jewish sages and scholars from Montpellier, Narbonne, Aix en Provence, and other cities became involved in the dispute.

Montpellier became a focal point in this controversy. Rabbi Solomon ben Abraham of Montpellier went further than his contemporaries: rather than just disputing the works, in 1232 he prohibited study of them on pain of excommunication. Rabbis in Lunel, Beziers, and Narbonne retaliated, declaring that Rabbi Solomon was himself excommunicated. In the search for allies, Narbonne sent the elderly scholar David Kimhi to Spain, while Rabbi Solomon tried to find support among the rabbis of northern France. Many others became involved, taking one side or the other; efforts to mediate, such as that of Joseph ben Todros in Spain, were ineffective. The famous scholar Nahmanides (1194–1270), also called Rabbi Moses ben Nahman or Ramban, tried to help find a compromise position among the various sides. Jewish intellectual freedom was severely impaired.

In *A History of Jewish Literature*, Zinberg gives much detail about these events. He quotes the letter of Rabbi Solomon, who defended his point of view—that the Bible is literally true—by saying of the Maimonideans: "Everything with them becomes a parable—the work of creation, the story of Cain and Abel; every verse in the Torah becomes for them an allegory, something fabricated" (Israel Zinberg, *History of Jewish Literature, Vol. 2: French and German Jewry in the Early Middle Ages; The Jewish Community of Medieval Italy,* Cleveland: Case Western Reserve University, 1972, p. 113).

The unfortunate result of this in-fighting was that Jewish open-mindedness came to the attention of the Catholic church, ever watchful for danger to their own monolithic views. Modern scholars still dispute whether anti-Maimonidean Jews actually invited Catholic intervention, or if church representatives acted on their own initiative. In 1233, at Montpellier the official censors of the church confiscated and burned Maimonides' works. Not long afterward, in the same spirit, a Talmud-burning took place in Paris.

Secular, objective examination of religious ideas and study of texts seems very compatible with modern attitudes, in contrast to the narrow traditionalism that characterized later Jewish response to brutal and confining persecution and hatred. In the more tolerant atmosphere that prevailed in earlier medieval times, Jews enjoyed much more freedom for this type of expression. Afterward, such activity was too dangerous— fear made Jewish scholars much more inhibited about intellectual controversy that might draw attention from authorities and endanger the entire community.

LUNEL AND ITS SAGES

Benjamin of Tudela wrote:

> From Montpellier it is four parasangs to Lunel, in which there is a congregation of Israelites, who study the Law day and night. Here lived Rabbenu Meshullam [died 1170] the great rabbi, since deceased, and his five sons, who are wise, great, and wealthy, namely: R. Joseph, R. Isaac, R. Jacob, R. Aaron, and R. Asher, the recluse, who dwells apart from the world; he pores over his books day and night, fasts periodically and abstains from all meat. He is a great scholar of the Talmud. At Lunel live also their brother-in-law R. Moses, the chief rabbi, R. Samuel the elder, R. Ulsarnu, R. Solomon Hacohen, and R. Judah the Physician, the son of Tibbon the Sephardi. The students that come from distant lands to learn the Law are taught, boarded, lodged and clothed by the congregation, so long as they attend the house of study. The community has wise, understanding and saintly men of great benevolence, who lend a helping hand to all their brethren both far and near. The congregation consists of about 300 Jews—may the Lord preserve them.

What You Can Find There Today

Lunel today is a small and rather insignificant town, lacking the overall charm of many villages in southern France and also lacking the vitality of the big cities and commercial centers. Since it hasn't been subject to much development, though, it quite astonishingly still has a few medieval streets. At one point, the road narrows as it passes under an arch of an old building. An old arcade stands near the center of the medieval town, and best of all, you can still see the building that housed the Jewish school—probably the famous medical school— and a synagogue in the twelfth and thirteenth centuries. This building is a private house, so you can see only its outer walls, of plain white stone, and a sort of garage door. I looked through the chinks in this door into a small garden where a child was playing, to see a couple of old stone doorways, trying to imagine the life lived there eight hundred years ago.

In the tourist information office where they supplied us with a map to this and various other attractions in Lunel, they told us that the archaeology institute in Lattes, a suburb in Montpellier, has all of the finds that have been discovered in past efforts to explore this site and that additional excavations may be planned in the basement of the building next year. We went to the museum of archaeology in Lattes, but found none of these items on display.

The historic Jewish building stands on Rue Alphonse Menard between Rue E. Zola and Boulevard St. Fructueux, less than ten minutes' walk from the tourist information office. To find it, go to the tourist office and obtain a free city map. As in most such places, the office location is well marked (with the signs containing an **i**) as you drive into the city. On your way, don't miss the medieval arcades that are incorporated in the tourist office building itself. Address: Office de Tourisme, Place des Martyrs de la Resistance, 34402 Lunel, phone 04-67-87-83-97.

The following map illustrates the main landmarks.

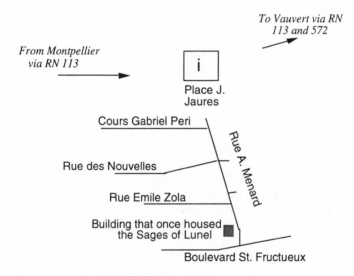

Fig. 2-2: Map of Lunel

Historical Background: Maimonides and His Translators

The *Encyclopedia Judaica* mentions an old Jewish tradition that claims that the city of Lunel was founded by residents of Jericho, fleeing after the city fell. The city's tourist brochure contradicts this, stating that Jews arrived in Lunel only in the eleventh century. From Roman times until the Middle Ages, the city was served by the old Roman Via Vinicilia, which connected more northern cities with the seacoast.

In any case, the Jewish community there grew and prospered until the Middle Ages. Benjamin mentions Judah ibn Tibbon, who came from Spain to Lunel in 1150. Judah was fleeing persecution by the Almohades, who then ruled one of the Spanish Islamic states. He founded an important family of scholars and translators who remained in Lunel. A testament that he wrote to his heirs has survived and provides a little insight into the life of the time. In it, Tibbon discusses how important it is to care lovingly for one's books.

In the last decade of the twelfth century, Lunel was a major center of Jewish study and was especially important as a site of great interest in Maimonides' works. Maimonides himself said that this community was unique and that he believed his salvation as an author depended on them and their well-founded critical activities. In the book *Maimonides: The Life and Times of the Great Medieval Jewish Thinker* (New York: Doubleday, 1982), Abraham J. Heschel has a chapter entitled, "The Sages of Lunel," in which he explains this relationship between Maimonides and this community. Presumably these sages worked and met in the building that we found in the city.

Heschel writes:

> Lunel had a Jewish community which, although numbering only a few hundred, had an extraordinarily vast sphere of influence. Both Talmudic learning, which was having a great upswing in France and Germany, and the versatile Jewish culture of Spain equally enriched the spiritual and intellectual life of the Jews in Lunel. Owing to the intermediary role of this community, the scientific literature of Jews and Arabs in the Pyrenean peninsula became a component part of medieval Christian learning. (*Maimonides,* p. 229)

The spokesman for the sages of Lunel, Jonathan Cohen, wrote a scholarly letter to Maimonides in 1195. Maimonides referred to the letter as "a comfort for my soul and a support for my old age" (*Maimonides,* p. 230). The Lunel scholars requested that Maimonides translate his renowned and controversial *Guide for the Perplexed* from Arabic into Hebrew; Maimonides, old and sick, was unable to do so, so Samuel ibn Tibbon, son of Judah, agreed to translate; he engaged in an exchange of letters with Maimonides in order to clarify various points, and sent a copy of his translation for Maimonides' approval.

After the death of Maimonides, the scholarly community of Lunel participated in the controversy over the appropriate role of Maimonides' thought in Jewish study, and they were involved in the excommunications and counter-excommunications exchanged with the rabbi of Montpellier. The school was important until the end of the thirteenth century; Joseph ibn Makir, who worked in Montpellier, studied astronomy and medicine there.

When the French expelled the Jewish residents of Lunel, some of them moved on into Provence, where they retained the last name Lunel; Armand Lunel, a French novelist who was well known in the early twentieth century, was born in Carpentras about one hundred years ago.

VAUVERT—POSQUIERES, HOME OF THE KABBALAH

Benjamin of Tudela wrote:

> From there [Lunel] it is two parasangs to Posquieres, which is a large place containing about forty Jews, with an Academy under the auspices of the great Rabbi, R. Abraham, son of David, of blessed memory, an energetic and wise man, great as a talmudical authority. People come to him from a distance to learn the Law at his lips, and they find rest in his house, and he teaches them. Of those who are without means he also pays the expenses, for he is very rich. The munificent R. Joseph, son of Menachem, also dwells here and R. Benveniste, R. Benjamin, R. Abraham and R. Isaac, son of R. Meir of blessed memory.

What You Can Find There Today

The town called Vauvert is very small, hugging the south side of a rather steep hill that was called Motte Foussat in the Middle Ages. Old medieval streets wind up to a small plaza with a fountain and a church; behind the church is another plaza, which adjoins the street called "Rue de Juiverie"—that is, the Jewish street. It has retained this identity, along with its very old buildings, despite the many centuries since the expulsion of the Jews. The private buildings have little to distinguish them but the knowledge of what might have been here. The town conserves the layout of the streets as well as the names; these streets zigzag beyond the church and plaza up to the hilltop site of the old fortress, now called the Castella. The hilltop is open green space with a few walls, park benches, and children's playground equipment.

The medieval name Posquieres is no longer used for the town, although a Rue Posquieres leads through a picturesque arch from the square in front of the church. The name Posquieres is old and, in Latin, referred to a wine-based beverage that the Romans made from the grapes that still grow on the hillsides and parts of the plains surrounding the town (perhaps like the old English *posset*, a medicinal beverage made from milk, wine, and spices, linguistic origin uncertain). The old medieval town center on the heights is surrounded by a large industrial area on the plains below, which probably replaced the old vineyards and agricultural areas of the past.

The main rush of the day in this tiny town seemed to be when the mothers picked up their children at the elementary school, also just behind the church and across from the Jewish street. The most dramatic moment of our visit was after we had walked around, and returned to the parking lot just as school was about to let out. Two waiting mothers dented each other's cars in trying to make room for us to exit from the lot.

The Tourist Information Office produces several brochures about the history of the town, including maps, which mention the old Jewish school. For information: Office du Tourisme, Place Ernest Renan, 30600 Vauvert, phone 66-88-28-52.

Historical Background: The Academy of Posquieres

Some time in the 1160s, that is, around the time of Benjamin of Tudela's visit, Abraham ben David (known by the Hebrew abbreviation *Rabad*) moved from Narbonne and established a school at Posquieres. Abraham ben David was the son-in-law of Abraham ben Isaac, the head of the rabbinical court at Narbonne. While to me this implies that there was a daughter/wife, her identity or even her existence is never explored by the very male-oriented scholars who write on this part of history.

Posquieres then (and ever since) was a small town, and rather rural, near the fortress of Vauvert, which now is the only name of the place. The Posquieres Jewish community was fairly new at that time. According to the *Encyclopedia Judaica*, the first record of Jews there is from 1121. They had their own quarter of town, the *Carriere des Juifs*, and Jews were employed in public office until forbidden in 1209. If Posquieres had been similar to other emerging communities throughout the region, the need for capital would have caused the local people to invite Jews to establish loan banks or other financial institutions and thus help jump-start the local economy and enable the middle classes in their inevitable rise. The

Encyclopedia Judaica lists a tax of one hundred sols per year for wealthy Jews. Evidently, at the same time that he was running the Posquieres school, Rabad continued to exercise his very lucrative family trade in textiles, or at least to receive the profits from it, as he supported much of the activity of the school out of his own pocket.

Rabad's school was evidently in a quiet and secluded environment with a peaceful country atmosphere. In a biography, *Rabad of Posquieres* (Cambridge: Harvard University Press, 1962), Isaac Twersky describes a "forest" setting—this seems a little odd, as at that time forests were viewed much more as threatening than peaceful, but I guess it's the spirit of peacefulness. The current tourist information mentions that even in Roman times, Posquieres was located among the vineyards that still grow on nearby hillsides and in the fertile valleys of the area. During Rabad's lifetime, the immediate area was peaceful and mainly friendly to Jews. Exceptionally, in 1172–1173, Rabad had to leave for a while and may have even been imprisoned, because the local count and the regional administration had a dispute over the rights of the Jews.

Rabad's son, Isaac the Blind, who invented certain facets of the Kabbalah, was born around the time of Benjamin's visit in 1165. He seems to have stayed in Posquieres for the rest of his life, including the nearly forty years after his father's death, continuing to develop his body of work, mainly transmitting it orally to the students at the school. His disciples, named Ezra and Azriel, returned to their native city, Gerona, Spain, where they continued his work. Although Isaac's life extended into the time of Simon De Montfort's Crusade against the heretics of Languedoc on behalf of the King of France, Posquieres was still a fairly peaceful and safe place for the Jews. The French Crusaders' campaign of 1217 appears to have included an invasion of Posquieres, but it seems not to have lasted long. Evidence that Isaac stayed in Posquieres includes a letter written in his old age saying that he was unwilling to travel to Gerona, to which his disciples had invited him, but would send his nephew Asher ben David to represent him (cited by Gershom Scholem).

The Jews of the Languedoc region, like the Cathars, had an ascetic or monastic tradition, adapted to Jewish customs—some young men, especially firstborn sons, would spend seven years in a cloistered, ascetic, and studious life. However, eventually Jewish men were required to marry—marriage was a prerequisite to the study of certain subjects. The school at Posquieres was evidently a place where men could choose such a Jewish cloistered life without financial difficulty.

Rabad had innovative theories about education, which presumably were tried on his own children. A contemporary Provencal syllabus listed seven years of education, which may provide a clue to the theory of Rabad's academy. For the time, its educational ideas were progressive, arranging small groups of students by occupational aptitude, and providing individual attention and fostering individual progress. Teachers encouraged discussion, reviewed students' accomplishments, and provided lessons in the vernacular. Above all, the document warned the teacher against "insincerity"—exhorting him "to be totally committed to his noble profession." This document also focused attention on the prevalence of intensely pietistic, partially ascetic Jewish groups called *perushim*, "an elite group of advanced students who isolate themselves almost hermetically in a special building for seven years, eating and sleeping there and refraining from idle chatter" (*Rabad of Posquieres*, pp. 25–26).

The specifics of Rabad's school are thus described:

> The school's success and reputation were direct consequences of Rabad's limitless attention and devotion. His intense love for learning and his total intellectual commitment to Talmudic studies motivated the establishment and maintenance of the school. He referred to his disciples as colleagues and friends. Even if this term suggests that they were well-advanced students, such modesty and spirit of comradeship is noteworthy. . . . He . . . often employed "modern" methods of visual aids to illustrate his lectures. For instance, Rabad encouraged the empirical study of animal anatomy, knowledge of which was basic for many aspects of the dietary law, by actually bringing into class parts of the animal. . . . (*Rabad of Posquieres*, pp. 31–34)

SAINT GILLES, A LOST COMMUNITY

Benjamin of Tudela wrote:

> [From Posquieres] it is four parasangs to the suburb (Ghetto?) Bourg de St. Gilles, in which place there are about a hundred Jews. Wise men abide there; at their head being R. Isaac, son of Jacob. . . . This is a place of pilgrimage of the Gentiles who come hither from the ends of the earth. It is only three miles from the sea, and is situated upon the great River Rhone, which flows through the whole land of Provence. Here dwells the illustrious R. Abba Mari, son of the late R. Isaac; he is the bailiff of Count Raymond.

What You Can Find There Today

Driving between Vauvert and St. Gilles, you cross the edge of the Camargue, a huge flat area formed by the delta of the Rhone river. Enormous fields and wetlands are everywhere, and much of the land is quite marshy, especially further south; flocks of flamingoes live in the marshes. The area is famous for particular species of horses and bulls; you can see them across the wide grassy spaces. There are a few isolated hamlets and farm houses. Finally, you reach the dusty, quiet town.

The cathedral of St. Gilles, described with great admiration in Aimery Picaud's guide, is recognized today for its early Romanesque sculptures and an unusual tower with a spiral staircase. You still have to go up narrow winding streets to get to the rather small hill on which the church stands, so there is a medieval flavor, and the open space in front of the church was probably as hot and deserted during early afternoons long ago as it was on the day we visited. Benjamin's description of "a place of pilgrimage of the Gentiles who come hither from the ends of the earth" corresponds to the description of the Christian pilgrim Aimery Picaud, quoted further on, which demonstrates how important this now-forgotten place once was.

By the next century, the city was apparently no longer important enough for the French to bother to convert the church into a Gothic structure or to do much of anything. Like several cities in the Camargue—the flat, well-watered area in the Rhone delta—St. Gilles today is the scene of various sorts of bullfighting. A branch of the Rhone goes through St. Gilles today, which might be different from the way it was nine hundred years ago—the frequent changes in the delta might leave a location high and dry! Other than the cathedral's treatment of Old Testament subjects and an allegorical picture of the synagogue, there are no traces of Jewish interest there.

The city of Aigues Mortes, not far from St. Gilles, is much more dramatic as a tourist attraction, as its late medieval walls were rebuilt in the nineteenth century by Prosper Merrimee, Viollet Le Duc, and their restorers. Aigues Mortes, farther south, replaced St. Gilles as a port city when the Rhone delta filled in; in turn, its port silted up and it, too, became frozen in a former time. Again, though there is no trace of Jewish history there, I recommend Aigues Mortes and various other medieval sites in the area (see your other guidebooks!) as a way to help imagine life in that distant time. Like many tourist attractions in France, it deserves its popularity. The famous annual gypsy pilgrimage to Les

Saintes Maries de la Mer takes place in a seaside village not far from Aigues Mortes.

Fishing, trans-shipment of agricultural and industrial products, and seaside activities still are important to the region, although the old ports are now defunct. The most active commercial and fishing port for that part of the Southwest now is the very modern city of Sete, a couple of hours away. It's bustling with refrigerator trucks carrying fish to inland cities, canals full of pleasure boats and fishing rigs, big hotels on artificially maintained sand beaches, and a long row of restaurants serving many local specialties, especially Mediterranean fish and squid dishes. Sete maintains its waterways by constant dredging to avoid becoming a literal backwater like the old medieval sites.

Historical Background

In Benjamin's time, the town of St. Gilles was beloved and important to its rulers and to pilgrims. One of the important participants in the First Crusade in 1096—Raymond IV of Saint-Giles, Count of Toulouse and Marquis of Provence—used the name in his title, because of the importance of this part of his domain. When leaving for the Crusade, Raymond enhanced the town's status by a lavish donation to its monastery.

In the eleventh and twelfth centuries, St. Gilles had great importance as a stop for pilgrims on the route to Santiago de Campostela. In 1150, Aimery Picaud, a Christian pilgrim and traveler, in his guide to this pilgrim route, described the religious experience available to Christian visitors:

> St. Giles should be venerated by everyone and loved by all. Oh, how wonderful and worthwhile to visit his tomb! . . . A large shrine in gold lies behind his altar and above are the sculptured images of the six apostles, with on the same level a likeness cleverly sculpted of the Virgin Mary.
>
> On another side of the shrine at the back there is a representation of the Ascension. In the first niche are the six apostles. In the second niche are the other six apostles in the same stance, but each one is separated by a column of gold. In the third niche Jesus is standing on a golden throne. Such is the tomb of the blessed St. Giles, confessor, in which his venerable body reposes with honor. (Quoted by T. A. Layton, *The Way of Saint James*. London: Allen & Unwin, 1976, p. 206)

St. Gilles also served as an important commercial center. The regularly scheduled fair at St. Gilles was one of the earliest centers of commercial activity for medieval Languedoc. Agricultural goods, textiles, and imports would have been traded there. Fairs in medieval cities were the most important methods of trade and contact between people from diverse places and represented important exchange of wealth. Although I have found no direct evidence of Jewish participation in these fairs, it's reasonable to speculate that they played a role in this commercial life.

Benjamin provides the names of a number of Jewish scholars of St. Gilles, which I have abbreviated. I suspect that they are not of much importance now because the *Encyclopedia Judaica* entry for this city states that these names on Benjamin's list are otherwise unknown to history. In 1215, Jews from other communities met at St. Gilles to discuss the Lateran Council and its anti-Jewish measures and to plan ways to try to forestall its effects.

Not long after Benjamin's visit, when its port silted up, St. Gilles fell into obscurity. The destructive French conquest also contributed to the loss of St. Gilles's importance to Christians and Jews alike, by disrupting the southern economy, encouraging the fairs of the preferred north of France rather than of St. Gilles, and promoting the pilgrimage shrines of more northern saints.

ARLES

Benjamin of Tudela wrote:

> Thence it is four parasangs to the city of Arles, which has about 200 Israelites.

What You Can Find There Today

After St. Gilles, the road goes past much more of the open, flat Rhone delta, crossing several small branches of the outlet of the huge river. When you reach Arles, you cross the Rhone, and now are in Provence rather than in Languedoc, a fact that had important meaning in the past and is still important to people who live in the region. As you approach Arles, you can see how the landscape flattens out as the Rhone slowly winds through the Camargues to the sea.

The published guide suggests the following important sites:

• The old street of the Jews, which is now called rue du Docteur Fanton

• The Lapidary Museum

• The Arlaten Museum, a museum of ethnicity founded by Mistral (ironically, an anti-Semite) in the earlier part of this century. It contains memories of daily life in Arles in the last two or three centuries.

For details you can contact the Arles Tourism Office, phone 04-90-18-41-20.

Arles is a busy modern city. Most people would associate it with Van Gogh rather than with earlier times. The bustling city center is full of traffic, one-way streets, and avenues lined with regular arrays of trees—a nineteenth-century feel. The cathedral stands at the top of a hill, inconvenient to reach by car. The main branch of the Rhone passes Arles today, and the bridge is imposing. I don't know what bridges would have been there in Benjamin's day, but most likely they would still have been using the structure built by the Romans.

Historical Background

Arles is one of the original sites of Roman Gaul, and thus the Jews settled there, as they did in Narbonne and Marseilles, during the dispersion that followed the destruction of the Second Temple in Jerusalem in 70 C.E. In fact, Arles is one of the legendary destinations of the three rudderless ships that left Jerusalem at that time and wandered the Mediterranean looking for a home. The first historical reference to the Jews of Arles is in 508, when they participated in the defense of the city, taking responsibility for part of the city wall during a siege. Occasional references to this community continue throughout the Middle Ages, until Benjamin's time. In 1215, three "rectors" governed the Jewish community under a constitution issued by the archbishop.

Arles is the first city on Benjamin's itinerary to be in Provence, rather than Languedoc. Because the expulsion of the Jews occurred much later, after the French assumed control of Provence in 1481, the Jewish community there has a longer history after Benjamin's visit. Throughout the fourteenth century, the community received many of the exiles who were fleeing from both the north and the southwest of France. In 1391, the city took in refugees from terrible persecutions taking place in Castile and Aragon. Many of the Jewish inhabitants in the fifteenth century had relatives in Spain, including many "new Christians" who had converted rather than flee.

The Jews of Arles lived in two small streets called Rue de la Grande Juiverie and Rue de la Petite Juiverie. Eventually these streets provided them with a secure area, as well as being a way to segregate them from the others. At that time, Jews owned vineyards and were making a living in commerce, medicine, and brokerage. The community paid a tax of sixty pounds of pepper.

The rulers often protected them from the fanaticism of the Christians: in 1478, the king and the governor of the city took the Jews' part in a court case accusing them of ritual murder, and the Jews were cleared of the accusation. In 1480, the town council allowed them to make the barriers to their quarter more secure, in order to protect themselves from the traditional Good Friday anti-Jewish rioters.

In 1493, Arles became the first Provencal city to expel the Jews, under the new jurisdiction of the King of France. The Jewish inhabitants moved on, some to the Comtat Venaisson, where the Pope permitted Jews to continue to live when they were no longer welcome in France.

Everyday Life: A Jewish Butcher of Arles

While elsewhere, historians provide us with the names of Jewish sages and rabbis, in Arles, we know the name of the Jewish butcher. Somehow, the records of the town reveal that in 1429, Samuel Bonsenhor, a Jew, and Antoine de Blandrat, a Christian, made a business arrangement. Antoine provided money. Samuel bought meat and arranged for kosher slaughter; he butchered the animals and sold the meat. Then the two of them shared the profit on what was left. Officially, this meant the hides. But perhaps it also meant the parts that Jews were not free to eat.

Now, you would think that Jews and Christians would have kept separate above all in matters of meat. After all, Christians ate pork more than any other meat, while Jews ritually refused to eat it. Jews required that a Jewish specialist employ a special techniqe to inspect and slaughter animals, while Christians had their own methods. Jews rejected the hindquarters of meat, while Christians ate them. Logic suggests that Jewish slaughterers would kill the animals and deliver the carcasses to Jewish butchers, who in turn would skillfully prepare meat according to the Law, distribute the acceptable parts to their community, and then quickly, in those old days without refrigeration, sell the rest to non-Jews.

It was more complicated than that. The older practice was to have a communal butcher's market, similar to the Halles that exist in some

French towns today (and were very common up to a generation ago). Various slaughterers or farmers who slaughtered their own animals would deliver the meat to these butchers. Imagine the smell of this place in the warm Provencal summer—full of hanging carcasses of lamb, mutton, pork, and occasionally beef, as well as partially cut up or cured meats, all unrefrigerated. Imagine the flies, and the sound of the butchers and probably their wives, calling out to the customers as French market sellers in Provence still do today. The Jewish butchers had their tables alongside the others, and the meat they could not sell to Jews was easily sold to the other butchers or to Christian customers.

However, as time went by, Christians more and more despised whatever Jews had touched; in this context, they were infuriated at purchasing meat that Jews considered unfit. New laws constantly dictated limits on Jewish butchers' activities. In 1306, when there were fourteen Jewish butchers out of a total of fifty-two in the city, there was a law requiring strict separation of Christian and Jewish butcher shops and prohibiting sale of meat from Jewish shops to Christian customers or even to Christian butchers. The numbers declined subsequently, but there were always means for profit-making activities to proceed despite the regulations. (The story of the butchers of Arles appears in Louis Stouff, *La Table Provencale*, Avignon: Editions A. Barthelemy, 1996.)

Other Occupations

Better records in the later part of the history of Arles allow additional glimpses of the ordinary people of the Jewish community there and what their occupations and concerns were. In 1414, a bookbinder named Jacob Stella lived there; in 1426, there were also a parchment maker and a number of scribes. Many Jews earned a living as ordinary laborers, hauling grain, cleaning sewers, repairing latrines, and other unglamorous tasks. Women in the community were recognized for their skill with clothing and textiles. At one point, all sixteen dressmakers in the city were Jewish. Women designed clothing, sewed household textiles, and made headgear and handkerchiefs. A woman named Vengessonne Nathan had a fabric business and also loaned money.

After the 1306 expulsion from Narbonne, one of the better-known refugees that came to Arles was Kalonymos ben Kalonymos, a member of the famous princely family. In Arles, he pursued his lifework of translating documents from the Arabic, and he also wrote original works of history concerning his experiences. He documented the anti-Jewish activity of the "Pastorals" in 1320 and mentioned accusations of well-poisoning in Provence, as well as a Talmud-burning that took place in Toulouse in 1319. He also reacted against some of the other exiles who were there: he complained about too many Jews from northern France in other parts of Provence. He also wrote about food—as I have noted in the section on what people ate.

MARSEILLES AND ITS CORAL WORKERS

Benjamin of Tudela wrote:

> From there [Arles] it is two days' journey to Marseilles, which is a city of princely and wise citizens, possessing two congregations with about 300 Jews. One congregation dwells below on the shore by the sea, the other is in the castle above. They form a great academy of learned men, amongst them being R. Simeon, R. Solomon, R. Isaac, son of Abba Mari, R. Simeon, son of Antoli, and R. Jacob his brother; also R. Libero. These persons are at the head of the upper academy. At the head of the congregation below are R. Jacob Purpis, a wealthy man, and R. Abraham, son of R. Meir, his son-in-law, and R. Isaac, son of the late R. Meir. It is a very busy city upon the sea-coast. From Marseilles one can take ship and in four days reach Genoa.

What You Can Find There Today

Despite a very long history as a Jewish site, Marseilles has preserved next to nothing from the Middle Ages; even the nineteenth-century synagogue, the oldest in the city, was damaged intentionally during World War II. It seems logical that only the sleepy little towns—where little has changed and there has never been real rebuilding—would conserve such old yet modest remains.

Historical Background from the
Romans to the French King

Marseilles, under the name Massalia, was an important Roman center. In 70 c.e., after the destruction of the Temple in Jerusalem, when the Jewish Diaspora began, Jews began to settle there. At that point, they

were in the process of defining a religion without Temple practices and
Temple sacrifices, and they focused instead on Sabbath observance, dietary
laws, compulsory circumcision, and a calendar of rituals and festivals. In
Marseilles, a tolerant atmosphere and prosperous environment lasted
several hundred years. With the Baptism of Clovis around 500, however,
restrictive laws began to be issued, such as a prohibition of intermarriage
between Jews and Christians in 535.

In 591, a letter from Pope Gregory the Great suggests the climate
of ideas. He wrote to the Bishop of Marseilles to express his disapproval of forcible conversions of Jews; instead, he recommended that the
bishop require Jewish attendance at sermons encouraging voluntary
conversion.

Nevertheless, a Jewish community continued to exist there until
Benjamin's visit and for several hundred years afterward. The two congregations that Benjamin mentioned included scholars on the hill
and merchants in the lower town; since 1257, they had enjoyed citizenship, although there were restrictions such as a prohibition of Jewish oaths
against Christians. These merchants dealt in wood, spices, textiles, metals,
pharmaceuticals, products for dyeing cloth, and slaves, and often entered
into partnership with Christians; few were moneylenders.

An important community of artisans in Marseilles worked in coral,
particularly polishing the stones and making necklaces; Benjamin of Tudela
may have been interested in them, as he might have been a merchant
dealing in such gems. In the fourteenth century, Jews dominated coral-
making throughout the Mediterranean, from Spain to Sardinia,
where the principal coral-fishing was done in boats funded by Jews.
The coral workers of Marseilles were very poor, although they
worked with precious stones. In 1380, their Christian bosses accused
them of substituting inferior coral for the top-grade material entrusted
to their workshops, and selling the better gemstones on the international market at Avignon. Despite their poverty, these workers sometimes managed to create small corporations, invest in the market,
and rise from being artisans to being entrepreneurs (Maurice Kriegel,
Les Juifs à la fin du Moyen Age dans l'Europe Méditerranéenne, Paris: Hachette,
1979).

Throughout the fourteenth century, Marseilles continued to make
official concessions to the customs of these Jewish citizens, allowing them
exceptions for flour for *matzoth*, lifting the requirement that they carry
lamps after curfew on Jewish holidays, and allowing them to sweep the
streets in front of their houses on Friday instead of Saturday, as Christians
were required to do.

There were also setbacks. In 1323, a violent anti-Jewish movement called the Pastorals attacked Jewish citizens in a number of French cities; King Robert of Provence wrote to the Marseillaise authorities, mandating them to protect the Jews under their jurisdiction. They also suffered when the Aragonese plundered the city in 1423. The French king annexed Marseilles in 1481, and expulsion followed by 1501.

WRAP-UP—ELSEWHERE IN LANGUEDOC

I have concentrated on the voyage of Benjamin of Tudela to the exclusion of various other sites in Languedoc. Here is a summary of some other sites, if you care to experiment:

Pezenas: the old arched entrance to the Jewish quarter, as well as its street and buildings, are still preserved. I have encountered little or no information about any famous people or records left by the Jewish community; I find only references to this traditional location. Tourism Office: Place Gambetta, 34120 Pezenas. **Mende, Sauve,** and **Peyrusse,** farther in from the coast, each have traces of historic synagogues. **Toulouse** and **Perpignan** have traces of the medieval Jewish quarter.

Tracing the Jews of Provence

Many Provencal towns preserve a few traces of the former Jewish population and illustrate how, historically, Jews arrived at various times, some with the Romans, some only after the expulsions from France. I have described what I found in two such places: Cotignac and Saint Maximin, from which the Jews were expelled in the late Middle Ages.

The Jewish presence in the four towns that belonged to the pope lasted much longer. Under the administration of the pope, who owned these territories until the French Revolution, Jews were allowed to remain until the new principles of equality restored tolerance of religions other than Catholicism.

The following map shows the relative locations of the places described further on, with arrows to indicate the order in which it might be convenient to visit them if you start in Marseilles. This is the most famous and picturesque part of Provence today, and you will find many wonderful things to see in addition to these towns. Among them are two restored Cistercian abbeys: Le Thoronet, near Cotignac, and Sylbecane, near the Durance River. Beautiful winding country roads link the towns; the straight-line arrows simply show a suggested order for a visit.

AFTER THE EXPULSIONS

As more and more countries in Europe persecuted and expelled the Jews, Provence became a refuge, which offered asylum and relative religious

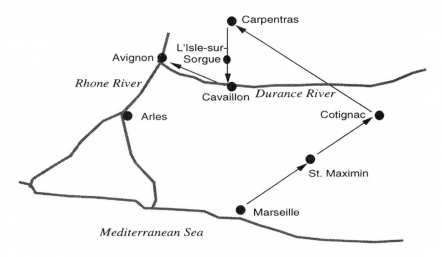

Fig. 2-3: Route for Visiting Towns in Provence

liberty. A few Jews from England had come there after their expulsion in 1290. Jews from Spain came during several centuries of persecutions, particularly after the Moslem persecutions that preceded Benjamin's voyage, and after the Christians destroyed many historic Sephardic communities in Aragon and Castile in 1391. Jews fled from the kingdom of France and from Languedoc to Provence during the persecutions of the thirteenth century and the expulsions of the fourteenth century.

The new arrivals sometimes settled in the places where Jews had lived for centuries, and sometimes in new places where economic conditions were right for them to practice their trades or to engage in money-lending. Jews arrived in Orange for the first time in the thirteenth century, receiving a charter from Prince Raymond in 1387. By 1283, they were first mentioned as owners of a synagogue in Aix, and their numbers grew in the fifteenth century. Fleeing Jews also joined long-established communities, such as Marseilles and Saint-Remy.

The Jews who joined these older communities often adopted their special customs and foods. In Avignon and other parts of Provence at the Jewish New Year, families placed plates of freshly planted grain or beans on a table, where they remained for the ten days of the holiday season. This custom may link the Jews of the region with worshipers of Adonis who once lived in the area, as it resembles fertility rites from the ancient times. Another New Year's dish was made from a ceremonial lamb's head or calf's head, which they may have associated with the sacrifice of Isaac. Other foods for the celebration included red apples, pomegranates, figs, white grapes, and honey.

Declining Tolerance

Many of these refugees, after coming and going during the cycle of expulsions and readmissions, stayed there after the final expulsion from France in 1396. Jewish life at the time was affected by a severe economic depression and by the plagues that affected the area early in the four-teenth century. In 1320 the violent group called the Pastorals terrorized Jewish communities across the region; their most extreme act was the massacre of five hundred Jews at Verdun-sur-Garonne. The Pastorals were headed for Avignon, where the pope lived, but were stopped before they arrived there. Other groups also often blamed the Jews for their mis-fortunes.

Increasingly fanatical rulers of other parts of Europe applied pres-sure counter to the Provencal tolerance of the time, and Jewish rights were more and more diminished. Finally, after the French kings took over in 1481, the Jews were expelled from Provence between 1500 and 1505, leaving only a handful of Jews under the jurisdiction of the pope in the area called the Comtat Venaisson.

At the end of the era, when persecutions became common, there were many conversions, both forced and willing. In some cases, entire families converted or left only a single member who remained Jewish; converts adopted new names and changed their lifestyles, so that unlike Spain, where secret Jews remained for several generations, their Jewish identity was often rather quickly forgotten and their descendants were assimilated. One very famous (or infamous) son of such a convert is the writer Nostradamus. Modern scholars study examples of the wills of the converts to try to understand the events; particularly interesting is the way that the remaining Jewish family member was often designated to inherit collections of Jewish and Hebrew books.

Making a Living in Provence

During this period, Provencal Jews practiced a variety of trades and professions. They made wax candles and supplied the candles to churches. They served as marriage brokers. They were accomplished in scientific fields such as astronomy and medicine, and were men of letters. Jewish scholarship, both religious and secular, flourished during the period. Scribes practiced a style of illumination of manuscripts that was related both to the Northern French and to the Spanish style. One surviving example, the Farhi Bible, dating from 1366–1383, contains a grammatical dictionary of Hebrew roots and elaborately illustrated "carpet pages" covered with geometric designs.

Orange was the home of the scholar Gersonides, who died there in 1344. He was a scientist, astronomer, and medical doctor. In 1444, Davin de Caderousse, a Jew from Avignon, made an effort to develop moveable type and thus print books; had he succeeded, he might have been ahead of Gutenberg. Davin contracted with a man named Procop Waldvogel of Prague, who agreed to provide twenty-seven matrices for Hebrew letters in exchange for instruction in the art of dyeing. (Since dyers, part of the active local textile industry, used a press, they were often involved in early printing efforts.) Somehow the contract didn't work out, and thus these entrepreneurs only earned a footnote in the history of printing—by the time Hebrew printing really developed, the Jews had been expelled. Around 1470, a highly educated Provencal family named Farissol moved from Avignon to Ferrara, Italy, where one member of the family, Abraham Farissol, wrote a treatise on geography that was famous in its day.

In fifteenth-century Provence, several families of medical doctors were particularly prominent. Members of this group intermarried among themselves. They shared manuscripts, translations, and methods, and in some ways formed a special class of individuals. Examples include a family named Borrion that was prominent in Arles, a family named Carcassonne in Aix and Avignon, and a family named Abraham in Saint Maximin; others lived in Draguignan, Pertuis, and Lattes. At one time during this period, the pope in Avignon had six physicians, all Jewish.

ST. MAXIMIN

The quiet and picturesque Provencal town of St. Maximin is located beside the major auto route heading for Nice or Italy. In the medieval quarter of the town, you can still see one arcaded house where the Jews lived in the fourteenth century. This house is on a winding street among a number of similar buildings, inside of what was once a small fortified town. Since there is no other information, it's anyone's guess if this one building once housed the synagogue or simply served as a private home. Most of the houses in the neighborhood have been covered with stucco

and paint, but a few neglected ones reveal their original stone construction—you can see occasional old stone lintels or doorways. Similarly, the
old stones paving the small streets, which probably once had a stone
gutter running down the center, have been resurfaced with asphalt, showing
only traces of their old form. The few times that a car or small commercial
van came along one of the streets, we flattened ourselves into the nearest
doorway, as the streets are barely wider than a modern vehicle.

While we were visiting, we also looked at the old cathedral with
its unfinished facade, Romanesque columns, and Roman marble crypt.
We were fortunate enough to hear an hour's recital on the cathedral
organ; we found it intriguing to hear J. S. Bach compositions played on
an instrument that was actually built during his lifetime. In the summer,
if you're interested, you can find many organ concerts, especially on
Sundays.

The Tourist Information office, in the town hall next to the cathedral, can give you a map of the town indicating the old Jewish quarter
along with the other streets and buildings of historic interest. The map
and information about the historic parts of the city also appear on placards
along the streets. Contact: Office du Tourisme, Couvent Royal, Place
Jean Salusse or write to Hotel de Ville, 83470, St. Maximin, phone
04-94-59-84-59.

The following map shows the major landmarks and the street leading
to the Jewish quarter.

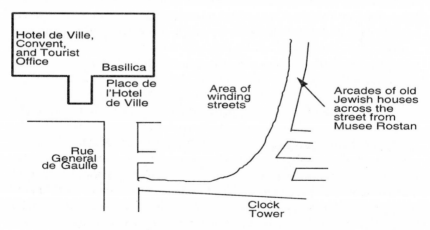

Fig. 2-4: Map of St. Maximin Streets

Historical Note

Neither the town of St. Maximin nor its Jewish community was ever of great significance. In 1283, the Archbishop of Aix collected tax on Jews in St. Maximin, Lambesc, Pertuis, and other localities; the tax had to be paid in pepper. Refugees came there from France in 1303, as the Jews were being expelled by the French king; others continued to arrive as the expulsions continued. The arcaded house that you can still see today dates from the twelfth century; its inhabitants added the arcades in 1320 and built additional rooms over the arcades. These arcades are unusual, as arcades at a certain point were forbidden in fortified cities in Provence. St. Maximin received special permission from King Robert of Provence in 1323, which allowed the inhabitants to preserve these. Arcades were dangerous in a fortified city, since one method of defense against intruders was to throw things down on them when they were wandering through the intentionally twisty little streets.

By 1330, the community received the right to have a synagogue and a school, while the archives mention that they enlarged the Jewish cemetery in 1335. In 1348, the community suffered because people blamed Jews for the devastating epidemic of black plague. A major riot in the town of Toulon caused many Jews living in very small towns to consolidate in larger cities, including St. Maximin. The principal occupation of the Jews there was probably moneylending, but at least in the fifteenth century, they also participated in a cloth trade with other Jews in Provence and practiced medicine. At that time, a Jewish doctor named Astruc Abraham treated a Christian patient who had leprosy. The Jewish community benefited from the tolerant views of the kings of Provence; for example, in 1435, King Rene protected a forcibly baptized Jewish woman in St. Maximin who wanted to return to her faith.

The expulsion of the Jewish community began shortly after the King of France acquired Provence in 1481. There are records of the sales of various Jewish properties. A formerly Jewish woman named Clareta, acting under her newly acquired Christian name of Madeleine, sold the Jewish school (perhaps the same building that stands there today) for twenty-five florins; perhaps she was acting for Jews who had already moved away. In 1503, a document that recorded the sale of the cemetery for sixteen florins made a note that the community was entirely gone from the town.

COTIGNAC—A BEAUTIFUL TOWN

Cotignac, a village not far from St. Maximin, is one of the many picturesque and intriguing towns in Provence. The location is not very close to the auto route, so the village keeps a kind of otherworldly personality about it; you drive along a beautiful, zigzag road through hills, vineyards, and surrounding hamlets before you arrive. Cotignac's narrow streets climb steeply up the sides of two adjacent hills that seem to embrace the town, and some of the houses are built directly into the steep slopes. One of the oldest remaining sites is the location where oil presses were built into the cliffs. The central square, small food shops, winding streets, and rural surroundings appeal to Europeans and Americans seeking a change from urban crowding.

In the main square, where you can find the one hotel and most of the town's restaurants, is a chipped stone fountain with four carved faces, which characterizes the village. At one side of the square we read a placard with a brief history of the town: this described how Jews, seeking refuge from persecution, were among the founders of the town. Two old medieval towers stand on the top of one of the hills, a reminder of less peaceful days; they bear the name "Tours Saracens" because they were supposed to have served as a defense or at least as watchtowers to warn against the Saracen invaders who threatened the region in the Dark Ages. (In actuality, they may or may not be as old as that.) At night from the hills you can see a panoramic view of all the small lights of the town. A church stands opposite the Saracen Towers, on another hilltop; we once saw a late-evening procession of pilgrims bearing candles from the old church in the town up the path along the cliff to this shrine.

Cotignac was once much larger and busier than it is today. By the turn of the century, the village had lost its former importance as a center of wine production, silk, and leather goods. The decline in its importance and population was a result of the microorganism phylloxera invading the grapevines, as well as the industrialization of leather manufacturing. The principal occupations of Cotignac's residents today are tourism and services to local farmers. Agricultural produce of the region still includes both wine and olives. Modern wineries and oil presses belong to various agricultural cooperatives, and local markets offer a variety of beautiful produce, locally grown meat, and fish brought in from the Mediterranean, making the town a good place to sample Provencal products.

Michelle, our friend and traveling companion on this trip, has a farmhouse in Cotignac. Her family lived there for several generations, and she still has cousins and family friends in the area. For this reason, we have spent brief visits there over the years and have enjoyed the beauty of the tiny paths between the vineyards, the twisting stream shaded by bushes and trees, and the gnarly olive trees with silver leaves in the fields around her farmhouse.

Photography studies and magazine articles often feature Cotignac's charm and state of unspoiled beauty. The coffee-table book currently available at many bookstores, *The Most Beautiful Villages of Provence*, contains a series of photos of the old fountain and the picturesque streets (Michael Jacobs, *The Most Beautiful Villages of Provence*, London: Thames & Hudson, 1994).

For information, maps, and other tourist help:

Service du Tourisme: 04-94-04-60-01

Syndicat d'Initiative: 04-94-04-61-87

History of Cotignac

A Celtic-Ligurian settlement occupied the caves in cliffs that tower over the village as early as 2500 B.C.E.; later, Greeks occupied the site, but this settlement may have been abandoned for a while during Roman times. The next stage of occupation began in about the fifth century, according to the placard that stood in the town and identified the inhabitants who came to the caves in this era as Jews seeking refuge. Other sources say that this story about Jewish settlement is only a legend, and document a history of descendants of the Roman inhabitants and conflicts with invading Moslem armies.

Michelle queried various people in town to help me reconstruct the obscure history of the Jews of Cotignac. She talked to one elderly acquaintance who makes a hobby of Cotignac's history and has done extensive reading about the residents of the town, including the medieval Jews. According to this friend, a rather significant Jewish community lived there at that time, showing the town's former importance. However, he says, there is little documentation about them, and in particular, he has found nothing in the town archives about them. Other sources that I have read specified two traces of the earliest Jews of Cotignac: a Rue de Jerusalem and a carving showing the head of Moses. Michelle queried some of the town's older inhabitants, who told her that the Rue de Jerusalem was renamed after the war and now has the name of a resistance hero, Rue Gabriel Phillis. While Michelle has not traced the location of the head of Moses, she also identified the place de la Liberté as the former site of Cotignac's synagogue.

This synagogue, or at least its building, survived until the 1950s or 1960s. Earlier in the twentieth century the building served as a meeting place for young people—among her historian-friend's memories, he told her that he had first met his future wife at a social event there. The site was razed to make the current open square. This development destroyed the walls of the medieval building, but the *mikveh*, underground, was conserved. The municipality owns the site now. In theory, you could gain access to it, with difficulty, through an iron gate, but I don't know how this is arranged. A local history book included a photo of this ritual bath, before the construction covered it up, identifying its date as fifteenth to sixteenth century. The bathing pools of the *mikveh* used the water from plentiful springs at the site (Jacques Seille, *Histoire de Cotignac,* Brignoles: Sovacom, 1990, p. 20).

In the fourteenth and fifteenth centuries Jews inhabited the Rue de Jerusalem and the nearby street. The gate that once stood nearby was built later, to keep in victims of the plague. This quarter of town was also the site of the tanneries at one time. The synagogue and ritual bath may at one time have been up in the higher part of town, near the Saracen towers. I assume that the expulsion of the Jews from Provence put an end to this community.

CARPENTRAS AND THE POPE'S JEWS

Carpentras is probably the best-known Jewish site in the south of France. The town has a very famous synagogue, about two hundred years old and still in use. On the outskirts of town is the still more famous Jewish cemetery. In 1990, an attack by some vandals on this cemetery caused a major outcry throughout France, inspiring something like a million people to march in Paris in protest against racism. (I was there.) Occasional newspaper articles still probe the roots of this medieval-spirited desecration and the efforts to bring the vandals to justice concluded very recently. A lasting result of the attack seems to be that the grounds of the cemetery are now kept locked at all times, and only family members of the dead may visit. Until recently, our friend Michelle often visited relatives in Carpentras; she remembers the shady alleys of the cemetery as a delightful spot to take a walk. On our recent visit, we looked through the bars of the sturdy iron gate down the green paths where only a few really old tombs seem to stand and through the branches of various evergreen trees.

Papal ownership of the town began when the Holy See acquired Carpentras in 1274. The popes retained control until the Revolution, allowing a small Jewish community to remain there throughout this time. The oldest Jewish location is the medieval Jewish quarter, with a street named for the old Jewish presence. At that time, the Jews lived near the city wall. At a certain point, the population became mistrustful of the Jews, and did not want them living in such a strategic location; therefore, they were moved to the center of town, where the synagogue still stands. Medieval Jews in Carpentras often made a living as grain merchants. When they could, they would grow vines in order to make wine, which they used for their own ceremonies: by 1444, they were prohibited from selling wine to Christians.

The synagogue, which the French government restored about thirty years ago, has regular visiting hours as well as religious services. (Like all official houses of worship, the synagogue is the property of the French government, and the congregation uses it under permission.) While the sanctuary is about two hundred years old and is built in the Baroque style characteristic of the eighteenth century, some parts of the building date from earlier times. The facade is intentionally unmarked. A Jewish community that lives in Carpentras today has primarily inhabitants who have immigrated from other places, particularly North Africa; the dispersion of the original Jewish community was nearly complete by the 1930s, when only thirty-five Jews were still living in the city.

For information, contact the tourist office, 170 allee Jean Jaures, 84200 Carpentras, phone 04-90-63-57-88. The oldest Jewish street is adjacent to this location.

Background: The Pope's Jews

Along with Carpentras, three other towns—Avignon, Cavaillon, and Les Isles sur la Sorgue in the Comtat Venaisson region—were the sole localities within the boundaries of present-day France in which Jews continued to live after the sixteenth century. In this era, the popes—who owned and ruled this region—were less bigoted than the kings—or the kings were more Catholic than the popes. Though the king expelled every Jewish community, the pope tolerated four ghettos, where Jews resided until the Revolution, when Napoleon granted them the rights of French citizenship and the freedom to choose their place of residence. Today, the four towns of the Comtat Venaisson, where Jews remained, are among the most dramatic Jewish sites of the south of France. Especially in Cavaillon and Carpentras, you can still see the street where Jews were required to live, as well as the synagogues with their associated bakeries, ritual baths, Succot porches, and study rooms.

The Jews had arrived in the pope's territories mainly after the expulsions by the kings of France in the fourteenth century and the final expulsions from Provence at the end of the fifteenth century. During this period, local residents made several attacks on the Jews of the Comtat Venaisson. In 1456, there was a day of such activity in Cavaillon. In 1459, there were sixty victims of anti-Jewish violence in Carpentras and also riots in Pernes, a small town that still had a Jewish community. At this time, local rulers at Mazan, a small town about twenty kilometers from Carpentras, prevented a massacre there. In the 1480s, the Jews of Avignon and Cavaillon suffered from attacks by artisans and students.

Initially, Jews lived in a number of other towns in the area as well, but over time, the pope expelled the communities of Jews that lived outside the four, where he established a regulation ghetto. (A more detailed history of the pope's role in developing a formal ghetto appears later, in the chapter on Italy.) By around 1600, Jews could live only in the officially designated ghetto areas in the four towns—very small areas surrounded by walls and gates that were locked each night. Conditions were very difficult in these inadequate areas, and diseases often spread uncontrollably among the very poor inhabitants, who came to be known, along with the Jews of Rome, as "The Pope's Jews."

The Jews of this region enjoyed few liberties and many restrictions. Beginning in 1524, the pope required all Jews to wear a distinguishing yellow hat, because they had been too discrete with the round red badge, which was too easy to conceal. All their prayer books and other books that preserved their Provencal rites had to be printed in Amsterdam: the Jews in the Comtat Venaisson were not allowed to have a printing press. They lived in painful isolation, with little opportunity to pursue the intellectual activities of their predecessors in Languedoc, Paris, Castile, and Provence, and they accomplished little in comparison to these earlier communities. Occasionally, a few Jews appear to have been rich enough to have helped both Jews and Christians. In the tiny country town of Mazan, near Carpentras, we stayed in a little hotel where we saw a brochure that told a story of how the town's Jewish community had once saved the town from famine by providing wheat for bread for all the town's residents. It's interesting to encounter such occasional faint memories or traces of the Jewish presence—in Mazan, the expulsion of the Jews took place in 1598, when the pope limited his Jewish subjects to the four ghettos I have mentioned.

These Jewish communities remained primarily confined to the ghetto throughout the eighteenth century, although Jews from the Comtat Venaisson began to settle in a few other French communities, such as Montpellier, just before the Revolution. At that time, besides the Jews in Avignon, Carpentras, and Cavaillon, there were a few thousand "Portuguese" Jews in the southwest and around thirty thousand Yiddish-speaking Jews in the east of France.

During the French Revolution, the situation changed completely. In particular, Abbe Gregoire, a revolutionary leader, actively promoted full rights for Jews. Though the Declaration of the Rights of Man was not considered to apply to Jews, he engineered a specific decree in 1790 that gave citizenship at least to Jews identified as "Portuguese," "Aragonese," and "Spanish." However, the violently anti-religious sentiment of the increasingly radical revolutionaries caused great difficulties for observant Jews. These revolutionaries were no more tolerant of Jewish rites than they were of Catholic practice. In Carpentras, annexed by France in 1794, the Jews were pressured to give up the worship that they had always enjoyed, and eventually, they "voluntarily" turned the synagogue over to the authorities. Subsequently, Napoleon strengthened the rights of Jews and extended to them a great many benefits throughout the rest of Europe, destroying the ghettos in Italy and elsewhere.

After the Revolution, there was no going back to the ghettos: the Jews of the region were citizens of France. They were free to choose a trade or a profession, to pursue an education, and either to practice their religion or assimilate, as they wished. They moved into a number of other places in Provence and the southwest, such as Arles, where they had been turned away earlier in the century. Although dispersed, the few descendants of the "Pope's Jews" retained their association with Carpentras. During the early part of this century, a local Jewish writer, Armand Lunel, wrote fiction and local historical guides and thus kept many of the community's memories and tales alive. Lunel collaborated on an opera, "Esther of Carpentras," with the composer Darius Milhaud, another descendant of the old Provencal Jewish community. The libretto was based on an old Purim tale that had been played in Carpentras in the eighteenth century.

CAVAILLON

Cavaillon still retains the old street, or *carriere*, where Jews lived from 1453 until the Revolution. The synagogue and museum of Cavaillon are located on Rue Hebraique; this tiny Jewish quarter provides a dramatic image of what the Jews' surroundings would have been like in the time of the pope's ghetto.

The museum is in the lower part of the building, on the site of the original fifteenth-century synagogue. The room in which the museum is housed served a number of purposes for the Jewish community, which had little space to spare. On one wall, you can still see the oven in which the community baked bread or *matzoths*; beneath that was the ritual bath, which used the same oven for heating the water. (The bath is not open to visitors.) On Saturdays and holidays, the same area served as the women's worship area; they were able to hear the services above through the wooden floor and also by way of a spiral staircase that connected the two stories of the building. Besides serving as a bakery and worship room, this room may also have provided space for the primary school. The main door of the synagogue on the second floor is on a sort of porch, with a balcony above it; the balcony was used for a communal Succot booth, as the individual families of the community had no space to build their own.

The small museum contains a number of fascinating books that the members of the community had considered unfit for further use and had placed in a sort of book cemetery in the attic, as well as other objects the community once used. It also contains the original Ark for the Torah scrolls from the fifteenth-century synagogue. There are also some Roman ceramic lamps stamped with the seven-branched candlestick that, in Roman times, was the symbol of Jewish identity.

The synagogue itself was rebuilt between 1772 and 1774, in a most startling pure Baroque style, with painted and gilded wood panels and elaborate decoration. The synagogue, too, served several purposes. It was the center for study as well as for worship. In one corner, far above the floor, a chair for Elijah is supported by a pediment in the form of baroque clouds. The tradition of the French Jews was that Elijah was symbolically present at circumcision rituals, which took place in the synagogue; the guided tour also includes display of the special chair in which the *moyhel* sat when performing circumcisions.

Although there seems to be no Jewish community in Cavaillon now, as the former members of the community had nearly all moved away by the 1930s, this is one of the most complete remnants of Jewish life in the Comtat Venaisson. In the 1960s, the government restored the synagogue (that's when they discovered the old books), and now provides guided tours of the synagogue and associated museum. There is also a gift shop, with a variety of books and pamphlets on the history of the Jews of the region.

For details and opening hours of the museum, contact the tourist office, 79 rue Saunerie, 84300 Cavaillon, phone 04-90-71-32-01.

L'ISLE SUR LA SORGUE

This is an extremely attractive town through which various branches of the Sorgue, a large mountain spring, run, making all of the town a sort of series of islands; there are old waterwheels everywhere and beautiful tree-lined streets. Although I didn't see it myself, I understand that there is an excellent antiques market in L'Isle Sur la Sorgue now. It's not far from the town of La Fontaine de Vaucluse, where the source of La Sorgue springs mysteriously bubbles up, at the foot of the imposing, solid rock mountains. The two towns have both been inhabited since Roman times. The popes valued the waterpower and picturesque views offered by the unique springs—a famous member of the papal court, Petrarch, lived by the side of the spring and wrote his sonnets there.

Although this was one of the four towns where Jews remained until the Revolution, the town currently has few remnants of the community. I'm not sure when urban renewal destroyed the synagogue, but the *Encyclopedia Judaica* entry for the town shows a photograph of the old and abandoned synagogue as it was before it was torn down. I understand that the town retains a Jewish cemetery, although it is said to be difficult to find, but its old Jewish quarter seems to have been destroyed; there may be just a placard at the former site. Ask at the tourist office for instructions on getting to the cemetery. Tourist office, Place de l'Eglise, 84800 L'Isle-sur-Sorgue, phone 04-90-38-04-78.

The nearby city of Pernes, where Jews were expelled by the end of the sixteenth century, also has a tradition of one Jewish building, perhaps the synagogue. For information, contact the tourist office, Pont de la Nesque, 84210 Pernes-les-Fontaines, phone 04-90-61-31-04.

AVIGNON

There is apparently little remaining of the medieval Jewish community of Avignon; the old synagogue burned and the building that one can see today was totally rebuilt in the nineteenth century. There is, however, much left of the old city, where Jews once lived; the ghetto was on Jacob street.

Avignon had a Jewish community from the earliest times, with archaeological evidence beginning in the fourth century and written evidence from the twelfth. In 1243, a record lists restrictions on the sale to Christians of animals killed by kosher butchers of the city. Jews were always severely limited as to how much area their community could occupy; by 1378, the Jewish area was inhumanely crowded, with a population density of more than one thousand persons per hectare.

Between 1353 and 1400, town records provide evidence of thirty-four Jewish doctors practicing in Avignon, despite various limitations and prohibitions ordered by church councils in the thirteenth century. In 1373, Abraham de Carcassone, whose family I mentioned earlier, took care of the convent of the Cordeliers; over the next century, three of the four physicians of this convent were Jews. The popes, too, often employed Jewish doctors. In the fifteenth century, sixty Jewish doctors practiced there. The popes who lived in Avignon made use of other Jewish services as well: both the tailor and the bookbinder of Pope Gregory XI were from the community.

As time went by, the condition of the Jewish community deteriorated, as the pope imposed the harsh restrictions of a standard ghetto with its gates locked at night. When Jews went into the streets outside their own quarter, they were often harassed. During Lent, in the fourteenth century, Jews caught on the street alone might have their beards forcibly shaved by unruly Christian youths. Needless to say, the pope required that all Jews wear the *rouelle*, or round Jewish badge, as well as other signs to ensure that they could easily be recognized wherever they went. Despite this treatment, however, this community was allowed to remain throughout the stay of the popes, who held the city until the Revolution restored Jewish rights to live anywhere in France.

As recently as the early 1930s, Avignon's medieval Jewish quarter may have been somewhat better preserved than now, as described in the now-obsolete guide *A World Passed By: Great Cities in Jewish Diaspora History* by Marvin Lowenthal (Malibu, CA: Joseph Simon/Pangloss Press, 1990; originally published 1933). Lowenthal wrote,

"Yet who of ten thousand English visitors that pour monthly through this southern world thrills at the name of David Kimchi? . . . Of the ten thousand monthly American visitors, is anyone found stricken before the synagogue in the Palace Jerusalem [nineteenth century], overcome with the realization that Gersonides must have lived nearby while he was devising his quadrant . . . which took Columbus safely to the new world? What Jews of these and other ten thousands give a thought to the Ibn Tibbons? . . . Instead, we thrill at the sight of the Papal Palace. . . . We are enchanted by fortifications and waterworks—the walls of Carcassonne and the Pont du Gard. (Lowenthal, pp. 104–105)

I conclude my visit to France with the words of this former Jewish visitor, whose efforts to promote Jewish time travel have long been forgotten, and most of whose recommendations in other parts of Europe no longer survive.

PART 3

Iberian Voyages

Introduction

The Jews of Spain were once a powerful minority, numerically more substantial than in any other European country. Jews coexisted with Christians and Arabs in an exciting blend of cultures. Their achievements were outstanding, and other Jewish communities viewed them as paragons of leadership and success. While visiting Spain, I tried to look for any remaining influence of these once-flourishing communities. I had a strong idea of the importance of Jews in the Middle Ages, and of their abrupt expulsion in 1492, and in visiting Spanish historic sites, I expected to find reasonable traces of the contribution of both Jews and Moslems.

I found that modern Spanish historic sites were uneven in reflecting memories of Jews in the medieval past, sometimes forgetting and sometimes memorializing Spain's multicultural history. The synagogue-museums in Toledo and Cordoba present Jewish history and artifacts. A fairly recent statue of Maimonides, also in Cordoba, his birthplace, suggests that the Spanish people honor the accomplishments of the medieval Jews. Elsewhere, the Jews are rather dramatically forgotten. A unique Roman-era synagogue, once visible in the town of Elche, seems to have disappeared. Madrid's museums of Spanish history downplay Jewish and Moslem contributions. The tourist agency in Segovia refused even to tell us that there were two streets still bearing the name "Juderia."

To understand the conflicts that Jews experienced during the last century of Hispano-Jewish history, I have followed several generations of one Castilian family: the Abravanels. As leaders of the community and

239

as court officials, members of the Abravanel family participated intensely in the last hundred years of Jewish life in Spain. Like masses of Jews of this time, each generation had to choose between hard options. If a Spanish Jew chose conversion to Christianity, he initially enjoyed material and social success; whereas if he chose to resist conversion, he and his family faced persecution, an increasingly diminished set of opportunities, and finally, in 1492, expulsion. The first prominent member of the Abravanel family, in the late fourteenth century, was the court financier Samuel Abravanel. He chose to convert. His son, Judah Abravanel, remaining a Jew, escaped to Portugal, where he became a court official. Judah's son, Isaac Abravanel, the most famous member of the family, in turn achieved success at the Portuguese court, but in 1483 circumstances forced him to return to Castile, where he repeated his success as a courtier. In 1492, all Jews in Spain had to make a choice: accept Christianity, become a refugee, or die. Isaac Abravanel chose to leave; he took his family to Italy, where he continued his illustrious career. In a later chapter, I will follow this subsequent history of Isaac Abravanel and his children.

MADRID, 1996

Before I continue with the detailed Abravanel family history, I want to share some impressions and experiences of my two-month stay in Spain. My travel journal begins in a small apartment on a very elegant street in Madrid. Even if you have never walked on this stylish street yourself, you may have seen it in the film *Women on the Verge of a Nervous Breakdown*. Although very small, dark, and filled with things that don't work quite right, this apartment is no more than a thirty-five-minute walk from anything we might want to see in Madrid, from the Prado museum to a variety of night life. We are surrounded by fashionable bars where local office workers drink beer and eat tapas every evening after work. One of the four restaurants within two blocks of our front door has a star in the *Guide Michelin*. A large indoor market offers a variety of food stalls, hardware sellers, dry cleaners, and other merchants in a sizable location on our street. A supermarket, a fancy fruit market, wine stores, and small toiletries shops also cater to local residents. Every corner seems to have a different international bank.

The primary function of the neighborhood seems to be upscale shopping. The English Marks & Spencer department store chain has a large store on a nearby corner, with a wide selection of tweedy clothing and packaged English food, for expatriates, I assume. A Spanish chain-store called Vips sells newspapers, books, lunch-counter meals, and small electronic goods twenty-four hours a day. Also close by are a huge choice of designer clothing stores—Chanel, Hermes, Rodier, Kenzo, Gucci, and many obviously comparable Spanish and Italian ones that I've never heard of. Incredible jewelry stores, including Cartier, present stunning display windows with multi-carat stones in huge rings and enormous gold chokers; uniformed guards stand at their massive glass doors. The crowds on the street and in the bars are generally dressed and groomed in high style, as if they all shopped at the top-of-the-line stores in the neighborhood. Even women carrying home their groceries wear wool suits, nylon stockings, and pumps.

The Retiro park, the best local attraction, is ten minutes from our deceptively elegant front entrance. Sycamore, linden, chestnut, and other European trees line the walks and shade the benches where I regularly sit to read my *International Herald Tribune*, work the crossword puzzle, or read a book. Among these trees live a strange breed of black or henna-colored squirrels with long tufts of hair on their ears, which at first glance make them resemble rabbits—until you notice their squirrel tails. In a corner opposite my usual entrance is a showy rose garden.

The park is of royal origin. The basic landscape architecture— fountains, formal gardens, a rectangular boating lagoon not much larger than a football field, wooded areas—dates to around 1630. A huge and elaborate white stone monument by the lagoon honors some king or other. In another area of the park, imposing statues of the rulers of various Spanish kingdoms line a formal avenue. I picked out Raymond Berenguer, Count of Barcelona, died 1162, who played a role in the history of Languedoc; other kings of Aragon, Castile, Navarre, or united Spain lived in the 600s, the 1300s, or the 1700s. The emphasis on kings reminds you that Madrid is a royal city, chosen and expanded to serve as a capital of the disparate kingdoms that existed in medieval times.

Individuals of all ages and social classes come to the park for their outdoor recreation. In this overpopulated city, people are eager to walk or run on its few paths, to enjoy a rare view of the sky, or to rent rowboats on the tiny lagoon. At the dock, huge crowds of children and parents enthusiastically wait in line to crowd onto a motorized excursion boat that takes perhaps forty passengers for a ten-minute tour. On Saturday mornings, a few kayaks join the rental boats. Once we even saw a regatta boat practicing with a crew of five rowers and a captain, chased by a smaller rowboat. In the morning every bench in the sun is full—I assume with escapees from cramped, sunless rooms like ours. Later in the day, park benches by the lagoon fill up with various sorts of entrepreneurs:

bead-stringers selling bracelets and necklaces, vendors of snacks like potato chips, and fortune-tellers sitting behind card tables with displays of Tarot cards, crystal balls, decorated boxes of colored stones and pebbles, small statues of witches or elves, palmistry diagrams, and other occult paraphernalia.

Sundays, alongside the fortune-tellers, entertainers set up portable stages and compete to attract the crowds to their presentations. One Sunday, a man in a colorful, asymmetrical jester suit was announcing a puppet show. He prompted the small audience of preschool children to jeer at a dragon and to beg the moon to rise, which it did, on a stick, a quarter moon with a face. Hand-made original puppets and the enthusiastic announcer made this more exciting than an officially sponsored show in a nearby amphitheater with bleacher seats and an admission charge. Normally, I hate mimes, but even one of them appealed to me: he had a small cat trained to close its eyes and strike a very still pose while sitting on its "frozen" master's shoulder. One Monday, when the park was almost empty, I saw a group of about ten young men with lutes, tambourines, and guitars singing for their own amusement in a grove of trees away from the main walks. They stood in a circle with their backs turned to the very few passersby, as if hoping for privacy.

People in these crowds are very unfriendly. Most individuals I spoke to were other foreigners, such as a few French junior high school students who were on a school trip to Madrid. The only Spaniard who engaged me in conversation was friendly, but eventually explained that she was taking drugs to make her more *pacifico*—because she was schizophrenic. One of my most interesting contacts occurred in a very old neighborhood as I was walking around, following one of my guidebook's itineraries. I heard a Dutch woman trying to get directions from two Japanese women who had one of those freebie maps that don't show all the streets. I joined the conversation, making use of my purchased map to try to help them.

I realized that the elderly woman had gone out of her apartment for a moment and become disoriented. I agreed to her dignified but clearly somewhat desperate invitation to walk back to her apartment with her through the winding medieval streets. She was staying on the fifth floor of an old ramshackle walk-up building for a week while visiting her daughter, a physician working for the European community. She mentioned that downstairs from her lived a unique artisan who made leather bottles and that she found the overcrowding in her building somewhat shocking.

As she led me up the many stairs that circled around a small central space hung with multiple levels of laundry, she kept repeating: "Forty families live around this tiny courtyard. A family with two children lived in my daughter's tiny apartment before the current owner." In fact, I found it quite interesting: other than our own place, this was my only exposure to Madrid living quarters. When we reached the apartment, I met her husband, who was pretty much stuck in the apartment because he is lame from his World War II injuries and couldn't go up and down the stairs. She was quite afraid that he would be very angry because she had been lost for an hour—my presence inhibited him from expressing his anger.

Their daughter was subletting from a Jewish-American flamenco dancer, who had furnished the small space in a simple, Bohemian style. An open beamed ceiling extended to the roof, and various household items such as a ladder were stored in the rafters. A few small windows above these rafters added to the light from the room's normal windows, which overlooked old tile roofs and a neighboring courtyard. The husband showed me one window whose frame was so poorly seated in the plaster wall that a crack of daylight was visible on the wrong side from the window opening. Over the small, low-ceilinged bedroom was a sleeping loft, accessible by a ladder from the living room. This loft appeared to be too low to stand up in, but afforded privacy. The Dutch couple couldn't wait to get home to their village in the north of Holland. I could easily understand their reaction.

What a contrast to five hundred years ago when Holland was under the yoke of Spain, terribly repressed but with a free spirit. In the sixteenth century, Holland became a haven on a sort of underground railroad for Spanish Jews making their escape from Portugal. Eventually, Holland revolted against Spanish tyranny and became the antithesis of Spain: tolerant in contrast to a country embroiled in the Inquisition, increasingly multicultural in contrast to Spain's obliteration of its past diversity, and growing in intellectual excitement while Spanish culture became stultified by its hostile environment. Economic contrast also emerged, as the Dutch fostered commercial and industrial skills while Spain relied on pillaged wealth from New World colonies. These Baroque contrasts still reverberate today.

MADRID'S WINDOWS ON HISTORY

I visited numerous museums and monuments in Madrid, but I found little there about Iberia's medieval multiculturalism. The Prado's main purpose is to commemorate the Golden Age after Spain expelled Moors and Jews. The superb Thyssen-Bornemiza museum expresses the taste of a modern German-Hungarian industrialist family that recently donated its remarkable collection to Spain. The Museum of the Americas mixes up all the cultures of the world in an odd post-modern view of culture. Its exhibits try to minimize the effects of Spanish colonialism that are inherent in the nature of its collection. The archaeology museum emphasizes Christian roots. One great Spanish monument might give you a faint hint of the dark spirit of that time, but for that, you must go an hour's train ride from the center of the city to El Escorial. The museums rarely refer to the history of the Jews or their converted descendants who helped form the literature and life of the country; they teach history, though it is a history almost without Jews. They lack Jewish artifacts because few survived, thanks to confiscation and centuries of intentional destruction; they lack consciousness of Jewish presence for their own reasons.

Discovery Plaza

One place where the sun can shine within this vast, sunless neighborhood of at least five-or-more-story buildings along narrow, periodically gridlocked streets is Discovery Plaza, a monument to Spain's sponsorship of the famous first voyage to the New World. A huge blocky concrete and stone sculpture dominates the plaza. The massive sculptural forms stand in small reflecting pools. Carved into each irregularly shaped block are many names—rulers, courtiers, voyagers, and the Indians who came in contact with Columbus. Stone benches face the monument across an expansive concrete space. Several covered stairways lead down into a vast underground parking structure under the plaza. Air pollution and traffic noise, along with the ultramodern concept of the sculpture, remind you that the events commemorated here are five hundred years distant. On all sides enormous overcrowded boulevards are always choked with cars, buses, and trucks.

Two names on the monument are Sanchez and Santangel. These high officials at the court of King Ferdinand and Queen Isabella were descendants of Jewish families—by the time Columbus sailed, Santangel and members of his family were having serious trouble, and were later hounded by the Inquisition. Santangel and Sanchez played a major role in support of Columbus's voyage. They helped to finance the voyage and oversee Columbus's preparations. Upon his return, Columbus addressed the report of his discovery to Santangel, with a copy to Sanchez, rather than directly to Isabella, requiring their intervention in his favor. Of course, by the time Columbus returned, his other patron, Isaac Abravanel, having refused to convert, was exiled from Spain—another side of life not reflected on the monument.

The National Archaeological Museum

One block from the Discovery Plaza is the National Archaeological Museum. Into this museum, for at least a century, Spanish archaeologists and treasure hunters have deposited their major finds—it houses all artwork and historic material before the time of the Renaissance, when the glorious era of Catholic unanimity began: at this point, the Prado takes over. Of all places, one would expect to find the Jewish presence reflected in the Archaeological Museum, but it is not the case. Experiencing Madrid's one-sided historical consciousness made me all the more determined to study these forgotten people.

Visitors enter the museum on the big boulevard, Calle de Serrano, through enormous iron gates in the impressive iron fence surrounding the museum. In a paved front yard with a circular drive, there are usually a few guards lounging and chatting with museum attendants on break. To the left, in a sort of bunker half-underground, there is a replica of the ancient cave paintings from Altamira. There is much gold in the museum: Visigoth gold, Classical gold, and some very primitive gold helmets. If you want to see more prehistory, the basement contains ancient rocks, skeletons of mammoths and other creatures, and small statues, bones, and tools remaining from the early human inhabitants of the peninsula.

Museum architecture being similar almost everywhere, you climb a monumental staircase and enter a large foyer, where you pay your admission fee. On this, the entrance floor, you find the artifacts dating from the early Celtic period until the early Gothic period—that is, the late Middle Ages, about the time that the Jews were expelled. The rooms are very spacious and light, with dramatic presentations of the most valuable archaeological finds from the entire country, presented in approximately historical order. The arrangement reflects geography, as the different areas of the country developed at different paces. The Mediterranean, under the influence of the early Middle Eastern traders, the Greeks, and then the Romans, became adept at the visual arts earlier than the northern parts of the peninsula, and thus, the first rooms contain the treasures from Mediterranean places. I have the impression that the policy for a long time was that any good archaeological find from anyplace in Spain ended up in this museum, so that you do not see the best things in the local museums where you could get a look at the sites during the same visit.

In the large exhibit halls beside the grand museum entrance, a collection of carved stone figures and other artifacts present the culture of the Celtic people of Spain, who lived several centuries before the Common Era. The culture of the original Celtic inhabitants emerges along with the influences from the more advanced parts of the Mediterranean. The Celts became the Iberians, contemporaries of the early Greeks. These people left interesting Greek-like sculpture. The centerpiece of the exhibit is called the Lady of Elche, one of the museum's masterpieces, a statue of a woman that combines Greek and Celtic motifs and artistic sympathies. Statues of fantastic beasts like lions also characterize this little-understood period of Iberian history. The images suggest a mythology and history that is more obscure than that of Greece or Rome. There are hints of barbaric practices, particularly infant sacrifice. When archaeologists in Elche discovered these works, they immediately sent them to Madrid, leaving Elche's own museum only a few second-choice items.

The Treasures of Elche (an Aside from the South)

The city of Elche, from which these treasures come, is now a large and touristically uninteresting industrial center just inland from the overbuilt coastal resort of Alicante. Like many ancient ports, it now stands rather far from the sea, thanks to a slow silting up of the marshy Mediterranean coast. On the outskirts of the modern urban sprawl, you can visit the vast though neglected archaeology site where the ancient city stood. In the center of the city, a small museum contains the less important material from the site, along with copies of the Lady of Elche and the other important ancient artifacts that now appear in Madrid. The museum shop is full of plaster casts and tourist souvenirs of the Lady of Elche. You constantly see her Celtic face with primitive hair, showing some Greek influence but not much.

We found Elche a crowded and unremarkable city, sprawling from a small and not even very old center. The main attraction of the town is its tens of thousands of date palms, rows and rows of them, now integrated into the ugly twentieth-century sprawl. They were planted during the Moorish occupation of Spain and seem to be replanted when necessary. It's not clear that dates are still commercially produced there. It was raining, so the palms looked rather droopy and we had no wish to walk in the long walkways between them. There was almost no place to park in the entire town center, which was full of impatient Saturday shoppers. When we left to go to the archaeology site, we found that the sprawl had almost reached Elche's neglected archaeology site.

This site contains the foundations of many buildings and displays of Greek and Roman mosaic pavement, coins, clay amphoras, lamps—the standard remains of a classical city. As we looked around, we learned that the Romans came to Elche and its surroundings in 200 B.C.E. and stayed seven hundred years. Archaeologists have discovered the impressive mosaics and also household goods, statues of gods, and representations of various famous emperors. One case shows startling artifacts having to do with Roman mining, including woven buckets and metal pipes, perhaps for ventilation. There are various early Christian-Roman burial sculptures as well.

The earliest material evidence of Jews in the peninsula is several centuries into this era, and one of the oldest Spanish-Jewish monuments ever found—though mentioned neither in the museums in Elche nor in Madrid—is the synagogue at Elche. During Roman times, Elche had become the destination of some of the Jews who left Judea and moved to Roman colonies. By the end of the Byzantine era, these colonial Jews became more significant than the occasional (and hypothetical) tag-alongs on the Phoenician and Greek ships. Jewish merchants, traders, and plain adventurers settled in southern Spain under the Romans, probably both before and after the destruction of the Temple. They enjoyed or suffered a variety of conditions of life during the Byzantine period, including the attacks of various "barbarians." In the Byzantine era, Christianity made many converts in Spain; according to legend, Spanish Christianity began with the arrival of the apostle Saint James, or, in Spanish, Santiago. The exact date when either Christians or Jews began to live in Spain is subject to debate, involving both scholarly and political partisanship. Evidence in the proceedings of quite early church councils points to coexistence of Jews and Christians throughout the early Byzantine period.

Jewish guidebooks explain that in the early part of this century, a mosaic floor from this synagogue was unearthed in the vast ruin of Greek and Roman Elche. It makes one speculate about the Jews, as they moved to new places and joined the far-flung outposts of the Roman Empire after the fall of the Temple and the defeat of Bar Kochba. Was this another mosaic of the zodiac intermingled with the symbols of the Temple and the Jewish festivals like the ones they left in Galilee? Was it primitive or

sophisticated in its execution? No one in the town museum, the archaeology display, or the city information center can tell what has become
of the mosaic from a synagogue that was excavated in the early part of
this century. The address given in the guidebook does not appear on
the map. Other tourists have also asked them about it, because it is listed
in the documentation for the Jewish Museum in Toledo.

This synagogue was probably destroyed in the urgent rush to develop
Spanish industry and economy in the 1970s, a victim of the same desperate greed that has also destroyed the beauty of the coast and turned
it into a forest of cheap concrete high-rise apartment buildings. In fact,
the mosaic floor of the synagogue at Elche, discovered in the early twentieth
century, was still visible in the 1960s, according to a guidebook listing
all of the surviving synagogues of Spain. The author describes it as being
in a lemon grove; he gives the size as thirty-four by twenty-three feet,
and states that the mosaic had Greek inscriptions. He also mentions an
exciting ruin of a still older Roman-era synagogue in the town of Sadaba,
which we did not search for (Don A. Halperin, *The Ancient Synagogues
of the Iberian Peninsula*, Gainesville, University of Florida Press, 1969).

In response to our efforts to find this site, none of the tourist-office
clerks or museum attendants in Elche could provide us with any information, though they admitted to having been asked the question before.
Tourist maps and brochures available in Elche do not mention it, although it is documented in the material distributed in the Jewish Museum
in Toledo. They seem more annoyed by the questions than troubled that
this attraction has disappeared, and we suspect that during the Franco
years, when Jews were less than popular, someone managed to build a
big ugly commercial building or apartment block on top of it. Unless
you think you can somehow find it, I don't recommend that you make
a special trip.

The Visigoths

Madrid's Archaeology Museum continues with the Visigoths, who invaded
the Roman Empire at the end of the Byzantine era. Their arrival definitively ended the Roman presence in Spain. The display of impressive
Visigoth treasures features several gold crowns from Toledo, which once
hung in ceremonial use in the Visigoth cathedral there. The Visigoths
buried treasures of many sorts in tombs and also in hiding places where
they hoped to protect their wealth from the next invasion. Besides the
crowns, the Visigoth galleries display incredible eagle brooches set with

red glass stones, elaborate buckles, axes, and swords. Again, the most beautiful and valuable treasures of Spain's past are in Madrid, not in the places where they originated. The Visigoth Museum in Toledo—once a Visigoth capital—displays only a copy.

Jewish inhabitants remained in the Iberian peninsula after the withdrawal of the last Roman forces. Initially, Jewish-Visigoth relations were good. Tolerance for the Jewish minority deteriorated when the Visigoth kings accepted Roman Catholicism rather than their own form of Christianity. King Recared was the first to convert, followed by other Visigoth nobles and bishops. As a consequence, the remaining Hispano-Romans accepted the Visigoth kings and ceased to hope for a reconquest from Byzantium. In the seventh century, troubled times characterized the reign of Wamba, who was deposed in 680, and his successors blamed the Jews for their troubles, giving them a choice of conversion or slavery. By the time they were in turn deposed from power, the Visigoths were engaging in significant persecution of the Jews. No Jewish artifacts appear in the museum in Madrid; the very few Jewish objects from this era are segregated into Toledo's Jewish Museum.

The obscure though important Visigoth period of history, with its varying treatment of Jewish inhabitants, is very complicated. The actions of Visigoth kings are significant for the later history of Spanish Jews because anti-Jewish Visigoth laws stayed on the books and were repeatedly reintroduced to justify anti-Jewish restrictions, continuing up until the expulsion.

Moorish Treasures

After the Visigoths, the Moors invaded Spain, defeating them and beginning a seven-hundred-year stay. Moorish galleries in the museum present a variety of magnificent architectural objects from Toledo on south, including the Alhambra. In my opinion, the galleries fail to capture the incredible splendor of this culture—you really have to go to Granada to grasp the marvel of the Alhambra. The repeated floral and geometric forms of Moorish Spain were faithful to the Islamic prohibition against human or animal images. While this was the Golden Age of the Jews in Spain, as well as the peak of tolerance and cooperation among the three religions, you won't learn about it here. I also feel that I didn't learn enough about the complex interactions between Moorish, Jewish, and Christian artisans.

Against the Moors, the more artistically and culturally backward

Christians struggled to create a religious art. The museum displays many objects from their various Romanesque and primitive churches built during the Moorish occupation. Wooden and ivory sculptures of saints and madonnas contrast to the sophistication and restraint of the geometric forms of the Moors. As the Christians pushed the Moslems back toward Africa, they also developed their own version of Gothic art, as well as elaborations on the Romanesque. There are some very interesting vivid-colored wood carvings and panels from this period, concluding the museum's tour of history. Although identifiably Jewish artifacts are absent, you could remind yourself that many Jews in this period were skilled workers in precious metal, textiles, and other materials, but you will never know whether any object on view was made, anonymously, by a Jewish craftsman. At end of the Middle Ages, the museum's collection ends, chronologically, where the Prado's collection begins.

Throughout the Moslem era, Christian kings or would-be kings were doing everything they could to drive the Moors out of Spain, defeating one Moorish kingdom at a time. When they finally prevailed, they made every effort to obliterate the past. The success of this effort to erase the accomplishments of the Moors pervades the Gothic section of the ar-chaeology museum. In a modern replay of the "Reconquest," the Chris-tian galleries emphasize the triumph of Christianity over the Moslem religion and culture. The emphasis on Gothic wood carvings of saints, church decorations, stained glass, and Christian ceramics expresses denial that Moslems or Jews are in any way the precursors of modern Spanish culture. Accepting only Christians as antecedents was a reasonable view for the still-medieval Reconquest leaders, but I find it strange, or maybe pathetic, that the museum organizers haven't rethought it recently.

The Prado

The cultural achievements of Christian Spain are the driving force in the Prado, the most famous of Madrid's museums. The collections reflect the taste of generations of Spanish royalty, beginning approximately in the time of Ferdinand and Isabella. The earliest work appears in an out-of-the-way gallery connected to a nearly hidden stairway. Here, the Prado has some remarkable Romanesque frescoes from the era of Spanish history primarily represented in the Archaeology Museum. The frescoes origi-nally decorated several churches in various provinces, including Segovia, in the thirteenth to fourteenth century. The predominant colors are red and yellow earth tones, in the case of the oldest, and a bright, vibrant range of colors in some of the others, all very well preserved. The people represented in the frescoes have the funny, cartoonish look of some Byzantine paintings and mosaics.

No other museum can match the Prado's collection of paintings by Hieronymous Bosch, the fifteenth-century Dutch master. It's tempting to view them as the expression of their collector: the strange king who combined a tormented religious life with terrifying persecutions of the Marranos through his unrestrained Inquisition. Bosch's *Haywain, Garden of Earthly Delights, Adoration of the Magi,* and *Temptation of St. Anthony* are remarkable works. The two versions of the *Temptation of St. Anthony* tempt one to interpret the collector. In one, the saint has a long beard, and his head, surrounded by his hood, rests on his folded hands, while he stares determinedly past the landscape and off beyond the viewer's shoulder. Right beside him rests a pig with a bell in his ear. In the other, he is large, younger, and sits beside a sort of house with a human face. It's not completely clear which things in these paintings are the temptations. Perhaps this represents Bosch himself, tempted by the incredible visions that distracted him, and all the strange hallucinations he painted, and trying to focus himself instead on his work. Perhaps it represents symbols of some obscure cult to which Bosch belonged. Interpreting outside the sphere of the artist himself, though, one can think of the tortuous mind of the king, and his willingness to preside at ceremonies where innocent descendants of Jews died in torment, accused of crimes such as refusing a bite of pork or changing their shirts on Friday night instead of on Sunday morning.

The Prado's most prominently presented works are by painters from the Spanish Golden Age of the sixteenth and seventeenth centuries. Huge works by Velazquez, El Greco, Goya, Ribera, Zuberan, and other Spanish artists fill numerous magnificent galleries. The dramatic masterpieces from spheres of influence outside Spain demonstrate the wide reach of the Hapsburg kings: the Northern European collection features works by Bosch, Breugel, and many early German Renaissance masters. The museum owns a small collection of Italian Renaissance painters, both originals and many copies: wonderful Titians, Lottos, Luinis, Georgiones, Del Sartos, a Mantegna, and even an early copy of the Mona Lisa. Three Botticellis I find baffling: each one shows hunters who seem to be chasing a nude young woman. I found two portraits by Sofronisba Anguissola (1530–1626), whose existence I learned about several years ago in Washington, D.C., at the National Museum of Women in the Arts. Sofronisba moved from Northern Italy, her home, to Madrid as the painting teacher of Isabel de Valois, a member of the Spanish royal family.

Painters of royalty represent the most splendid and prominent parts of the collections. Velazquez gives eternal vibrancy to the personalities and quirks of the kings, queens, princesses, and even court dwarfs. Goya's paintings, particularly, present a wide range of themes. You see paintings of the royal family dressed in the clothing of the time of the American Revolution, the king in a wig like that of George Washington. Next to that you see the famous painting of the eighth of May executions, from the invasion of Napoleon. The French soldiers line up, their lantern illuminating the man who has a few seconds to live. His arms are spread out in fear, and his face shows that he comprehends but doesn't fully accept; his eyes are wide and not quite vacant. Nearby is a tonsured priest in a futile pleading posture. Not far from these works, Goya's famous naked and clothed Majas occupy a place of honor. In contrast, a long series of almost insipid pastel-colored scenes show peasants and nobles, bucolic landscapes, women tossing a figure in a blanket, women on a swing, haystacks, cats arching at each other on a roof. Some of these paintings look a lot like wallpaper. Another gallery groups Goya's private paintings, in which the old man expressed his visions or nightmares. Before your eyes, Saturn devours his son's bloody trunk, the head already eaten. Two giants with brutal faces battle each other, their legs buried up to the knees in the earth. A Satanic goat, shown in profile, leads depraved old women with bare feet in a witches' Sabbath. A procession of old women celebrates a saint's day. The shadowy hooded leaders of the Inquisition suggest evil embodied in human form. Goya must have experienced the maximum contrast between his public and his private art.

The Prado boasts of Spain's former wealth and grandeur, flaunting ownership of colonies throughout the New World and power over much of Europe. The ensemble is meant to overwhelm the viewer with power and grandeur. It takes determination to remember the other side: the rejection of the cultural variety preceding this empire, the horrors of the Inquisition, the torment and extermination of Indians and other enslaved peoples, suppression of the free-minded Dutch, and lack of economic development of the peasants of Spain itself.

Medieval Spain

To understand the final century of Jewish life in Spain, we must look at the background that the museum exhibits hint at: Moslem Spain and its destruction. The Moslems conquered most of the Iberian peninsula from the Visigoths in the seventh century, forming several rich multicultural states populated with Moslems, Christians, and Jews. Almost immediately, Christians—not necessarily Visigoths—began to try to take this territory, a process that ended in 1492 with the Moors' final defeat and the expulsion of the Jews from Spain. Besides defeating the last small Moorish kingdom of Granada, King Ferdinand and Queen Isabella, by marriage and politics, unified all the Christian kingdoms of the peninsula, leaving only Portugal and Navarre outside their realm. With this, Spain emerged from the Middle Ages as a coherent European and colonial force. From the Spanish point of view, the political unity of Catholic Spain, the expulsion of the Jews and Moslems, and the discovery of the New World transformed the country into a new and splendid place. From the point of view of Jews and Moslems, it represents the end of a tolerant and productive era, where Spanish scholars helped to bring Classical knowledge back to Europe to feed the birth of the Renaissance.

JEWS, CHRISTIANS, AND MOSLEMS IN SPAIN

The Moslems, new kids on the international block, conquered Spain in the eighth century. Almost immediately after Mohammed invented their religion, he energized the formerly primitive Arabs and began a vast campaign of conquest and forced conversions. First, the Moslems captured the Middle East and north Africa from the Byzantines and other local rulers, and then, increasing in strength as more and more peoples joined them, they crossed the Strait of Gibraltar. In seven years, they took nearly the entire peninsula from the weak and unpopular Visigoths, extending Moslem domains up to the Duro river on the Atlantic side. Though Christian, these Visigoths were ethnically different from the native Spaniards, and the so-called "Reconquest" was the responsibility of other Christian groups. Later, however, the Christians would say it took seven hundred years to recapture what was lost in seven.

After the conquest, a persistent view held that the Jews had betrayed the Visigoths, who had recently been persecuting them, and had helped the Moslems to conquer Spain. Specifically, later polemics held the Jews responsible for the loss of Toledo. Actually, several competing Visigoth factions had engaged in a continuing struggle to rule, and ultimately, one faction invited the Moors to join on their side, only to find themselves also deprived of power. Jews made alliances at one time or another with most of the various factions, enabling later antagonists to blame them for anything. Moreover, at the time of the conquest, Jews in Africa and the Middle East had already developed a relationship with the Moslem juggernaut, which reinforced the conviction that they sided with the Moslems. Later, anti-Jewish writings popularized the tale of Jewish betrayal, and, true or not, this became an element in rationalizing the Christians' inhumane treatment of the Jews. Anti-Jewish churchmen and laymen continued to cultivate this impression throughout the Christian struggle over Moslem Spain and its aftermath.

Moslem Civilization

The Moslem rulers created a great civilization in Iberia. They built huge, splendid cities from which to rule. In about the year 1000, when the Caliphate of Cordoba dominated the region of Andalucia, the city of Cordoba occupied an extensive area, with a large population, a substantial ruling class, vast palaces and public buildings, and an advanced infrastructure. The pleasure gardens of the Alhambra of Granada employed a clever water system to run numerous cooling fountains and to irrigate fruit trees and decorative plantings. Inhabitants of the palaces enjoyed a rich diet and wore luxuious clothing and exotic gems. Stimulated by improved economic conditions, artisans and shopkeepers prospered. Other cities throughout Moslem domains similarly exceeded the wealth and luxury of medieval Christian Europe.

The Moors invested in many projects to increase the prosperity of the country. Improved agricultural techniques; numerous new crops like oranges, sugar cane, rice, and dates; and cleverly designed irrigation systems contributed to the agricultural wealth of the Moslem areas of Spain. This development resulted in groves of date palms in Elche; rich, irrigated orchards, vineyards, and farmlands around Murcia; rice fields in coastal Aragon; pastures in the central plateau of Castile; and much more. Merchants traveled across the Mediterranean, following trade routes throughout the Orient and bringing the Spanish kingdoms a variety of goods and foodstuffs unknown in the primitive Christian countries of the rest of Europe. Throughout this time, the Jews were especially active in this international commerce. Within the Moslem kingdoms, Jews also attained exceptional levels of respect, wealth, and intellectual achievement, and Jewish courtiers often rose to high political office.

During the seven hundred years when Moslems and Christians competed for dominance, the Moslem-held territories became subject to groups from various national and ethnic backgrounds, with roots in North Africa and the Near East. The relationships between the various dynasties and their Christian and Jewish subjects changed over time. The major trend that affected the Jews was a constant erosion of Moslem power and territory by means of Christian war and conquest, one by one, of the Moorish realms.

Memories of Moslem Rule in Cordoba Today

The city of Cordoba was one of the major capitals of Moslem Spain. Today, Cordoba preserves a few reminders of the way it looked under medieval Moslem rulers. However, it has never achieved the population or the level of greatness that existed there under its Moslem rulers.

The city's mosque, called the Mesquite, is a massive structure whose architectural elements preserve the history of all the city's rulers—long rows of Roman and Visigoth columns are united by means of Moorish-style arches. The first cathedral on the site re-used Roman columns from the city that the Visigoths conquered. The Moslems converted the structure to be a mosque and altered and added to the immense building. Finally, after the return of Christian rule, the new kings built a Gothic church in the center of the old structure. This building is still surrounded in a spooky way by the huge rows of Moorish arches and more ancient columns. Baroque chapels hide in fenced-off niches within this vast structure, all under a huge roof. Date palms in the gardens within a wall surround the structure, a further reminder of the Moslem contribution to the city's past.

Cordoba's synagogue, which the Jewish community built around 1300 and used until 1492, has been restored and made into a museum, containing art and ritual artifacts of Hispano-Jewish life. Books, a special chair used during circumcision ceremonies, textiles, and other items appear in the former community buildings. A statue of Maimonides, put up in recent times, reminds us that his family fled Cordoba and the Almohad persecution, when Moslem tolerance failed for a while. The synagogue has a stucco interior with white inscriptions and Moorish-style traceries. Its flower-filled courtyard had a cooling effect, which made our visit there very pleasant. Anything cool would have been welcome, as our day in Cordoba was the hottest day we have ever experienced; people told us that the temperature reached 50 degrees Celsius: 120 Fahrenheit!

Additional reminders of the period when Moslem, Jew, and Christian lived together are numerous in Cordoba. The narrow streets are lined with buildings that present nearly blank walls to the street, as they probably were in those days. Stout wooden doors sometimes gave glimpses into winding tile-lined stairways or inviting courtyards. These courtyards, with their small tile-lined fountains, tile floors, potted plants, and shade-producing vines or canvas sun-awnings, were at their most appealing in this heat, made muggy by the proximity of the river. Overlooking the city walls, a complex ruin of a fortified castle also suggests the atmosphere of medieval times.

Multiculturalism in Moslem and Christian Spain

Spanish Jews under Moslem rule experienced a Golden Age of culture, literature, religious and secular learning, political accomplishment, and overall prominence. As the Christians gained a kingdom or territory at a time from the Moslems, the Jews found the means to serve under the new Christian kings, extending the Golden Age in time and space. Jews brought their political and cultural awareness to the new Christian kingdoms, serving as a conduit of new ideas from Moslems to Christians. With the contribution of Jewish cultural and linguistic flexibility, Christian Spain came under the influence of Arab and Jewish learning. A dramatic contrast emerged between the Spanish enlightenment of the time and the Christian Middle Ages elsewhere in Europe.

The Moslems never outlawed the practice of Judaism or Christianity
in their Iberian territories, a policy that enabled Jews to flourish in many
ways. Under Moslem rule, Jews, Christians, and Moslems were different
social classes and had different economic contributions to the country.
Tolerance of monotheistic minority groups is supported by the Koran,
as Mohammed was personally familiar with Jewish communities of Mecca
and Medina. Formation of special, separate, highly taxed minority communities was part of Islamic rule in North Africa, and it also developed
in Spain. The conventional assessment is that the Moslems ruled, the
Christians were peasants, and the Jews provided the urban, financial class:
a very small part of the population in the Middle Ages. Actually, Moors
were often outnumbered by Christians; Jews were often in a sort of
intermediary relationship. The communities were distinct: recall that the
Moslems invented distinctive dress to separate members of different groups,
including the Jewish badge.

During the seven-hundred-year Moslem rule, some Moslem groups
canceled tolerance, notably the Almohads who ruled in the 1100s. This
was the persecution that forced the Maimonides family to leave Cordoba
and caused other well-known families to flee to Narbonne and other parts
of Languedoc. In addition, when the Christian kings were repopulating
the conquered lands and establishing a new kind of Christian society,
Jews were too valuable in helping to establish the new rulers, who ignored
Catholic theory and law prohibiting toleration of a Jewish presence. Jews,
Christians, and Arabs in Spain thus had a complicated relationship and
prospered through mutual acceptance.

In the end, the Jews made much more cultural impact in Spain
than that left by the Jews of France. While the French Jews were a small
and relatively isolated community, Spain had large and prominent one,
perhaps once 10 percent of the population, whose destiny was intertwined
with that of the Moslem rulers of the peninsula. When the Jews left
southwestern France, they sold their property, packed up their families,
and essentially disappeared. No identifiable converts were left behind,
and time erased the identity of the descendants of the exiles. While the
Hebrew term *Zarfat*, in reference to the medieval French Jewish community, has no modern applications, the term *Sepharad*, the Spanish
community, remains important today, especially in Israeli politics.

Perhaps besides, a myth of an Iberian Jewish Golden Age has grown
and persisted despite violent Jewish riots in Spain in the 1390s, despite
the expulsion of Jews in 1492 in Spain, and despite their forced conversion of 1497 in Portugal. Somehow, the Jews of Eastern Europe, living
lives of extreme deprivation in ghettos of the most confining sort may

have romanticized the freedom and wealth that Jews experienced in Christian Spain and in Moslem lands so long ago, before all these catastrophes.

JEWS UNDER THE "RECONQUEST"

During the Golden Age of Spanish Judaism, Moslems, Christians, and Jews occupied well-defined places in society. In the Moorish kingdoms of Spain during the eleventh and twelfth centuries, Moslems dominated the ruling class; most Christians were peasant-farmers, urban craftsmen, or laborers; and Jews formed a kind of urban middle class. Jews engaged in wholesale and retail sales, they owned land, and they dealt in bulk agricultural commodities. They had an important role in secular scholarship, especially in the sciences, medicine, and map-making. They made fortunes dealing in gems such as coral, precious metals, wax candles, perfumes, spices, and other luxury goods. Many Jews held high and respected positions at court, reflecting Jewish literacy, education, and ability with languages. They served as diplomats, translators, tax farmers or tax collectors, financial managers, scientific advisers, astrologers, and personal physicians. Needless to say, many Jews were also poor and less accomplished, working as artisans or manual laborers, but their perceived status in society was one of privilege.

As Christian rulers conquered these Moslem kingdoms, they found it impractical to displace Jews from these positions immediately—in fact, Jewish know-how played an important role in their strategy for empowering Christians to take over the administration and ownership of land. However, Christian policy against Jews worked against the continution of their power. Although, at first, the Christians found them as useful as court officials and financial managers as the Moslems had, the Christian kings quickly looked for other ways to accomplish these tasks. Within a few generations, the Jews' economic and social advantages eroded, due to restrictions mandated by the church and slowly implemented by the conquerors. Their mobility was restricted, their roles limited, and their taxes increased. Above all, church teaching and Christian prejudice demanded an end to Jews as a privileged group.

Legends, Forgeries, Claims, and Counter-Claims

In the Middle Ages and particularly during the last century of both legal and lawless persecution, it became important to Jews in Spain to prove

that they had a long history in the region, and it became important to
Christians to demonstrate that the Jews had always been their enemy and
thus deserved persecution. Historic accuracy in these matters becomes
problematic, because later centuries reinterpreted, distorted, or at times
falsified such matters. These documents sometimes are used in writing
history in modern times, but the authors always have to be careful to
evaluate the sources.

One such source was a purported eighth-century document stating
that when the Moors had attacked Toledo, the Jews had made a deal
with the attackers and enabled their entry into the gates, causing a massacre
of the Christian residents. In developing legislation in Toledo in 1449,
legislators found "proof" in this seven-hundred-year-old document to justify
legal restrictions on recently converted Jews, citing ancestral guilt. This
citation neglected several facts: the document was not historically based;
a portion of the Christian population had also supported the entry of
the Moors into the city; and the Visigoth rulers had ruthlessly persecuted
the Jews. In other justifications of persecution and restriction of Jews and
their descendants, Christians claimed to have documents showing that
rabbis in Istanbul encouraged disloyal acts among the Jews of Spain and
documents showing other similar treachery (B. Netanyahu, *The Origins
of the Inquisition in Fifteenth Century Spain*, New York: Random House, 1995,
pp. 377–378).

Jews, in their own defense, managed to discover a variety of documents that "proved" such things as the arrival of Jews in Toledo just after
the First Temple was destroyed, which showed an ancient right to be there
and demonstrated their innocence with regard to the crucifixion. They
also fostered a memory that an exceptional number of the Jewish nobility—
descendants of the House of David—had come to Spain in Roman times,
particularly immediately after the destruction of the Second Temple, a
claim that supported their sense of superiority. Alternate documents showed
that other Jewish communities had been in Spain from the time of the
Maccabees. It is my understanding that none of these documents is accepted
by modern scholarship and that the material evidence and other "hard"
information sets their arrival in the first centuries after the destruction
of the Second Temple.

It was of particular importance to Spanish Jews in the late Middle
Ages to demonstrate that their ancestors had already settled in Spain
before the crucifixion, because this absolved them from the Christian
accusation that they were "Christ Killers." For a modern logical mind,
it's hard to understand the medieval obsession with the guilt of contemporary Jews, who were born over one thousand years after the crucifixion
but were held personally responsible for these events, or the importance

of a detail like whether the actual personal ancestors of Jewish individuals were in Jerusalem that day. Associated with these Christian beliefs were accusations that Jews in the Middle Ages continued to "crucify" Jesus by defaming the consecrated host. These accusations were the center of many anti-Jewish sermons.

Anti-Jewish Thought

Throughout the Middle Ages, anti-Jewish theories and myths developed. Theoretical or philosophical degradation of Jews joined with popular myths to create a strong aversion to Jews and their religion. Peasants and townsmen believed rumors of many evil things: Jews were in league with the devil; the Kabbalah was a dangerous magic practice; Jews caused disastrous fires or poisoned whole communities by putting noxious substances in town wells; Jewish organizations kidnapped Christian children, tortured or killed them, and used their blood for ritual or Satanic purposes; Jews made diabolic use of stolen crosses, consecrated hosts from Catholic mass, or church icons; Jews could be hired to murder or poison Christians; and many other stories.

The intellectuals amplified popular beliefs. Beginning around the twelfth century in a number of European centers of Christian learning, Christian thinkers were working on justifications for the more irrational parts of Christian belief. Jewish dogma rejected these very beliefs, and thus these philosophers also condemned Jews and their faith. Specifically, scholastic Christian thinkers had problems rationalizing church doctrines such as transubstantiation (the literal, not symbolic, change of bread into the body of Christ and wine into the blood of Christ) or Jesus's virgin birth and resurrection. At the same time, church teachings became increasingly dogmatic, as in the case of the Lateran Council of 1215, which formalized the requirement to believe in physical transubstantiation. To preserve belief, these intellectuals took several approaches. One method was to suppress the rational approach, another was to accept the irrational as a matter of authority, and another was to stress an intellectual commitment to Christianity. Each of these allowed them to despise the Jews for their rejection of the most difficult Christian doctrines, such as the condemnation of Jews by Peter the Venerable of Cluny: he expressed doubt that Jews could be human because they did not "yield to human reasoning nor find satisfaction in authoritative utterances" (cited in Joshua Trachtenberg, *The Devil and the Jews*, Philadelphia: Jewish Publication Society, 1983, p.18).

The Franciscan and Dominican orders, beginning in the thirteenth century, assumed much of the responsibility for anti-Jewish theory. They refocused scholarly attention from an earlier respect for biblical Judaism to a concern with the practice and beliefs of Jews of their own day. They challenged the rationale, first articulated by St. Augustine in the fifth century, that "God preserved [the Jews] for the sake of the Church, so that in adhering to the Old Testament they might witness the truth of and historical basis for christological prophecy." The Franciscan and Dominican participation in the Jewish dispute over the validity of the works of Maimonides led to the burning of the Talmud in the 1240s; both the Talmud and the works of Maimonides were taken as evidence of the failure of Jews to adhere to true biblical Judaism, as they interpreted it. Over time, leaders of these orders began to argue that Jews must either be converted or expelled from Christian Europe; to this end, they arranged to force Jews to hear polemic sermons and to appear at rigged disputations where the errors of the Jewish faith could be demonstrated to the unwilling participants (Jeremy Cohen, *The Friars and the Jews: The Evolution of Medieval Anti-Judaism,* Ithaca, N.Y.: Cornell University Press, 1982, p. 20).

Scholarly anti-Jewish theory merged well with populist sentiment, making it easier to accuse the Jews of rejecting Christian morality as well as doctrine. Fantasies about Jewish atrocities corroborated the philosophical view of Jews as recalcitrant or incapable of the higher thought that enabled Christian philosophers to make their religious commitments. One important fantasy was ritual murder, also called blood libel—the accusation that Jews murdered Christians, especially children, to obtain blood for their own rituals or magic practices, or that they crucified Christian children in a travesty of Easter. Another fantasy was host desecration—the accusation that Jews stole consecrated bread, the host, from churches, and then tortured it in an effort to repeat their alleged crimes against the historic Jesus. Fantasies and rumors easily gave rise to accusations that Jews had done these things at a specific time and place. Mob violence as an emotional response to such rumors could be tolerated or even encouraged on the basis of the new intellectual grounds. The result was that this combination of scholastic views with popular anti-Judaism allowed society to marginalize the Jews. It helped to promote and justify the growing number of expulsions (Anna Sapir Abulafia, *Christians and Jews in the Twelfth-Century Renaissance,* London: Routledge, 1995, p. 5).

Rumors, stories, sermons, and fears about Jews were highly effective in inspiring violence. Jews were accused of kidnapping and killing children even when no children were missing, and they were suspected of other crimes. Sometimes the truth was stranger than you could imagine. A repeated claim alleged that consecrated or pre-consecrated hosts in the coffers of Catholic priests would begin to bleed—or at least, be covered in a blood-red substance. Jews were accused of causing this by torturing the host, in an evil effort to repeat the crucifixion. This sounds like a made-up story inspired by a variety of anti-Jewish motives. However, in the nineteenth century, scientists were able to identify a bacteria that caused blood-red stains to appear on various foodstuffs, particularly bread, under warm and moist atmospheric conditions. Thus, there was an actual phenomenon that provided a basis for some of the hysteria, though the accusation against Jews was clearly unfounded. (The phenomenon of the bacteria and its nineteenth-century discovery are described in H. E. Jacobs, *Six Thousand Years of Bread*, New York: Lyons and Buford, 1997, p. 168.)

In the late 1200s, blood libel cases occurred in Spain as well as in other parts of Europe. An interesting case in 1301 concerns an effort to frame the Jewish community of Barcelona of such a crime by putting the rotting corpse of a baby under a Jewish butcher's stall. A few Jews found the body on a Saturday night. They called together the heads of the community, who managed to alert the Christian authorities. The Jewish alliance with authority went into action, with the unspoken aim of preventing a riot from breaking out in the morning. Armed with an official permission and accompanied by a chosen Christian witness, the Jews buried the body quickly and secretly in the middle of the Jewish cemetery. Thus, the matter was kept from being used as an incentive for mob action.

Subsequently, twenty-nine witnesses testified at a hearing. They described a foul-mouthed fishwife—a tall, blond Christian woman who detested her Jewish customers. She was angry because a Jew had given her a counterfeit coin. In revenge, it appeared that she had planted the baby's body under the stall. According to the witnesses, she had been in the right place the previous evening, though the inquiry never achieved complete identification of the perpetrators and their motives. The Jews' actions and their testimony illustrated the terror and fear in which this community lived. Jewish existence in Spain was far from idyllic, even a century before the most famous and wide-ranging riots began (Elena Lourie, *Crusade and Colonisation*, Hampshire, England: Variorum, 1990).

Several similar episodes in Spain helped to inspire the riots of the 1390s. A century later, manipulated accusations of such Jewish crimes helped to fuel popular support for the expulsion order. The Jewish attitude was always desperately fearful. The accusations were so often repeated that some Jews may even have feared that their fellow Jews could have been guilty, at least in some respects, although they knew with certainty that the religion did not require such crimes.

The Consolidation of the Peninsula

From 1300 until the 1470s the Christian parts of the Iberian peninsula consisted of the kingdoms of Castile-Leon, Aragon, Navarre, and Portugal. The Moslems held only the kingdom of Granada, including Gibraltar, facing across the strait to Africa. In the 1470s, the marriage of Ferdinand of Aragon to Isabella of Castile joined the two principal Christian realms, and in 1492, their conquest of Granada completed their ambitions for expelling the Moors. By arranging a marriage of one of their daughters to the king of Portugal in 1497, they tried to consolidate still more; Navarre, too, was added within Ferdinand's lifetime.

Between 1391 and 1492, Spain's Christian kingdoms were involved in several kinds of change. In Catalonia, civilization and culture were ahead of Europe. Maybe because of the Arab and Jewish contacts that had been there until recently, Catalonia had early on become an influence on Italy, as shown by Dante's respect for Catalan troubadours. Also, the ruling family from Aragon at the time also ruled Naples and intermarried with Northern Italian families such as the Este, ruling family of Ferrara. The development of humanism was counterbalanced by the development of the Inquisition, and the power of reason was counterbalanced by the insatiable power of the Church. Similarly, the church figures like St. Domenic counterbalanced the classical influence of Arab and Jewish thought.

During this time, Jews played an important role in finance in both Christian and Moslem kingdoms. They were tax collectors and financiers when Christian kings reconquered Moslem territory. They also filled a valuable niche as traders and negotiators, because they had cultural flexibility and contacts in both camps. The rulers considered them direct citizens, not indirect vassals like the middle-class urban dwellers who answered to the nobility. They and their profitable activities were directly taxed, bringing important revenues to the kings, and consequently enjoyed the kings' protection. This direct relationship with monarchy consistently engendered hostility toward the Jews.

Politically, there was a great deal of unrest in all the principalities of the peninsula. Under weakened and distracted rulers, anti-Jewish violence could easily flare out of control, as people expressed their hostility toward the monarchs through attacks on their perceived allies: the Jews. Riots reflected the level of civil tension and unease. In 1391, the instigators of anti-Jewish riots took advantage of the terribly weak boy-king's uncertain grip on power. In 1412, the kingdom of Aragon was becoming accustomed to its first outsider king, Ferdinand I of Castile, who had obtained power as a result of the "Compromise of Caspe." At the same time, the Church sponsored the Disputation of Tortosa, a popular theatrical event—Jews versus Christians, which increased anti-Jewish sentiment and demoralized the Jews. In Castile in the 1470s, while various factions contended violently over the succession, popular anti-Jewish and this time also anti-converso violence became part of the overall disorder. With the backing of her husband, Ferdinand of Aragon, the winner was Isabella.

Eventually, a new kind of monarch, perhaps a modern one, emerged. Ferdinand and, to some extent, Isabella exemplified this ideal: a ruler who took power from people and kept formerly powerful nobles in check. The resulting stability changed the whole peninsula and by 1492 enabled them to wage a successful war against Granada, to subsidize the discovery of the New World, and finally, to definitively rid the kingdom of its Jewish presence. The map in Figure 3-1 illustrates the political divisions of Spain at the time of the expulsion of the Jews, with Granada newly conquered, and with Castile and Aragon still ruled separately despite the marriage of the two monarchs.

Ferdinand and Isabella's expulsion of the Jews and their slightly later expulsion by Navarre and Portugal meant that by the early 1500s, the peninsula was free of any officially practicing Jews: all remaining Jews had to be converted or were subject to the death penalty. In sum, Jews were a victim of the consolidation of power at least in part because they represented the enemies of the people and thus were a convenient scapegoat, especially as practiced by Ferdinand and Isabella.

Jewish–Christian Relationships and the Decline of Convivial Living

A myth exists that the Jews in Christian areas of Spain during the reconquest period experienced an idyllic time when they were not merely tolerated but were actually in some sort of state of peace and harmony with both Christian and Moslem neighbors. *Convivencia* is a name historians use for a kind of peaceful coexistence of the three religions under medieval kings. Under Alphonse the Wise and other kings, there were schools of

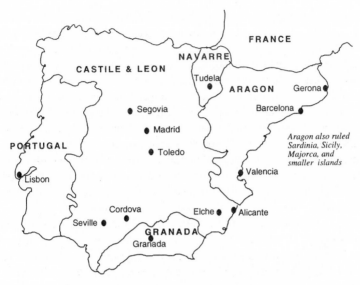

Fig. 3-1: Spain in the Fifteenth Century

translators whose activity was based on cooperation among all three groups, with the goal of translating from Arabic and classical Greek into Latin or vernacular languages. By combining the knowledge and talent of Jews (who knew Hebrew, Arabic, the vernacular, and, in some cases, a little Latin) with the skill of Christians (who knew the vernacular and much Latin), they could orally translate manuscripts. Jews held high office, sometimes served in the army or at least contributed to defense of the cities, and served as diplomats and real-time translators. Jewish networks of friends and relatives were loosely linked for commercial purposes, and always in communication about religious decisions. With this network of contacts, Jews could be useful to culturally diverse Moslem and Christian governments around the Mediterranean.

However, the day-to-day life of Jewish communities may not have always been so idyllic. A variety of evidence shows that the Jews were very defensive about their position in Christian society. By 1391, when hostility turned into an unremitting series of anti-Jewish riots led by fanatic churchmen, mass conversions of Jews to Christianity resulted. This is usually the date used as the end of *convivencia*, but it goes much further back. The conflict usually lined up like this: Jews and officials against fanatic preachers and common people, at times fired up to mob action. Jews served the needs of the rulers and were thus hated because they often did their dirty work—especially contracting to collect taxes, loaning money at interest, and paying much of their gains to the crown.

Jews in Spain had a long tradition in which their differences from the mainstream had both positive and negative consequences. Their variant tradition of learning, literacy, and financial experience made them valuable, especially in the economically developing urban areas, where these skills were needed. They had more international contacts, a wider grasp of languages, and a broader sense of the world beyond any specific political borders than the rest of the population, especially in Spain, and were thus often useful as official representatives of various governments. Jewish diplomats and translators for centuries had worked for Christian and Moslem rulers at various Spanish courts, as their own differences prepared them to cope with alien customs in unfamiliar situations.

Up until the fifteenth century, shared cultural interests, business deals, family relationships, and social ties continued to allow dispersed Jewish communities to maintain many links. Over time, Jewish bankers developed more reliable ways to place money on deposit with other Jewish bankers elsewhere, in case of an expulsion or other disaster in their native locality. Business travelers such as Benjamin of Tudela or the brother of Maimonides continued to cover all of the world's trade routes using Hebrew as a common language, as well as other languages. Religious scholars also interacted and communicated widely, quickly spreading Jewish religious decisions among various schools of prominent rabbis. As the Renaissance increased interest in secular learning, Jewish physicians, scientists, map makers, and other scholars similarly shared their discoveries among themselves and with non-Jews, often translating new works and classics from Arabic into Hebrew or into European languages. To further these diverse relationships, Jewish marriages would sometimes be arranged between families as far apart as Spain and the Middle East.

All these skills could elicit a variety of reactions. While the kings of Castile and Aragon or the dukes and princes of small Italian states found Jewish science, medicine, linguistic abilities, and diplomacy useful, common people became hostile. The uneducated masses and even the uneducated nobility of Spain tended to confuse international contacts and consciousness with disloyalty or conspiracy. Medieval thought even at its most sophisticated frequently associated both scientific erudition and theological differences with a range of evils: white magic, black magic, sorcery, witchcraft, devil worship, blasphemous practices. Multiple sources of anti-Jewish feeling were emerging by the end of the Middle Ages as Christian scholastic rationalism began to blame Jews for their "irrational" rejection of what they considered to be iron-clad arguments.

Another part of the situation may be rooted in many of the larger Jewish communities, where internal competition and disagreements deeply divided the Jews of higher status from those of the artisan classes. These internal problems were a source of danger when perceived by the Christians. Jewish courts in the past had had jurisdiction over Jewish affairs, but they were losing it to Christian courts, which especially wanted to try Jews accused of secular criminal acts.

THE INTERNATIONAL CONTEXT

Between 1400 and 1500, the outlines of western European countries were beginning to resemble the modern map. England slowly ceded territorial claims in France. The French consolidated the smaller units that now lie inside their boundaries. Italy remained divided into many small states, including the Papal States, but its people possessed a sense of being Italians. The Austrian empire united portions of current Austria, Hungary, and the Balkans, though there were ethnic differences among these groups. The various German states at least had a common language. Wars and re-alliances were a permanent way of life for kings. Reconfigurations especially strengthened centralized rule in Spain and France.

Overall, the atmosphere of consolidation, shifting alliances, and recurring conflicts had a substantial impact on the Jews. They seemed to be perceived as alien in all countries, and pressure mounted to expel them or curtail their choices for making a living and organizing their worship. Expulsion became more problematic as kingdoms became larger and places to flee became more distant and scarce.

These general trends were strong in the Iberian Christian kingdoms. Aragon, in the South, had been formed from the old kingdoms of Catalonia, Barcelona, Aragon, and Valencia; the royal family of Aragon also controlled Naples, Sicily, and parts of what is now southwestern France. During this consolidation, fewer and fewer Jews had continued to participate at the highest levels of government. While Aragon, on the Mediterranean, interacted with Italy in matters of style, the arts, and commerce, Portugal and Castile were somewhat more isolated. Portugal joined with England in alliances against France and Castile; the Jews often suffered in the course of various conflicts. The Christian kingdoms of Navarre and Portugal were separately ruled. By the end of the century the marriage and political alliance of Isabella's Castile with Ferdinand's Aragon, and their conquest of Granada, the last

Moslem kingdom, created a strong and confident Spain, which promptly expelled the Jews.

In the eastern Mediterranean, the Ottoman Empire was growing— a critical date during this period is 1453, when the last Byzantine Christians of Constantinople were overrun by the Ottoman Turks. The families of heads of state in Italy, France, England, the Iberian peninsula, the old Byzantines, and the Holy Roman Empire constantly intermarried to further their constantly changing alliances. In addition, they continued to acknowledge the feudal relationships of various kings and their vassals, who might be kings, princes, dukes, or other nobles. In Spain, during most of the Middle Ages, the counts of Barcelona and kings of Aragon directly or indirectly (by feudal alliance) ruled parts of Provence and Languedoc. In the late fourteenth century, the English duke of Lancaster, better known as John of Gaunt, arranged to have one daughter marry a king of Castile and another marry a king of Portugal, while his son eventually usurped the throne of England, making all those rulers cousins. In the mid-fifteenth century, Henry IV of Castile and his uncle King Juan of Aragon were lifelong rivals and often at war, a condition going back to 1412, when Ferdinand of Antequera, a brother of the king of Castile, had obtained the throne of Aragon. Through the Naples branch of the Aragonese branch of this family there were intermarriages with the dukes and marquises of northern Italy as well. There were lots of French royalty and nobility also engaged in this game.

Few popes missed a chance to intervene in the affairs of everyone else's states, though they were generally unable to join in the marketing of eligible daughters (except for Lucrezia Borgia, acknowledged daughter of Pope Alexander III, whom he married to three different men). A royal marriage in those days scarcely ever could take place without a dispensation from the pope, because royal spouses were generally too closely related for ordinary, dispensation-free Catholic marriage. When divorce or annulment became dynastically or personally convenient, the popes wielded even greater power. The popes used religious requirements to advance their own political manipulations. In fact, at the beginning of the era, two contending popes represented different alliances; one of them directly ruled the territories around Avignon, the other, the Italian papal states.

The alliance of Jews with rulers was an old medieval tradition. Taxation of Jewish activity was an important source of revenue for wars and dowries. During the fourteenth century, Jews in Castile were continually increasing their dependence on the king and on royal protection against growing public hostility. Because of the restrictions on other activities, they relied more on employment as royal financiers or royal charters as money-lenders, which caused still more public hostility. In the third quarter of the fourteenth century, a civil war between Pedro the Cruel (he got his epithet from his victorious and usurping successor) and Henry of Trastamara had brought new attention to the position of court Jews. Henry, in a successful campaign that in our time would be called disinformation, accused Pedro not only of cruelty but also of being too soft on Jews in his administration. In fact, Jews were the most skillful of administrators, and new Jews were immediately hired and used by Henry, the accuser, in the same way. The anti-Jewish pressure had started to build. The Jews' customary access to power and wealth through service to the king soon came to an end.

In this changing world, the traditional ways that Jews had coped with the nationalism of Europeans may have started to be obsolete. In Spain and elsewhere, rulers' reliance on Jews as tax collectors and financial agents began to harm the kings' reputation with the common people, who were stirred up by neo-Christian theories of Jewish evil and by rabble-rousing, power-hungry priests. Old advantages that had served when principalities were numerous and volatile were diminishing, as strong central governments replaced weak ones and as new political theories justified violence against Jews. In this context, we will begin to look at the Abravanel family, who depended on such a relationship with kings for at least five generations, from the fourteenth until the sixteenth century.

WHAT IS REMEMBERED

The history of the Spanish Jews is full of questions about interpretation. How do I know that a particular conclusion is correct, when supporting evidence came from the Inquisition? What makes any sources reliable? What was a writer's motive or point of view? Did scholarly and political controversies affect the reasoning? Does pride or prejudice motivate a proof that a historic figure was Jewish or secretly Jewish? Did the scholar live or work under Franco's watchful eye and write to serve the Spanish Fascist version of history? Was the scholar a Zionist? A patriotic nineteenth-century Spaniard? A self-hating Jew? A religious Jew who sees God's hand in these events? An anti-Semitic Englishman? A pious Catholic who wants to defend the Inquisition?

A major contrast distinguishes the memory of the expulsion of the Jews from Spain in 1492 from the memory of the expulsion of the Jews from France in the fourteenth century. The Jews of Spain left behind numerous converts to Christianity, while the French Jews left few heirs. In Spain, synagogues, homes, streets, cemeteries, and businesses often remained in the hands of the converts, while in France the rulers usually confiscated goods and property and disposed of them by making gifts to subordinates or by holding auctions. Most important, the convert community in Spain could never lose its distinctiveness because of three hundred years or more of the infamous Spanish Inquisition. In France, once the faithful Jews were gone, the few converts completely assimilated. In Spain, extensive documentation remains from the records of the Inquisition and from Jewish writers searching for meaning and responsibility in their history. In France, very little was said. Thus, the Spanish expulsion has been the subject of continuous reinterpretation. Questions such as why Ferdinand and Isabella agreed to the expulsion, whether the Inquisition had broad-based support in Spain, and which individuals may have been secret Jews often have no answers, but speculation has never ceased.

The question of "Jewish blood" became an obsession. In Spain by 1500, a document called the *Green Book* circulated among Jews, former Jews, and Old Christians. The *Green Book* listed prominent conversos among Spain's nobles and men of letters. The motive for the creation of this book is extremely unclear. I have seen the origin of the *Green Book* attributed to conversos who wanted to demonstrate their contribution to their country and express pride in their heritage. I have also seen it attributed to anti-Jewish interests, who wished to show that Spanish nobility was degraded by despised Jewish blood. In either case, the Inquisition found it a convenient source of victims for its relentless probes into the sincerity of Christian practice by descendants of Jews. Later on, the "taint" of Jewish blood also restricted individuals from many paths of advancement. Any modern scholar who uses this document must ask: Were its authors motivated to include prominent people out of pride or out of spite? Thus, how much can one trust it?

Under these conditions, every historical fact can be questioned, and a writer could become paralyzed. As I don't want to write about scholarly quarrels and modern politics, I have tried to research and present a story about people who interest me, and only bring up the controversies if I don't see how the facts can be decided. If you want to know how the memory of these five-hundred-year-old events was preserved, altered, used, distorted, loved, hated, and how it still perplexes, you can read the various sources for yourself.

About Women

Another problem with historical memory is this: I would like to know more about the Jewish women who took part in these histories. When I read history, I feel as if historians inhabit several parallel universes. There is "standard" history, usually written by men, which deals with rulers and wars and whatever men think is important. In a parallel universe there is Jewish history, usually written by Jews about Jews and their struggle to retain an identity. In another parallel universe, there is the history of women, usually written by women, often in recent years for feminist motives, usually outside the mainstream of power and glory. Occasionally, an author will find that another universe has made an impact on "his" universe. Even when old-fashioned historians adopted a variety of patronizing attitudes, they couldn't omit coverage of the accomplishments of royal women, such as Isabella of Castile, Elizabeth I of England, or Eleanor of Aquitaine. Similarly, Jewish figures or Jewish ideas sometimes make an appearance in histories of mainstream phenomena—as the Kabbalah's influence on the development of Renaissance ideas played a role in Umberto Eco's book *The Idea of the Perfect Language*.

To learn about Jewish women, the problem is compounded. Jewish men writing history have always appeared phenomenally uninterested in the women of the era. Isaac Abravanel had a low opinion of women's intellectual and moral capabilities, according to Netanyahu's biography. Abravanel agreed with St. Augustine and most medieval theologians, who interpreted the biblical creation story to mean that only Adam, the man, reflected God's image. "Woman was created for the propagation of mankind and also—which seems quite unnecessary under the conditions of primordial nature—to care for the material necessities of man and enable him to concentrate more freely on the achievement of his rational perfection" (B. Netanyahu, *Don Isaac Abravanel: Statesman & Philosopher*, Philadelphia: Jewish Publication Society of America, 1953, p. 136).

As a result of this late medieval attitude, I doubt if the names of Isaac Abravanel's mother, wife, or daughters have been preserved. Even the family names of his wife and mother do not appear to have been of enough interest for scholars to mention them, if there is still any historical record of them. How frustrating.

Feminist medieval historians usually prefer to discuss saints, peasants, and a few other types, rather than Jewish women. Exceptionally, the book *Women, Jews, and Muslims in the Texts of Reconquest Castile* associates the marginal position of women with the attitude toward Jews during the Middle Ages in Spain. In questioning the accuracy of claims as to how convivial was *convivencia*, the author contrasts the few works written by women to works by male authors of the time, and also to uncritical modern interpretations that accept them at face value. She suggests the significance of the contrast in women's own views with that of men. When it comes to Jews, she does not, however, discuss the considerable body of contemporaneous Jewish writing, but only explains how Christian sources marginalized Jewish and Moslem characters by such techniques as making Jewish male characters in epic poems into feminized and stereotyped figures, and depicting Jewish and Moslem female characters as beautiful women of easy virtue (Louise Mirrer, *Women, Jews, and Muslims in the Texts of Reconquest Castile,* Ann Arbor: University of Michigan Press, 1996, p. 163).

A final, ironic exception to the general omission of Jewish women from the chronicle of Jews in Spain is the record of women victims of the Spanish Inquisition. Inquisitors tried many women and kept very detailed archives. Women apparently preserved a secret adherence to Judaism more loyally than men did, or at least, in their responsibility for food and household affairs, they implicated themselves more frequently in crypto-Jewish practices. For whatever reason, women became important targets for questioning, including questioning under torture. The consequent revelations provide details about the lives of otherwise unknown women of various social classes. Unfortunately, the intentions and methods of the Inquisitors created rather doubtful testimony, and the evidence is not much use here, as I am most interested in events before the Inquisition.

In sum, I will do the best I can, and I will try to mention the slightest scraps of information about the women in the families that I have studied. But if I ignore women, it's because I can't find even scraps. I hope that there are additional primary sources about these families and that someone with the right skills might write about them someday, preferably in my lifetime.

The Abravanels

The highly successful Abravanel family descended from King David—true or not, this story suggests how they viewed themselves and how their contemporaries viewed them. In the Middle Ages, a high level of accomplishment implied a noble heritage. In addition, the Abravanels continued in high positions at the Christian courts of Castile and Portugal long after the Hispano-Jewish golden age under Moslem rulers during the eleventh and twelfth centuries. Although some family members accepted Christianity, those whom we remember today stuck to Judaism and prospered even when they faced expulsions and temporary losses of fortune.

The Significance of a Name

In modern times, the name Abravanel (or one of its many alternate spellings, resulting from various transcriptions from Hebrew characters) connotes Jewish fame and high achievement. Writers during the past hundred years or so have referred to the name with reverence, assuming instant recognition from the Jewish reader. While instant recognition may have become exceptional among contemporary American Jews, Abravanel remains a well-known name in Israel. One indication of this view: many Israeli cities have a street named Abravanel. The name is often a kind of touchstone for the highest achievements of Sephardic Jews. I found it used this way in an Italian novelist's history of the Venetian Ghetto (published around twenty years ago) and in a cookbook published this

year by Claudia Roden, whose origin is in the Sephardic community of
Alexandria, Egypt.

A French author, Jean-Christophe Attias, has published various studies
of the Abravanel reputation and myth. He cites a Sephardic saying that
indicates the strength of the symbol: to be respected, the saying goes,
"It would be enough if my name were Abravanel"—or, he quotes in
Ladino, "*basta mi nombre sea de Abravanel.*" Attias has also traced the popular
and scholarly image, symbol, and reputation of Isaac Abravanel, citing
numerous texts, plays, family newsletters, and other places where the
name has appeared (J-C. Attias, *Isaac Abravanel: La Mémoire et L'Espérance*,
Paris: Editions du Cerf, 1992, p. 11).

A. B. Yehoshua's novel *A Late Divorce* offers a more extended example
of how this stereotype works out. Yehoshua uses a Sephardic Jewish
character's awe for the name Abravanel to highlight how he differs from
mainstream Israeli characters of Ashkenazi origin. The novel explores
Israeli concepts of self-identity and individualism, in the context of a tense
and violent family of selfish, problem-ridden individuals. The long internal monologues of the family members scarcely mention that they are
Ashkenazi—it's a given, an element of their identity that they don't seem
to obsess about. Quite the contrary, the novel's one Sephardic Jew has
a great deal to say about the differences between his and their ethnic
backgrounds. At a certain point, he learns that the family has one Sephardic
grandmother; the following conversation, in which three people take
part, indicates how this is important to him. The Sephardic man begins
the conversation:

> "Mr. Kaminka told me that on your mother's side . . . that you . . . I mean
> that you have a bit of us in you . . ."
> "A bit of who?" [answers the narrator, a member of the family]
> "Of Abrabanel." He pronounced the name grandly. "That you're part
> Abrabanel . . . I mean that you have their blood . . ."
> When did they meet and what made Yehuda tell him about Grand-
> mother Abrabanel?
> "He was very glad to hear that we're part Sephardi," explained Tsvi.
> "Does that seem important to you?" I asked softly.
> He squirmed redly. "It's another way of looking at yourselves . . .
> a different bloodline . . . the Abrabanels are of very fine stock. . . . It's
> something intangible." (A. B. Yehoshua, *A Late Divorce*, San Diego: Harcourt,
> Brace, 1984, p. 272)

Yehoshua here plays on the significance of the name. To the character,
it means everything—it has great symbolic status. This modern signifi-

cance of the Abravanel family, about whom the details may be somewhat vague, is another reason why I have chosen to study them, to visit some of the places associated with them, and to learn what is mythical and what may be true.

THE ABRAVANELS IN SPAIN AND PORTUGAL

The first Abravanel name clearly preserved in the historic record is Judah Abravanel, who served at the court of Ferdinand IV of Castile as early as 1310. Half a century later, Samuel Abravanel became a high financial official, especially succeeding in service to the Trastamara monarchs of Castile. Samuel's son, a second Judah Abravanel, achieved a high position in the Portuguese court in the mid-fifteenth century. Samuel's grandson, Isaac Abravanel, who is now the best-known family member, was born in Portugal in 1437 and lived in Portugal, Castile, and Italy, working for a number of rulers in Portugal, Spain, and Italy, amassing a substantial fortune, and creating an important body of religious writings. Because he served at the court of Ferdinand and Isabella of Spain but refused to convert to Christianity, Isaac Abravanel is especially remembered as a Jewish leader during the expulsion of the Jews from Spain in 1492. In the sixteenth century Isaac's oldest son, a third Judah Abravanel, was famous as an Italian Renaissance poet and philosopher, appreciated by both Jews and Christians, as we will see in the later chapter about Jews in the Italian Renaissance. Generations of this illustrious family participated in major events in Castile, Portugal, and Italy.

The following Abravanel family tree shows the major family members and relationships discussed in this chapter and a time line of major events that affected them.

Samuel Abravanel in the King's Service

A devastating civil war disrupted Castile in the 1360s; in its course, Henry Trastamara usurped power from his brother, Pedro the Cruel. At approximately the time of this civil war, Castilian court records first show the name Samuel Abravanel. In 1379, his name also appeared on the tax records. Samuel Abravanel held significant responsibilities during this era. As a "citizen of Seville," he attained, for a time, the position of *almoxarife*, chief tax officer for the entire kingdom. Two other times, he wanted this high position, but members of another Jewish family outbid

The Abravanel Family

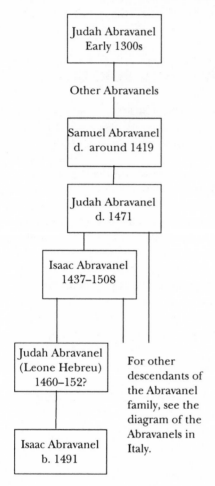

Time Line

- From the thirteenth century, Abravanels serve the Castilian kings.
- 1360s: Castile torn by civil war between King Pedro and the usurper Henry Trastamara, who uses anti-Jewish sentiment to advance his cause.
- 1360s until his death: Samuel Abravanel serves the victorious Trastamaras as tax farmer and financial wizard.
- 1380s: Samuel converts to Christianity.
- 1391: Anti-Jewish riots in Castile and Aragon create difficult environment for Jews.
- 1410s: Samuel's son Judah Abravanel and other family members go to Portugal.
- 1430s-1471: Judah serves Portuguese royal family and establishes family fortune.
- 1470s: Judah's son Isaac Abravanel becomes financial official for Duke of Braganca.
- 1483: Under a death-threat from the new king of Portugal, Isaac and his children flee to Castile. His brothers remain in Portugal.
- 1483-1492: Isaac serves at the court of Castile; encourages Columbus. Isaac's son Judah Abravanel studies, marries, has a son also named Isaac.
- Spring 1492: Spanish monarchs announce that Jews must convert, leave, or die. King plans to kidnap and convert the year-old child (young Isaac), hoping thus to force his valued official Isaac Abravanel to convert also and remain in Castile. In desperation, the family sends the child to relatives in Portugal, where he becomes a hostage of the king.
- August 1492. Abravanel family flees to Italy.

Fig. 3-2: The Abravanel Family in Spain and Portugal

him—in those days, a tax officer received his appointment on the basis of his ability to pay the king the value of the entire tax burden up front, and then to squeeze whatever he could out of rural villagers, peasants, urban poor, and the middle classes. Contenders needed two things: a vast fortune to support their bids and the ability to organize subordinate collectors to recoup this sum plus a profit.

Samuel Abravanel's exercise of wealth and achievement of a position at court at this early stage of his life suggest the earlier importance of the family. In 1380, Abravanel received as surety the sum of 30,000 maravadis (a substantial value) from a count Don Alfonso, probably Albuquerque. The admiral of Castile paid a similar sum, probably for taxes. Abravanel, also the treasurer of the queen at that time, paid the king the sum of 153,191 maravadis for debts and other expenses (Norman Roth, *Conversos, Inquisition, and the Expulsion of the Jews from Spain*, Madison: University of Wisconsin Press, 1995, p. 118).

In the 1390s, Abravanel continued to serve the courts in Castile; by this time, however, he had converted to Christianity and held various offices under the Christian name Juan Sanchez de Sevilla. He became the Contador Mayor and Treasurer of King Henry III and the Queen of Castile, Catalina (or Catherine) of Lancaster. He held office for almost the entire time that Henry reigned: 1390–1406. An indication of Abravanel's importance is that, in 1391, the archbishop of Santiago and the duke de Benavente engaged in a conflict, which included armed engagement, over Abravanel's appointment. They disputed where he would be more useful: as a tax assessor or a tax farmer, but felt that his holding both offices would create a conflict of interest. In around 1391, a popular poem accused a renegade Jew or converso of buying an office, and of having extended his power as far as Fez. This might have been Abravanel.

Historians are unable to fix definite dates for either Abravanel's birth or for his conversion. He was already at court in the 1360s, indicating that he was probably born in the 1340s. The name Abravanel, his Jewish name, appears on the record of 1379 and thus suggests that his conversion was not before this date. Norman Roth dates Abravanel's conversion to around 1391, which would suggest that he yielded to the pressure of the riots and mass conversions that took place at that time. Netanyahu and other writers believe that he converted earlier than this. Netanyahu speculates that his conversion was as early as 1380. He attributes Abravanel's motivation to an otherwise undisclosed loss of all his fortune and to his disagreement with the Jewish community about a particularly ugly affair, the execution of Joseph Pichon, the treasurer of Castile, just after the death of Henry of Trastamara (B. Netanyahu, *Toward the Inquisition: Essays*

on Jewish and Converso History in Late Medieval Spain, Ithaca: Cornell
University Press, 1997, p. 99).

The character and leadership of Samuel Abravanel were evidently
appreciated by his fellow Jews, at least in the years before his conversion.
According to Roth,

> Manahem Ibn Zerah who was in Toledo at the time, wrote of the kindness
> of Samuel Abravanel, who assisted him in moving to Toledo, adding: "I
> saw that those who walk in the court of our lord the king [Enrique III],
> may his glory be exalted, are a shield and protection to the rest of the
> people, each person according to his need and position." However, he
> noted, many of these Jewish courtiers are lax in their religious observance,
> prayers, and the like (perhaps a foreboding of Abravanel's conversion).
> (N. Roth, *Conversos,* p. 119)

Netanyahu also mentions Zera's work, written in 1374, during
Abravanel's service at court. Zera wrote how Abravanel had saved him
when he was the victim of the sack of Alcala de Henares toward the end
of the civil war, finding him a permanent teaching position in Toledo,
as well as helping other Jewish scholars, providing protection to the Jews
through his position at court, and becoming a leader of the Jews of Spain
and France (Netanyahu, *Toward the Inquisition,* pp. 99–100).

Abravanel served at court during difficult times, especially difficult
for Jews. The habit of using Jews as tax collectors and moneylenders and
making them a front for funding royal needs had always kept the heat
off the kings. However, this habit meant that Jews became increasingly
hated by the masses, a situation that intensified throughout the fourteenth century. Anti-Jewish rhetoric played a part in Henry II's campaign
for power: he attacked the legitimate ruler, Pedro the Cruel, for his use
of Jewish officials, particularly as tax collectors and financial officials, thus
trying to stir up populist opposition. Like the effective invention of the
nickname "Pedro the Cruel," this rhetoric was part of Henry's skillful
public relations campaign.

On both sides, a variety of anti-Jewish actions, as well as rhetoric,
occurred during the civil war. One disaster took place when the English
prince, John of Gaunt, Pedro's ally, marched against Henry of Trastamara.
Gaunt had the blessing of the pope, and claimed to be crusading rather
than invading. Naturally, he demonstrated this by attacking Jewish neighborhoods and killing Jews as he marched through Castile to challenge
Henry. Later, small localized attacks on Jews and their communities broke
out in the 1370s, along with accusations of Jewish blasphemy, like host
desecration and blood libel.

Although Henry of Trastamara, in forcibly attaining the throne, had used anti-Jewish propaganda, once he was in office, he needed financial expertise and willingness to commit funds, which only Jews could provide. He appointed Abravanel and Pichon as his head tax collectors, leaving out the Jews who had served and remained loyal to Pedro. When Henry died, Jewish tax collectors from the pre-Trastamara regime, jealous of their former position, took swift action. The method that they employed to destroy Pichon was unbelievably coldblooded. First, they essentially tricked the newly enthroned king into signing an order for Pichon's execution. Using this document, the plotters convinced the official executioner to accompany them to Pichon's house early one morning. They woke him up, took him outside without a word, and had the executioner immediately *cut off his head*. The particularly underhanded way in which they tricked Henry of Trastamara's heir into signing the execution papers, and the stealth with which they had the execution performed, created terrible divisions in the Jewish community. Predictably, they also activated anti-Jewish feelings that were always present among the rest of the population—with the inevitable result of having Jewish officials thrown out of office. In the course of these events, Abravanel suffered the rejection of his fellow Jews, whom he criticized for their brutal methods. Possibly in response to all this, Abravanel converted to Christianity and continued to serve the Trastamara kings through the next several administrations.

Under King Henry III, Abravanel served as the Contador Mayor. Henry was a minor when he came to the throne in 1391, and his weakness left a vacuum in place of the normal leadership of a medieval king. Up to this point, Castilian kings had generally protected Jews when they became the target of social and religious attacks, but this power vacuum caused a breakdown of royal policy, and churchmen began to incite the mob against the Jews. The most militant of these was Ferrand Martinez, a priest who had been urging the destruction of all synagogues since 1378. In early June 1391, Martinez, finding himself unopposed, preached anti-Jewish attacks from his pulpit in Seville. While there was a pretense of spontaneity, Martinez and his allies had actually strategized in advance to ensure that the walls of the Jewish quarter would yield to the mob and to maximize damage. The resulting mass sentiment turned to a full-scale riot. Mob action forced Jews to convert, looted Jewish property, and killed many people.

Within two weeks of the riots in Seville the violence continued with the pillage of Jews in nearby cities and towns. Increasingly uncontrollable anti-Jewish violence, supported by careful planning among the core anti-Jewish forces, quickly spread throughout Castile and over the border to

Aragon. In Toledo most Jews converted. Communities in Ciudad Real and Burgos disappeared. Copy-cat rioting, looting, and killing broke out in Alicante and Valencia in July and in Barcelona in August. For the first time in history, large numbers of Jews showed little resistance to forcible conversion. Many hoped to revert to Judaism at a later date—that is, they were set up for a long history as crypto-Jews. The Jewish communities never really recovered.

Henry's minority, troubled by nobles who were pursuing their own gain, as well as by the widespread anti-Jewish violence, ended when he reached the age of fourteen, after which he slowly restored order in the kingdom. He used the supreme court and the magistrates to consolidate and restore royal power. During this period, the services of a highly skilled financial official were no doubt valued, although only speculation can tell us what now-Christian Abravanel might have thought, as order returned and the vast damage to the former Jewish quarters, Jewish property, Jewish life, and all that had been there must have been assessed in terms of its implications for taxation and finance. As the Jews had always paid very high special tax assessments, their material decline must have been important in the finances of the king, even if there was no sympathy from the treasury. Abravanel followed the court to Toledo and Segovia, as well as to his native Seville. He seems to have put down at least some roots in Toledo, where extreme damage had almost destroyed the Jewish community. He owned property there—the will of a man who died in 1407 mentions that certain houses and gardens had formerly been Abravanel's property.

Besides serving King Henry III, Abravanel was also treasurer to Henry's wife, Queen Catalina of Lancaster, another important figure in the international struggle over the Trastamara succession. The English-Castilian-Portuguese connection created by their marriage had helped to secure Henry's firm recognition in Castile. Queen Catalina's father was John of Gaunt, the English prince who had participated in the civil war. Gaunt, after fighting on Pedro the Cruel's losing side, had married Constanza, Pedro's daughter. Based on his wife's inheritance rights, Gaunt subsequently challenged the Trastamara's claim to the throne of Castile on his own behalf. Earlier, Gaunt had allied himself with Portugal through the marriage of another daughter, Philippa, thus also giving Portugal a claim to the throne of Castile. However, when Gaunt arranged for Henry to marry Catalina, he relinquished his own claim and also arranged for the king of Portugal to relinquish his claim. In sum, Henry III could derive legitimacy via his wife and could also depend on the powerful backing of John of Gaunt. However, the price of these concessions was that Henry III had to pay an annual indemnity to Gaunt. Thus, Henry was always in desperate need of money—and he probably found Abravanel's talents as a financial official all the more valuable. (You probably recognize John of Gaunt from Shakespeare's history plays, which deal with his son's usurpation of the English throne from Richard II; he was also a friend and patron of Geoffrey Chaucer.)

Henry, who came to the throne as a weak boy, never became a healthy man. His nickname, in fact, was "Enrique El Doliente" or "Henry the Sufferer." When he died in 1406, Catalina competed to be regent for their minor son, the heir to the throne. Catalina had been brought up in the anti-Jewish atmosphere of England, from which Jews had been exiled one hundred years earlier, and evidently continued to act consistently with this background. In 1412, while acting as regent, she became responsible for some of the most repressive anti-Jewish laws that had ever been passed in Castile, the "Laws of Catalina." Working for this queen must have been a challenge for Abravanel, the former Jew.

Samuel Abravanel's family turned up in Portugal a generation later, but there is evidence that he remained in Castile and continued to serve the rulers until at least 1419. While some sources make references to his reversion to Judaism, other scholars argue that he remained a convinced Christian convert until the end of his life. They suggest that he had a large family, so that some of his sons, including Judah Abravanel, and possibly also his wife, did not convert but went to Portugal, while a number of other descendants intermarried into the Castilian nobility. Although Jews throughout the Diaspora eagerly mention any possible claim that they have to Abravanel ancestry, I have never seen any sign of similar pride among the Spanish descendants—I guess they were either wiped out during the Inquisition or learned, from the Inquisition, to shut up about it.

A Century of Conversion Begins

The anti-Jewish riots of 1391 marked the beginning of a century of problems for the Jews in all of Spain: for those who remained Jewish, for those who were violently forced to convert, and for those who converted willingly. Militant proselytizing by churchmen like Ferrand Martinez and Vicente Ferrer was followed by conversion of prominent Jews who joined the ranks of the proselytizers. Violent riots, urged and skillfully organized by Martinez began in Seville in 1391 and spread throughout Spain. Any traces of a golden age of tolerance for the Jews disappeared, and within a century, a new racism emerged, giving rise to the expulsion of faithful Jews and relentless persecution of those who had converted.

The wave of conversions that began in 1391 represented a new trend among Jews. Violence, prejudiced laws and actions, the persuasion of passionate churchmen, and the influence of recent converts all contributed to the pressure on Jews throughout Castile and Aragon. Additional causes may be found in the special history and outlook of Spanish Jews. While Jews elsewhere had preferred flight or death to baptism, between 1391 and 1415, tens or hundreds of thousands of Spanish Jews, including prominent rabbis and civic leaders, chose Christianity. As we have seen, Samuel Abravanel was one of these converts, although there is no record that he participated in the religious dialogue between passionate converts and equally passionate and loyal Jews.

Some of the converted Jews, perhaps including Abravanel, immediately began to assimilate fully into Spanish life and the Christian religion. The rich and ambitious rose quickly, once free of restrictive anti-Jewish laws and customs. The success of some formerly Jewish families, who not only rose rapidly, but also intermarried with Spanish nobility, inspired resentment or jealousy, and anti-Jewish racism began to evolve among their competitors and the Spanish lower classes.

Many new converts didn't attain such instant social status but continued to live in the Jewish community, never feeling committed to their new religion, and culturally and socially retaining a Jewish identity. Some felt that they could be inconspicuous until they found an opportunity to leave Spain. Others, convinced that times would change and tolerance would return, continued to practice some Jewish customs and wait for an opportunity to revert to their former religion. In some cases, the newly converted Christians were ignorant that some of their customs and manners of prayer marked them as Jews rather than Christians, and they preserved traditional dietary habits and festivals without self-examination. Great difficulty strained both the ex-Jews and the Christians, in understanding how these "others" could become a part of the mainstream. Among faithful Jews, they posed serious social and religious problems.

The passionate dialogue between Jews and recent converts became a "live" enactment in 1413 in Tortosa in the kingdom of Aragon, at the event now called the Disputation of Tortosa. Although far from Castile where Abravanel lived, these dialogues had wide repercussions throughout the Iberian peninsula, and Jewish communities, probably including the recent converts, paid careful attention to the proceedings.

The political side of the dispute involved Pope Boniface, who was a party to the church conflict over the schism between Rome and Avignon: he took the opportunity to make himself look like a savior of souls. During the Disputation, church efforts to convince the Jews to convert were only slightly less coercive than riots. Christians, under the leadership of a convert named Joshua Halorki focused on theological and psychological weaknesses in Judaism, applying every possible pressure on the unwilling Jewish participants short of immediate threat of death. These participants represented a selection—made by the Christians—of the most wealthy, prominent, and intellectually respected Jews of Aragon. While many of them argued well, some did convert, thus receiving a great deal of attention. Most critical, their absence caused suffering and problems in the communities and families from whom they were forcibly separated.

Joshua Halorki, the ex-Jew who organized the whole show, managed to set up a situation that would lead to defeat of the Jews. The Christians, led by Halorki, presented the argument that Jesus fulfilled the Jewish prophesies concerning the Messiah. From their position of power, they insisted that this was the only reasonable argument for Jews to consider. Jews were not permitted to set or to change the terms of the discussion, though they tried. Among Halorki's methods were the introduction of forged documents that were supposedly representative of Jewish tradition, a refusal to argue when it did not suit him, and many other unreasonable tactics (Y. Baer, *History of the Jews in Christian Spain, Vol. 2: from the Fourteenth Century to the Expulsion,* Philadelphia: Jewish Publication Society, 1992).

Halorki forced the Jews to answer questions which entrapped them; Hanne Trautner-Kromann summarizes their reaction: "Since they *had* to answer they resorted more and more to declaring that they were not learned enough to explain the disputed Talmud passages." This apparent indecision discouraged many of the Jewish observers and helped bring about their conversions (Hanne Trautner-Kromann, *Shield and Sword: Jewish Polemics against Christianity and the Christians in France and Spain from 1100–1500,* Tübingen: J. C. B. Mohr, 1993, p. 163).

Baer vigorously praised the Jewish scholars, despite the demoralization of the outcome. He wrote: "The replies of the Jewish scholars . . . were among the very best ever given by defenders of Judaism to Christian arguments in the whole course of the Middle Ages. They interpreted the messianic doctrine of the *Mishnah* and the Talmud more explicitly and comprehensively than any of their predecessors or successors; and it is a great pity that they did not publish their statements in a Hebrew work for their own generation and for posterity." In another passage, he said: "Throughout the whole protracted and despairing struggle, the Jewish scholars strove to defend their right to interpret the literature of their faith in accordance with the explanation and principles of their own tradition. They fought for freedom of worship—as far as such a fight was possible . . . and for the right of a persecuted faith to remain loyal to its ancestral heritage and historic destiny. This task they performed with exemplary perseverance and steadfastness" (Baer, p. 195 and pp. 209-210).

What Were Jews' Motives to Convert?

Throughout the riots and civil disorders, fanatics subjected unwilling Jews or their children to baptism against their wishes. Many conversions, however, took place without direct violence and thus were in at least some sense voluntary. Those who converted had several types of motives—fear, convenience, ambition, or conviction could all contribute to an individual's decision. Many converts were convinced that things would improve and that eventually they would be able to again practice Judaism openly.

Fear is the easiest motive to comprehend—there were several large-scale riots where Jewish homes were looted and burned and Jewish men, women, and children were raped, mutilated, and murdered. Before or during these riots, many converted to try to protect themselves from the violence. Historians sometimes compare this reaction to that of the Jews in Germany at the beginning of the Crusades, who preferred death to conversion, and who killed their children and then themselves when the mob outside threatened them. Of course, during a riot, conversion didn't always save Jews from the mob, but the motive was powerful. Over time, indirect threats of force provided a motive.

During the early fourteenth century, economic fears and pressures had caused many Jews to convert. As laws and restrictions proliferated, Jews accepted Christianity as the only way to avoid the loss of their homes and livelihoods. Such fears intensified in 1391 throughout Spain, as well as in Toledo and Segovia in the middle of the fifteenth century. Such economic motives were not trivial—laws forced Jews to move out of their houses to comply with restrictive laws about a Jewish quarter, laws affected Jews who didn't want to wear distinctive clothing or otherwise be singled out, and old and new restrictions on Jewish occupations were newly enforced. Christians were forbidden to employ Jewish medical professionals, while Jews were not allowed to sell various products to Christians or practice various trades that they had practiced in the past. Converts no longer owed their former contribution to the tax on each Jewish community.

Improved political opportunities and social advancement rewarded almost any convert, while opportunities for Jews eroded steadily. The upper-class Jews who had been tax farmers and government officials were more and more restricted—unless they converted. As new converts began to rise in the professions that opened up to them and to intermarry with Spanish nobility, their choice looked more plausible to those who had not yet converted, especially those whose faith in Judaism was already weak. A continuum of motives began with fear of violence and continued with fear of hardship from loss of professional opportunity; convenience of a better social situation; and desire for wealth, advancement, and power. Needless to say, Christians became jealous and turned against the successful converts, leading to the later development of racism and persecution of their descendants.

Disappointment of Jewish expectations caused serious doubts. Messianic promises didn't come true. Promises of happiness or other rewards failed to materialize. Constantly being the target of persecution was demoralizing. Christians claimed to be enjoying God's favor. Introspective Jews began to turn to Christianity from deep religious motives, particularly as new converts tried to influence them. Before the fifteenth century, Christian polemics had generally presented the evidence of the New Testament as a reason to convert. In this new atmosphere, Christians, particularly new converts from Judaism, based new argument for conversion on the Talmud, on reinterpretation of Jewish biblical traditions, and eventually on the basis of Kabbalah. The effective sermons by Vicente Ferrer, and later by converted Jews, received credit from many converts. So did the introduction of arguments that used the Talmud as a proof text rather than using the Old Testament, which had been traditional. Thus, a number of Jewish thinkers began to consider Christianity—several of them documented their struggle to make this decision.

From the time of the conversions onward, there was also a tendency of faithful Jews to blame freethinking ideas for making Jews lose their commitment to the old religion. They called these ideas "Averroism," in reference to the philosopher Averroes. The *Encyclopedia Britannica* defines Averroism in the Christian context, calling it "the teachings of a number of Western Christian philosophers who, in the later Middle Ages and during the Renaissance, drew inspiration from the interpretation of Aristotle put forward by Averroës, a Muslim philosopher. The basic tenet of Latin Averroism was the assertion that reason and philosophy are superior to faith and knowledge founded on faith" (Online *Britannica*, "Latin Averroism"). Or, in another summary: "God is not a manipulator who sticks his nose into everything at random; he established nature in its mechanical order and in its mathematical laws, regulated by the iron determination of the stars. And since God is eternal, the world in its order is eternal also" (Umberto Eco, *Faith in Fakes: Travels in Hyperreality*, London: Minerva, 1997, p. 264).

The faithful Jews feared that the motive to convert arose from an indifference to religion rooted in this philosophy. They often associated Averroism with Maimonides, whom you may recall had been the subject of much criticism because he tempted faithful Jews—particularly intellectually inclined ones—away from orthodox beliefs and encouraged them to detach their view of reason or science from their view of religion. Baer offers a particular example of this reasoning on the part of a man named Solomon Bonafed. In a work written during or shortly after the Disputation of Tortosa, Bonafed stated that "the hand of faith has been weakened" and cited "Aristotelian metaphysics," based on the work of Maimonides. Bonafed was aware of many Jews whose general philosophical background seemed to make it easy for them to reject the Jewish part of their background, and accept Christianity without an apparent struggle or spiritual crisis. He saw their identification with Averroism as having undermined any conviction that the Jewish religion offered them something unique and irreplaceable: "Their attitude toward their persecuted people, composed as it was of artisans and simple folk, was one of contempt, and they had lost all desire to be a partner in its common destiny" (Baer, pp. 223-224).

Understanding the many individual and socially based motives for conversion is a challenge. In reading the current best-selling memoir *The Color of Water*, I thought about parallel pressures and social influences on individuals in our own society. *The Color of Water* requires an entire book to explore the reasons and consequences of one woman's conversion from Judaism to Christianity, written with the assumption that readers will bring to the book an understanding of many aspects of our own culture. I wonder how we could ever achieve any confident grasp of the thoughts of those people so long ago (James McBride, *The Color of Water: A Black Man's Tribute to His White Mother*, New York: Riverhead Books, 1996).

What Were the Faithful Jews' Motives?

At this distance, it's no easier to understand in detail what maintained the faithful Jews in this period than to understand what motivated others to convert. Moreover, if they documented their own inner struggles, many of their works were no doubt destroyed in the aftermath of flight and persecution. Explicit comparisons of the Jewish and Christian faiths would have been dangerous to themselves and to other Jews, and would have been disguised or hidden. In addition, a large number of the unconverted Jews were poorer and less educated, and thus of non-writing classes. In seeking their motives, I have tried to look for Jewish statements that were not forced by Christian events such as the Disputation of Tortosa, where the terms of the argument were determined by the Christians who were intent on proving that the Jewish faith itself requires the acceptance of Christ.

In the critical years from 1390 to 1416, two Jews wrote about their commitment to Judaism: Hasdai Crescas and Profiat Duran, also known as "Ephodi." Both writers made a strong effort to persuade other Jews to preserve their beliefs, and they expressed their strong loyalty to the traditions of the religion. The two motives, belief and loyalty, were the major positive motivation of the faithful Jews of that time, as far as I can determine. Duran, in fact, expressed these beliefs despite having formally undergone conversion.

Profiat Duran's expression of belief, written in 1396, is called "Be not like unto Thy Fathers." This document, in the form of a letter to a converted friend, David Bonet Bongoron, expresses ironically a number of reasons to preserve both belief and loyalty. The irony allows the pretense that he is actually favoring Christianity, thus ostensibly staying on the safe side of the extreme censorship of Jewish ideas; as a result, it's nearly impossible to summarize the content without seeming dense.

I use Duran to try to discover contemporary beliefs that motivated the faithful Jews. Here is a brief quote to illustrate his ironic handling of the topics of faith and loyalty to tradition:

> Be not like unto thy fathers, who believed in one God from whose unity they removed any plurality. They have erred indeed, when they said "Hear Israel, the Lord is One!" when they understood this unity in the purest sense without inclusion of species, kind or number. Not so thou! Thou shalt believe that one can become three and that three united make one. Lips will never tell it, ears never take it in. . . .
>
> *Be not like unto thy fathers,* upon whom the holy Torah of Moses was bestowed as heritage and possession, when they strove after spiritual perfection in thought and deed . . . and kept faithfully the commandments and prohibitions . . . *Not so thou!* For this would be shameful. If thou beget sons, do not introduce them into the covenant of the fathers. . . . Eat leavened bread on the Passover; eat also milk and meat together! . . . Eat of pork, of all animals in the water, on the earth, and in the air, which

have been interdicted to thee once. ("Be not like unto Thy Fathers," *Disputation and Dialog: Readings in the Jewish-Christian Encounter,* Frank Ephraim Talmage, ed., New York: KTAV Publishing House, 1975, pp 119-123)

In addition to positive belief and loyalty, Jews also found a powerful deterrent to conversion: they feared that they would never be fully accepted. Duran expressed this as follows, in advising his audience to be different from their forefathers: "Do not be put out by the humiliation and contempt and shame that will cling to your soul and the disgrace that will be on your brow. Your enemies will insult you and your personality will go to pieces in their presence when they say to you all day long: *newly-baptized, apostate or circumcised Jew*" (quoted in Hanne Trautner-Kromann, *Shield and Sword,* p. 156). This motive—fear that they could never truly be accepted—became stronger as the Inquisition took on its racist character in the 1480s.

Finally, there is evidence that Jewish doubts of Christian beliefs prevented some Jews from accepting conversion. These Jews found Christian "mysteries," such as the doctrines of transubstantiation, resurrection, and virgin birth at odds with their concept of natural laws. Others could not go along with the idea that God gave the law to Moses and then changed his mind.

Debates on various philosophical positions raged among Old Christians, faithful Jews, and New Christians (that is, converts or their descendants). The rigidity of Christian doctrine was an issue, but the existence of force and hatred was more important than subtleties. As I have said, rationalist Christians who also found these doctrines hard to reconcile were particularly critical of Jews for refusing to accept their faith, and they developed a variety of hatreds and myths about Jewish stubbornness and about the Jewish habit of stealing and "torturing" the Host, that is, the literal body of Christ. It may be relevant that these beliefs had relatively recently been cast in concrete by the Catholic church: the requirement that the conversion of the Host during the mass be taken literally and not symbolically dates from the Lateran Edict of 1204.

Economic Consequences of Mass Conversions

I have mentioned that Samuel Abravanel's success, influence, and wealth, first as a Jew and later as a convert, were exceptional. By the end of the fourteenth century, the life of the Jewish community was dramatically worse than it had been in earlier centuries. As more and more Jews converted, the economic and social status of the faithful declined even further. Not only were the faithful Jews more likely to be workers and artisans, at the same time the authorities were constantly increasing the restrictions on allowable occupations and commercial activities for those who refused to convert. Jews were more and more successfully barred from the court and tax collecting occupations that had enabled a few highly placed community members to advocate on behalf of less fortunate members of the community. The civil war and the execution of Pichon had made things even worse, as mentioned earlier. As time went on, the Jewish community became steadily poorer and less powerful. And in contrast to faithful Jews—although their success was a source of dissatisfaction and jealousy among lower classes and competing Christian bourgeoisie—converted Jews were in a particularly good position during the main part of the century.

Before 1391, Jewish physicians, courtiers, and secular scholars had been leaders of the community, along with scholars and rabbis. Among faithful Jews, these occupations all declined rapidly in the fourteenth century. Jews who had been farmers, landowners with tenants, or dealers in luxury goods were forced out of business by increasingly restrictive laws about Jewish occupations, or they simply gave up the struggle and converted. Poorer Jews, who had always followed trades as cloth makers, bookbinders, copper or tin smiths, or shoemakers, seemed to resist conversion better and were less likely to be legislated out of a job. By the end of the period of rapid conversion, a growing number of Jewish workers were limited to lower-paying and often marginal jobs, such as dealing in used clothing, lending small amounts of money or running pawn shops, dealing in small goods or foodstuffs, operating market stalls, acting as innkeepers or tavern keepers, and continuing in trades such as metal working, cloth working, shoemaking, tailoring, and the like. Obviously, Jewish workers continued to serve as Jewish ritual slaughterers and butchers, kosher wine makers, bakers, and other exclusively Jewish trades, but even these were less profitable as the wealth of their fellow Jews declined. Throughout the fifteenth century the higher-level activities declined or were performed by converts only. In Aragon, the royal courts had practically no Jews, although in Castile, Isaac Abravanel and Abraham Senior served as important court officials up until the expulsion, when Abravanel left and Senior converted.

In housing, Jews particularly suffered. Some towns and regions expelled the Jews altogether. Others forced them to move into exclusively Jewish neighborhoods, often with a loss of valuable property outside the new restricted areas. Jewish communities lost communal property, as converts "gave away" synagogues, to be changed into churches, and as other properties were confiscated. The synagogues that one sees in modern Toledo were lost in this way. Mid-century riots forced more and more Jews to sell or abandon property in areas where they had once been allowed to own land or buildings. For instance, in Segovia, in the fourteenth century, the Juderia, or Jewish neighborhood, was forced to move from one part of town to another, settling in a less desirable location in the red-light district. In the medieval area of modern Segovia you can still see the two streets marked with the names of the "old" and "new" Juderia.

Eventually, in the 1480s, royal decrees required all Jews to reside and work in separate quarters from Christians, often far from their workshops and markets. The bureaucrats overseeing the Jews' evictions assessed former Jewish property at low values and set substantial purchase prices for the buildings in the new neighborhoods. Furthermore, the Jews had to fund the construction of security walls or gates around these frequently inferior quarters. Failure to comply could result not only in penalties, but also in attacks or mob violence. The process of separating Jews from Christians was still underway when the expulsion of 1492 made it unnecessary (Haim Beinart, "Order of the Expulsion from Spain," *Crisis and Creativity in the Sephardi World 1391–1648*, ed. Gampel, New York: Columbia University Press, 1997, p. 85).

Taxes were a major factor in the impoverishment of the Jewish communities. The special tax assessed on each Jewish community was a fixed sum. The king demanded payment of this amount, no matter how many community members converted, died in riots, lost their jobs or their fortunes, or fled. In addition, special taxes applied to kosher meat and wine, and communities became liable for costs associated with the removal of Jews to new quarters, as described earlier. This high tax burden became more and more difficult for the remaining Jews, as their misfortunes and poverty increased. Often, the richest of the Jews converted—the tax policy intentionally encouraged them to do so—and thus escaped from the Jewish tax obligation, continually leaving fewer, poorer community members to share the debt. Ironically, at court, Jews and New Christians, still the most skilled financial analysts and the most experienced tax farmers, were in the process of restructuring taxes on the rest of the population and thus compensating the treasury for the loss of Jewish revenues.

Jews, converts, and non-Jews were all affected by major changes to the economy as a whole during this time. Between 1391 and 1492, a more modern capitalism was slowly replacing feudalism. The monarchs of Castile and Aragon were engaged in the consolidation of power and attacks on the powers of the nobility. Enclosure of peasant land and restrictions on previous privileges, such as the right to walk sheep across private fields or farms, changed the economy for everyone. Movement to urban areas, changing demographics, and the development of new tax and financial organization were all important contributing factors to general economic evolution. Iberian trade in the Mediterranean region was spreading, with ongoing competition with other powers such as Venice and Turkey. Aragon was a major power—members of its royal family also ruled Naples, Sicily, Majorca, and part of Greece, and its representatives competed in eastern trade routes. Portugal was opening up new routes in the direction of Africa, which provided competition for the Spanish trade routes. These conditions provided many opportunities for the converted Jews, who already had skills demanded by growing job markets in the emerging urban, financial, and commercial sectors.

TOLEDO, 1996

Toledo, Spain, in 1996 still invites you to connect with the 1400s. Built on a dramatic site, the city occupies a craggy hilltop. On three sides, a natural moat, formed by a bend in the Tagus river, protects the historic quarters of town. Medieval buildings, towers, an old city wall with three-story-high gates that once could keep out armies, and several fortified bridges have changed little in five hundred years. While Madrid, in contrast, has a minimum of streets, buildings, and squares from the fifteenth century, the entire old city of Toledo today allows a much more concrete grasp of life at that time, particularly for life in the Jewish community. Many of the city's streets and monuments already were in place when Samuel Abravanel was here, particularly the two synagogues that remain today.

Upon approaching Toledo, you see its silhouette against the impressively clear and vivid sky. After you enter the main gate, narrow streets wind in an impossible maze-like pattern. Even an attempt to follow a simple city map to a prominent destination gives you a strong impression of what it must have been like to be an unwelcome stranger there in distant times. Streets climb at odd angles, dead-end at private locked gates, or lead to the edge of high cliffs that drop down into the canyon-like river valley. The locals don't seem very helpful to strangers, just as it must have been in the Middle Ages.

From a vantage point in a comfortable hotel on the cliffs across the Tagus, we observed the skyline for hours, relieved at a temporary respite from our unfortunate Madrid apartment. Changing sunlight created beautiful effects from daybreak to dusk, and floodlights kept it visible throughout the evening. One morning, as I watched the slightly pink light of dawn and sunrise, a cloud almost immediately appeared behind the Alcazar. Within fifteen minutes, mist hid everything, even the Parador Hotel, which was just across the road from our hotel. Perhaps a memory of this rugged beauty contributed to the passionate love expressed by generations of Jewish exiles from Spain. Everyone recognizes Toledo's special light, blue sky, and dramatically outlined clouds in the works of El Greco.

We started our walking tour of the city at the main gate and walked up and down the narrow streets to reach the two surviving synagogues, in the heart of the old Jewish quarter. The first synagogue, now called the Transito, was completed in 1356, and served the Jewish community until the expulsion in 1492. The Church owned and used it for three centuries. After the Napoleonic era, it fell into decay, but restorations began in the late nineteenth century. In the former sanctuary, the plaster medallions and ornate arabesques represent some of the best of Hispano-Jewish design. The high, multicolored, ornate ceiling is particularly famous and attractive. Hebrew inscriptions commemorate the builder, Samuel Ha-Levi, and Pedro I, King of Castile in the mid-fourteenth century. The inscriptions interweave with elaborate geometric designs in Hispano-Moorish style. I find it remarkable that in the centuries when Christians made other uses of the building, Hebrew inscriptions survived. The exotic Moorish architecture illustrates the continuing influence of the Arab occupants of Spain even after the reconquest.

Since 1964, the Transito's sanctuary, women's gallery, courtyards, supplementary rooms, and gardens have served as the Sephardi Museum of Toledo. The museum had been undergoing renovations on our previous visit, so we were particularly happy to find it accessible. The first part of the museum presents a general overview of Jewish history, with biblical times represented by archaeological specimens loaned by the government of Israel. There are several cases about the Jews of Spain and what happened to them; in particular, the museum owns several Jewish artifacts from the Visigoth and Moslem periods of Spanish history. The garden includes several ancient Hebrew-inscribed tombstones and a modern monument with a poem by Judah Ha-Levy. In the women's gallery, cases of ceremonial objects illustrate the celebration of various holidays throughout Jewish tradition. I was fascinated to see a book about the High Holy Days printed by Solomon Usque in Mantua in the 1550s. Many photos, contributed by a variety of people, enrich the exhibit.

Toledo's other synagogue, called by its later church name, Santa Maria la Blanca, dates from 1205. During the early fifteenth-century anti-Jewish outbreak, in 1411, this building became a church. Eventually, neglected and ignored, it served as a carpenter shop and a military barracks, but now restored, it is also a civic monument. Its decoration is a wonderful variety of Arab-inspired aisles and floral-decorated arches and columns. Beams of sunlight from high windows cut through near-darkness inside the former worship space, illuminating an occasional Moorish capital or archway and creating a dramatic effect in the quiet, whitewashed building. The first time I saw this beautiful interior, it was a revelation to me because the decoration of the Reform Jewish temple that I attended as a child was obviously based on the style of this synagogue; ironically, my former congregation has replaced the old Moorish-style inner-city building with a 60s-modern suburban facility; that is, the copy is gone but the original, in Toledo, endures. Visitors to the synagogue come from Jewish communities throughout the world, creating a sense of connection of present and past; for example, we began talking with an Israeli couple, who invited us to have dinner with them when we later spent time in Israel.

Finally, we visited a church, San Juan des Reyes, not far from the synagogue. The church dates from the time of Ferdinand and Isabella and no doubt was intentionally situated in the old Jewish Quarter. In a beautiful Gothic cloister, the late afternoon light was shining on the white marble floor and reflecting on the Arab-style coffered ceiling, allowing a clear view. The sun illuminated Gothic drain spouts, including one with a long-faced, helmeted knight that reminded me of Don Quixote, wearing a real helmet, not a barber's basin, and another that had a realistic baby cupid or angel hanging upside down from the spout, as if it were a jungle-gym.

On the second day of our trip, we again walked through the city to visit several museums. The winding streets make it very difficult to find the Visigoth museum, at the highest point in the city. This museum has a small collection compared to the Archaeology Museum in Madrid, where the major treasures are always deposited. We also visited a major museum of historic and artistic collections. As in Madrid, these suppos-edly general museums emphasize Christian Spain and provide little clue to the once-important Jewish and Moslem presence. At the end of our walk through Toledo, we toured the huge Cathedral, which is in-your-face Gothic, my least favorite kind, another reminder of the attitude of Ferdinand and Isabella's triumphant conquest and Catholic unification.

Just before driving back to Madrid, we parked at the old pedestrian bridge, which is flanked by guard towers on either end, and we briefly walked on the bridge that was the site of various struggles as mobs attacked the city in 1449. Because it gave access to the Jewish quarter, bitter and violent attacks on conversos were launched here throughout the fifteenth century, a major contrast to the peaceful and pleasant stay we enjoyed.

Note: Be sure to check opening hours before you attempt to visit Toledo's monuments. The Jewish museum and synagogues close during the midday lunch hour, and re-open late in the afternoon. Standard guidebooks describe how to reach the two synagogues. If these synagogues intrigue you, but you are visiting Tel Aviv rather than Spain, you can see scale models of the buildings and partial reproductions of the plaster decorations in the Diaspora Museum.

THE ABRAVANELS AT THE PORTUGUESE COURT

We left the Abravanel family at the time when they were about to leave Castile to resume the practice of Judaism in the more tolerant atmosphere of Portugal. The details are quite unclear. There are two scenarios for the end of Samuel Abravanel's life:

- According to some sources, Samuel Abravanel moved to Portugal with his family by 1412, during a temporary period of tolerance by the Portuguese. He entered the service of King John I in Lisbon and remained there until the end of his life, training his son Judah in finance and management and introducing him to the court.

- Other sources say that Samuel Abravanel never returned to Judaism. Netanyahu identifies possible references to Samuel Abravanel's Christian name, Juan Sanchez de Sevilla, as Contador Mayor of Castile up until 1419, by which time he may have been over eighty years old. In this case, only Samuel's family went to Portugal— possibly including his wife and sons. The family members either returned to Judaism (which was tolerated in Portugal despite church prohibition) or had never converted when their father converted.

Like the date of his birth and that of his conversion, the record of Samuel Abravanel's death seems to have been lost. Besides the general obscurity of the historical record from this time, later family members probably concealed the details of which family members converted, returned to Judaism, or remained in Spain. Jewish family members experienced embarrassment for a temporarily Christian ancestor. The Inquisition later threatened New Christians, who therefore would have had a strong motive to conceal this history.

Background: Fifteenth-Century Portugal

Before 1400, there were very few Jews in Portugal. Their numbers increased as the massive persecutions, beginning with the riots in Spain in 1391, drove the Jews from Castile. The Portuguese welcomed the refugees, beginning with John I of Portugal, also called John of Aviz or João I, who became king in 1385. He resisted social, political, and international pressures to put more restrictions on the Jews of the kingdom and to refuse to allow reversion by converts. Although he put new laws on the books, such as a mandate that Jews wear the badge, declared in 1391, and a prohibition against Jews holding office, declared in 1404, these laws were unenforced. Until 1412, he welcomed Jews and converts who fled from the persecutions in Castile. He allowed them to practice Judaism and to make use of their valuable financial skills. Like earlier medieval kings, he regarded Jews as a valuable royal resource. Portugal's late hospitality to Jews could be viewed as evidence that it was a backward place—the more advanced countries of Europe had already committed to persecutions and expulsions!

The Abravanel family, in a sense, was in the avant garde, arriving in Portugal ahead of the trend, which became a major effect only in 1492 when Jews had to choose between conversion, exile, and death. You could view this Abravanel action as a part of their exceptional, imaginative lifestyle. If Samuel Abravanel served the Portuguese king, it's clear how his extensive experience in finance in Castile could have been adapted to the new situation; his son and grandson certainly became important figures in the court life of their new country.

Portugal was a good place for an ambitious, talented family. John I was ambitious and determined to improve the overall position of Portugal internationally. He had attacked the neighboring kingdom of Leon around 1390 and skirmished with Castile until 1411. John's wife, Queen Philippa, was the daughter of John of Gaunt, the English duke who frequently became involved in affairs on the Iberian peninsula. Philippa exerted a cultural influence at the court, introducing new trends in style and architecture. John and Philippa's five sons became men of diverse accomplishment.

Under the leadership of his third son, Prince Henry the Navigator, John also undertook ambitious programs of exploration and conquest in Africa. These activities required increasing amounts of money, and new and imaginative ways to raise it. Furthermore, while developing as a strong king, developing cultural institutions, and building up his external affairs, John had granted vast land holdings and estates as sources of wealth to the nobles, thus leaving him in need of alternate sources of income. No doubt for these reasons, the king was delighted to welcome the financially trained exiles from his rival, Castile.

Prince Henry the Navigator is the family member who remains most famous in the twentieth century. Born in 1394, Prince Henry's first notable deed was an expedition against the North African city of Ceuta, which he conquered in 1415. He served his brother, who became King Duarte after John I's death. Until his death in 1460, Prince Henry sponsored map making, exploration of new routes along the African coast, discovery of new commercial opportunities, new technology for navigation, and innovation in the rivalry between Christian Europe and Moslem North Africa. In 1437, Prince Henry, accompanied by another brother, Fernando, mismanaged an attack on Tangier. He had to leave Fernando as a hostage, and Fernando eventually died at Fez in 1443, a victim of the enemy's mistreatment. King Duarte died in 1438, shortly before Henry returned from the war. Duarte's son and heir, Alfonso, was a child, and in the ensuing period Portugal suffered the predictable fate of a medieval kingdom with an underage ruler: rivalry over the power of the regency leading to weak government. This was bad for the Jews, as it had been in similar circumstances in Castile in 1391.

Alfonso V became legally of age in 1446, when he was fourteen. Despite his early kingship, he developed good qualities. Among other things, he was curious about learning and committed to the emerging principles of Renaissance humanism. At times he even expressed curiosity about Judaism. Alfonso also had weaknesses; he was subject to being heavily influenced by others, often granting them extravagant favors. In 1449, there were anti-Jewish riots in Lisbon. The Jewish quarters of the major towns were well fortified, though, and the mob was unable to break into them. When Alfonso V, then seventeen years old, tried to put them down, the uprising turned against him. The regent, another uncle, Pedro, was killed in the resulting conflict, which some historians consider to have been a civil war. Henry the Navigator—also Alfonso's uncle—tried to be a peacemaker, siding with the king. Later in his reign, Alfonso engaged in territorial adventures, as had his predecessors, conquering a city in North Africa in 1458, trying again and failing at the conquest of Tangier in 1463, and finally succeeding in its conquest and that of Arzila in 1471.

The Life of Judah Abravanel

Judah Abravanel, Samuel's son, seems to have been born about 1400; Samuel, already an old man, also may have had much older sons. If the family went to Portugal before 1412 during the window of opportunity when Jews were welcomed, one would assume that older family members accompanied the boy and his mother. This is definitely a mysterious area.

Judah Abravanel apparently developed financial and administrative skills that were characteristic of his family and somehow received an introduction to the Portuguese court, but a gap in the family record until the 1430s leaves the details unclear. By the 1430s, Judah Abravanel began to turn up in high positions, working for members of the Portuguese royal family. He developed as a courtier and leader, first becoming the treasurer of the ill-fated Prince Fernando, who died as a hostage in Fez in 1443.

Judah's service to the royal family and the Jewish community continued after 1433, when King John died and his oldest son, Duarte, succeeded him, and his career continued until around 1471, the apparent date of his death. He became the leader of the Jewish community of Lisbon. This community was small but showed signs of activity, such as the demand for manuscripts and books. Beginning in the 1460s, an exceptional workshop for creating illuminated Hebrew manuscripts flourished there, producing prayer books, Bibles, and works of scholarship for the local Jews. Shortly after Judah's death, the establishment of one of the first Hebrew printing presses also demonstrated the strength of interest in Jewish books in Lisbon. During Judah's lifetime, the Abravanel house is said to have been a meeting place for the intellectuals of Lisbon, though this was no doubt hampered by various restrictions on Jewish activity, particularly by curfews on the Juderia and its inhabitants. Because Judah's accomplishments included no writing or scholarship, he failed to establish a permanent reputation like that of his son Isaac Abravanel or his grandson, also named Judah Abravanel. Nevertheless, he was important in Lisbon's Jewish community.

The Early Years of Isaac Abravanel

Judah's son Isaac Abravanel was born in 1437; other sons and possibly daughters were born later. The year of Isaac's birth was also the year of Henry the Navigator's expedition against Tangier, which ended in disaster for the Portuguese. Shortly afterward, the early years of Alfonso's reign were difficult times for Jews. The exact survival strategy of the Abravanels during this time doesn't seem to be known, nor is Judah's method of coping with the loss of his patron Fernando.

During Alfonso's struggle for power and the attacks on the local Juderias, the youthful Isaac Abravanel lived in Lisbon, the principal city and port of Portugal. He is said to have been "a precocious child, quick to learn, with an absorbing and penetrating mind. He grasped everything, understood matters far beyond his years . . . He was endowed with an extraordinary memory, retaining to a fault everything he had ever read or learned." While Lisbon at this time had a university, as a Jew, Isaac Abravanel was not allowed to study there, but studied with his father and with Joseph Hayyun, "the erudite rabbi of Lisbon" who had "an ideal blend of Jewish and secular knowledge." He also studied with unnamed secular scholars who were employed through his father's court connections. He learned "Latin, Spanish, and Portuguese and became familiar with the treasures of Christian and Muslim literature, as well as with the ideas of the ancient philosophers." Abravanel's work "The Crown of the Elders" appeared when he was twenty; it showed the influence of Judah Halevi. In an age when university training was beginning to be highly valued as an attribute of a courtier, Abravanel was able to compensate through his own efforts and through the value of this exposure to important elements of secular and classical knowledge.

Soon after Judah Abravanel died in 1471 or early 1472, Isaac began to rise at court, succeeding his father as minister of finance to Alfonso V of Portugal. He wrote "Happy was I in the palace of Don Alfonso . . . under his shadow I loved to dwell. I stood near him and he leaned on my hand." Not long after this, Isaac Abravanel also began to serve the Duke of Braganca, who was very powerful at the king's court. Both this service and his investments began to make him enormously wealthy. He also developed Portuguese and foreign connections that served him later in life. (Quotes in these two paragraphs are from S. Gaon, *The Influence of the Catholic Theologian Alfonso Tostado on the Pentateuch Commentary of Isaac Abravanel*, Hoboken, NJ: KTAV, 1993, pp. 2–5; the first citation is attributed to an author named Minkin.)

Despite the rivalries between royal factions, Portugal was at this time a major power. The trade routes and African conquests developed under Prince Henry's leadership were beginning to pay off, and the Portuguese rivaled the Mediterranean mercantile powers—especially Venice, former owner of a trade monopoly with the Far East. Unfortunately for Abravanel, his alliances did not allow him to continue to profit from this situation. The king died, and the duke lost power to rivals as the new king was establishing his administration. As a result, Abravanel had to flee from Portugal to Castile in 1483 when the new king passed a death sentence on the duke and his followers, including Abravanel, judging them as traitors to his realm. Isaac Abravanel's son Judah, in his autobiographical poem, later presented his view of the family's experience of the feud of the royal family of Portugal. The poem states that after the usurper defeated those whom he considered traitors and killed his own brother, he also tried to kill Isaac Abravanel, forcing him to flee to Castile, and seizing the family wealth. Abravanel's wife and sons, including Judah, escaped with him. However, at least one Abravanel brother and the sons of this brother appear to have stayed in Portugal, where they continued to represent the family's interests for a number of years; we will meet them again.

PORTUGAL SINCE 1483

For me, a trip to Portugal is still a dream, just as all the trips in this book used to be dreams. The place where I believe I would find the most important memories of the fifteenth-century Jewish presence there is Tomar. It has one of the only medieval synagogues in Portugal, now a museum that houses a number of artifacts from Tomar and other Jewish communities of Portugal. The city's architecture currently includes important examples of decoration from the age of King Manuel, the man responsible for the forced conversion of the Jews in 1497.

The Tomar synagogue and the Abraham Zacuto Luso-Hebraic Museum stand on the street that once was Tomar's Jewish Quarter, or Juderia, a few blocks north of the grand square. The synagogue is small: the sanctuary is 31 by 27 feet, supported by four slender columns topped by pointed arches. The style includes elements of late French Gothic and Italian Renaissance. The exterior is simple stucco, probably not original. (Since I have not been there, I base my descriptions on the report of my friend Michelle, on the documentation and photos she brought back, and on Don A. Halperin, *The Ancient Synagogues of the Iberian Peninsula*, Gainesville: University of Florida Press, 1969.)

The brochure from the Tomar synagogue gives its construction date as 1430 to 1460—that is, just at the time when the Abravanel family lived in Lisbon. This makes it the oldest in Portugal. While the community never totally lost the tradition that this building had been the synagogue, the ritual bath was only rediscovered and excavated in 1985. Coins and pottery vessels from the excavation also date it from the mid-fifteenth century. Evidence about the Tomar Jewish community is based on excavations of the synagogue and the ritual bath and on various grave markers. The brochure cites the gravestone of a Rabbi Joseph of Tomar who died in 1315, suggesting that the community predated the synagogue by at least half a century.

The history of the synagogue after the forced conversion of 1497 begins when it was converted to a prison. Later, it may have been a part of the town hall or a chapel. In 1885, it was a hay loft and by 1920 was a grocery warehouse. At this point, preservationists identified it and managed to make it into a national monument; their efforts were supported by the efforts of Samuel Schwartz, a German engineer who rediscovered evidence of secret Judaism in Portugal early in the century. Schwartz began to clean and restore the building at his own expense, and a little later, in the 1930s, the building became a museum.

I know of no detail that directly represents the presence of the five generations of the Abravanel family (Samuel, Judah, Isaac, Isaac's sons Judah and Samuel, and Judah's son Isaac) in Portugal. The closest items listed in the Tomar Museum's brochure are a stone from the fourteenth-century Great Synagogue of Lisbon, where one would assume that the Abravanels worshiped, and a few partially readable gravestones. Today, in Lisbon, there are traces of the Jewish Quarter, but the current Lisbon synagogue dates only to 1902. The major fifteenth-century earthquakes in Lisbon sometimes triggered anti-Jewish riots; destruction of Jewish buildings not accomplished by the earthquakes was accomplished by the mob.

Above all, Tomar is famous as a center for the order of the Knights Templar, whose fortified castle is the major attraction of the town. Do the Knights Templar have anything to do with the Jews? According to the Templar-obsessed hero of *Foucault's Pendulum*, "The Templars have something to do with everything." Eco balances this idea with the statement: "If someone brings up the Templars, he's almost always a lunatic" (Umberto Eco, *Foucault's Pendulum*, New York, 1989, pp. 312 and 354). In my own defense, I wouldn't have thought of this if a Spanish acquaintance hadn't connected Jews with the Templars in a rather startling way: hearing that we were Jewish, he looked at us in amazement, having never laid eyes on a Jew, and then asked if we knew about the Knights Templar, considering both us and the Templars to be strange and exotic sorts, hanging on from the conspiracies of the Middle Ages. Even in view of this interchange, I wouldn't try to link Jews and Templars outside the context of Tomar, combining best-in-class Templar castle and oldest Portuguese synagogue. Since I have decided to do this lunatic thing, here are a few reasons why Jews might be associated with Templars:

- First, the Templars' original claim of ownership and exploration of Solomon's Temple may give a boost to any theory trying to connect them.

- Second, following the characters in Eco's novel, who seem to serve as ironic mouthpieces for his very well-researched though rather oddball theories, you can also associate Templar philosophy (secret and perhaps lost) with the esoteric cabalistic speculations first of Jews and later of Christians.

- Third, the Knights Templar, and their entire organization, like the Jews and their religion, were victims of Inquisitorial politics, in a persecution just as ruthless and just as self-seeking as Torquemada's Inquisition. In the early fourteenth century, at the time of this persecution, the Templars may have been wiped out— but they continue to exist in legend, theories, and fiction such as *Foucault's Pendulum.*

If you follow Eco, you can consider it significant that the Rosicrucians and the Masons borrow both from cabalistic sources and perhaps from the Templars. You can trace common threads in alchemy, Byzantine mystery religions, Catharism, Arab mysticism, and Templar contacts during their years in Jerusalem. You can consider it significant that several centuries after the Templars lived in the Marais quarter of Paris, the same neighborhood became the Jewish quarter. For some lovers of the occult and the obscure, these and similar coincidences may be enough to prove a connection. Odd bits of lore with a partially historical basis seem to receive plenty of attention. Above all, since the late eighties, when Eco's fictitious conspiracy brought together the numerous devotees of Templar associations and theories, the World Wide Web has provided vast resources linking the lovers of similar theories, so that simple Web searches now allow access to new speculations and manias with every scan. Enough of this—I'd love to see both the Templar castle and the synagogue of Tomar.

The trickle of Jews into Portugal developed into a major stream of immigration in 1492, as Jews exiled from Spain settled there. The hopes that they had of continuing Jewish life in an Iberian setting quickly disappeared in 1497, when the king forced their conversion and drove Jewish practice underground. The people of modern Portugal conserve a memory of secret Jews, who either gradually escaped to other environments or gradually lost most of their knowledge of their ancient religion.

Some individuals and families in Portugal up until this century, especially in out-of-the-way villages, preserved a tradition of being crypto-Jews, though they retained little actual Jewish belief or ritual; by most definitions they practiced the Catholic religion. A brief effort to reconvert them to modern Judaism took place in the 1920s, but failed in the face of twentieth-century totalitarian government. Current Portuguese consciousness of their country's past relationship with Judaism is apparent on the World Wide Web. Some Web sites describe Portuguese activities and publications that took place in 1997 to memorialize the forced conversions five hundred years ago.

THE CASTILIAN COURT AND
THE JEWS IN SEGOVIA

Isaac Abravanel and his family fled from Portugal back to Castile, his family's land of origin, in 1483. After escaping the wrath of the King of Portugal, he expected to retire, watch his investments, and become a full-time writer. For a while, he lived near the border, evidently tending his Portuguese finances via secret messengers, possibly transferring assets to safer places, and concentrating on the biblical commentaries that he had neglected in favor of the life of a court official. However, his administrative skills were not a secret in Castile—within a few months of his arrival across the border, Queen Isabella summoned him to her court at Segovia.

Isabella was in need of all the fund-raising she could find. She had debts left over from the civil wars that preceded her inheritance of the crown, and she and King Ferdinand were engaged in an expensive war to take the territory of Granada from the last Moorish rulers on the peninsula. Abravanel joined several Old and New Christian court officials (by this time, several generations removed from Judaism) and one important Jewish figure, Abraham Senior, on her staff. During the years from 1483 until 1492, he helped raise money for debt payment, for financing the successful campaign for Granada, and for support of the voyage of Christopher Columbus. His vast fortune played an important role in his effectiveness: remember that in this era, distinctions between private and public funds were nothing like those we have today. Monarchs accepted loans, supported speculative joint ventures, and solicited cash gifts. In return, the royal recipients of these private funds dispensed the right to collect taxes or conferred other unlimited powers over lands, money, or people that our government today would retain for itself, to be performed openly with due process of law.

Growing Anti-Jewish Sentiments

Between the Abravanel family's departure in the early 1400s and their return to Castile in 1483, the situation of Jews and of New Christian descendants of converted Jews had steadily deteriorated. I have described how the economic situation of faithful Jews suffered under high taxes and reduced opportunities, and how Christian tolerance for Jews steadily decreased. Conversion at first opened opportunities for New Christians, but jealousy of their rapid political, social, and business successes quickly transferred religious antipathy into a new racism. Toward the end of the reign of King Juan II, riots against New Christians broke out in Castile. His son King Henry IV, whose reign began in 1453, was weak, unpopular, and perceived to favor the New Christians over established noblemen.

In 1449, riots began in Toledo in response to an act by the prime minister, Alvaro de Luna, a New Christian. Luna had levied new royal taxes. Old Christians attacked the property of another New Christian, a tax farmer, who was responsible for collecting these taxes. Pedro Sarmiento, the commander of the castle of Toledo, tortured confessions from several prominent New Christians and burned them at the stake for secretly practicing Judaism. Sarmiento then stated vastly generalized accusations against the city's New Christians, claiming that they had infiltrated city administration and achieved terrifying power over Old Christians. His statutes, which the King later revoked, were the first laws that restricted legal privileges to those who demonstrated purity of blood— that is, freedom from any Jewish ancestry. "These events firmly underscored the popular conviction that conversos were secret Jews and that their heresy was appropriately punishable by both church and civil authorities" (David M. Gitlitz, *Secrecy and Deceit: The Religion of the Crypto-Jews,* Philadelpia: Jewish Publication Society, 1996, pp. 13–15).

During attacks on the Jewish community during Holy Week of 1452, Juan's heir Henry listened to complaints from two representatives from the Jewish community and attempted to order the protection of the Jews from the mob. Despite his goodwill, he never seems to have been stro enough to effectively shield them. Furthermore, Henry IV had a liki for underdogs, and this included not only Jews, but also Moors and oth outsiders.

The growing demand for tests of racial purity was hotly debated in Castile at this time. Old Christian nobles insisted on racial purity. An alternate view was held by the churchman Juan Torquemada and was generally accepted by theologians elsewhere. Torquemada said that injustice and heresy characterized the trials of New Christians in Toledo in 1449. He blamed those who set up the trials: their racist actions, he stated, amounted to heresy because in their distinction between different classes of Christians, they failed to accept the power of baptism. He pointed to a fundamental doctrine that baptism could change any person, even a Jew, into a Christian, with equal opportunity for salvation and all the spiritual benefits of the religion. He thus described the trials and other attacks on New Christians as the work of "agents of the Devil" who "used the Devil's tactics." The trials were unjust and illegal, he pointed out, because the judges personally hated the conversos and had something to gain from convicting them. Furthermore, the judges trusted testimony from clearly biased witnesses, accepted involuntary confessions extracted by torture, reached their verdicts in haste without appropriate delibera-tion, and then hastily executed the victims. (The arguments of Torquemada, who was incidentally the uncle of the later Inquisition leader Thomas Torquemada, are summarized from Netanyahu's *Inquisition*, pp. 235–238.)

During Henry IV's reign, many nobles rose up against him, intrigu-ing with foreign enemies and opportunists. At times Castile experienced outright civil war; rebels fought the king's men and destroyed and sacked Castilian cities, especially the king's favorite, Segovia. The civil war had another root cause: disagreement over the successor of the king. Henry IV had two half-siblings, Alfonse and Isabella, and a daughter, Juana. First his half-brother became the pawn of the nobles who challenged his authority by attempting to recognize the half-brother as king instead of Henry. After Alfonse's death in 1468, Isabella challenged Henry and his daughter. After military and personal humiliations, Henry finally gave in and recognized Isabella as his heir, bypassing his daughter. Simulta-neously, various challenges shook the power of the kings of neighboring Aragon. Neither faithful Jews nor New Christians could achieve a state of security in this atmosphere, where no stabilizing leadership was avail-able to counter mob violence and racism.

Segovia in the Fifteenth Century

Throughout the century, Segovia was an important seat of the court, as it had been in many previous eras of Spanish history—Roman, Visigoth, and medieval rulers had all appreciated the security of its special geography. Segovia underwent much building, especially under Henry IV, who considered it his favorite city, and later, under Isabella. Segovia had been a place where Jews lived and served. The Jewish community had suffered in the riots of the 1390s. In 1412, under the notorious anti-Jewish laws of Queen Catalina, the Juderia moved from one location to another, which also caused financial hardship.

A new situation emerged after 1416, as Jewish life was suppressed: at least one of the synagogues was confiscated as early as 1420. As in other Jewish communities, conversos were mixed up in the Jewish quarter with Jews who remained faithful. At first, there was little notice taken of the semi-committed way that recently converted Christians practiced their new religion mixed up with their old religion. Many families actually had both Jewish and Christian members, who often still viewed themselves as Jews. Intermarriage with Christians occurred mainly between wealthy Jews and Spanish upper classes. New Christians over time began to enjoy their freedom to rise, and among them the preponderance of tax farmers and administrators led to fear.

Segovia, as Henry IV's favorite city, was much affected when the nobles attempted to depose him and put Alfonse on the throne. In a major campaign, the rebels violently took the city and, by destroying important buildings and quarters, took revenge on Henry. Jews, as always, were a target, because they seemed to back the legitimate ruler and then be the victim or scapegoat of the rebels. After the succession was settled, anti-Jewish violence nevertheless continued uncontrolled. Riots in 1473 burned New Christian neighborhoods of Segovia. "When the Marquis of Villena took advantage of the 1473 riots to take control of the city of Segovia, the converso and Jewish leadership assisted in turning the city, with its castle and resources, over to Isabel, and in trying once again to make peace between her and her half-brother Enrique. Once again Jews and conversos were caught in the middle" (Gitlitz, p. 16). More restriction on Jewish freedom led to the closing of walled-off ghettos, badges, social restrictions, and barring from civil office. This situation also probably paved the way for Isabella's acceptance of the Inquisition a few years later, when her power was fully cemented.

By the 1480s Segovia experienced terrible violence against native

Jews, converts, and Jewish refugees who had come there to escape from persecution elsewhere on the peninsula. The high court officials Abraham Senior and his son-in-law Meir Melamed, who lived in the community, attempted to protect the Jews and refugees. Among those living as Christians, the secret practice of Judaism was no longer as easy as it had been: "Occasionally, particularly in the years just prior to the Expulsion, groups of Judaizing conversos joined a particular religious house (such as the Jeronymite monasteries of Guadalupe near Caceres or La Sisla in Segovia) so that they could maintain some measure of crypto-Jewish community life in the shelter of the monastery walls" (Gitlitz p. 87).

When the politically motivated marriage of Ferdinand of Aragon to Isabella of Castile finally consolidated power in both kingdoms, there was at last an unchallenged monarchy. After Henry IV died in 1474, Ferdinand and Isabella began with a mop-up of the residual problems caused by the independence that strong rebel nobles had been enjoying. Under the influence of strong church leaders, they were beginning to agree to the institution of a national Inquisition, directed at the suspected unfaithful among the ranks of New Christians. They set a goal of strength and conquest, attacking Granada and developing commercial potential in their own realms.

In this atmosphere, Isaac Abravanel, a refugee from Portugal, was called out of his contemplative life as a writer to serve at court. He started with an appointment as a tax farmer, for which he needed both the experience to do the accounting and organize the collections, and also a large fortune to back up his promise to the throne, as he had to commit to paying the agreed-upon taxes whether or not he actually collected them. Either he had escaped from Portugal with a substantial fortune or his nephew Joseph, who came out later, had brought his uncle's money out for him.

Although the monarchs had a single court, there were various separate governments for various separate political kingdoms of which they were together or separately the rulers. In Castile, particularly, Ferdinand developed new economic policies and practices to improve the country. He relied on Abraham Senior, Senior's son-in-law Meir Melamud, Luis Santangel, and later Isaac Abravanel, who had the know-how to change the accounting system and impose heavy taxation in new and creative ways. General economic changes had enabled the growth of taxes from the beginning of the reign—changes that were partly due to the actions of the monarchs and partly to trends beyond their control. In the north, the sheep and wool industry was the focal point of change, particularly in the area of new policy for the enclosure of land, in restrictions on associated common rights to graze and to move sheep between seasonal pastures, and in industrial development of better-quality wool weaving. Royal control of huge fairs, development of new roads connecting important cities, new power over the collection of funds from the church, and new regulations and systematic development of uniform commercial codes all contributed to the centralization of power.

Most important, the ability to run this expanding enterprise derived from enormous improvement in the systems of royal revenue tracking and tax collecting. While tax increases are never popular, the monarchs inspired grass-roots support by stressing the need to fund the enormously expensive campaign against the Moors in Granada. In order to tax the clergy, they obtained the pope's blessing, both spiritual and financial, for the endeavor. (This coincided with other direct powers, such as the right to appoint churchmen and to direct certain church activities, particularly, replacing the church-based Inquisition with the Spanish National Inquisition.) They reorganized the treasury and improved the collection of both "ordinary" taxes on large landowners and industry and "extraordinary" taxes, which were mainly collected from the poorest sectors of society. They expanded the number of fairs and cities that had to pay excise tax on cloth; they taxed grain, wine, and oil; and they regulated the movement of sheep. The monarchs made use of the skills of Senior and Abravanel in carrying out this major restructuring. The changes were so effective that from 1479 through 1504, collections increased by 377 percent. In sum, the monarchs revolutionized the treasury to their own advantage and to the terrible disadvantage of commercial interests and poor, ordinary people. Senior, Melamud, and Santangel had already made a lot of these improvements in the tax system when Abravanel arrived. (Information on the new Castilian economics is based on Stephen Haliczer, *The Comuneros of Castile,* Madison: University of Wisconsin, 1981, pp 50-55.)

A MODERN TOURIST'S SEGOVIA

Ferdinand and Isabella's success at combining the various kingdoms of Spain, taming the often-rebellious nobility, and moving toward a more modern state all contributed to marginalizing Segovia's importance—and thus preserving much of its medieval charm and character, and making it a good choice for a trip in search of historic places. Segovia's two streets with the name "Old Juderia" and "New Juderia" reinforce the impression that you can guess how it was when Isaac Abravanel walked here.

Like Toledo, Segovia stands on a hilltop, its old city walls intact and
many other features just as they were in the fifteenth century. Its numerous Romanesque churches remain as they were then. Henry IV lovingly
beautified the city—though his vengeful enemies destroyed much that
he had built. The most dramatic monument today was already ancient
when Isaac Abravanel arrived in Segovia: the Roman aqueduct, which
obviously stood there throughout the Middle Ages. The aqueduct carried
water across the deep valley that protects the town on the west, spanning
a huge open plaza now a part of the lower town. The keystone arches
appear to stay up by some sort of magic: no mortar holds the huge dressed
stones in place, and the tiers of arches are astonishing in their solidity.
Guidebooks mislead you that this aqueduct has been in continuous use
for two thousand years. While it was in use until twenty or thirty years
ago, this was not without interruption. Specifically, in 1072, a Moslem
raid pulled down thirty-six of the aqueduct's arches, and as a result, the
ancient structure was little more than a ruin throughout the time that
I am writing about. Queen Isabella, at the end of the fifteenth century,
had it repaired and restored to working order, but this was after the
departure of the Jews.

The tourist attractions of this city stabilized long ago; since many
of the narrow streets of the high, walled center continue to be for
pedestrians only, you feel a kinship with previous generations of sightseers
whose goals were the same as yours. In the cathedral museum in Segovia
were a collection of views of the city at various times in the past, which
I suspect were meant as souvenirs for tourists before the invention of
postcards, compact cameras, and camcorders. These etchings reinforce
the sense that little has changed.

We spent a day walking around the town, starting at Segovia's bus
station. The bus ride from Madrid had been a pleasant hour and a quarter
trip. First, the road led us through city traffic and then on into rougher
and rougher country, until we went through a tunnel and emerged in
a land of very rocky pastures with sheep and horned cattle, but little
vegetation. Finally, we reached the bus station in the lower town, which
appears newer than the medieval city on the hill. Actually, the population
of Segovia today is slightly less than it was five hundred or six hundred
years ago, suggesting that little of the area is newly urbanized.

Segovia's cathedral is elaborate, very late Gothic with three stories
of stone carvings. The cathedral's three-tiered design uses symmetrical
buttresses, each topped by a decorative peak. Its large bell tower seems
almost out of proportion to the soaring Gothic structure. The cathedral
walls and towers glow in Segovia's clear and extraordinarily beautiful light,

which enhances the natural reddish-gold color of the stone. Inside, the chapels are rather uninteresting, painted in white and gold baroque or rococo elaboration, and separated from the aisles by heavy metal grilles. Instead of a row of columns, the cloister has Gothic tracery in the form of a series of arches, like church-aisle windows without the glass, all very lace-like and graceful. Also in the cathedral museum we saw three Incunabula: fifteenth-century printed books. They occupy a glass case below a wall display of elaborate churchmen's vestments. One book is elaborately hand-illuminated, one decorated with blue and red capital letters, and one illustrated during the printing process with simpler woodblock images. Their pages are cream-colored, not at all as yellowish and fragile as I would expect. Later, we walked past a building not far away on which a plaque marked the site of Segovia's first print shop, with commemorative dates: 1482–1982.

The early monarchs of Castile evidently loved Segovia, not only for its beauty but also for its security. The Alcazar, or castle, stands at the craggy east end of town, separated from the main town by a startling crevasse that serves as a moat. The walls of the town would have been only one of its many defenses, and it would have been very difficult for anyone to climb into this castle. It has been frequently remodeled to meet the taste of its numerous regal owners. Deep in the cellars are stones said to resemble those of the first-century B.C.E. Roman aqueduct that supplied water to the walled fortress-like city until twenty or thirty years ago. One guidebook suggested that even before the Romans, Celtic inhabitants used this site. The latest remodeling was apparently after a fire around one hundred years ago.

The castle's tallest point is an ancient keep with a flat roof and crennelations. After a rather strenuous climb up taller-than-normal stairs, we looked over the castle's courtyards and turrets, the walls of the city, the cathedral and church towers, and off into the stark, mountainous landscape in the vivid October sun. These turrets are mainly roofed by pointy slate peaks, which give it a romantic fairy-tale look; perhaps this style was exaggerated to meet the expectations of travelers on the nineteenth-century grand tour, or perhaps it was due to the taste of the renaissance monarchs, who continued to use it even after they moved the capital to Madrid. Inside, there are rooms with *mujedar*, or Arabic plaster carvings, and gilt decorations, Flemish tapestries, Renaissance chests, beds, and chairs, a number of suits of armor for men and horses, and a nineteenth-century pair of thrones. Both from a distance and close up, I think it's in the spirit that romantic writers intended when they talked about castles in Spain.

Segovia has somewhere between twelve and thirty Romanesque churches, depending on which guidebook you read; most use the same warm stone in shades of peach, rose, and pink. Several of them have impressive multistoried bell towers and unusual wraparound side porches with rows of columns. The capitals appear once to have been beautiful and imaginative but have mainly crumbled. In the late afternoon as we hurried to make the 6 P.M. bus back to Madrid, one wall of a yellowish building was reflecting the late afternoon sun onto the wall of a church, causing it to look positively golden.

Now I see the beauty of the Romanesque churches differently than I did at times in the past because I know more history, especially Jewish history, and sometimes I look at the carvings of saints and the holy family while imagining how Jewish beholders—or new and diffident converts— may have seen them at the time when they were made. I have always seen them with my father's eyes. He said that he could never appreciate Christian art because each church procession in his village, when displaying icons and saints' statues, was a potential time for an attack on the Jews, particularly any Jew who looked at the statues. I wonder if the Jews of the Middle Ages similarly viewed the artistic spirit springing from the same church sources as the terrifying threats of anti-Jewish violence.

Five synagogues once served the Jews of Segovia, but today not a single building serves as a monument or museum to commemorate the medieval Jews of the city. In 1899, a fire totally destroyed the thirteenth-century Corpus Christi church, once a synagogue, and the subsequent renovation destroyed any remaining evidence of what it had been. Now the only trace of the Jews seems to be in the names of the two streets, the old Juderia and new Juderia. These streets are still steep, narrow, and winding, as they must have always been.

While we were searching for the Jewish streets, at the end of our day of seeing churches, Roman monuments, armor, and slate-roofed turrets, we started to talk to an anglo-Australian couple who were also tourists and who were moderately knowledgeable about medieval Jews in Spain and England. The woman, who repeatedly classified herself as an atheist, felt that all religion was harmful, and that all people should intermarry and, as she put it, have coffee-colored children. She compared forced conversions of Jews in the eleventh through nineteenth centuries to the forced removal of Australian aboriginal children up until twenty years ago, intended to make them western as well as Christian, and intended to do them good—an insightful end to our walk through this beautifully preserved city.

Note about the two Juderías: The tourist office will offer you no help in locating them! Consult a detailed map and follow it. The churches named La Merced and Corpus Christi may have been synagogues, though they show no traces of it now.

The Sacrament of Pork

Our commitment to searching for evidence of the former Jewish presence in Segovia did not stop us from going to a restaurant in the Plaza Mayor, across from the cathedral, and trying Segovia's most famous special dish: suckling pig, which guidebooks extol as the most characteristic local specialty. We chose to eat at what I call Anglo-Saxon lunch time: 1:30, rather than 2:30 or 3:00, when the Spaniards stop their morning work, close shops and offices, and take two hours off. As we ordered our meal, only English-accented tourists seemed to be in the beamed-ceiling dining room, which was decorated with heads of deer and mountain goats and attended by uniformed waiters and waitresses. By the time we left, it was filling up with Spanish people; I couldn't tell if they were local or tourists. Only a few tours were in town, and they seemed to leave before lunch time. Besides these, we saw a few scattered small groups. October, though beautiful, is not the season for touring, and we enjoyed a sort of freedom of the streets and monuments.

As for the suckling pig: we received an earthenware dish on which a quarter of the animal—small, but nevertheless rather fat—had been cooked over very high heat. The first bite was delicious: crisp and tender, not stringy like pork from an older animal. No spice or added flavoring or garnish accompanied the tender and rich meat. The other diners around us seemed to be eating it in the same manner; Spanish restaurants do not typically serve vegetable side dishes. As the centerpiece of a meal, though, the dish seemed rather boring, like many unspiced Spanish specialties.

As a curious eater with totally American habits, my decision to order pig was untroubled by the history of the dish. But as I ate, I thought of the symbolism of eating pork in public, which developed first as a symbol of Jewish observance, and later as a kind of test of New Christians of Segovia and other parts of Spain. Before the mass conversions and resulting social pressure, Christians already had used pork as a way to taunt observant Jews. During anti-Jewish riots, Jews caught by the mob might be forced to eat pork (of course, this wasn't the worst the mob could do). Before the violent conversions and Inquisitorial activities of the fourteenth and fifteenth century, medieval laws in some Spanish areas targeted Jewish financial activity by the specification that certain contracts became valid only when all parties had shared a dish of pork. During the Inquisition, Christians began to perceive pork as a kind of litmus test of sincere conversion—when the observant Jews were gone, Jewish food attitudes remained as a way to recognize and persecute unfaithful converts, and avoiding pork became the most widely recognized of these attitudes.

The cookbook author Claudia Roden suggests even further connections between my lunch and the history of Spain: she attributes the special Spanish way of cooking suckling pig to Marranos, who demonstrated how Christian they were by applying the traditional Jewish way of preparing a lamb to cooking a pig instead. She describes a further Marrano tradition of hanging a ham out in front of the house to emphatically demonstrate their assumed faith (C. Roden, *Book of Jewish Food.* New York: Knopf, 1997, pp. 223 and 386).

For most of the Middle Ages, Jewish food in Spain was much like the food I have discussed in my description of contemporary France. Within ritual restrictions, Spanish Jews' food resembled their Christian neighbors' food. Poor Jews naturally ate basic local food, using grain and bread as staples and rarely enjoying meat. The Jews of both Islamic and Christian Spain acquired a taste for many of the foods brought to Spain by the Moslems: rice, citrus fruits, almonds, dates, and the expensive, increasingly popular sugar cane. They incorporated typical Mediterranean produce such as olives, pomegranates, quinces, eggplant, chick peas, and other fruits and vegetables. However, they viewed the staples as a rather simple list: Rabbi Solomon ben Adret, who lived in Barcelona in the thirteenth century, listed a Jewish diet as "meat—even if the latter was not a daily food—fish, bread, cheese, eggs, and soup" (Cooper, *Eat and Be Satisfied*, p. 127).

Wealthier Jewish merchants participated in the spice trade and thus no doubt used the rare and valuable black pepper, cinnamon, and ginger. Saffron was a preferred spice and always a luxury, as it still is in today's southern Spanish rice dishes. Rabbi Adret, in the passage quoted here, warned that some shops might adulterate it. Poorer salesmen sold a few spices in marketplaces or at fairs; one was Diego Arias, a convert who later rose to be the chief financial officer of Henry IV in mid-fifteenth-century Castile, but who began his life as an itinerant spice salesman.

"To draw his crowds, he juggled and sang Moorish songs," according to Henry's biographer (Townsend Miller, *Henry IV of Castile*, Philadelphia: Lippincott, 1972, p. 17).

Among the more ordinary Spaniards, food habits attained new symbolism as indicators of Jewish identity and Jewish background after 1391. After the mass conversions to Christianity, the majority of converts at first continued to eat as they had in the past. No one seems to have told these inexperienced converts to do differently: conversion sermons dealt with loftier topics of dogma and theology, and thus former Jews continued to maintain the seemingly unimportant differences. They observed familiar customs, such as ritual slaughter, food taboos, or special holiday and Sabbath meals, which derived from Jewish laws, and continued to buy food and wine from observant Jewish merchants. Functionally, these distinct eating habits had separated members of the Jewish community from their neighbors by preventing shared meals, and thus they continued almost incidentally to distinguish the converts and their descendants. One New Christian told the Inquisition that while he practiced Christianity and even prayed "to the pot of pork," he could "never wipe out the lineaments of a *confeso (converso)* or lose the name of a common old Jew'" (Y. Baer, *A History of the Jews in Christian Spain*, v.2, p. 311).

Sabbath customs and meals were especially important in the relationship between Jews and converts. As in modern-day Judaism, Friday was a day of preparation, cleaning, and cooking, while Friday night and Saturday were times of ritually imposed rest. The traditional Saturday noon meal in Jewish medieval Spain could not involve lighting a fire. Its contents varied among several choices: hard-boiled eggs, a chicken stuffed with "minced meat, meatballs, and kneaded dough, all garnished with the yolks of eggs and well cooked under the ashes," or some type of stew, often in an earthenware or iron pot that could be kept hot or reheated, following the practice considered to respect the Sabbath (Cooper, p. 104). There were many variations of Sabbath stew, some using dairy products and some using meat. Many included onions, oil, chick peas, and grain. These stews, often called *adafina* (from an Arab word), became a kind of touchstone in the Christian view of Jewish behavior.

New Christians frequently continued to eat these traditional stews without lighting a fire, and might eat meat when their new Christian faith ordered Friday to be a fish day. Before the expulsion, converts could share Sabbath meals with unconverted Jewish friends or relatives. The backsliders also continued pre-Sabbath observances such as bathing, putting on clean clothes, or blessing their children. When zealous Christians took issue with these practices, a number of measures could conceal the "Judaizing" practices. Some families prepared two meals, a fish meal for their public/Christian friends, servants, or neighbors to see, and a secret Jewish meal with associated rituals. During the fifteenth century, various satires made consumption of *adafina* a distinguishing Jewish trait and used it to caricature Jews or Judaizing New Christians.

A variety of rabbinic discussions of food issues illustrate the relationship of faithful Jews and converts during the years before the expulsion. A number of these texts deal with kosher wine, because converted Jews often attempted to continue to use kosher wine in their secret or semi-secret Jewish practices. By the 1400s, the laws about kosher wine very specifically prohibited non-Jews from participation in its preparation or even from handling it, thus leading to many questions about whether, by contact, a converted Jew caused it to no longer be kosher. The record of concern with kosher wine seems to have been more on the Jewish side than on the Christian side, although a few references from the Inquisition mention Jewish wine makers who visited New Christian homes to make wine or to converts' consumption of kosher wine (Gitlitz, p. 549).

The cooking of royal Catalonia and Aragon, like their other high cultural achievements, was particularly recognized during the fifteenth century. At the court of Ferdinand and Isabella, the Abravanel family would have enjoyed a standard of cuisine that rivaled that of Italy, the world's leader in splendor and luxury—that is, if they ate with the court. Elaborate Renaissance banquets provided huge numbers of dishes, elaborate preparations of meat, and a wealth of rich pastries. Aragonese and Catalan cuisine of the time probably surpassed the French, who had not yet achieved the culinary leadership that they later developed. I have never seen any indication of whether the Jewish courtiers separated themselves at royal banquets, whether there were concessions made to their dietary laws, or whether they refrained from dining with the rest. In any case, the monarchs ate well, and Isabella believed in good food—she may have been the first mother in history to succeed in spoiling her children with too much sugar. This came about because sugar was such an expensive luxury at the time, that her expenditures for sugar for the children figured as a notable line item in her household budgets—the crown prince alone ate sweets each year whose cost would have maintained a soldier in arms during that time. Few other mothers of the time could afford such indulgence of their offspring.

Inquisition and Expulsion

To begin this section, I want to consider how the memory of the Spanish Inquisition persists in our current popular culture. On TV and in the movies, characterizations of the Inquisition play on underlying popular associations of torture and cruelty, but usually in a glib sort of way. In a magician act I saw on TV, the patter about a card trick began: "I am Torquemada, and I will torture this card." In film, Mel Brooks's *A History of the World Part I* (1981) has a musical-comedy treatment of the Spanish Inquisition with Yiddish-speaking victims, the synchronized swimming nuns, and a singing Grand Inquisitor who quips: "Torquemada—you can't torque 'im outta anything."

An episode of *Monty Python's Flying Circus* (BBC, 1970, still playing on PBS) invokes the Spanish Inquisition repeatedly. Each few-minute skit ends with someone, taken unaware, saying, "Well, I wasn't expecting the Spanish Inquisition," at which point three men in red capes (two wearing Cardinal's hats, one in a World War I aviator's helmet) abruptly appear, saying: "Nobody expects the Spanish Inquisition." The skits themselves are totally unrelated to one another or to the Spanish Inquisition, in typical Monty Python style.

In a more serious Hollywood history film, *The Captain from Castile* (1947), the evil and self-serving Inquisitor of Jaen accuses the captain, played by Tyrone Power, and his family of "heresy." In the name of religion, the Inquisitor then has them all arrested, tortures and kills Tyrone Power's little sister, steals all his money, marries his beautiful fiancée, and pursues him as he escapes from prison and joins the

315

exploration and conquest of Mexico. The plot is not entirely inaccurate, the drama holds your attention, and the photography on location in Mexico is magnificent. However, the film carefully avoids any mention that the Inquisition may be persecuting characters because of a current or former relationship to Judaism.

In spite of such references, the Inquisition occupies a rather small place in popular imagination today because it is too complicated. The evident fact that the most cruel and barbaric acts were done in the name of a religion that is now respected just doesn't lend itself to popular treatment. In the eighteenth century, the Inquisition persecuted English Protestant sailors taken prisoner by the Spanish, as well as various mystics and members of dissenting Christian, especially Protestant, sects. At this time, in Protestant countries, the Catholic church was hated and feared. A hundred years ago, when the term "the Black Legend" was still a recognizable reference to horrors that English and Frenchmen had faced, it was easier for the Inquisition to have a strong popular notoriety. Edgar Allen Poe's story "The Pit and the Pendulum" plays on this stereotype of the Inquisition. These much later stories and impressions diverge from the subject of my story.

Modern Jewish literature on the Inquisition, especially scholarly literature, has as a goal to know the following: Were most Inquisition victims secret Jews, and thus martyrs? Or were most of them sincere in their Christianity, and thus victims of racial bigotry? In the first case, the Inquisitors were right, even if over-zealously cruel. In the second case, the Jews of the time were right in considering the converts to be lost to Judaism. Isaac Abravanel warned the converts that they would never be accepted as Christians, that their Jewish heritage would haunt them forever. His sad words seem almost to demonstrate hindsight from his experience in Spain, instead of foresight about the following centuries.

A compromise position suggests that the converts were sincere at the beginning of the 1400s, but returned to Jewish self-identification when the Inquisition re-opened the question of their sincerity, around the 1480s. Another view suggests that the converts were sincere but were given inadequate instruction into important Christian practices like eating pork, crossing themselves, and praying as Christians. Some scholars are more credulous about confessions obtained under torture; others dismiss them. Some say that in Spain, where faithful Jews had a chance to leave, there was less crypto-Judaism, while in Portugal, there was more crypto-Judaism, because the Inquisition was postponed for around forty years after the forced conversions of 1497. The more I read scholarly debates—which use both the evidence of the Inquisition itself and the evidence from contemporary Jewish sources—the more I think these questions will never be resolved. However, I don't admire the Spaniards' jealous preoccupation with destroying the successful New Christians, for acting out their greed for the New Christians' wealth, for begrudging their social and economic position, for wishing to overturn their political successes, and, above all, for looking on them as permanent aliens in an emerging nation.

THE CONTEXT OF THE SPANISH INQUISITION

The Spanish Inquisition was run as an organ of the government. The institution experienced considerable change when national interests replaced the original church interests. It was often out of line with official Catholic doctrine. The first stage of the Spanish Inquisition developed under Ferdinand and Isabella, whose title "Catholic Monarchs" was awarded by the pope to recognize their dedication. The monarchs' loyal churchmen loosely based the new institution on the earlier version of the Inquisition from the early thirteenth century. This had begun with the goal of eliminating the Cathar religion, as described in a previous section about Languedoc. The big change in the 1480s was to make this a national institution, under control of the Spanish monarchy and Spanish churchmen working more or less independently of the pope. While the official motivation of the Inquisition was to be a tool for returning wayward Christians to correct Catholicism, without prejudice, the Spanish fanatics quickly made it a tool for extreme racist persecution outside the boundaries of due process. They violated the norms that set standards of fairness for judicial actions even in that age. The authorities of the church in Rome failed to prevent the Inquisition from becoming a travesty of justice and a tool of the most fanatic Spanish churchmen. Busy with other concerns, they allowed it to serve Spain's national policy rather than church policy.

The Inquisition was obsessed with the slightest symptom of "Judaizing"—that is, any hint that converts, particularly among those who still lived close to Jewish communities, preserved traces of Jewish behavior. As the racism of the Inquisition developed, it viewed all descendants of Jews as still Jewish and attempted to make its point by proving that they engaged in secret or even unconscious Jewish practice. The Inquisition's official purpose was to clarify the religious faith and practice of converts. There is some reason to believe that by its fanatic persecutions, it drove them back to Jewish identity, and thus to Jewish practice, but this cannot be proved. Because of the gap between its rationale and its implementation, the Spanish Inquisition embodied an incredible number of perverse incentives:

- The Inquisition encouraged the naked power of the strong against the weak and provided an incentive for ambitious, politically motivated, and self-serving Inquisitors.
- The Inquisition served the financial needs of the government and monarchy. The fact that all the money, goods, and property of convicted heretics became the property of the state provided a horrendous incentive to the judges to deliver a quick guilty verdict on virtually everyone whose name came up. Such greed gave rise to practices such as convicting dead people in order to obtain their estates from heirs who were themselves innocent of heresy.
- The Inquisition called on the population to offer information without fear of public disclosure or serious critique of truthfulness and thus encouraged denunciations from anyone harboring a grudge against a friend, relative, or neighbor. Pre-expulsion, this opportunity to settle scores and express grudges especially enabled practicing Jews to attack those who had become converts. Both resentful Jews and jealous Christians could get even with converts who enjoyed their new economic and social advantages.
- The Inquisition fed on the sheer racial hatred of the Old Christians. In the terms of medieval Christianity, the Inquisition motivated people to hate the sinner rather than to hate the sin—a violation of Church teachings. In more modern terms it rewarded false testimony based on self-serving prejudice, religious fanaticism, or personal animosity.
- In particular, the Inquistors' hatred of the people whom they tried was unconcealed. A ghastly love of cruelty provided a major motivating force in continuing and expanding the Inquisition over the centuries, as the victims became less and less likely to be crypto-Jews, according to Netanyahu's study, *The Origins of the Inquisition.*

Earlier, I summarized the views of Cardinal Juan Torquemada (the Grand Inquisitor's Uncle) about the injustice of the earlier persecution and false trials of the conversos. Each "work of the Devil" of Juan Torquemada was in effect a perverse incentive; these were repeated and amplified as the Inquisition matured. Overwhelming pressure to convict every accused person gave the whole inquisitorial process a perverse incentive to ignore all contemporary standards of evidence, due process, and justice; to employ torture; and to accept testimony from biased witnesses. Underlying this was the need for the Inquisition to ignore long-existing church policy that once a person became a Christian, he or she was equal to all other Christians, and that to act otherwise was to undermine the foundations of Christianity—that is, to participate in the heresy defined by Juan Torquemada.

Reasonable evidence shows that the Inquisition was the major driving force behind the expulsion, particularly because of the influence of the Grand Inquisitor Thomas Torquemada, Isabella's confessor and strong religious influence, on the monarchs. Thomas Torquemada was responsible for the definition and the shape that the Inquisition assumed. He suggested that it was practical and logical to expel the Jews, who could provide converts and their descendants with a link to their guilty past.

Jewish tradition particularly held Thomas Torquemada responsible for the cold-blooded expulsion. According to a later book of Jewish chronicles by Elijah Capsali, he prevented Isabella from listening when Isaac Abravanel begged her to soften the decision. Capsali reported that Abravanel saw Torquemada hold up a cross and ask if Isabella wanted to repeat the crucifixion by canceling the Edict of Expulsion. Once the faithful Jews were gone, there was nothing left but Torquemada's racism and belief in the taint of "blood." Torquemada's continued role in defining the scope and implacable logic of the Inquisition is undisputed; he ensured that conviction was motivated by the fact that the Inquisition kept the fortunes of the convicted and that even the dead could be dug up, prosecuted, and their heirs deprived of the estates they had left. He defined any opposition as heresy. His obsession was to find "Judaizers"— New Christians who observed any Jewish practice, no matter how seemingly insignificant.

Food and the Inquisition

By the 1480s, the Inquisition became fanatical about every detail of the converts' lives and interpreted personal choices as intolerable evidence of "Judaizing" among the New Christians. The Inquisition and its inform-ers particularly observed converts' behavior at meals on Passover and on major fast days such as Yom Kippur. Before the expulsion, some faithful Jews were even convinced to turn in converts who had asked for help with Jewish rituals. Both Jews and Christians had doubts about whether an individual could belong to both religions, which enabled the Inqui-sition to use the Jews this way. Faithful Jews may also have hoped to keep themselves safe by cooperating with the Inquisition. According to the pronouncements of the Inquisition, a major habit that distinguished Judaizers was whether they cooked and consumed the Sabbath *adafina*, a special stew that I described earlier. Inquisition records disclose that Sabbath food was a commonly confessed sin among those accused of Judaizing, particularly among the women who commonly preserved their old religion by continuing their existing household practices. Refusing to eat pork was another critical sign of heresy, as I have noted.

Continuation of Jewish food habits often involved Jewish festivals. For Passover, some converts continued to eat unleavened bread, which they had to make or obtain from other Jews. Like the other Judaizing, this was tolerated in the early part of the fifteenth century, identified as a dangerous continuation of Jewish practice toward the end of the century, and became grounds for severe penalties when the Inquisition got into full swing—especially after the practicing Jews were expelled from the country. The sixteenth-century Jewish historian Elijah Capsali described such permissiveness toward the crypto-Jews under King Don Juan, who ruled from 1406 until 1454: "Even the Marranos had great freedom. . . . During Passover, they would bake *matzot*, . . . keeping secretly the laws of Passover. . . . All the people, including the king, were aware of this and said nothing" (*The Expulsion 1492 Chronicles*, David Rafael, ed., North Hollywood, CA: Carmi House Press, 1992, p. 3).

In later years, Inquisitors continued to investigate the persistent Jewish practice, during bread-baking, of throwing a small piece of dough into the fire. For more than a century after the expulsion, the Inquisition charged the descendants of Jews with doing this, imposing the most serious of consequences. The Inquisition also questioned servants, family members, and other witnesses about whether those accused of Judaizing had practiced ritual slaughter of birds or beasts, or had removed the blood from their meat or dissected the vein that caused the hindquarter to be unkosher.

The annals of the Inquisition document numerous cases where New Christians denied that an obviously Jewish practice proved that they were reverting. Consider the following converso's story:

> On June 23, 1485, during the "period of grace," a *converso* . . . confessed that when occasion offered (for example, in the course of a journey), he had visited Jewish homes and partaken of Jewish food. He had also observed the Jewish mourning customs by sitting on the floor and eating eggs and fish. [He] asserted that he did not regard this as a specifically Jewish rite: "It was the general custom in the city to do so without concealment, and

no one objected." The inquisitors were not satisfied with this interesting confession. . . . After a trial which lasted six months the accused was burned at the stake in August 1486. (Baer, p. 351, v. 2)

The chronicle of Andres Bernaldez, who lived at the time of the expulsion and was a secretary to the Inquisitor General, illustrates how the Christian hatred of Jews incorporated perceptions of their eating habits. Bernaldez particularly discusses the Jews' "earthen jars of stewed meats, onion and garlic dishes, fried in oil"—that is, the slow-cooked Sabbath meal. He points out that cooking in oil instead of lard is an indicator of Jewish practice—later, this became one of the tests that Inquisitors used to ferret out crypto-Jewish activity. Bernaldez continues: "The meat with oil is a thing that causes a very bad odor to one's breathing. Thus their houses and doors stunk very badly with these dishes. They themselves had the odor of the Jews because of the dishes and because of not being baptized. And given that some were baptized, the character of baptism was so mortified by their credulity, and by their Judaizing, that they stunk like Jews" (*The Expulsion 1492 Chronicles*, pp. 63–64; Cooper, p. 127).

Jewish food and its influence on New Christians became such an important issue that the Edict of Expulsion specified that Jews were guilty of supplying converts with "the unleavened bread and the ritually slaughtered meats with their ceremonies, instructing them on the things they should stay away from, thus in foods as in other matters, for observance of their Law . . ." (*The Expulsion 1492 Chronicles*, p. 190).

GRANADA, 1492

The scene of the final drama of the Jews' expulsion was not in the capital, Segovia, but in the newly conquered city, Granada. Symbolically, the monarchs relocated to their newly conquered territory soon after driving out the Moslem ruler, Boabdil, on January 2, 1492. On March 31, 1492, the Catholic monarchs, Ferdinand of Aragon and Isabella of Castile, signed the official edict of expulsion, giving the Jews until the end of the following July to convert or to conclude their affairs, dispose of their possessions, and depart from the country.

It does not take much imagination to understand that the Jews experienced enormous hardship from the moment the edict was announced—approximately a month after its official signing, or three months before they had to convert to Christianity, to face the death penalty, or to terminate their continued presence in the homes and occupations they had always known. Even the Abravanel family, although one of the most powerful and best-placed in the land, faced great difficulty. The king applied enormous pressure on Isaac Abravanel and his family to convert, in order that Isaac could continue to serve at court. In desperation, the family sent Isaac's grandson to Portugal, where they still had connections. Their intention was to send for him after finding refuge somewhere. Like most of their fellow Jews, they were not certain which country would take them in.

A variety of personalities and interests converged at Ferdinand and Isabella's court. In learning about them, we can see how truth and myth might be mingled in stereotypes and preconceptions about Jews, Christians, and their relationships. It's particularly interesting to understand the extent to which the earlier conversions had led to the presence of many persons of nobility with at least a distant Jewish ancestor—sometimes intentionally concealed. When an individual's ancestry is ambiguous, the lack of knowledge itself can perpetuate a variety of speculation.

The Monarchs

The court of Ferdinand and Isabella in 1492 was triumphantly celebrating the conquest of Granada from Boabdil. They believed in a process of purification of the country, now entirely under Christian rule. Machiavelli discussed the expulsion of the Moors as evidence of Ferdinand's power consolidation. The expulsion of the Jews was a logical next step.

King Ferdinand was an extremely effective administrator and by 1492 had total control of the recently chaotic Castile, as well as of his own ancestral kingdom, Aragon. His challenge was further consolidation of his support among the nobles. Netanyahu suggests that the expulsion of the Jews at least improved Ferdinand's credibility and power base among the common people and thus aided him in controlling the nobles.

Ferdinand himself, according to Jewish tradition and a few other sources, had a Jewish ancestress. Contemporaneous stories told how Isabella manipulated him with taunts about his Jewish antecedents and thus accused him of being a bad Christian. At least some recent scholars feel that the story is credible. Despite this story, most analysts believe that Ferdinand was the driving force behind the Edict of Expulsion.

Queen Isabella had seemed unlikely to become queen during her youth. King Henry IV was her half brother. His daughter was ahead of her in line, followed by her own brother Alfonse. The years before Isabella became queen were filled with violence and civil war. Alfonse, with the support of many nobles, had usurped the throne and then died. Henry IV subsequently was recognized as king again, at least grudgingly, for the rest of his life, but he had to repudiate his daughter in Isabella's favor.

Because of the improbablity that she would be queen, Isabella had not received a regal education and was thus unprepared for all of the responsibilities of administration and decision making. What education Isabella received caused her to have habits of guilt and piety, and she was easily influenced by pretentiously religious men such as her confessor Thomas Torquemada. She believed that the welfare of the kingdom, her personal interests, and the welfare of Christianity were identical. Legend says she promised to rid Spain of the Jewish heretics if ever she did come to power (Roth, *The Inquisition*).

From all evidence, Isabella was a pure Old Christian. Her ancestry included a long series of intermarriages between the various regal houses of the Iberian peninsula with occasional imports from other kings and emperors of Europe.

Jews in the Service of the King

Employing Jews in the service of the king was an old habit of the Spanish Royals: a habit that this administration was trying to break. By the start of the monarchs' joint reign in 1480, Ferdinand, in Aragon, had already almost disposed of the need for Jewish help in this area. In Castile, though, the tradition had not completely gone away, particularly because enormous economic development was occurring and the war in Granada was creating a gigantic demand for funds. At least three Jews were still at court in 1492:

Abraham Senior and his son-in-law Meir Melamud were the most powerful court Jews in 1492. They worked with Abravanel to try to convince the monarchs to back out the expulsion decree. Senior, a man of eighty, gave in at the end and became a Christian, along with his son-in-law. Jewish tradition was generous to Senior and attributed his conversion to a threat that if he insisted on flight, other Jews would be viciously punished. It's a believable story. His role had been enormously important. Though he held the title "Court Rabbi," making him the nominal head of the Jews of Castile, his real importance was in taxation and finance.

Isaac Abravanel. in 1492, had been eight years at the court. His responsibilities had been limited to tax collection, for which he had had ample experience in Portugal, and at which he was apparently quite adept. He had been important in raising funds and using his own funds to assist with the conquest of Granada. While he worked hard, according to his autobiographical notes, to convince the monarchs to change their policy of expulsion, his three audiences with them were unsuccessful, and despite their hope that he would convert, he remained faithful to his religion and departed with all the others.

During Isabella's reign, enormous economic changes had supported the consolidation of power in Castile. Senior had been a major player in the development of better accounting information, which allowed tax farmers to know more exactly who owed and how much. When Isaac Abravanel joined him, he also participated in the development of these new tax-collecting measures.

Explorers and Scientists

Christopher Columbus, too, was at the court of Castile occasionally throughout the spring of 1492, arranging for his voyage and raising money with the assistance of Santangel, Sanchez, and others. Major modern Columbus scholars now refute a former interpretation that he descended from either Spanish or Genoese Jews, insisting that the record of his lower-middle-class Christian Genoese family is indisputable. A few still raise questions; for example: Columbus's immediate descendants destroyed his papers—does this suggest that they wanted to hide something? A generation ago, Cecil Roth offered the following explanation: "Modern Spanish scholars, in a frenzied attempt to vindicate Christopher Columbus as a child of their own country, have evolved the theory that he was in fact a Marrano, and for that reason somewhat secretive as to his origin: and they point to the significant fact that in his will he left money to a Jewish beggar in Lisbon" (Cecil Roth, *The Spanish Inquisition*, London, 1964; originally published 1937, p. 208).

Abraham Zacuto was an important Jewish scientist whose work contributed to the discovery of America. Columbus used Zacuto's astronomical tables during all of his voyages, in order to calculate latitude and predict eclipses; by Columbus's account, on one of his voyages he used the information from these tables to impress the natives in Jamaica by threatening them with an eclipse, which he said was about to punish them for hostile acts toward his crew. When his life as a Jew at court became difficult, Zacuto became the court astrologer and astronomer to the King of Portugal.

As an aside: Zacuto, Santangel, and Abravanel appeared on a medal issued by the Jewish-American Hall of Fame in 1986, for the anniversary of Columbus's first meeting with Ferdinand and Isabella in 1486. According to the *New York Times*: "The new medal commemorates this anniversary and focuses on three Sephardic friends of Columbus who helped make the venture possible: Luis de Santangel, Don Isaac Abravanel and Abraham Zacuto" ("A Medal for Christopher Columbus," Ed Reiter, *The New York Times*, October 12, 1986).

Conversos in the Service of the King

The names Santangel and Sanchez appear on the Discovery Monument in Madrid because of their critical support of Columbus and their efforts in helping the monarchs raise funds for Columbus's first voyage.

Luis Santangel was a descendant of conversos who had served the monarchs of Aragon for several generations and had developed a successful business enterprise in Spain and abroad. In 1492, he was the secretary of the household, a high official with great influence at the court, especially in matters of finance. His family's commercial interests in Genoa had made him an early contact for Columbus: they had been communicating about the proposed exploration since 1486. Santangel became the chief fund-raiser for the voyage; at the last minute, he managed to convince Isabella to support Columbus and to find support, including money from his personal fortune. For this reason, Columbus addressed his first report of the New World to Santangel. The Santangel family exemplifies Jews who had converted in early fifteenth century and thus had experienced a century of Christianity but little or no intermarriage with old Christians. Like other successful New Christians, the Santangels already faced the Inquisitors' fanatic desire to "purify" Spain.

Gabriel Sanchez was also a descendant of a converted Jewish family. His great-grandfather, Alazar Golluf, a Jew, had been the treasurer of the queen of Aragon in the fourteenth century. Shortly after Golluf's death, in 1389, Gabriel Sanchez's grandfather had converted and changed his name, first receiving assurances that the king would not exercise his right to confiscate the property of a Jew who converted to Christianity. (I have mentioned the medieval law that technically defined all the property of Jews as actually belonging to the king, to be confiscated upon their conversion.) The Sanchez family remained a powerful force at court for the next hundred years, and Gabriel Sanchez became a distinguished courtier of Ferdinand of Aragon, accompanying him to Castile to serve the joint court of the Catholic monarchs. By 1492, the Inquisition had already begun to investigate a variety of accusations against Sanchez and his brothers—one of them had escaped and had been burned in effigy.

Thomas Torquemada, another possible descendent of a New Christian grandmother, was the queen's confessor and later Grand Inquisitor. Some say Torquemada was of partial Jewish descent, others deny it. Since he and his family would have had very strong reasons to destroy the evidence, little material remains for scholars and historians today; moreover, their motives for wanting him to be one or the other sometimes overpower the facts. Some Jewish scholars insist that converted Jews were never vicious persecutors and thus feel they must defend his pure Christian blood. Some Christian scholars—especially those under the sway of twentieth-century Spanish totalitarianism—feel it would be unseemly for such an ascetic and religious paragon to have been of Jewish descent and thus defend his pure Christian blood. Other Christians prefer to see him as a Jew and thus blame the victim; other Jews see him as the ultimate traitor among the traitorous unfaithful. In his comprehensive book about the Inquisition, Netanyahu makes a convincing case that at least Thomas Torquemada's uncle, Juan Torquemada, had a Jewish grandmother, who was reasonably well known to his contemporaries.

The Inquisition and the Santangel Family

To define the effect and scope of the Inquisition in its early days, I will describe how it affected the powerful and immensely rich Santangel family, including Columbus's most important supporter, Luis Santangel. Although one of the most influential officials in the court of the Catholic monarchs, Santangel had much to fear in 1492.

The Santangel family became Christians when Jews were hastily converting, in the period from 1391 to 1413. Already rich, prominent, and powerful in their native Aragon, their story demonstrates how conversion conferred enormous benefits. In accumulating wealth and power, they had an advantage over faithful Jews, who had the skills to excel in a changing society but weren't allowed to employ these skills. They also had an advantage over Old Christians, who had social standing but lacked the skills to adapt to new economic conditions. By mid-century, the Santangels were a major banking power, with representatives in Aragon and many of its possessions and trading partners. Individual family members served as royal advisers and financial officials, judges, lawyers, ambassadors, and were beginning to send sons into the Church and to obtain titles of nobility. They arranged marriages with most of the other famous converted families of the realm and, like many families, used only a few first names, so any detailed account becomes confusing as you try to distinguish one Luis or Jaime from another.

The Santangels often had the nerve or influence to ask favors from the crown, which leaves interesting royal documents as a witness to their lives. In one document, dated 1459, the king granted them special permission to dig up the ground beneath a house that had formerly belonged to their grandfather, because they believed that their ancestors had buried their gold and other treasurers there. The Jew who currently owned the house was not offered a share of the loot—this would be shared by the Santangels and the crown. They were, however, supposed to pay for the excavation and restore the house when they were done.

Their power continued to accumulate, but with built-in risks—at least some of the members of the family appear to have maintained ties with their Jewish past. The Inquisition records about the family include both men and women victims. Tradition has it that the original matriarch of the family had in fact resisted the original conversion around 1400. Like all accusations of the Inquisition, we can never know if the unnamed and well-protected accusers were inventing their claims out of spite or political motives, or if the family indeed continued to pray, eat, and act as if they still believed in their old religion.

In any case, members of the family were in trouble with the Inquisition almost as soon as it started in 1480. From 1486 to 1488, Santangels named Martin, Mosen Luis, Gabriel Goncalo, Gabriel, Jaimie Martin, Dononsa, Simon, and Clara Lunel were burned at the stake. Simon and Clara Lunel Santangel were betrayed by their own son. Other family members fled to France, which wasn't persecuting converts at this point, but they were burned in effigy. Dead family members were exhumed and burned as corpses. Needless to say, the Inquisition realized enormous proceeds from all this activity, since the state took a convicted person's property whether the person was living or dead, available for punishment or in exile.

Luis de Santangel himself had one or two rounds with the Inquisitors and even had to appear once in the *Sanbenito*, or hooded garment
of a penitent—that's the one you can see in the Goya painting that looks
like a Ku Klux Klan outfit (not entirely by coincidence). However, the
monarchs valued Luis de Santangel's services enormously: all this time
he was serving at the court of Ferdinand and Isabella as a chancellor
of the royal household, as a tax and custom-duty farmer, and also pursuing
his own financial and banking interests. He was helping to organize the
treasury to fund the war in Granada. He was promoting and funding
the proposals of Christopher Columbus and personally advancing money
to the king—enormous sums of money. He definitely earned his position
on the monument in Madrid!

Evidently, Ferdinand was worried when the Inquisition got closer
and closer to this trusted councilor. During this time, he granted the
Santangel daughters special royal gifts for their marriages and granted
Luis additional high offices and titles. Luis de Santangel's final reward
for all his service was a royal document, dated 1497, exempting him and
his descendants from the Inquisition and guaranteeing their right to
inherit his property. This was a rare exception to the infinite power that
the Inquisition was to have for several centuries to come. Santangel died
in 1505. (The Santangel story is based on Meyer Kayserling, *Christopher
Columbus and the Participation of the Jews in the Spanish and Portuguese
Discoveries*, North Hollywood, CA: Carmi House Press, 1989, Orig. from
1893, and on *The Christopher Columbus Encyclopedia*, v. 2, pp. 600–601.)

Isaac Abravanel was at court with Santangel for most of these years.
In the summer of 1492, as Abravanel prepared to leave Spain, it was
Santangel who paid him 1,500,000 maravadis that the monarchs owed
to him. Abravanel must have known about the trials and persecutions
of members of the accomplished and seemingly successful Santangel
family. His view that converts could never be accepted, and thus could
never be safe, could easily have been influenced by Santangel's difficulties. Perhaps his success at resisting conversion—and accepting all its
short-term material benefits—was strengthened by witnessing what happened to the Santangel family.

THE EXPULSION

The expulsion from Spain was the most important event of the era for
Sephardic Jews, and probably for all Jews. This importance is the focus
of vast amounts of scholarship today. First of all, there is the question

of why Ferdinand and Isabella decided to expel the Jews. In their edict of expulsion, they presented a totally clear reason: they stated that Jews were having a disastrous influence on converts, both by luring them back to Jewish belief and by enabling them to continue in Jewish practice. The expulsion presents the previous remedies that the rulers had tried, such as segregation of Jewish communities, expulsions from particular locations, and the early activities of the Inquisition, and states that these efforts have not been sufficiently effective. The edict held that the community had to take responsibility for the actions of all members and thus all Jews and Jewesses were expelled three months from the announcement, which was dated March 31, 1492. This statement of religious motivation fits into the historic reality in which various churchmen had characteristically been able to become powerful in Spain and in which the Inquisition, under the jurisdiction of the monarchs rather than directly answerable to the pope, was beginning to become a serious force.

Political and social reasons take account of the civil unrest that resulted from the frequent anti-Jewish riots in Spanish cities and of the rulers' desire to consolidate power and decrease the leverage of the various persons of nobility in the kingdom. Jews had been allied with the rulers and the nobility, an alliance that continued to apply to converts; several previous kings—as well as ambitious churchmen—had manipulated anti-Jewish sentiment to control the mob or to sway public opinion. Association of Jews with the previous and unpopular Moslem rulers, and hatred of Jews for other reasons, facilitated such propaganda, which at times diverted attention from injustices propagated by Christian rulers. Without Jews, the Catholic monarchs—who had just conquered the last Moslem kingdom—might have a much more absolute power over their other subjects. By increasing the loyalty of the anti-Jewish lower classes, they may have hoped to reduce the power of the noble classes. In several European societies emerging from the Middle Ages, a regrouping of the power structure between kings and common people increased the ability of kings to rule more absolutely.

An analysis of financial reasons for expelling the Jews or forcing Jewish conversion is complex. While some people then and now have held the view that the rulers wanted Jewish wealth, others have perceived that expulsion would cause economic problems rather than solve them. Fernando del Pulgar, the royal chronicler, regarding the earlier expulsion of Jews from Seville and Cordoba, recorded that "even though the absence of this people depopulated a great part of that land and even though the Queen was notified that commerce was diminishing, she regarded with little concern the diminution of her revenues." She preferred to "cleanse the land of that sin of heresy" rather than worry about money (*The Expulsion 1492 Chronicles*, p. 58).

Contrasts between the various personalities and their influences are also striking and contribute to the sense of drama that surrounded the expulsion. One such contrast differentiates the personalities and philosophies of Isaac Abravanel and Thomas Torquemada: "Torquemada advocated 'cruelty out of love for the human race in order to save it from damnation.' Abravanel, however, believed in the inherent good in men; he was convinced to the last moment that the conscience of the Spaniards would be stirred and that they would try to prevent the expulsion of the Jews" (Gaon p. 9).

Jewish historians writing shortly after the expulsion, as well as modern writers, have noted that Ferdinand and Isabella borrowed heavily from Jews in order to fund the war against Granada and Columbus's expedition. However, the monarchs' exhortations to the high financial advisers Isaac Abravanel and Abraham Senior to convert demonstrate that they had some expectation of keeping them there and somehow paying off the debt. The seizure of Jewish property, both from individuals and from the collective community, did profit the crown, but the loss of a highly productive (and high-tax-paying) part of the community offset this; in fact, departing Jews were forced to pay their taxes for the entire year before being allowed to leave, in order to reduce the loss to the treasury. A relevant comparison: when the king of Portugal was faced with the same choice a few years later, he didn't allow the Jews to leave but converted them forcibly. He specifically stated the financial advantage that he would obtain by keeping them. Historians, in fact, are not in agreement about the long-term impact of the expulsion on Spanish commercial life, which was shortly afterward so greatly affected by the wealth of the New World. If you are looking for a neat historical retribution for a cruel act of thoughtless monarchs, you won't find it here.

The Expulsion from Segovia

As the end of the Jews' stay in Spain neared, Segovia continued to be important to the Jews and played a role in the final drama of expulsion. First, Segovia, in 1490–1491, was the site of an important staged event known as the case of El Nino de La Guardia. In 1490, in Astorga, Benito Garcia, a New Christian from Toledo, was accused of stealing a consecrated host. He confessed under torture and accused others. The trial was held in Segovia, home of Thomas Torquemada, the first Inquisitor General, rather than in the normal jurisdiction of Toledo. A suspect named Yuce Franco was tortured for a year and confessed to killing a child. The prosecutors were undisturbed by the evidence, which was quite sketchy, particularly since *no* child was missing. However, Yuce and alleged accomplices were burned in the "first great auto de fe" in Avila, November 1491. This was a lead in for the expulsion, intended to stir up anti-Jewish feelings in the time just before the expulsion order was made widely known (Gitlitz, p 24).

When the expulsion decree gave Segovia's faithful Jews no choice but to leave, the pain of separation from their roots caused the Jews much suffering:

> . . . a historian of Segovia described the moving scene of "those miserable ones" who filled the fields of the Hosario (site of the Jewish cemetery) visiting and praying at the graves of their ancestors before leaving. Even at such a time "certain zealous religious and secular" Christians could not resist the temptation of going there to preach to the Jews in a last effort to convert them. Some few, indeed, were baptized on the spot, which henceforth was called Prado Santo, but the rest chose exile. (N. Roth, p. 309)

Aftermath

After the expulsion, converts, cut off from practicing Jews and their written traditions, lost practically all detailed information about the practice of Judaism. Ultimately, a few Sabbath rituals, abstaining from pork, eating *adafina* and unleavened bread, a vague memory of kosher slaughtering practices, and a few fasts replaced previous meaningful rituals. The Inquisition itself kept traces of knowledge alive by warning informers of what to look for. The telltale signs of Judaizing appeared in the public announcements of the Inquisition called the "Edicts of Grace." As a result, information about crypto-Jews is somewhat circular. First, crypto-Jewish practice itself relied only on clandestine oral tradition and on the Inquisitor's lists of prohibited and suspicious practices, and kept no records of its own. Second, the Inquisition seems to have directed accused victims to confess to specific "crimes"—often under threat or torture. They also prescribed the content of the testimony of witnesses, who often had dubious motives for offering their cooperation. These questionable Inquisition archives often provide the only source by which modern scholars can construct the practices of the later crypto-Jews. Almost all conclusions about these post-expulsion practices thus rely on testimony that may be true and may be false.

GRANADA TODAY

Granada is a city of contrasts of every period of Spanish history. Moorish, Gothic, modern, and the typical stucco "Mediterranean" architecture that was replicated in colonial California are all present, in famous buildings and in vast hill-hugging neighborhoods of beautiful white homes and hostels. Granada offers the wine bars along the ravine in which the river flows; the memories of Garcia Lorca, the now-revered poet assassinated there by the fascists in the 1930s; the gypsy camps and gypsy cafes with loud music and dancing; and shops selling Washington Irving's *The Alhambra*. While I have always loved French Gothic buildings such as Chartres cathedral, I found the Gothic church where Ferdinand and Isabella are buried to be aggressive and rather unimaginative compared to the graceful beauty of the stucco work, courtyards, stone carvings, hedges, and gardens of the Alhambra, a vast palace that climbs the hills and uses the rushing water of the natural mountain streams to run amazing water effects in a vast array of fountains.

In Granada we suffered from the full fury of summer heat. My daughter and I spent two days in the summer gardens of the upper Alhambra, picking shady spots near bubbling fountains. We experienced the same pleasure as the royal families once did, using the gardens and fountains to relax and escape the heat of the town and its sun-baked pavements. We brought along a book and we simply sat by the fountains and read. From time to time a guided tour with fifty or sixty people would file past us, looking hot and harried, but we enjoyed ourselves. This is another way to gain insight into history if you can: put yourself in the place of the ancient inhabitants. It's particularly important here, as evidence of daily life in a Moorish palace or home has been almost entirely obliterated. While the Moors during their seven hundred years of Spanish experience no doubt built similar palaces for the rulers, and simpler versions for common people, these do not remain. I imagine the wives and daughters of Jewish courtiers and wealthy merchants enjoying similar quiet times next to Moorish fountains.

THE SEPHARDIC DIASPORA

The next centuries were a process of both forgetting and remembering. While those former Jews who remained in Spain slowly forgot Judaism, they held onto small and sometimes ironically insignificant shreds of the tradition of their ancestors. While the exiles always remembered Spain, the details also became more myth than documented historical fact.

After 1492, as the faithful Jews went into exile, the Inquisition continued with terrible consequences for the New Christians. From then on, the term *Marranos* becomes more and more common as a term for New Christians, while the term *Sephardi* applied mainly to the exiles. *Marranos* meant "pigs" in both Spanish and Portuguese. Various writers have come up with clever and well-researched demonstrations that the word may have additional or different roots, but as far as I understand, when the Old Christians called converts or their descendants *Marranos*, they thought they were calling them pigs.

As mentioned earlier in this chapter, faithful Jews found desperate refuge in North Africa, Turkey, Italy, and the Balkans; many died in seeking a place that would have them. The Abravanel family was among a minority who resettled themselves with reasonable success. In addition, some converted families also determined that escape was in their interest, as the Inquisition became more capricious.

A large number of Jews fled to Portugal in 1492, where the king grudgingly accepted a large sum of money to admit them. In 1497, this community had scarcely begun to adapt when the king gave in to pressure from Ferdinand and Isabella and forced all Jews in his realm to convert— both refugees from Spain and long-term inhabitants. The new conversos were thus the most-committed Jews from Spain, who had resisted conversion in 1492 and who had much more determination to try to preserve a secret Jewish life. A defining moment for this Portuguese community was a disastrously violent anti-convert riot in Lisbon in 1506. At this point, Jews who had expected Portugal to be a haven for crypto-Judaism began to seek opportunities to leave the country, often by developing international businesses and planning their escape for years. Their desperation increased in the 1430s, after additional anti-convert events and the institution of the Inquisition in Portugal. In describing the Italian Jewish communities of the next century, we will meet some of them.

Over several hundred years, these former Jews slowly obtained permission to remain in other countries and then to revert to more and more Jewish practice, away from the national Inquisitions of Spain and

Portugal. The identification of Portuguese merchants and financial wizards as Jews became commonplace in the sixteenth century. Individuals coped with political events and international conflicts of the era, offering a variety of skills to emerging nations such as Holland and to colonial endeavors in the New World and Asia. When they were able, they also fled to Moslem lands, especially the Turkish Empire, then at its peak. Portuguese New Christians started out as the richest and most able members of Spain's former Jewish community, and as they fled from Portugal, many became famous. Members of these "Portuguese" families often became well known. Through their contacts with other secret Jews, they developed international banking and trading organizations throughout Europe and in the New World. Portuguese Marranos included a physician of Elizabeth I of England; the Montifiore family of England who came by way of Italy; early Portuguese settlers on the island of Curacao and in other American colonies; the family of the philosopher Spinoza in the Netherlands; and many other Jews who went to Holland or France. While some actively returned to Jewish practice and married only within the community, others assimilated, practiced Christianity, and intermarried.

The history of Marranos in France is particularly interesting. Even before the final decree of expulsion from Spain in 1492, the French King Louis XI had permitted foreign merchants—particularly converted Jews— to live and work in Bordeaux. One successful family of converts named Lopez settled in this region at this time. Most of them were physicians. One woman from this family married a French nobleman and became the mother of the French writer Michel de Montaigne (1533–1592). Nowhere in his famous essays does he mention his Jewish connections, but several passages suggest that he perhaps thought about the experiences of distant cousins who were suffering under the Spanish Inquisition.

During the fifteenth century, the Bordeaux foreign community grew and prospered, because the Inquisition was much less active in France than in Spain. Between 1550 and 1604 a number of official documents recognized the Spanish and Portuguese Marranos' rights to live and own property in this area. At the same time, people called "Portuguese merchants," but in fact known to be secret Jews, began to settle in Bayonne, Biarritz, and elsewhere. By 1632, the Inquisitor of Pamplona issued a complaint about this tolerance for his intended victims. In various French cities, openly Jewish commercial travelers and merchants were allowed back in from time to time. In 1670, there was a brief relaxation, and a few Jews settled in Marseilles but were expelled again in 1682. In 1760, there was again a relaxation, and by 1768 the Jews built a small synagogue and by 1783, founded a cemetery. Jews from the papal territories traded in Montpellier throughout the sixteenth and early seventeenth centuries; they were expelled in 1653, readmitted in 1714, and then allowed to remain.

A few crypto-Jewish families slowly became established in Montpellier. Some had their sons become Catholic priests in order to provide the outward show of compliance with the official religion, while secretly celebrating Jewish marriages, funerals, and holidays. They used a variety of strategies to appear to be Christian—they kept shops open on Saturday, but they would leave a child in charge, who commonly told customers that his father would be back later, and thus they avoided commerce on the Sabbath. Gradually, they dropped various pretenses of Christian life; by 1705, they ceased to have public church weddings before their customary private Jewish ceremonies. After the revolution, the Jews received the rights of citizens, and the separate, secret customs of the Sephardic communities were absorbed into the much more numerous Ashkenazic communities or were assimilated into the mainstream.

In my travels, it has not been my goal to trace the history of the many places where the exiles settled or to interview distant descendants of the Sephardic Jews. If this interests you, I recommend Howard M. Sachar, *Farewell España: The World of the Sephardim Remembered* (New York: Vintage Books, 1994).

The Labels Sephardic and Ashkenazic

One legacy of the expulsion still has importance for modern Jews. What does the term *Sephardi* or *Sephardic* mean? The simple national-origin meaning—Jews whose ancestors lived in Spain before 1492 and followed the Jewish religion with the rituals and practices of this area—doesn't cover the current usage. Conflicting stereotypes of Sephardic Jews exist today, in the modern world:

- First, there is a surviving stereotype of the Sephardic Jews as a kind of aristocracy, possessing education and wealth greater than that of the poor Jews of Eastern Europe, such as my own ancestors. This clearly harks back to the minority of Jews who had the money to escape Spain. It also recalls the forced converts from Portugal who, in the sixteenth and seventeenth centuries, gradually made their way to more tolerant places such as Amsterdam, England, France, Italy, the Turkish empire, and the New World, where they returned to Judaism. The richest and most prominent Jewish families in eighteenth- and nineteenth-century England, America, and France had such a background. In the early twentieth century these superior Sephardic Jews disappeared as a prominent factor in the West (some having converted and assimilated to Christianity, others having intermarried and assimilated with the more numerous Ashkenazim).

A few wealthy and well-educated communities with clear Spanish roots also survived in Moslem cities such as Istanbul, Alexandria, Aleppo, and Baghdad, until the 1950s, when hostility to the foundation of Israel reduced or destroyed them.

• A conflicting stereotype points to the impoverished and backward Sephardic communities that have immigrated to modern Israel from North Africa and Asia Minor. This stereotype originated in the nineteenth century, with the vast fall of the fortunes of Moslem lands and all the inhabitants, including Jews. A century ago, when European charity efforts began to target these communities with educational and other assistance, the distinction between those in need of aid was ignored. Along with descendants of Iberian Jews, they also helped Jews from North Africa, Turkey, Greece, the Balkans, Yemen, Iraq, and so on, whose origins were non-Spanish. The term *Sephardim* was applied indiscriminately to the members of these communities.

• The term also sometimes simply refers to any non-Ashkenazi Jew, thus including modern Italian Jews and others who have no roots in Spanish culture. This also confuses the root meaning of the term *Ashkenazi,* meaning a Jew from Germany or Eastern Europe. In Israel today another term, *Mizrachi,* or Easterners, refers to Jews from places in the Near East, such as Yemen or Iraq.

A reflection of this complexity and possible confusion is the change in customs and culture even among stable, openly Jewish Sephardic communities. Between 1492 and the present, simple cultural practices have experienced many transformations. Modern attempts to reconstruct Sephardic music from before the expulsion must trace the melodies of Jews in places like Turkey and Syria and try to find common elements, or must rely on a few written melodies. Similarly, medieval Spanish cooking formed a base for later Sephardic cuisine; however, modern cookbooks that present Sephardic foods are not a clear indication of pre-Exile cooking. They reflect not only what existed in Spain but also five hundred years of exile from Spain along with enormous influences from European,

North African, or Middle Eastern cooking. Current recipes have adopted many modern foods, such as New World beans, chocolate, tomatoes, jalapenos, and bell peppers; Asian tea and coffee; and the use of refined sugar as an abundant ingredient rather than as a rare condiment. In sum, the modern term *Sephardic* reflects the cultural and historic currents experienced by the Diaspora of Jews from Spain.

REMINDERS OF THE INQUISITION

No tourist site in Spain advertises a connection to the Inquisition, although guidebooks to Madrid sometimes mention the pyres where "heretics" were burned in the presence of the Inquisitors in Plaza Mayor. Detecting the ghosts of the Inquisition in modern Spanish monuments is an exercise for the observer. In this short section, I will describe my own thoughts about this amnesia. The Spanish today have a capacity to question their history, but all the energy goes to their twentieth-century totalitarian experience. Well, the inner life of Spaniards is none of my business.

The Plaza Mayor is at the center of the Renaissance and older quarters, which are architecturally the most interesting of the city. Every guidebook will remind you that the Plaza Mayor was once the central location where the *autos de fe* took place for many centuries, and will remind you of the hooded executioners and tormentors dragging the helpless broken bodies of the tortured prisoners to their final terrestrial judgment in the name of racial and religious purity. Etchings in old books and in the Prado show the bleacher seats erected in front of the now-historic buildings, to enable privileged noble spectators to watch the victims suffer and die.

When guidebooks describe the modern-day flea market in the colorful Rastro neighborhood, their authors sometimes note that it's built over the former Juderia, where pious street names cover up its former identity. After the expulsion, this became the New Christian quarter where artisans and workers, descended from converted Jews, lived marginal though imaginative lives in sordid poverty. Consider the guidebook's hint that the Rastro flea market today occupies the streets of the New Christian quarter: some of the victims of the Inquisition thus must have come from the picturesque and well-preserved streets leading from this part of Madrid. I wonder where the jails and Inquisitors' torture chambers were located— probably near today's Royal Palace. I picture the processions of victims in their special penitents' garments coming through the oldest part of town and into the impressive tunnel-like entrances to the large open Plaza.

Madrid: Museum of the Americas

The Museum of the Americas tells the history of Spanish colonialism, and indirectly recalls the extent of the Inquisition in the Americas. The series of paintings of life in colonial Mexico that appears in one room of this vast museum seems out of place in the resolutely postmodern, anthropology-oriented museum. Who were these colonials? Many were descendants of Jews who hoped to escape from the Inquisition, but the Inquisition followed them almost immediately. It was well in place by the 1520s, ferreting out hints of Jewish rituals, lapses of pork eating, and excesses of cleanliness.

Unlike the other museums, the Museum of the Americas doesn't reflect any consistent taste at all. It has a great collection of Indian, mezo-American, and colonial objects but has far too many points of view. I have seen the term *politically correct* translated into Spanish in the newspapers here, and I think that's what is at work in the slick presentations installed in the museum for the 1992 celebration of Columbus's voyage.

Originally, the collections seem to have reflected a joy in Spain's successful colonial past, including many paintings of glorious conquerors, a variety of early maps of the New World, and documentation of colonial life. But now the Indian artifacts have center stage, and the European/colonial paintings seem to be an afterthought in rooms or cases dedicated to themes like death, marriage, religious life, the tribe, and so forth. The problem is that each theme is almost randomly exemplified by objects from any and all New World cultures and colonial times—Eskimo, Tlingit, and Plains Indian ceramics displayed next to Mayan or Peruvian, Amazon mixed with Hopi, and so on. I just tried to look at each thing for itself. The documentation is all in Spanish anyway, so I stopped even trying to make it out. And in the end, gold provides a powerful and impressive part of the presentation: when they talk about treasures, they aren't exaggerating. Some of the gold masks, foot-high gold statues, and heavy decorative brooches are amazing.

The modern ambiguity, hiding behind political correctness that levels all cultures, seems a fitting way to avoid the common problems of Jews and Indians with cultural tyranny.

El Escorial

On a beautiful Sunday morning we left our apartment and headed for the train station to go to El Escorial. By the time the train emerged from its center-city underground tracks, the sky was clouded over with foreboding gray, much more solid than the El Greco style puffy white and gray clouds we had seen during the first ten days or so of our trip. From the railroad station in the town, we walked through a beautiful formal garden with a high wrought-iron fence, up a considerable hill, to approach the dramatic setting of the monastery-palace.

El Escorial deserves its sinister and mysterious reputation as the morbid, though architecturally remarkable, retreat of King Philip II. His obsessions with death and salvation are visible throughout the palace. The austerity of spirit seems perfectly captured in austerity of forms. Clean lines and curves, severe expanses of unadorned stone, and simple geometric forms characterize the sixteenth-century construction. The unusual size of the palace, with a large basilica, numerous cloisters, gardens, and catacombs, contributes to the crushing atmosphere.

A vast mausoleum occupies a place of honor in one wing of the palace. The tombs contain the bodies of kings, queens, princes, and dead children; a whole chamber is dedicated to royal children who died young. Philip arranged the royal apartments so that his bed stood beside an interior window looking directly down at the altar of the huge baroque basilica, like a sort of Piranese dream scene. His wife's bed was all the way on the other side of the altar, and also looked down through a symmetrically placed window. I would think this would be a rather nightmarish place to wake up in the night. Not to mention privacy—even though the monks in the services did not have a view back to the royal beds. The king's exterior window faced the cold, barren, rock-strewn mountainside. When we walked through the palace's many summer apartments, arranged around courtyards with formal gardens, we found that many of the windows in this wing also look away from the small trees and plantings toward stark mountain landscapes. The views included barren crags and rocks and, during our tour, plenty of dark clouds.

El Escorial's architect, Juan de Herrera, trained with Michaelangelo in the construction of St. Peter's in Rome. The basilica design, in particular, is in a similar style, with the lofty series of domes that Michaelangelo invented, but all the joy is gone. The dome seems to be prevented from soaring by its heaviness and geometric perfection. Michaelangelo did not leave huge gray stone expanses so unadorned. In this cruel starkness,

I even missed the overblown Rococo white and gold add-ons that I so often wish had never been added to Italian Baroque churches.

A big part of the palace still serves its original function as a monastery. The monastic meeting and dining halls, as well as the King's private quarters, were decorated with many paintings by Titian, Veronese, Ribera, Velazquez, and Bosch, though he's scarcely mentioned in any of the guidebooks. These and many other masterpieces now appear in the picture galleries of the palace. Many of El Greco's paintings here depict skies full of brooding clouds just like the ones that threatened us outside— the Escorial's Grecos are much more brooding than those in the Prado. Many of the Escorial's religious paintings were commissioned or selected particularly for the palace, and for the monastic atmosphere that the king was creating. Some works of Bosch are contemporary copies of works now in the Prado, but at least two seem to be unique: both are of Jesus just at the time of his crucifixion. One shows Jesus surrounded by cruel-looking men, especially one with a wispy white mustache. In another, Jesus is carrying the cross surrounded by his tormentors, also looking evil but not surreal. The depiction of the Passion by Bosch and others emphasize the ugliness and brutality of the faces of the Jewish tormentors of Jesus. I think the choice of these paintings reflects the racist views that continued to blame the descendants of Jews and persecute them. Nothing could erase the idea that all Jews and their descendants were forever responsible for the crime of the few distorted Jews depicted in these paintings. I am very unhappy with this interpretation if it condemns Hieronymous Bosch, because I am utterly fascinated with his work and have enormous admiration for his imagination. In the context of the Prado, along with the numerous other paintings and lavish court scenes, the intention—whether it is due to the painter or to the king—does not stand out so much as it does in the weird Escorial setting.

By the time we emerged from the monastery the matching clouds were pouring rain, and we missed seeing the Escorial's famous library in order to try to get back to the railroad station without being soaked. I thought about King Philip II on the train on the way back. What a nut. I would have thought that the perpetrators of the Inquisition would have led a calm life, knowing how much they were doing for religious conformity. Why not have a happy carefree balance to the monstrous cruelty of the persecutions of so many innocent people? But, in fact, it seems that there was a joyless cold existence for all, from top to bottom— so different from the Italian Renaissance exuberantly going on across the Mediterranean.

Other Hints

Small towns in Spain are less postmodern than Madrid, with its frantic lifestyle. Some still betray a spirit of repressed ancient diversity. In one tiny town called Bocairent, we were told that we would find a Jewish quarter. In the tourist office, they said they knew nothing of this. However, in a picturesque square in the medieval part of town, we found a plaque commemorating the spot where Saint Vicente Ferrer preached. We knew what that meant: a Jewish community had lived on this spot, and Ferrer must have been participating in the campaign to convert them. In fact, our Spanish friends in Alicante considered any little town with a well-preserved medieval quarter to be a witness to the ancient Jewish presence here.

Throughout Spain, there are such hints. You think how Jews left the big cities in the 1390s and settled in these small towns. They had another century of prosperity even in the face of increasing persecution. The memory of the dark days of persecution and Jewish fears contrasts to the physical environment. The sun shines as you drive through the orange groves. When I arrived back home, I found a reminder even in American grocery stores: the splintery wooden boxes full of sweet clementines for Christmas bearing obscure names—Murcia, Tortosa—recall the forced disputation, the unwilling conversions, and the cruelty with which the Inquisition later persecuted the descendants of the Jews who once lived there. Only hints, no monuments.

Keys without Doors

As Sephardic Jews grew more and more distant from Spain, memories of the regretted Iberian homeland often involved a key. A key meant something different than another sort of physical object. A key could keep alive a belief that there was still a door waiting, which the exiled family could really open and somehow regress to that long-lost life. In old pictures or dusty museum cases sometimes one sees enormous keys, of the old-fashioned kind, not like a small, metallic-gray key to a Yale lock. The business end of a medieval key might be several inches long and might have small carved animals, letters, or other figures incorporated in the mechanism. Keys to doors of synagogues long since torn down or made into churches or stables, keys to heavy gates that once protected a Jewish community from an angry mob, keys to houses or castles, all offer much to the imagination. Even earlier, in Seville, inhabitants had symbolically preserved a silver key that the Jewish community had presented to King Ferdinand III upon his conquest of the city from the Moors in 1248 (Cecil Roth, *The Spanish Inquisition*, New York: Norton, 1996, p. 19).

The Lazaro Galdiano Museum in Madrid began as a rich man's private museum but is now open to the public. It's full of eccentric collectibles, impressive furniture, and art masterpieces (many reclassified from originals to copies, such as a Leonardo da Vinci). It has a display of a whole case of keys from Moorish occupation times, including one that claims to be from the house of Boabdil—you know, the defeated king of Granada who, as he fled from Ferdinand and Isabella, is known for sighing the Moor's last sigh. These keys are huge and the projections that turn the lock are intricately formed with little geometric patterns or tiny molded animals. An old engraving of such keys appropriately serves as the frontispiece to the reprint of the 1851 translation of Don Adolfo de Castro's *The History of the Jews in Spain, from the Time of Their Settlement in That Country till the Commencement of the Present Century* (reprint published Westport, Connecticut: Greenwood Press, 1972).

Keys sometimes even link contemporary Sephardic Jews with their distant past. A friend once told me that her family, after five hundred years in Morocco, still possessed the key to their house in Barcelona. Stories—collected as folk tales—preserved Sephardic families' beliefs in houses with false floors where secret mystic documents wait for them, or fables about hidden coffers rich with treasures that had to be abandoned, with only a key separating the tellers from wealth or power, or simply promising a return to what was lost.

PART 4

Italy, Renaissance Voyages

Introduction

Beginning in the late Middle Ages, open-minded rulers of various small Italian states offered Jewish refugees a haven from troubles elsewhere. In the 1200s and 1300s, Jews from Rome established communities in newly hospitable areas: Tuscany, Ferrara, Mantua, Milan, Umbria. Persecutions in Germany and France sent victims to join these Italian Jews in the 1300s and early 1400s. In the 1470s, Provence created refugees, such as Abraham Farissol, a writer, manuscript copyist, and religious leader from Avignon. The expulsion of 1492 drove a new wave of exiles from Spain, including the Abravanel family, whose members came to Genoa, Naples, Venice, Florence, and Ferrara. In the mid-1500s, Portuguese men and women of Jewish descent escaped the Inquisition via northern Europe and proceeded to Ferrara, Mantua, and Venice. Some Portuguese Marranos openly or secretly returned to the practice of Judaism; these included the printer Abraham Usque, the writer Samuel Usque, the physician Amatus Lusitanus, the financial wizard Joseph Nasi, and the philanthropist Gracia Nasi.

From 1450 until 1600 the Jews in Italy enjoyed a wide range of participation in mainstream cultural and intellectual pursuits, as well as in Jewish religious life. Unique attitudes of the Italian Renaissance enabled Jews to create works of religious and secular literature, philosophy, music, and science, and to be unusually full participants in secular culture. Jewish scholars helped to transmit Jewish thought to Christian philosophers, who were especially intrigued by Jewish mystical traditions. Giants of Renaissance art, science, music, architecture, engineering, and medicine dominate the intellectual history of this time, while Jewish figures justifiably remain in their shadow; nevertheless, the Jews' lives and accomplishments are worth studying. Both intellectual achievers and ordinary Italian Jews of the time had unusually diverse origins and international contacts. In cities that tolerated diversity among the Jews, different synagogues served Italian, German, Spanish, and French communities. Unfortunately, as this period drew to a close, the institution of the ghetto shut the Jews off increasingly, preventing involvement outside their own communities, and the vibrant achievements even of a few exceptional people no longer seemed possible.

INTRODUCING THREE FAMILIES

I have selected as the focus of this chapter three families who made a contribution in the Italian Renaissance period: the Abravanels, who came from Spain; the Soncinos, who originated in Germany; and the Norsa family, whose ancestors had been in Italy since Roman times. I chose these families because of their interesting and varied accomplishments and because they each represent a different Jewish ethnic origin. I visited several cities where one or more family members lived in order to visualize the physical surroundings in which they led their lives. To summarize who they were and where they came from:

- The Abravanel family arrived in Italy after their expulsion from Spain in 1492. Isaac Abravanel, after leaving the service of Ferdinand and Isabella, served the king of Naples and, during his last years, worked for the interests of the Republic of Venice. The most famous Italianized members of this Sephardic family were Judah and Samuel, the sons of Isaac Abravanel. Judah Abravanel, a poet, lived in Genoa, Naples, and possibly Florence. Samuel Abravanel and his wife, Benvenita, who was his cousin, lived in Naples; later they, their children, and other Abravanel descendants lived in Ferrara.

- The Soncino family originated in Speyer, Germany, and immigrated to the Italian town of Soncino, near Milan, during the first half of the fifteenth century. They eventually adopted the town name as their surname. This Ashkenazic family achieved recognition in the emerging trade of printing and were responsible for important innovations in Hebrew book production. The most famous family member, Gershom Soncino, published books in Hebrew, Italian, and Latin between the 1480s and the 1530s. He worked in a number of other Italian cities besides Soncino, and with his sons, he eventually moved on to the Turkish empire, where they continued the family printing business.

• The Norsa family's roots went back to the first Italian Jews of ancient Rome. In the Middle Ages, members of the family became rich bankers in the principalities of Mantua and Ferrara and patronized the Jewish cultural life of those cities. In the fifteenth and sixteenth centuries, Norsa family members enjoyed the exceptional tolerance of Mantua's and Ferrara's rulers, in a time after ghetto walls suffocated Jewish participation in the Renaissance elsewhere. Descendants of the family have remained in those cities until the present.

Venice is the most famous Jewish tourist site in Italy. Understanding the diversity of the Venetian Ghetto is the goal of my final narrative. Isaac Abravanel and Gershom Soncino, the most famous members of their families, each lived in Venice early in the sixteenth century, when few Jews were permitted to live there. The first ghetto, established in Venice in 1516, gave the concept of the ghetto its modern meaning. During the early years of the Venetian Ghetto, Jews from Germany, Portugal, and Turkey established trading operations there. As more and more Jews came to Venice, the Ghetto became a focal point for entertainment, gambling, and other low-life experience, as well as housing respectable businessmen, middle-class workers, poor rag-pickers, and conventional rabbis and scholars.

Travel in Italy

Travel in Italy is ideal whether you are interested in the ancient Etruscans, Greeks, Romans and Byzantines, in medieval or Renaissance humanism, or in more recent culture and technology. Painting, sculpture, and architecture; fountains, gardens, mountains, vineyards, and seacoasts; film festivals and opera; racing cars and industrial design; fashionable clothing and shoes; high-tech plumbing, kitchen gear, and furniture; imaginative and traditional cuisine—all compete for your attention.

Sometimes the styles appear distinct, and at other times they become a kind of pastiche. Ancient but honorable hotels have renovated bathrooms with the most modern of Italian fixtures tucked into huge or tiny pre-bathroom spaces. Nineteenth-century grand opera performances take place in the old Roman amphitheater of Verona. A wildlife refuge in the Po delta greets hikers at a visitor center in a Renaissance castle. At cafes, you can order the world's best espresso, local vintage wine, or Coca Cola. You can eat fresh seafood and handmade pasta in pure Mediterranean style, snack on crisp pizza, or find a McDonald's tucked into a medieval corner of Venice. Even small, completely obscure towns possess layers and layers of history: their museums or churches may display locally dug-up Neanderthal tools, Bronze Age pottery, Etruscan gravestones, Byzantine mosaics, medieval altarpieces, or Renaissance frescoes. In Ferrara, within a few hours, we visited the early modern synagogue and Jewish museum, the Romanesque cathedral, and the medieval ducal palace. We climbed down stone stairways into the palace's cellar dungeons, in which the sixteenth-century duke locked up his younger brothers for fifty years; moments later, beyond the palace moat, across the street, I window-shopped at boutiques selling stylish knits, steel and glass kitchen gadgets, and colorful sandals.

Italy's countryside includes sedate, snow-covered Mount Blanc; currently erupting Mount Etna; rolling hills planted in grapevines and olive orchards; marshy, rice-growing deltas; wide sandy beaches; craggy cliff-lined coasts; and picturesque villages. Urban scenery varies from Roman triumphal arches to medieval and Renaissance palaces and fortifications to postmodern steel and glass. The landscape is fascinating, and my fascination increases because it reminds me of the work of the many Italians who have depicted or described it. I have had the impression of seeing outdoor vistas, cityscapes, or human forms through the eyes of Da Vinci, Di Chirico, Raphael, Umberto Eco, Italo Calvino, Italo Svevo, Primo Levi, Georgio Bassani, Giacometti, or Modigliani. I thought of finding myself in the set of a Fellini or DeSica film or a Rossini opera.

On earlier visits to Italy, I learned little or nothing about Italy's two thousand years of Jewish tradition. The first time I was in Italy, in 1964, I was interested only in its mainstream history, particularly art history, which I had studied in college. I wanted to see the early Renaissance paintings in the Uffizi in Florence, the Roman treasures in the Vatican museum, the Sistine Chapel, the architecture of the Tuscan countryside, and the jewel-like ports on the Mediterranean. I still love Italy for all of this. It was years later before I ever thought of wondering if any Jews had lived there. As everywhere, you can learn all kinds of things about a European country without ever hearing anything about Jewish history.

In my efforts to discover the Italian Jews, I read several books by Italian-Jewish writers: Italo Svevo's *Zeno*, Primo Levi's horrifying memoirs of the holocaust, Carlo Ginzburg's social observations, Natalia Ginzburg's novels, Georgio Bassani's *Garden of the Finzi-Continis*, and Carlo Levi's memoir *Christ Stopped at Eboli* with its few, indirect references to the Jewish background of its socialist author. Modigliani's long-faced portraits contain no specific references, but he's also known as a Jewish painter. A few cookbooks describe the long history of Italian Jewish food and how it influenced other Italians. These themes also appear in films based on Bassani's *Garden of the Finzi-Continis*, on Carlo Levi's *Christ Stopped at Eboli*, and on some of Primo Levi's works. Later, I began exploring the role of Jews in the Italian Renaissance. The books of Cecil Roth and many others showed me the richness of Italian Jewish history. Some aspects of this culture have recently appealed to modern Americans, such as two recent CDs of the work of the Jewish composer Salamone Rossi, who was born in Mantua in the sixteenth century.

As I traveled and read guidebooks, I realized the unequaled riches remaining from the Jewish past in Italy—and the tragedy of the final years of World War II when Hitler's troops destroyed individual lives, uprooted whole communities, and intentionally pillaged and burned the riches of Italy's Jewish past. Increasingly, I learned that I had been missing the high points of Italian Jewish tourism. Synagogues and Jewish neighborhoods or former ghettos existed in huge numbers of small Italian towns, particularly in the North. Postwar events resulted in the removal of many Jewish religious items to Israel. Holy Arks, Torahs, *menorahs*, and carved-wood desks from many Italian synagogues now serve religious communities in Israel or appear in museums there. However, many still are in Italy in their native context. The major Jewish sites in Ferrara, Mantua, Venice, and Rome particularly offer a variety of memories of their long-term Jewish communities. I have barely begun to explore what is there.

The twentieth century has utterly changed the world of Italian Jews. You can't visit any synagogue or ghetto without becoming conscious of the enormous loss that Nazi destruction caused. Though major historical sites still link the past and present of Italian Jews, there is a crucial break in the chain of tradition. In these pages, I hope to make you aware of the vivacious past of these places, and I will suggest a few ways that you can see these links.

ITINERARIES IN ITALY

The places that appear in the following travel descriptions lie in a triangle between Milan to the northwest, Venice to the northeast, and Ancona to the southwest down the Adriatic coast. Florence lies just outside this triangle as well. To organize them into a single voyage, you can begin at one of several places, depending where you are coming from and where you are going afterward. If you don't care to stay in a different location each day, it's also possible to select some convenient locations and to make various trips to the cities and towns you wish to see.

Unfortunately, the attraction of the smaller secondary roads, which take you through fields and really tiny places, is badly marred by the fact that commercial traffic makes major use of these roads, probably to avoid the high Autostrada tolls. The first time that we planned to enjoy a leisurely drive on a two-lane country road, we expected an idyllic route but found the road overcrowded with fast cars, large tankers, and other trucks carrying all kinds of cargo, up to enormous concrete I-beams. Instead of enjoying the scenery, we found our attention riveted on the oncoming traffic, waiting for impatient passing drivers who expect you to move onto the shoulder when they speed toward you. Though the rather flat fields and farm hamlets are picturesque, with occasional medieval-looking churches and bell towers, we would have been more relaxed if we had remained on the toll way. After we had been traveling for a day or two, we determined to stick to the Autostrada even if the resulting route was somewhat longer.

Assuming that you begin in the Milan area and travel toward the east, the logical progression (as shown on the map immediately following this) is Milan, Soncino, Mantua, Ferrara, Venice, Rimini, Pesaro, and Fano. Ravenna and Urbino are easily added to this itinerary. Florence is a slight detour. There are major international airports near Milan, Bologna, Pisa, and Venice, which can serve as starting/ending points. The descriptions further on follow the lives of several Italian Jewish characters and thus do not appear in convenient geographical order; however, all the Jewish sites and museums thoroughly complement one another.

If you decide to see the Jewish sites of Italy, a superb and very detailed series of guidebooks on the subject is in the process of being published and translated from Italian into English. Each one intensely and in a scholarly way covers a single region, describing what is present now and what was there in the past, and identifying the current location of Jewish artifacts from the town, such as the Torah Arks and woodcarvings from the synagogues. Tracking down all the sites listed in these books would take months or years of effort; each has a separate author who seems to live in the local area and to have extensively explored the potential Jewish sites. Consult the Appendix to this book for information on these guides and other practical travel information.

A Note on Cemeteries

Several Jewish cemeteries offer travelers a different sort of look at the traces of the ancient Italian Jewish communities. The ancient cemetery of Venice near the Lido has recently been the object of a preservationist campaign. The tourist-office map of Jewish Ferrara shows the location of several cemeteries there. Because my time was limited and because I find cemeteries less appealing than most other sorts of tourist sites, I didn't visit them and thus will not describe them. If you have time to arrange a visit, you might find them interesting, particularly if you can read the Hebrew on the grave markers. Recent anti-Jewish acts by the extreme right in France have included desecration of historic Jewish cemeteries; this alarming trend already makes it difficult to visit Jewish cemeteries in France and may also affect the accessibility of those in Italy now or in the future.

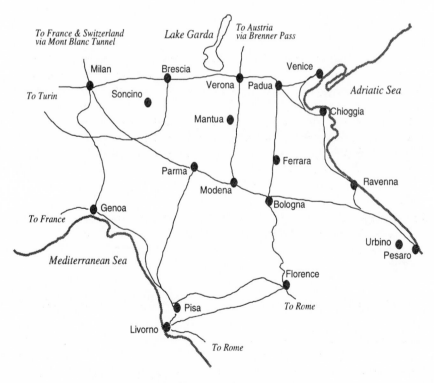

Fig. 4-1: Map of Northern Italy

From Roman Citizens to Ghetto Dwellers

The oldest known Italian Jewish synagogue stands at Ostia Antiqua, near Rome. Possibly built before the destruction of the Temple, the synagogue served immigrants or children of immigrants from the Roman colony of Judea. These first Italian Jews had reached Rome at least a century before the fall of the Temple, as described in the first part of this book. Most of them began Roman life as slaves, but interactions between Jews and Romans provided a few with other motives or excuses to go to Rome. Herod came to make political contacts; he sent his sons to be educated; later, Jewish-Roman citizens achieved a special status and were free to move to Rome from Jewish enclaves in other colonies such as Alexandria or Carthage. The Jewish wars of 70 and 132 augmented the number of free Jews fleeing the deteriorating conditions in Jerusalem, as well as providing a source of war captives to add to the slave population.

ITALIAN JEWISH COMMUNITIES BEFORE 1500

Jewish-Roman slaves eventually became free men, adopted Roman ways, and achieved Roman citizenship. Modern knowledge of the Roman-Jewish community comes from traces of burial catacombs, from other archaeological remains, and from documentation in Roman literature, including

Flavius Josephus. As did the Greeks, many Romans found Jewish philosophy intriguing, and Roman sympathizers appear to have participated in a limited way in Jewish rituals without actually accepting full Judaism or being accepted fully by Jews. Special legislation permitted Jews to maintain their religion and Roman citizenship simultaneously, exempting them from Roman worship but requiring payment of extra tax. Jews also inhabited other Roman and, later, Byzantine cities, as we have noted in the histories of Jewish communities in Spain and France.

History and surviving records quickly shifted their focus to the rapidly emerging presence of Christians. As Christianity prevailed, traces of Jewish communities became vague. Ravenna, the seat of the empire for a while in the fourth through eighth centuries, offers at least some evidence of Jewish inhabitants. In Ravenna's museum, we saw a single fragment of a Roman-style amphora with the Hebrew word *Shalom* on it, among hundreds or thousands of archaeological finds. (Based on our guidebook, we expected to find a second item, a sarcophagus, in the museum as well, but failed to identify it.) During the Byzantine era, the Jewish presence was overwhelmed by the wide success of Christianity—which had a good motive to cause the Jews to be forgotten. Although Christian emperors set limits on Jewish behavior and activity, and continued the special tax on Jews, they did not legally confine Jewish citizens to a single quarter of cities or restrict them to particular professions or occupations.

In the Dark Ages, as the papacy assumed power, every pope created his own policy toward the Jews of Rome. Although papal policies frequently imposed intolerant and crushing handicaps on Jewish life, the Roman-Jewish community never seems to have been entirely eliminated. Jews also continued to inhabit certain Italian cities. Benjamin of Tudela visited several northern and central Italian cities with small Jewish populations. During this time, the center of Jewish life in Italy was Sicily, where the population numbered in the thousands. By their expulsion in 1493, there were forty to fifty thousand Jews there (H. Beinart, *Atlas of Medieval Jewish History*, Jerusalem: Carta, 1992, p. 81).

In the Middle Ages, to work or live in a town, Jews required specific permission from city authorities, often with the concurrence of the church. When Jews spread to more cities in Italy, they most often began with a permission, or charter, to open a bank for a set period of time, with a number of negotiated conditions for lending. When the charters expired, they sometimes had to leave the town. In more favorable circumstances, their charters were renewed and they slowly obtained other economic, social, and religious privileges in the towns. The Norsa family is typical. They started in Rome, settled in the town of Nurzia, and later, becoming richer and richer, settled as bankers in Mantua and Ferrara. Some family members periodically made brief trips to nearby towns where they didn't have a residence, to loan money. Other banking families with a similar history were the Da Pisa family, who had banks in Umbria and Tuscany, and the Finzis, who often were partners with the Norsas.

Where the Jewish community was sufficiently numerous, Jews may have chosen to live or have been encouraged to live in a single Jewish street, similar to the custom in France or in Spain in the Middle Ages. Because they were bankers, and hence responsible for pawned items from Christian borrowers, the security of their homes and businesses against robbery was a concern to the rest of the community as well as to themselves. The Jews' streets often were located in the town center, near the marketplace and cathedral, for the convenience and security of the borrowing public. When you find the medieval Jewish neighborhood of an Italian city or town, you are seeing the result of these trends; as we will see in a moment, it is not completely appropriate to refer to these early Jewish neighborhoods as ghettos, because they lacked the extreme restrictions, such as guards and curfews, of the later institution. Also, the formal ghettos of the sixteenth century and later were often established in a different and less desirable area than these more ancient Jewish quarters.

Immigration became an important factor in increasing the size of Italy's Jewish communities, as Jews elsewhere in Europe experienced new disasters, making Italian cities appear to beckon with opportunities. At the start of the Crusades in 1096, Crusaders attacked Jewish communities in Germany and Eastern Europe, causing many to flee. Expulsion from England occurred around 1290, from France and its territories in the fourteenth century. German and Eastern European Jews came through the Alpine passes, Jews from southern France traveled across the Mediterranean, Jews from England made the slow trip overland, and even a few Jews from Babylonia joined the Italian community. Spanish Jews came to Italy during the persecutions of 1391 and continued through the 1492 expulsion. Some Jewish optimists at the time even came around to the opinion that expulsions were a normal part of Jewish life; they classified rulers as unreasonable only if the expulsion was done brutally, with heavy loss of Jewish life or property.

New immigrants found homes among small Jewish communities with a nucleus of bankers, as well as in larger cities, bringing skills that were accepted and integrated into the Italian scene. Because Italian commerce was growing, they were able to incorporate traditional Jewish skills. They became merchants, financial organizers, dealers in cloth and clothing, medical practitioners, and other sorts of professionals and entrepreneurs. Their varied national origins and differences, though, helped contribute to the isolation of Jewish communities.

In 1490, the population of Italy was about 12,000,000, and there were about 120,000 Jews (according to the *Dictionary of the Middle Ages*). Larger Jewish communities existed in a few cities such as Rome with 25,000 to 30,000, and several cities of Sicily, though Sicily expelled them in 1493. Venice at this point allowed only a few Jews to live outside the city proper. Jewish communities also lived in Florence, Naples, Mantua, Ferrara, and Genoa. Most of the Jewish community was dispersed, a few families at a time, among many small towns and cities.

Throughout the 1490s, a series of wars and invasions disrupted life for both Christians and Jews in Italy. The invasion of the French, under Charles VIII, devastated many cities from the French border down to Naples. As Charles led his troops toward Florence, the panic-stricken departure of the Medicis enabled the fanatic monk Savanarola to take power; his theocracy lasted for several years. The French sack of Naples led to anti-Jewish riots. Toward the end of the decade, Pope Alexander and his son Cesare Borgia were just beginning an effort to unify Italy by conquering the smaller states adjacent to the papal territories. By 1500, wars and expulsions had virtually eliminated the Jewish communities of Milan, Sicily, and Naples. The large and small cities ruled by Genoa, the papal states, Tuscany, and Umbria permitted Jews to live relatively freely; however, changing attitudes and conditions in the church and in the political situation threatened the continuation of tolerance.

Medieval Jews before the Ghetto

By the end of the fifteenth century, prominent Jews in Italy included rich bankers, respected medical professors, influential philosophers, poets, and others in positions of community leadership. The first wave of refugees from Spain in 1492, such as the Abravanel family, belonged to a similar class and quickly joined these leaders. Throughout the sixteenth century, a number of wealthy and well-educated Jews and Conversos from Portugal continued to arrive.

Middle-class Jews in cities and small towns in Renaissance Italy included all kinds of craftsmen and small merchants dealing in leather, cloth, clothing, grain, metal, used or new manuscripts or books, and other products or commodities. Many of the Jewish loan bankers were little more than operators of pawnshops and made no more than a middle-class income. Successful actors and musicians belonged to the middle class, as did the Soncino printers. Descending the social scale, there were Jews who worked as tavern keepers, wine makers, old-clothing dealers, itinerant performers and dancing teachers, dealers in playing cards and dice, and many Jews involved in the less respectable forms of gambling. Among the most impoverished people were Jewish peddlers, failed craftsmen, and even poor and degraded beggars. Sometimes the marginal personalities were depressing in sheer poverty, but others displayed colorful personalities or perpetuated engaging con games.

The bankers' families were generally the first to move into Italian towns. Under the initial terms of most bank charters, the number of Jews who were permitted to reside with the contracting banker was limited; however, by modern standards, the banker ran a substantial household. Besides his children and his adult relatives, who probably shared his business, the "family" could include teachers, scribes, doctors, kitchen servants to prepare food and even slaughter small fowls or make wine according to Jewish law, and sometimes also the spouses and children of these people. Such a household might or might not have had per-mission to employ local Christians in other domestic roles, such as wet nurses or manual laborers. In many cases, the banker's household, once established, would manage to expand its economic and professional activities: the family doctors would practice medicine while the entre-preneurs in the household would expand their dealings in books or clothing or grain. A few Jews with other skills might join this nucleus, and a small Jewish community could emerge.

Under the terms of the charter, the banker and his associates loaned money with certain restrictions on the interest rate, on discretion about rejecting borrowers, and on the type of items the bank could accept as pledges—generally, no religious objects or weapons. The charter might mandate lower-interest loans to rulers, to Christian students, or to the municipality. Bankers had to comply with required record keeping, though they often kept the books in Hebrew instead of Italian, as the rules specified. Customers were normally unable to read at all; the implication is that the bankers leveraged traditional Jewish literacy. Most important to the rulers, the charter determined the tax rate, ensuring that the banker shared his gains with the rulers. Thus, the rulers' hands were always clean of the terrible sin of usury, but the ruler and his subjects enjoyed access to capital for their endeavors and funds for dealing with temporary crises. Whether the banker was successful or not, the people perceived him to be very rich—at their expense.

Relations between Jews and Christians in small Italian communities were among the best in all of Europe. Jews lived and traveled freely among Christians, engaged in joint business ventures, bought and sold goods, and learned trades from them. Jews might employ Christian servants or helpers, or work for Christians, as local customs and laws allowed. Enlightened rulers made the Jews welcome in many cities; even when they were taxed excessively, restricted in activity, or intermittently expelled, they generally prospered. Because Jews tended to be dispersed, including some communities with little more than a few families, they usually lived side by side with Christian neighbors and often shared many aspects of life in the small towns, including the pursuit of leisure time activities such as tennis, playing cards, theater attendance, and musical performances.

Over time, laws requiring Jews to be visually distinct from Christians became more common in Italy, as they already were elsewhere. In various times and places, Jewish men were required to wear a round yellow badge, a special red cloak, or a distinctive hat, and Jewish women to wear hoop earrings or special-colored aprons. Still, tolerant rulers often made exceptions of time and place when these signifying items could be hidden or omitted, and Jews, even in such distinguishing clothes, continued to have a variety of freedoms and interactions with others.

Among the Jewish professions, besides bankers, craftsmen, and doctors, entertainers ranged from wandering street performers to recognized professionals. Jewish musicians, actors, and dancers were popular with both Jews and Christians. Dancing teachers were often Jewish, such as the dancing teacher of Isabella and Beatrice d'Este. Around 1500, a Jewish theater troop presented plays to the courts in Mantua and Ferrara, and later in the century, Jewish playwrights and musicians worked for the Dukes of Mantua. Jewish musicians in Florence and Mantua performed and composed for many Jewish religious events, such as weddings, circumcisions, and minor holidays when performance was not prohibited. Dancing was a popular activity during the Italian-Jewish all-night celebration before a circumcision, when friends and family gathered for a vigil to keep away the evil spirits that were feared as a threat to the new baby. Musical education appeared in some Jewish educational records. Diamante, wife of the banker Jehiel da Pisa, played the lute, and many Jews owned musical instruments and books. Jewish musicians and teachers had a role in all of these personal activities.

Jewish card players, playing-card makers and sellers, and keepers of gambling houses will be mentioned in the various histories that follow. In 1418, a meeting of important rabbis in Forli attempted to prohibit

Jewish gambling; such prohibitions are a key to social problems. Many individuals were engaged in a range of activities from professional gambling to casual card-playing at many events, including the pre-circumcision vigil. The gambling-addicted and those who took advantage of them came from all social levels. The most famous case of a compulsive gambler is Leone Modena, rabbi of Venice, who documented his struggle to give it up. Also, a Jewish engineer, inventor, and sometimes con man from Mantua and Ferrara, Abraham Colorni, according to Cecil Roth, was an early inventor of card tricks (Cecil Roth, *The Jews in the Renaissance*, New York: Harper & Row, 1959, pp. 26 and 240).

In Rome, where there was a larger and poorer Jewish community, many Jews became low-life characters, especially in neighborhoods where Spanish converts half-returned to Judaism. These were often tavern owners, prostitutes, con men, and providers of other dubious entertainment. These activities appear in a novel from the 1520s, *La Lozan Andaluz*. The Spanish-immigrant author describes the adventures of a marginal semi-converted Jewish woman in a lower class Roman Jewish/Marrano neighborhood.

Jewish religious life was able to develop freely in places where the communities were large enough, especially in the major concentrations of Mantua, Ferrara, Bologna, and later Venice. Religious observances in homes and synagogues and attendance at sermons preached by educated rabbis became important elements of Jewish social life. Even these were not entirely segregated. Some well-known Jewish preachers attracted not only Jews but also Christian listeners; the formal sermon became a kind of literature that could come from either a Jewish or a Christian clergyman. Also, when Jews put on some types of happy religious celebrations such as weddings, circumcisions, and Purim plays, they often invited Christian neighbors or business associates.

Many communities incorporated a diverse mixture of native Italian Jews and representatives of the continually arriving immigrants. Synagogue rites varied with nationality: Ashkenazic, Italian, Sephardic, and Zarfati (French) synagogues and schools maintained differences in the order of prayers, practices of covering the head, and pronouncing and writing Hebrew. Sometimes Hebrew manuscripts had to be recopied in order to be readable by groups other than those that had copied them. In some cases, the established Jews opposed admission of the newcomers, leading to feuds or bad feelings and intensifying the tendency to maintain their separate institutions.

In small Italian towns, where the middle-class or poor Jews were often very assimilated into local life and customs and isolated among the Christian population, ordinary Jews didn't have a completely set way to follow Jewish laws or a solid education in religious traditions. Rabbis and other individuals who knew the traditions lived mainly in bigger towns with a larger Jewish population. The small-town Jews often became lax about holiday observances and dietary laws, particularly about kosher wine; in some cases, despite good intentions, this situation eventually resulted in intermarriage and conversion. Even in somewhat larger communities, the isolation of families complicated the arrangement of desirable Jewish marriages, and a wedding thus was always a major event.

Conversion was always an issue in Jewish communities. There were reasons for both rich and poor to convert. Rich people converted to preserve fortunes, in times when they were faced with expulsion or loss of commercial rights. Poor people converted to get attention or improve employment opportunities. When Catholic priests convinced a Jew to convert, Christians were often very solicitous and offered the person clothing for his or her Baptism and other gifts, sometimes including money, another incentive to the poor. If a Jew wanted to marry a Christian, as often happened, conversion was mandatory. Motives also included zeal for the new religion or a simple desire to stop being different. Among the lowest and least-respectable Jews, one specialized type of rogue exploited the Christian desire to make Jewish converts. Such a Jewish con man would travel from town to town with a long story about having been a Jewish usurer and then seeing the light, renouncing his evil ways, even sometimes claiming to have seen visions and miracles. He would publicly ask to become a Christian and lead a new life and thus attract a lot of attention for the ceremonious conversion—a form of entertainment for Christians—collecting lots of gifts every time. Since being baptized more than once was heretical, the Inquisition sometimes investigated and recorded the antics of these characters (B. Pullan, *The Jews of Europe and the Inquisition of Venice, 1550–1670,* Oxford, England: Basil Blackwell, 1983, pp. 244 and 300).

Italian Jews of various classes had a reputation for a separate cuisine, beyond the simple application of dietary laws. Some dishes in Italy even today are labeled "Jewish style"—though the basis for association with Jews may be lost. Jews in the Renaissance are alleged to have been the main consumers of artichokes, eggplant, and beets, though this may be a myth. Jewish physicians as well as others improved herbal medicines by adding sugar, pepper, lemon, chicory, fennel, coriander, or bitter almonds. Perhaps the rich Jews imitated the taste of Isabella d'Este's kitchen, which valued good bread, cheese, olive oil, and game birds or stuffed geese with sweet stuffing. The record of a Jewish marriage mentions gifts of sugar and honey, "also pepper, cane-sugar, spices, powdered sugar, flour, wine, firewood and salted fish" (Pullan, p. 239).

Italian Jews, like the other residents of cities and towns in the fifteenth and sixteenth centuries, were partial to eating meat. Beef and mutton were the most popular choices. One family for whom there are records appears to have eaten meat at every lunch and dinner. Many felt deprived—or even in danger for their health—if they could obtain only chicken or other fowl.

> Forced for nearly three years to eat only poultry and wildfowl, the Jews of Todi were driven to despair, and by 1438 they were obliged to address an urgent protest to Francesco Sforza which was to prove highly convincing: "We are no longer able to provide sustenance for ourselves or our families, because we have been forced to eat only poultry for too long." A long-enforced diet of salami made from goose and the insipid flesh of chickens, wildfowl, capons, and pigeons had made the Jews of Todi desperately crave good food and a more varied and appealing menu, including ossobuco, tripe, and rump-steak. (Ariel Toaff, *Love, Work, and Death: Jewish Life in Medieval Umbria*, London: Littman Library of Jewish Civilization, 1996, p. 73)

To satisfy their need for meat that they could eat, a Jewish community needed trained ritual slaughterers, butchers who knew what parts of the animal were permitted under Jewish law, and butcher shops to process and distribute the kosher meat. They needed permission to sell the unkosher parts of the animals to Christians and therefore to make meat affordable. Jewish communities engaged in repeated negotiation about these activities. There were fights because obligatory placement of butcher shops in Jewish quarters of the towns caused filth and bad smells. There were conflicts with butchers' guilds that jealously guarded their exclusive rights to the profession. The archives record the ups and downs of these arrangements for a supply of kosher meat.

The Italian taste for wine captivated Jews across the social scale. In those days when water in general was unsafe to drink, tea had scarcely become known, and coffee was entirely unknown, wine was the principal beverage for everyone. The average Jewish consumption was 1.5 to 3 liters per person per day, and they often neglected to restrict their consumption to wine handled only by other Jews. Wine was also considered to have therapeutic value and was prescribed by doctors and used in preparing medicines. Some doctors even made and sold wine. With all this exposure, Jews were sometimes accused of being drunkards, and sometimes ran taverns of bad repute (Toaff, pp. 82–83).

When settling in a new place or even when continuing to live there, Jews entered negotiations about rights to produce and sell their own wine. Often, Jewish grape-stompers needed to use the vats of Christian peasants to press the juice from grapes just after the harvest and then to make kosher wine. Sometimes there were efforts to prohibit them, but they usually failed. In principle, Christians weren't supposed to use what was left in the vat or to drink kosher wine. In practice, they often drank with Jewish friends, bought wine from Jewish tavern-keepers, and were unconcerned about Jewish wine. Some Jews also owned small vineyards and could make their own wine. Reciprocally, as Jews were not always concerned about kosher wine, they often simply bought wine from Christians.

Restrictions on grapes could also be associated with restrictions on other produce: effectively, Jews weren't supposed to touch or contact food that would be consumed by Christians. One regulation to this effect states: "No Jew or Jewess may purchase or cause to be purchased any quantity of must in the city or region of Perugia, unless they purchase the whole vatful . . . Jews may not in any way touch any type of fruit unless they have purchased it first, excluding melons, garlic, onions, and walnuts, and all fruits with hard skins" (Toaff, p. 78).

Christian suspicion of Jews, as reflected in these food worries, was especially strong when times were bad, especially during epidemics. Encouraged by various demagogues, people were more likely to attack Jewish communities during plague years than during normal years, when violence was rare. Because Jews were often doctors, they were in a precarious position. Medieval medical practice was helpless against plague, and the Jews suffered its devastation along with the others, but Jews were nevertheless frequently blamed for the plague. In the earliest epidemic, around 1348, Jews all over Europe suffered from mob violence and expulsions. In the sixteenth century, this attitude was still common: Portuguese Jews were expelled from Ferrara during an epidemic at mid-century. As Jewish doctors knew no more than anyone else, some Jews resorted to magic and Kabbalah to try to cure themselves.

Needless to say, if standard histories record any Jews of Renaissance Italy at all, they primarily document their influence on the Christian philosophers of this richly creative period. The majority of Jews, in contrast to these few, were relatively poor and politically powerless, and suffered from the additional burdens and restrictions placed on them. Jews, particularly those who made small loans to the poor, often made a convenient target that enabled rulers to redirect mass hostility away from themselves.

THE RENAISSANCE CONTEXT

The moment of the Spanish Jews' arrival in Italy was the peak of the Italian Renaissance and also the last moment before the institution of the ghetto first in Italy, and then in many other places. The last decade of the sixteenth century was the age of Leonardo da Vinci, Machiavelli, and the Renaissance popes in all their decadence. The world was full of explorers, religious leaders, philosophers, politicians, humanists, soldiers, and artists. The recently invented technology of printing was making an enormous impact, word of Columbus's voyage was spreading, and new ideas were everywhere.

The extraordinary hope and promise in Europe in general is in extreme contrast to the condition of life for Jews, particularly for those who had just become exiles from Spain. While Christians were expanding their horizon, Jewish philosophers were in a mood of despair. Isaac Abravanel's effort at comfort was to predict that the Messiah would arrive in 1503. We will discuss his philosophical point of view a little later, but for the moment let's take a look at the world into which he thought this change would come. Here is a summary of some famous men and women and what they were doing at that time.

Modern memory tends to dwell on the voyages of exploration and discovery that energized this age.

Christopher Columbus (1450–1506), made his fourth voyage of exploration and colonization to the newly discovered "Indies" from 1502–1504.

Fernando de Magellan (1480–1521) was in the service of the king of Portugal by 1502; by 1504, he participated in a voyage to India with the first Portuguese viceroy. He died during his most famous voyage, the first circumnavigation of the world, which began in 1519.

The science of astronomy was also achieving some major discoveries.

Nicolaus Copernicus (1473–1543) lectured on astronomy in Rome for the jubilee year, 1500. In 1502, Copernicus was in the process of studying medicine in Padua. In 1503, he also received a degree in canon law at Ferrara. His astronomical experiments began in 1513. His famous work, which challenged the commonly held theory that heavenly bodies revolved around the earth, dates from 1530. Note that while virtually everyone before Copernicus believed that the earth was the center of heavenly motion, it is a misconception of our own day to think that Renaissance men viewed the earth as flat.

Abraham Zacuto (c.1450–c.1522), a Jewish astronomer, worked for Ferdinand and Isabella until 1492 and had advised them to support Columbus. He developed and published important navigation tables, the *Perpetual Almanach*, used by Columbus and other voyagers. After 1492, he became an exile, moving from Spain to Portugal and then from Portugal to Italy.

The arts and humanities were flourishing, and I will mention more of the famous artists later.

Aldus Manutius (1450–1515), an innovative printer and humanist publisher, saw how to use the new technology of printing to serve the humanist cause. By 1503, his press in Venice was producing a breakthrough series of small-format classic texts in Latin and Greek, as well as a Hebrew grammar. He had commissioned the design of the first italic typeface from Griffo, who later worked for Gershom Soncino. Aldus's successors continued to publish important humanist texts through much of the sixteenth century.

Niccolo Machiavelli (1469–1527), the playwright and political theorist, served as one of the Florentine representatives negotiating with Cesare Borgia in 1502; it was at this time that he made many of the observations that he incorporated in his famous work *The Prince*, which was written several years afterward. Like Isaac Abravanel, he turned his practical experience to philosophical study of government and the practical conduct of rulers. Machiavelli's description of the successful "prince" praised those who consolidated power, administered through some sort of middle-class bureaucracy, and rendered the old nobles superfluous in the power structure. This indicates the big change from the Middle Ages when the nobility, with many feudal characteristics, had enjoyed a much bigger role in administration, economic affairs, and national policy. In *The Discourses*, Machiavelli cites France and Spain as successful at consolidation, Italy as a failure (Bondanella and Musa, eds., *The Portable Machiavelli*, New York: Penguin, 1979, p. 212).

Machiavelli particularly described **Ferdinand of Aragon** (1452–1516) and **Isabella of Castile** (1451–1504), who were responsible for the expulsion of the Jews from Spain, as discussed in the previous chapter. Machiavelli cites Ferdinand as a king who started out head of a small, weak principality, and by his own talent and by taking every opportunity, controlled the power of the nobles of Castile. He says: "from being a weak ruler he became, through fame and glory, the first king of Christendom; and if you will consider his accomplishments, you will find them all very grand and some even extraordinary" (*Portable Machiavelli*, p. 151). From the Italian perspective, by 1503 their international impact depended not only on the potential of the New World, but also on their diplomatic corps, highly sophisticated by the standards of the era. Their ambassadors were cultivating commercial and political relations with European rulers, Moslem rulers of North Africa, and with the newly discovered rulers of the New World. One of their tactics was to arrange their children's marriages to the inheritors of other European kingdoms, including Portugal, the Holy Roman Empire, and England.

King Manuel I ruled Portugal from 1495 until 1521. While his immediate predecessor had allowed the Jews to enter the country in 1492, he did not continue to tolerate their religious practice. In 1497, negotiations with King Ferdinand and Queen Isabella over his marriage to their daughter initially forced him to issue an expulsion order for Portuguese Jews and recent Jewish refugees from Spain. However, he was a practical man and didn't want to lose these extremely valuable citizens—instead he forced them to convert and then forbade them to leave. The resulting situation was volatile; in the Lisbon Massacre of 1506, the highly identifiable New Christians were attacked by the populace, and the government was temporarily destabilized. Ironically, his marriage to the heiress of the Spanish kingdoms did not result in the hoped-for combination of territory because the Spanish princess died in 1500.

Louis XII (1462–1515), King of France, was involved, at the start of the sixteenth century, in his invasion of Italy—one of a series of efforts by France to take over Italian territories, which had started with invasions by his predecessors.

Henry VII (d. 1509) was the reigning king of England at the beginning of the century. His more famous son, **Henry VIII** (1491-1547), succeeded him and soon became an important contender on the international scene. Later in the 1520s, Henry's prolonged negotiations over divorcing Ferdinand and Isabella's daughter, Catherine of Aragon, were important to the religious and political history of England, as well as to English relations with Spain and Italy. His claims to a divorce from Catherine were based on passages in the Old Testament, and as a result, Jewish scholars were called as expert witnesses during the proceedings in Rome.

The **Hapsburgs** ruled Austria and received a certain level of feudal loyalty from some of the principalities of northern Italy. They played a role in some of the wars in Italy during the period, and they soon became more important when they inherited Spain, thanks to another of the marriages arranged by Ferdinand for his children.

Bayezid II (1447–1512), sultan of Constantinople, was winding up an important war with Venice in 1502–1503, winning several important possessions for Turkey. Throughout the next century, as the conflict with Venice continued, Turkey offered refuge to many Jews who were trying to escape the Inquisition. The capital, Constantinople, and the city of Salonika, in what is now Greece, both developed as important centers of Jewish life, and we will see many of the individuals in the following stories end up in the realm of the sultans.

In Mexico, **Montezuma II** (1479–1520), became the Aztec king in 1502. The Aztecs were just completing nearly a century of conquest, expanding their territory throughout Mexico. These Indian conquerors enjoyed a short rule: the Spanish conquered Mexico in 1519, established total power over the Mexicans, and utterly changed the cultural atmosphere. The Italians, along with the rest of Europe, were receiving accounts of the New World eagerly, and its existence was changing their perspective, as well as reducing the importance of Mediterranean powers in favor of those who looked toward the bigger oceans. As for the Jews, recent Spanish converts participated in the Mexican campaigns, and the Spanish established the Inquisition right along with their colonies, burning accused heretics in Mexico City shortly after the conquest.

Notable Italians

During the Renaissance, Italy was a patchwork of independent or semi-dependent principalities. In northern Italy most of the states and principalities belonged to several ruling families with remnants of feudal allegiance to the pope or the Holy Roman Emperor. Venice was a republic. Rome and the papal states of central Italy belonged to the pope, though some also had local noble rulers. Naples and Sicily were kingdoms affiliated with Spain. Despite the political divisions, the Italians visualized a greater entity: Italy. Dynastic marriages constantly realigned local noble families and foreign rulers, but intermarriage and kinship did little to stop the numerous conflicts or to enable effective action against foreign opportunists.

The decade beginning in 1492 was of critical importance to the

three Jewish families under scrutiny in this chapter. The ambitions of
the Sforzas of Milan, the republican leaders of Venice, and Pope Alexander
in Rome came into deadly conflict. Their local and foreign alliances
brought on invasions of Italy by various French kings, anxious to obtain
a share of the wealth and splendor of Italy. Battles, sacks of cities, pillaging
by soldiers, and concurrent attacks on Jewish quarters in the besieged
cities all caused great suffering for Jewish communities and disrupted
the lives of individual Jews. The political events and relationships of this
decade had important consequences in the lives of Jews throughout the
next century.

In 1492, when Isaac Abravanel fled from Spain, members of the
house of Aragon, cousins of King Ferdinand of Spain, were the kings
of Naples, King Ferrante I and then his son, King Alfonso. Only Abravanel
praised them: all the other chroniclers considered them petty and despotic,
and they fell to the French invasions.

The city of Rome at this time was ruled directly by the pope, and
the large papal territories politically answered to Pope Alexander VI—
by birth a Spaniard named Roderigo Borgia who became pope in 1492
and died in 1503. For several years prior to his death, he and his son
Cesare Borgia had been waging a campaign to conquer Italy or, as they
claimed, to unify Italy under the sway of the church. The armies of the
Borgias affected the lives of many Italians, Jews included, as they attacked
numerous small cities and conquered various territories from their
hereditary rulers. Cesare Borgia's methods and character, particularly as
Machiavelli presented them, have been notorious ever since the peak
of his power in 1503; he lost his hold on Italy as soon as his father died.
The Borgias' infamy may have at least partially been a later Protestant
invention, designed to highlight Catholic excesses and place the papacy
in disrepute—fairly recent books are still disputing the Borgias' true
character. (It's not only Jewish history that becomes cloudy due to the
motives of the chroniclers.)

Florence, the major city of Tuscany, was temporarily a republic,
recently emerged from the theocracy of Savanarola. Very soon there-
after, the famous Florentine Medici family made a comeback. They
not only resumed the rule in Florence, they also achieved power
through a Medici pope and through the marriages of their daughters,
such as Marie de Medici and Catherine de Medici, who married kings
of France.

In the north, Venice was a major power: Venetian territory occupied
much of northeastern Italy and included several Mediterranean islands.
The Venetians, or at least a noble minority of them, had traditionally

designated their leader, the Doge, in regularly scheduled elections, and no predominant personality characterized this government. Three families dominated the rest of northern Italy. The Sforza family ruled Milan, Pesaro, and other principalities. The d'Este family ruled the territory of Ferrara, and the Gonzaga family ruled Mantua and surrounding lands. As models of Renaissance nobility, they patronized the arts and humanities, and equally provided military leadership in the wars that swept Italy in their time. Tolerance for Jews made Mantua and Ferrara particularly important locations in Italian Jewish history. Several memorable personalities from this era were:

Isabella d'Este, known as the "First Lady of the Renaissance." (In Italian, she's the *prima donna.*) She was the daughter of Ercole d'Este, duke of Ferrara, granddaughter of the king of Naples (through her mother), and wife of the marquis of Mantua. Her passion was to collect artworks, books, sculpture, ceramics, beautiful clothing and jewels, and most other decorative items.

Gianfrancesco Gonzaga, Marquis of Mantua, Isabella's husband. He was a rather boorish military officer who offered his services to various sides, depending on the way the various conflicts were going.

Elizabetta Gonzaga, sister of Gianfrancesco Gonzaga, and her husband, Guidobaldo Montefeltre, duke of Urbino. They were patrons of humanists such as Castiglione and hosted at a model court. Guidobaldo was also a military officer, though he was better known as the proprietor of a famous library, originally assembled by his father.

Beatrice d'Este, Isabella's sister, married to Ludovico Sforza, the duke of Milan. Duke Ludovico patronized the arts and intrigued to increase Milan's power. Now he is remembered particularly for employing Leonardo da Vinci as a military engineer, monument designer, theater artist, and painter of *The Last Supper.* Beatrice died very young, the French conquered Milan in 1499, and Ludovico fell from power by 1503.

Lucrezia Borgia, Pope Alexander's daughter, married to Alfonso d'Este, Isabella's brother, in 1502. Lucrezia's father arranged this and two previous marriages for her in order to ratify his alliances with powerful families. Her first husband was the Sforza ruler of Pesaro. Using his papal powers, Alexander arranged her divorce when he wanted to make a new alliance. When divorce was inconvenient, with her second husband, he evidently had the man murdered. After the death of her father, Lucrezia spent the rest of her life in Ferrara, in comparative obscurity.

In brief, this was the Italian world that began the era in which the three Jewish families—Abravanel, Soncino, and Norsa—spent their lives.

THE INVENTION OF THE GHETTO

In 1500, the world looked wide open for art, culture, exploration, commerce, and many other things. At least, that's how it looked to Christians—and perhaps to recently converted Jews. The fortunes of Jews and Christians at this point, though, could not have been more different. The promise of the Renaissance, if it originally offered any hope to Jews, was soon lost. Ghetto walls and gates enclosed an increasingly poor and isolated Jewish community and alienated Jewish life from the culture and the economy of the Christian majority.

The term *ghetto* often refers to any Jewish neighborhood. In modern times, we have extended the term to any socially isolated and underprivileged ethnic area whose inhabitants have little flexibility to choose another home. Israel Zangwill described this later, more familiar ghetto: "People who have been living in a Ghetto for a couple of centuries, are not able to step outside merely because the gates are thrown down, nor to efface the brands on their souls by putting off the yellow badges. The isolation imposed from without will have come to seem the law of their being . . . . Such people are their own Ghetto gates" (Israel Zangwill, *Children of the Ghetto: A Study of a Peculiar People*, Detroit: Wayne State University Press, 1998, p. 61).

The first literal ghetto was built in Venice in 1516. In Italian history, the term *ghetto* thus refers to a particular social institution, an institution that built the physical gates that segregated and stigmatized Jews and gave rise to the conditions in Zangwill's description. The Venetian Ghetto did more than simply extend the treatment of Jews in the Middle Ages, because it much more thoroughly canceled the freedom of association between Jews and Christians that had existed earlier, even when there were separate Jewish streets and Jewish badges.

The background of the Venetian Ghetto goes back to the Middle Ages. In the fifteenth century, as the church promulgated anti-usury policies, anti-Jewish sentiment grew. Venice had always objected to Jewish inhabitants, and Venetian regulations often had required Jews to live on the mainland away from the center of commerce. Political and military

Noble Families

The Gonzagas of Mantua Established 1328	The Estes of Ferrara Established Twelfth Century	The Borgias
Marquis Ludovico Gonzaga, ruled 1448–1478; m. Barbara Hohenzollern	Duke Ercole d'Este, b. 1431; ruled 1571–1505; m. Leonora of Naples (1455–1493)	Pope Alexander VI (born Roderigo Borgia in Aragon, 1431; Pope from 1492–1503)
1. Marquis Gianfrancesco Gonzaga, b. 1466; ruled 1484–1519; m. Isabella d'Este (see next column) 2. Elizabetta Gonzaga; m. Duke of Urbino; three other children	1. Isabella d'Este (1476–1539) 2. Beatrice d'Este (d. 1493); m. Ludovico Sforza, Duke of Milan 3. Duke Alfonse d'Este, ruled 1505–1534; m. Lucrezia Borgia (see next column); three other sons	1. Cesare Borgia (1476–1507) 2. Lucrezia Borgia (1480–1519)
Children of Gianfrancesco and Isabella: 1. Marquis Federico II, ruled 1519–1540, promoted to Duke, 1530 2. Cardinal Ercole Gonzaga (1505–1565); six other children	Children of Alfonse and Lucrezia: 1. Duke Ercole II of Ferrara, ruled 1534–1559 2. Cardinal Ippolito d'Este	

Fig. 4-2: Connections among Italian Nobility

conditions, such as a growing rivalry with the Turkish Empire and with Portugal's new extra-Mediterranean trade routes, created a motive for Venice to allow more Jews in, but popular prejudices demanded control of these newcomers. In 1516, the Venetian ruling body, the Serinissima, allowed Jews, particularly German Jews who were numerous there, to occupy a location beside the new foundry—which in Italian, is called a ghetto. Thus, the neighborhood was called the "Ghetto Nuovo." Later, the governing body allowed small expansions to the Ghetto Nuovo. One of these included an area near the old foundry, giving the *newer* part of the neighborhood the name "Ghetto Vecchio," or old ghetto.

By decree, the Venetian Ghettos had walls, gates, and guards. Inhabitants were required to observe a curfew, and Christians were not allowed to enter during restricted hours. The residents had to employ and pay Christians to guard the gates—which officially protected them but more realistically jailed them. In Venice, patrol boats in the canals that surrounded the Ghetto also controlled entry or exit. Authorities could thus easily scrutinize activities of the inhabitants to ensure compliance with a variety of restrictions. In particular, the local Venetian Inquisition dealt with former Christian converts. They were especially concerned when individuals presented themselves as Jews when it was useful for aims like obtaining charity in the Ghetto, and as Christians when it gave them privileges like staying outside the Ghetto at night or following a restricted trade.

After the first Ghetto in Venice, at the growing insistence of the church, other Italian cities founded their own ghettos: like Venice, they gathered up Jews who lived under their jurisdiction and forced them to move to a few central locations under severely restricted circumstances. The Venetian Ghetto thus had wider influence, as the social and political climate of Italy was changing and becoming less tolerant and more cranky (partly thanks to the Reformation and counter-Reformation). As most Italian cities and small states instituted their own regulations, based on the system of Venice, a few towns resisted such measures, but over time, virtually all Jewish communities were either confined or expelled. Jews who had owned land or buildings outside the delimited ghetto usually lost their property, along with the right to inhabit their former homes or engage in agriculture or real estate rental. Also in imitation of Venice, the new Jewish neighborhoods became known as ghettos. The institution and the word *ghetto* also appeared in other countries, being applied retroactively to medieval Jewish neighborhoods and developing a more general meaning, especially in Eastern Europe, where Jews were numerous and very restricted.

As more and more cities in Italy and Europe at large isolated the Jews, they experienced increasingly disappointed goals and limited professional opportunities. Sometimes Jews resorted to conversion in order to keep family property and land that were outside the restricted ghetto territory. The continuously declining choices for making a living increased poverty, especially in the face of anti-Jewish laws restricting Jewish occupational categories. Finally, extreme crowding and poverty led to nearly total loss of the vigor and accomplishments of the medieval Jewish community. In the makeshift buildings, crowding caused fire hazards, health hazards, and psychological hazards. Contagious diseases and pests spread more rapidly than in places with more space, light, and sanitation. Consequently, despite the efforts of its residents to counter these tendencies, the ghetto became an unhealthy and unclean place, and Christians began to view the degraded state of the residents to be a confirmation of their preconceived ideas about Jews.

The End of the Ghetto

The physical ghettos of Italy and Western Europe also experienced a distinct end. The ideals of the French Revolution created a change in the treatment of Jews, as Napoleon and others insisted that liberty, equality, and fraternity should apply to Jews as well as to Catholics and Protestants. As he conquered the cities of Italy, Napoleon specifically ordered the destruction of the gates and walls of the ghettos. In Venice itself, the original Ghetto walls fell in 1797. Despite the nineteenth century backlash against Napoleon and what he stood for, the ghetto never fully recovered as an institution in Italy. The Italian Jews rapidly moved into mainstream society; many of them became successful professionals and civic leaders, and participated actively in the historic unification of the Italian states.

Ultimately, new attitudes and general acceptance of Jews into society in Western Europe had the same effect on ghettos elsewhere as well. As Jews in France, England, and Germany received official emancipation, the ghetto retained only the symbolic aftereffect that concerned Zangwill, who wrote: "For better or for worse, the Ghetto will be gradually abandoned, till at last it becomes only a swarming place for the poor and the ignorant, huddling together for social warmth" (*Children of the Ghetto*, p. 62).

The Abravanels in Italy

In August of 1492, just as Columbus's three ships were leaving Spain, the Abravanel family left their ancestral homeland, as mandated by Ferdinand and Isabella's order outlawing the practice of the Jewish religion in their realm. The family had already lost its youngest member, the son of Judah Abravanel and grandson of Isaac Abravanel. A panic evacuation of this baby to Portugal resulted from a royal campaign to force Isaac Abravanel to convert and thus remain in royal service. There was a plot to kidnap and baptize the child, and once baptized he would never be returned to unconverted family members. Judah Abravanel's autobiographical poem, written a decade later, described this event. It described his two sons, "precious, noble, handsome boys," both lost. The younger had died at the age of five. The elder was named Isaac Abravanel, after his own father, whom he praised lavishly, comparing him to King David. The poet described his own expectations, at the birth of this son, of continuing this proud family tradition. He told how the king of Spain, upon issuing the expulsion order, ordered a watch to be set so that he, Judah Abravanel, couldn't escape through the mountain passes of Spain. To deter him, the king ordered his men to seize the child, but, he says, "I sent him with his wet-nurse in the dark of midnight—just like smuggled goods!—to Portugal." This put the child into the control of the Portuguese king, who had already almost ruined the family. (Judah Abravanel's poem appears in Constable, *Medieval Iberia: Readings from Christian, Muslim, and Jewish Sources*, Philadelphia: University of Pennsylvania Press, 1997, p. 357).

With the loss of the child hanging over them, the Abravanel family prepared to flee from Spain to Italy. Everything that Isaac Abravanel could do at court had been done, such as offering his fortune to the king and attempting to reason with the queen. Between the expulsion order and the deadline for departure, Abravanel and his colleague Abraham Senior begged and exhorted with the monarchs to show leniency to the Jews. A variety of stories in Isaac Abravanel's own works and in the works of others describe the resolute refusal of the monarchs to weaken their determination that no unbaptized Jews would remain inside their borders. Some later accounts say that Senior was in fact threatened that if he did not convert, and thus continue to serve the king as a critical financial official, there would be even worse things done to his fellow faithful Jews. For whatever reason, Senior and his son-in-law, the highest Jewish officials in Spain, converted and remained behind.

In August, the final deadline, the Abravanels traveled to the Mediterranean coast, and although their money and power made their flight easier than that of the less fortunate, it must have been terrible. Desperate columns of now-homeless people were walking through the rugged Spanish country roads to reach ports where ships might take them to some land, somewhere, that would accept them. These refugees had given up all but a few possessions and abandoned their established ways of making a living; the expulsion decree prohibited the export of money and valuables by departing Jews. Along the road, well-meaning Christians begged the fleeing Jews to save themselves by accepting baptism; less friendly Christians abused the refugees. Beside the road, women gave birth to babies for whom there was no hope, and men, women, and children who were unable to keep walking faltered there. Many who found a place on a ship were robbed, sold as slaves, abandoned on deserted stretches of North African coast, or simply thrown overboard. Others, unable to find any ship at all, or unable to liquidate property into legally portable assets, lost hope for departure and unwillingly converted. Historians classify this as the worst catastrophe for the Jews between the destruction of the Second Temple and the Holocaust of the 1940s. The Abravanels understood the weight of what was happening, though they fared better than the others and arranged transport on a ship with at least a reliable captain.

In later generations, chroniclers called Isaac Abravanel the leader of his people on the exodus from Spain. However, the departure was much too disorganized, harassed, and chaotic to have had any real leadership. In their respect for Isaac Abravanel, they must have recalled how he had struggled and how he resisted the pressure to which Abraham Senior and his son-in-law capitulated.

Spanish Exiles Join the Italian Jews

The expulsion from Spain shook the Jewish world of 1492. Although the Jews in Spain had experienced a century of pogroms, had seen many of their community give in to the pressure to convert, and had experienced the founding of the Spanish Inquisition and its persecution of converts, they did not expect expulsion. Jews elsewhere, lulled by the confidence of the Spanish Jews, continued to view Spain as a kind of Jewish homeland and still looked with admiration on the accomplishment and leadership of Spanish Jews. The separation from Spain and their real or imagined life in the Spanish environment seemed more painful than any previous expulsion. Both Spanish and non-Spanish Jews viewed it as a new exile, and the victims identified with the captive Jews who lost Jerusalem when the Babylonians leveled Solomon's Temple and with those who fled from Judea after the Romans destroyed the Second Temple. There was no other precedent for the loyalty and the nostalgia of Spanish Jews, and few precedents for their difficulties in finding somewhere to go.

Several factors distinguish the experiences of earlier refugees—from France, Germany, and Moslem Spain—and the experiences of the refugees of 1492. Earlier expulsions had sometimes made more exceptions for talented or valuable Jews, while the edict of Ferdinand and Isabella was unwavering: convert, leave, or die. Abraham Zacuto expressed a major geographic difference: this time, instead of crossing a border to find a less-hostile environment, Jews had to choose either a long voyage on dangerous seas or doubtful refuge with unwelcoming neighbors. In Navarre and Portugal, attainable by land, the few who were admitted paid heavily for a temporary right to enter.

Only the richest, canniest, and luckiest of Spanish Jews managed to obtain passage on ships leaving Spain in the desperate spring and summer of 1492. Onboard the ships in which most of them headed for Italy, disease broke out in the overcrowded quarters, and provisions, sanitation, and medicines were in short supply. As a result, the refugees arrived in terrible condition. Some ships were turned away from Genoa and only accepted reluctantly in Naples. Admission of Jewish refugees to other Italian cities, such as Rome, Ferrara, and Mantua, occurred later. Genoa, Rome, and Naples accepted a very small number of refugees at first, and later, as more and more fled from Portugal, retained a very exclusive policy. It is far from clear that Italian and other Jews already established in Italy welcomed the refugees; in fact, they were often very reluctant to take risks in order to accommodate them. Isaac Abravanel, who was able to exploit his financial contacts in the Jewish community in Italy as well as to appeal to the king of Naples with his expertise from the courts of Spain, was extremely unusual.

The Spanish edict of 1492, combined with various military campaigns in Italy, also touched off the expulsion of Jews from other kingdoms. Within a decade, the kings of Portugal, Naples, Navarre, and Majorca (which included cities in present-day France) emulated their Spanish cousins and required the conversion or departure of the local Jewish communities, including any Spanish exiles who had joined them. Another upheaval thus affected their lives. The Abravanel family first settled in Naples and was forced to move on after experiencing the loss of more of their remaining possessions. One member of the Soncino family had established a branch of the family printing press in Naples and disappeared during the sack of the city by France. By 1500, only converted Jews (some still practicing Judaism in secret) lived in Portugal and Spain, while the faithful Sephardic Jews concentrated in the Balkans, Turkey, North Africa, and the Middle East. The total number that reached northern Italy was small, though it later increased as the Sephardic Jews of Portugal slowly escaped.

While the Italian rulers and Jewish communities did not consistently welcome the exiled Sephardim, Italy became important as a place where Sephardic culture managed to survive. Prominent Spanish Jews, such as the Abravanel family and Abraham Zacuto, found a home in Italy and managed to establish or join existing synagogues with the Spanish ritual, preserve their learning and traditions, and gain the respect of their fellow-Jews and of openminded Italians.

The Abravanel Family: A Summary

In 1492, Isaac Abravanel brought four sons with him from Spain to Italy. He had left several brothers, nieces, and nephews behind in Portugal; within a few years, many of them also joined the family, especially in Naples. The following family tree shows the major family members of the Abravanel family who are discussed in this chapter, and how they are related, particularly by cousin marriages.

The Abravanel Family in Italy

The following represents the names of family members who played a significant role in the text. Isaac Abravanel's daughters' names are not known.

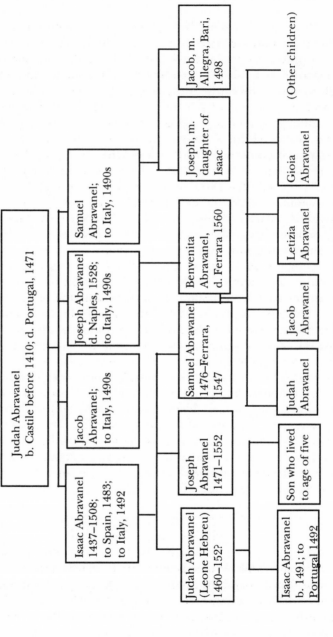

Fig. 4-3: Abravanel Family Tree

NAPLES—ISAAC ABRAVANEL ARRIVES IN ITALY

Isaac Abravanel arrived in Naples, Italy, in much better shape than most of his fellow Jewish refugees from Spain. The monarchs, in gratitude for his former service, had granted him a special dispensation of the rule against Jews' removal of liquid wealth, leaving him able to take some of his capital out of Spain. Moreover, he had managed to obtain places for his family on one of the first ships to leave Valencia and arrive in Italy; although conditions on board were not great, the ships that arrived later experienced disease and starvation. Thanks to his vast fortune, his international connections, and his foresight, he also had letters of credit with Jewish bankers in Italy; that is, he had deposited money with them earlier and could therefore retrieve it without formally carrying it out of the country. As a result, he reached Naples with his dignity and many of his goods intact, and quickly found a job at the court of the Aragonese King Ferrante of Naples and was able to support his brothers and sons who had arrived with him or shortly after.

In Naples, the situation for the Jewish refugees became desperate soon after Abravanel's arrival. Many had been on boats that had been refused entry to Genoa and other ports because the plague had broken out on board the ships. Under the influence of Abravanel, King Ferrante permitted the Jews to leave the ships, providing temporary quarantine camps, in hopes of protecting the city from the plague. Obviously, they were also set up for the traditional attribution that Jews caused plague, a bad start in a new place. These recently prosperous people looked like walking skeletons, having spent months at sea on unsanitary, under-provisioned, and crowded boats in a hot climate, suffering as well from the evident toll on their pride and self-respect. When Abravanel later reviewed the situation of these Jews, he identified the curse of exile as the lack of three things: courage, honor, and a government (B. Netanyahu, *Don Isaac Abravanel: Statesman & Philosopher,* Philadelphia: Jewish Publication Society of America, 1953, p. 231).

Naples and Monopoli

Isaac Abravanel's talents were snapped up by the Spanish rulers of Naples. His statesmanship and his financial knowledge made him valuable. He first served King Ferrante, a nephew of King Ferdinand. Despite the relationship, Ferrante had not chosen to implement Ferdinand's anti-Jewish policies. In 1494, upon Ferrante's death, his son Alfonso succeeded him as king, continuing to depend heavily on Abravanel's services. The war against Naples by the French King Charles VIII disrupted the lives of Alfonso and his court. Along with them, Isaac Abravanel fled to Mazzara, Sicily. Although Sicily was officially part of the Spanish territory from which Jews were expelled, Abravanel was now loyal to his new master and accompanied him. The Sicilians gave him temporary immunity from the expulsion order, as long as he was directly serving Alfonso.

Soon after they left Naples, the French invaded. The Jewish community, including the recently arrived Spanish Jews, suffered terribly in the devastation and pogrom that accompanied the invasion. The French troops' actions inspired the Christians of Naples to join them and to sack the Jewish quarter, loot Jewish property, and kill large numbers of Jewish inhabitants. Essentially, the Jewish community of Naples never recovered from the events of 1494, although individual Jews, particularly members of the Abravanel family, returned at times after the invasion, and huge numbers of refugees from Spain remained there. Over time, the expulsion order from Spain was similarly applied to Naples as well, though it did not become final until 1540.

When Isaac Abravanel had accompanied King Alfonso's flight, he had left the other members of his family in Naples; although they survived the pogrom, much of his property was lost again, including his valuable book collection and works in progress. After this, his sons went on to other cities, and when Alfonso no longer needed him, Abravanel could not remain in Sicily and thus moved on. From early in 1496 until 1503, he spent a very quiet interlude in Monopoli, a city on the Adriatic. Monopoli belonged to Naples, halfway between Brindisi and Bari, but had recently been captured by Venice in a campaign in the ongoing wars.

During his Monopoli years, Abravanel spent his time writing and completing various philosophical works, in a kind of retirement from the extraordinarily active political life he had led until then. In these writings he reviewed the sorrows and misfortunes of the Jews and reflected on events of his lifetime, writing in context of various battles he had witnessed. Although well into his sixties, Abravanel did not succeed in retiring for good. In 1503, he moved on to serve again in Venice.

Meanwhile, Isaac Abravanel's adult sons Judah and Samuel were also establishing themselves in the new Italian environment. Judah first went north, became associated with philosophical movements in Genoa and Florence, and later returned to Naples as the physician of Gonsalvo of Cordoba. Samuel married his cousin Benvenita, the daughter of Isaac's brother Jacob. He studied in Salonica, later returned to Naples, and finished his life in Ferrara, where his sons continued his successful financial business, as I will describe later. Cousin marriages and re-use of the same few masculine first names—Samuel, Joseph, Judah, Jacob, Isaac—seem to have been a common practice in the Abravanel family.

VENICE—AN IDEAL CITY?

In 1503, Isaac Abravanel went to Venice; again, he offered to apply his talents in a major international endeavor, suggesting that he would help the Venetians to set up a trade agreement with Portugal. Venice and Portugal had become trade rivals because of the new Portuguese trade routes that circumnavigated Africa. The Venetian Council of Ten, the main rulers of the republic, accepted Abravanel's plan and designated him to act as a mediator. They sent Joseph, his nephew (and also his son-in-law) to Portugal as a Venetian emissary. In view of the Venetians' policy restricting Jews, and in view of the recent forced conversion of every Jew in Portugal, this seems rather odd. The Venetians' potential loss of their former monopoly on spice and other Eastern precious goods must have left them desperate to formalize an arrangement with the Portuguese.

Venice was at the time an extremely important Mediterranean power, with many colonies in the islands and along both the east and west coasts of the Adriatic. The rivalry with Portugal was only one Venetian conflict of the time. The growth of the Turkish empire since the Moslem Turks conquered Constantinople in 1453 had eroded Venetian power. Venice was also involved in the constantly changing alliances within Italy, including the repeated invasions by the French and the wars involving the Borgias. Venetians were also beginning to see the potential of Spain's New World.

The trade negotiations ended in 1505, after which Isaac Abravanel could pursue literary goals, publishing several new books. As usual, he acted both as a political man and as a philosopher, and his observations of Venice found their way into his political philosophy. He had high praise for the Venetian republican government, where no hereditary prince, but rather a council of individually chosen people, controlled the municipality; he interpreted certain biblical passages to promote such government as the ideal political arrangement. His son Judah—by then a recognized poet—wrote prefaces for some of these works.

I will discuss what remains to be seen in Venice today at the end of this chapter. I have very little information as to the details of Isaac Abravanel's life and experience there; I don't know whether he had an exception to the prohibition, then in effect, against long-term Jewish residents.

Venice and Isaac Abravanel's Philosophy

Isaac Abravanel was one of the most famous Jewish thinkers of the period. His innovative works of biblical commentary were used by both Jewish and Christian scholars for several centuries. His main legacy was a messianic view that contributed to Jewish messianic expectations and paved the way for the subsequent recognition of various false messiahs. Abravanel developed a utopian view of political activity, based on both biblical interpretation and on his experiences as a hands-on administrator. In his writings, Abravanel constantly used historical and biblical parallelism; thinking along such lines, he was the first writer to set the date of the expulsion from Spain as the ninth of Av, the date of the destruction of both Temples and other catastrophes of Jewish history. (Evidently, this date is slightly inaccurate.)

During his years in Venice, Abravanel idealized the Venetian republican form of government that he encountered there and integrated a number of its elements into his view of an ideal, biblically based city. Abravanel reinterpreted certain biblical verses about the way that Moses governed in order to idealize the republican method of governing Venice, which he called "The Princess among the States." He explained the separation of the Jews from all other nations by his belief that Hebrew was the original and perfect language. During construction of the tower of Babel, he claimed, the creation of artificial things had caused newly invented vocabulary to factionalize and divide humanity into differing nations, a process that eventually led to this separation (Netanyahu, *Abravanel*, pp. 141–142).

He combined these views with what he found in Venice. The Venetian ruling body, the Council of Ten, made the supreme decisions. Less powerful governing bodies in Venice had larger numbers of members and apparently worked in an advisory or less important capacity. Abravanel compared this to the government of the Jews under Moses, though, according to Netanyahu, he interpreted the biblical passages in a nonstandard way in order to support his views of Venice. He also favorably compared Venetian government to the rule of the Greek and Roman republics of antiquity. His praise was also based on the high esteem and power Venice enjoyed in European politics of the time. Abravanel clearly felt that success in a political system, even if was unjustly or tyrannically managed, was a mark of God's favor. For this reason, he disapproved of overthrowing even the worst tyrannical kings (Netanyahu, *Abravanel*, pp. 166–169).

Abravanel's utopian government, as described in various political works, differed in some ways from the Venetian model. He wanted more democratic election of the councils of state. This represents another departure from more standard interpretation of the government under Moses: usually, it is supposed that Moses made appointments, not that the Israelites had elections. Netanyahu describes how Abravanel's ideal government had lower courts in cities and towns, elected by the people; regional units, also elected, to deal with judicial, political, and military matters; and the highest court (Sanhedrin) with the highest authority in these matters, over the entire nation, coming from the aristocracy and not elected. Another modern analyst of Abravanel says: "Of all the medieval and early Renaissance Jewish philosophers, Abravanel alone revived the biblical ideal of a theocratic state and condemned Israel's longing for a monarchy as an example of assimilative tendencies" (Martin Cohen, "Usque and Isaac Abravanel," in Martin A. Cohen, *Samuel Usque's Consolation for the Tribulations of Israel*, Philadelphia: Jewish Publication Society, 1965, p. 275).

Abravanel paralleled other Jewish humanists in writing biblically based political works, summarized as follows: "Writings on moral philosophy, which Jewish writers tended to call political philosophy, have always been part of Jewish teaching, so that the most obvious innovation during [this] period was the use of new literary forms, often narratives, to present the goods and virtues. As in the other fields . . . Hebrew writers tried to derive their compositions from the most ancient Hebrew texts." The biblical book of Proverbs, attributed to King Solomon, was used as a source, in particular by Johannen Alemanno, who associated with the Christian humanists. Alemanno wrote a biography of Solomon between 1488 and 1492 for Pico della Mirandola, about whom more information appears further on. He presented Solomon as the Jewish model of a perfect sage and ruler (Arthur M. Lesley, "Jewish Adaptation of Humanist Concepts," in Ruderman, *Essential Papers*, New York: New York University Press, 1992, pp. 57–59).

Abravanel's contemporaries, such as Machiavelli, thought quite differently about politics. The humanists were intensely interested in the day's rulers and in a view of what effective government and good governing philosophy would be—holding the view that men, especially those in power, have a large measure of control of their own destiny. Italy was an interesting laboratory. Its governments included the papal territories, republics, hereditary dukedoms owing allegiance to the Holy Roman Emperor, and other dependent and independent principalities. Powerful states preyed on less-powerful neighbors, with lots of intrigue and the formation of alliances. Some families or individuals had risen from obscurity and stayed in power a long time, such as the Medicis in Florence or Gonzagas in Mantua. Others rose and fell rather rapidly, such as the Sforzas in Milan and Cesare Borgia. Some families inherited power rather quietly over many generations (such as the d'Estes in Ferrara or the Picos of Mirandola). Others came and went obscurely in a stable oligarchy, such as the Doges of Venice or pre-Medici republican leaders in Florence. The Italian political philosophers of 1500 also looked to Spain, regarding Ferdinand's successful consolidation of Aragon, Castile, and other parts of the country. As I mentioned earlier, these philosophers ultimately admired Ferdinand's expulsion of the Jews as a successful power move.

Abravanel's view of kings is problematic, as he condemned opposition to even the worst tyrants. He held a deterministic view, that God put kings there even if they were not good, which he applied to the kings in Italy and Spain. And while he praised individual kings, he disapproved of the institution of kings in general. Dynastic permanence and inheritance were not necessarily good things, in his view. He felt that good and just laws and customs should limit absolute power, as he felt had been the case in mosaic times. In addition to Venice, he praised the other non-monarchies in Italy of his day. He felt that kings abused power, but even where their power was limited, he didn't think it was ideal. Besides biblical sources, he may have used Plato, Cicero, and the humanists of his own time to develop this ideal.

Messianic Predictions

The year 1503, when Isaac Abravanel arrived in Venice, was also the earliest date that he had predicted as the beginning of the messianic era. His prediction specified that critical, foreboding occurrences and astronomical events in this year would create the conditions for the destruction of Rome some thirty years later. The destruction of Rome would herald the arrival of the Messiah, the return of the Jews to Israel, the restoration of Jerusalem, and the fulfillment of traditional prophesies. The biographers whom I have read give no indication that Abravanel reacted particularly strongly when his first year in Venice came and went without apparent change in worldwide conditions. Evidently, he was confident that one of the later dates that he had predicted would turn out to be the beginning of the desired chain of events.

Abravanel's mix of messianic belief, humanistic sympathy for the suffering of his fellow Jews, and wide learning in Jewish and classical areas cause some critics to focus on his traits as a late medieval thinker and others to stress his Renaissance tendencies. His philosophy had elements of medieval scholastic rationalism, mystical sources inspired by kabbalists, and Renaissance sources. Some modern writers classify him as original, others trace numerous influences on his major ideas.

In his messianic speculation, Abravanel seems to have more in common with medieval thinkers. However, Abravanel was not the only person in his time to choose the date 1503 or to hedge with alternatives. Both other Jews and Christians based messianic predictions on social and historic events, on astronomical or astrological reasoning, or on kabbalistic speculations. The planetary line-up of 1503 drew everyone's attention and inspired a variety of predictions. Like Abravanel, these prophets did not lose face when this year came and went without earthshaking changes, and both Christians and Jews continued to make predictions and explain their reasons without revising their assumptions. Abravanel continued to share and amplify the messianic hopes and superstitions of Jews. His conviction that the Messiah's arrival was an immediate possibility strengthened the impact of various "false" messiahs on Jewish communities in his own time and for some time afterward (Ruderman, "Hope against Hope: Jewish and Christian Messianic Expectations in the Late Middle Ages," in Ruderman, *Essential Papers*).

The explicitness of Abravanel's prediction seems rather strange to a modern person. The views of that time differed considerably from modern views; in the words of Netanyahu: "Any man who would make such a statement in our time would be considered a lunatic or a charlatan." He contrasts our attitude with the medieval attitude toward such people, comparing the medieval view of messianic prophesy to modern attitudes toward political predictions, which we judge by evaluating the argument and its presenter. He continues:

> The mere fact that messianic predictions involved a superhuman, miraculous element was not considered sufficient reason to diminish their prospects for realization. People everywhere were inclined to believe in miracles and the line of demarcation in man's mind between the possible and the impossible was very thin. Messianic predictions, moreover, were based upon the words of the prophets, and their materialization was therefore considered likely to the extent that it seemed reasonable to accept the interpretation on which they relied. (Netanyahu, *Abravanel*, p. 219)

Abravanel extended the standard speculation of the age by adding the specific motive of improving the psychological condition of the demoralized refugees. In fact, the major focus of Abravanel's later writings and predictions centered on the consolation of the Jews for the loss of their hopes and of the Spanish homeland. The writer Menachem Kellner described Abravanel's motives in comforting the victims of the greatest calamity in their recent history. He points out that Abravanel considered conventional religious leaders a failure for not giving Jews an orderly explanation of "what Judaism demanded of them. . . . All of Abravanel's post-Expulsion literary activity was connected in one way or another with his attempt to encourage and console the shattered people." Kellner also writes:

> Abravanel sought to console and encourage his fellow Jews primarily by instilling in them the fervent belief in the imminent coming of the Messiah. Aside from his three explicitly messianic works . . . we find the theme of redemption dominating his commentary on the Passover *Haggadah* . . . and many of his biblical commentaries. . . . [Abravanel] sought to justify the ways of God in the light of catastrophes like the Expulsion, [and he] encouraged Jews to remain faithful to the "inheritance of their fathers." (Menachem Kellner, *Dogma in Medieval Jewish Thought: From Maimonides to Abravanel*, London: Oxford University Press, 1986, pp. 179, 193–194).

ISAAC ABRAVANEL'S DEATH

Isaac Abravanel died in Venice in 1508. He couldn't be buried in Venice, because the few Jews who lived there had no right to establish a cemetery. His body was removed to Padua, though his grave, along with the Jewish cemetery to which his body had to be taken, disappeared within a year after his death, during one of the invasions and wars that continually affected Italy in the first quarter of the sixteenth century. Perhaps this lack of final respect was a preview of how this ideal republic would soon treat Jews, by confining them within the newly invented Ghetto. In any case, it was not unusual for Jews in Italy at that time to have difficulties burying their dead; even when they did have permission to maintain a cemetery, it was frequently located far away from the Jewish residential area, and municipal authorities—or a mob—sometimes prevented mourners from conducting a timely and dignified burial for their dead.

JEWS AND HUMANISTS

Isaac Abravanel was a mature thinker when he arrived in Italy. Many of his most important works were completed or at least planned before he left Spain, and he wrote in Hebrew for a Jewish audience. Thus, he only marginally joined in the intellectual life of the Italian Renaissance. His son Judah, however, participated actively in Italian intellectual life. He became acquainted with non-Jewish philosophers and their works, and wrote an influential poem, the *Dialogues of Love*, that was published in Italian and translated into many European languages. Before continuing with Judah's life, I want to pause to consider the wider context in which intellectual Jews interacted with the Italian humanists and influenced Christian thinkers of the period. Humanism focused interest on ancient languages, including Hebrew. Humanists were interested in broadening their perspective, and one way they saw to expand was to study various other religions. Both humanists and other Christians also became interested in Jewish mystical traditions, particularly in their kabbalistic developments.

A simple description of humanism defines it as a philosophy that is centered around human beings, as opposed to preoccupation with an afterlife, a spirit world, or other superhuman or nonhuman concerns, particularly those that were most important to medieval philosophy and Christian thinkers. Humanist thought first flourished in the twelfth century, when the rational philosophy of classic authors such as Cicero, Seneca, and Aristotle initially returned to the European arena of intellectual endeavor. Religious humanists at this time made efforts particularly to visualize Jesus, his parents, and his followers as human beings. Further, humanists began to value human curiosity, intelligence, and accomplishment for their own sake.

In the Italian Renaissance in the fifteenth and sixteenth centuries, the combination of Christianity with a focus on humanity was still developing. At least two other definitions applied to these Renaissance humanists. A humanist was a scholar who acquired a wide knowledge of classical languages and literature of the ancients—Latin, Greek, and Hebrew. More broadly, a humanist was any one of the erudite men who, in the course of the fifteenth and sixteenth centuries, by their lessons and publications, restored the reputation of the masterpieces of classical antiquity. (Definitions cited by G. Weil, *Elie Levita: Humaniste et Massorete [1469–1549]*, Leiden: E. J. Brill, 1963, p. 213.)

Humanist thinkers often served as teachers to the noble families of Italy. The d'Este family of Ferrara employed humanist tutors for several generations of their children, including Isabella d'Este. Pico della Mirandola sent Aldus Manutius as a tutor to his nephews, heirs of a very small town called Carpi. (Later, we will explore the subsequent humanist activities of Aldus as he transferred his efforts to the arena of printing classical literature and thus making it more accessible to further humanists.) In Florence, the Medicis patronized a humanist academy, where numerous important interactions occurred between scholars from various traditions, including Greek and Hebrew. Humanists also became teachers at the emerging universities, such as Padua, where Jewish scholars joined Christian humanists, who valued the Jewish contribution toward one of the reviving areas of study, Hebrew literature and traditions. The Medici popes, the rulers of northern Italian cities such as Florence, Milan, and Ferrara, and many other prominent men and women of the era were influenced by these humanist thinkers and teachers.

Leonardo da Vinci's notebooks, an exciting source of Renaissance ideas, offer further insight about the scope of humanism. Leonardo wanted to expand human knowledge by observation and experiment. He recorded what he learned as he dissected bodies, looked for the beautiful and the grotesque in human faces, sketched from life and from cadavers, studied the motion of birds and horses, tested how the human eye perceived landscapes and natural scenes, analyzed mechanical systems and imagined new ones, invented military and engineering projects, created plans for paintings and sculptures, and experimented with new techniques in paint (unfortunately, very often unsuccessfully). His modern position as *the* Renaissance Man idealizes this combination of art and science and captures this spirit of humanist inclusiveness.

How well do these various definitions and questions about humanists apply to the Jewish thinkers and scholars of the Renaissance? A twelfth-century definition of the humanist who tries to see Jesus as a man is clearly inapplicable. The definition of someone who revives classical languages is also a problem, as Jewish scholars never lost their connection with Hebrew knowledge; moreover, in Arab and Iberian countries, Jewish scholars had participated in study, translation, and preservation of the Greek and Latin classics. Even much later, Isaac Abravanel studied Latin classics as part of his early education in Lisbon. Jewish humanists couldn't easily be accepted for their Hebrew learning, because of the present and growing distrust of Jewish material, seen as dangerously obscure or subversive by Christian establishment figures who couldn't read it. The Talmud and kabbalistic material, in particular, were constantly suspected of containing overt or hidden anti-Christian sentiments. In the early fifteenth century, the church combined humanist interest and anti-Jewish fear by encouraging Christian printers, rather than Jews, to produce the Hebrew-language books they considered important. By mid-century, this distrust led instead to book-burning and severe censorship.

In general, Jews as humanists differed from Christians because they had never lost the love of learning that was being revived by the Italian Renaissance. According to the definition of humanists as erudite restorers, as well, Weil suggests, a Jew can't be classified as a humanist, because the masterpieces of Jewish literature never ceased to be witnesses of the reality and tribulations of his community. Later, we will discuss how this Jewish-humanist approach distinguished Gershom Soncino, the foremost Jewish printer of the time, from other printers and other humanists.

Humanists in the Visual Arts

Today visual arts are much more familiar than literature. In keeping with traditional Jewish views, Jews seem to have completely abstained from participation in the visual arts, rarely even voluntarily having their own portraits made; the only exception is the illustration of books, a much more modest endeavor than the huge altarpieces and palace decorations of the major painters and sculptors of the time. Nevertheless, I wish to introduce the following summary to suggest how you might relate the most famous images of the era with these more obscure chapters of history, and particularly how they may help you to relate to the most famous tourist sites and museums of Italy that you will experience on a well-rounded visit to Florence, Milan, or Rome. Here are some famous artists and what they were doing in the first years of the sixteenth century:

Michelangelo (1475–1564) was in Florence, working on the statue *David*, which very much reflects the influence of ancient Greek sculpture.

Raphael d'Urbino (1483–1520) was in Perugia as an apprentice in Perugino's studio, where he was just beginning to produce independent works.

Sandro Botticelli (1445–1510) was in Florence—having fallen under the spell of Savonarola, he had virtually renounced painting. His works had broadly included a number of Greek and Roman mythological subjects, such as his famous *Spring*, as well as many Christian religious subjects. His last work dates from 1500.

Andrea Mantegna (1431–1506) was the court painter to the Gonzagas, rulers of Mantua, as he had been for most of his life. He executed many commissions for Isabella d'Este and Gianfrancesco Gonzaga. In *Parnassus* he depicted Isabella d'Este as a dancing nymph among the worshipers of the god Apollo. The Louvre now owns this and also owns his work *Madonna of the Victories*, which has a special significance in the history of the Jewish community of Mantua, to be explained later.

Albrecht Durer (1471–1528) spent most of the early part of the century in Nuremberg, Germany. Slightly earlier, on a youthful visit to Italy, he had been influenced by Mantegna and later visited Venice. Although he eventually favored Luther's reaction against humanism, he was heavily influenced by the Italian Renaissance and its interests.

Hieronymous Bosch (1450–1516) probably spent his entire life in Holland, which belonged to Spain.

Leonardo da Vinci (1452–1519)—probably the most famous painter of the time—traveled semi-rootlessly around Italy after the French conquered his employer, Ludovico Sforza, the duke of Milan. He had been Milan's court engineer and painter, and after the war, during a short stay in Mantua, he sketched pictures of Isabella d'Este. In 1500, he entered the service of Cesare Borgia. In 1504, he returned to his native Florence, where he competed with Michelangelo in making murals (now lost) for the town hall of the Florentine Republic. In 1505, Leonardo painted a portrait of a Florentine woman named Mona Lisa (born around 1480, date of death unknown). This portrait made her the most permanently famous woman of the era—though in 1500 she was merely the second wife of an obscure merchant.

Pico della Mirandola and Jewish Philosophers

Count Giovanni Pico della Mirandola lived from 1463 to 1494. As a Renaissance humanist, he valued diverse ideas and thus studied with several Jewish thinkers. At the age of fourteen, Pico began to study at the university of Bologna, where the faculty included the Jewish scholars Elijah del Medigo and Johannan Alemanno. Along with many other topics, Alemanno introduced him to kabbalistic philosophy. Pico established a personal goal of the study of Kabbalah in order to synthesize its teachings with that of Catholicism—a thankless task that soon got him in trouble with the establishment, especially when he tried to present a major treatise on world religions to the pope.

The synthesis of various intellectual endeavors was important to all humanists. Before Pico's arrival in Florence, the Medicis and other patrons had founded seminars and an "academy" in Florence, where Italian philosophers, Greek scholars from Constantinople, artists, and others discussed their work. Pico continued to set up dialogues between scholars and to commission manuscripts and new translations of works he considered important. He arranged to have Aldus Manutius, a would-be humanist philosopher, become the tutor of his nephews, who lived back in Mirandola, the small and isolated territory near Ferrara where his family were the rulers. A few years afterward, Aldus became an entrepreneur in the new and growing field of printing, innovating many ideas for publishing the texts to advance humanist studies. Pico or other members of his family may have continued to patronize Aldus. Along another line, it is said that a Jewish philosopher consulted with Ghiberti and the humanist Ambrogio Traversari to choose the biblical symbols for the famous *Doors of Paradise* for the Baptistry. I have mentioned the all-encompassing view of Leonardo da Vinci, who was also in Florence at the time.

The influence and accomplishments of Pico illustrate the nature of humanism and humanists. He collected books and manuscripts, assembling one of the great private libraries that didn't belong to the church or a major ruler. He joined the circle of Florentine humanists led by Marsilius Fincino, who had introduced many humanist ideas. He gathered a circle of widely varied thinkers to discuss humanist issues and to teach him about diverse philosophies, inviting prominent Jewish philosophers, possibly including Judah Abravanel, and his former teachers to symposia at his home in Florence.

Pico believed that his synthesis of all previous philosophy was the way to full understanding that he and other scholars of the day were seeking. Like many of his contemporaries, he looked to existing occult knowledge as a source of objective truth and, like them, made little distinction between a secret process that was owned by a guild such as the masons (the literal bricklayers, not the cult) and some other secret process that was owned by mystics such as the Hebrew kabbalists. He wrote: "The dignity of the liberal arts . . . and their value to us is attested not only by the Mosaic and Christian mysteries but also by the theologies of the most ancient times" (Pico della Mirandola, *Oration on the Dignity of Man,* Chicago, transl., Robert Caponigri, Chicago: University of Chicago, 1956, p. 25).

When Pico presented his ideas about the unity of many religions

in Rome, he tried to influence the church to have an open discussion—
but was quickly silenced. Eventually, history favored the empirical and
rational approach of science, and Pico's kabbalistic studies turned out
to be a blind alley, although he called them "science." The deductive
systems of physics, mathematics, and natural observations were developed
successfully by Kepler, Copernicus, and Bruno (J. L. Blau, *The Christian
Interpretation of the Cabala in the Renaissance*, Port Washington, NY: Kennicat
Press, 1965).

Evidently, Pico was a religious, not a secular, humanist and was very
committed to religious enlightenment. This led him, among other things,
to make efforts to convert the Jews to Christianity. He suggested that ideas
from the Kabbalah would provide a good starting argument to persuade
the Jews of Christian truth, analogous to the talmudic arguments that
had worked at the Disputation of Tortosa and the polemics of Spanish
churchmen earlier in the century. He wrote:

> [Oral communications of wise men since Moses were to be collected by
> scribes into seventy volumes; these books] are the books of cabalistic wisdom.
> In these books . . . resides the springs of understanding, that is, the ineffable
> theology of the supersubstantial deity; the fountain of wisdom, that is, the
> precise metaphysical doctrine concerning intelligible and angelic forms;
> and the stream of wisdom, that is, the best established philosophy con-
> cerning nature. . . . There was to be found the mystery of the Trinity, the
> Incarnation of the Word, the divinity of the Messiah; there one might also
> read of original sin, of its expiation by Christ, of the heavenly Jerusalem,
> of the fall of the demons, of the orders of the angels, of the pains of
> purgatory and of hell. There I read the same things which we read every
> day in the pages of Paul and of Dionysius, Jerome and Augustine. In
> philosophical matters it were as though one were listening to Pythagoras
> and Plato, whose doctrines bear so close an affinity to the Christian faith
> that our Augustine offered endless thanks to God that the books of the
> platonists had fallen into his hands. In a word, there is no point of controversy
> between the Hebrews and ourselves on which the Hebrews cannot be
> confuted and convinced out of the cabalistic writings, so that no corner
> is left for them to hide in. (*Oration on the Dignity of Man*, pp. 63–65)

The Christian humanists' attitude toward the Jews was also reflected
in their assessment of Ferdinand and Isabella's expulsion of the Jews from
Spain. The consensus of Christian opinion, including that of Pico, quickly
accepted the Inquisition as an unchallengeable fact in law and history.
In 1493 Pico wrote that he "found pride and solace in the victory of
their Church, the exaltation of their faith and the divine judgment meted

out to Jews through the 'Most Christian King who is beyond all praise.'
... In the famous polemical work in which Mirandola attacked astrology,
he referred with much satisfaction to the Expulsion of the Jews from
Spain as having disproved the astrological calculations of the Jewish
scholars." Similar anti-Jewish sentiments include the humanist historian
Guicciardini's praise of Ferdinand and Isabella and Machiavelli's com-
mendation for Ferdinand's seizure of Jewish property for his own political
purposes (Baer, *History of the Jews in Christian Spain*, pp. 440–441).

Compartmentalized Medieval Philosophies

Jewish philosophy, kabbalistic studies, and theories of the mystical quality
of the Hebrew language were unknown to mainstream Christians for most
of the Middle Ages; in fact, Jews made every effort to keep them secret.
The secrecy itself made this appealing to Renaissance seekers of new
truth. By 1500, Pico and others began to adapt the Jewish thought stream
into their Christian philosophy. Afterward, a continued tradition of
Christian Cabala (the spelling differs for the Christian and Jewish versions) achieved a life of its own without Jewish participation.

In the Renaissance, the practice of alchemy became tied up with
Christian philosophy and mysticism. Earlier, it had been a more straight-
forward effort to find the "philosopher's stone" that would extend life
and allow the transmutation of base metals into silver and gold, and had
been respectably linked with the medieval study of natural science. In
the Middle Ages, Jews had participated in these efforts. They served as
royal physicians, astrologers, and alchemists. Many of them had methods
that convinced both themselves and their royal masters that they could
produce gold from other substances. The same person often combined
what we now view as both science and non-science. Even at the end of
the fifteenth century, Abraham Zacuto, relying on what we now see as
solid science supplied Columbus's astronomical tables and informed him
about the patterns of storms he might encounter in his voyage. But Zacuto
later held an appointment as astrologer to the king of Portugal. Judah
Abravanel held a chair of medicine *and* astrology at the University of
Naples (Roth, *Jews in the Renaissance*, p. 129).

Although anti-Jewish sentiment increased rapidly during the period
of the Reformation and counter-Reformation, at the same time, a sort
of respect for the wisdom of the Jews emerged. Most of the proponents,
fearing the Inquisition or similar Protestant thought police, preferred
to keep their distance from real Jews. They defined Jewish wisdom as

coming from ancient sages and magicians, not from the current persecuted minority seen as impoverished rag pickers who lived in the ghetto.
A few Jewish scholars still managed to participate in humanism or medicine,
to have occasional positions in Italian universities, to be music teachers
or composers, or to continue in ancient Jewish traditions of mysticism
and scholarship. In contrast, popular imagination included ancient Jewish
astrologers, mystic-magicians, alchemists, and general mysterious ancient
figures. During the sixteenth century, several manuscripts from Jewish
alchemists were republished, perhaps partly fictionalized, by Christians,
with appropriate commentary to update their attitudes. At the same time,
theoretical ideas about Hebrew as a perfect language increased the
perception of the Jewish mystics' importance. I find it paradoxical that
as the Jews became more and more marginalized, legends about their
mystical and magical abilities seemed to become more important and
direct knowledge of medieval Jewish accomplishments faded.

JUDAH ABRAVANEL AND RENAISSANCE LITERATURE

Judah Abravanel, the oldest son of Isaac Abravanel, made a significant
contribution to Italian Renaissance humanism. After the family's arrival
in Naples in 1492, he lived in various parts of Italy. He apparently made
contact with many Italian intellectual leaders and humanists with whom
we moderns are more familiar, and eventually his work *Dialogues of Love*
earned a place—though minor—in the history of European secular
literature and philosophy.

To review his earlier life, Judah Abravanel was born in Lisbon in
approximately 1460. At the time of his birth, his grandfather (and
namesake) was an official at the royal court of King Alfonso V of Portugal,
and his father, Isaac Abravanel, was rising as a financial official. The
family's high status continued until Judah's early manhood, and he was
probably beginning a similar career to that of his father. In 1484, a
struggle for the throne destroyed the family's position. Abravanel appeared to have backed the king's opponent, and the king threatened
his life. Judah, whose role in the struggle is not documented, escaped
from Portugal to Castile with his father. In his autobiographical poem
he specified that in this flight from Portugal, he lost all his possessions,
saying that the king of Portugal had nearly ruined him. While his father
found a position at the court of Castile, Judah settled in Toledo in order
to continue his studies. His interests appear to have included medicine,
traditional Jewish studies, and classical studies. Sometime after 1484, Judah

married and his first son, named Isaac Abravanel, was born shortly before Ferdinand and Isabella's expulsion order.

The expulsion order became known to the courtiers of Castile, including the elder Isaac Abravanel, in the spring of 1492. Along with Abraham Senior, Isaac Abravanel negotiated with Ferdinand and Isabella to try to persuade them to rescind the expulsion order, and they negotiated with their courtiers to try to persuade them to convert. Ferdinand wanted his trusted financier, the elder Isaac Abravanel, to remain at court after the expulsion, but only as a convert, not as a Jew. The child became a pawn in this affair; the family became aware of the king's plan to take the child from them. Knowing the strong ties that connected all the family members, the king hoped that if he could baptize the child, he would also force the conversion of the grandfather. A Christian child would never be returned to a Jewish family unless they, too, converted.

To avoid the loss of the child, the Abravanels had to act quickly, and in response, as the poem describes, the family sent the child to Portugal with his wet-nurse, on the expectation that he would be safer. Their own fate was in peril at this point, as they had little time to find a refuge or find better alternatives. Portugal offered two advantages: it was a land trip that they knew well, and they still had family connections and possibly even money there, probably with an uncle or cousin of Isaac Abravanel. However, the Portuguese king, João II, immediately detained the child and his caretakers in order to exercise power over the Abravanel family. Shortly afterward, along with their fellow Jews, the Abravanel family went into exile from Spain. Few other details about Judah's life before this point have survived.

With hindsight, Judah bitterly blamed himself for having chosen to send his son to Portugal. In 1497, João's successor Manuel I forcibly caused all Jews in the country to be baptized, starting with children; many of these children were brutally exiled to a nearly deserted island, where they were never heard from again. The king prevented the departure of these converts, including the remaining members of the Abravanel family. Historical documents suggest that by the time Judah wrote his autobiographical poem, the child had almost certainly been baptized with the majority of Portuguese Jews, but his poem does not deal with the forcible conversion and brutal exile of the children. Young Isaac became less likely than ever to be able to rejoin his family, and by 1502 Judah seems to have lost hope. Further certain information about the child is unknown, including how long he lived and whether he and his family were ever reunited. A Jew named Isaac Abravanel was recorded in Salonika in 1558, according to one source. Elsewhere, I read that Portuguese members of the Abravanel family, including the younger Isaac, eventually emigrated to the Netherlands, becoming the ancestors of Abravanels who eventually lived in Eastern Europe.

After reaching Italy in 1492, Judah Abravanel lived or spent time in a number of places; he maintained his family connections throughout his travels. He was in Naples until 1495, remaining even after Naples was attacked by the French. He left Naples for Genoa for a while, but returned in 1501, when he taught briefly at the University of Naples. During much of the time, his father, his brothers, and his sisters were also in Naples. His brother Samuel, whom we will discuss later, lived or visited there; possibly also another brother (or brother-in-law), cousins, and uncles. After 1501, he went to Barletta and then to Venice, where he visited his father in 1505. Judah's wife accompanied him during his travels in Italy. During this time, she gave birth to a son, who died at age five, according to the poem. The family had many business contacts— a major one was the da Pisa banking family in Florence. Perhaps Judah Abravanel's various travels also served the family's financial interests.

Another area where little hard evidence survives is that of Judah Abravanel's contact with humanist philosophers. Abravanel's fame among Christian humanists came much later, and there is no clear contemporaneous record of his actual presence in Florence or at the Florentine philosophic academy. The beginning of the Savanarola influence on Florence at this time, and especially on Pico, might possibly have caused the record of a Jewish Platonist's participation to be erased—like many religious fundamentalists, Savanarola was particularly hostile to philosophy, especially to the influence of Plato. There is one specific item: Cecil Roth cites a document from the mid-sixteenth century that mentions the relationship between Judah Abravanel, Pico della Mirandola, and other Christian humanists in Florence. According to this, some time between Judah's arrival in Italy in 1492 and Pico's death in 1494, Judah may have spent some time in Florence (Roth, *The Jews in the Renaissance*, pp. 130–131).

Judah Abravanel deployed several sets of skills during his life in Italy. He was widely recognized as a classical humanist author and philosopher, and he appeared to have studied the traditional Jewish religious body of knowledge, including Bible, *Mishnah*, Talmud, and the works of Maimonides, as he wrote introductions to some of his father's religious works. He may also have participated in the family financial endeavors. He evidently used his medical skills as his major source of income; in particular, he served as the personal physician of the viceroy of Naples, Don Gonsalvo de Cordoba, known as "the Great Captain." The last record of him is in 1520, when he received an exemption to paying the Jewish tribute, in gratitude for his service in Naples; he probably died in 1523.

Judah Abravanel, Humanist

Judah Abravanel participated in various circles of Italian humanists, probably in Genoa and Florence, as I have mentioned, and made contact with the Jewish humanists Johannan Alemanno and Elijah del Medigo. He noted that he had participated in the academies of the gentiles, where he met Pico della Mirandola and others. His secular education probably went back to his early experiences in the then-open environments of Lisbon and Toledo. Under these influences he wrote about celestial harmony, a work now lost. His most famous work is the *Dialogues of Love*, which he probably wrote while living in Genoa. All the dates vary depending on which source is giving them.

In the *Dialogues of Love*, Judah Abravanel developed ideas based on Platonic thought and philosophy. He expressed his own ideas and reflected his connections with Platonic philosophers in Italy at the time, particularly with the Platonic Academy of Florence. The work contains references to all the broad cultural interests of a Renaissance humanist, including Greek mythology, biblical stories and characters, and more recent philosophers and writers, both Jewish and non-Jewish. He could have been inspired or influenced by various contemporaries and associates of the Academy such as the Christian Pico della Mirandola, and the Jewish mystic Johannan Alemanno, who wrote about the concept of love expressed in the *Song of Songs*. Roth points out that many other humanists also wrote on similar topics, such as Marsilio Fincino, who wrote a commentary on Plato's *Symposium*; Mario Equicola of Ferrara, and Bembo. Another influence, of course, was Judah's father, although there were vast differences in their intellectual approaches and attitudes. Their relationship is suggested by the fact that Judah wrote prefaces or appreciations of his father's works that were being published in the years 1502–1508 and visited his father in several places, particularly Monopoli and Venice.

After Judah Abravanel completed *Dialogues of Love* in about 1503, the work circulated in manuscript until after his death, and thus began to have an influence before its first publication in print in 1535. Scholars question whether he intended to address a Jewish audience or a more general audience. This dispute is connected with the issue of whether Italian was the original language for his work. A manuscript version in

Judeo-Spanish still exists in the British Museum (according to Cecil Roth's introduction to the 1937 English translation), suggesting that even the "original" Italian may have been a translation from Judah's real native language. Other scholars believe that the original language was Hebrew, and that the initial circulation was thus the same as the learned Jewish audience for the works of Isaac Abravanel. Arthur M. Lesley says that a Hebrew-language audience is indicated by early reactions to the *Dialogues* among Jewish scholars, particularly in 1506 by the scholar Saul Cohen Ashkenazi, who expressed questions about the practice of both Isaac and Judah Abravanel of combining ideas from Greek philosophy, Jewish learning, and Kabbalah (A. Lesley, "The Place of the *Dialoghi d'Amore* in Contemporaneous Jewish Thought," in Ruderman, *Essential Papers*, 1992).

Judah Abravanel's reputation as a mainstream writer grew when the initial 1535 printed edition of the *Dialogues of Love*, in Italian, appeared in Rome. Many later editions in Italian and other languages followed, notably French, Spanish, and Hebrew editions. Translators included interesting people, such as one of the French poets belonging to the "Pleiade" and a man named Garcilaso de la Vega, El Inca (1539–1616), who immigrated from the Americas to Spain and became a man of letters. Throughout the sixteenth and seventeenth centuries, the *Dialogues of Love* remained famous and influential. Writers and philosophers who are still famous today—including Cervantes, Spinoza, Castiglione, Montaigne, and Francis Bacon—made references to the *Dialogues*. A modern scholar of Judah Abravanel also credits his philosophical exploration of the various forms of love with influence on John Donne and Shakespeare, particularly on the character of Cordelia in *King Lear* (T. Anthony Perry, *Erotic Spirituality: The Integrative Tradition from Leone Ebreo to John Donne*, University, Alabama: University of Alabama Press, 1980.) Later, interest in the work dropped off, until today he has become virtually unknown.

Several areas of mystery or confusion remain about the author and his work. I have mentioned that no definitive proof exists about which were the cities where Judah Abravanel and his family resided, about which Italian humanists he knew personally, about the exact date of his death, and about the language of the original manuscript of the *Dialogues*. Editions of his work, published only after his death, leave other uncertainties. Various versions of his first and last name appear on the title pages. His Hebrew name, Judah, alternates with the Italian versions, Leon or Leone. Also, instead of his family name, his publishers simply called him "the Jew"—that is, Ebreo or Hebreo. Thus, he was known by the following names: Leone Ebreo in Italy; Leon Hebreo in Spain; and Leon l'Hebreu or Leon Hebreu in France; as well as Judah Abrabanel or Abravanel, Giuda Abarbanel, or Judah ben Isaac Abravanel among Jewish sources. (Remember this if you want to look him up in an encyclopedia, a library catalog, a database, or the Worldwide Web.) A final area of doubt arises because, in the 1540s, the title pages of two editions of the *Dialogues* from the Aldine press identified the author as a convert to Christianity. Neither the content of the book nor other historic evidence supports this claim, which probably was meant to reassure purchasers in an increasingly anti-Jewish environment. Editions published earlier and later said nothing about this, leaving the name "Ebreo" to speak for itself.

FLORENCE, PAST AND PRESENT

I try to picture the Jewish philosophers, authors, bankers, and merchants as they walked the arcaded streets and entered the palatial houses of their contemporaries in Florence, and to imagine them in the neighboring towns of Tuscany, such as San Miniato with its surrounding countryside, where once Jewish bankers lived. I try to imagine the Florence of Pico and of Johannan Alemmano as I walk the medieval streets, cross the historic bridges across the river, and explore the ancient gardens of Florence today. I picture Benvenita Abravanel, several decades later, perhaps in the newly refurbished ducal apartments of the Palazzo Vecchio, as she visited her former pupil, Eleanora of Toledo, wife of Cosimo di Medici, Duke of Tuscany. I regret that the actual streets and buildings where the medieval and Renaissance Jews of Florence lived and worked are no longer identifiable.

The history of the Florentine Jewish community parallels the histories of other Jewish communities of northern Italy. In the fourteenth century, Jewish bankers established a small community, invited by the government, which desired to take advantage of the capital that they could import. The extremely wealthy banker Jehiel da Pisa, who lived at the end of the fifteenth century, was a friend, correspondent, and business associate of Isaac Abravanel; their relationship began while Abravanel was still at the Spanish court.

During the last quarter of the fifteenth century, anti-Jewish preachers, particularly Bernardino da Feltre, and the fanaticism of Savanarola caused hardship, persecutions, and a few cases of anti-Jewish rioting. In the sixteenth century, when other Italian cities were confining the Jews to the ghetto, Cosimo di Medici employed Jacob Abravanel, son of Samuel and Benvenita Abravanel, as an adviser. Under Jacob's influence, he permitted an expansion of the Jewish community in Florence and Tuscany and privileges for Jews fleeing from Portugal. Subsequently, in 1567, a Venetian-style ghetto was established, Jews were required to wear the Jewish badge, and within a few years, new restrictions forced all the Jews of Tuscany to move to the ghettos of Florence and Siena. After Napoleon's reforms, fewer and fewer Florentine Jews lived in the ghetto, which became a slum.

In the 1870s, the Jews of Florence built a new synagogue, far from the site of the ghetto; this is the Jewish site that you can see today—nothing remains of the medieval or Renaissance Jewish areas of the city. The ghetto, which had developed in stages since 1567, was destroyed in the nineteenth century, replaced by the Piazza della Repubblica. Today, the Piazza della Repubblica is dramatically in contrast with the older plazas, such as the Piazza della Signoria or the Piazza del Duomo. In the late 1860s, during the unification of Italy under the House of Savoy, Florence briefly served as the capital of Italy. The old Jewish marketplace and the medieval ghetto houses that had stood there were leveled to create the new public space, conforming to the needs of the new government. One medieval synagogue survived, at Via dei Ramgalianti, the former Via dei Giudei; the German army blew it up during their retreat in 1944 because of its strategic location beside the Ponte Vecchio.

The synagogue and associated Jewish museum are located at 4, Via Farini, near Piazza d'Azeglio; to visit, you must call the secretary of the Jewish community. I recommend consulting with the tourist information office to obtain up-to-date information on this.

Any number of standard guidebooks can direct you to the famous and wonderful art museums, sculpture gardens, plazas, bridges, palaces, churches, bell towers, and fortified castles of Florence. The Uffizi and the other museums in Florence offer a wide choice of paintings that illustrate the contrast between the humanity of figures in Italian Renaissance art and the stiff, formalized images of earlier times. You can't miss the progressive replacement of Saints and Madonnas with subjects from Roman and Greek myths and scenes—such as Botticelli's *Birth of Venus*. In expressing appreciation of the beauty of the human form, painters and sculptors explored new ways to portray humans as individuals, rather than as religious types or allegorical figures; Raphael's Madonnas display the same signs of inner life as images of Greek goddesses or contemporary portraits. Mathematical perspective geometry and careful observation of nature enhanced their ability to direct your attention around the painting and turn a static scene into a drama where every detail counted. The Italians were the undisputed leaders of this artistic era, and European

Renaissance artists from elsewhere, such as Durer, often spent at least some time in Italy.

The humanism of Jewish philosophers leaves its major memorial in the works rather than in physical objects; these works are far less accessible today than the visual masterpieces that you can see in Florence. Architecture and art collections in Florence can provide a perspective on their environment, as you enjoy the progression from medieval painters to the painters of the Renaissance such as Botticelli, Leonardo, and Raphael.

FERRARA AT MID-CENTURY—BENVENITA AND SAMUEL ABRAVANEL

Ferrara is a small city in the region of Emilia Romanga. The dukes of Ferrara, members of the Este family, were leaders in patronizing the Renaissance arts and literature, and from the fourteenth through the sixteenth century, a number of artists and humanist intellectuals spent some time at their court. The ducal palace, which you can still visit, was furnished and designed in Renaissance luxury, though the brick walls and moats around both city and palace were also built to protect against hostilities from outside. Because of the exceptional tolerance of the Este dukes, the Jewish community of Ferrara developed a special life in both Jewish and secular culture.

Ferrara became the home of Samuel Abravanel, his wife, Benvenita Abravanel, and their children in 1532. Samuel was the son of Isaac Abravanel. Benvenita was the daughter of Isaac Abravanel's brother Joseph. At this point in history, both Jewish and non-Jewish women began to receive more recognition and to attain higher levels of education, so that Benvenita was not alone in earning a reputation as an active, philanthropic, intellectual woman. I believe she is the first woman in her family whose personal name and achievements are not forgotten.

Background: Jewish Life in Ferrara

Jewish life in Ferrara was bound up with the attitudes of its rulers and with their political and social position in the complex Italian scene of many small principalities. The rulers of the city-states of Ferrara, Mantua, and Milan had particularly close relationships; in particular, two daughters of Duke Ercole d'Este—Beatrice and Isabella—married the rulers

of Milan and Mantua in the 1470s, touching off a generation of social
and political interaction among these families. The Jewish communities
of these areas were also in close contact, and individuals sometimes lived
or ran banking businesses for a time in several municipalities in the
territories of Mantua, Milan, and Ferrara.

Various archival documents demonstrate a Jewish presence there.
An early record tells how Salamone from Assisi established a banking
partnership with Dattilo di Abramo da Norcia around 1385; by 1437, his
family moved to Ferrara and was also active in Florence and San Miniato.
In the first quarter of the fifteenth century, the rulers employed a Jewish
physician named Elijah ben Sabbetai Beer, who also served popes and
lectured at the University of Pavia. In the 1440s in Ferrara, a Jewish poet
named Salomone wrote several love lyrics. Another Jew named Solomon
worked as an engineer for Lionello d'Este in 1444. By 1451, Ferrara had
a Jewish cemetery, showing the presence of a community in good standing. In a safe-conduct granted to Noah Manuele Norsa in 1469, Borso
d'Este paid him the compliment of calling him a noble (Toaff, p. 245,
and Roth, *The Jews in the Renaissance*, p. 237).

The Norsa family (the subject of a later part of this section) played
an important economic role throughout this history. In 1454, Marquis
Ludovico d'Este signed seven contracts setting conditions, interest rates,
and taxes on banks to be operated by Jewish bankers including Leone
(Judah) and Jacob Norsa. In 1458, he received a request to allow the
Jews to set aside a special building for a synagogue, and again, in 1466,
Duke Borso formally received such a request. Solomon Noah Norsa, in
1461, received not only a license to operate a bank in Ferrara, but also
an exemption from wearing the yellow Jewish badge. Duke Ercole I
reinstated these privileges a decade later. The Ferrara Norsa family and
other bankers of the time engaged in various feuds about their banking
activities. In 1503, Emanuel Norsa of Ferrara and his former partner
Abraham Finzi of Bologna were embroiled in a legal controversy. In 1518–
1521, records describe a dispute between Abraham Raphael Finzi of
Bologna and Immanuel Norsa of Ferrara over a partnership.

By the 1470s, when Ferrara's major Jewish community records began,
there were a number of Jewish residents. About this time, Ferrara's dukes
practiced an exceptional tolerance. In 1474, Duke Ercole went so far as
ordering his officials in the nearby town of Reggio to behead a citizen
convicted of murdering a Jewish banker named Zinatan. By 1476,
mandatory attendance at conversion sermons was a fact of life for the
Jews of Ferrara, but the dukes continued to discourage anti-Jewish attacks of the sort that were common elsewhere. In 1479, when anti-Jewish

hostility broke out during Ferrara's celebration of Lent, Duke Ercole sent his wife, Leonora, instructions to protect the Jews. He told her to caution the preacher not to touch off violence. On February 26, 1479, Ercole wrote:

> It sometimes happens in seasons like this, that the preachers who preache in the churches of the city urge and excite the people to hunt the Jews, and to make them go to hear the Word of God against their will, in such wise that, on account of what these say, they are sometimes attacked. Therefore, your Ladyship had better have them told beforehand that they must behave themselves in their preaching in such a way that these Jews of ours who dwell in our city be not molested nor forced, by their persuasions, to go to hear sermons, and that they be not interfered with in any way through words of theirs. (Edmund G. Gardner, *Dukes and Poets in Ferrara*, New York: Haskell House, 1968, pp. 152–153)

The common people didn't always agree with the rulers' tolerant views. In 1480, during carnival, Solomon Noah Norsa was wounded in his home by a student —Giovanni Guazimano of Forli—who was disguised in a costume. By orders of the duke, when Norsa died, Giovanni was publicly executed by being hanged in chains from a window of Palazzo della Regione. Defiantly, the other students gave the murderer a very honorable funeral and buried him in a dignified location, in protest against the duke. In October, Duke Ercole's men investigated and denied a rumor of a Jewish murder of a Christian child, protecting the Jewish community again.

In 1481, a large mob in Ferrara attempted to assault a Jewish bank, the Banco della Ripa. They accused the Jews of ritual murder and again directed the violence against the Norsa family, the richest Jews in the city. The same year, Solomon Noah's sons made an effort to consolidate their interests, working with the duke, who protected them and insisted that he alone could tax them. The pope complained about this policy, because Duke Ercole didn't let him collect tithes from the Jews. In 1482–1483, attacks, forced conversions, and accusations continued as part of Bernardino da Feltre's campaign against usury, but the dukes again pacified their subjects. In Duke Ercole's territory of Reggio in 1488, another expression of his tolerance occurred when his captain, Boiardo, substituted a fine for the usual death sentence (and even remitted the fine) for a Jew accused of having intercourse with a Christian woman.

In 1487, the Jews of Ferrara dedicated their first permanent synagogue, which followed the Italian rites. In 1492, the Spanish Synagogue of Ferrara was founded, reflecting the arrival of the first small group of

Spanish exiles, whom the duke admitted that same year. (The building was used until its destruction in 1944.)

Life in Ferrara under such protection enabled Jews to develop talents and skills. Around 1500, Duke Ercole employed a Jewish metalsmith, who converted to Christianity; the duke served as his godfather. Under the Christian name Ercole dei Fidele, he made beautiful decorative swords for the courtiers of Ferrara and Mantua. Jews excelled at acting, dancing, and music in both Ferrara and Mantua. Jewish performers and instructors were often found at the courts, like the Jewish dancing master, Guglielmo da Pesaro, who taught Isabella and Beatrice d'Este. From the 1480s on, local Jewish theater troops performed for both courts. Mantua later became a center for Jewish theater and music, and at the end of the century there is at least a tradition that Shakespeare, and possibly Queen Elizabeth of England, witnessed a Jewish-Italian theater performance.

A number of events illustrate the culture and organization of the Jewish community in Ferrara and, in particular, the community's demand for both manuscripts and books. An early printer named Abraham the Dyer worked in Ferrara for a time. During the last quarter of the 1400s, the Jewish community included an important scribe named Abraham Farissol, who had come from Avignon to Ferrara. Besides being a highly skilled manuscript copyist, Farissol was the *hazan* of Ferrara's synagogue. Appointed in 1478, he held this position for over fifty years; he also played musical instruments, using melodies appropriate for both the Italian and the Provencal religious services, and was the author of several books on a wide variety of topics, including a commentary on the ethics and economics of moneylending at interest. Abraham Farissol may have also participated in a famous seminar held by Pico della Mirandola in Florence in the 1480s, where several Jewish scholars explained various occult sciences to Christian humanists in Pico's circle. Wealthier Jews often bought manuscripts from Abraham Farissol. Records for a manuscript include a payment, in 1472, from Eliezar ben Solomon Norsa of Ferrara to Abraham Farissol and in 1494–1496, Emmanuel Norsa, also of Ferrara, commissioned manuscripts from Farissol. Another Ferrara member of the Norsa family, Benjamin ben Emmanuel Norsa, was himself an author; he wrote a study of the calendar in 1477.

The Jewish community of Ferrara had the luxury of sharing the successes and life-cycle events of its members. When a banker's family celebrated a wedding, Jewish banks closed, and all the community joined the festivities. When a boy was born, Jews who could afford it often made rather long journeys to attend the circumcision ceremony, undertaking difficult travel and obtaining special permits to join friends or family.

They managed this even though a circumcision could be scheduled only eight days in advance, at the birth of a healthy boy. The arrangement of weddings involved a great deal of negotiation between the concerned families, including delicate financial transactions over the bride's dowry, and thus also called for major festivities. These celebrations reflected how births and weddings represented hope for the continuity of the Jewish community.

From 1490 until the early 1500s, a number of trends reduced the comfortable state of the Jewish communities of Ferrara and its neighbors. The preaching friars led by Bernardino da Feltre continued to stir up anti-Jewish actions by the people and the rulers of northern Italy. In the Duchy of Milan, this trend caused the end of some of the Jewish communities in the various towns in the Duchy. When the French defeated Milan and ended the Sforzas' power, the Jewish community came to an end. The climate of intolerance also disrupted Ferrara's openmindedness. Duke Ercole's wife died, and in the late 1490s the grieving duke came under the influence of Savanarola, the famous priest from Ferrara who was now the demagogue ruler of Florence.

Ferrara did not follow Florence to the extremes of the famous bonfires of the vanities, where people burned frivolous objects, fancy clothing, and forbidden books. However, the duke backed off from his former enlightened policies. He cracked down on prostitution, gambling, sodomy, shops opening on feast days, married men with concubines, and other lapses of his Christian subjects. He decreed that Jews in his territory had to wear the distinguishing yellow badge on the front of their clothes, observing a church regulation he had formerly refused to implement. He forced Jews to attend sermons in the cathedral, another papal requirement that he had previously ignored. Ercole's cruel enforcer of these laws, Zampante, was murdered by two medical students and a converted Jew, but the public supported the perpetrators, who fled to the Venetian border.

Between 1500 and 1502, all Italy suffered from the effort of Pope Alexander and his son Cesare Borgia to unify the peninsula by violent conquests. In Ferrara, capitulating to the ambition of the powerful Borgia family, Alberto d'Este, son and heir of the aging duke, married Lucrezia Borgia, daughter of the pope, in an incredibly elaborate ceremony involving enormous display of the pope's questionably gotten wealth. Isabella d'Este wrote back from the festivities that one of her retainers had won a substantial sum from a Ferraran Jew, suggesting another of the activities of Jews at court: gambling. Earlier, before the influence of Savanarola, the duke had himself enjoyed betting on card games with some of "his" Jews, such as Abraham Norsa, who lost three thousand ducats to the duke in a single card game in 1477.

After the death of Duke Ercole, Ferrara experienced an outbreak of anti-Jewish violence, touched off by a blood-libel rumor, resembling more severe violence that, some years before, had been put down by Ercole's brother Sigismundo. In May of 1506, thugs attacked Jewish houses. Lucrezia Borgia at this time was acting as regent for her husband, Alphonso, the recently installed duke. Upholding the tradition of her husband's family, she instructed the municipal officers to punish those who injured Jews in any place and in any way just as if they had injured fellow Christians; she called it "iniquitous" to harass and injure the Jews under her responsibility (Rachel Erlanger, *Lucrezia Borgia: A Biography*, New York: Hawthorn, 1978).

In 1524, Jews throughout Europe were overwhelmed with the claim of David Reubeni, who came to Italy from Egypt, claiming to be the Messiah. Messianic expectations were strong—possibly inflated by Isaac Abravanel's widely known predictions. Upon his first appearance, in Venice, Reubeni said that he was the brother of a King of the Jews somewhere in Arabia and that he had paid a visit to Prester John. His extravagant claims, amplified by the publicity stirred up by his sidekick Molcho, caught the imagination of both Jews and Christians. His proposal to mount a Jewish Crusade to recapture the Holy Land received improbable levels of acceptance. Many Jews believed uncritically that he was the Messiah. In Rome, he enjoyed invitations from Rabbi Daniel de Pisa and the pope's representatives, and the pope received him personally.

In March of 1525, with the pope's support, Reubeni made a triumphal progress through Italy on the way to his crusade, which was to start in Portugal. Many Jews in Ferrara and Mantua reacted dramatically to Reubeni and to his companion and promoter Molcho. Abraham Farissol, the scribe and scholar in Ferrara, recorded that he was "short of stature, thin of flesh, courageous, a great prayer, swarthy-skinned" (cited in Roth, *The Jews in the Renaissance*, p. 310). In Naples, people welcomed him with enthusiasm; Benvenita Abravanel, at this time a companion of the daughter of the king of Naples, sewed a beautiful banner for his campaign, embroidered in gold and displaying the ten commandments. After many adventures, in 1533, in Mantua, Molcho was condemned to death. He appeared to be burned, "miraculously" reappeared, and finally died at the stake. Reubeni, though with less acclaim than he had previously enjoyed, traveled to Regensburg to meet with Emperor Charles V, to many cities in Italy, to the papal territory at Avignon, to Portugal, and to Spain, where he died in prison in 1538.

Meanwhile, in 1531, the populace blamed insincere converts for a devastating earthquake in Lisbon, and many of these former Spanish Jews began desperately trying to leave. A quote from John Florio's 1600 Italian-English dictionary defining the word *Marrano* suggests the attitude that already applied to these Portuguese rejects. He defined *Marrano* as "a nickname for Spaniards, that is, one descended of Jews or Infidels and whose Parents were never christened, but for to save their goods will say they are Christians" (Pullan, p. 206). Once they had been identified as former Jews, they would never be accepted as Portuguese Christians but also had no right to worship as Jews. The Portuguese situation was becoming more and more like the one in Spain, encouraging the victims to face new but acceptable risks to get to a place where they would be accepted.

In 1536 the Inquisition was established in Portugal, after a futile struggle by Marranos to prevent it. As endangered Portuguese crypto-Jews, or Marranos, left to seek other homes, they found Italy to be culturally similar enough to be a real attraction. The Venetian ghetto, under pressure from the Sultan of Turkey, offered one refuge, where the Inquisition was mild and Marranos were tolerated. In 1538, the duke of Ferrara allowed Portuguese Marranos, fleeing the Inquisition and other forms of persecution, to live there and revert to Judaism; for many years, he and his successors defied papal prohibitions on this policy. To escape the Spanish and Portuguese Inquisitions, Portuguese refugees slowly established a secret route, traveling through English ports, to Antwerp and other locations in the Spanish Netherlands, and through Lyons, France. Their escape became possible particularly under the leadership of Gracia Nasi and her family, who will be discussed a little later. Destinations were Ferrara and Venice, and ultimately the entirely tolerant Turkish Empire.

The intellectual and economic situation remained good for Ferrara's Jews for several more decades. The Abravanel family enjoyed the open atmosphere and the commercial opportunities. Several synagogues flourished, serving the various Jewish communities. Portuguese refugees, as we will see, established printing presses and produced their own literature. In 1556, a Jew named Solomon Riva received a patent to allow establishment of a school of Jewish learning where both Jews and Christians would study—one special provision offered immigrating students and teachers duty-free import of their goods. Fewer restrictions applied in Ferrara than in most Jewish communities at mid-century. After Samuel and Benvenita died, their sons and nephews prospered, continuing their good relationships with the d'Este rulers.

Samuel and Benvenita Abravanel

Samuel Abravanel had come from Spain with his father, Isaac Abravanel, in 1492. He received an education in the growing Jewish community of Salonika, in the Turkish empire, and remained there through the late 1490s while the other members of the family lived in Naples and Corfu. Eventually, Isaac Abravanel decided definitively not to go to Turkish territory, and so Samuel returned to Italy and his family. Samuel became a figure at the court in Naples. During this time, Samuel had married, and his first wife had died, leaving him with one son. Subsequently, while at the court of Naples he married Benvenita, his cousin, daughter of Isaac's brother Jacob. During her stay in Naples, Benvenita served at court as the tutor of Eleanora of Toledo, daughter of the Spanish viceroy of Naples, who later became the duchess of Tuscany.

Samuel followed the career path of his father, serving as a financial official of the king and also earning money in private financial dealings. Eventually, the Jews of Naples were forced to wear the Jewish badge and threatened with expulsion; at first, Samuel seems to have convinced the authorities to postpone the expulsion, upon a ransom payment to the king. The final expulsion of the Jews from Naples was complete in 1541, although the Abravanel couple—perhaps themselves expelled earlier—may have moved to Ferrara in 1532 (various sources disagree on the date when they moved). After their arrival, Samuel continued his financial activities in Ferrara, working with Marranos from Portugal in investment endeavors in partnership with the ducal treasury; he also exploited his financial contacts in Tuscany and investment opportunities in the papal states. He bought a mansion and spent significant amounts to repair and restore it for their large household, which included Jewish servants and professional aides such as a valet and an accountant. His fortune was thought to be very large, though most of it, according to his will, was the result of his successful investments of Benvenita's dowry.

In Ferrara, Benvenita and Samuel, continuing family tradition, joined a circle of cultured Spanish and Portuguese Jews, as well as interacting with the Italian-Jewish community and with Christians of similar interests. Benvenita was active in civic and benevolent activities in Ferrara, as well as in intellectual life. Samuel Abravanel had inherited his father's library and some of his unfinished or unpublished manuscripts, which he and later Benvenita made available to scholars, such as Samuel Usque, who lived in Ferrara. "Dona Benvenita, . . .was a typical grand dame of the Italian renaissance, cultured, gracious, and beloved by Jew and non-Jew alike. . . . Her home, both in Naples and Ferrara, became the center of a circle of Italy's intellectual elite. Learned Jewish and Christian aristocrats flocked thither to discuss the arts and philosophy and even to delve into the mysteries of the Kabbalah" (Cohen, *Samuel Usque*, p. 16).

Samuel and Benvenita had at least two sons, Judah and Jacob (also called Leone), and two daughters, Letizia and Gioia. One of the daughters married a cousin, another descendant of Isaac Abravanel. In addition to his son, Samuel may also have had other children with his first wife, and he was the father of an illegitimate son. Cecil Roth characterizes Samuel's evident indiscretion as "very much in the spirit of Gentile society in his beloved Ferrara" (Roth, *Jews in the Renaissance*, p. 45).

The death of Samuel Abravanel, in 1547, was a result of accidental poisoning, due to an overdose of a drug called scammony, which left him paralyzed and then killed him. Due to this paralysis, he was not able to make a will on his deathbed. He had made an earlier will six years before, upon his undertaking a long voyage, and this became controversial; the rabbinical discussions of the will preserve a number of its terms. The dispute and a subsequent long-term family feud occurred for several reasons:

- First, he left all his money to Benvenita, making her the head of the household, and left only a gift to his younger sons. He stated that some of the sons had a gambling problem and thus feared that they would "destroy everything in a single moment." He requested that in her will, Benvenita, acting alone, should determine how the remainder of the funds should be distributed. A few years afterward, one of these sons, Judah, was even arrested at the request of Benvenita, because he had married a Portuguese girl in Pesaro; in Benvenita's will, he was disinherited. (Samuel's treatment of his daughters was not recorded in the rabbinical documents; a daughter's share of her family's fortune would have been transferred as a dowry, not as an inheritance.)

- Second, he cut his oldest son—named Isaac—out of the will entirely. I believe that this was the son of Samuel's first wife, who lived in a separate household in Ferrara. Samuel may have disapproved of this son's ties with Portuguese converted Jews, especially the members of the Nasi family and their associates. The illegitimate son seems to have received a small gift that was unchallenged. (The distinction between the elder son and the illegitimate son is sometimes not made clear.)

- Third, the will was notarized and witnessed by Christians, in the non-Jewish legal system, rather than by Jews. In spite of this, a driving force behind the entire family feud seems to have been the unacceptable relationships between the sons and the Portuguese converts.

After Samuel died, the younger sons and the daughters may have continued to live at home with their mother, Benvenita, and thus appeared to be favored. Although they didn't inherit money, one of Benvenita's sons received gifts such as a diamond ring, a silver jar, and the books that had belonged to Samuel's father; the younger ones received one thousand scudi each. The oldest son, who was cut out of any inheritance, challenged the will. The dispute lasted for several years, and rabbis from a number of places gave their opinions of the various elements of the controversy and attempted to conciliate the parties to the dispute. The eldest son finally accepted a negotiated settlement. (Information about the will and the family feud is from David Malkiel, "Jews and Wills in Renaissance Italy: A Case Study in the Jewish-Christian Cultural Encounter," *Italia*, Vol. 12, 1996, p. 7; and Renata Segre, "Sephardic Refugees in Ferrara," *Crisis and Creativity in the Sephardi World 1391–1648*, B. R. Gampel, ed., New York: Columbia University Press, 1997, pp. 164–185.)

After her husband's death, Benvenita, as well as administering the family estate, assumed his financial and intellectual commitments and helped her son Jacob to become better established. She jointly ran the loan business in Tuscany with her sons, and exploited her earlier connection with her former pupil Eleanora of Toledo, wife of Cosimo di Medici, duke of Tuscany. Taking advantage of Benvenita's visits to the court while they were on business in Florence, her son Jacob later became an adviser to Cosimo di Medici and influenced the decision to permit Portuguese Jews to settle in Florence, as I have mentioned in the discussion of the Jews of Florence. The family's luxurious lifestyle continued as well; in 1549, when a plague was raging in Ferrara, Samuel's oldest son, Isaac, took refuge in a house in the countryside that was equipped with a "courtyard, orchard, hatchery, granary, and stable" (Segre, p. 182). Benvenita also continued to be a hostess for the intellectuals of Ferrara and a patron of learning.

Samuel Usque, Intellectual Heir of Isaac Abravanel

Among the members of the Jewish community of Ferrara, Samuel and Benvenita Abravanel had an ongoing relationship with the writer Samuel Usque. The Abravanels and Usque had met before 1532 when they were all in Naples. Usque's book, *Consolation for the Tribulations of Israel,* mentions this relationship with the Abravanels and his admiration of them. Usque may even have used, as a source for his work, one of the now-lost, unpublished works of Isaac Abravanel that he borrowed from Benvenita and Samuel. Thus, Usque was a very strong intellectual heir of Isaac Abravanel and possibly also of Judah Abravanel. According to Martin Cohen, the translator and commentator who published the English translation of Usque's work: "Abravanel's relationship to the writings of Samuel Usque lies not so much in his brilliant biblical commentaries . . . nor in many areas of his philosophical contributions. It lies primarily in three major areas of his writings and thought— in his Messianic writings, his philosophy of Jewish history, and his abortive history, whose manuscript never saw the light of day . . ." (Cohen, p. 275).

Usque's life story is practically unknown but very intriguing. He was born after the forcible conversion of the Portuguese Jews and thus inescapably was raised, at least nominally, as a Christian. However, his parents had evidently been among the Jews who escaped from Spain to Portugal in 1492 to preserve their religion, so he was evidently raised as a secret Jew. How he left Portugal and came to Naples is not clear. His activities can only be inferred from his major work, the *Consolation,* and its sources. Cohen provides an analysis, suggesting what Usque's sources might reveal about his previous life. By his references to the works of Saint Augustine, de Espina (a virulent Spanish anti-Semite), and a large repertoire of classical sources, Usque may imply that his pre-Ferrara Portuguese life included a period spent as a Christian divinity student. Knowledge of such material would have probably been available to a young man of Jewish descent only in a religious order or at least a religious institution of higher learning. Usque's work makes it clear that he returned to Judaism sometime before or during his stay in Naples. Between 1532 and 1552, Usque traveled in Israel, Salonika, and perhaps elsewhere. After these voyages, Usque found refuge in Ferrara, thanks to the unusual tolerance and generosity toward Jews of the Este rulers of the time, and had the opportunity to write and publish his work, addressed to other secret Jews and hoping to encourage them.

Usque's personal view is often compelling. My own impression is that this is the first document since Flavius Josephus that I can read with comfort (although I can read it only in Cohen's translation from the original Portuguese). Usque writes all of Jewish history in the first person. One persona named Ycabo (anagram of Jacob, Y = J) narrates the entire history. Ycabo tells of each catastrophe as his own experience, starting in biblical times, continuing with a detailed history of Maccabees, Herod and Roman times, and European pogroms and persecutions up until Usque's own time, the 1550s. The most recent event that he describes is the painful expulsion of Portuguese refugees from Ferrara in the early 1550s, at a time when the population became terrified that they might be carriers of plague. He describes the agony of those refugees, cast out without adequate food or protection from the elements and scorned even by fellow Jews in more fortunate circumstances. In reading, I was convinced that this was a description of his own experiences. These references to the thought of Usque's contemporaries or very personal statements keep it lively.

Ycabo's narrative makes me think of a sort of Jewish Everyman. He asks you to join him in experiencing Jewish history: "Why do you not put freedom above any kind of torment as the Israelites did at Masada, the impregnable fortress of Judah?" Or he relates each thing that happened to him: "Under the wicked trees of Ahab and Jezebel, I suffered many calamitous periods of long famine." After telling the story of Herod's rise to power, he says: "Thus was the iron net being woven which would imprison my liberty until this very day." And he suffers each torment: "The fire of my punishment burned so brightly". . . "my children suffered the cruelest and most frightful famine". . . (Usque, *Consolation*, pp. 56, 76, 132, and 146).

At the end of his historical narrative, Usque presents a formal "Consolation" in which stylized figures directly offer comfort to the reader, attempting to console them despite the catastrophes of Jewish history. The comforters make reference to the redeeming qualities of Benvenita and Samuel Abravanel as an indication that God has not stopped offering such members of society to the Jewish exiles. In discussing how Usque followed in Isaac Abravanel's tradition, Cohen concludes: "Not only did Samuel Usque carry to fruition Abravanel's dreams of a theologically oriented history of the Jews, but he also presented this history in such an appealing, artistic and popular form that it could reach and move an audience of far greater scope than any of Abravanel's works . . ." (Usque, *Consolation*, pp. 210, 277).

One area in which Samuel Usque did not reflect the teaching of Isaac Abravanel was in Abravanel's condemnation of Marranos and his prediction that by converting, the Jews who remained in Spain would never be able to find the acceptance they hoped for. Usque's own experience as a Marrano and observations among the forced converts of Portugal left him much more sympathetic and tolerant than the teaching of Abravanel, who addressed the Marranos with the statement: "You are considered as heretics and Epicureans and disbelievers in both religions—

i.e., in the teachings of God and of the gentiles as well" (quoted by Pullan, p. 206).

During the same time period in Ferrara, there were two other men named Usque. The first, Solomon Usque, was a writer as well and was also known by the name Salusque Lusitano, which stood for Salomon Usque, the Portuguese. He wrote various works in Italian, such as a Purim play presented in Venice in 1558 and a translation into Spanish of Petrarch's verses. Little information exists about the interactions between the Usque writers and the other members of the intellectual circles of Ferrara.

The final Usque in Ferrara was Abraham Usque, who ran a major printing press from 1551–1558, publishing over fifty books. In 1552, the press published a Spanish translation of the Jewish prayer book in Ferrara, an indication of the toleration of a Spanish-Portuguese Jewish and Marrano presence. The next year, Usque's press published the Ferrara Bible, a work in Spanish in two separate editions with different title pages, one for Jews, dedicated to Dona Gracia Nasi, signed Abraham Usque; one for Christians, dedicated to the duke of Ferrara, signed Duarte Pinel. Abraham Usque in Portugal, as a Christian, had been called Duarte Pinel. In September of 1553, he published Samuel Usque's *Consolation*, also dedicated to Dona Gracia. In 1555, Usque published an edition of the *Itinerary of Benjamin of Tudela*, of interest in the context of the earlier chapter of my book. This was the second printed edition of the *Itinerary*. On the title page was Usque's printer's mark, a globe encircled by the ecliptic and zodiacal marks, supported by an anchor, his initials, and his printer's motto, "I wait for the Lord; my soul doth wait, and in His word do I hope" (from the 130th psalm, cited in David Werner Amram, *The Makers of Hebrew Books in Italy*, London: Holland Press, 1963. p. 282).

On September 27, 1553, the decree mandating the confiscation of Hebrew books and the burning of the Talmud took place in Rome and Venice, with serious consequences for Jews throughout Italy and the rest of Europe. Individuals and schools had to turn in all copies of the Talmud. Two members of the Abravanel family in Ferrara, a son and a nephew of Samuel Abravanel, were listed among those Jews who turned in copies of the Talmud to the local inquisitor.

In 1554 the leaders of the Italian Jewish communities, including members of the Abravanel family, met in Ferrara, in an effort to respond to these events. Rabbi Meir Katzenellenbogen of Padua was president and delegates represented Rome, Mantua, Ferrara, Romagna, Bologna, Reggio, Modena, Padua, and Venice. This group issued a decree concerning Jewish publication:

Printers shall not print any book not before printed without the license
and approbation of three Rabbis ordained by three Rabbis, nor without
the approbation of the heads of the congregation near to the place of
publication if the press be in a small town. If it be in a larger city then
the approbation of the heads of the congregation of this city together with
the said three ordained Rabbis shall suffice. (Amram, p. 286)

There were penalties for anyone who purchased a book that did
not list the names of these rabbis and community heads—an attempt
to protect the community against the bad judgment of a few. Unfortunately, pressure was mounting more and more against Jewish privileges,
no matter how small, and Hebrew printing was suppressed in large measure
in spite of the efforts at self-censorship.

Gracia Nasi

Benvenita Abravanel also had opportunities to become acquainted with
the much more famous Portuguese Marrano woman Gracia Nasi and her
large household. During the 1550s, various members of the Nasi family
lived in Ferrara, where the duke's generous policy enabled Gracia Nasi
to revert to Judaism. The Abravanel and Nasi business interests sometimes
coincided and sometimes competed. Later, the Nasis made their way to
Turkey to find freedom, finally, from the Inquisition. Gracia Nasi, as we
have mentioned, was a friend or patron of Samuel Usque as well.

The Nasi family used more than one name, which was typical of
reverting Jews. As Portuguese secret Jews, her husband's family used the
Christian name Mendes, and her family used the name Luna. The Mendes
family included the two Mendes brothers, Diego (or Diogo) and Fran-
cisco. Gracia and her sister married the Mendes brothers; she was also
called Beatrice de Luna; her sister, Brianda de Luna. Their daughters
had the same names in the opposite order; that is, each Mendes couple
had one daughter, and each named the daughter for her aunt, in a plot
to drive historians crazy. The women also had two nephews, named Miches
or Micas, perhaps children of their brother, probably also deceased. When
they reverted to Judaism, the sisters chose the name Nasi, probably their
traditional Jewish name from before the expulsion. In my narrative, to
be consistent, I have used the name Gracia Nasi for the woman who
became the head of the family, and the name Joseph Nasi for the nephew
(earlier Joao Micas) who later became very prominent and was appointed
Duke of Naxos. I will call her sister Brianda Nasi.

In the early part of the century, Gracia Nasi and her husband remained in Portugal while her husband's brother and his family went to Amsterdam. Their presence in Portugal reassured the authorities that their intentions were acceptable and also allowed them to transfer much more of their unimaginable fortune out of Portugal. Her husband died, and she fled from Portugal to Amsterdam via England. Shortly after her arrival, her brother-in-law also died, leaving Gracia Nasi in charge of the family and, particularly, leaving her, rather than his wife, in sole charge of the vast family fortune. Under her leadership, the family continually moved toward safer locations, where Judaism was better tolerated. This long voyage took them from Amsterdam on a flight through Lyons and eastern France to Ferrara and Venice and then, finally, to Turkey. As they traveled, they slowly became more open about the practice of the old religion.

In Venice, Gracia Nasi didn't openly declare her Jewish beliefs, but her behavior was risky, and she almost met with disaster because of her sister. Gracia Nasi's full responsibility for the family's extensive fortune made her sister, a rather small-minded person, extremely jealous. During a quarrel, her sister tried to get the upper hand by reporting to the Inquisition that Gracia Nasi was a secret Jew, asking the authorities to transfer control of the money to herself. Needless to say, the authorities thought of other pockets into which the money might go. By properly applying her political influence and talent, Gracia Nasi bought her way out of the problem, but it was expensive, and she was no longer comfortable in Venice.

In 1550, in Ferrara, defying papal rulings, the duke had declared that he would tolerate a return to Judaism by Portuguese refugees such as Gracia Nasi. Thus, in 1550–1552 Gracia and her daughter, sister, niece, and nephew lived in Ferrara, and she reverted to open Jewish practice. It was at this point that she took back the name Nasi, which means "prince" or "leader" and which had presumably been in use in her family before their conversion. In 1551, people in Ferrara blamed an outbreak of plague on Marrano newcomers, forcing them temporarily to flee the city. At this time, Gracia Nasi may have returned to Venice, where she had further difficulties, and she soon returned when accepted again in Ferrara. Soon afterward, Gracia Nasi and her nephew departed for Turkey via Ancona.

In 1556, the city of Ferrara received an envoy from the court of Suliman the Magnificent. His wealth and the gifts he brought impressed the people and the rulers. He came in order to request that the duke allow Samuel Nasi, Gracia's nephew, to leave Ferrara, where he had remained after her departure. By this time the money, the political savvy, and the forceful personalities of Gracia Nasi and Joseph Nasi had already begun to influence the sultan, who thus agreed to help obtain the freedom of the last relative remaining in Christian territory. Gracia and Joseph Nasi's business representatives retained at least their outward Christian behavior and continued to do business on their behalf in a number of Italian cities, as well as in some of the northern ones. As the conflict between Venice and Turkey escalated later on in the century, these representatives were sometimes perceived to be dangerous double agents.

In Istanbul, Joseph Nasi became very successful at the sultan's court. In particular, he received a monopoly on the Turkish wine trade, which was prohibited to Moslems, and he maintained his influence by presenting the best wines to the sultan, whose tastes didn't conform to the restrictions set by his religion. As a wealthy man and associate of the sultan, Joseph Nasi received the title Duke of Naxos and the authority to govern the island of Naxos and profit from its trade in agricultural products, especially wine, and resources such as emery.

As their wealth and power grew, Gracia Nasi and her nephew began to dream of a Jewish return to Palestine, which was a part of the Turkish empire. At this time very few Jews remained in or near Jerusalem. They had long ago been killed or forced to convert during the centuries of persecution, first by the Moslem conquerors, then by the Crusaders, again by Arabs, and most recently by Turkish rulers. Jerusalem was too daring to propose, but the Nasis influenced the sultan to allow establishment of Jewish colonists in Tiberias and the expansion and improvement of the small existing Jewish colony in Safed. With large contributions of money, the Nasis arranged for recruitment of Jewish settlers in Europe, especially Italy; subsidized Jewish agricultural developments; encouraged Jewish artisans; and funded the rebuilding of the walls of Tiberias.

After the death of Gracia Nasi in 1569, Joseph Nasi continued his court life and the project of a Jewish settlement in Palestine, although his influence declined when the next sultan came to power. The early Zionist dream did not long outlive Joseph Nasi, though the colony of mystics of Safed continued to hang on until the arrival of the nineteenth-century waves of immigrants and still exists now.

Ethical and Charitable Behavior

The biographies of Benvenita Abravanel and Gracia Nasi repeatedly emphasize their charitable activities. Their contemporaries seem to have seen this as especially appropriate praise for women who gained recognition. Benvenita was recognized in Ferrara, and Gracia Nasi was recognized in each of the diverse places she lived, including Ferrara, as a model of charitable behavior. To better understand their motives, here is a summary of what they and their contemporaries viewed as the high points of ethical and charitable Jewish behavior.

Samuel Usque expressed the view—generally in agreement with Renaissance Jews—that the highest obligation was to remain faithful to Judaism, implying that an admirable form of charity was to facilitate such acts of faith. Usque valued the activities of Samuel and Benvenita Abravanel, noting how Abravanel "provided for the marriage of countless orphan girls, maintained many needy people and distinguished himself preeminently in the freeing of captives. He gave his help so extensively that all the qualities needed to receive prophecy were present in him" (Cohen, Introduction to Usque's *Consolation,* p. 15). Benvenita Abravanel, in her own right, maintained a place where an intellectual elite could discuss arts, philosophy, and even Kabbalah. People thus called her "a munificent patroness of learning" (Roth, *The Jews in the Renaissance,* p. 54).

In longstanding Jewish tradition, charity had originally been associated with the behavior of landowners and involved the provision of food to the poor. The Bible suggested idealistic prescriptions for observing Sabbatical years by leaving fields fallow, for performing crop rotation, and for allowing the poor to glean in the corners of fields. "No less idealistic were the provisions for the poor, particularly widows and orphans. We also recall the extremely liberal demand that, upon manumitting his Hebrew slave, the master should also provide him with some necessaries for a fresh start in life." Beyond this, rabbis made a wider interpretation to include the shared use of property and stressed the responsibility of relatives for each other beyond the requirement of the redemption of captives (Salo W. Baron et al., *Economic History of the Jews,* New York: Shocken Books, 1975, pp. 49–50).

Gracia Nasi engaged in several different types of charitable endeavor. She apparently funded Usque's efforts with the *Consolation,* in which Usque encouraged Marranos to come back to or remain faithful to the religion they had been deprived of, receiving his dedication of the book. "In literature, as in other realms of life, she supported activities that would return the New Christians to Judaism and to a useful and productive life" (Cohen, p. 15). Earlier, she had helped secretly practicing Jews to escape from Portugal by organizing an "underground railway" that enabled hundreds or even thousands of Marranos to leave the Iberian peninsula through "stations" in England and the Spanish Netherlands.

These "were helped on by her agents from place to place and station to station until they arrived in some haven of refuge" (Roth, *The Jews in the Renaissance*, p. 55).

Gracia Nasi's husband, Diogo Mendes, had upheld the Jewish charitable tradition in his will even though he publicly lived and died as a Christian. Diogo died in Lisbon before her departure in the 1530s. Her brother-in-law, who died in around 1542, similarly left money to charitable endeavors. Cecil Roth writes:

> His will, in its public version at least, was a model of orthodoxy as well as of benevolence. He left the sum of 1,600 Flemish pounds for the poor, out of the income of which one hundred pounds were to be distributed in charity each year for all time in Portugal or (if it proved impossible to arrange this) in Flanders—one third for the relief of needy prisoners, one third for clothing the naked, one third for dowering orphans. (It is perhaps significant that these were considered among the Jews to be the three primary social obligations after the promotion of study.) (Roth, *Dona Gracia Nasi*, pp. 39–40)

The Jewish communities of Italy in the fifteenth and sixteenth centuries developed their own code for charitable behavior:

> There can be little doubt that the community organization found its justification in the will of the Jews to survive as a group, in their collective awareness of the need to perpetuate their different social, religious, and ethnic identity. We find an extremely simple . . . formulation of this idea on the first page of the volume that records the decisions handed down by the leaders of the Jewish community of Verona . . . in 1539, we find summarily defined the goals . . . "to make provision for all dangers that may eventually threaten the community, and for matters of public utility, as well as for the individual misfortunes to which any member of the community may fall a victim."

The group was the highest priority, then individuals. This reflects the point of view generally held in Italy at this time. The Jewish community was modeled on the Italian city. Cities with few Jews had a few representatives to the local authorities. Larger communities had commissions for special purposes, such as assisting the poor or keeping up synagogues and cemeteries (Robert Bonfil, *Jewish Life in Renaissance Italy*, Berkeley: University of California Press, 1994, pp. 187–191).

The provision of dowries to orphans was an important charitable act because it was perceived to prevent poverty from condemning them to a sterile life or even driving them to a life of shame and degradation. Dowries for poor girls might result in new members for the endangered Jewish community and would help the parents who would otherwise have had to support the unmarried daughter at home. Often the girls who benefited from gifts or legacies were relatives or servants, not strangers.

De'Sommi, a Mantuan playwright from the late 1500s, describes several types of ethical and moral behavior. His modern editor, Golding, writes of his best-known play:

> The theme of *A Comedy of Betrothal* resonates with the complex ethical and legal issues that were the traditional subject of Jewish scholarly debate. . . . Implicit in the play are such Talmudic imperatives as: contracts are not to be broken, young women are not to be manipulated for private gain or selfish ends. Moreover . . . there is also present an over-arching social theme: if there is to be redemption from Gentile oppression, the Jewish community must itself be free of domestic wrongdoing. (A. S. Golding, Introduction to Leone De Sommi, *A Comedy of Betrothal*, Ottowa: Dove House Editions, 1988, p. 24)

Jewish history included numerous cases of communities that collected money to ransom other Jews who had become slaves or captives. Benvenita Abravanel was "said to have ransomed over one thousand Jewish captives out of her private means" (Roth, *The Jews in the Renaissance*, p. 54). A century later, the Jews of Urbino helped ransom Polish Jewish captives sold into slavery at a time of Cossack Wars in 1641. "Special bodies in Venice and Leghorn, supported by a tax on imports and exports, organized the ransoming of Jewish travelers captured and sold into slavery by the Knights of Malta or Barbary corsairs, equally pitiless where Jews were concerned" (Roth, *History of the Jews of Italy*, pp. 363 and 365).

Many Jews engaged in the charitable habits of paying for oil for the synagogue lamps, other synagogue expenses, alms for the poor, and payment for those who would say *Kaddish* for the deceased. The bequest of oil resulted from associating the continuous burning of the lamps with a benefactor's own soul, who wanted them lit on his behalf. Toaff gives an entire passage from a will of Mose di Abramo from Terni, living in Spoleto: "when he should come to die in Spoleto, his body shall be buried at Valiano in the Jewish cemetery, according to the Jewish rite. Furthermore, in accordance with the Jewish custom, he leaves a florin for his tomb. For the love of God, he leaves a florin to be distributed among the poor of Spoleto. He leaves a florin for the purchase of the oil which shall burn in the lamps of the synagogue of the Jews of Spoleto. He leaves a florin for the purchase of the oil . . . Perugia." He left money for oil for numerous synagogues (Toaff, pp. 46–48).

Bequests to hospitals or other institutions for caring for the sick augmented the more usual gifts. Toward the end of the sixteenth century, rabbinic sermons sometimes made special appeals for charitable gifts to the impoverished sick, who were not included in the standard charitable gifts and synagogue collections (D. Ruderman, *Preachers of the Italian Ghetto*, Berkeley: University of California Press, 1992, p. 33).

Charity in those days incorporated an undercurrent of belief that poverty (along with other misfortunes) was either a test or a punishment that God has ordained, although this view was not used to justify callousness toward the poor. In many cases, the commitment to support study was higher than the commitment to help poor or deprived people, although this could result in support for poor students, including meals. At times, Italian Jews even left property or money to the Catholic church and to civil institutions, perhaps to attempt to buy good treatment for their heirs, perhaps out of actual charitable intention (Toaff, p. 48).

In sum, Renaissance Italian Jews such as Gracia Nasi and Benvenita Abravanel supported Jewish learning, they observed the traditional obligation to help fellow Jews with basic essentials (including dowries for poor or orphan girls), they contributed to ransom for Jewish captives or slaves, and they were committed to ensure smooth social functioning, especially within the community where they actually lived.

1998—THE JEWISH MUSEUM OF FERRARA

We traveled to Ferrara to see the synagogue and Jewish museum. Although we drove along the fifty kilometers of highway and then walked from the car through the streets of Ferrara in pouring rain, the rain stopped by the time we finished our tour of the synagogue, and by noon the sun came out again. We seem to have been lucky—elsewhere in Italy there was far more rain. Ferrara's Jewish sites are unusually easy to locate because the central tourist information office, in the courtyard of the ducal palace, offers brochures about the community and the synagogue with photos, a street map, and a description of the museum—a convenience that few Jewish sites in Italy offer to prospective visitors.

The three synagogues and museum occupy a complex of buildings around a courtyard. The Jewish community has owned these buildings continuously since Sr. Melli (from Rome) willed them to the community in 1485—as commemorated on a plaque on the wall. The community maintains the museum, with an attendant who takes visitors on a guided tour. In addition to the tourists, schoolchildren from the Ferrara region come to the museum to learn about Judaism and about its local history.

On Fridays, Saturdays, and Jewish holidays, the museum closes, and community members use the building and synagogues. Their rabbi comes in from Turin every Thursday night. He takes the ritual objects such as Torah crowns out of the museum display cases for use in the services. The regular Saturday services take place in the smaller, Italian synagogue, while holiday services require the larger space of the Ashkenazic synagogue. About eighty Jews remain in the city, most of them women, some nonobservant. Though the rabbi comes each week, they find it difficult to assemble ten men for the services.

The German synagogue is the best preserved. It dates from the eighteenth and nineteenth centuries. Large stucco murals on one wall replaced former large windows when the final ghetto orders came in the 1730s, because the windows opened toward the outside. A rule of all ghettos stated that Jews were not allowed to have windows piercing the external walls, as this would conflict with the goal of full isolation. The women's gallery above the main seating area has satin-covered benches with backs. On the back wall there is a wood cupboard with Torah covers and binders and books. A quite high square lattice separates the gallery from the area below. Women are no longer required to sit upstairs: at present, the men sit on one side of the aisle, the women on the other side.

On display in the museum are a wealth of beautiful ritual objects, arranged according to the holiday or custom during which people used them. Quite a few of these objects came from other towns around Ferrara that no longer have any Jewish community at all, such as a beautiful small Torah Ark. There are many Torah ornaments and covers, ornate plates for celebrations held in honor of a baby's birth, various Hanukkah lamps, Sabbath spice boxes, prayer shawls, and other similar ritual objects. I enjoyed seeing one very fine silver noisemaker for Purim, along with several scrolls of Esther and some cookie molds for the local Purim food tradition. Two of these molds had pictures of an artichoke (a vegetable especially associated with Jewish food). The attendant told us of plans for an enlarged museum, which will display objects from the daily life of the Jewish community, as well as religious articles.

The other synagogues—Italian and Sephardic—are reconstructions, as the Nazis destroyed them almost totally. The events of the 1550s, when the Estes allowed crypto-Jews from Portugal to revert openly, are not commemorated, but the site of the Sephardic synagogue, now marked by a plaque on an otherwise private building, is where they would have worshiped, and the traces of the Spanish synagogue show where their neighborhood was; the narrow street with arched doorways and high buildings with few windows facing the street, is probably what their neighborhood was like. One photo exists to document the prewar appearance of the big and magnificent Sephardic synagogue, originally about a block away from the museum. It was founded November 20, 1492, when Duke Ercole invited Spanish Jews to settle; the plaque commemorating its site dates from November 20, 1992.

The memory of this community seems to be kept alive even though it now has such a small membership. The synagogue and museum are marked on direction signs along the city streets in the same way the authorities mark palaces, churches, and other tourist attractions. The nice brochure map is available in the tourist information office. There are reliable hours for opening and touring: as of now, you are supposed to arrive at ten, eleven, or noon each morning Sunday through Thursday for a guided tour; however, on the day we toured, we were the only ones. A surveillance camera watches anyone who rings the bell at the museum, though its door is clearly marked. The young woman in charge speaks good English and seems well informed about the explanations of Jewish history and practices, though she told us that she is not Jewish.

This is also the community of the modern author Georgio Bassani, and the site of his book and of the film *Garden of the Finzi-Continis.* Concentrating on Renaissance monuments, we didn't go to look at his house (which is not a museum) or at the school building where he taught Jewish children in the early days of the war. As I viewed the museum and the once-grand synagogues, Bassani's words about the sadness of the loss of so many people in World War II seemed to echo in my mind. I thought about the descendants of the Renaissance, lives destroyed, as I also tried to picture the presence of the Abravanels, the three men named Usque, the early generosity and unusual tolerance of the Este Dukes, and events of more recent history. But it's all very remote and not yet brought into the displays. In the museum's future extension about daily life in the Jewish community, I hope they will add some material on the illustrious people who lived there and on their generous and tolerant rulers.

While in Ferrara, we also toured the ducal palace, most notable for its still damp and claustrophobic dungeons and a charming rooftop garden of potted orange trees. In 1504, a quarrel between Ippolito and Gulio d'Este, half-brothers, over Angela Borgia saw Guilo imprisoned in this dungeon, from which he emerged only fifty years later. Isabella d'Este, their sister, tried to intervene from Mantua, making this a widespread episode, as noted on the dungeon wall. Occasionally, Jews from Ferrara must have been imprisoned here, too. We glanced at the fortification wall surrounding the city—one of its engineers was Jewish, as it happens. The entire city is open, the castle and its moat on a broad straight street, which must date from later! The people are stylish, even when riding on bicycles. Nice shops line the streets, though they all closed on this Thursday afternoon, illustrating that you can never predict what the hours of things will be. We found Ferrara to be much more pleasant, though artistically less appealing, than Mantua.

LATER ABRAVANELS AND LATER MYTHS

In the beginning of the family history, I described how the name Abravanel was a touchstone of Jewish respect, especially to the Sephardic Jews, ever since the days of Isaac Abravanel. It seems fitting to give a brief summary of what happened to the family and why the name is still around. The first question: In the light of what I have said about the family, can I explain why the memory is so powerful? In the book *Isaac Abravanel: La Mémoire et L'Espérance,* J-C Attias summarized the biographical elements that may have created the myth, allowing the family to be a totem.

The main appeal of Isaac Abravanel, said Attias, was his promise of the immediate arrival of the Messiah, an idea that permeated Jewish thought for several centuries afterward. At that time, such an idea, according to Netanyahu, received acceptance on the basis of the credibility of the proposer and on the strength of his arguments; obviously in our time, such a specific prediction would be considered crackpot. Abravanel's contemporaries respected the man and his arguments. They respected him because he escaped Spain without converting, while still retaining his wealth, his political power, and the respect of Christian kings. While the others were in camps in Naples, Abravanel was at court— and the other escapees were almost certain to have had wealth and power in Spain or they never would have made it onto the boats. Moreover, the less fortunate exiles perceived that he used his political connections to try to help them, and they remembered that he had tried to talk Ferdinand and Isabella out of the expulsion. Ultimately, the failure of his specific prediction—that the Messiah would come in 1503 or 1531, and no later than 1573—was not an issue.

The work of Isaac Abravanel further contributed to his mythic status later. He tried to comfort the survivors and possibly also the converts who were left behind by putting the Exile in a religious context. He was the first to associate the Exile with the fall of the Temple by claiming that the departure had occurred on the ninth, rather than on the seventh, of the Hebrew month of Av (that is, Tishabav). He connected the drama of expulsion with other biblical dramas, such as the Exodus and the story of Esther. This rationalization was also probably helpful to the survivors in sorting out the catastrophe that they had suffered and created a way for their descendants to deal with the past in the context of the faith they had sacrificed for. His myth started early. In 1551, Rabbi Baruch Uziel Forte of Mantua published the first modern Jewish biography— of Isaac Abravanel.

Who were the later Abravanels, and where did they go? Evidently, some Abravanels were left in Spain in the early 1400s. Isaac's brothers remained in Portugal when Isaac and Judah Abravanel left in 1483. Despite forced conversion, the Portuguese relatives appear to have communicated with Isaac Abravanel in his Venetian days, when they may have helped with his negotiation over Portuguese-Venetian trade arrangements. Some Abravanels, including at least one voluntary convert, remained in Ferrara. Some possibly escaped from Portugal via Amsterdam and became Ashkenazic Abravanels. Others eventually moved from Spain or Italy to Salonika and Turkey, retaining the name in eastern communities such as that of Alexandria, Egypt, until the early part of the twentieth century. Now, many people still have the name Abravanel, the most famous recently being the musician Maurice Abravanel. They appear in fiction such as A. B. Yehoshua's story, which I quoted in the previous chapter. In his study of this question, Attias even mentioned an Abravanel family newsletter, which appeared at some time in the last decade.

The Soncino Family—
Jewish Printers

Gershom Soncino worked with his hands as a printer. His innovations, beginning with his first independent work in 1488 and continuing until his death in 1534, contributed to the development of the art of the printed book. He traveled in Italy and beyond the Alps to find manuscripts of rare Jewish books, which he edited and prepared for publication at his press. He was committed to the advancement of his religion through the preservation and dissemination of its written heritage. He often had to move his business and became an official printer to several municipalities that were suffering from the wars and disruptions of the early 1500s. When he couldn't earn enough from printing Hebrew books or town archives, he also printed editions of Latin and Italian classics. Considering this variety of accomplishment, you could say that he fit the modern ideal of a Renaissance Man.

For several generations before and after Gershom, the Soncino family coped with the difficulties of contemporary Jews. Early in the fifteenth century, his great-grandparents became refugees from Speyer, Germany. The family had lived for centuries in Speyer's significant Jewish community, but conditions in Germany changed, compelling them to find a new home. They settled in the Duchy of Milan, in a small town whose name they later used: Soncino.

The lives and professional successes of the family demonstrate the potential that Jews could realize in the more tolerant atmosphere of Italy. Under Gershom's grandfather, father, and uncles, the initial family print shop produced extraordinary early Hebrew books. After working in Soncino for several years, Gershom had to leave Soncino. He traveled for a time, perhaps rootlessly, and subsequently established print shops in a number of other cities in Italy. Gershom and his sons finally settled in the Turkish Empire, a haven for Jews from Christian Europe.

To introduce the family, here is a chronological description of the major locations where they lived and worked:

- *Speyer.* The family later called Soncino came to Italy from Speyer, in the current state of Rhineland-Palatinate, Germany, in approximately 1435. By legend, Jews had lived in Speyer since Roman times; in fact, the community probably had been there since the early Middle Ages. The family had been there for at least several centuries; their ancestors included Moses of Speyer, a prominent member of the family in the mid-thirteenth century.

- On several occasions, times had been difficult for Speyer's Jews. During a series of massacres of Jewish communities in honor of the first Crusade in 1096, rioters had attacked Speyer's synagogue and killed ten Jews. Another round of persecutions accompanied the 1349 plague year. In the fifteenth century, Jews experienced a series of expulsions: the Soncino family's departure apparently occurred in response to an edict of expulsion in 1435. The Jewish community of Speyer subsequently declined, resuming only in the nineteenth century. While little information suggests continued communication with their former home city, it's interesting to note that within decades of their departure, Speyer became a center for early printing, and in 1469 two brothers from Speyer, John and Wendelin (non-Jews, of course), founded the first press in Venice and obtained a temporary monopoly on printing there.

- *Soncino, Duchy of Milan.* Soon after expulsion from Speyer, the family moved to Italy. On May 9, 1454, Francesco Sforza, duke of Milan, gave formal permission to Samuel of Speyer that allowed him to live in the city of Soncino, a small fortified town between Milan and its enemy to the east, Venice. Samuel was the only Jew admitted, and his permission to settle in Soncino required him to open a bank and make loans to virtually anyone who needed money, including poor shopkeepers or peasants. The dukes of Milan were more tolerant than the rulers that the family had known in Ger-

many, and the Soncino family, who lived there for several generations, became very loyal to the dukes. After Samuel's death, his son
Israel Nathan Soncino continued the bank and also practiced
medicine. Earlier, I described the life of a Jewish banking household
in a small town in Italy; evidently, the Soncino family formed such
a household, living as the only Jewish family in town.

By the 1470s, the family also included Israel's sons Joshua and
Moses. At this time, anti-Jewish Franciscan friars and other demagogues were preaching in many Italian cities in support of the
church's prohibition of loaning money at interest, using this as a
reason to call for expulsion of Jews. From time to time, they also
accused Jews of crimes—notably, during a major persecution in 1475
in Trent, where Jews were charged with the ritual murder of a child
called Simon. Incendiary sermons stirred up anti-Jewish violence,
as people responded to the call to replace every Jewish pawnshop
and bank with a Christian Monte da Pieta, or philanthropic lending
institution. The hope stirred up was that no Christian would any
longer be required to pay interest on loans. It was difficult to found
alternative loan banks, particularly if no interest was to be charged,
but occasionally the Monte da Pieta also managed for a while by
soliciting Christian donations of cash to meet expenses and sustain
losses. In some places, the friars succeeded in closing Jewish banks
and even in driving out the Jews.

As elsewhere, when the preaching monks and priests came
to Duchy of Milan, they convinced the town of Soncino to found
a charity bank, with the goal of driving out the family from Speyer.
This bank opened in 1478. (Today, a plaque on a building a few
houses from the Soncino print museum reads "Monte da Pieta,"
commemorating the location of this charity bank.)

Having lost the family's once-prosperous moneylending business, Israel Nathan Soncino evidently looked for other options and
realized the value and business potential of the new technology of
printing. He decided to change his trade rather than try to move
on—clearly, the town had taken to heart the message against moneylending at interest but had not proceeded with the virulent anti-
Jewish sentiment that the friars often stirred up.

A big question is where Israel Nathan learned the new techniques needed for this change of activity. There are several possible
sources. The first Italian press was located near Rome, where
Sweynheym and Pannartz, two German printers under Gutenberg's
influence, had introduced printing in the 1460s. Two brothers from

Speyer had established a print shop in Venice in 1469. A few Jews were printing Hebrew books in Italy by the 1470s as well. Any of these could have been a source of ideas, direct or indirect, for the Soncinos. The environment in Italy at the time fostered business relations between Jews and Christians, so that such transfer of technical knowledge was evidently possible.

The Soncino Hebrew press began publishing in 1480, jointly operated by Israel Nathan, his sons Moses and Joshua Solomon, and eventually Moses' sons Solomon and Gershom. The first book that they printed was a yearly prayer book. Throughout the 1480s, the Soncino press continued to provide for what was clearly a pent-up demand for Hebrew religious, philosophical, and secular books, designing their product to please not only Italian Jews, but also those from other countries.

Some of the publications: the *Blessings* of the Babylonian Talmud appeared in December 1483, along with another talmudic treatise, *An Egg*. For this, they had the help of the printer Gabriel ben Aaron of Strasbourg. In 1484, they printed the books *Choice of Pearls, Investigation of the World,* and *Chapters of the Fathers*. In 1485 appeared the *Earlier Prophets*—their first biblical text—and Joseph Albo's *Book of Roots*. For this, they hired Abraham the Dyer, who formerly had had a printing press in Mantua. The first complete edition of the Bible with vowel points and accents came from their press during this period.

While a very small number of Hebrew books appeared earlier than theirs, the Soncino endeavor lasted longer and accomplished more than its predecessors. From a collector's standpoint, the date— before 1500—gives the books the status of *incunabula,* rare and desirable. A variety of events from the sixteenth through the twentieth centuries caused the loss or destruction of many Hebrew volumes and thus contributed to their scarcity. Above all, the Soncino press had exceptional standards and innovative ideas for use of the new technology of printing.

• *Castelmaggiore.* In 1486, the family had to flee for a time to Castelmaggiore, where they published another volume of the prayer book. The exact reason for this flight is unclear.

• *Soncino.* The family returned to Soncino in 1486–1487, and published the Talmud. In 1488, Gershom Soncino put his name on the *Great Book of the Commandments* by Moses of Coucy, the first time he took full credit for a publication. At this stage in the history of printing, this means that he would have set the type, would probably have done some of the work that an editor in a modern printing house would do, and would also have run the press to produce the final printed pages. Only the bookbinder may have had his own separate workshop. This began Gershom Soncino's long and accomplished career. Soon after, he also published some fables with decidedly untraditional animal decorations and initial letters, a suggestion of the innovation that he brought to the emerging craft of printing.

• *Naples.* In 1489, Israel died, and the same year, Lodovico Il Moro, the usurping duke of Milan, instituted a persecution of the Jews. Joshua Soncino fled to Naples, where King Ferrante allowed Jews to enjoy a more tolerant atmosphere. Between 1490 and 1492, Joshua published several books, including a Bible and a *Mishnah*, at his press in Naples. There were already Hebrew presses there, founded by Germans named Ashkenazi and by an immigrant from Aragon. Non-Jewish tradesmen worked for Jewish printers, who printed non-Jewish as well as Hebrew works, such as a work by Avicenna. Unfortunately, the invasion of the French and the ensuing pogrom destroyed the Naples Jewish community. After this disaster, which, as usual, was worse for the Jews than for the rest, Joshua Soncino disappeared from the historical record, almost certainly dead in the chaos. While no historical record preserves Gershom's reaction, it's inconceivable that he was unaware of the fate of his uncle.

• *Soncino.* In 1490, in Soncino, Moses died. Gershom was now the head of the family press. He seems to have been committed to spreading his work to Jews in many lands: "Make haste so that East and West may abound with thy books," he wrote in his printer's message at the beginning of Maimonides *Mishneh Torah*, published in 1490 (Cited in L. S. Gold, *A Sign and a Witness,* New York: New York Public Library, 1988, p. 86).

• *Brescia.* In the 1490s, Gershom's life in Soncino evidently became difficult, as French invaders conquered the territory and deposed the dukes of Milan. Around 1490, the family moved the press to Brescia, not far from Soncino. Brescia was ruled by Venice, which was at war with Milan in 1491–1492. The same war led, in 1492, to the French invasion of Naples, where Joshua Soncino disappeared. Among many other things, the war destroyed the ability of the Jewish community to buy books: the printer's epigraph to the Brescia Bible expressed Gershom's complaint that bad times were making it hard to sell books and that copyists had ceased work because of persecution and suffering.

Gershom continued at Brescia until 1495; his publication list included both religious books, particularly an important edition of the Bible (the edition later used by Martin Luther), and secular Hebrew poetry by Immanuel of Rome. The exact whereabouts of other family members during this time are not completely clear, as their situation was deteriorating. The press at Soncino may have continued under the direction of Gershom's brother Solomon until 1495, but the evidence is not definitive. The press at Soncino permanently ceased production at some time in the 1490s.

• *Barco.* In 1497, Gershom spent a brief period at Barco where he published three books, including the Talmud. The Talmud from Barco had certain problematic changes, especially to portions that had offended Christian censors.

• *Chambery and Geneva.* At the end of the 1490s, Gershom spent some years traveling. During this time, no family press was running—in fact, there was no production of Hebrew books anywhere during part of this period. Gershom later gave a brief view of this part of his life: "With great labor I have found books which have, since days of old, been concealed dark and obscure, and I have made them as clear as the light of day. . . . I traveled to France, to Chambery [in the Savoy] and to Geneva, to the places of their origin . . ." (title page of his Constantinople edition of a work by David Kimhi, published in 1533, and quoted by Moses Marx, "Gershom Soncino's Wander-Years in Italy, 1498–1527," in *Hebrew Union College Annual,* Vol. 11, 1936, p. 486). As Jews were not formally permitted in all of these places, perhaps he traveled in the clothing of a Christian; any further data on his travel is pure speculation.

• *Venice.* Around 1500, Gershom returned to Italy. He spent some time in Venice, where he interacted with the famous Aldus Manutius, to be described in greater detail later.

• *Rimini, Pesaro, Fano, Ancona.* By 1501, Gershom began to accept contracts to print Latin and Italian books in various small towns, particularly in the Papal Marches. He worked at first for the governments that answered to Cesare Borgia, who was temporarily in control of varying amounts of Italian territory. Upon the death of Pope Alexander (a.k.a. Roderigo Borgia), the Borgia family lost power, but Gershom continued to work in various towns along the Adriatic coast: Rimini, Pesaro, Fano, and Ancona. The varied origins of the books he printed during the fifteenth century suggest that he became a wandering printer, who could move his entire rig from place to place when new opportunities arose.

- *Salonika, Istanbul, Cairo.* Gershom's sons were also printers, and they moved on to the Turkish empire, founding presses in the Turkish cities of Salonica, Greece, and Istanbul. At the very end of his life, Gershom joined these sons and worked in their printshops. Also, one son who was not a printer left his mark in Istanbul—he was a rabbi who participated in the Jewish debate over the boycott of the city of Ancona. The last recorded Soncino family members were printers in Cairo in the mid-sixteenth century. A modern press in England uses the Soncino name but can claim no connection, other than symbolic, with the original family.

Gershom Soncino worked for many years in many cities. He was responsible, in his lifetime for ninety-six Hebrew works and over one hundred non-Hebrew works. Before following him through this distinguished career, I want to describe the modern town of Soncino, and to survey the condition of early printing and its impact, in order to illustrate the environment in which Gershom Soncino developed his craft.

MODERN SONCINO

On June 9, 1998, we visited the very small town of Soncino to see the Museum of Hebrew printing. I think Soncino is unique in its recognition of a Jewish native son by the establishment of this museum and by the sponsorship of occasional seminars and publications about Hebrew printing and the life of the Soncino family. (For tourist information, maps, and brochures, the office is in the Rocca. Contact Associazione pro Loco, Via IV Novembre, 14, Soncino [Cremona], Italy. Phone 0039-374-84499; fax 039-374-85333.)

The town is small and alive but still very medieval. It's not particularly easy to get there, as no autostrada is nearby, requiring one to drive on the two-lane back roads that link many north Italian locations. While these roads are reasonably wide, gigantic trucks frequent them, and the Italians are all challenged to pass these trucks at the earliest possible moment, making it a little hair-raising. You see, the drivers expect you to move over onto the shoulder so that they can pass even if there are oncoming cars. (I was fortunate enough never to see two eighteen-wheelers try to pass each other with additional oncoming traffic in the road.)

Despite the challenge of heavy traffic, the route is very beautiful, winding through fields and open spaces, and approaching the tiny walled city through its still-existing gates.

There are basically three attractions in town: the Museum of Hebrew Printing, the Rocco (fortified palace), and the beautifully intact city wall from the thirteenth century. The Rocco is a superbly solid brick building integrated into the brick city walls. The printing museum is in an old building, also brick, that was traditionally associated with the printers, though it's not certain to have been their actual house. It's the traditional neighborhood where the Jewish printers lived. A building right down the street commemorates the location of the old Monte da Pieta, which, of course, put the family out of the moneylending business and drove them to become printers.

Soncino's Museum of Hebrew Printing dates from around 1991. Although it displays various old printing presses, none actually dates from the first century of printing, when the Soncino family worked at the site, though one of them is a reproduction of fifteenth-century technology. (I am not sure that any press from that era survives at all.) The museum displays some reproductions of the books printed in the original shop, although, of course, such a small and recent museum would own none of the now very rare and valuable products of the press. The museum has one attendant, who collects the admission fee, provides a guided tour, and sells various printed items.

Each floor of the museum has one single room. On the ground floor, a poster on the wall shows the Hebrew alphabet. In his presentation, the guide explained to us the need to set type with Hebrew vowel points, with the letters going from right to left, and a number of other basics of how Hebrew differs from Italian. He summarized the history of the Soncino family and their accomplishments—all in a very simple Italian that we marginally understood by reference to French. The guide seemed to be a craftsman. He demonstrated the use of these old presses, pulling some smudgy reproductions of a page of the Soncino Bible, an old drawing of the town, and so on.

The first floor of the museum simultaneously functions as a bookshop and souvenir shop. You can buy the products of the press: the inky pictures of the town or the Bible page, or a set of postcards showing early printers at work. Among the books for sale, a number are by academic scholars, some of them the result of the museum-sponsored academic workshops or meetings about the Soncino family. Unfortunately, most of them are in Italian. Although the museum offers scholarly works, the guide himself seems to have little deep expertise.

Upstairs, the guide showed us collections of memorials to Gershom Soncino—for example, some postage stamps commemorating him. A video provided additional information. We did not have time to watch the entire video, because we had to rush back to view the Rocca, which, like the museum, was open only from 10 A.M. to noon on the day of our visit.

The Rocco has high ramparts overlooking the town and the open fields beyond; its defensive function is clear. It was built under the Sforza domination of the town, in the mid-fifteenth century, at the time when the Sforzas also permitted the Soncino family to settle in the town. The Sforzas also strengthened the city wall, as they needed strong defenses for the town, which had always stood on the frontier between various warring regions and which had been destroyed a number of times—initially by Charlemagne's army, and later several times in the twelfth century. Viewing these fortifications helps you to understand the conditions under which the Soncino family lived.

In addition to impressively high brick walls, dry moats surround the Rocca. You can walk up and down winding stairways, through the inner and outer courtyards, and enter or look into lots of little doorways with stairs that go up or down, looking mysterious. Up on the walls you can climb to each of the defensive towers and look out through the arrow slits or down through the openings that were no doubt planned for dumping your sewage or else for spilling boiling oil and hot tar on unlucky attackers. The museum of this fortress is rather anachronistic: it features helmets, canteens, and other soldiers' memorabilia from the nineteenth century and the two World Wars. There's even a little toy model of a Sherman tank, though most of the World War II stuff is fascist. The objects seem to have belonged to local men—this museum is not part of the appeal of the town.

Beyond the Rocca, sloping city walls continue around the town, and the streets that enter the town go through white-pillared gates in the wall. Two interesting churches are in town, one with a very high brick bell tower. Most of the old buildings are brick, and the overall look is very appealing. The very nice sunlight of an early summer day helped to make the whole town very attractive.

It was market day in the town so there was a lot of activity, but no other tourists as far as we could tell: one school group in the fort, just us in the printing museum. The modern town has many evidently medieval buildings but somehow doesn't have the stultifying atmosphere that we experienced in Mantua. Perhaps the streets are just a little wider, the arcades a little more spacious—although Mantua's squares have quite a lot of space, just very tall piled-onto-each-other churches and so on. I think the atmosphere in Soncino and its state of preservation are really exceptional—it's a more unspoiled part of Italy than we had expected. It takes little imagination to picture the life five hundred years ago, because other than cars and parking problems, life has probably changed rather little. The Rocca, the streets around the church, the market square, and the sale of produce, fish, and meat, were all probably similar to the daily events witnessed by the members of the Soncino family who lived in the neighborhood and walked on the same streets where we could still walk.

The freeway that we took to return to Mantua (where we were staying) skirts around Brescia, where the family spent a short time. Travel by freeway makes the distances between these once very distinct places seem insignificant, but if you consider the distance through open countryside and the number of small towns in between, you can see that Gershom Soncino's move from Soncino to Brescia must have been a significant change in his life. Every modern tourist appreciates the beauty of the countryside and of these small villages. I wondered if they seemed equally appealing to men of the fifteenth century.

We stopped at Lake Garda for lunch. Once, this portion of the shore was in the territory of Mantua, and Isabella d'Este was fond of the trout and pike that lived in the lake, and relied on citrus orchards that were painstakingly developed to withstand the cold climate by taking advantage of the situation of the lake. As we enjoyed lake fish and local wine for our lunch, the lake provided a cool breeze. Our table stood on a grass terrace with a stone walk leading to a dock between beds of reeds in the lake. Early in the morning we had seen the snow-covered peaks of the Alps as we drove along the freeway near the lake, but a foggy layer had settled by lunchtime, so we could only see the opposite shoreline up to a few hundred feet above the shoreline opposite us. Having picked the restaurant for its view and its location only, we were delighted to have such a perfect meal.

A JEW AS A RENAISSANCE PRINTER

When Gershom Soncino took over the family press in 1490, he began a mature life as an important innovator in the new field of publishing. The Soncinos had already made advances by printing the first Hebrew Bible, developing Hebrew typography and vowel markings, marking signatures (groups of pages) to assist readers to find their place, and particularly by creating printed books of unprecedented beauty. In books from the Soncinos' press, whole pages were filled, leaving no blank space, following the Hebrew scribes' tradition; they also derived other printing innovations from Hebrew manuscript conventions. Gershom Soncino, extending the family tradition, was the first Hebrew printer to place woodcuts on title pages and in text. Along the same lines as other early printers, he began to offer the reader or prospective buyer expanded information on title pages and in colophons, giving the printer's name, his assistants' names, the city of publication, and dates of publication.

Wars, invasions, and political changes in Italy in the 1490s caused hard times for Jewish communities and small businessmen. When Gershom Soncino, victim of these conditions, could no longer make a living on Hebrew books, he entered the world of Italian and Latin printing. At this time the atmosphere and technological environment for the new invention were as hot as any modern computer technology—throughout his lifetime, print publication speedily increased from a kind of extension of manuscript publication to an important factor in European culture, with new features and new consequences all its own.

To clarify the environment in which he worked, the following discussion presents the issues faced by Gershom Soncino and his fellow printers—both Jewish and Christian and both religious and secular. I have concentrated on both early printers and their customers, using examples where possible from the specific accomplishments of the Soncino family. Gershom Soncino was a particularly interesting participant in the development of printing because he worked in several fields of Jewish, secular, and occasionally Christian printing. Soncino retains the reputation as a leader in printing Hebrew books, though in most mainstream, secular histories he receives only a footnote concerning the affair of Griffo's italic type.

I believe that obvious parallels relate the emergence of printing to the current emergence of electronic media. Computer technology has recently enabled anyone to become his own editor, typesetter, layout artist, and publisher—disrupting formerly secure job categories that were established in Soncino's day. Physical reference books, magazines, newspapers, catalogs, and bookstores now must meet the challenge of electronic production and distribution—obsoleting the speed and efficiency of print that itself obsoleted hand-copied manuscripts. Electronic distribution techniques are straining modern concepts of intellectual property and copyright—concepts that emerged to deal with printing. The capability of electronic media to accelerate ideas may dwarf the revolutionary ability with which the press spread ideas in Gershom

Soncino's time. The potential of the new revolution is still unknown, as the full potential of print was unknown in 1500. Though I will not explicitly refer to these parallels again, you may find them throughout the following discussion.

Background

Print culture as we know it today was created in the fifteenth century. The technological advance of Gutenberg in the first half of the century revolutionized cultural communications, and changed intellectual life in many ways. In the 1450s, soon after Gutenberg received wide recognition, early books appeared in many countries, and in all European languages including Hebrew. Italy quickly became a central location for the rapid development of the new technology, which fit perfectly into the cultural and intellectual atmosphere of the Italian Renaissance. By the time Gershom Soncino was on his own, this was a free-for-all atmosphere where "the Republic of Letters . . . resembled a newly liberated state where every citizen felt he had an irresistible vocation for serving as prime minister" (Elizabeth Eisenstein, *The Printing Press as an Agent of Change*, London: Cambridge University Press, 1979, p. 228).

Like many Jews of his time, Gershom Soncino felt that printing Hebrew books was a special Jewish mission that his trade enabled him and other Jews to fulfill. Once, a man named Abraham Esquerra Zarfatti, who gave him a subsidy for printing the Talmud, put this sense of mission into words. Zarfatti explained that as a Jew, he had a duty to study, but his business prevented this obligation. As a result, he said, he wished "at least to support the production of books." Soncino in his will mentioned his dedication to editing texts in order to make clear "what is obscure, as God in his goodness has enabled me to do" (Marx, "Gershom Soncino's Wander-Years in Italy, 1498–1527," pp. 490–491).

By 1500, the Italians widely appreciated the value of printing, but printers' skills were rare. Possession of the knowledge and tools of the trade afforded opportunities that even a Jew—Gershom Soncino—could exploit. After the family lost its moderately secure status as Hebrew printers in Soncino, he became an itinerant printer, spending a few years here and there in towns whose rulers were anxious to make use of the new technology. Although he clearly wanted to print Hebrew books in the family tradition, he applied his trade to town archives and to Italian and Latin books in order to continue to make a living. He fits the definition of the printer as "an urban entrepreneur who substituted machine-made products for hand-produced ones, who had to recoup large investments and secure trade networks beyond the limits of late medieval guilds and towns; . . . and who confronted constant competition from profit-driving rival firms" (Eisenstein, p. 22).

New Technology Required New Skills and Led to New Enterprises

Gutenberg became the first commercially viable printer by successfully combining a number of existing ideas with original improvements. He developed a way to make large batches of metal type: the process started with carved "punches" for each character in a font; with these punches, he made multiple indentations in molds; and in the molds, he cast the type. He devised an efficient way to set this type for production on a press and invented a new formula for ink. He adopted from other printers the press used at the time for woodblock and fabric printing, wine extraction, and many other purposes (oddly, the press was the least radical of the new inventions). Later, others made minor improvements —one, in the 1470s, was Nicholas Jenson, who had begun as a metalworker in a mint. He invented a way to hold the type in the forms with iron bands, instead of using threads to hold each line of type in place.

In Germany, where a number of printers began the trade, political problems curtailed commercial activity shortly after Gutenberg's early efforts. Holland and Provence (today's southern France) were also sites of earlier experimentation, so the new enterprise took root there quickly. In fact, Jews in Avignon had been in the technology race before Gutenberg, but for various reasons they didn't win. Caxton, the first English printer, spent a number of years in Holland, where he founded his first printing business, and printing also spread rapidly in Italy. Hebrew printing developed in Spain and Italy not long after Gutenberg, though German guild restrictions had shut out German-Jewish craftsmen.

In Italy, Sweynheym and Pannartz, two German printers, first introduced printing in the 1460s. Intellectual and economic conditions in Italy encouraged the rapid growth of the industry; a number of other Germans established printing houses in several Italian cities—such as the brothers John and Wendelin from Speyer who were prominent in Venice. Natives quickly picked up the required skills. These early printers in Italy evidently allowed some of the early Jewish printers to become their apprentices, and these men in turn began to cut Hebrew type and to train other Jews; this route probably allowed the Soncinos to acquire the technology in the 1480s. Although there were formal restrictive laws in force in some places, there was a great deal of openness toward Jews in trades at the time (it went away during the sixteenth century). Jews worked for Christians and Christians for Jews—a Christian typecutter, Francesco Griffo of Bologna, worked first for Aldus Manutius and later for Soncino, as we will see.

Printing required different combinations of skills than previous book-creation efforts by scribes working for stationers. New possibilities for skilled craftsmen and for editing attracted different types of people to become printers. The exciting atmosphere also appealed to entre-preneurs like the older generation of Soncino printers. Early printers thus came from a variety of professions, especially skilled metalworkers, cloth-dyers (who used techniques of block printing), and academics such as Aldus Manutius. As it happened, Jews were active in these professions; Abraham the Dyer, who took over for Conat, was the first Hebrew printer in Mantua and briefly worked on one of the Soncino classics. By 1500, print shops had their own specialized workers: the employees of a Hebrew press included the owner, compositors, printers, a foreman, a proofreader or corrector, and possibly a distinct publisher who furnished money; the assets included a supply of type in necessary sizes and the presses.

Another development in Italy: itinerant printers who traveled from town to town, printing what was needed in the way of legal or other documents, and then moving onward. Full equipment for a master-printer could be packed up with surprising ease. The wood press, a supply of type adequate to set around sixteen pages, a wooden frame for composing type, tools, and other necessities could fit into a cart that two horses could pull. Supplies of paper and ink could be purchased or imported when needed. Gershom Soncino, as we mentioned, ap-pears to have worked this way during the early 1500s. Two other such printers were Enrico da Colonia who printed at Brescia, Bologna, Mantua, and elsewhere, and Porro of Turin who printed for a bishop in Corsica—neither of them Jews (Marx, "Gershom Soncino's Wander-Years," p. 429).

Once introduced, Italian printing grew rapidly. By the 1490s there were two hundred printers in Venice alone, with a quickly growing market for their products. For Jews, acceptance accelerated even more rapidly, due to a sort of natural "backlist" of popular Jewish books for which there was instant demand, and Jewish print shops, including the Soncino press, had produced a number of Hebrew editions by 1490.

New Conventions and a New Look

Before the invention of printing, specialized copyists had employed various styles of handwriting—Christians had different scripts for legal works, secular poetry, and religious commentary, and Jews used various Hebrew scripts, depending on their national origins: Italy, France, Aragon, Catalonia. At first, typecutters imitated handwritten alphabets. Later, as their skill increased, they developed more readable typefaces. Hebrew type required attention to ensure distinctions between similar letters and to clarify vowel markings. Conventions for using Sephardic or Ashkenazic Hebrew also emerged during the early years of printing: the Soncino family employed Sephardic alphabets to attract Spanish buyers in the early days of their press, before the Jews' expulsion from Spain.

Aldus Manutius, around 1500, was especially important in employing new typefaces. He based his fonts on humanist writing styles, which earlier humanists had derived from Roman inscriptions rather than from following medieval manuscript conventions. For a publication of Petrarch's sonnets, Aldus hired the typecutter Francesco Griffo to create a new font. As a model, he provided Griffo with a two-hundred-year-old manuscript handwritten by the poet himself, as well as with samples of his own cursive handwriting. The result was *italic* type. Griffo also designed a still-popular typeface called etna or bembo for Aldus's edition of Pietro Bembo's now-obscure work about Mount Etna. Aldus was one of the first to produce a Hebrew grammar directed at a non-Jewish audience.

Gershom Soncino attempted to compete with Aldus over type innovation. During his visit to Venice, Soncino may have contributed to the production of the Hebrew alphabet that Aldus used in this work, though he received no recognition. Later, in direct competition with Aldus, Soncino hired Griffo to produce another set of italic type and contested Aldus's ownership of the italic typeface. Griffo—a prickly character—was particularly resentful that he had done the work but that Aldus had obtained a copyright, and he transferred his loyalty to Soncino.

Paper-making technology, which had made important advances just before Gutenberg, also affected the difference in the appearance of books and manuscripts. Manuscripts had traditionally been written on vellum, made from animal hides, while the printing press from the start used paper. Development of paper more suitable for the printing press altered the look of books (as well as helping to drive down prices). Supplies of good-quality paper concerned early printers: Fano, where Soncino had one of his presses, was a paper-producing city, which may have attracted him there.

Book illustration became adapted to the new constraints and freedoms of printing as well. When a scribe copied a manuscript by hand,
he left room for ornate capital letters, borders, miniature or full-page
decorations, or technical diagrams and maps, which a specialized illus-
trator later added to the manuscript. Some Jewish scribes employed
Christian illustrators for this purpose, as demonstrated by many very
beautiful illuminated Hebrew manuscripts of the Middle Ages. Early
printers at first continued to leave similar spaces, hiring illustrators to
complete each printed copy separately. It didn't take long to streamline
this process. Printers quickly figured out how to incorporate woodblock
illustrations directly. Also, they developed stock metal engravings for ornate
capital letters and prefabricated borders, as well as custom engravings
for a particular text. A printer named Radolt innovated a variety of book-
illustration methods; in the 1480s, he produced an edition of Euclid's
geometry with the first printed mathematical diagrams. At about the same
time, the Soncino press added woodcuts to a text and produced the first
illustrated Hebrew printed book. The end result was not only aesthetic
but also improved technical consistency.

During the first century of printing, page design for printed books
in Italy, England, and France assumed a characteristic appearance, including conventional combinations of roman and italic type, surrounding
white space, and so forth. German book design, with its Gothic script,
took another direction. The Soncino press contributed a great deal to
the appearance of Hebrew books, augmented in the following century
by the work of Daniel Bomberg, a Christian printer of Hebrew in Venice,
who developed the still-current tradition of organizing text and commentary on the pages of the Talmud and other Hebrew sacred writings.

New Job Definitions

Printing demanded a revolution in existing job definitions. It created
a new distinction between a book-producer and an editor or author.
Manuscript culture had blurred the line between the author, the physical
producer of a manuscript, and even the user who copied to meet his
own needs. An author might make copies of his own works, thus doing
everything. Proofreading or critical editing of manuscripts was rare among
Christian copyists, and although Jews had slightly higher standards, copyists
often introduced changes to make works conform to their own opinions.
In a pinch a scholar might borrow a book and copy or summarize as
much as he could before its owner wanted it back, and thus accidentally

create a new version. When stationers—who dealt in manuscripts—hired several scribes to meet demand for many copies of a work, errors were likely.

At first, printers continued to do all the jobs. Aldus Manutius himself wrote the Hebrew grammar book that his press published. In England, William Caxton not only was a hands-on printer and editor, he also created material, translating heroic tales from French into English and writing a new volume to update a historical work. At the same time, printers began to hire out their press capability to produce works needed by someone else, especially legal documents: Gershom Soncino made such a contract with the municipality of Fano. Overall, print culture required a new author-producer-user relationship and fostered specialization in areas that previously had been mingled.

Print shops could be large or small. The Soncino family enterprises, which varied at different times from a reasonable-sized shop to a small itinerant business, were usual in the fifteenth century. Aldus represented a new trend of large, well-funded shops, with several presses and many specialized employees. Such a well-capitalized endeavor was possible in a place such as Venice, where printers and their backers had been more numerous since the introduction of the trade.

Women often participated in every activity of print shops. In Venice, the widow of John of Speyer, named Madonna Paola, successfully took over her late husband's business and was an important figure in printing for a number of years. Aldus, who was the brains of his operation, married his partner's daughter, seemingly as part of the business deal. In Mantua, in the 1480s a couple named Abraham and Estellina Conat both were printers of Hebrew books—her name appears on the title page of an early Hebrew edition as the fully responsible printer of the book. Thus, it is very likely that in addition to sons, Soncino's business employed his wife and any daughters, who all nevertheless remain unnamed in historic record.

Printed Books: More Manageable and More Affordable

Manuscripts were always rare and hard to obtain, even when demand allowed Christians to have mass-production copying shops and when wider Jewish literacy and values made it possible to find men like Abraham Farissol of Ferrara, who would copy books to order. Before print, Christian scholars, especially those with limited means, had great difficulty obtaining important documents, even just to read them. Experts often taught from memory, which meant that students might learn about an important thinker without a firsthand look at his works. The result was dependence on authority, limited critical development, and a rather cloudy apprehension of the integrity of masterpieces from the past. Printed books freed scholars from these limitations by allowing careful study of earlier scholars' arguments from accurate texts.

Jewish readers had always demanded and valued books and had maintained higher standards for copyists, though there were always challenges in obtaining manuscripts. While Christian printers quickly began to introduce new literature to their audience, Jewish reading tastes were already formed, and Hebrew printers were "merely enabling what was already well known to be circulated more freely and at less expense. The Christian printers gradually introduced a non-Christian literature very different from the martyrologies and saintly biographies dear to the Middle Ages; the Jewish printers made no breach in the tradition of Jewish learning, but merely made accessible books studied by generations of scholars." However, Jewish printers also began to print books by living authors and to produce popular editions (Amram, p. 18).

When books were rare, bulky, and expensive, even rich and interested men could own very few of them. Count Pico della Mirandola, the humanist scholar, dedicated a combination of a personal fortune and enormous determination to creating a major philosophical library. By his death in 1493, his efforts had yielded a collection with no more than 1200 printed and manuscript books. Leonardo da Vinci, at about the same time, owned only 116 books. In 1475, the Vatican library had 2,527 volumes. The Venetian collector Sanudo owned 500 volumes in 1500; by the 1530s, he increased his collection to 6,500, presumably as prices dropped. At the end of the fifteenth century, a few exceptionally large collections existed elsewhere in Europe as well, such as that of the King and Queen of Hungary or Oxford University. Italian Jewish collectors included Menachem of Volterra, Baruch da Peschira, and Solomon Finzi, whose 200 volumes were a large collection for his time. The Da Pisa family had the largest Jewish collection of the era. Within a century, printing revolutionized ease of ownership of books for Christians, while censorship and crowded conditions in the ghetto handicapped Jewish book ownership, even among those who could afford the price.

At first, printed books cost almost as much as handwritten manuscripts, because early printers felt compelled to imitate many manuscript features. They left room for hand-drawn illustrations in the text, they used very expensive paper, and they found ways to add color to make printed documents more like manuscripts. As a result, it took some time .

before they achieved economies of scale. Eventually, standards adjusted
to the capability of the technology, and thus prices dropped and the
market grew enormously. Scribes simply couldn't compete with the speed
of printing: Sweynheym and Pannartz, the first Italian printers, produced
12,000 volumes in five years. To produce equal output in the same time
period in a mass-production copying shop would have required one
thousand scribes. These economies also caused excessive confidence. In
Venice, where printing took off rapidly, a shake-out occurred around
1473, and the weak or overextended shops went out of business.

Creating a market for the new, affordable product was more of a
challenge for non-Jews than for Jews, who instantly knew that printing
would facilitate the dream of every Jew: to own books. Christian scribes
attacked printing and encouraged connoisseurs to insist that manuscripts
were more pleasing or more beautiful and that mass-produced books were
inferior to their handiwork. Further, the Christian establishment quickly
grasped the danger of easily available information, scripture, and works
of opinion and began to oppose printing. Jews found few arguments
against printing—the traditions that still enforce hand-copying of the
Torah and other ritual documents.

A lag in getting the majority of existing works into print forced
scholars and collectors to continue to rely on copyists during a transition
period, although eventually most reasonably known works became available in print. Well beyond the introduction of printing, Federigo da
Montefeltro of Urbino continued to employ thirty to forty scribes to copy
manuscripts for his exceptional library; some of these were Jewish copyists, as his library included Hebrew manuscripts. His library included early
printed books along with the manuscripts (though an often-repeated
myth has it that a printed work would have been ashamed to be in the
finer company of his manuscript collections). Similarly, members of the
Norsa family of Mantua and Ferrara continued to order handwritten
manuscripts from the copyist and scholar Abraham Farissol, despite the
existence of local Hebrew presses.

The size and value of manuscripts also affected the reading methods
of individuals. A scholar normally read while standing or seated at a high
lectern, of the type now used for an unabridged dictionary. Handmade
books didn't travel far from the library; at most, a rich person may have
owned a small prayer book to use in private. Maybe reading a paperback
of *Jaws* at the beach and reading in the bathtub are modern diversions,
but portable books were an early convenience. Print made small type
practical—scribes don't easily write in 10-point letters, and thus the
manufacture of small, easily handled books other than a few prayer books

became possible. The first printer to make these early pocketbooks consistently was Aldus Manutius, who issued humanist classics in the new format in around 1500. (The invention of reading glasses had occurred a few centuries earlier, so middle-aged or myopic readers didn't necessarily cringe at the new small type.)

The immediate Jewish reaction to the vast new potential of print: "No religious community made so widespread a use of the press as the Jews, who saw in it a perpetual guarantee against monopoly of knowledge by the rich, who alone could afford to buy manuscripts. In the mechanical process of printing they had an assurance that after careful editing and correction of proofs the correctness of texts would no longer be dependent on the skill, knowledge and scholarly accuracy of the copyist; and literature was saved from the danger of fire and water and secure against destruction by fanaticism and ignorance" (Amram, pp. 36–37).

Market Savvy Determined the Choice of Subjects and Method of Distribution

An early printer had a wide field—ancient literature in classical languages, recent prose and poetry in the vernacular, popular tales, scholarly documents of academic interest, vanity-press type publications at a rich author's expense, church documents and prayer books, law codes and legal documents, mariners' maps, astronomical tables, political or literary commentaries, short broadsides or pamphlets, music, and many more topics. William Caxton, who published in England from the 1470s to the 1490s, printed heroic tales and histories that were a commercial success with upper-class English readers. In Venice in around 1500, Aldus introduced affordable scholarly editions of humanist classics. While Christian printers experimented to discover which books would sell, how fast they would sell, and what extras, such as illustrations or editorial commentary, would enhance their appeal, early Hebrew printers knew which Jewish books were already in demand. The Soncino press produced editions of the Bible, Talmud, prayer books, popular tales, and philosophical books.

Printers began to advertise. Nicholas Jenson in Venice in the 1470s publicized his use of several experts who ensured high-quality texts. Gershom Soncino provided compelling information by enlarging on the previous standard for the colophon and title page. Two generations later, at the press run by the heirs of Aldus, the title page of Judah Abravanel/ Leone Ebreu's *Dialogues of Love* made deceptive use of this type of publicity.

The title page of one particular edition claims Leone as a convert to Christianity, though this is without foundation and was probably intended to make him more acceptable in the anti-Jewish atmosphere of the time.

Competition became a big issue. Around 1502, in one of his revealing colophons, Gershom Soncino bitterly challenged Aldus Manutius over their editions of Petrarch's Sonnets in Griffo's italic type. A wide variety of pirate or counterfeit Aldine editions from the sixteenth century exist in modern collections, along with the originals. Many imitative grammar books included a copy of Aldus's Hebrew grammar—which may have resulted from collaboration with Gershom Soncino. Later, competition among several publishers of Hebrew books in Venice (none of them Jewish) attracted the attention and then the wrath of the church and led to the burning of the Talmud in St. Mark's Square on the Jewish New Year in 1553.

Another issue for editors and for living authors was how to get paid. When the only way to disseminate your work was one handmade copy at a time, you were delighted when anyone wanted to copy it. If you were a nobleman or a monk, you didn't need income from another source; otherwise, you could dedicate your work to a duke, prince, cardinal, or rich merchant to see if he would patronize you—that is, give you some money to encourage your efforts. You didn't expect to get paid by your readers, since you didn't have direct contact with them. Printing made this arrangement obsolete. Poor authors began to expect payment from publishers, who then profited from the work, while richer authors began to pay publishing costs—that is, to make vanity editions. Methods of compensating editors also evolved—at first, they received an agreed-on number of copies of the book or payment by the job. Later they became salaried employees of the publisher. In some cases, the publisher had to wear all the hats because he couldn't afford the expense of a good editor. Aldus, with several rich backers, could pay top-quality editors such as Bembo, while the poorer Gershom Soncino at times overestimated his capability to edit his own Italian editions.

Distribution practices also had to change. Printing made it easier to locate and purchase printed books. To obtain a printed book, you could look in a publisher's catalog—another printed innovation from Aldus—instead of tracking down and borrowing a private copy and hiring a scribe, hiring an agent to find an available copy, or finding a dealer to send a work on approval. This also helped to cause both private and institutional collections to grow rapidly (although the public lending library did not develop until Benjamin Franklin invented it in the eighteenth century). At the same time, books began to be sold in stores. The

Giunta family of Florence first became printers, around 1497, and eventually founded a "chain" of bookstores in several European cities.

The changes in distribution of Christian or secular books affected Jewish book dealers, who had traditionally bought and sold used books and accepted books as security for small loans (sometimes despite prohibitions against their activities). Jewish dealers were often active in university towns like Padua. In contrast, Hebrew books appealed to a much smaller market, and their distribution continued to be less institutionalized.

Printing Created New Issues for Government

An early printer had many reasons to seek legal protection for his efforts. Before publication a printer had to expend his effort and money to find a salable manuscript and an editor to create a good text, or had to contract with a living author for his work; then he designed a layout and set the type. The result, once this printer had created such an edition, was much cheaper to duplicate than to originate. Sometimes an insider at a print shop would steal a work-in-progress and sell it to a pirate printer, who could get a cheap imitation on the market before the originator sold even the first copy. In response to this situation, printers asked government bodies to grant them exclusive rights and protection of their efforts. The first such privilege went to John of Speyer, guaranteeing his exclusive right to be the only printer in the Venetian Republic, but this right expired at his death. Later, the Venetian Senate granted a copyright to Aldus Manutius, not for a text, but for the italic typeface he had commissioned from Griffo. Aldus's copyright only applied in Venetian territory, perhaps explaining why Griffo and Soncino both ended up in Fano, which was papal territory. By 1517, the authorities in Venice began creating specific legal codes to regulate printers' privileges, such as limiting copyright to new works.

Censorship became an issue more than ever before. When books existed only in manuscript, few people could expect to have access to them. Church and civil authorities soon noticed that printed books were reaching a much broader audience, and the implications didn't escape them: censorship arose quickly, from a variety of sources. At first, scholarly organizations debated what should be allowed. When printing was new, Florence became a center for light popular literature, but Savanarola's bonfires in the 1490s consumed the books. In 1501, the pope ordered prior approval for books to be printed in Germany and ordered inspection of existing printers' catalogues for conformity to church doctrine; a thorough policy of censorship developed, and the Catholic church created the index of banned books, backed up by the Inquisition. As the Reformation spread, Protestant states developed their own methods of controlling books. Later in the sixteenth century, the Jewish community also responded defensively to a few books considered dangerous to Jewish dogma or dangerous to the well-being of the Jewish community. In this spirit, rabbis in several Italian cities prohibited Jews from reading a controversial work by the historian Azariah de Rossi. Remember—the freedom-of-the-press amendment to the U.S. Constitution was a radical idea in the 1790s, in response to centuries of suppression.

The summit meeting of Jewish leaders, held in Ferrara at this time, made an attempt at self-censorship to satisfy the scrutiny and avert external pressure, and called for prior approval of Jewish publications by local rabbis, but the pressure continued. Many other Jewish books, including the standard prayer books, were censored by Christian authorities, although when a part of the prayer book was left out, the Jews would memorize it and use a word as a symbol for a suppressed passage, continuing the old way via oral tradition. Another consequence of the campaign against Jewish books was that many editions of Hebrew books survive in only one example, while others have evidently been 100 percent lost. (Sadly, some of these rarities, which were once in German or Russian collectors' hands, disappeared as recently as the 1940s, for obvious reasons.)

As for the Talmud: since the thirteenth century, a series of Christian attacks had constantly increased Christian hostility and suspicion of its content and intentions, although no irreversible ban on its use had been promulgated. In the late 1400s, a combination of factors—including available printed versions—attracted Christian scholars, such as Reuchlein, to study the Talmud for its wisdom, not merely to search for material with which to condemn the Jews. In the 1500s, more editions appeared, such as those published by Daniel Bomberg, the non-Jewish Venetian printer of Hebrew books. The church got worried (they also had Martin Luther on their hands, which made them skittish). In the mid-1500s, Rome retracted permission it had given for publication and ordered all copies of the Talmud, whether in use by Jews or Christians, to be burned. In the bonfires in Venice, which consumed the banned Talmud, some printers lost their entire investments in typesetting, ink, paper, and labor.

A Renaissance Man

The printer became one of the models of a Renaissance Man, performing and mastering many tasks in varied disciplines. While written about Aldus Manutius, there are many ways that the following description applies, with limitations, to Soncino:

> The humanist printer is by definition a Renaissance-era scholar, a professional who printed his own works or had some hand in the editorial content of the books that issued from his press, either as editor, commentator, or translator; moreover he was thoroughly trained in the classical languages and printed classical and Biblical texts from manuscripts that he himself edited, emended, or translated into Latin from Greek, occasionally writing commentaries on them; finally, he is someone whose reputation in typography is as great today as is his renown in scholarship. (H. George Fletcher, *In Praise of Aldus Manutius*, New York: Pierpont Morgan Library, 1995, p. 19)

GERSHOM SONCINO'S WANDERINGS

Let us move from the professional life of Gershom Soncino to his travels and explore what still remains of the places where he lived. Having participated in what may be the initiation of the most revolutionary invention of the West, Gershom left Soncino and began a period of wandering around 1492. Gershom Soncino's activity in Soncino, Brescia, and Barco account for only a few years of the 1490s.

From 1495–1497, Soncino was the only Hebrew printer in existence. The presses in Spain and Portugal had been silenced, the Turkish Empire had no Hebrew press until 1503, and Prague had none until 1513. Between 1497 and about 1502, even the Soncino family had no press; no Hebrew books whatsoever were published in those years. As mentioned, Gershom traveled north of the Alps to Chambery, Geneva, and other places, collecting manuscripts for later projects, but he recorded next to nothing about the details of these voyages.

Since the colophons to his books are a major source of information about his life and locations, this leaves the time when he was not active in printing relatively undocumented, meaning one can only speculate about his search for manuscripts, about his stay in Venice from around 1500, and about the nature of his interaction with the great humanist printer Aldus Manutius.

In Venice with Aldus

Around 1500, Gershom spent some time in Venice. He may have actually worked on the Aldine Introduction to Hebrew, as a compositor, and interacted with various Venetian Christian-humanist scholars who were in Venice at the time, particularly in their early studies of Kabbalah. Aldus and his partners had ups and downs in their printing activity in Venice; the period around 1500 was a peak of innovation and productivity for the Aldine press. About this time, Aldus published the edition of Petrarch edited by Bembo, with type cut by Griffo, which was the source of the later feud between Aldus and Gershom.

If Gershom Soncino had tried to work as an independent printer in Venice, he would have experienced difficulty as a competitor of Aldus, who had the backing of a wealthy father-in-law and the favor of the rulers. Aldus and his partners founded the Aldine press in an extremely competitive atmosphere; many other printers had already folded. Gershom seems at that time to have had few resources but his own skill, and perhaps not even to have owned a press, type, or tools. Unless he lived as a Christian, he would additionally have suffered from the anti-Jewish attitudes and laws that existed in the Venetian Republic of the time, limiting a Jew's stay in the city and prohibiting him from permanent commercial activity: formally, Jews were allowed only fourteen days per year as residents of Venice proper—that is, the city on islands in the lagoon, at that time accessible only by boat.

At the end of this chapter, I have discussed the condition of Venice today, and I have pointed out the places where you can visit streets and buildings that may have been known to Gershom Soncino and to Aldus Manutius.

Cesare Borgia and Gershom Soncino in Pesaro and Fano

After Venice, Gershom Soncino found a way to take advantage of his skills and to leverage the constantly changing political rivalries between the powerful rulers of the day. From 1497–1502 Cesare Borgia was conquering the towns of former papal states. With the support of his father, Pope Alexander, he directly seized power from minor nobles who had been feudally connected to the pope. In particular, he expelled the rulers of Fano, Pesaro, and Urbino. In Fano, the people in fact asked Borgia to take over from the old, corrupt lords of the town. When Soncino arrived, Cesare Borgia was also treating the Jewish community of Fano favorably. Under his sponsorship, the civil and ecclesiastical Council of Fano declared in January 1502 that Soncino should undertake the printing of the town statutes as a permanent commission.

Thus, Gershom Soncino set up his print shop at Fano during this period of occupation, with the blessings of the conquering Borgias. In 1503, Soncino published Petrarch's poems, dedicated to "most illustrious and most excellent Prince Cesare Borgia" and in a poem called him "godlike." His first publication, earlier in 1503, he had dedicated to Franciscan father Francesco Georgi, a Christian Hebraist interested in Kabbalah. During the first year the new Soncino press published only non-Hebrew books, including some containing attacks on the Jews. Gershom managed to develop various relationships with the intellectuals of Fano. Lorenzo Astemio, the former librarian of Duke Guidobaldo of Urbino, was working as a grammar teacher in Fano and also worked for Gershom's new press, editing and correcting Latin and Italian books. He wrote nice dedication letters, suggesting that people with unpublished manuscripts should have them published by "Hieronymous Soncinus." Lorenzo also mentioned Gershom in the dedication of the "Life of Epamindonas," published in 1502.

In his publication of Petrarch, Gershom's introduction praised the atmosphere of Fano, as well as the wit of its inhabitants. Along with the dedication to Borgia, he also attacked Aldus and revealed the quarrel involving Griffo:

> To the most illustrious and most excellent Prince Cesare Borgia . . . Two years, most excellent and invincible Prince, have passed since being pleased with the air, the site and the fertility of your most devoted city of Fano and the friendliness and wit of its inhabitants, I decided to come and live in it and practice the art of printing. At that time I met here the Reverend Apostolic Legate . . . a man truly worthy of his dignity and a lover and patron of all learning. I recommended myself to his Eminence and made known to him my full intention to take up my perpetual domicile in this city and to bring here typecutters and printers, not ordinary and inferior but such as excelled all others . . . a most noble cutter of Latin Greek and Hebrew type, called Messer Francesco da Bologna [Griffo], whose skill I certainly believe to be unequaled in this work. For he not only knows how to cut fonts most perfectly but he has invented a new form of letters called cursive or chancery, which neither Aldo Romano nor others who cunningly have tried to adorn themselves with the plumes of others, but this very Messer Fancesco first invented and deigned, and it was he who cut all the fonts of letters from which the said Aldo ever printed, as well as the present font with a grace and beauty that speak for themselves. . . . (Amram, p. 97–98).

The following historical events might help to understand the situation in which Gershom Soncino undertook his professional activities there. Several of these events, such as the events at Sinigaglia and Fano, figure in the eyewitness reports of Machiavelli, who was a negotiator representing Florence during this time. Another famous member of Cesare Borgia's entourage was Leonardo da Vinci, who was serving him as a military engineer during this time.

According to a contemporary source, Collenuccio, Cesare entered Pesaro, triumphant, on October 27, 1500. The citizens welcomed him and freely gave him the city. The smaller city of Fano made the same offer, and when he refused, the citizens insisted on being included in his state. By the end of October, Cesare Borgia held the entire stretch of coast and delegated the governing of the state to Ramiro de Lorqua. In 1502, Borgia launched the famous campaign in Sinigaglia, where he lured the condittori from Fano to their deaths.

> On December 10 [1502] Cesare left Imola, still accompanied by Machiavelli, to join the attack on Sinigaglia, a small city on the Adriatic coast. The force at the duke's immediate disposal was impressive. . . . The company halted at Cesena, and Cesare was immediately inundated with complaints against his governor, Ramiro de Lorqua. The Spaniard had ruled energetically in Cesare's name but simultaneously had indulged in an orgy of cruelty surpassing that of the most depraved Romagnol tyrants. One of the many tales told against him was of how he had thrust a clumsy page boy into the fire, pressing him down with a foot while the boy burned alive. (E. R. Chamberlain, *The Fall of the House of Borgia*, New York: Dial Press, 1974, pp. 284–286)

Cesare was indifferent to cruelty as such, but de Lorqua's habits had seriously undermined his control in the areas he governed. While no government was democratic, popular support was always useful to a conqueror, and in this case, the people had welcomed Cesare's rule only as a means of escape from the arbitrary cruelty of their previous overlords. Hence, Cesare summoned de Lorqua from Pesaro to account for his stewardship. His accounting was deemed inadequate. On the morning of December 26, the people of Cesene found a carefully arranged horror show. The headless corpse of de Lorqua still clad in its Christmas finery lay in the marketplace below the castle. His head was stuck on a pike not far from a bloodstained cutlass. The body remained in the marketplace when Cesare left the city shortly afterward. He proceeded with additional plots to depose his opponents and to consolidate his power, as made famous in Machiavelli's eyewitness account.

After Borgia: Fano and Pesaro

The Borgia family's power in Italy lasted only as long as Roderigo Borgia was pope. Not long after these events, his sudden death and the illness of Cesare Borgia gave their opponents the upper hand. Conquered territories and some (though not all) of the looted artworks and valuables were returned to the former ruling families. The unification of Italy would have to wait several more centuries. Ironically, the marriage of Lucrezia Borgia to the Duke of Ferrara lasted and produced children, so that Roderigo Borgia's descendants ruled in Ferrara for another century and subsequently ruled in Modena. Throughout this time, these were among the most tolerant European rulers with respect to their treatment of the Jews.

After the Borgias' fall, Gershom Soncino continued to publish in Fano for a few years more. He dedicated works to the now-restored duke and duchess, Guidobaldo Montrefeltre and Elizabetta Gonzaga, of Urbino and to Ramberto Malatesta of Fano. During this time, he printed in Latin and Italian as well as in Hebrew. He continued publishing in Fano through 1506, the date of publication of an especially beautiful illustrated book, *The Christian Ten-Stringed Harpsichord*, by Marco Vigerio. In 1507 he began to publish some books at Pesaro, though some work continued at Fano; this is the date of publication of *Decachordum* by the Bishop of Sinigaglia, published at Fano.

After the Borgias' fall from power, Pesaro was ruled by the families Sforza and Rovere. Giovanni Sforza, the ruler, married Ginevra, daughter of Gershom's Venetian patron Marco Tiepolo, and she may have been responsible for inviting Gershom to Pesaro. He started to dedicate books to this couple at about the time of her arrival. Also, in 1508, Gershom returned to Fano where he contracted to print the town's statutes for the priors of Fano. In a contract dated February 21, 1508, he agreed to print eighty copies of these statutes in the same type that he had previously used for the *Decachordum*. In return, the priors promised to supply him with a house for his press, a corrector for the work, and a stipend of eighty gold florins (Amram, p. 108).

Between 1507 and 1520, Gershom Soncino printed a number of books at Pesaro, which had a library that rivaled that of Urbino. Both libraries collected the works of the Soncino press. A few were Hebrew books, though bad times for Jews had made Hebrew publishing a difficult market. One of Gershom's Hebrew publications in this period was a grammatical work that included a commentary published anonymously but which was, in fact, by Elijah Levita. This seems to have been published without permission: Levita later complained that it had been stolen from him while he was imprisoned at Padua. It appears that Soncino cheated Levita out of credit and financial reward for his work. During this time, Soncino was also a bookseller and had business connections in various places, including Ancona. He published two happy books on the subject of Purim, other Hebrew books, and also a chivalrous romance for not-necessarily Jewish readers.

Pesaro already had a Jewish community at this time. Jews participated as craftsmen. Some worked with the Christian ceramists of the town, which was traditionally known for its painted pottery. Later in the century, several were known by name, particularly the Azulai family who worked there from 1532 to 1570 and produced ceramic works for Jewish uses, such as Passover plates.

By 1515, Christian competition in the area of Hebrew printing emerged, because of humanist interest in the Talmud and other Hebrew texts, and because it was easier for a Christian to be trusted with permission to print them. Daniel Bomberg, the famous printer in Venice, began to obtain the service of Jewish workers, as well as establishing a copyright (later lost) to make Hebrew books. He published a Bible in 1517–1518 and later employed Elijah Levita.

Political events continued to affect Gershom's circumstances. In 1515, the situation in Italy was destabilized by another French invasion, this time by King Francis I. In 1516, the Rovere family was expelled from Urbino and Pesaro, making a bad situation worse. In 1518, Soncino moved on to Ortona, where he published four books, including one in Hebrew. Ortona is in Abruzzi, part of the kingdom of Naples. Gershom never appears to have really established himself here, and returned, at least briefly, to Pesaro.

In 1521 Gershom published at Rimini, just up the coast between Fano and Ravenna. He had petitioned Rimini for permission to print in 1518, and they encouraged him, offering favors and exemptions. They assigned him a location on the old Roman Bridge, where artists and craftsmen had shops, gave him tax exemptions, and paid a year's rent. Gershom was able to go back to Hebrew printing, and he adopted as a printers' mark the tower of Rimini. Also, he developed a well-known Soncino-press title page depicting two twisted columns.

In 1525 Gershom somehow offended the printers of Venice, including Daniel Bomberg and Cornelius Adelkind, by some hasty verses that he spoke or read at a meeting where they were all present. Adelkind, a converted Jew of German descent, and later from Padua, denounced him. Bomberg employed several members of the Adelkind family, who knew the business well, including enough scholarship to help with editing some Hebrew texts. At the time of this visit to Venice, Soncino visited Bomberg's print shop, a busy Venetian workplace with many employees and lots of activity, probably in contrast to his much smaller operations. Bomberg had a great deal of money at his disposal and was turning a profit, while Soncino was doing badly by then. This episode is the last, and perhaps least pleasant, of Soncino's career in Italy; he left soon after to join his sons in the Turkish empire.

MODERN PESARO, FANO, AND URBINO

On a June morning, after a night of rain, we walked on the beach at Chioggia, a seaside resort across the bay to the south of Venice. The day before, coming from Venice, we had crossed various causeways and canals to get out to the beachfront, where all the hotels are located. In its natural state, there isn't a mainland beach here. Our walk took us from our hotel to a wide jetty made from huge stones and topped with a cement sidewalk. Chioggia is out on the spit of land extending into the bay, so its beach is really on the sea, and there are small waves: the tide was going out. Large numbers of people were also walking with babies in strollers, old people, little kids, and teenagers all included. The number of people increased steadily between 8:30 and 9:30 during our walk, and it was getting crowded when we went back to the hotel, checked out, and drove south.

We drove from Chioggia to Pesaro, finding a way to take the autostrada for more of the distance than we expected. We went around Ravenna, avoiding the worst of the traffic, and then turned south, past Cesena. This was the route taken by Cesare Borgia and his troops around 1502, when he was going toward Fano and Pesaro for his showdown at Senigallia, where he had his unpopular governor dramatically executed. The landscape changes near Ravenna, as you leave the Po valley and thus the mountains nearly come down to the sea. The wide beaches with fringing islands that are the characteristic from Venice down to near Ravenna give way to sand beaches directly on the sea, and the water appears cleaner than it does near the Po delta. Making good time, we were in Pesaro by lunchtime and ate at a seaside place: salad and sandwiches. We observed an odd phenomenon—ladybugs were swarming all along the seaside, covering the railings that separated the public walks from the sea.

Our hotel room in Pesaro was on the fifth floor, with windows looking up and down the beach toward the east and the south. If Italy is a knee-boot, we were on the bulge of the calf. We had a particularly nice room with a couch and chairs and a little anteroom with a counter over the minibar and safe. The floors even in the bathroom were dark wood, the first wood floors I saw in Italy: all the other hotels had tile or marble. We had made four phone calls to find a hotel with a vacancy: according to the clerk in Chioggia, the Italian school year had just ended, and for the first time, we were experiencing the full summer demand on the beaches. The hotel stood on a small circular seaside park called Piazza Liberta, with a sea wall right on the water, very charming. In the center of the grass circle of the park stood a very modern brass sculpture, more or less spherical. The wide beach contained the usual stretch of long rows of umbrellas, usually rented to the vacationers, though they were all furled around their poles, as little rain squalls with lots of wind were blowing in from the sea. This beach had the most beautiful sea view we had seen so far in our stays along the Adriatic coast, though we weren't expecting it.

A few minutes' walk away from the seaside, with its entirely modern developments, we found the old medieval center of Pesaro, where Gershom Soncino must have had his print shop. Alessandro Sforza built the ducal palace on the main square, Piazza del Popolo. He finished in 1465, around fifty years before Gershom Soncino arrived. I found the palace a very nice example of Renaissance Italian: not too huge and massive, and not fortified like the Rocca. It has an arcade, some very severe windows, and a decorative roof edge visible at the top of the facade. The courtyard (finished later) also looks interesting. Today, it is the temporary home of the Ceramics Museum, whose usual building is being renovated.

Costanzo Sforza married Camilla d'Aragona at Pesaro in 1475, just as he was starting to build the Rocca. The streets through which their bridal procession passed may have looked much the same as they do today, and no doubt the procession marched to the main square where the palace—then nearly new—still stands. For the festivities, the Jews of the town presented a special pageant. They dressed in costumes and pulled three wooden elephants in a procession through these streets. The first elephant, topped with a canopied gold throne, carried the "Queen of Sheba"; on the others rode young women carrying lilies. The queen presented a formal speech in Hebrew and delivered the Jewish community's wedding gifts to the couple. Afterward, young people presented a dance choreographed by Guglielmo Ebreo, also called Guglielmo of Pesaro, who was renowned as a dancing master. He had earlier worked for the duke of Milan, Costanzo Sforza's relative, and composed a document called "Treatise on the Art of Dancing." It was he who also, in 1481, gave dance lessons to Isabella and Beatrice d'Este in Ferrara (Roth, *Jews in the Renaissance*, pp. 276–278).

The old Sephardic synagogue from the seventeenth century was also being restored when we were there. The synagogue is on Via Scuolo and Via Levi-Nathan. Via Scuolo goes around a corner of the building, as far as we could guess. Though the information center office (next to our hotel on the Piazza Liberta) tried calling and making arrangements for us to see it, they couldn't accommodate us—the synagogue is open only in July and August. My disappointment was mitigated because I was aware that the main synagogue furnishings were long ago removed to Livorno, Ancona, and Jerusalem—only the architectural elements remain. Among the many documents that the tourist office gave me was a brochure about the synagogue (ironic, in Mantua, with an intact and active synagogue, the tourist office had nothing but the phone number). The seventeenth-century Jewish community, who built the synagogue and lived in the few narrow streets around it, had a different ethnic composition than the Jews who lived in Pesaro in Gershom Soncino's time. He most likely lived near the church, which has been restored to a rather plain medieval brick facade. The exterior of the church is probably what Gershom Soncino saw, but the interior is nineteenth-century Baroque. In the fifth or sixth century, an earlier church on the site had a mosaic floor; according to the brochures, this mosaic is currently in the process of being restored.

A few blocks from the center, the Rocca, a fortified castle, has four very heavy brick towers and a moat, built between 1474 and 1505. Costanzo Sforza started the project, and Giovanni Sforza finished it. Now, a pleasant walkway goes all the way around the moat. We found that the bridge to the castle gate was blocked by construction work, with a large crane and piles of building stone in the moat further demonstrating substantial renovation. The modern crane and piles of materials were no doubt different from the construction methods at the site when Gershom Soncino arrived; however, he probably also saw it in an unfinished state. With its stout walls and moat, finished or not, the Rocca was almost sure to have been involved in the various fire fights between Cesare Borgia and his local enemies. Good luck if you get there in the future, when the current construction is complete—perhaps it will become a tourist attraction. In any case, the streets around it clearly have much of a similar look to when Gershom Soncino lived here, even though there seems to be no memory of his stay.

As for the details of the life of Gershom Soncino in Pesaro, the woman in the information office didn't know about him. I doubt that there is clear documentation identifying the street and house where he lived and worked. However, there are quite a few winding, narrow streets off the main street (Via Rossini), and you can imagine his presence. I assume that in the Middle Ages, there was a town wall at approximately the place where you can see the medieval town change to a modern beach resort. Medieval people would probably have ignored the sand and sea, though the port must always have been important.

From the Piazza Liberta we walked the length of the beach, staying in front of the umbrellas where the lifeguards were watching adolescent girls playing with Frisbees or beach balls in the gentle waves. At the end of the beach, a breakwater protects the port, which is relatively small but appears very busy with Adriatic commercial transport vessels, sailboats, and pleasure yachts. Dry-docks, cranes, guard huts, and chain-link fences reduced my appreciation of the picturesque quality that the deep blue water and bright sky seemed to promise. Some serious dredging seems to have taken place since the Renaissance.

The overall ambiance of the town, which prides itself on being both Giacomo Rossini's and Frederico Fellini's birthplace, was really pleasant. Bookstores were everywhere. An opera house across from Rossini's birthplace—now a museum—presents Rossini operas and celebrations. A film festival was going on at two movie theaters on the main street; since all the announcements were in Italian, I didn't figure out exactly what the film events were. Another surprise: the town has many beautifully preserved Art Nouveau houses, called Liberty Style in Italian. I particularly admired one that stands beside the circle next to the hotel. A ceramics factory here made Art Nouveau ceramic ware around a hundred years ago, and its owner designed and commissioned this magnificent building around 1907. Every detail is consistent, including incredible decorations of vines around the balcony and roof supports under the eaves made in the form of lobsters. It's more ornate than Hector Guimard's style, probably influenced by Austrian and German Jugendstyl. A book that the tourist office showed me (their copy, not available) illustrated the furnishings inside, which were also made for the same overall perfect consistency. This house is still owned by the same family, who recently restored its pale greenish yellow paint and white trim.

The Michelin *Green Guide* is not overly enthusiastic about Pesaro, though the *Red Guide* recommends quite a few hotels, including ours, and several restaurants, awarding one star to two of them. On our first night in Pesaro, we had a very good meal at Da Teresa, one of the restaurants with a star. One entire dinner on the menu is based on recipes by Rossini, a noted gourmet. The decor was postmodern, with basket chairs, windows, and tables all draped in heavy white cotton fabric. I regretted the window coverings, which obscured a view of the magnificent Liberty-Style mansion, which is just across the street.

The next morning, we drove up from Pesaro to Urbino, approaching from the east, and then down toward the south, going back to Fano on the Via Flaminia—now a four-lane limited-access highway linking to a main autostrada. The Via Flaminia follows a wide river valley between rather craggy mountains. I don't know if it's like that all the rest of the way to Rome, but, on the whole, one gets a sense of how these various places were connected in the days of Caesar Augustus (whose arch marks the entrance to Fano) or in the days of Cesare Borgia and Machiavelli.

Urbino is remarkably isolated, and it's hard to see how its dukes amassed the wealth and power they once possessed. Urbino is also remarkably alive and active today, with excellent art and architecture: I find it quite easy to understand why people make the effort to go there as a part of a serious tour of Italy, even though it's difficult and out of the way.

The mountains in Italy really make a difference, which is quite apparent here: Pesaro and Urbino are almost due east of Florence, but there was never any traditional connection between this region and Tuscany. Urbino is up the mountain from this coast, Rome is around three hundred kilometers due south. The Romans did have a road from Fano, the Via Flaminia—it's on the map. As usual, lots and lots of history, but the interesting parts were a long time ago.

The walls of Urbino are incredibly high, fortifying its hilltop location, and one walks up an almost vertical street to get from the edge of town up to the plaza, where the palace and the cathedral are located. The side streets are picturesque, with roof overhangs that almost touch or arched connectors between buildings. The entire center seems perfectly preserved from the Middle Ages; however, all appears to be in excellent modern condition, with little squares full of cars and even vans or small trucks whose access routes seem a mystery. We saw a workman trying to back up a truck and spinning his wheels on the steep granite street. The main street passes by not only souvenir stands and cafes, but also numerous buildings belonging to the modern university: faculties of law, sociology, science, and languages. We not only visited the ducal palace and its art collections, we also found the museum of ancient physics experimental equipment! It is closed because of damage from the earthquakes a few months ago, but the researcher in charge allowed us to look around.

The ducal palace is huge and in extremely fine Renaissance taste.

The rooms are lined up one after another. Most have rather Gothic arches and pilasters under the arches, and a few retain some fresco work. The art is mainly from the fourteenth to early fifteenth centuries, from the collections of the discerning Duke Federico Montefeltre. There are quite a few pictures of him—he's the one with the notch in his nose, always depicted in profile to avoid showing his destroyed right eye. Especially appealing is his portrait with his little son, who became the duke, married Elizabetta Gonzaga, and later was defeated by Cesare Borgia, who looted the palace. The father, a warrior, art collector, and manuscript collector, was a model Renaissance Man.

Duke Federico's *studiolo*, or study, has extraordinary inlaid-wood paneling. The inlay designs were by Botticelli. They depict a number of scenes and motifs, and many of them use dramatic perspective to trick the eye into "seeing" objects protruding from the panel, or "seeing" that the doors are actually open. In one panel, very foreshortened musical instruments appear to come forward from the panel. Other rooms in that part of the palace have inlaid wood of similar quality, though not with such clever designs. The famous paintings in the collection, displayed throughout the palace, include many great works of the early Renaissance, notably some by Piero della Franchesca and a very beautiful portrait of a mute woman by Rafael—Urbino's native son.

I was particularly anxious to see Ucello's *Profanation of the Host*, a rare presentation of the life and hardships of Jews in Italy in the Middle Ages. The painting's panels tell the story of a woman who pawns a consecrated host to a Jew. In the most interesting panel, you see this Jew behind a high counter, in a rather large public room with a black-and-white checkered floor—a revelation of what the Jewish money lending establishment might look like. In the next panel, by a miracle, the mistreated host begins to bleed, although the Jew tries to destroy it. The following panels show how, as punishment, the woman is hanged and the Jew and his entire family are burned at the stake. As propaganda this painting is horrifying; as art, it's excellent; as a historical testament, it's unique, especially in depicting a Jewish pawnshop and a Jewish family of the fourteenth century.

The rooms of this palace have seen many events of cultural and historic significance. In which room, I wondered, did Elizabetta Gonzaga sit on the floor, overcome with grief when her husband died? How can I picture Cesare Borgia as he pillaged the magnificent art collections and unique library? I wish Leonardo da Vinci had recorded his thoughts on this subject. The people, who loved the deposed duke and duchess, must have been sad to watch the lines of donkeys packed up with ducal treasures file down the steep mountain road toward Rome. I prefer to picture Castiglione, a few years later, as he observed the polite conversation in the huge castle drawing rooms, with occasional glimpses into rose-filled gardens behind high protecting walls. Castiglione presented his observations of life at the court of Urbino in his famous work *The Courtier,* making the Montefeltres and their guests famous, at least for a few generations.

After walking around the town, we drove down the mountain to Fano, a rather depressing little town, especially compared to its upscale neighbor Pesaro. The medieval buildings seemed rather derelict, though the city wall has many fairly intact sections. The streets are drab and narrow. The Augustan arch and a small area of archaeological interest are at one edge of the medieval city. In the center is a large palace, the "theater of fortuna." The railroad runs just below the old city wall facing the sea, thus separating the modern bathing resort from the medieval center (in contrast to Pesaro, where the old and new parts of town meet at a series of traffic circles, making the center inviting and lively.)

In one corner of town is the old Rocca, the fortified castle, dating from the late fifteenth century. Like that of Pesaro, it was made of brick and consisted of a number of massive towers seriously intended to fend off the expected unfriendly guests. It's in worse condition, as far as I could see. The sixteenth-century ghetto appears to have been located nearby, but as far as I can ascertain, it disappeared long ago. Presumably Gershom Soncino's print shop was among these mean streets, but no details appear to have been preserved. The library, it says, owns a number of his works as well as seventeen *incunabula,* but this is not a public display.

Poor Gershom Soncino—he had to move from Venice to Fano! It's no mystery that he was glad to have a chance to work in Pesaro a few years later. Fano and Pesaro are only eleven kilometers apart by a road that now runs alongside the Adriatic just inside the railroad right-of-way. Because of the tracks, an exceptional stretch of beachfront between the two towns is quite unspoiled (though not very accessible). As you approach Pesaro, the sand dunes and natural vegetation disappear, and a really unsavory trailer campground takes over the beach. Finally, the railroad tracks head inland, and the road goes over a bridge and heads back toward Pesaro's medieval center.

In Pesaro, my Gershom Soncino voyage ended. I pictured him loading his presses, his type, and his household goods onto a boat in one of these small harbors and departing across the Adriatic for Salonika and

Constantinople, sad to leave the land that had been his family home for three generations, but optimistic about joining his sons, who had already established branches of the family business in the more friendly realm of the Sultan.

THE FINAL YEARS—ISTANBUL AND SALONIKA

In 1520, two sons of Gershom, Moses and Eliezer, left Italy and opened a press at Salonika. Very little is known about their lives, as they left even less of a personal trail than their father. Finally, after a series of discouraging events, in 1527 Gershom Soncino left Italy and joined his sons in the Turkish empire. At first, he worked in their shop in Salonika. In 1530 he completed his first publication at the Soncino press at Istanbul. In 1534 he returned to Salonika to join his two sons, and he died there that year.

In Salonika and Istanbul, the family preserved the tradition of beauty and quality that had characterized the press from the start. One publication at this press—of interest in the present context—was the first printed edition of the *Itinerary of Benjamin of Tudela*, published in 1543, with an introduction assembled from the works of Isaac Abravanel. Until 1547 the press in Istanbul was almost constantly publishing new works, either under Gershom's direction or under the direction of his sons. Many of these works have title pages and colophons that provide clues to the life of Gershom Soncino.

Summary: The Life of Gershom Soncino

Born into a family that developed one of the first Hebrew print shops, Gershom Soncino—sometimes also known as Gerson, or Hieronymus in his Latin and Italian publications—published actively for approximately fifty years. His output numbered approximately two hundred books, and he made numerous innovations in Hebrew and in non-Hebrew printing. He competed with the best, including Aldus, though he could never obtain the financial backing or political permissions to really challenge the Christian printers of the time. His taste in books displayed an appreciation for both Renaissance Italian humanism and Jewish tradition. His dedications display an appreciation for his political situation: he dedicated works to various Sforzas, to Duke Ercole of Ferrara, to Duke Guidobaldo of Urbino and his wife, Elizabeth Gonzaga, and to Cesare

Borgia. He had many other powerful friends and patrons, including various churchmen. His early success was possible because of the exceptional openness of fifteenth-century Italy, while his departure from Italy was a symptom of the deteriorating conditions of Jewish life at the beginning of the sixteenth century.

Rabbi Joshua Soncino in Istanbul

While Moses and Eliezer Soncino continued the family printing business, another son of Gershom, named Joshua Soncino, became the rabbi of the Great Synagogue, or Sinagoga Mayor, of Istanbul. This was one of the oldest places of Jewish worship in the city, as it had existed even before the Turkish conquest. Rabbi Soncino was involved in several controversial endeavors in Istanbul in the later part of the sixteenth century. In the course of events, he tangled with the very wealthy and powerful Gracia Nasi, whom I have already described. She and her nephew Joseph Nasi had arrived in Istanbul in great splendor, established an influential relationship with the rulers, and lived in a great palace. Because of the large amounts of money that they distributed to the various Jewish congregations in Istanbul, they expected automatic support for their endeavors from all rabbis and all other Jews. The following episode shows how Rabbi Soncino stood up to them.

The events that engaged Rabbi Soncino and Gracia Nasi began with the election of Pope Paul IV in 1555. This pope's fanatical attitude toward the Reformation in northern Europe spilled over into actions against Jews. During this time, throughout Italy, Jewish communities were being moved into ghettos, synagogues were attacked and destroyed, and a variety of restrictions threatened Jewish livelihoods. The persecution of Portuguese Marrano refugees who had reverted to Judaism was particularly violent. In the papal territory of Ancona, the Inquisition began proceedings to bring such apostates back to Christianity. The pope's representatives arrested all of Ancona's Jews, confiscated vast amounts of Jewish property, and rescinded all previous guarantees of tolerant behavior toward them. Some escaped, but around fifty were subjected to public punishment consisting of "Acts of Faith" before a hostile crowd. Finally, the church announced the death sentence for those who refused to retract their Jewish faith, though they spared Jews who had never been Catholic or Portuguese. Some of the Marranos accepted death and "sanctified the name" with the martyr's blessing. Others recanted and were sent to the galleys. While such zeal on the part of the church was common in Spain and Portugal, Italy had not previously been the site of such fanatical persecution. Jewish public opinion in Italy and in Turkey was stirred up, but the Jews had little or no influence.

There was one exception: Gracia Nasi and Joseph Nasi, former Portuguese Marranos themselves, had the sympathy of the Sultan of Turkey and were thus in a position to exert some influence. The Sultan had already taken strong action to protect Portuguese and Turkish Jews who traded with the Venetian Republic. With the encouragement of the Nasis, he determined to protest the papal persecution in Ancona. The Sultan's special envoy went to Ancona to demand the release of Jewish prisoners under Turkish protection. He backed up his demand with threats of reprisals (Cecil Roth, *The House of Nasi: The Duke of Naxos,* Philadelphia: Jewish Publication Society, 1948, p. 148).

In coordination with the sultan's envoy, the Nasis instituted a Jewish trade boycott against the city of Ancona. First they diverted their own numerous ships to other ports, particularly to Pesaro, which belonged to Urbino. They persuaded other Turkish merchants to do so as well. In response, the Ancona merchants asked the pope to stop the persecution so that their trade could continue, expressing the fear that the papal states were at financial risk, but the pope refused. Another demand came from Rustam Pasha, a Turkish official and a buddy of Joseph Nasi. In Turkey, orders were executed to impound any of the papal states' trading vessels found in Turkish waters. Michel de Codignac, French ambassador to Turkey, tried to intervene, but the pope kept burning Marranos. By the time the boycott got into full swing, it was too late— the Marranos were dead, and the principal victims were the surviving Italian Jews of Ancona, who were suffering economic losses from the boycott, along with the other citizens.

Gracia Nasi, despite these problems, was determined to organize a truly effective boycott to punish the pope and demonstrate Jewish economic power. For this, she needed the support of the entire Jewish community of Istanbul, and she asked the leaders to sign a declaration committing to the boycott. The main rabbi who supported her, Ibn Leb, tried to recruit Rabbi Soncino, who initially went along with the plan. However, Rabbi Soncino was in sympathy not only with the Marranos, but also with the Italian Jews of Ancona. He began to reconsider. He presented both political and talmudic objections to its continuation and said that he was obliged to withdraw support unless there was physical danger to Jews. Because the Marranos' deaths had occurred already, physical danger was hard to demonstrate. When Gracia and Joseph Nasi learned about his position, they summoned him, along with the leaders of his congregation, and ordered him to sign the boycott declaration. He offered conditional support, based on fuller disclosure to the Istanbul Jewish community, but the Nasis refused to promise to communicate his objections to the rest of the community. In the end, Rabbi Soncino didn't sign. Gracia Nasi tried again, through the president of the synagogue. The congregation met. They tried to explain the objections to her. She stood firm.

"Now the grand tussle began, Dona Gracia becoming more and more determined, Rabbi Joshua more and more stubborn. He suggested that a special messenger should be sent to Venice and Padua at his expense (he did not intimate that some merchants who sympathized were willing to pay their share) to enquire the view of such Jewish notables and scholars as Meir Katzenellenbogen, the venerated rabbi. . . . But the matter was too urgent to brook delay" (Roth, *The Duke of Naxos*, p. 166). Other Sephardic rabbis agreed to proclaim the boycott as if it was universally agreed, ignoring Rabbi Soncino. The Portuguese and Castilian rabbis threatened their congregations with excommunication if they didn't observe the boycott. The Ashkenazis were getting money from Joseph Nasi, who threatened to cut off their allowance. One rabbi gave in.

Rabbi Soncino then issued a document showing that Jewish law was opposed to boycott, citing "talmudic principle that a man must not protect himself at another's expense" (Roth, *The Duke of Naxos*, p. 169). He said the supporters were motivated by sordid considerations and that he was being threatened. He pointed out that there had been an anti-Jewish outbreak at Pesaro, too. The synagogue had been desecrated and no one was avenging this act. He stated that Portuguese Jews should not expect to continue to live in Christian countries "with the sword hanging continuously over their heads." Opposition spread throughout Turkish Jewry. Despite Gracia Nasi's further efforts, the boycott received incomplete support and therefore failed. Among Italian Christians, support for the pope concurrently increased. Urbino gave in and also banned the Portuguese Jews, as the pope had required. The pope also put pressure on the duke of Ferrara, who didn't expel the Marranos, but did use this reason to close down Abraham Usque's press. In the end, the effort to demonstrate Jewish strength failed.

Rabbi Joshua, son of Gershom Soncino, died in Constantinople in 1569. His brother Moses had died in 1530 and Eliezer had died in 1547. The last Soncino printer was in Cairo. Any further descendants of Gershom Soncino are undocumented, as far as I know.

Modern Istanbul and Modern Salonika

From the time when the Turks became firmly established in Constantinople in 1453, the Turkish empire offered a home for large numbers of Jewish refugees, both Italian and Sephardic. Shortly after the expulsion of 1492, some Spanish Jews were reluctant to go there, feeling as the Abravanels evidently did, that they would have difficulty adapting to the severely different life in a Moslem country. However, the Sultan's policy favored them in many ways, particularly as he allowed tens of thousands of Jews to settle in Salonika, Greece. And as time went on, Portuguese Jews escaping from the widening net of the Inquisition, like Gracia Nasi and her nephew Joseph Nasi, spent years of their lives arranging their escape to the Sultan's lands.

The modern traces of the Empire's Jewish communities in Greece and Turkey differ vastly from one another. Although a voyage to Turkey and Greece is not a part of this book, I will provide you with a summary of what might be found there.

The remains of Jewish life in Greece are mainly ancient synagogues in Athens and a few islands. Although Salonika was a majority-Jewish city until the early part of the twentieth century, it's virtually useless to search for the once-vibrant community. Two political trends destroyed this community. First, early in this century, Greek policy dictated the eradication of all traces of Turkish occupation, which involved major population resettlements and changed the ethnic make-up of the city, marginalizing and impoverishing the Jews. Second, most devastatingly, the Nazi occupation in World War II resulted in the deportation and extermination of virtually all the Jews of the city.

Although I have not been to Salonika, I have heard about the current state of things there from a friend who works with the survivors of the Salonika community in Israel. She has attempted without success to find any traces of Jews in present-day Salonika. Her impression, in fact, is that the people who live there now prefer to forget. She found that the Jewish cemetery, which served a major community for centuries and was obviously quite large, had been entirely razed to make way for the modern university campus. Theoretically, there should have been a memorial on campus. One or two Jewish gravestones were supposed to have been saved for this purpose. My friend, with the help of a faculty member, was unable to locate such a memorial or even an acknowledgment of it; the authorities had evidently forgotten even this one token. Disastrous fires and earthquakes have destroyed much of the old city as well, making it unlikely that one could obtain even an impression of the life of the sixteenth-century Jewish community.

Turkey is a different story from Greece. Jewish communities existed in many Turkish cities besides Istanbul, and I understand that various synagogues and other institutions still remain. Jews in Turkey became impoverished at the end of the nineteenth century, though. The Holocaust did not reach Turkey, but nevertheless, a majority of Turkish Jews moved to Israel. Although I have visited Istanbul, I have not made specific efforts to find Jewish sites. However, the shape of the city from the time when the Nasi family lived there is well preserved, and the skyline and major architectural monuments are very accessible. The neighborhood near the Golden Horn where the Nasi family lived retains various palaces; more important, the geography, with imposing architecture by Sinan, which must have been in the process of being built in their day, still creates the look of the city. I hope some time to go and attempt to find more details of the family, as I have done in Italy and elsewhere.

The Norsa Family
of Mantua

For hundreds of years almost every member of the Norsa family of Mantua made a living by loaning money and by related commercial enterprises. Their profits enabled many of them to collect books and manuscripts, patronize scribes or scholars, donate money to beautify their synagogues, support the Jewish musicians and theaters of the city, or engage in other idealistic activity. The Norsas were leaders in Ferrara and in Mantua, the two most stable Jewish communities in Northern Italy. Their history illustrates how such native Italian Jews lived, interacted with their communities, and handled periods of wealth or adversity during states of war or of peace.

Family tradition identified the Norsa's ancestors among the Jewish slaves or free men who had arrived in Italy in ancient Roman times and then established themselves as Roman citizens. Thus, the Norsas had been Italians at least since the destruction of the Second Temple in the days of the early Caesars. By the early Middle Ages, the family had moved from Rome to a small town named Nurzia, which provided their family name, Norsa. Like many banking families in the 1200s and 1300s, they expanded their territory by obtaining new charters that enabled family members to move to new cities; in some of these cities they may have replaced Christian bankers driven out of business by the solidifying anti-usury policy of the church.

The Norsas ran small-loan banks, lending mainly on the pledge of small items left as collateral. In order to obtain a charter, the Norsas must have demonstrated substantial means, to set up the required establishment and begin loaning money. Each charter specified rates of interest, conditions of loans, maintenance of secure storage areas to protect the pledges, agreement to loan money to virtually any prospective borrower, and an obligation to pay tax at a set rate, thus sharing the profits with the Gonzaga rulers of Mantua or with the Este rulers of Ferrara. Such access to money met the needs of the rising middle class and the working poor, who were always desperate for capital to fund their endeavors, especially in the emerging prosperity in Mantua and Ferrara. They also received charters in other towns in the domains of Ferrara and Mantua, where they may not have lived, but where they might spend a set day per week or per month to make loans available to the small-town residents. Modern economic analysis of these conditions suggests that the typical interest rates (around 18 to 25 percent per year) were reasonable in view of the required risks and commitments. The Norsas and other banking families of Mantua and Ferrara prospered.

Both the Gonzagas and the Estes were always in need of cash, so they generally maintained good relations with their town bankers, especially with the Norsas. However, members of the lower classes, who were often in debt to the bankers, were hence more hostile and thus easily stirred up by churchmen denouncing Jewish usury. Tensions always existed between bankers and customers, between commoners and rulers, and between church teachings and day-to-day goodwill between Jews and their Christian neighbors. These tensions sometimes flared up despite the rulers' efforts to keep their domains calm. In my introduction to the Jewish history of Ferrara, I mentioned that the people, stirred up by preaching friars, had attacked the Norsa bankers who lived there on several occasions.

Background: The Gonzaga Rulers

The Gonzaga family of Mantua were involved in Renaissance art and humanism from the start. The Gonzagas, like the Estes of Ferrara, had espoused humanist education for several generations. They participated in an early humanist experiment with education for lower classes as well as for the ruling family, for which they hired a famous humanist educator named Vittorino da Feltre (1378–1446). Vittorino's school was considered to be the first great humanist school of the Renaissance. He taught Latin authors, whose works had formerly been feared because the authors were pagan, but he presented them as having no conflict with Christian values like church loyalty or personal purity.

Vittorino's pupil, Gianfrancesco Gonzaga's father, put his teacher's ideas into practice. His most memorable action was to hire Mantegna as the court painter. The agreement gave Mantegna a stipend to live in Mantua, in a house that he had designed. In return, he had painted a series of family-portrait frescoes in the ducal palaces and provided both decorative and religious paintings. (Only a few of these frescoes remain in Mantua today; anything portable has long since been sold or looted.)

In some ways, humanism was rather wasted on Gianfrancesco himself. He was more dedicated to military prowess and horses than to culture. (One of the rooms of the palace was decorated with portraits of his favorite horses.) However, after his marriage in 1488 to Isabella d'Este, his wife kept up the traditions of both families. Her background as daughter of the duke of Ferrara had established her taste for art and culture, and the atmosphere of Mantua quickly expanded her horizon. From Isabella's marriage at the age of fourteen and her arrival in Mantua, she appreciated Mantegna's work. She ensured his continued employment as court painter and commissioned many of his now-famous paintings.

During her long life, Isabella expressed her tastes to whatever extent her husband, the Gonzaga Marquis of Mantua, could afford. She furnished their palace with as much art as they could afford and continued to commission paintings not only from Mantegna but also from other Renaissance painters. She collected precious stones, gold and silver objects, coins, medals, ceramics, books and manuscripts, classical and contemporaneous sculpture, and other curios. Her agents searched for items that she wanted in many places—particularly Rome and Venice. She was most anxious for Leonardo da Vinci to paint her portrait, in addition to some sketches he had made of her when he stopped in Mantua briefly in the 1490s. Though she never succeeded in convincing him to return, she constantly sent letters urging her agent to pressure the great and independent artist, and the agent replied with letters telling her about Leonardo's activities—thus greatly enriching the information available to later historians of art! In another historically interesting letter, she wrote to decline to purchase a book on offer from the Aldine press, complaining about its excessive price.

Cynics sometimes accuse Isabella of being more acquisitive and jealously competitive with other collectors, like her sister, than really cultured, but that's quibbling. Perhaps it would simply be decent to compliment her on being one of the great shoppers of all time. In 1527, she narrowly escaped during the sack of Rome, where she had gone to shop for classical statues and other things that she wanted for her collection.

Sixteenth Century Events That Affected Jews in Mantua

Current events continually made an impact on Mantua and on the Jews of Mantua. At the start of the century, in 1500 Cesare Borgia began his campaign to conquer and unify Italy, which ended in 1503 with the death of Pope Alexander VI, his father. Pope Julius II succeeded Alexander and reigned until 1513. During this campaign, the marquis of Mantua lay low, although he opposed the Borgias. Isabella attended the wedding ceremony of her brother Alfonso d'Este, future duke of Ferrara, and Lucrezia Borgia alone because of the politics of the situation.

The French repeatedly invaded Italy. In 1512 the Italians drove them out of Italy, at least temporarily, and held the "Congress of Mantua" to decide various remaining questions. Soon after, in 1515, Francois I became king of France and once again decided to invade Italy. Another struggle between Francis I of France and the Holy Roman Emperor Charles V over the spread of the Reformation was going on in 1520.

Alliances constantly shifted. The following brief summary shows the complexity of the situation and the fragility of Italy's small states, which were always threatened by the ambitions of their much more powerful neighbors. Early in the century, Charles V (Holy Roman Emperor) and Pope Leo made an alliance. At the death of Pope Leo, Adrian VI became pope, and in 1523 Pope Adrian made an alliance with Charles V, Archduke Ferdinand of Austria, Henry VIII of England, and the rulers of Siena, Lucca, Florence, Genoa, and Milan. This coalition opposed France and Francois I. Mantua sided with the allies. France was defeated at Pavia but came back in 1526; Francois I tried to regroup. Pope Adrian died and Clement VII became pope. The League of Cognac united France, Venice, the Sforzas, and Pope Clement VII against the emperor. The pope was soon in trouble when Ferrara and Urbino joined the imperial armies and invaded Tuscany. The duke of Bourbon, a Spaniard on the emperor's side, marched toward Rome and was killed. In 1529, Mantua's Marquis Federico was promoted to be a duke of the Holy Roman Empire—to his mother Isabella d'Este's satisfaction. At this point, the Italian wars became less complicated and foreign rulers carved up so much of the power that things became a little calmer.

After Gianfrancesco Gonzaga died, Isabella d'Este continued to have a great deal of influence on their oldest son, who succeeded him as marquis, and she continued to be involved in the complex wars and alliances between Mantua and other states. In 1521 the writer Castiglione represented Mantua and Isabella at the Vatican as an envoy charged with the question of making one of her younger sons, Ercole Gonzaga, a cardinal. In 1525, Isabella was in Rome to shop for antiquities when war began between France and the alliance under the leadership of Charles V. In 1527 when Charles V invaded and sacked Rome, Isabella was caught there but rescued by another son, Ferrante.

The pressure of the Reformation and counter-Reformation and the struggles of religion in northern Europe dominated politics, affecting the Jews as more and more ghettos prevented their freedom and economic well-being. Throughout the sixteenth century, Mantua offered a refuge to Jews and at times even to escaping Marranos from Iberia (though less than Ferrara). We will return, in a moment, to the cultural flourishing of this Jewish community during the century. Unfortunately, the economic condition of the rulers was deteriorating, and at the beginning of the next century, wars and plague cast them into a ruinous state. Pressure from outside finally caused the rulers to capitulate and institute a walled and confining ghetto in 1610–1612.

Both the Christian and Jewish populations grew during the sixteenth century. In 1500, Mantua had 32,000 residents, of whom 200 were Jews. In 1591, the total population was 50,000, and there were about 1,600 Jews. The prosperity of the city and its rulers' tolerance and openness to Jewish immigration are reflected in these numbers, which followed the city's fortunes and misfortunes. At its peak, around 1620, when Mantua was at the end of its wealth and power, there were around 3,000 Jews in the city; the war, plague, and destruction that followed reduced the community. By 1930, when the city was a backwater, the Jewish population had dropped to around 600. The community has never recovered from World War II, and today 80 Jews live there. (Numbers are from Donald Beecher and Massimo Ciavolella's introduction to Leone De'Sommi, *The Three Sisters*, Ottowa: Dovehouse, 1993, and from the guided tour of the synagogue.)

MANTUA'S RENAISSANCE MONUMENTS TODAY

We arrived in Mantua on a Monday, when many tourist sites are closed. Although the guidebooks agreed that the main ducal palace is open on Monday until 2:00, they were all wrong. We found people in the ticket offices, but the palace was closed. We wandered around the numerous courtyards and entryways of the immense rambling and poorly maintained structure, hoping to find some rooms open. But we gave up and visited the Palazzo de Te, and looked around the outsides of the several other palaces in this rather small area. On Tuesday we returned to the Ducal Palace and successfully joined a tour. Warning: When you travel, have lots of flexibility in your plans!

Our first impression is that Mantua's past is a lot brighter than its present. The entire city seems to be middle-class people making do with ancient palatial structures that are rather poorly adapted to the life they are now leading. Today, Mantua is so small and out of the mainstream that it seems impossible even to buy one of the international papers that are easy to find in most Italian cities and resorts.

Around the old city, the Mincino river forms two lakes. Like the palace at one end, the city seems to look inward, avoiding any view over the attractive water. Alongside the bigger lake, the shore is a mess of railway lines, railyards, and depots. On two other sides, a busy road and a series of parking lots divide the city from the lake shore. The peripheral roads follow the top of a sort of dike, and at the water level, there is a strip of grass and trees and a wide gravel path, with a few pedal boats, excursion steamers, and (on the larger lake) some sailboats. We spotted one outdoor cafe with chairs, tables, the French-cafe game of baby-foos, and a pleasant view. The causeway that Mantegna painted (in a painting I saw in Madrid but was unable to find a reproduction of) is gone in its old state of Renaissance beauty, replaced by modern auto-bearing bridges and roadways. The palace moats—probably they were originally serious as defenses—use the river water, but in them it looks ugly green and smells putrid.

We obtained some maps and information from the tourist information office in Piazza Erbes, explored the city a little bit, and then chose a restaurant across the plaza from the tourist office. At lunch we talked briefly to some British tourists who were on a tour organized to attend a huge Pavarotti concert that was about to take place in nearby Modena, his birthplace. Otherwise, there seemed to be very few tourists.

We walked the entire length of the old city, arriving at the Palazzo de Te in about a half an hour. Toward the center of the city, pedestrians can walk under arched colonnades in front of the buildings, which come right up to the edge of the street. The long arcades use graceful columns of varying styles but consistent proportions: plain capitals, ornate capitals with floral or grotesque figures, Corinthian capitals in marble or red stone, Romanesque columns in white stone. This may be a secondary use of the columns; perhaps they originated in one of the earlier

Romanesque churches that were replaced in the fourteenth and fifteenth centuries. On this route is Mantegna's house, a square brick building constructed around a beautifully proportioned circular courtyard. The house is huge—as *houses* go. The open streets of modern suburban houses set back from the street which are near our hotel, also seem much more appealing. We ate dinner at a pizza place that seemed like an American pizza place trying to be Italian.

Two Ducal Palaces

Everything is "Ducal," beginning in the center of town, which is dominated by the immense rambling Ducal Palace of the Gonzagas. We stayed in a suburb of Mantua named Porto Mantovani in a hotel called the Ducale, four kilometers from the historic center of Mantua.

The Ducal Palace of Mantua is bigger than it was possible to imagine, and much of the interior is better preserved than we could see at first impression. This palace occupies around one quarter of the old city center. Some loggias and windows look toward the lakes around the city, but the palace cuts the city off from the lake. We knew that Isabella d'Este's collections departed before the 1620s, when the last Gonzagas turned the duchy over to the Austrians, but we were surprised to find the substantial collection of art that still remains.

Though nowhere near all of the palace is on the tour, we spent about three hours walking through only the preserved portions. Other sectors of the palace seem to be used as government offices, for other administrative functions, or as a gallery for temporary exhibitions; some parts seem to be closed off, perhaps in ruins. The guidebooks rate the palace as having five hundred rooms.

The Gonzagas, who built most of the palace, seem to have been individualists and collectors, but they didn't want to be rude about their forbears' collections or tastes. The family seems to have had no will to change things, they just kept building on new wings each generation. In spite of neglect and looters after the fall of the Gonzagas and occupation by the Hapsburgs and by Napolean's armies, much remains to visit. We saw chapels, vast ballrooms and staircases, lavish tapestries, Isabella d'Este's *studiolo*, the Mantegna paintings of the Gonzagas in the Cameri di Sposa, and vast numbers of rooms from Mantua's entire history, from the Middle Ages to Marie Teresa of Austria and finally Napoleon and Eugenie. There are several extremely long corridors comparable to the

Uffizi in Florence. Larger-than-life paintings of Gianfrancesco Gonzaga's horses decorate the walls of one large hall. A hall of mirrors has painted tromp l'oeuil medallions and friezes of cupids modeled in 2-D to look 3-D.

At the door of this vast hall, a modern information panel mentions that Monteverdi and his musical company performed here for the duke and his court in the first quarter of the seventeenth century. I tried to hear in my mind the echoes of that ancient music. Madame Europa, the beautiful singer and sister to the Jewish composer Salamone Rossi performed in the premiere of Monteverdi's opera *L'Arianna*. Rossi composed the intermezzos for this presentation, which celebrated the marriage of the Prince of Mantua, one of the last of the Gonzagas. I wonder whether Madam Europa sang here in this room.

Isabella's *studiolo* was the most beautiful of the suites, which we visited at the end of our tour. It's clearly based on the earlier *studiolo* of Duke Federico Montrefeltre in Urbino. The rooms of this suite are very small compared to most of the palace rooms. Adjacent to her rooms, she had a tiny garden surrounded by high walls where flowers, trees, statues, and so on created an ambiance for polite and courtly conversation (as described by Castiglione). A few tiny private rooms once held her collections. The rooms have coffered ceilings in green, gold, and inlaid wood panels. One room in particular had beautifully inlaid wood cabinets, similar to those in Urbino. The doorway between two of the rooms has delicately carved marble panels about eight inches square around the doorposts and lintel. Throughout the rooms, the decorations incorporate her initials. The locations where the paintings like Mantegna's *Parnassus*, now in the Louvre, once hung are simply filled by blank canvas. The rooms contrast extremely with the scale of the palace, where one room had such exaggeratedly large doors and surrounding moldings (though proportioned like regular doors) that I felt like Alice in Wonderland.

Beyond some of the rooms of the palace are various gardens in the many palace courtyards, including one that's on a second-story level, presumably on a rooftop or built-up area. Some of the rooms and furnishings on display have been rescued or moved from other locations, such as some small rooms that once belonged to Maria Paleologus but were destroyed to restore an older wing of the castle. A set of tapestries based on cartoons by Raphael depict biblical themes—another set based on these cartoons belongs to the Vatican. The Mantuan examples were obtained by the Gonzaga cardinal.

I never managed to develop the slightest sense of how our guided routes through this and that area of the palace interconnected, or what its floorplan must be, though I'm sure we occasionally came back to the same place and then started in a different direction. It's really several palaces built at different times. I tried to put myself in the place of the outsiders, such as Jewish bankers, actors, musicians, or other visitors, on whom the reception areas would have made a crushing impression.

Just when we thought we were done, we were led through a long series of rooms with artistic white mannequins wearing carefully reproduced period costumes, including one of Isabella d'Este in a massive black and gold dress with her famous hairdo full of pearls. She looked small and fat in this rendition, without the flattery of the artist. There must have been around one hundred other mannequins, very beautiful in brocades, velvets, ermines, and long trains, even models of full-scale, elaborately clad horses. They were preparing for some sort of pageant where, I guess, actors were going to wear the costumes.

The Palazzo de Te, the second ducal palace, is in the process of being beautifully restored, resulting in vividly colored frescoes or stucco decorations in nearly every room. A young woman in a white coverall was on a scaffold painting in one room as we toured. The palace was originally a sort of hideout for Isabella's son, who had a mistress whom his mother didn't like. The designer, who made it very artistically unified, is Julio Romano.

The most impressive room in the Palazzo de Te is a large room with high ceilings and walls entirely covered with frescoes in bright colors of the giants and titans from classical myth. Its arched ceiling makes it possible for people in diagonally opposite corners to whisper and be heard by one another, but not by someone in the nearer corner. The giants are huge and colorful. They seem to be inside caves and the mouths of the caves have views off into the distant Italianate countryside. Other rooms also have mythological or biblical themes. One loggia has David slaying Goliath and then playing his harp over the head. Another room has portraits of the marquis's favorite horses, larger than life about twenty feet above the floor. Plaques give credit to industries and corporations that funded the restorations for the various rooms.

The rooms all open into a central courtyard, with another garden outside closed off by a high wall of gated arches and columns. Though the palace mainly looks inward, it's still delightfully light and airy. In the outside garden, two square pools come right up to the palace wall, dividing it from the open, green space. From the balconies above the ponds, you can see lots of small and medium-sized fish in the ponds. A walkway from the palace to the garden separates the two ponds. Today you can see the design of flowerbeds and walks, but only grass grows in them. The Palazzo de Te, despite being quite large, seems much homier than the five-hundred-room Ducal Palace, which was fortified and built over numerous generations.

Before continuing with the Jewish sites of Mantua, let's take a closer look at the history of the Norsa family, which has the longest continuous presence among Jewish families in the city.

THE NORSA FAMILY

Members of the Norsa family participated in the first charter agreement for a Jewish loan bank in Mantua in 1390. The charter, signed by Count Francesco Gonzaga (1366–1407), permitted up to twelve bankers to move to the city and allowed interest of 20–25 percent—a fair rate, considering the risks, taxes, and scarcity of capital. The parties renewed or expanded the charter as each new ruler took office in Mantua and as new generations of Norsas entered the banking business. In 1428, a subsequent charter allowed eleven Jewish bankers at Mantua to loan money to all comers for one year only—that is, they agreed not to turn away poorer borrowers or those wanting very small loans. They promised to maintain a warehouse to store pledges and agreed to clean it twice per year and to keep a cat, then an uncommon house pet, in order to prevent mice from destroying pawned clothing or textiles. This time the interest rate was specified as no higher than 25 percent, which was lower than the rate that the law set for Christian moneylenders. In 1434–1435, Immanuel (Menahem) of Norcia and two Finzis of Bologna received a ten-year contract. In 1444, Marquis Ludovico, upon coming to power in Mantua, confirmed the charter of the Norsa heirs and of Bonvinus ben Samuel Dattilo.

Subsequent charter renewals continued, except between 1462 and 1466, when Mantua forbade the Jews to loan money. Immediately afterward, two Norsa bankers and Isaac ben Abraham Finzi received permission to operate a bank in Mantua and also to loan money in Castel Giuffre, another town in Mantua's domain. A 1493 charter specified that Norsa family members Deodato (Nathaniel) ben Shabbetai, and sons of Leone (Judah) named Daniel, Simon (Samuel), and Moses, could continue the family business. These charters also demonstrate that the completely Italian Norsa family maintained a habit of giving their sons both a Hebrew name and an equivalent Italian name.

The good relationships that existed between the Norsa bankers and the ruling Gonzaga family, the counts, marquises, and later dukes of Mantua, included helping the Norsas with difficulties with other Mantuan citizens and even with their own deputies. In 1497, for instance, Moses Norsa lodged a complaint about officials behaving too strictly and thus depriving bankers of their pledges and allowing borrowers to evade their debts. In response, the marquis ordered the officials to stop this behavior. Similarly, in 1495, "Absolution" (for something unspecified) was granted by the marquis of Mantua to Deodato (Nathaniel) Norsa and his sons, to the sons of Leone Norsa, and to the sons of Immanuel Norsa. (A note on the Gonzaga's titles: Count, Marquis, and Duke: the Gonzaga family owed its title to the Holy Roman Emperors. By a combination of service and monetary bribes, they had the title first upgraded from Count to Marquis, and then, in the 1530s to Duke. As in a lot of modern corporate name games, the job was the same whatever the title.)

The Gonzagas not only collected taxes, they also borrowed money directly from the local Jewish bankers. When the Gonzagas renewed the moneylending rights of Leone (Judah) Norsa in 1490, the record shows that Leone and Daniel Norsa also received a receipt for the return of jewelry pawned by the marquis. Isabella d'Este was in debt all the time, thanks to her habits of collecting art, musical instruments, jewels, fine furniture, books, manuscripts, antiquities, pottery, interior decorating, and so on. She seems to have also been a potential customer for loans, especially for loans against her jewelry. Her eagerness to spend more money than she could afford was also fed by jealousy of her sister Beatrice, married to the richer duke of Milan; of her husband's sister Elizabetta Gonzaga, married to the duke of Urbino, who inherited one of the premier art and manuscript collections of Italy; and of her brother's wife, Lucrezia Borgia, whose wedding clothes were purchased with the riches of the church because her father was pope.

Through their tenure in office, the Gonzagas continued to renew and enlarge the Norsas' contracts and permitted them to make various other legal agreements, to the profit of both the bankers and the rulers. In 1504, the marquis specified permission for Isaac ben Daniel Norsa to loan money and allowed Moses ben Leone Norsa to lease his bank to Abraham ben Moses of Vigevano. At this time another record shows that Moses and Jacob, sons of Nathaniel Norsa, and one of the sons of their brother Rafael received "absolution" for various unspecified crimes. In 1505, Isaac ben Daniel Norsa served as the guarantor of a financial agreement concerning the daughters of his uncle Moses ben Leone: Allegra (Simha), Stella, Diamanta, and Bellaviola. On the death of Rafael

Norsa, the marquis formally allowed his six sons to lend money; they were listed in the agreement as: Bonaiuto (Hebrew name, Azriel, age twenty-one), Gabriel (twenty-one), Beato (Asher, eighteen), Speradio (Heftzia, fourteen), Joseph (twelve), and Asdra (Ezra, eleven). Allegra (Simha), Rafael's widow, served as their guardian from 1510–1515. Stella, widow of Moses Norsa and guardian of their son Solomon, received permission in 1517 to lease her bank in Mantua. At the same time, the marquis granted special absolution to Jacob ben Deodato Norsa and his wife, Rosa, daughter of Solomon of Pontremoli. When Federico, the son of Isabella d'Este and Gianfrancesco Gonzaga, became marquis of Mantua, he confirmed the rights of Jewish bankers, including Daniel Norsa, Solomon ben Moses Norsa, Jacob ben Deodato Norsa, Benvenuta Norsa, and Joseph ben Abraham Finzi.

Earlier, we surveyed the Jewish history of Ferrara and the relationship of the Jews with the Este family, Ferrara's rulers. The Norsa families in Ferrara and Mantua had parallel histories in the two places and continuously interacted with each other. In 1503, Isaac, the only son of Emanuel Norsa of Mantua, attended a circumcision in Ferrara, for which he required a special travel permit. Other records show similar communication between the Norsa and other families, including intermarriages that served to combine fortunes. After the death of Moses ben Leone Norsa of Mantua, in 1504, his widow, Benvenuta, married Benjamin ben Joseph Finzi of Reggio, an inhabitant of Ferrara.

A HOSTILE ENVIRONMENT?

Every Jewish family in Italy in the 1470s and later was affected by the friars' preaching campaign against Jewish banks and by the emergence of anti-Jewish sentiment that increased as a result of their polemical sermons. In Italy, the anti-usury message carefully exempted the many Christian banks, such as the financial empire of the Florentine Medici family. Italians had generally ignored church regulations against usury unless someone found it convenient to bring them up; suddenly, the preaching friars found it very convenient.

Jewish banks made a good target because they usually received permission to deal in unpopular and less profitable small business and consumer loans, while Christians made much more money on large financial activities, such as the Medici's lending to the popes or investing in their endeavors. The redirection of populist sentiment away from the rulers and toward this convenient and visibly different group was generally not accidental. The church and rulers at all levels found it useful in maintaining their political and economic power.

A few Jewish bankers, such as the Da Pisa family and the Norsa family, had become rich, though Jewish fortunes never rivaled those of big-time Christian bankers. As I have pointed out, Jewish lenders received all of the hostility, but only a share of the profits—the rulers also took a share of the profits but never dirtied their hands; when things got too hot, they could always side with the hostile masses. Leveraging this situation, demagogues instituted the church campaign that promised to replace Jewish banks and pawnshops with *monte de pieta*, or interest-free Christian banks. When church authorities set up such banks, few Jewish bankers showed themselves as creative or flexible as the Soncino family with its switch from banking to printing. Often, the Jews simply tried to stay in business. At times they couldn't compete, at times they were expelled from the towns where they had lived, but sometimes their patience worked, when the charity banks were unable to capitalize enough unprofitable loans.

Violence and destruction of entire Jewish communities resulted from the friars' preaching. Under their influence, formerly tolerant Italians began to blame Jews for various dreadful practices and crimes. Old legends were revived, such as stories of bleeding hosts as depicted in the painting by Ucello now in the Ducal Palace at Urbino. In 1475, in the most violent case, a blood-libel accusation concerning the death of the child Simon of Trent caused a number of Jewish deaths and destroyed the Jewish community of Trent.

The rulers of both Mantua and Ferrara remained unusually tolerant and protective of the Jews who lived in their domains—at least, considering the standards of the day, which included large numbers of expulsions. We have seen examples of the tolerance of the dukes of Ferrara. In Mantua in 1484, the year that Gianfrancesco Gonzaga became the marquis, Bernardino da Feltre preached against the Jews there. "In an impassioned series of sermons delivered before enormous crowds in the cathedral square, the friar pleaded fervidly on behalf of his cherished idea [establishment of a charity bank, or Monte di Pieta] and assailed the ruling house for the favor shown to the Jews and their 'perfidy'" (Cecil Roth, *The History of the Jews of Italy*, Philadelphia: Jewish Publication Society, 1946, p. 174).

The next year, 1485, a Monte di Pieta was set up in Mantua with the approval of the pope. Thus, the Jewish loan-bankers, including the Norsa family, lost some of their economic power, at least for a time. The economics of zero-interest loans did not lead to long-term stability, so the charity bank was unable to compete with the Norsa family in the long term, and their bank eventually resumed its activities.

In 1494, the persecutor of Italian Jews, Friar Bernardino da Feltre, died. Roth cites that there followed the "heyday of some of the greatest Jewish capitalists of Renaissance Italy, such as Asher Meshullam (Anselmo) del Banco of Padua, reckoned the wealthiest of all, the overbearing Immanuel Norsa of Ferrara, the Da Pisa family in Tuscany, or Salamone di Bonaventura of Ancona. . . . For rather more than half a century, the communities of central Italy enjoyed a reprieve" (Roth, *The History of the Jews of Italy*, p. 176).

The determination of the rulers of both Mantua and Ferrara to prevent the expulsion and impoverishment of their Jews became even more unusual as the sixteenth century proceeded and the Reformation and counter-Reformation whipped up anti-Jewish feelings throughout Europe.

Daniel Norsa's House in Mantua

One episode in the Norsa family history particularly illustrates the treatment of Mantua's Jews. The privilege of buying a house was not automatic, and Jews had to obtain the permission of the ruler. Moses Norsa had obtained such a privilege in Mantua uneventfully in the 1490s. Similarly, before 1495, Daniel Norsa bought a very fine house from a Christian, after obtaining appropriate privileges. Unfortunately for him, on an exterior wall of the house he found a painting of the Madonna, which he considered inappropriate for a Jewish residence. With the permission of a subordinate to the bishop, he had the painting removed.

At the same time as he was doing this, the war between the Italians and the French was in full swing. In 1495, as Charles VIII of France invaded Italy, his armies habitually plundered Jewish communities. His victims included the Jews of Reggio, Rome, and, as we have seen earlier, Naples. Although theoretically Duke Ercole of Ferrara sided with the French, his territories were also invaded—nothing personal, this was the only way to get through northern Italy conveniently. In Reggio in the Duchy of Ferrara, certain priests rescued Jews who were in personal danger, and a representative named Boiardo, in Duke Ercole's name, suppressed the preaching against the Jews; that is, he continued the policies that we have earlier described. However, in this climate of anti-Jewish sentiment and actions, Daniel Norsa's removal of the Madonna in Mantua was bound to touch off an angry public reaction.

The inevitable anti-Jewish violence broke out against Daniel Norsa during a major campaign of the war. Gianfrancesco Gonzaga, marquis of Mantua, was away at the front, serving as a military leader on the side of the Italian allies against France. His wife, Isabella d'Este, was left as ruler of Mantua. Isabella, following the example that her father had set by many of his actions, ordered the police to put down the violence and restore order and the safety of the Jewish community—an action that the local clergy criticized.

The marquis returned in triumph after the Battle of Fornovo between the French and Italians. In fact, both sides claimed a glorious victory. Hearing of the anti-Jewish outbreak and its resolution, the marquis and his advisers determined that Daniel Norsa was liable for the replacement of the missing painting and ordered him to pay Mantegna, the court painter, for a replacement. The marquis's advisers recommended that Daniel Norsa not be let off only with the replacement of the painting. They also required him to give up his house and fund the construction of a chapel on the site where the house had been. The chapel was designed to commemorate the victory and to house the painting that celebrated its glory.

The dediction of the Chapel of the Victories in 1496 celebrated the victory of their marquis. From Mantegna's house, at most a kilometer distant, the people carried his new painting, *Madonna of the Victories*, through the streets in a gala procession, and the gathering at the chapel was a great social event. The people expressed their appreciation of Mantegna and his art, and participated in the public humiliation of the Norsa family, who were forced to attend the ceremonies. Details of the treatment of the Norsa family are not preserved; however, it was not violent or severely degrading—at least not compared to many abuses of the Jews in that era.

MANTUA'S JEWISH MONUMENTS TODAY

Much evidence of the events surrounding the purchase of the *Madonna of the Victories* and the associated chapel exists in modern Mantua. You can see the Chapel of the Victories, the building that replaced Daniel Norsa's house. The tourist office in Piazza Erbe can give you directions—it's less than a five-minute walk from there along Via Domenico Fernelli, at the corner of Via Claudio Monteverdi. The building is well-marked with a plaque that notes that it was built in 1495 to house Mantegna's famous *Madonna of the Victories*, which adorned the chapel between 1496 and 1798, and now hangs in the Grand Gallery of the Louvre in Paris.

The chapel has been closed for many years, but the exterior has the simplicity of the early Renaissance: plain arched doorways, sparse decoration. The side door has two columns. The woman in the tourist office told us that she has never seen the interior of the chapel, though she thought it might still be in shape for restoration some day. The doorways are closed by ugly metal shutters of the sort used on shops when they are closed, and trash has accumulated under the doors.

You can follow the route of the procession that carried the painting from Mantegna's house, still intact and now a museum, to the chapel. You can walk now along still medieval streets with arcades and cobblestone paving. You can follow the procession's deviation toward the ducal palace, where Isabella d'Este was in the last term of one of her numerous pregnancies and thus unable to leave the palace. Picture the gala procession passing by her balcony to show her Mantegna's painting.

Our route from the Palazzo de Te, past Mantegna's house, to the square in front of Sant Andrea's church and down the narrow street to the now-closed chapel, was probably the route that the procession walked for the formal and important dedication ceremony. In 1496, the columns were all hung with garlands. Banners and flowers could have been draped across the street as well, so that the procession filed underneath them.

In the Basilica Sant Andrea in Mantua you can see a contemporary portrait of four members of the Norsa family, painted by an anonymous student of Mantegna. The principal subject, the Madonna, sits on a throne above the four highly individualized Jews. This painting commemorated the dedication of the chapel, presenting another version of the Madonna of Victories and a symbolic representation of the role of the Jews. Like Mantegna's painting, it is large, vividly colored, and visually interesting.

This painting is unique in its portrayal of a fifteenth-century Jewish family. The Jewish men wear the circular yellow badge of Jewish distinction or shame, also a rare depiction. Another mark showing their religion is the red bonnet-like hats of the men. I think the women look sad. An inscription above the Madonna calls attention to the shame of the Jews.

An Oriental rug hangs as a backdrop behind the four figures; perhaps it is intended to suggest their origin in the exotic East, though the Norsas' ancestors, in fact, had been Italian citizens for fifteen hundred years at that point. Similar rugs appear in Mantegna's earlier painting, *Enthroned Madonna* (in San Zeno, Verona) and in contemporary paintings by Messina and Carpaccio, so it may not have any symbolic significance.

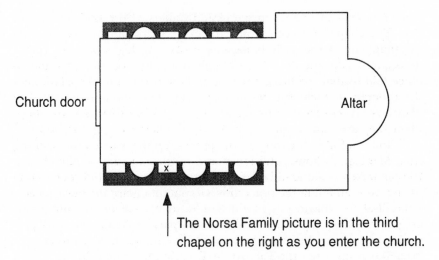

Church door

Altar

The Norsa Family picture is in the third
chapel on the right as you enter the church.

Fig. 4-4: Floor Plan of Sant Andreas, Mantua

When we visited Mantua, we were very anxious to see the painting
of the Norsa family. We waited until late afternoon when the church re-
opens after its long lunch break. We peered into every chapel on both
sides of the church (see Figure 4-4) and finally managed to make out
the painting in the third chapel on the right. The gate of the chapel
was locked and the painting was in nearly total darkness behind the iron
grille. However, the church attendant (who was folding up chairs that
had apparently been set out for mass) was willing to open it and to go
and get an electric floodlight for us (he said we would have to give him
an offering, which we did, 10.000 lira or around $7, which seemed okay
with him). The painting is extremely beautiful, I was surprised to see.
Note that the Basilica itself is of great architectural and artistic interest.

Beyond Mantua, in the Louvre in Paris you can see Mantegna's
masterpiece, *The Madonna of the Victories.* Ironically, it stayed in the Chapel
of the Victories until Napoleon, another French invader, took it to France.
A huge canvas, it shows Marquis Gianfrancesco worshiping at the feet
of a stunningly beautiful Madonna, holding her child. Above her head
a brightly colored coral branch hangs from a chain, a talisman to ward
off the evil eye. Garlands of flowers and oranges surround her. In the
other place of honor at her feet, facing the marquis, stands a nun, a
portrait of a locally revered holy woman. In the same gallery, you can
also see all of the paintings from Isabella d'Este's studio and other works
by Mantegna.

The Ghetto and Synagogue of Mantua

While Mantua originally had six synagogues, built in 1513, 1530, 1546, 1588, and 1595, only one remains. Two were destroyed in the 1920s and 1930s, and their furnishings, such as holy Arks, are now in Israel; others were destroyed earlier.

Even in tolerant Mantua, sumptuary laws prohibited Jews from expressing themselves or showing their wealth by unrestrained personal displays of fine clothing or jewels. The reaction seems to have been a profusion of fine work in religious objects for use at home and in lavish donations to the synagogues. Behind the plain facades of the crowded ghetto, *menorahs*, spice boxes, *seder* plates, candlesticks, Purim noisemakers and cookie molds, and citron boxes in ornate Renaissance forms appealed to families who could afford them. The synagogues built during the sixteenth century were all adorned with beautiful carved-wood Arks, railings, desks, light fixtures, and precious-metal decorations. The rich people of Mantua, such as the Norsa bankers, often seem to have indulged their love of fine fabrics and gold or silver thread and jewels by dressing up the Torah with beautiful brocade covers and elaborate precious metal finials. Only a few of these riches remain in Mantua, but many of them appear in Jewish museums around the world today; in particular, you can see several examples in the Italian Jewish Museum and the Israel Museum in Jerusalem.

In exploring the town the first afternoon when we arrived, we walked around the streets where the ghetto was located from the seventeenth until the nineteenth century. From 1400 until 1500, Jews lived in several quarters of the city, including near Sant Andre, the site of the Norsa's former house, currently the site of the Chapel of Victories. In the sixteenth century, the Jews began to move voluntarily to the east side of town, somewhat south of the Ducal Palace. In 1610–1612, when the ghetto was first built, Jews were 7 percent of the population. After the sack of the ghetto in 1630, the population declined, one of the four gates was destroyed, and the area allowed to the remaining Jews was reduced. No trace remains of the ghetto gates, destroyed in the nineteenth century and replaced by large squares. The old streets and houses have been repaired and renovated, so that only the winding narrowness of the streets themselves remains. During the nineteenth century, when the Jews of Italy returned to the mainstream of social and political life, people preferred to forget where the ghetto had been.

The ghetto of Mantua must have been particularly destructive of the open relationships that Jews formerly had with the neighbors, in spite of occasional violent episodes. Salamone Rossi and his music, the famous Jewish dancing teachers, and Leone di Sommi and his theater troupe seem to have left no memories with the locals, other than in the educational display in the entry of the synagogue. The well-stocked bookstore of the Palazzo de Te carried many disks by Monteverdi and his contemporaries, but not by Rossi—also a native son. Elsewhere, the Jews may have felt that the ghetto walls and gates did offer at least a little protection from mobs or thieves, but in Mantua, their introduction couldn't have seemed like anything but a way for them to be cut off from mainstream culture, crowded, and prevented from leading the full life that they had formerly enjoyed.

The Norsa synagogue, the only one that remains, is a little to the south of the old ghetto area we saw, at #13 Via Govi. (Number 11, usually the entrance, seems to have been under renovations.) This is not a museum or tourist site, simply the synagogue for the eighty or so Jews who still live in Mantua. It's behind a totally unmarked door on an unpretentious street; the door to the synagogue is inside the building, through a long entrance hall. Sadly, in the current climate of European society, most synagogues must keep a very low profile unless they can afford serious security measures (like the synagogue-museum of Ferrara), so there is no sign on the door or anywhere.

The synagogue is called the Norsa synagogue because the family donated it to the community in about 1515. I believe that many of the fittings date from somewhat later. Although the inside of the building was moved and reconstructed around 1900, it is faithful to the original. The design represents the Italian tradition and system of organizing the layout of synagogues (see the floor plan in Figure 4-5).

The entire synagogue is very beautiful, and the design makes a fine impression as you enter by the door from the hall. Carved wood benches face the central area, with lecterns having a lift-up top in which to store prayer books. The Ark, covered by a brocade velvet curtain, backs up to a window so that daylight comes from behind it. Its supports are twisted columns in baroque style. The reader's platform, against the opposite wall, also has natural light behind it, creating a very beautiful atmosphere. The Ark and the platform are in little niches. Above the center of the room, between the niches, is a dome, and elaborate metal chandeliers hang from the ceiling and dome. On the walls, interesting molded plaster decorations in geometric-floral baroque designs alternate between plaster panels with Hebrew inscriptions, forming an overall pattern. A beautiful carved-wood lattice separates the women's gallery upstairs from the entrance to the main area. Opposite the entrance, a large brass *menorah* of very plain design stands on the facing wall.

The woman who showed us around the synagogue identified herself as a member of the Norsa family. She was very interested in the history of the city and of her family, and expressed a hope that her children would continue that history. She told us about her adolescent son's trip to a kibbutz in Israel, by which she hoped to cement his relationship with his ancestors' religion. She also told us how the community is constantly declining in numbers, particularly due to intermarriage; many of the eighty remaining Jews of Mantua are not observant, because their spouses are non-Jewish. Some Norsa family members now live in Milan, she said.

At the suggestion of the woman in the tourist office we went into the "Casa di Bianco," a linen store belonging to a Mr. Norsa, a descendant of the ancient Norsas. The store is directly across from the tourist office in the Piazza de Erbe. He was friendly but not particularly interested in discussing the history of his family with us. "That was a long time ago," he explained. I saw a more historically inclined woman named Imanuella Norsa being interviewed in a video about Salamone Rossi, but, of course, I have no introductions to anyone and, speaking no Italian, can't do much in that line.

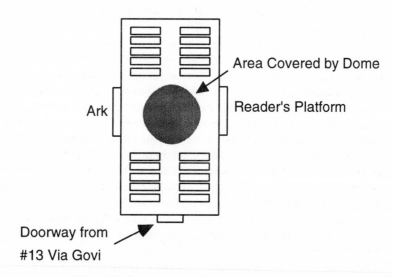

Fig. 4-5: Synagogue of Mantua, Floor Plan

> *Note on finding the synagogue: The tourist office and some guidebooks specified that we would find the synagogue at #11 Via Govi, rather than at #13, but a helpful passerby told us which doorbell to ring. The synagogue has a listed phone number, 0376-321-490, but when we tried to call, it was attached to the fax machine. When we were in Mantua, the opening time included only a few hours in the morning on some week days. I suggest that the most effective way to contact the synagogue is through the tourist office, which does keep in touch with the visitors' policies and can call for you or inform you of any day-to-day scheduling issues.*
>
> *The synagogue attendant, the day we were there, was a woman, Mrs. Norsa, who appeared to be a secretary or perhaps a volunteer. While she was interested in telling us about it, she was also in a hurry to go out on her errands (if we had been a little later, in spite of the hours the tourist office told us, we would have missed her, so don't count on it being easy to see this synagogue). All these difficulties aside, the synagogue is well worth seeing, and if you are an observant Jew, you might want to arrange to attend a service there.*

Mantua's Other Synagogues

Six synagogues once stood at various locations in the ghetto: three Italian rite synagogues, and three German synagogues, reflecting the origins of the Jews in the community. The most impressive was the Grand Synagogue, which was the major Italian synagogue. Along with the other Italian synagogues the Grand Synagogue stood on Via Scuola Grande; as the community declined, the Grand Synagogue fell out of use and was destroyed in 1938. Another impressive Italian synagogue, the Cases synagogue, was built in 1595 and destroyed in 1929. The third, the Norsa synagogue, is now the only survivor. The most notable German synagogue was in use from 1588 until 1846; I'm not sure about the dates of destruction of the other two.

At least three Torah Arks and many of the other beautiful and lavish religious objects from these synagogues are now in Israel. I particularly recommend the Nahon Museum of Italian Art in Jerusalem, which owns a Mantuan Torah Ark and a pair of throne-like chairs dating from 1543; it also has a number of objects from the Veneto, Pesaro, and Ferrara.

A WELCOMING ENVIRONMENT?

In spite of a few hostile incidents, Mantua during the fifteenth and sixteenth centuries provided an amazing atmosphere for Jewish accomplishments. The beauty and richness of the synagogues suggest how remarkable the Jewish success in Mantua was, in a time when the life of Jewish communities elsewhere was steadily deteriorating. Although the Italian Renaissance Jews continued to excel as writers, linguistic scholars, medical practitioners and teachers (mainly at the openminded medical school in Padua), and financiers, Mantua had an exceptional concentration of such activity and attracted accomplished people from elsewhere. Jews in Mantua even spoke a unique version of the Mantuan language, adding a variety of Hebrew words to the Italian-based dialect.

Mantua's special atmosphere received support from the rulers, who resisted enforcement of a locked ghetto and curfew until the beginning of the seventeenth century, and who actively patronized Jewish performers, intellectuals, and writers. Only when the city itself was devastated by plague and invasions, this tolerant and welcoming environment failed. The Gonzagas made many exceptions to increasingly harsh rules set down by the pope and the Inquisition. They often exempted individuals from the requirements that Jews wear the special round badge, that Jewish publication be severely censored, and that Jewish professions be strictly limited. In 1516 Ezra ben Rafael Norsa of Mantua was accused of having sexual relations with a Christian woman and fled the city. Despite the apparent seriousness of this offense, the marquis granted him "absolution" and allowed him to return.

In the fifteenth century, Jewish scholars, music teachers, musical and theater performers, and Hebrew printers lived and worked freely in Mantua. One of the first Hebrew printing presses, slightly earlier than that of the Soncino family, belonged to Abraham and Estellina Conat of Mantua. She was one of few women to identify herself on the title page of a Hebrew book as the independent printer of the work. The scientist, sociologist, economist, scribe, and geographer Abraham Farissol immigrated from Avignon to Mantua, where he lived for a time before settling in Ferrara; the Norsa family in Mantua patronized his scribal services, as did those in Ferrara. A historical record shows that in 1470 in Mantua he completed a manuscript for Judah and Jacob Norsa, brothers, who were wealthy bankers and silk manufacturers.

At mid-century, the Jews of Mantua had a place in the life of the city and shared a variety of experiences with prominent citizens. In 1464, after becoming Mantua's court painter, Mantegna painted his early painting the *Circumcision and Presentation of Christ* (now in the Uffizi in Florence). He may have obtained technical details of the circumcision, such as the tray of bandages and medical tools depicted in the painting, from members of the Jewish community or even from directly witnessing such a ceremony, to which Christians were sometimes invited. This operation was, of course, generally unknown to most Christians of the time.

After her marriage in 1488, Isabella d'Este adapted to the cultural offerings of Mantua. Besides her continued patronage of Mantegna, she evidently enjoyed the presentations of Jewish theater troops: in 1489, a troupe of Jewish players staged a presentation about Judith and Holofernes for the wedding of the duke of Urbino to Elizabetta Gonzaga. At one time, Isabella employed a Jew to translate psalms for her so she might be sure to have a correct text. Isabella, known for her original style of dress and for imaginative perfume recipes, augmented her store of knowledge by buying cosmetics from Jewish women, who had a reputation for a Renaissance combination of beauty secrets and magic. Her reliance on loans from Jews, including the Norsa bank, was thus only one of her points of contact with this community.

Jewish Life in Mantua in the 1500s

Mantua's Jews built a number of institutions with the permission of the Gonzagas. In 1511 they established a sort of a guild called a "university," which indicates a high level of social organization and acceptance by the town and the rulers. Throughout the sixteenth century, under the protection of this organization, religious and cultural activities continued. The Italian and German communities among Mantua's Jews built synagogues for their individual traditions of worship.

The specific achievements of Jewish residents of Mantua in the sixteenth century have for the most part been forgotten; however, the following information might help you picture the atmosphere of Mantua in the sixteenth century, when it was a leader in Jewish culture. Besides Hebrew scholars, rabbis, and printers, outstanding members of the Jewish community included medical doctors, philanthropists, philosophers, musicians, actors, a still-famous composer, and a playwright-theater writer. Throughout Italy, Jews continued to achieve in many of the same fields; thus, Jews in Mantua were in contact with others from Padua, Rome, Florence, and other communities, as well as with leaders outside of Italy; the Mantuan community was widely recognized at the time.

Moses Provinciali (1503–1575), a man of diverse talents, was born in Vicenza and lived in Mantua, where he served as the main rabbi. His new ideas and interpretations caused friction between him and other rabbis, and the rabbinic authorities of Venice banned him from his post, though he and the community of Mantua appear to have ignored the ban. In one rabbinic decision, he specified the conditions when Jews were allowed to play tennis on the Sabbath—no betting, no rackets, and not during the sermon. Besides religious works, he wrote a mathematical treatise on a theorem of Apollonius that had been of interest to Maimonides. (As far as I have been able to discover, this treatise was of no great importance to the history of mathematics.) In 1550, the Mantuan printer Joseph ben Jacob Shalit published an Italian translation of this work, and it was appended to some editions of the works of Maimonides.

Among Jewish immigrants to Mantua was Rabbi Provencali's student Jehudah Moscato, who was born in the mid-1540s, near Ancona. After the Ancona persecutions in the 1550s, he settled in Mantua, where he studied with Provinciali and became a literary stylist, poet, preacher, rabbi, head of a talmudic academy, a connoisseur of music, and a scholar of the Kabbalah—more famous than his teacher (Amram, p. 323, Roth, *Jews in the Renaissance*).

Judah Leone ben Isaac Sommo (also known as Leone de'Sommi or de'Sommo or Portaleone, 1527–1592) wrote verses, a theatrical how-to-do-it manual, plays, and theater sketches, and translated poetry from Hebrew into Italian. He directed a successful theater company that performed for both Jews and Christians. Sommo was born and died in Mantua and did most of his work there, although he may also have been associated with the Jewish theater of Ferrara. His favor with the dukes resulted in his being allowed to participate in activities of the otherwise all-Christian Mantuan Academy, dedicated to humanist arts and letters. His work, the *Art of the Stage*, continues to serve as a major source of information about the theatrical production of sixteenth-century Italy, including interesting suggestions about stage lighting and its uses.

Sommo's Hebrew plays include *A Comedy of Betrothal* and *The Three Sisters*. The works depict rather ordinary people and their everyday lives. He directed and produced his troupe's popular presentations, which included his own plays (in Italian and Hebrew), light sketches, and mainstream Italian plays of the day. They performed for the court of Mantua to celebrate the duke's birthday, court weddings, or other state occasions; out of respect for his religion, the court arranged that these performances didn't conflict with the Sabbath or Jewish holidays. Unfortunately, in 1904 a fire in the library of Turin destroyed the unique remaining manuscripts of many of his works. A few surviving plays, of which copies existed in Mantua's library or elsewhere, have recently been revived and translated into English. (Information on De Sommi is from I. Zinberg, *History of Jewish Literaturee, Vol. 4: Italian Jewry in the Renaissance Era*, Cincinnati: Hebrew Union College, 1974, p. 97–99; *Encyclopedia Brittanica Online;* and Donald Beecher and Massimo Ciavolella's introduction to Leone De'Sommi's *The Three Sisters.*)

Azariah de' Rossi (1511–1578), another recognized figure of the time, was a scholar, classicist, and humanist; in his work, he mentioned his family's tradition that their ancestors had come from Jerusalem with Titus after the fall of Jerusalem in 70 c.e. Azariah de' Rossi lived at times in Mantua, Ferrara, Ancona, Bologna, and Sabionetta. Between 1573 and 1575 in Ferrara he published a controversial historic work. This work began with an eyewitness description of the Ferrara earthquake of 1571 and a review of extant literature on earthquakes. It continued with studies of a document about the ancient translation of the Pentateuch into Greek, and of Jewish history and chronology. His critical methods and his wide variety of Christian and classical sources gave unusual results— he demonstrated that the widely accepted historical work *Jossipon* was a medieval compilation based on the original work of Josephus rather than an authentic work of Roman times. Because he challenged current beliefs in the traditional view of the Jewish calendar, rabbis banned his book in Venice, Rome, Ferrara, Padua, and elsewhere; in more openminded Mantua, the prohibition only extended to persons under twenty-five years old.

In 1548–1549 in Mantua, Azariah de' Rossi—himself also a physician—suffered an illness and underwent treatment by the Marrano physician Amatus Lusitanus. In one of his case histories, Lusitanus recorded de' Rossi's course of treatment. Before treatment de' Rossi was emaciated, according to Lusitanus's account, and he suffered from "quatran fever, a dermatological disorder, digestive distress, chest constriction, melancholic insomnia, and various other maladies." As a course of treatment, for four months the patient successfully followed a "comprehensive dietary, physical, and psychological regimen." Lusitanus was also known for being the physician of Gracia Nasi (a sort of hypochondriac) while she lived in Italy; his voluminous case studies provide scholars with an important source of social and medical history (Lester A. Segal, *Historical Consciousness and Religious Tradition in Azariah de Rossi's Me'or 'Einayim*, Philadelphia: Jewish Publication Society, 1989, p 14).

Other medical practitioners in Mantua during this period included representatives of the Portaleone family, who also practiced in Urbino,

Ferrara, and elsewhere, treating rulers, commoners, Jews, and Christians; the writer Sommo belonged to this family.

The composer and performer Salomone Rossi (born 1570) lived at the end of Mantua's most productive artistic period and died or disappeared during the invasion, plague, and expulsion of the Jews in 1630. He was a younger relative of Azariah de Rossi (at one time, thought to be his son, but no longer so considered). He composed both secular music for Mantua's court and religious music for performance in Mantua's Jewish community, where a strong tradition of music and dance existed. His popularity with the dukes led them to grant exemptions to many restrictions on Jewish activity. In 1606, they exempted him from wearing the Jewish badge. Many other Jewish musicians composed and performed in Mantua at about this time, including Rossi's nephew, the son of his sister, the popular opera singer known as Madame Europa.

Music historians recognize Rossi for his innovations—in particular, the invention of the trio sonata. His secular works include five collections of madrigals. He developed a way to coordinate music notation, written left-to-right, with Hebrew words, written right-to-left, by placing each correctly written Hebrew word under its corresponding musical note. His religious works belong to an effort to introduce contemporary polyphonic music into synagogue ritual; the Venetian rabbinical assembly had specifically approved this modernization, though it didn't catch on widely and was lost after his death. His works, in a style similar to that of his contemporary Monteverdi, have recently been performed and recorded. His best-known Jewish work, called *Songs of Solomon*, was published in 1623. (This information is from the notes by Gabe M. Wiener to a two-volume recording of the *Songs of Solomon*, PGM Records, 1996–1997. My inexpert opinion is that Rossi's music is very wonderful to listen to— I recommend these recordings.)

Printing had had a very early beginning in Mantua with Abraham and Estellina Conat and others in the 1470s. After them, printing ceased until the mid-1500s, when several printers began to work there. The duke at that time had prohibited Jews from the pursuit of agriculture and from renting out real estate, and had turned the Jewish cemetery over to an order of monks; nevertheless, he protected the Jews who were occupied in business and the professions, including printing. Printers included Joseph ben Jacob Shalit, a leader of the Mantuan German-Jewish community. Joseph printed Provencali's work and also an edition of Isaac Abravanel's commentary on Deuteronomy.

In 1545, Venturin Ruffinello, a Christian printer, arrived in Mantua from Venice; he printed Hebrew books in association with Meir the Scribe and Jacob of Gazolo, who worked in Mantua from 1556 to 1563. The *Zohar*, which appeared in 1559, and the *Bahur* of Elijah Levitas were the principal works from this press. Condemnation of Jewish books under scrutiny of the Inquisition began to cause major problems for all Hebrew printers in this era, but in 1572, Meir the Scribe obtained permission to print an edition of Maimonides' works in Mantua. Plague and increasing persecutions put an end to his activities; he died shortly afterward. Also in the mid-1500s, Samuel Norsa and his sons Isaac and Solomon Norsa were patrons of presses run by various others and later became printers themselves. Even after the ghetto's establishment in 1610, a few determined Jews in Mantua attempted to reestablish printing of Hebrew books. One press published intermittently under difficult conditions until the 1670s (Amram, pp. 320–337).

In Mantua throughout these centuries, the Norsa family played an active role in civic affairs, in Jewish community leadership, occasionally as rabbis or scholars, and as patrons of Jewish art and culture. They supported the synagogues, sponsored Hebrew printing, and collected manuscripts and printed books. There are numerous records of their activities. One documents that in 1496 Moses ben Nathaniel Norsa of Mantua purchased an illuminated manuscript from Baruch ben Joseph Cohen. Family members, as noted, also frequently commissioned manuscripts from Abraham Farissol. In 1513, Moses ben Nathaniel Norsa of Mantua made such manuscript purchases. Around 1516, the Norsa family paid for the creation of a beautiful small synagogue for Mantua. At the time, the community also had many others, mostly larger, but today it remains the last synagogue in Mantua. In the early 1600s, Jedidiah Solomon Norsa renewed a method of biblical scholarship in order to produce a good text of the Bible. He assembled ancient codices and other sources of variants, and traveled to obtain texts and meet other scholars (Roth, *Jews in the Renaissance*, p. 313).

Private Jewish collectors of the time purchased elaborate decorations and ritual items to use at Jewish festivals and special celebrations. Festivals and Sabbath dinners demanded lavish table covers, wall tapestries, and embroidered cloths to cover bread or *matzos*. For Sabbath dinner at the Norsa family home, the woman of the house probably covered her dark-wood, richly carved table with a many-colored cloth embroidered in precious-metal threads and laid the table with beautiful plates, candelabra, table ornaments, and vessels made from ceramics, glass, and precious metals.

Besides the familiar Jewish festivals and feasts, Italian Jews practiced a ritual the night before the circumcision of a newborn boy. Women gathered with the new mother and close female relatives in a vigil, because there was a fear that evil spirits, such as the demon Lilith, threatened the newborn. Elaborate platters with traditional decorations were in use for many generations to serve food to the mother of the newborn. Also, brides received gifts in precious inlaid or carved chests, which became part of the family treasures. In the Israel Museum in Jerusalem you can see a fifteenth-century tiny metal casket intended for a woman's use in holding the household keys.

The Norsas must have had collections of beautiful religious objects, such as those that appear in synagogue museums in Israel today. They appreciated secular art and decoration as well. Against their will, the family had played a role in the history of mainstream art by their subsidy of Mantegna's *Madonna of Victories*, and figured in the anonymous painting now in Sant Andreas in Mantua, illustrating the dedication of Mantegna's painting. Their family coat of arms, a usually Christian sort of representation, depicted the heads of three blindfolded black men. In 1557, Abraham Emanuel Norsa of Mantua commissioned a portrait medal of himself, made by the fashionable Ferarran artist Pastorino de Pastorini. Similar medals often served as a means for Christians of the upper middle class to memorialize a family member. A medal showing the niece of Gracia Nasi is by the same artist; a few other Jewish families also had such portraits made.

The creation of the ghetto in Mantua in 1610–1612, wars, plagues, the disastrous defeat of the Gonzagas, and the expulsion in 1630 of a large number of Jews put an end to much of the cultural activity. There was even a prohibition on Christian employment of Jewish music teachers—with an exception for the duke. As they had done earlier in other cities, the Jews had to turn inward, losing their former close relationship with the rest of the community.

Ordinary Italians in the Venetian Ghetto

In the introduction to Part 4, I summarized the founding of the Venetian Ghetto in 1516, what features made it new and important, and its impact on Italian and European society. Now I will expand on my impressions of Venice, with a bit of speculation about the experiences of Gershom Soncino and Isaac Abravanel, who lived there just before the founding of the Ghetto. I will describe more detail about the history of the ghetto, introduce a few colorful characters who lived there in the sixteenth century, and describe several synagogues and historic buildings that still stand in the Venetian Ghetto, which may be the most famous Jewish tourist attraction in Italy today.

VENETIAN IMPRESSIONS

For a visitor to Venice today, the inevitable first impression is your introductory boat ride down the Grand Canal, beginning at the railroad station or the parking terminus where you enter the city and following its s-shaped route to St. Marks' square and the Doges' Palace at the opposite end. Along the way you see dozens of medieval, Renaissance, Baroque, rococo, and nineteenth-century palaces, some in a state of well-preserved grandeur, some decayed and boarded up, and some surrounded by scaffolds and construction equipment. They serve as hotels, private residences, government offices, museums, or headquarters for banks or private foundations. Many have private docks to tie up a small yacht or rowboat or to allow a water-taxi to dock. The family names associated with the palaces of Venice may have a familiar sound: they are also the names of great Venetian admirals, doges, thinkers, and artists.

As you travel the Grand Canal, you also have the opportunity to glance quickly up the many side canals. A typical scene—irresistibly picturesque—is a still strip of water with high buildings crowding both sides of it, with a high arched stone bridge across it, not far from where it joins the Grand Canal. Sometimes several small rowboats, power boats, or gondolas park along the banks of these side canals.

In addition to the waterways, Venice has a network of small pedestrian streets, not in the least like a grid, which wind between buildings and into a variety of dead ends, widen into plazas where open-air markets can take place, accommodate sidewalk cafes and shop windows, and cross the canals on the many attractive bridges. Private homes, grocery stores, churches, and schools seem to be on these small streets, leaving the Grand Canal for museums, splendid office environments, and private palaces.

Unlike most European cities, no nineteenth- or twentieth-century urban renewal has cleared acres of old buildings and created wide boulevards and peripheral highways. Once you traverse the causeway across the lagoon, you must leave your car in a large garage (costing almost as much as a night in a hotel elsewhere) and go on foot or by boat. Public transportation consists of large motorized boats called *vaporettos*, with a covered seating platform and a central open platform. Each *vaporetto* has a set route with a number, and takes on and discharges passengers at regular stops every few hundred feet along the Grand Canal, continuing to other destinations such as the Lido. Smaller water taxis provide individual service, and porters with wheelbarrows or dollies are available to carry tourists' suitcases through the pedestrian streets for a fee. Commercial loads ride on motor barges, which you can particularly see in the early morning. One may be loaded high with boxes of produce and groceries, another with building materials or with dozens of suitcases for a tour group. We noticed one special barge equipped with a gas-powered freezer; it was decorated with the Motta logo and a picture of some of the most popular ice cream bars.

Everything helps you to feel the lack of modernization: the old, arched bridges, stagnant canals, antique storefronts, lack of large Eurostyle supermarkets and department stores, even the placement of a MacDonald's in a yellowish aging building on a narrow street. You can't shake the impression of age, although all the other accustomed modernity is right there: cellular phones in use in the street; fax machines, cash machines, and computers in hotels and banks; warnings on restaurant menus that the pizza ingredients were previously frozen; modern plumbing in bathrooms (though the sewage goes right into the canals); air conditioning and global TV stations in bars and hotel rooms; security cameras and alarms in museums; occasional high-tech cranes and scaffolds on building projects. There are occasional ambiguities—is the fear of pickpockets in a crowded public boat ancient or modern?

As a modern American city dweller I find the narrow streets and lack of front yards in Venice to be somewhat stifling. The occasional sight of a few bushes or flowers behind courtyard walls or outside a restaurant's back door, or the tantalizing glimpse of a water-side garden as my motorboat rushes me by, only increases my sense of being confined by the Venetian atmosphere. One good way to see Venice is to make a trip down the Grand Canal seated in one of the few seats outside the front or rear of the *vaporetto*. From these seats, you can look up the canals, into gardens, and see things that are inaccessible by foot, as far as I can tell. To see the gardens and interiors of the water-side palaces, you can check your guide for those that are museums. My favorites are the Peggy Guggenheim Museum and the Ca D'Oro.

The most unusual feature of the cityscape is the complete absence of motor vehicles. To be sure, the major boat transport is motorized, meaning that the sound and sight of the traffic along the Grand Canal has utterly changed. Nevertheless, tourist demand preserves the ancient craft of building and rowing gondolas, which have a unique asymmetrical design that enables the oarsman to use a single long oar for propelling and steering them in a forward course.

The city is almost always packed with Italian, American, German, Japanese, and who-knows-what other tourists. I often had the impression that only tourist-related businesses are really viable in this strange atmosphere; real industry moved out when the lack of easy access became an issue. The often-repeated complaints about high tides and motorboat wakes undermining the canals don't really affect you when you are a simple tourist. At high tide, though, you can see that the water comes up above the older stone porches and docks, such as that of the famous Ca D'oro, and at low tide, you can smell the sewage and garbage that the Venetians continually dump into their watery surroundings.

Gershom Soncino's Venice

Many spots in Venice still resemble the streets and canals that Gershom Soncino must have seen around 1500. Though fewer fine palaces lined the Grand Canal, the opulent wealth that now is faded was then new and stunning. Venice was a major trading center—the real "Queen of the Adriatic," and the palaces represented the profits of centuries of far-flung enterprises and maritime conquests. The owners of the palaces were rich merchants and noble families who shared in the ruling of the Venetian republic. Ordinary though prosperous craftsmen, such as Aldus Manutius and his father-in-law, lived on the pedestrian streets and small squares in the more obscure and crowded parts of the city. Aldus's home and press, in those years, was on a square at Sant Agostino, at the corner of Calle del Pistor, in a building that currently has the address San Polo 2343. Other than this ancient history, the building, now private, has nothing else to recommend it, though the area can give you an idea of what things were like five hundred years ago.

The continuity of appearance of streets and canals in Venice is impressive. The atmosphere of pedestrian streets without motor vehicles and the need to travel by water (even by motorized boats) gives one a strong impression of being in another era. Perhaps the challenge of building on such watery foundations, of bringing in materials and laborers from the mainland by barge or carrying everything in wheelbarrows, and of carrying out debris from renovations puts pressure on owners to leave ancient buildings standing. Of course, some have been demolished: the second workshop of the Aldine press was torn down in 1871, although its neighborhood, Sant Paternian, retains its Renaissance appearance. (Information about Aldus and his homes is from H. G. Fletcher, *In Praise of Aldus Manutius*, New York: Pierpont Morgan Library, 1995, p. 15.)

Gershom Soncino, according to one account, lived in the house of the noble family Tiepolo, presumably on some sort of retainer, while he was in Venice. The Tiepolo family was one of the ruling families of Venice; earlier there had been at least one Tieoplo Doge. Gershom's relationship with them also was evident later, when a member of the family patronized Gershom's press at Pesaro. Gershom's actually living at their palace, however, seems to conflict with his religion and consequent low social status. The story, which everyone quotes, appeared in Amram's book ninety years ago. Amram specifically describes the Tiepolo house as a palace on the Grand Canal with two obelisks on the roof.

I followed up this lead to see if I could actually find a location clearly identified with Gershom Soncino. Riding on the open platform of the *vaporetto,* I discovered that three obelisk-topped palaces stand beside the Grand Canal. Each of them is surrounded by narrow winding streets and ancient buildings that could date back to the early 1500s, and I hopefully explored each neighborhood. I compared these three possible suspects to photos of the specific Tiepolo palace in the Italian Encyclopedia and in the book *Venetian Palaces.* This book describes the "Palazzo Coccina Tiepolo Papadopoli," a palace on the Grand Canal, a little after the Rialto on the way toward St. Marks, which has two slender obelisks on its roof, as described in histories of Gershom Soncino. However, the text says: "The palace was built in approximately 1560 by Giangiacomo de'Grigi for the Coccina family. . . . When the Coccinas died out, the residence passed on to the Tiepolos in 1748, and in 1837, to Valentino Comello . . . Since 1922 the palace has belonged to the counts Arrivabene" (Raffaella Russo, *Venetian Palaces,* Paris: Hazan, 1998, p. 30).

Isaac Abravanel's Venice

I have no information about where Isaac Abravanel lived during his years in Venice, but I know that his presence as a practicing Jew required an exception to the law and custom then in effect in Venice, and that it is probable that on the Sabbath and on Jewish holidays he made his way out of the canal and lagoon city and onto the mainland, where he could find a synagogue in which to participate in Jewish worship. Creating a mental image of the Venice where Isaac Abravanel lived seems easy, due to the appearance of old buildings and lack of motor vehicles, but in fact, his memory can only be rather distant, as a shadowy figure who walked these streets and visited the doge's palace and city offices.

Venice in 1515

At the beginning of the sixteenth century Venice was desperately hanging onto its position as the cultural center and most powerful trading nation of northern Italy. The growing international trade capabilities of Spain, Portugal, and the Turkish Empire were all eroding the former Venetian dominance. The Turks were taking over sea power in the eastern Mediterranean, ending the Venetian monopoly on many commodities. The Spanish and Portuguese were developing new trade routes that went west, going around Africa and toward the New World and discovering new products to compete with the old luxuries from Asia and the Arab world.

The struggle against this loss of greatness occupied the Serinissima, Venice's republican government, for the entire sixteenth century.

One of the early policy changes was to increase the number of international merchants allowed to live in the city. The formerly exclusive policies appeared no longer viable—they realized a need to tolerate more Turkish merchants in Venice, hoping to ensure that Venetians would be welcome, reciprocally, in Istanbul. As they questioned their exclusive policies, they considered the contribution of Jewish traders who lived or had formerly lived throughout their competitors' territories and considered how they could balance a greater tolerance of Jews against ancient public antipathy toward them.

This latent popular anti-Jewish sentiment had always prevented a large number of Jews from settling in Venice, a republic. The Serinissima had historically responded to public sentiment in ways that hereditary rulers, such as the Gonzagas and Esteses, did not have to do. People's concerns included worries about sexual relationships between Jews and Christians, which were feared too likely if Jews had freedom of residence. The Venetians were traders and financial dealers themselves and thus were hostile to Jewish competition in financial activities. And as elsewhere, under the influence of the church, populist anti-Jewish sentiment had a fundamental basis in the distrust of a people who continued for centuries to deny the central beliefs of Christianity (S. Haliczer, *Inquisition and Society in Early Modern Europe*, London: Croom Helm, 1987, p. 19).

The history of Venetian Jewry included repeated changes of policy. The few Jews who lived in Venice proper or its immediate surroundings are poorly documented. By around 1500, Venice was becoming somewhat more openminded, as indicated by their employment of Isaac Abravanel. At this time, Jews were permitted to stay in Venice for temporary periods up to fifteen days to transact business such as making loans. Isaac Abravanel's permission to work for the government had been exceptional. Gershom Soncino's method of working or observing the print business in Venice is mysterious (he may have posed as a Christian). Some Jews lived on the mainland, in Mestre, and managed the long and inconvenient commute across the water; other Jews, particularly German Jews, may have exceeded the time limit in spite of the policy, and the authorities may have looked the other way.

Increasingly, Venice faced a choice: bow to economic conditions, which demanded that Jews be allowed more active participation in the changing trade situation, or continue to follow public opinion, opposed to expanding rights for Jews. While medieval Jewish quarters in the cities of Spain and France by this time had ceased to exist, people still remembered the walls and gates that had protected Jews from the mob and protected the Christians from Jewish influences. Although Milan, Naples, and the cities of Sicily had once had a more fluid Jewish quarter, with fewer restrictions on residence, they had already expelled their formerly substantial populations of Jews. Throughout Italy, the motive for special regulation of living quarters for Jews had been protection of the interests of their Christian customers: when Christians pawned their goods with Jewish moneylenders, they wanted these goods to be safe—from fire, water, riot, or theft—for when they eventually would redeem them. Often the methods of protection were written into the charters that admitted Jews to Italian cities. Over time, the church had added restrictive laws as well, but the Italian communities had often ignored them.

The Venetian Ghetto implemented a more rigorous version of some of these medieval restraints on Jews. Its organization was a compromise designed to find a way to allow useful Jewish occupants to move to Venice while still catering to local fear, hatred, and other anti-Jewish sentiments and also complying with church policy. When first proposed in 1515, the proposal for a segregated and regulated Jewish quarter was rejected, but local sentiment changed. A year later, in 1516, the rulers created the first ghetto. The rules of this new ghetto applied a number of church proclamations that had rarely been observed in northern Italy. The Jews, particularly the German Jews, had been dodging the Venetian regulations for years anyway; for them, the new rules afforded recognition of a previously irregular situation. Despite the restrictions, it was better than being an illegal alien or going back and forth from Mestre—now wives and children could also stay in Venice with their trading fathers, brothers, or husbands. Skeptical Venetians were initially comfortable with the segregation of Jews into a canal-ringed quarter behind locked gates.

Thus, the founding of the Venetian Ghetto had both positive and negative consequences: formally admitting Jews but keeping them at an economic and social disadvantage. On the positive side, the Ghetto offered the first opportunity for establishing a Jewish community there. The synagogues in the ghetto were the first officially permitted in Venice. The freedom to establish non-Catholic houses of worship and to organize public prayers was a major privilege for Jews. While Moslems and later Protestants sometimes had freedom of conscience (that is, they weren't prosecuted for non-Catholic affiliations), they were denied freedom of public, open worship and were never allowed to build churches or mosques. In fact, merchants of other ethnic groups were jealous of the Jewish privilege of living indefinitely in Venice and having more or less permanent status rather than temporary quarters for visiting merchants only.

Over time, a vigorous, ethnically diverse, and socially active community life developed. Population numbers increased, as the original Germans were joined by Jews from many other groups. In 1516, Jews were only 0.5 percent of the Venetian population—a few hundred people. In 1552, the population of the Ghetto was 1,300 Jews. By 1586 the Ghetto had 1,694 inhabitants. In the year 1642, the Ghetto housed 2,671 inhabitants; this amounted to 2.25 percent of the population. (Percentages from Haliczer, *Inquisition and Society*, p. 22; population for 1552, from R. Calimani, *The Ghetto of Venice*, New York: M. Evans and Co., 1987. p. 2; population for 1642, Pullan, pp. 156–157.)

Anyway, it was an idea whose time had come: within a century, virtually every Jewish community in Italy, willingly or unwillingly, was confined to a walled part of town. Jews who had formerly enjoyed many freedoms no longer had permission to occupy or use real estate that they owned outside their quarter; they lived in crowded and inadequate housing; they lost the freedom to choose occupations and found businesses; Jewish and Christian scholars found increasingly fewer opportunities for the exchange of ideas; and the gates—literally and figuratively—began to close on Jewish participation in the general course of life.

THE GROWTH OF THE GHETTO

After the Ghetto's initial establishment in 1516, international trends and local customs caused constant evolution of the life within the Ghetto's confining walls. Externally, Luther's reformation, the counter-Reformation, and the devastating power and influence of the Spanish Inquisition on Catholics everywhere contributed to growing unease about non-Christian ideas and "heresies." Continued medieval-style hatred caused people to blame Jews directly for such disasters as an earthquake in Lisbon or a plague in Ferrara. The introduction of the Portuguese Inquisition in the 1530s created Jewish or crypto-Jewish refugees who eventually showed up in Venice. Book burning, such as the general attack on the Talmud in the 1550s, affected the freedom of Ghetto residents to own or print books. Ghetto residents in Venice were occasionally threatened with expulsion during the 1560s, but they nevertheless remained. A local Venetian Inquisition represented more of these tendencies; it was founded in 1547.

Immigrants were a major force in Ghetto life, contributing to a vibrantly diverse atmosphere. Colorful characters on the lam from the Spanish or Portuguese or Roman Inquisitions frequently tried to hide in the Venetian Ghetto. Occasional Christians, attracted by the exciting life or by opportunities to work for a Jewish bookkeeper, goldsmith, or school, even sometimes tried to live in the Ghetto, though the Venetian Inquisition often caught them. Merchants who had lived as Christians when they were in Amsterdam or elsewhere, put on Jewish clothing and lived in the Ghetto when they were in Venice. Turkish Jews brought their exotic customs, as well as profitable trade connections. Some Portuguese Jews claimed to be Turkish citizens and by one means or another received "protection" from the Turkish government—the Turks throughout the century put a high value on the contribution of Jews and had insisted that the Venetians respect the rights of their citizens in Venice.

The Jews in the Ghetto were formally or informally divided into "Germans" meaning people from Germany, Poland, and so forth—that is Ashkenazi; and "Levantines," that is, Jews from Turkey. The latter in many cases were originally Marranos from Spain or Portugal who had stopped in Ferrara to be accepted into the faith of their ancestors and to be circumcised, and then had gone to Turkey for a while and put on a turban, coming out "Levantine." Secret Jews from Portugal, such as Gracia Nasi and her family, also came to Venice, though they didn't live in the Ghetto, but continued to behave as Christians. Italian Jews from other Italian cities arrived later, but also began to contribute to the atmosphere. Marranos from Portugal and occasionally Spain joined the community by claiming that their parents had never allowed them to be baptized, even though it was required. Jews like these, or others who reverted from Christianity, found it possible to quietly move into the Ghetto, often without attracting notice of the Inquisition unless they were indiscreet. When in the East, some Jews may even have disguised themselves as Moslems—their experiences contributed another perspective to the Ghetto. Ghetto residents were always engaging in trade and traveling to all kinds of other places: Portugal, Spain, England, Amsterdam, Istanbul, Salonika, Ragusa, and the other cities on the eastern Adriatic coast, the Near East, and all the other Italian cities.

Jews in the Ghetto had many skills, although restrictions limited their activities mainly to dealing in used goods, especially used textiles, and lending money. One impoverishing set of regulations forced the community as a whole to fund a moneylending organization. This organization essentially was required to make relatively unprofitable loans to any Christian who met extremely minimal qualifications. In some cases, Jewish craftsmen worked around limitations by forming partnerships with Christians to camouflage the pursuit of restricted occupations.

Thus, the Ghetto housed people speaking all kinds of languages, with varying experiences, customs, costumes, skills, and food. The sights and sounds of the Ghetto must have been remarkably diverse and colorful; the buildings and synagogues also reflected the diversity, with synagogues representing several rites—German, Italian, Spanish. As the Ghetto of Venice increased in population, it constantly needed new territory, but it received only two very small additions after the 1516 allocation.

The number of inhabitants continued to grow until the population far exceeded any realistic capacity of its few buildings. Italians from Rome and the papal territories became more numerous as the popes instituted new and increasingly repressive anti-Jewish policies; German Jews fled from the fallout from Catholic-Protestant battles; and the Inquisition drove more and more Portuguese to Venice. Even the wealthiest residents had extremely tiny living spaces. Strict laws and absentee Christian owners limited the changes or enlargements that residents could make, so they added gerry-built subdivisions between floors to cram more people into rooms in which a man could scarcely stand up. They put in odd windows and winding stairways. They partitioned rooms and divided former apartments into smaller and smaller units. The buildings began to tilt and assume odd angles above unstable foundations. Furthermore, for these deteriorating quarters, inhabitants were obliged to pay high rents to the owners who already had title to the land and buildings, as well as special taxes. Most of these exorbitant rents went to a single family, which owned most of the real estate, but the deeds were complicated and sometimes there were deals where Jews improved or restored buildings and then executed leases with other Jews.

The situation became much worse in seventeenth century, as the amount of space allocated was never increased during continuing growth of the population. Overcrowding, filth, disease, noise, and lack of privacy made life in the Ghetto unhealthy and unpleasant for rich as well as for poor Ghetto dwellers. Clearly, the alternatives were worse or non-existent, and despite the problems, immigration increased throughout the existence of the Ghetto. The creation of beautiful synagogues must have been an important source of hope in this stifling atmosphere.

Ordinary People

Christians in Venice viewed the Ghetto as a sort of continual costume party. They came to the Ghetto to patronize gambling houses, taverns, and establishments offering entertainment and prostitution. Purim carnivals, where everyone wore masks to the Ghetto, usually occurred during

Lent. They attracted Christians who wanted to have fun when they should have been fasting and behaving themselves. These big street parties became so popular that it was difficult or impossible for the authorities to enforce the usual curfew and send the Christians out of the Ghetto during the night.

Most books focus on famous Jews, especially the many rabbis who led the community, but I want to introduce the more marginal characters who gave the Ghetto its strange appeal. First of all, gambling, particularly with dice and cards, was common among both Jews and Christians and had been so for centuries, as I have mentioned in other contexts. Gambling accounted for 8.5 percent of the offenses charged against Jews in Umbria between 1320 and 1520; presumably, this indicates its incidence elsewhere as well. When representatives from various Jewish communities of Roman origin held a congress at Forli in 1418 to discuss Jewish affairs, gambling was on the agenda. Rabbis would have liked to prohibit gambling and, with optimism, decreed that "no Jew living in . . . communes, walled towns, or villages should venture to play games of chance with cards or dice, even indirectly, with other Jews or Christians in his own home or those of others." They specified a penalty of one ducat.

Anti-gambling efforts by Jewish authorities paralleled Christian opposition, which often singled out Jews for gambling. Public disapproval had parallels in private struggles. In the 1470s, the anti-Jewish preaching of Bernardino da Feltre specifically attacked the Jews of Perugia, Siena, and Florence for manufacturing cards and dice. In the 1540s, as mentioned earlier, Samuel Abravanel's son displayed gambling tendencies that led Samuel to leave his money to his wife, Benvenita, and allowed her to decide whether the sons should later obtain control of his fortune. In 1548: "the well-known and wealthy medical officer of Perugia, Laudadio de Blanis, thought nothing of hauling up his own four sons . . . before a notary and making them solemnly promise to give up games of chance, on pain of losing the huge paternal fortune."

Besides the underworld, gamblers came from all strata of society—"beggars, bankers, and merchants." The famous Venetian rabbi Leone Modena wrote about his struggle to give up gambling. Names of flagrant encouragers of gambling appeared in the Venetian archives. David Pas was recorded as proprietor of a gambling house, and Noah the Jew was charged in 1576 with keeping a gambling house frequented by both Jews and Christians. Legal cases elsewhere also record Jews who ran gambling dens and taverns, and Jews who participated in a "jaded night-life" with "vagrants, pimps, foot-pads, and prostitutes."

Both the gambling and the wide travel experiences of Jews, and especially of Marranos, appear as elements of the story of a Marrano who used the names Anrriquez Nuñes, Enriques Nuñes, Abraham, Righetto, and Righetto Marrano. Records of the Inquisition show that this Righetto was probably born in the 1530s and that he squandered fortunes, gambled, and also created a variety of stories to explain himself. He was a picaresque character, wandering sometimes alone, sometimes with his family, from Flanders, Spain, and Lisbon to Venice and Ferrara, and eventually to Salonika. He probably was born in Lisbon in a village whose baptismal records were destroyed, so that by Venetian and papal law, he had been baptized there and thus was not allowed to practice Judaism. The family lived in Ferrara in the 1550s and 1560s, and his brother made a will in Ferrara in 1552, but the trail of their travel from Lisbon to Ferrara is obscure.

Righetto's own account of his life may have been embellished, in order to win sympathy or impress the Inquisitors. He insisted that Ferrara was his birthplace—and thus, saying he had been born Jewish, he claimed not to be subject to the Inquisition. He admitted to disguising himself as a Christian when it was convenient—as when he decided to woo a rich Christian woman in Antwerp, where he had gone to seek his fortune. By his late teens, Righetto rebelled against his family. He described how his father had become angry and beaten him because he had run away from Ferrara and had gone to Mantua to see the festivals. In response to his father's punishments, he stole two thousand crowns from the family and began his travels, which included a voyage to Italy, Augsburg, Flanders, and Spain as a participant in the court of Prince Philip during 1551, and subsequently a visit to Lisbon by himself. In all, he visited the Iberian peninsula three times.

During this time, Righetto was becoming increasingly addicted to gambling. In 1552, he became the administrator of the family's extensive fortunes, which enabled him to gamble with wealthy Christians. In particular, he became notorious for losing seventy thousand ducats in one gambling session at the salons of Cosimo de' Medici, Duke of Florence. Besides gambling with Christians, he also lived and ate with them. Eventually, he attracted the attention of the Inquisition because in Venice he sometimes wore Jewish clothing and associated with Jews in the ghetto. When he was in jail in Venice, in serious trouble with the Inquisition, he played cards with his jailers and tricked them into trusting him so that he could escape. He's no doubt one of the most colorful characters that they investigated.

Contact between Jews in various communities was not limited to marginal figures such as Righetto. Important scholars and cultural figures also communicated extensively, and events that were controversial in one place often had consequences elsewhere. The daringly modern religious music of Salamone Rossi received approval from a body of Venetian rabbis, though it was rejected elsewhere. The controversy over the advanced ideas of Mantuan rabbi Moses Provencali inspired negative judgments from the councils of Padua and Venice. Rabbinic institutions in a number of Italian cities, including Venice, participated in banning Azariah de Rossi's controversial book. Similarly, in 1566, a widely discussed conflict in Venice over a contested divorce resulted in an actual fistfight in Mantua between individuals arguing on the two sides of the dispute, and the authorities had to be called. Eventually, the case caused Jewish communities all over northern Italy to take sides. Frequently, the rabbis of Venice took a more conservative side, while the rabbis and Jews of Mantua seemed to be more adventurous.

Most Jews in Venice worked as clothing merchants, dealt in used goods, and—as an obligation—ran special low-interest pawnshops. These ran at a loss to the entire community, and all were required to help support them. Also, some Jews worked for Christians, for instance, in printing; they could be typesetters and editors for the Venetian Hebrew printers in the years before the suppression of Hebrew printing, but could not be printers and own the shop. Jews were always in textiles: weavers, embroiderers, lace makers, and bookbinders, as demonstrated by the handworked textiles in museums of Jewish life in Venice and elsewhere.

Suffering from the limited economic opportunities of the Ghetto, Jews could be very poor and yet still men of learning. In 1545, a non-Jewish typecutter, Guillaume le Bé, who worked for Giustiniani's Hebrew press, described such a Jew, named Master Leon. In his diary, he recorded that Leon was "a queer person, possessed of a great knowledge of the finer points of Hebrew calligraphy and literature, although by calling he was a dealer in second-hand clothing." Although they were poor and in no position to command respect, Ghetto dwellers were often called upon to teach Hebrew and Jewish learning to Christians. The liberal and inquiring atmosphere of Christian Venice outside the Ghetto seemed to overcome the consequences of its degrading atmosphere. Also in 1545, a Ghetto physician named Elijah Halfon defended the appropriateness of sharing Jewish knowledge with Christians, though he opposed the communication of secret mystical lore to outsiders.

(Quotes and previous examples above are from Toaff, pp. 113, 115, 116; Roberta Curiel and Bernard Dov Cooperman, *The Venetian Ghetto*, New York: Rizzoli, 1990; Roth, *Jews in the Renaissance*, pp. 186, 142. Information about Nunez is from Pullan, pp. 217 to 220, and from Pier

Cesar Ioly Zorattini, "Anrriquez Nunez alias Abraham alias Righetto: A Marrano Caught between the S.Uffizio of Venice and the Inquisition of Lisbon," in *The Mediterranean and the Jews*, Toaff & Schwarzfuchs, eds., Tel-Aviv: Bar-Ilan University Press, 1989.)

The Inquisition

Eventually, the church pressured Venice because of the increasing presence of diversity. In response, Venice developed its own Inquisition. The biggest problem for the Inquisition was people who dressed and acted like Jews in Venice and like Christians in other places—the Marrano Righetto, as we have noted, was such a person. They noticed things like black slaves who had been purchased in the slave markets of the Turkish empire and converted to Judaism and were living as Jews in the Ghetto—a situation totally forbidden by the church, which didn't want any avenue for the increase in the total number of Jews in the world. The Inquisition also gained motivation as a result of conflicts between Catholics and Protestants: all the coming and going spurred by Venetian commerce and leadership in the book trade meant that visitors often knew too much about Luther's ideas and all the religious diversity emerging north of the Alps.

The Venetian Inquisition involved several bureaucratic organizations. These variously constituted bodies had responsibility for a variety of suspicions. The highest level were responsible for heresy—that is, irreligious acts by baptized Christians. Magistrates were in charge of blasphemy, a lesser offense than heresy, but more logically applied to Jews. Another class of officials supervised the Ghetto Nuovo and had the responsibility to maintain social distance between Christians and Jews. They enforced dress regulations—mainly, distinctive Jewish headgear, and observed social contacts, whether they involved Christians who worked as domestic servants for Jews or involved Jewish service to Christians. Despite restrictions, Jews still managed to follow traditional service occupations as physicians, music teachers, or performers, but they were watched.

Jews who merely failed to observe the rules about dress and residence were less strictly treated than Jews suspected of heresy, especially those who dressed alternately as both Jews and Christians. There was no tolerance for disrespect of one's allegiance to Christianity. Other possible avenues of investigation involved suspicion of a sexual relationship between Christian and Jew, particularly if it violated the Christian sacrament of marriage or threatened that the Christian member of the relationship might convert to Judaism. The Inquisition recorded occasional accusations that Jews had seduced Christians or had engaged in prostitution, although these accusations did not lead to any trials. Family members or close friends involved in feuds, such as between Jews and converts, sometimes denounced rivals to the Inquisition. This was the case in the feud when Gracia Nasi was accused as a secret Jew by her sister, and they almost lost their fortune to the Inquisition.

The Venetian Inquisition offered fewer perverse incentives for false denunciations or for hasty convictions than the Spanish. First, the Venetians lacked financial incentives to persecute and convict accused heretics: neither the state nor the Inquisitors necessarily confiscated all the goods and money of those they convicted. Second, they recognized that denouncers might be perversely motivated. They looked for evidence that an accuser might be seeking revenge or money, and didn't necessarily follow up all accusations as the Spanish did. Finally, since it was legal to be Jewish, the basis of investigation wasn't racist in the same way— no persecution occurred in Venice for the simple lack of "pure blood." Unlike in Spain and the Spanish colonies, victims of the Venetian Inquisition included very few women, suggesting that it was less intrusive on purely private behavior. In spite of the Inquisition, Venetians were much more openminded about reversions to Judaism. They consistently opposed or ignored church rulings and practices under which secret Jews elsewhere were rigorously watched and persecuted for "Judaizing" (Pullan, pp. 79–80; 204–205).

The Jews: Loyal or Disloyal?

After about 1550, many Venetians of all classes tended to view the Jews as disloyal and to suspect them of having sympathy for the Turks, their enemy. The use of Hebrew, Spanish, and German in the Ghetto had already begun to worry the Venetians, who regarded these languages as secret ways to send messages to enemy powers. The sultans of Turkey included their Jewish subjects when they negotiated privileges for Turkish traders and government representatives in Venice. In the course of these negotiations, they defined Portuguese New Christians as belonging to this group, the "Levantine" Jews; thus, they also protected the Portuguese Jews against discrimination in Venice and, in so doing, increased the Venetians' suspicions of Jewish loyalty. The Papal Bull called *Cum Nimis Absurdum*, dated 1555, reinforced suspicion of Jews by increasing their social isolation, limiting their residential choices, and restricting their employment opportunities in all Catholic countries.

The Venetians also had another sort of religious reasoning that led to mistrust of Jews. They interpreted Jewish messianic longings to imply a course of action that threatened Christianity. Specifically, they believed that Jews and Turks had made an alliance whose purpose was to destroy Rome, the Church, and all Italy, and in so doing to fulfill a necessary prerequisite for the Messiah's predicted arrival in Jerusalem. The belief that destruction of Christianity was a religious precept of the Jews enabled them to interpret any possible evidence as a conspiracy between the Jews and the Turks, who were often at war with Venice. They suspected that Jews were spying, providing information about Venetian military plans and preparations, and supplying arms and ammunition to Turkey (Haliczer, *Inquisition and Society*, p. 24).

Another basis of Venetian suspicions centered around the family of Gracia Nasi and her nephew, Joseph Nasi. While in Venice, Gracia Nasi, her sister Brianda, her daughter, and her niece had lived as Christians. During their well-known feud over control of their vast fortune, Brianda accused Gracia of secret Jewish practices. Furthermore, Gracia Nasi had gone on to Ferrara and reverted openly to Judaism. Meanwhile, Joseph Nasi had established a substantial international financial business based in Venice, including a number of agents, also Marranos. None of them lived in the Ghetto or practiced Judaism; however, they were suspected and often attracted attention from the Inquisition, which conducted a number of investigations and interrogations of the Nasi family retainers, although there were no definitive convictions.

After Joseph Nasi left Venice for Istanbul, he was tried in absentia and condemned to hang between the two columns of St. Marks' Square. Since he didn't return to face this punishment, he was considered a traitor. To make matters worse, in Venetian eyes, not long after arriving in Istanbul he reverted to the open practice of Judaism. Moreover, he became a favorite of the sultan of Turkey and achieved a high level of visibility and power at the sultan's court. Venetians viewed his actions on behalf of the sultan as a reflection of loyalty to Turkey among all Jews, particularly those in the Venetian Ghetto. Soon afterward, the Ancona boycott, held under Gracia's and Joseph's leadership, intensified the fear that powerful Jews were engaging in an international conspiracy against Italian—if not Venetian—interests.

The suspicions intensified when the sultan appointed Joseph Nasi as duke of the island of Naxos, which the Turks had taken in the course of the ongoing armed struggles for domination of the eastern Mediterranean. Venetians found two reasons to deplore Joseph Nasi's actions in Turkey:

- His improving position as the sultan's trusted deputy increased the Venetian conviction that he was a leader among their Jewish enemies. The extension of the sultan's power was a bitter pill for Venice, and anyone who participated was suspect, especially someone who continued to profit from a significant economic organization within Venice at the same time. In 1568, a secret report to the Venetian authorities specifically described how Joseph Nasi was a leader of the Jews against the Venetians (Report cited in Calimani, p. 100).

- They considered Naxos to be theirs. Before the sultan's conquest and appointment of Joseph Nasi, a Venetian family had held the dukedom and had enjoyed the income from the island's resources for generations. The Venetians may especially have resented the way that the new duke actually did not live in the ducal palace at Naxos, but continued to live in his much more luxurious and convenient palace beside the Golden Horn, in Istanbul, and to further his relationship with the sultan. On Naxos, Joseph Nasi appointed a representative to govern and exploit his franchises; this representative was a descendant of Spanish converts, who continued to practice Christianity and thus reduced the resentment of the Catholic natives. Every action of this sort provided evidence to favor the conspiracy theory in Venice.

Shortly after appointing Joseph Nasi as duke of Naxos, the sultan of Turkey began to challenge Venetian rule in Cyprus, which the Turks overpowered in 1570. All-out war soon began. In the Battle of Lepanto, in October 1571, the Venetians had one of their few military victories against the sultan's forces; however, their success was short-lived. One Venetian response was once again to discuss the possibility of expelling all the Jews in the Ghetto; Venetian religious authorities pressured the republican leaders to view the Ghetto as an affront against God and therefore urged cancellation of the Ghetto charters. Like other similar efforts, this one soon reversed, as the Jewish role in Venetian trade, especially in the East, was becoming a necessity to their economic survival. Indeed, it is in their contribution to international commerce that Jews from all national backgrounds demonstrated their loyalty to their adopted city of Venice.

A generation later, the English theater echoed repercussions of the many stories about Joseph Nasi and of Venetian anti-Jewish suspicion. Christopher Marlowe's play, *The Jew of Malta*, written in approximately 1590, may contain distorted references to his history, though I find the similiarities unimpressive—a Jew, an island in the eastern Mediterranan, a lot of stereotypes about Jewish greed and deviousness. A bit later, the overall Venetian antipathy to Jews may have also influenced Shakespeare's portrayal of Shylock in *The Merchant of Venice*.

THE VENETIAN GHETTO TODAY

When you visit the Ghetto of Venice and the synagogue and museum, you will find the emphasis on the religious life of the various ethnic communities. The ornate objects on display nearly all relate to religious holidays and religious life-cycle events. The vibrant secular life, the enforced distinguishing badges and special clothing, the low-life gamblers and taverns, Jewish makers of cards and dice, theatrical events, costumes, and Purim carnivals, all seem to take a distant place in the background. Scant reference is made to them at all in the documentation, guide books, and museum displays. One must make the best of the context of the religious displays and the atmosphere of the existing streets, squares, and buildings to imagine the color and rhythm of daily life in the Ghetto.

The Tourists' Ghetto

Venice today promotes tourism to the Ghetto and its museum and synagogues. The placard at the public motorboat stop announces the Ghetto, both in Italian and in Hebrew. The area around the Ghetto offers a variety of clues to its former status. The houses are tall and narrow, the entryways tunnel under buildings, and there are odd window placements. The shops all over Venice that sell artistic carnival masks to tourists could also be a reminder that once Purim carnivals brought disguised revelers to share the Jewish celebrations.

The modern Jewish community of Venice lives on the mainland, back again in Mestre as before 1516, reflecting the modern reversal—Mestre is now the living center of activity, finance, and industry. Thus, religious visitors have to stay at local hotels, because the majority of inhabitants in the Ghetto today aren't Jewish at all. In the Ghetto, hasidic Jews from New York or Israel have established a kosher restaurant named

Gam Gam to cater to the tourists who want kosher food. Religious Jewish visitors can arrange to attend services held in the Ghetto on Saturday—they walk to services, but one assumes that local participants must ride from their rather distant homes.

We visited the Ghetto on a Saturday and a Sunday. We observed relatively few local people in the main square. While we saw groups of Israeli, American, and German tourists and a few individuals, in its busy days, both Jews and Christian shoppers must have crowded the space. A few shops and cafes now serve these tourists—I imagined the Ghetto alive with activity and vastly overcrowded. Centuries ago, the square would no doubt have been crowded with shops, food vendors, and temporary market stalls selling the goods from which Ghetto Jews made a living. Even during the night, after the gates should have been locked, I imagined the intense activity during festivals and religious holidays, which attracted even Christian participants. Today, the single cafe with its few tables and the little knots of tour groups that stand in the square scarcely compare to what was once there. One similarity is that today, as of old, many languages can be heard. Italian, Hebrew, Spanish, and German are the tourist languages today and were the languages of commerce in the past. Now, in addition to these, you hear English; two hundred years ago, you would have heard Yiddish.

Bridges and long, narrow passageways lead to the Ghetto, forcing you to walk thorough the same small and restricted entryways that served the residents centuries ago. You can't see the old warehouse doors that once opened onto the canals, allowing transfer of the goods, particularly used clothing, in which Ghetto residents were allowed to trade. Like the gates, now taken down, these were also locked at night and guarded by Christians whose salaries, by law, came from the Jewish community that they incarcerated. You can still see the very narrow and damp passages cutting through the ground floors of the buildings on the periphery of the Ghetto. You can imagine bricked-up windows, narrow fire-prone wood stairways, and the extreme overcrowding by looking at the old and crooked buildings that remain now. Plaques on the street or in the museum memorialize the Nazi roundups and the bravery of the last rabbi, and note the locations of various institutions and events of the long history of the Ghetto.

An open, white-paved square is at the center of the Ghetto; in it stand a few trees and three wells decorated with coats of arms with lions. The houses around the square, tall and shambling, reach a height of seven or eight stories, but you can observe how each story has much less than the normal vertical rise. The guide explained that construction in the square was forbidden, and that the huge population had to squeeze into the available building room that was allowed, therefore subdividing vertically and horizontally. The old-folks home that stands on one side of the square is a modern addition, but the other buildings and the synagogues date from the Ghetto days.

Five synagogues survive in the Ghetto of Venice. Most of the synagogues occupy the upper floors of buildings whose general purpose was living and commerce. They were located upstairs out of respect: people felt that it was inappropriate to occupy quarters above the house of God. Besides, space was so scarce that the community had no locations that could be exclusively dedicated to use as synagogues. One result is that most of the synagogues have little or no outdoor indication of their presence; there are no facades to compare to the facades of Baroque churches and grand Venetian palaces.

Among these synagogues, some remain in use for religious purposes and others serve as museums. In a single visit to Venice, you can see a few of them; you must be content to hear about the others or to return another time. Like the synagogue of Mantua, the Venetian synagogue walls are decorated with plaster medallions or scrollwork in which Hebrew inscriptions and biblical quotations appear, and they lavishly use ornate and costly wood and metal work, candelabra, and beautiful textiles.

To visit the synagogues, you purchase a ticket at the museum in the square. At scheduled intervals, groups of approximately thirty visitors gather in the foyer to receive a guided tour in Italian or English. Before or after the tour, you can look at the exhibits in the museum and at the books and other items for sale in the museum gift shop. The Jewish community of Venice reserves one of the five synagogues for religious services, alternating the choice according to the season or other requirements. Whatever their original dates, all of the synagogues have repeatedly been restored, improved, and beautified over the centuries.

The guide who led our tour seemed reasonably well informed about the history and artistic interest of the synagogues. The following summary describes my experience and observations on the tour of the synagogues, as well as some additional background about the synagogues.

The five synagogues:

• The German Synagogue, or Scuola Tedesca, dates from 1529. Currently, this synagogue is being renovated and has therefore been removed from the tour. Our guide told us that the planners are uncertain of the date of completion, as they haven't identified the source of all needed funds for planned improvements. The interior of this synagogue is said to be very beautiful, with an asymmetrical floor plan that makes use of the available space and with an especially interesting women's gallery.

• The Scuola Canton, dated 1532, was probably built by Provencal Jews; it stands in the oldest part of the Ghetto, adjacent to the museum. I found it particularly magnificent, perhaps because it has already undergone a major restoration, which lasted from 1989 until 1992. All the synagogues, particularly this one, show a lot of influence of contemporaneous Christian churches. The readers' platforms are raised and have elaborate stairways and columns. The readers' platform of the Scuolo Canton resembles a Catholic high altar: it has Baroque twisted columns like St. Peter's, with columns and canopy all covered with fruit and vegetables. The reason for this apparent influence is that Jews were not allowed to do crafts; thus, designers, builders, woodcarvers, and architects all had to be Christians. Jews weren't allowed to manufacture anything, even for their own use. This included wood and metalwork that would be required to decorate the synagogues, so they hired members of the guilds of Christian artisans whose jobs and guilds this law protected.

• The Scuola Italiana, next door to the museum, was built in 1575. Its floor plan changed later: a central readers' platform was the original design, by Italian tradition. However, support for the floor carrying the weight at the center of the room became a problem, our guide explained, and the tradition at all the synagogues changed, so that the platform was to one side and the holy Ark at the other side. The walls of the Scuola Italiana display a series of wood-inlay depictions of the Exodus, entirely shown by symbolic nonhuman representations, such as Moses' hand smiting rocks: only a hand. Or the falling Manna, a lot of little pieces. This artwork represents a compromise between the Jewish prohibitions and the representational inclinations of the non-Jewish artists.

• The Scuola Spagnola originated between 1555 and 1584 and was extensively remodeled in the 1640s. It stands in the neighboring plaza, the Campiello delle Scuole. Built by Sephardic Jews, it was intended to be used for the Spanish tradition of services. Our guide took our tour to this synagogue after we had seen the synagogues adjacent to the museum. The lower floor includes an entranceway and a wide, marble stairway. The synagogue has a gray and white tiled floor and is paneled with dark wood; the guide pointed to one area where a secret panel allowed the community to conceal a few of their religious treasures from the Nazis.

• Finally, the Scuola Leventina, which was built in 1538, stands across the Campiello delle Scuole from the Scuola Spagnola. This synagogue has an identifiable facade with high second-story windows facing the square. During our visit, this synagogue was taking its turn as the active house of worship for the community and observant visitors, and therefore, I did not visit it. I saw a glimpse of the entrance hall, similar to its neighbor, on Saturday, as the worshipers were leaving for lunch. They evidently had a prior arrangement with Gam Gam, the hasidic restaurant, for a Sabbath meal.

The Jewish museum has a few objects mainly from the seventeenth through nineteenth centuries: *menorahs*, Hanukkah lamps, spice boxes, Torah decorations, and beautiful fabrics of various ritual uses. As usual, the majority of items relate to religious practices. Much of the material goods of the dwellers of this ghetto was lost when the community was deported in the war. The Jewish cemetery is at the Lido.

The Jewish guidebooks to Venice (listed in the appendix) elaborate what we saw in fairly great detail. I'm trying to communicate to you the idea of the ghetto, not a full architectural description of the synagogues. The hardest challenge is to imagine the Jews of Venice when Soncino and Abravanel were there, before the ghetto or the synagogues. Much of what is in Venice now is probably only from a hundred years ago, mainly preserved by absence of the automobile, which, of course, creates reality in the modern city. Frozen in time, yes, but I am afraid not really in the fifteenth century.

The names and contact information for the local Jewish community appear in most standard guidebooks. They also appear on the community's Web page; search under "Ghetto of Venice" for their current Web address, as there are always changes of servers as well as changes in the schedules. Here are the most useful phone numbers, along with other information from the "Ghetto of Venice" Web site as of November 1999:

• Jewish Museum: Campo di Ghetto Nuovo 2902b, phone 041/715359; fax: 041/723007. Opening hours: June 1st to September 30, 10 A.M. to 7 P.M.; October 1st to May 31, 10 A.M. to 4:30 P.M. Closed Saturdays and Jewish holidays.

　Guided tours of the synagogues: Tour departure and information from Jewish Museum. Guided tours in Italian and English begin every hour starting at 10:30 A.M. (last tour begins 5:30 P.M./

summer and 3:30 P.M./winter). Reservations required for groups and schools.

- Community Secretary's Office: Campo di Ghetto Nuovo 2899, phone 041/715012; fax: 041/5241862
- Rabbi's Office: Campo di Ghetto Vecchio 1189, phone 041/715118
- Cemetery: Via Cipro 70. Lido of Venice; phone 041/5260142.

The Sadness of These Synagogues

While the synagogues of Venice are beautiful, they make one sad because they remind one of the fate of the Jews of Venice: five thousand before the war, five hundred now. When I think about Italy, I remember the continuous Jewish presence, which is so fascinating, the people who were so accomplished, the history that is so varied, and the destruction of so much of this by events of our century. I wonder if this community will come back to life. Just after our tour there were thirty-five Israelis about to take the tour of the synagogues. Perhaps they represent the future.

I end my book with my visit to the Ghetto of Venice, outside of Israel the biggest Jewish tourist attraction I have described in this book. The book began when I wondered what was meant by saying that Jews had no history. It began in my experience that Jews had no place in the history that I studied in school for lack of interest on the part of the Christians who wrote the history books. It began in Jewish Sunday school, where Jewish history never seemed in the least connected to mainstream history or to anything else. This Sunday School history consisted of very boring and badly written accounts of authors whose books I couldn't imagine anyone wanting to read and of Jewish participants who hadn't made any difference in historical events. For years, I never looked into whether these impressions were true, but in this book, I have tried to check it out. I feel lucky that the modern ideas of social history and writers such as Cecil Roth, Yizak Baer, Yosef Hayim Yerushalmi, and Gershom Scholem have opened up my perspective on the history of Jewish communities. I feel lucky to have had wonderful traveling companions in my husband and in the many friends that I have mentioned in the text.

Practical Information and References

APPENDIX 1

General Suggestions

Even if you are inexperienced in making your own way without a tour group, I encourage you to consider independent travel in order to find sites of Jewish historical interest. I have collected some tips for this kind of independent travel in this section. Europe and Israel are very civilized countries, and it's not very difficult to get around.

Consumer information for travelers is useful wherever you can get it from an unbiased source. I recommend the *Consumer Reports Travel Newsletter* and the *New York Times* Sunday Travel Section for level-headed and timely information on good deals and on protecting yourself from travel rip-offs or disasters.

MONEY AND PRICES

In the past, travelers' checks were the essential way to carry money abroad. You had to find a bank or a currency exchange office to change them to local currency. You had to be aware of who charged a flat fee for a transaction and who gave good rates. This has changed. Credit cards can be used for major purchases, hotel bills, and meals (though you obviously have to ask before you buy/check in/order).

Automated Teller Machines (ATMs) in Europe and Israel now accept most American ATM cards, making travelers' checks almost obsolete—but not totally. Warnings:

- You must carry some cash or travelers' checks in case the ATM computer line to your bank is temporarily down or in case some other problem occurs with the system.

- You must note any time that a transaction is interrupted in the middle, with the result that you don't get your money. At least twice, when I have noted such an event, my bank debited my account, and I had to call them and tell them that the money was not delivered; they were able to straighten things out so that I didn't lose the money. In other cases, the aborted transaction did not appear on my statement.

Once you have some money, how much will things cost? The relative value of different currencies changes all the time. Anything I write could easily be out of date before you read it. Value Added Taxes and other taxes make many consumer goods relatively expensive in other countries, compared to the United States. By policy, tolls on the toll roads and gasoline are characteristically much higher outside of the United States. Hotels in big cities are quite costly—but that's the same in Manhattan.

HOTELS AND LODGING

Europe and Israel offer various lodging options. With the widespread availablity of the fax machine, reservations have become very easy—most guidebooks list a fax number. You send a fax inquiring about price and availability; in the response, the hotel will tell you if you are expected to confirm and send a credit card number to hold the room.

To find hotel or bed and breakfast names, see the guidebooks in the list in Appendix 2. Hotel reservation services on the Web are also developing into a reliable service.

The Kibbutz Hotel Chain, which I recommend, can be reached at:

1 Smolanskin Street, P.O.B 3193,
Tel Aviv, Israel 61031
Phone: 972-3-524-6161. Fax: 972-3-5278088.
E-mail: yael@kibbutz.co.il

When to Reserve a Hotel Room

You may wish to reserve all hotels in advance. However, I have found that in fall, winter, and spring, it is possible to travel in Europe or Israel without a set itinerary and to phone or fax only a few days in advance, leaving more flexibility in the schedule. During the high summer season, advance planning becomes necessary if you want to get your first choice of hotels and destinations (or in places like Venice, if you want any choice at all).

Exceptions:

• Major cities—Venice, Florence, Paris, and so forth—require that you reserve at least weeks in advance to obtain rooms convenient to the tourist attractions.

• European holidays that include a long weekend cause tourist attractions to fill up with local people. Check a calendar—some of their holidays differ from ours, particularly All Saints Day (November 1), May Day, and Pentecost (early June—date variable).

• Israeli tourism varies depending on the international situation; however, the Israelis themselves travel on Jewish holidays, and thus accommodations can become overcrowded. The period from Rosh Hashana until Simchat Torah, Hanukkah, and Passover are the most crowded.

MEALS

The four countries described in this book each have a distinctive cuisine, and you can enjoy enormous variety as you travel to these places. And if you aren't adventurous, MacDonalds' has outlets in all four countries. The guidebooks listed in Appendix 2 offer information and many specific restaurant recommendations.

Suggestions:

- Walk around the area near your hotel and find where local people are eating. Try the restaurants that are most popular with locals.
- Try local fast food, especially for lunch: falafel in outdoor stalls in Israel, tapas in the bars in Spain, pannini in sandwich shops in Italy, small savory pastries such as quiche at bakeries in France.
- Breakfasts tended to be included in the rates quoted by most hotels in Italy and Israel. In Israel, this seems to be standard, and the breakfast buffets are worthwhile. In Italy, the posted prices on the back of the door of the room implied that the charge was separate and thus perhaps breakfast wasn't obligatory. If you are on a seriously limited budget, you might try discussing whether you can pay for a room only, in which case you could save money by breakfasting in a cafe, as the breakfast charge is high. In France, the hotels seem to serve breakfast as a convenience to guests, but in my opinion, the coffee in cafes is always better.

Dinner Hour

Every country has its own meal times. In Spain, dinner is almost unbearably late—we usually saw the restaurant begin to fill up around 10:30 P.M. when we were exhaustedly eating dessert. In Italian cities and in France, restaurant guests tend to arrive between 8 and 9:30 P.M. In Italian seaside resorts, the hotel dining rooms seemed to serve somewhat earlier.

In Israel, kosher restaurants are closed on Friday night and Saturday. Some reopen after sundown Saturday. Hotels serve meals to guests, arranging payment to be made before or after Sabbath, in accordance with religious custom. Although I spent several months in Israel, I was never certain of the expected dinner hour in restaurants, and I suspect that it varies depending on whether you are in a city like Tel Aviv or a resort like Eilat or Tiberias. Please consult the restaurant guidebooks or ask when you reserve a table.

When to Reserve a Table

Highly recommended restaurants in European and Israeli cities usually require a reservation. The guidebooks note when the number of tables is particularly limited. Holidays and peak seasons that cause hotels to be crowded also affect restaurants. Except for those most in demand, you can usually arrange the reservation a few hours before lunch or dinner. If you don't speak the language, the hotel desk can often make the call for you; very fancy restaurants sometimes accept fax reservations.

DRIVING AND CAR RENTAL

Outside the United States, the right of way belongs to the boldest driver with the biggest or fastest vehicle. Speed limits are for the faint-hearted. In big cities and even some smaller ones, traffic jams can be major and can last for hours. You can, however, get used to driving in other cultures. You have to watch how other drivers operate and accommodate your expectations as well as your driving.

Check with the travel agent or the rental company regarding current drivers' license requirements (U.S. or international), age limits (some companies don't rent to under-twenty-five or over-seventy customers), or other restrictions. For example, cars we rented in Israel couldn't be driven across the border into Jordan or PA territory.

Notes on cost and economy in car rentals:

• Rental prices, insurance surcharges, taxes, and supplementary costs vary in different countries and with different rental firms. When you reserve a car, be sure to ask if the amount quoted is inclusive of all charges and taxes.

• You can arrange rentals via a U.S. 800-number for all of the big American rental companies. For Israeli rentals, an alternative is El Dan, the Israeli car rental company. El Dan's 800-number is available from the *Jerusalem Post* or the Internet.

• Travel agents sometimes find good car rental deals, but it pays to do a little research for yourself, calling several companies on their toll-free numbers or checking rates on the Web.

• It is often cheaper to reserve a car from the United States than to make arrangements directly with the rental firm in Europe or Israel. Even if you are already in the foreign country, you may save hundreds of dollars on a weekly or monthly rental (and even save a bit on weekend rentals) by calling or faxing the United States. This fact is so strange that I would expect it to change in the future, but it's been this way for some time.

- For weekend car rentals at the last minute, you can sometimes find local special deals. Always ask for the special; they may not volunteer!

- You may be entitled to a discount because of your employer, AAA, Frequent Flyer clubs, or membership in some other organization.

- One-way drop arrangements are possible. Between European countries, these may be expensive, though you have to compare them to the cost of a comparable rail or air ticket for each passenger. Within some countries, certain drop-offs incur no charge. This is true between some Italian cities and in Israel, where there is no drop fee between Ben Gurion airport and the cities nearby (Tel Aviv, Rehovot). But policy is always subject to change.

- Some airports charge a pick-up or drop-off fee or tax, which is added to the rental price.

- Rentals billed to some credit cards issued in the United States cover the deductible damage you will incur in case of accident, making it unnecessary to accept discretionary damage insurance. Check with your credit card company to find out what your card covers. We found that this coverage changes often, without any clear warning. For example, one of our credit cards cancelled insurance coverage for car rental in Israel but not in Europe, while the other credit card retained both. Staff at car rental desks are not usually well informed about this issue and sometimes are motivated to pressure you to accept the extra coverage, at prices up to $15/day, whether you need it or not.

Parking

We have consistently found parking to be the most difficult challenge in travel to European and Israeli cities. When you reserve a hotel room in a city, it's essential to know if you will have a safe, legal space in which to park your rental car. Finding a parking place while sightseeing can also be difficult and worrisome, as public lots are very often full, and European parking restrictions, like those in the United States, are often enforced by tow trucks.

Cautions:

- Our understanding is that items left in a parked car, even in the trunk, are very vulnerable to theft anywhere in Italy, Spain, parts of Israel, and many other places. Surely you would never leave your passport, purse, wallet, credit cards, laptop computer, onward bound air or rail tickets, or other irreplacable items in a parked car, would you?

• Italy and France often offer public spaces where a machine in the center of the lot requires you to have large numbers of coins to put in a slot and get out a little piece of paper with a date and a time based on how much you paid: maybe a few minutes or hours in the future. You must be sure to pay the whole amount before you push the button.

• Many indoor garages in Europe and Israel require you to pay for your parking, with coins or a credit card, at a machine located in the stairwell or other access space, before you pick up your car. Your ticket is then valid for several minutes, and you insert it in the control gate as you leave. Sometimes this is explained in English as well as the local language.

• Hotels in Italy that are supposed to have parking (according to the guidebook) sometimes simply have you leave your car at a public parking garage. Although there may be a discount for hotel guests, it's not particularly convenient to do this. In Florence, we once stayed at a hotel with valet parking, meaning that bell boy took your car at the door of the hotel and drove it to the public garage, and you had to leave a lot of time when you wanted him to get your car back. You can inquire about this when you reserve a hotel room.

• If you drive to Venice, you must park your car at a quite expensive garage at the entrance to the city, as the city has only canals and pedestrian streets. In peak periods, it may be necessary to reserve a space in these garages.

A Word about Restrooms

• First and foremost: always carry tissues.

• The public facilities and restaurants on the European autoroutes generally have acceptable restrooms, subsidized, I assume, by the very high tolls.

• A hamburger chain restaurant is almost always a good place to find a relatively clean public restroom, though some McDonalds' in European cities keep them locked.

• Cafes in picturesque old buildings in Europe often have antique toilets of the pit variety. Public accommodations in subway stations are often appalling.

• The French are more openminded about pay toilets than Americans, and there are often kiosk-like self-cleaning pay toilets on city streets. I have not tried them.

• The Israelis have built decent public restrooms at strategic points in Jerusalem and other major tourist sites. In the Old City, one is on the Via Doloroso. Another is at the top of the stairway leading from the Western Wall to the Jewish Quarter. These unfortunately close after business hours, so they aren't available at night.

ALTERNATIVES TO CAR TRAVEL

Alternatives in Israel

• **Egged**, Israel's national bus company, offers both scheduled buses and special tours to parks and historic sites. At bus stations you can obtain current schedules and brochures. Caution: No buses run on major Jewish holidays and no buses run from Friday afternoon until Saturday night, due to the Sabbath. And the situation changes all the time.

• **Touring organizations**, such as one run by the daily English-language *Jerusalem Post,* sponsor tours in English. These are advertised in the daily issue of the *Post* and on its Web site. As I have traveled only by private car, I cannot say which organized tours are the most enjoyable or best presented.

• **Private guides** sometimes advertise in the newspapers; a few are named in the Fodor guide. If you hire a private guide, be sure he or she has a government license. Assuming that you make sure that your guide is licensed, you are certain to have a qualified person who has at least learned the basics of history and recent archaeological discoveries. The ones I have encountered could answer reasonable questions—they didn't just have a memorized speech, without any further information. I believe they also have to know the languages in which they lecture. This is in contrast to experiences I have had elsewhere.

  Warning: Above all, avoid the self-proclaimed guides who aggressively force themselves on you at places like the Jaffa Gate or the Temple Mount in Jerusalem—they may be some type of con men and are certainly not licensed. For more warnings, see the *Lonely Planet Guide.*

Guided Tours to European Sites

Many people prefer to have all arrangements taken care of. There are many historic tours of Israel sponsored by a variety of organizations. As I have not experimented with them, I cannot specifically recommend them.

European tours or cruises that cover the material in this book are rare, but I can give you one name. I have not traveled with this tour operator, but I received the following name from friends who have taken one or more of the tours. The tour organization, as of August 1998, is:

Ziontours Jerusalem Ltd.
19 Hillel St.
P.O.B. 2726
Jerusalem 91025, Israel
Phone: 972-2-625-4326
Fax: 972-2-533-7552

This organization arranges bus tours to historic Jewish sites, with lectures in English. The tours include participation in local synagogues' Sabbath services each Friday and Saturday. Tour destinations include Provence, Spain, Portugal, Italy, Greece, and Turkey. They offer a few of these each year.

APPENDIX 2

Obtaining Information

This book does not claim to be a complete source of information to enable you to travel to Jewish historical sites in Europe and Israel. This appendix suggests sources of information that will help you make your way.

TOURIST INFORMATION OFFICES

In Europe, the tourist information office is a particularly important resource for any traveler. The staff can help you to find lodging accommodations, points of interest, and opening hours of the town's attractions. They often offer city maps and small historical pamphlets that are extremely well researched (sometimes these are even free of charge). There is often an English-speaking staff member.

Most towns have clearly marked signs to help you find the tourist office. They are frequently marked by a sign with the letter i in a box.

In France, people in tourist offices often helped me to identify many of the obscure Jewish streets and otherwise unmarked buildings that I mention here. In Italy, several of the synagogues have brochures, which the local tourist office usually stocks. In Spain, they were somewhat less helpful and often didn't speak English, but they did provide maps. I also found, in various offices, excellent photo collections, biographies of local writers or historical figures, and other very detailed information. Needless to say, a local book or pamphlet is sometimes less rigorous in accuracy about ancient times than would suit a serious scholar.

The only drawback is that for commercial offerings, locally written guides and free maps from the tourist office are often a form of paid advertising, and the hotel and restaurant information they present may not be objective. In Italy, however, the government rates hotels with a variable number of stars, which depend strictly on the facilities that they offer, such as in-room bathrooms, English-speaking staff, and other objective measurements. More stars mean more amenities.

THE WORLD WIDE WEB

Every form of information about every country is available on the World Wide Web, and the number of sites and type of information is growing all the time. Airline and hotel reservation systems, tour and charter operators, individual hotels and restaurants, archaeology digs that want volunteers, and many individuals who want to share their experiences all post information. You can obtain practical information like currency exchange rates and museum hours. You can search library catalogues, booksellers' catalogues, online encyclopedias, back issues of daily newspapers, and other reference materials for geographical and historical background. I encourage you to keep up to date, as all travel details are in great flux and there are no reviews of quality or accuracy.

I have used a number of Web sites for a variety of purposes. I have not placed exact electronic addresses in the text because they change continually. Especially relevant sites to search for:

- Archaeology sites in Israel maintain Web sites that describe current research and potential for travel that includes volunteering as an assistant on the digs. The magazine *Biblical Archaeolgy Review* maintains a site with links to some of these digs.
- The Israeli National Park Bureau maintains a Web site, with detailed information on each park.
- French cities, towns, modern Jewish communities, and universities are the subject of many Web sites in French and English.
- Venice, the Venetian Jewish community, and other Italian cities

maintain useful Web sites.

• Travel agents and tour brokers maintain Web sites about many other cities and towns that appear in this book.

GUIDEBOOKS TO EUROPEAN JEWISH SITES

Most easily available Jewish guides are targeted to travelers concerned with kosher food and with finding synagogues and religious functions, not with historical sites. The following books focus on Jewish tourist sites in Europe. They may not be easy to find in bookstores, though several of the following titles are listed by the online bookseller amazon.com.

• M. Aguilar and I. Robertson, *Jewish Spain*, published (in English) by Altalena Editores, Cochabamba 2, 28106, Madrid, describes Jewish monuments and traces of the medieval Jews of Spain, including the location of the house of Benjamin in the modern city of Tudela!

• Annie Sacerdoti: *Italy Jewish Travel Guide*, New York, 1993. A good overview of Italian Jewish sites.

• Umberto Fortis, *Jews and Synagogues: Venice, Florence, Rome, Leghorn*, Storti Edizioni, 1973. Although this is old, it has additional useful details about the synagogues. It is still sold in places such as the Jewish Museum in Venice.

• Alan M. Tigay, *The Jewish Traveler: Hadassah Magazine's Guide to the World's Jewish Communities and Sights*, Northvale, NJ: Jason Aronson, 1995.

• A series of excellent guidebooks by various authors covers the many Jewish sites of Italy, region by region. A few English versions have been released very recently; perhaps more are forthcoming. All are published by Marsilio Editori, Venice / Marsilio Editions, New York. Titles:

  Emilia Romagna Itinerari ebraici

  Lazio Jewish Itineraries

  Lombardia Itinerari ebraice

  Marche Itinerari ebraici

  Tuscany Jewish Itineraries

  Venice and Environs: Jewish Itineraries

• Marvin Lowenthal, *A World Passed By: Great Cities in Jewish Diaspora*

History, Malibu, CA: Joseph Simon/Pangloss Press, 1990 (originally published 1933), covered many of the European sites in this book and many more that are now tragically lost.

- The French Ministry of Tourism, Caisse Nationale des Monuments Historques et des Sites, provides a guidebook to Jewish sites called *The Road to Jewish Heritage in the South of France*. Published in Vaucluse, France, 1993.

> Addresses: B.P. 147, 84008 Avignon Cedex, phone: 90-86-43-42;
> 6, rue Jeune Anacharsis, 13001 Marseille, 91-5492-66;
> Avenue des Moulins, B.P. 306f, 34034 Montpellier Cedex, 67-84-71-70

- Another French government publication (in French): "Les Synagogues du Comtat." by Elizabeth Sauze. Number 98 in "Itinerares du Patrimoine," published in 1995 by Direction regional des affairs culturelles de Provence-Alpes-Cotes d'Azur.

GUIDEBOOKS AND MAPS TO GENERAL SITES

Before a trip, you might look over this list and obtain at least basic atlases and guidebooks. (I give no dates—obtain the most up-to-date editions!) Most large bookstores and booksellers on the Web in the United States offer a selection of guidebooks to Europe and Israel. Bookstores in large cities in Europe and Israel offer a selection of material in English; in smaller cities, there may be less material available in English. Museums and monuments often run giftshops with unusual books and guides. In France, a bookstore chain named the FNAC offers a large selection of maps and guidebooks at favorable prices.

You will need these guides for general sites. Besides Jewish sites, every country in this book offers enormous numbers of other tourist attractions. Most people, in fact, would classify the other attractions as superior to the ones documented here. Besides guidebooks, newspaper travel sections and travel magazines offer lots of other ideas for travel themes besides Jewish history.

Guidebooks

- **Michelin Red Guides** to France, Spain, and Italy. Essential for finding hotels and restaurants. Updated often and reliably.

• **Michelin Green Guides** to France, Spain, and Italy. Excellent overviews of major tourist sites. Michelin publishes general guides to each country as a whole and more detailed regional guides.

• **Gault-Millau restaurant guides**. The guide to France offers a different perspective on French cuisine than the Michelin guides. The guide to Israel offers a non-Israeli perspective on finding interesting places to eat.

• **Berlitz Guides and Fodor Guides.** These are often good and cover all of the relevant territory. Fodor's includes information on accommodations. The Berlitz guidebooks usually incorporate a very useful phrase book if you don't know the local language.

• **Lonely Planet Guides** to cities and countries including Europe and Israel provide a different perspective about people and places, less historically oriented, more in tune with city life, nightlife, cafe life, and the like. The City Guide to Jerusalem is very useful.

• **Guides Bleues** (Hachette), or Blue Guides (Norton) give a general guide to European cities, towns, and interesting natural attractions.

• **Cadogan Guides,** published in England, offer a more historical and cultural outlook than other tourist guides. See: *The South of France: Provence, Cote d'Azur, Languedoc-Roussillon; Lombardy, Milan, & the Italian Lakes*; and others.

• **Israel Handbook**, Dave Winter and John Matthews, Passport Books. Good overall guide to the country. Not excessively political in either direction. Limited information on accommodations. May not be updated very often.

Maps and Atlases

Maps and atlases are essential for car travel. You need a combination of a large atlas with maps of the entire country, and more detailed maps of the regions where you will spend more time. The following have served me in finding the sites in this book:

• **Michelin maps and atlases** to France, Spain, and Italy. For the obscure towns in the south of France, the very detailed regional and local maps are essential. The atlases are usually available in the United States; for the more detailed maps you may have to go to a bookstore in the country where you are traveling.

- **Carta** road maps, atlases, and city maps to Israel. These can provide you with very complete detail for car travel, including the road to every small town, every National Park, and even the location of gas stations. Carta's historical atlases, often available in museum shops, can help you to connect today's geography with historic borders and ancient cities.

ISRAELI NATIONAL PARKS AND NATURE RESERVES

Two organizations own most of the historic and natural sites in Israel. The **Israel National Parks Authority** manages most of the archaeolgical sites. The Society for Protection of Nature in Israel, or **SPNI**, owns many other sites. National Parks include Sepporis, Bet She'an, Bet Alpha, Bet She'arim, Nimrod's castle, and a variety of sites surrounding the Sea of Galilee. Nature reserves include Banias, the Hula Valley, and Tel Dan. Certain sites in the Palestinian Authority territories have ceased to be administered by the National Parks Authority.

Because of rapid change in the park situation, I have only given the names of parks in the text, leaving it up to you to check hours, fees, and interesting temporary or new exhibits. This can be done on the Israel National Park Web site, as well as by consulting an up-to-date guidebook. Also note:

- Be sure you obtain up-to-date opening information, particularly concerning policy for holidays and the Sabbath.
- Admission fees, set in Israeli currency, can vary with the exchange rate.
- The National Parks offer an annual pass or a two-week pass— you might reach the payback point for one of these even on a short trip, just by touring the major archaeology sites.
- The SPNI offers a membership that includes free (or reduced-price) entrance; you can get the terms at the entry to their reserves.
- Most of the parks have some sort of museum or documentation center designed to help you learn about what you are seeing and other on-site facilities such as marked trails, parking lots, bookshops, picnic areas, refereshment stands, and restrooms.

Active archaeology digs constantly discover new items, which are often highly publicized and shown elsewhere—the Israel Museum in

Jerusalem seems to have priority on high-profile finds, large or small. For example, when archaeologists find mosaics, the experts at the Israel Museum restore them and reset them in portable frames, making it possible to transport them to off-site museums or traveling exhibits. By law, the Israeli government Antiquities Authority controls all ancient artifacts and determines where to display them. In any case, some parks have no secure space to exhibit valuable items; for example, mosaics at Beth She'an had to be removed after a serious theft from the nearly open park. Besides, constant improvements and changes are being made to the national parks. For example, a celebration called Nazareth 2000, commemorating the life of Jesus of Nazereth, includes plans for additions and improvements to the park at Sepphoris, a few miles from the modern city of Nazareth. As a result of these factors, you can never be sure where you will find specific artifacts or whether a particular artifact will be on display at all.

THE JEWISH MUSEUM, PARIS

In December 1998, a new museum of Jewish art and history opened in Paris. It displays many objects of relevance to the topics in this book.

Museum of Jewish Art and History
Hôtel de Saint-Aignan
71, rue du Temple
75003 Paris
tel: 01-53-01-86-60

APPENDIX 3

References

In the following lists, I have specified the major books that I used as sources for the historical material in each chapter. I also used the entries in the *Encyclopedia Judaica* for virtually every city and town and every major person mentioned in the text.

REFERENCES FOR CHAPTER 1

Barclay, John M. G. *Jews in the Mediterranean Diaspora from Alexander to Trajan (323 B.C.E.- 117 C.E.)*. Edinburgh: T & T Clark, 1996.

Ben-Dov, Meir. *In the Shadow of the Temple: The Discovery of Ancient Jerusalem.* Jerusalem: Keter Publishing House, 1982. (English translation: Ina Friedman, 1985).

Ben-Yehuda, Nachman. *The Masada Myth: Collective Memory and Mythmaking in Israel.* Madison: University of Wisconsin Press, 1995.

Cohen, Shaye J. D. *From the Maccabees to the Mishnah.* Philadelphia: Westminster Press, 1987.

Cohen, Shaye J. D. and Ernest S. Frerichs. *Diasporas in Antiquity.* Atlanta, GA: Scholars Press, 1993.

Cooper, John. *Eat and Be Satisfied: A Social History of Jewish Food.* Northvale, NJ: Jason Aronson, 1993.

Davies, Philip R. *In Search of "Ancient Israel."* Sheffield, England: Sheffield Academic Press, 1992.

Feldman, Louis. *Jew and Gentile in the Ancient World: Attitudes and Interactions from Alexander to Justinian.* Princeton, NJ: Princeton University Press, 1993.

Feldman, Louis, and Meyer Reinhold. *Jewish Life and Thought among Greeks and Romans: Primary Readings.* Minneapolis: Fortress Press, 1996.

Fenn, Richard. *The Death of Herod.* Cambridge, England: Cambridge University Press, 1992.

Geva, Hillel. *Ancient Jerusalem Revealed.* Jerusalem: Israel Exploration Society, 1994.

Goodman, Martin. *Mission and Conversion: Proselytizing in the Religious History of the Roman Empire.* Oxford: Clarendon Press, 1994.

———*The Ruling Class of Judaea: The Origins of the Jewish Revolt against Rome A.D. 66–70.* Cambridge, England: Cambridge University Press, 1987.

——— *State and Society in Roman Galilee, A.D. 132–212.* Totowa, NJ: Bowman & Allanheld, 1983.

Holum, Kenneth G., et al. *King Herod's Dream: Caesarea on the Sea.* New York: W. W. Norton, 1988.

Israel Exploration Society. *Jerusalem Revealed: Archaeology in the Holy City 1968–1974.* Jerusalem, 1975.

Israeli, Yael and Uri Avida. *Oil-Lamps from Eretz Israel.* Jerusalem: Israel Museum, 1988.

Jacob, H. E. *Six Thousand Years of Bread: Its Holy and Unholy History.* New York: Lyons & Buford, 1997.

Josephus, Flavius. *The Jewish War.* Trans. G. A. Williamson. London: Penguin, 1981.

——— *The Wars of the Jews.* Trans. William Whiston. London: J. M. Dent & Sons, 1915.

Nagy, Rebecca Martin, et al. *Sepphoris in Galilee: Crosscurrents of Culture.* Raleigh: North Carolina Museum of Art, 1996.

Netzer, Ehud, and Zeev Weiss. *Zippori.* Jerusalem: Israel Exploration Society, 1994.

Neuser, Jacob, et al. *Judaisms and Their Messiahs at the Turn of the Christian Era.* New York: Cambridge University Press, 1987.

Oppenheimer, Ahron. *The 'Am Ha-Aretz.* Transl. I. H. Levine. Leiden: E. J. Brill, 1977.

Otzen, Benedict. *Judaism in Antiquity: Political Development and Religious Currents from Alexander to Hadrian.* Trans. F. H. Cryer. Sheffield, England: JSOT Press, 1990.

Price, Jonathan J. *Jerusalem under Siege: The Collapse of the Jewish State 66–70 C.E.* Leiden: E. J. Brill, 1992.

Richardson, Peter. *Herod, King of the Jews and Friend of the Romans.* Columbia, SC: University of South Carolina Press, 1996.

Roitman, Adolfo. *A Day at Qumran: The Dead Sea Sect and Its Scrolls.* Jerusalem: Israel Museum, 1997.

Russell, D. S. *The Jews from Alexander to Herod.* Oxford: Oxford University Press, 1967.

Schäfer, Peter. *The History of the Jews in Antiquity.* Australia: Harwood Academic Publishers, 1995.

Talmon, Shemaryahu. *Jewish Civilization in the Hellenistic-Roman Period.* Sheffield, England: Sheffield Academic Press, 1991.

Vermes, Geza, and Martin D. Goodman. *The Essenes According to the Classical Sources.* Sheffield, England: JSOT Press, 1989.

Weiss, Ze'ev, and Ehud Netzer. *Promise and Redemption: A Synagogue Mosaic from Sepphoris.* Jerusalem: Israel Museum, 1996.

Yadin, Yigael. *Bar Kokhba: The Rediscovery of the Legendary Hero of the Second Jewish Revolt against Rome.* New York: Random House, 1971.

———— *Masada: Herod's Fortress and the Zealots' Last Stand.* Jerusalem: Steimatzky, 1988.

Yerushalmi, Yosef Hayim. *Zakhor: Jewish History and Jewish Memory.* New York: Shocken, 1989.

Zerubavel, Yael, *Recovered Roots: Collective Memory and the Making of Israeli National Tradition.* Chicago: University of Chicago Press, 1995.

REFERENCES FOR CHAPTER 2

Adler, Marcus Nathan. *The Itinerary of Benjamin of Tudela: Critical Text, Translation and Commentary.* New York: Philipp Feldheim, Inc., 1907 (reissue of original London edition; only the original date given).

Benjamin of Tudela. *The Itinerary of Benjamin of Tudela: Travels in the Middle Ages; Introductions by Michael A. Signer, 1983; Marcus Nathan Adler, 1907; and A. Asher, 1840.* [no city specified]: Joseph Simon, 1983.

Benjamin, Sandra. *The World of Benjamin of Tudela.* Cranbury, NJ: Associated University Presses, 1995.

Carmoly, E. *Notice Historique sur Benjamin de Tudèle.* Brussels: Kiessling et Compagnie, 1852.

Cooper, John. *Eat and Be Satisfied: A Social History of Jewish Food,* Northvale, NJ: Jason Aronson, 1993.

Heschel, Abraham J. *Maimonides: The Life & Times of the Great Medieval Jewish Thinker.* New York: Doubleday, 1982.

Hollander, Anne. *Sex and Suits,* New York: Kodansha International, 1995.

Iancu, Carol, ed. *Les Juifs a Montpellier et Dans Le Languedoc A Travers l'Historie du Moyen Age A Nos Jours.* Montpellier: Centre de Recherches et d'Etudes Juives et Hebraiques, 1988.

Kriegel, Maurice. *Les Juifs à la fin du Moyen Age dans l'Europe Méditerranéenne.* Paris: Hachette, 1979.

Layton, T. A. *The Way of Saint James.* London: Allen & Unwin, 1976.

Leguay, Jean-Pierre. *La Rue au Moyen Age.* Rennes: Editions Ouest-France, 1984.

Marcus, Ivan. *Rituals of Childhood.* New Haven: Yale University Press, 1996.

Metzger, Therese and Mendel. *Jewish Life in the Middle Ages: Illuminated Hebrew Manuscripts of the Thirteenth to the Sixteenth Centuries.* Secaucus, NJ: Chartwell Books, 1982.

Oldenbourg, Zoe. *Massacre at Montsegeur.* New York: Pantheon Books, 1961.
Roth, Cecil. *Gleanings: Essays in Jewish History, Letters, and Art.* New York: Bloch Publishing Company, 1967.
Scholem, Gershom. *Jewish Mysticism in the Middle Ages.* New York: Judaica Press, 1964.
——— *Major Trends in Jewish Mysticism.* New York: Schocken, 1971.
———*Origins of the Kabbalah.* Jewish Publication Society: Princeton University Press, 1987.
Stouff, Louis. *La Table Provencale.* Avignon: Editions A. Barthelemy, 1996.
Toussaint-Samat, Maguelonne. *A History of Food.* Cambridge, England: Blackwell, 1994.
Twersky, Isadore. *Rabad of Posquieres.* Cambridge, MA: Harvard University Press, 1962.
Zinberg, Israel. *History of Jewish Literature, Vol. 2: French and German Jewry in the Early Middle Ages; The Jewish Community of Medieval Italy.* Cleveland: Case Western Reserve University, 1972.
——— *History of Jewish Literature, Vol. 3: The Struggle of Mysticism and Tradition against Philosophical Rationalism.* Cleveland: Case Western Reserve University, 1973.

REFERENCES FOR CHAPTER 3

Abulafia, Anna Sapir. *Christians and Jews in the Twelfth-Century Renaissance.* London: Routledge, 1995.
Armitage-Smith, Sidney. *John of Gaunt.* New York: Barnes & Noble, 1964.
Attias, Jean-Christophe. *Isaac Abravanel: La mémoire et l'espérance.* Paris: Editions du Cerf, 1992.
Baer, Yitzak. *A History of the Jews in Christian Spain. Vol. 2: From the Fourteenth Century to the Expulsion.* Philadelphia: Jewish Publication Society, 1992.
Beinart, Haim. *Atlas of Medieval Jewish History.* Jerusalem: Carta, 1992.
Benbassa, Esther. *Memoires Juives d'Espagne et du Portugal.* Paris: Publisud, 1996.
Castro, Don Aldofo de. *The History of the Jews in Spain, from the Time of Their Settlement in That Country till the Commencement of the Present Century.* Westport, Connecticut: Greenwood Press, 1972 (reprint of original 1851 translation by Rev. Edward D. G. M. Kirwan. Orig. publ. Cadiz, 1847).
Cohen, Jeremy. *The Friars and the Jews: The Evolution of Medieval Anti-Judaism.* Ithaca, NY: Cornell University Press, 1982.
Constable, Olivia Remie, *Medieval Iberia: Readings from Christian, Muslim, and Jewish Sources.* Philadelphia: University of Pennsylvania Press, 1997.
Cutler, Allan Harris, and Helen Elmquist Cutler. *The Jew as Ally of the Muslim: Medieval Roots of Anti-Semitism.* Notre Dame, IN: University of Notre Dame, 1986.

Dillard, Heath. *Daughters of the Reconquest: Women in Castilian Town Society, 1100–1300*. Cambridge, England: Cambridge University Press, 1984.

Dolader, Miguel Angel Motis. *Los Judios en Aragon en la Edad Media (Siglos XIII–XV)*. Aragon: Caja de Ahorros de la Inmaculada, 1990.

Eco, Umberto. *The Search for the Perfect Language*. Oxford: Blackwell, 1997.

Faur, José. *In the Shadow of History: Jews and Conversos at the Dawn of Modernity*. Albany: State University of New York Press, 1992.

Fernandez-Armesto, Felipe. *Ferdinand and Isabella*. New York: Taplinger, 1975.

Gampel, Benjamin R., ed. *Crisis and Creativity in the Sephardi World 1391–1648*. New York: Columbia University Press, 1997.

Gaon, Solomon. *The Influence of the Catholic Theologian Alfonso Tostado on the Pentateuch Commentary of Isaac Abravanel*. Hoboken, NJ: KTAV, 1993.

Gerber, Jane S. *The Jews of Spain: A History of the Sephardic Experience*. New York: The Free Press, 1994.

Gitlitz, David M. *Secrecy and Deceit: The Religion of the Crypto-Jews*. Philadelpia: Jewish Publication Society, 1996.

Goetschel, Roland. *Isaac Abravanel: Conseiller des princes et philosophe*. Paris: Albin Michel, 1996.

Haliczer, Stephen. *The Comuneros of Castile: The Forging of a Revolution, 1475–1521*. Madison: University of Wisconsin Press, 1981.

Halperin, Don A. *The Ancient Synagogues of the Iberian Peninsula*. Gainesville: University of Florida Press, 1969.

Kamen, Henry. *Crisis and Change in Early Modern Spain*. Hampshire, England: Variorum, 1993.

Kamen, Henry. *The Spanish Inquisition*. London: Weidenfeld and Nicolson, 1965.

Kayserling, Meyer. *Christopher Columbus and the Participation of the Jews in the Spanish and Portugese Discoveries*. North Hollywood, CA: Carmi House Press, 1989.

Kedourie, Elie. *Spain and the Jews: The Sephardi Experience, 1492 and After*. London: Thames and Hudson, 1992.

Leroy, Béatrice. *Les Juifs dans L'Espagne Chrítienne avant 1492*. Paris: Albin Michel, 1993.

Lourie, Elena. *Crusade and Colonisation*. Hampshire, England: Variorum, 1990.

Miller, Townsend. *Henry IV of Castile: 1425–1474*. Philadelphia: Lippincott, 1972.

Mirrer, Louise. *Women, Jews, and Muslims in the Texts of Reconquest Castile*. Ann Arbor: University of Michigan Press, 1996.

Netanyahu, B. *Don Isaac Abravanel: Statesman & Philosopher*. Philadelphia: Jewish Publication Society of America, 1953.

———— *The Origins of the Inquisition in Fifteenth Century Spain*. New York: Random House, 1995.

———— *The Marranos of Spain: From the Late XIVth to the Early XVIth Century, According to Contemporary Hebrew Sources*. New York: American Academy for Jewish Research, 1966.

———— *Toward the Inquisition: Essays on Jewish and Converso History in Late Medieval Spain*. Ithaca, NY: Cornell University Press, 1997.

Raphael, David, ed. *The Expulsion 1492 Chronicles: An Anthology of Medieval Chronicles Relating to the Expulsion of the Jews from Spain and Portugal.* North Hollywood, CA: Carmi House Press, 1992.

Roden, Claudia. *The Book of Jewish Food.* New York: Alfred A. Knopf, 1997.

Roth, Cecil. *Gleanings: Essays in Jewish History, Letters, and Art.* New York: Bloch Publishing Company, 1967.

——— *The Spanish Inquisition.* New York: W. W. Norton, 1996.

Roth, Norman. *Conversos, Inquisition, and the Expulsion of the Jews from Spain.* Madison: University of Wisconsin Press, 1995.

Ryder, Alan. *Alfonso the Magnanimous: King of Aragon, Naples and Sicily, 1396–1458.* Oxford: Clarendon Press, 1990.

Sachar, Howard M. *Farewell España: The World of the Sephardim Remembered.* New York: Vintage Books, 1994.

Talmage, Frank Ephraim, ed. *Disputation and Dialog: Readings in the Jewish-Christian Encounter.* New York: KTAV Publishing House, Anti-Defamation League, New York, 1975.

Tobiass, Marc, and Maurice Ifergan. *Crescas: Un philosophe juif dans l'Espagne médiévale.* Paris: Les Editions du Cerf, 1995.

Trachtenberg, Joshua. *The Devil and the Jews.* Philadelphia: Jewish Publication Society, 1983.

Trautner-Kromann, Hanne. *Shield and Sword: Jewish Polemics against Christianity and the Christians in France and Spain from 1100–1500.* Tübingen: J. C. B. Mohr (Paul Siebeck), 1993.

Verdon, Jean. *Voyager au Moyen Age.* Cher, France: Perrin, 1998.

Waddington, Raymond B., and Arthur H. Williamson. *The Expulsion of the Jews: 1492 and After.* New York: Garland Publishing, 1994.

Yerushalmi, Yosef Hayim. *Zakhor: Jewish History & Jewish Memory.* New York: Schocken, 1989.

Zagorin, Perez. *Ways of Lying: Dissimulation, Persecution, and Conformity in Early Modern Europe.* Cambridge, MA: Harvard University Press, 1990.

REFERENCES FOR CHAPTER 4

Altmann, Alexander. *Jewish Medieval and Renaissance Studies.* Cambridge, MA: Harvard University Press, 1967.

Amram, David Werner. *The Makers of Hebrew Books in Italy.* London: Holland Press, 1963.

Attias, Jean-Christophe. *Isaac Abravanel: La mémoire et l'espérance.* Paris: Editions du Cerf, 1992.

Baron, Salo W., et al. *Economic History of the Jews.* New York: Shocken Books, 1975.

Beinart, Haim. *Atlas of Medieval Jewish History.* Jerusalem: Carta, 1992.

Blau, Joseph Leon. *The Christian Interpretation of the Cabala in the Renaissance.* Port Washington, NY: Kennicot Press, 1965.

Bonfil, Robert. *Jewish Life in Renaissance Italy.* Berkeley: University of California Press, 1994.

Calimani, Riccardo. *The Ghetto of Venice.* New York: M. Evans and Co., 1987.

Chamberlain, E. R. *The Fall of the House of Borgia.* New York: Dial Press, 1974.

Cohen, Martin A. *Samuel Usque's Consolation for the Tribulations of Israel.* Philadelphia: Jewish Publication Society, 1965.

Curiel, Roberta, and Bernard Dov Cooperman. *The Venetian Ghetto.* New York: Rizzoli, 1990.

Damiens, Suzanne. *Amour et Intellect chez Léon l'Hébreu.* Toulouse: Privat, 1971.

De Sommi, Leone. *A Comedy of Betrothal.* Trans. Alfred S. Golding. Ottowa: Dove House Editions, 1988.

———*The Three Sisters.* Ed. and trans. Donald Beecher and Massimo Ciavolella. Ottowa: Dovehouse, 1993.

Ebreo, Léone (a.k.a Leon Hebreu or Judah Abravanel). *The Philosophy of Love.* Trans. F. Fredeberg-Seeley and Jean H. Barnes. London: Soncino Press, 1937.

Eisenstein, Elizabeth. *The Printing Press as an Agent of Change.* London: Cambridge University Press, 1979.

Fletcher, H. George. *In Praise of Aldus Manutius: A Quincentenary Exhibition.* New York: Pierpont Morgan Library, 1995.

Gampel, Benjamin R., ed. *Crisis and Creativity in the Sephardi World 1391–1648.* New York: Columbia University Press, 1997.

Gaon, Solomon. *The Influence of the Catholic Theologian Alfonso Tostado on the Pentateuch Commentary of Isaac Abravanel.* Hoboken, NJ: KTAV, 1993.

Gardner, Edmund G. *Dukes and Poets in Ferrara.* New York: Haskell House, 1968.

Goetschel, Roland. *Isaac Abravanel: Conseiller des princes et philosophe.* Paris: Albin Michel, 1996.

Gold, Leonard Singer. *A Sign and a Witness: 2,000 Years of Hebrew Books and Illuminated Manuscripts.* New York: New York Public Library, 1988.

Haliczer, Stephen. *Inquisition and Society in Early Modern Europe.* London: Croom Helm, 1987.

Hébreu, Léon (a.k.a. Léone Ebreo or Judah Abravanel). *Dialogues D'Amour.* Ed. T. Anthony Perry. Chapel Hill: University of North Carolina Press, 1974.

Kellner, Menachem. *Dogma in Medieval Jewish Thought: From Maimonides to Abravanel.* Oxford: Oxford University Press, 1986.

Machiavelli. *The Prince.* In Bondanella and Musa, eds. *The Portable Machiavelli.* New York: Penguin, 1979.

Marx, Moses. "Gershom Soncino's Wander-Years in Italy, 1498–1527." *Hebrew Union College Annual,* Vol. XI, 1936, pp. 427–501. Reprinted New York: KTAV, 1968.

Netanyahu, B. *Don Isaac Abravanel: Statesman & Philosopher.* Philadelphia: Jewish Publication Society of America, 1953.

Perry, T. Anthony. *Erotic Spirituality: The Integrative Tradition from Leone Ebreo to John Donne.* University, AL: University of Alabama Press, 1980.

Pico della Mirandola, G. *Oration on the Dignity of Man.* Trans. Robert Caponigri. Chicago: University of Chicago, 1956.

Posner, Raphael, and Israel Ta-Shema. *The Hebrew Book: An Historical Survey.* Jerusalem: Keter, 1975.

Pullan, Brian. *The Jews of Europe and the Inquisition of Venice, 1550–1670.* Oxford, England: Basil Blackwell, 1983.

Roth, Cecil. *Gleanings: Essays in Jewish History, Letters, and Art.* New York: Bloch Publishing Company, 1967

———— *The House of Nasi: Dona Gracia.* New York: Greenwood Press, 1969.

———— *The House of Nasi: The Duke of Naxos.* Philadelphia: Jewish Publication Society, 1948.

———— *The History of the Jews of Italy.* Philadelphia: Jewish Publication Society, 1946.

———— *The Jews in the Renaissance.* New York: Harper & Row, 1959.

Ruderman, David B. *Essential Papers on Jewish Culture in Renaissance and Baroque Italy.* New York: New York University Press, 1992.

———— *Kabbalah, Magic, and Science: The Cultural Universe of a Sixteenth-Century Jewish Physician.* Cambridge, MA: Harvard University Press, 1988.

———— *Preachers of the Italian Ghetto.* Berkeley, CA: University of California Press, 1992.

Russo, Raffaella. *Venetian Palaces.* Paris: Hazan, 1998.

Sabatini, Rafael. *The Life of Cesare Borgia,* New York: Brentano's, 1912.

Sachar, Howard M. *Farewell España: The World of the Sephardim Remembered.* New York: Vintage Books, 1994.

Segal, Lester A. *Historical Consciousness and Religious Tradition in Azariah de Rossi's Me'or 'Einayim.* Philadelphia: Jewish Publication Society, 1989.

Simonsohn, Shlomo. *History of the Jews in the Duchy of Mantua.* Jerusalem: Tel-Aviv University, 1977.

Tamani, Giuliano. *L'attivita editoriale di Gershom Soncino: 1502–1527; Atti del convegno (Soncino, 17 Settembre 1995).* Soncino, Italy: Edizioni de Soncino, 1997.

Toaff, Ariel. *Love, Work, and Death: Jewish Life in Medieval Umbria.* London: Littman Library of Jewish Civilization, 1996.

Toaff, Ariel and Simon Schwarzfuchs.*The Mediterranean and the Jews.* Ramat-Gan: Bar-Ilan University Press, 1989.

Weil, Gérard. *Elie Levita: Humaniste et Massorete (1469–1549),* Leiden: E. J. Brill, 1963.

Yerushalmi, Yosef Hayim. *The Lisbon Massacre of 1506 and the Royal Image in the Shebet Yehudah.* Cincinnati: Hebrew Union College, 1976.

Zangwill, Israel. *Children of the Ghetto: A Study of a Peculiar People.* Detroit: Wayne State University Press, 1998.

Zinberg, Israel. *History of Jewish Literaturee, Vol. 4: Italian Jewry in the Renaissance Era.* Cincinnati: Hebrew Union College, 1974.

Index

ABOUT THE AUTHOR

Mae E. Sander was a technical writer and marketing specialist. Her interest in history and the mystics of small Jewish communities in the South of France began in 1994. *Jewish Time-Travel* is her first book.